EZRA POUND : POET

EZRA POUND : POET

A Portrait of the Man and his Work

I : THE YOUNG GENIUS
1885–1920

A. DAVID MOODY

The events of a life like mine are of course fantasmagoria,
but the events working inward—I mean the effects of
events on whatever in genius takes the place of the 'self'
in a human being are even harder to follow.

Ezra Pound to Margaret Cravens, 30 June 1910

OXFORD
UNIVERSITY PRESS

OXFORD
UNIVERSITY PRESS

Great Clarendon Street, Oxford ox2 6DP

Oxford University Press is a department of the University of Oxford.
It furthers the University's objective of excellence in research, scholarship,
and education by publishing worldwide in

Oxford New York

Auckland Cape Town Dar es Salaam Hong Kong Karachi
Kuala Lumpur Madrid Melbourne Mexico City Nairobi
New Delhi Shanghai Taipei Toronto

With offices in

Argentina Austria Brazil Chile Czech Republic France Greece
Guatemala Hungary Italy Japan Poland Portugal Singapore
South Korea Switzerland Thailand Turkey Ukraine Vietnam

Oxford is a registered trade mark of Oxford University Press
in the UK and in certain other countries

Published in the United States
by Oxford University Press Inc., New York

© A. David Moody 2007

British Library Cataloguing in Publication Data

Data available

Library of Congress Cataloging in Publication Data

Data available

Typeset by SPI Publisher Services, Pondicherry, India
Printed in Great Britain
on acid-free paper by
Clays Ltd, St Ives plc

ISBN 978-0-19-921557-7

JOANNA, JOANNAE

CONTENTS

PART TWO : 1911–1920, LONDON

ILLUSTRATIONS

TEXT ILLUSTRATIONS

PREFACE

Genius can be troublesome, can be liable to break out of the common conventions and to make outrageous demands. Ezra Pound, a profoundly original poet, was like that as a young man. He wanted a humane renaissance, nothing less, in Georgian London, and in his own brash USA; he wanted poets to be originators; he wanted people to reject convention, to come into their full individuality and to find what their intelligent hearts desired; he wanted universal enlightenment, and a city in which even the doorways of the houses would be a pleasure to contemplate. He demanded all this with exuberant gaiety and good humour. In his calling for energy to be released from repression he was himself a figure of energy delighting in life's abundance. He could attack fiercely, savagely, the moribund and those who would in any way snuff out the flame of life—but always, in these early days, the dominant effect would be of generous energy about its work of creation.

Even as a youth Pound was certain that he was called to be a poet, and in his idealism felt that his life was being shaped by a kindly fate to enable him to answer to that high calling. He believed that poetry would serve, as organized religion no longer could, to maintain an awareness of the vital universe, and of human civilization as one flowering of its energies. He held that the genius of poets and artists consisted in their acting as the intelligences and mediators of those natural energies; and that by their truth-telling and their visions they would set men free from blind error and inhumanity, and open their minds to the possibility of a paradise on earth. However, the realities of the 1914–18 war made him begin to attend to the human powers in immediate control of his world, especially its financial powers. When he left London at the end of 1920 he knew that in his time and culture any earthly paradise would have to be forged in the inferno of imperial capitalism.

There is a great deal more to the full story of Ezra Pound than is allowed for in the received ideas which would make of him simply an outcast or an icon, or both. There is more of the human comedy; and in his end there is a tragedy to arouse horror, compassion, and awed comprehension. He was in his own way a hero of his culture, a genuine representative of both its more enlightened impulses and its self-destructive contradictions. And his poetry is prophetic, at once revealing something of the mystery of the contemporary money-dominated and market-oriented Western world, and envisioning a wiser way of living.

This book is devoted to recovering a sense of the complexity of the man, and to engaging with the challenging originality of his poetry, and the disruptive, regenerative force of his genius.

Ezra Pound exists now in what he wrote, in his poetry, and also in all the thousands of pages of his published writings and the tens of thousands of pages of unpublished letters and drafts. That hoard is the form in which I have studied and contemplated him, and I have taken his words as the material and the medium of this portrait—as both what I have had to work from and what I have had to work with. Nearly everything that matters here has behind it some document—I have refrained from speculation, and I have ignored hearsay. My interest has been to weave the varied threads of Pound's life and work into a patterned narrative, and to present the drama of this egregiously individual and powerful vortex in the stream of his language and culture.

A.D.M.

Alleins, 14 July 2006

CHRONOLOGY

1632   William Wadsworth, a Puritan refugee and ancestor of Mary Parker Weston, EP's grandmother, sails from England to Boston on the *Lion*.

1635   Edmund Weston, another Puritan refugee ancestor, sails from England to Duxbury, Mass.

*c.*1650   John Pound, a Quaker, sails from England to New England; dies in New Jersey 1690.

1802   Elijah Pound III (1802–91), EP's great-grandfather, born.

1832   Thaddeus Coleman Pound (1832–1914), EP's grandfather, born in Elk, Pennsylvania.

1847   Elijah Pound and family move to farm at Catfish Prairie, Rock county, Territory of Wisconsin; move on to Chippewa Falls, Wisconsin in 1856.

1855   Thaddeus marries Susan Angevine Loomis of Oneida County, New York State.

1858   Homer Loomis Pound, EP's father (1858–1942), born. Mary Parker, daughter of Hiram Parker and Mary Wadsworth, and EP's grandmother, marries Harding Weston.

1860   Isabel Weston (1860–1948), EP's mother, born.

1864–9   T. C. Pound State Assemblyman and Speaker, Wisconsin.

1870–1   T. C. Pound Lieutenant-Governor of Wisconsin.

1876–84   T. C. Pound US Congressman for northwestern district of Wisconsin.

1883   Homer Pound opens Government Land Office, Hailey, Territory of Idaho.

1884   Homer Pound marries Isabel Weston.

1885   Ezra Loomis Weston Pound born 30 Oct., in Hailey.

1887   Homer Pound and family remove from Hailey to New York city in the winter of 1886-7, and stay there for some time with Isabel's Uncle Ezra Weston and Aunt Frank.

1889   Homer Pound appointed Assistant Assayer in Philadelphia Mint— family lives first in West Philadelphia, then moves after about two years to 417 Walnut St., Jenkintown, and in July 1893 buys 166 Fernbrook Avenue, Wyncote.

1892–7   Ezra's first schools: in 1892 Miss Elliott's school in Jenkintown; in 1893 the Misses Heacock's Chelten Hills school in Wyncote; in 1894 Florence Ridpath's private school, which in 1895 became Wyncote Public School.

1898   Enrols in Cheltenham Military Academy. European tour with Aunt Frank.

1900   Did not graduate from the Academy—may have attended a high school to prepare for university.

1901   EP enrolls in College of Liberal Arts, University of Pennsylvania. Meets Hilda Doolittle.

1902   Second European tour with Aunt Frank. Meets William Carlos Williams.

1903   Transfers to Hamilton College, Class of '05. Meets Viola Baxter.

1904   Meets Katherine Ruth Heyman.

1905   Graduates Bachelor of Philosophy from Hamilton. Enters Graduate School of Arts and Sciences, University of Pennsylvania.

1906   Obtains MA; awarded Harrison Foundation Fellowship in Romanics for research towards Ph.D.—spends May and June researching in libraries in Madrid, Paris and London.

1907   Abandons Ph.D. Meets Mary Moore of Trenton, NJ. Appointed Instructor in French and Spanish and Chair of Department of Romance Languages, Wabash College, Crawfordsville, Indiana.

1908   Feb., resigns from Wabash College. Travels via Gibraltar and Venice to London. In Venice publishes *A Lume Spento*; in London publishes *A Quinzaine for This Yule*.

1909   In Jan. and Feb. gives short course of lectures at Regent Street Polytechnic. Elkin Mathews publishes *Personae* and *Exultations*. Begins to meet writers and people in literary society, among them Ernest Rhys, May Sinclair, T. E. Hulme, Ford Madox Hueffer, Olivia Shakespear and her daughter Dorothy, W. B. Yeats. In September finds a room at 10 Church Walk, Kensington. In October begins course of 21 weekly lectures at Regent Street, Polytechnic—to be published as *the Spirit of Romance* in 1910.

1910   Leaves for Paris and Italy in March. In Paris meets Margaret Cravens. Goes on to Sirmione on Lake Garda, returning to London in June. Sails on 18 June for US, spends six weeks with parents at Swarthmore, then rooms in New York.

1911   *Canzoni* published.
Leaves US in Feb.; March–May in Paris; June–July at Sirmione; July–Aug. with Hueffer in Germany; back in London by end of Aug.
In Oct. meets Alfred Orage and begins to write for his *New Age*.

1912   *Sonnets and Ballate of Guido Cavalcanti*, and *Ripostes*, published by Swift. May to mid-July walking tour in Southern France; returned to Paris 8—27 June following Margaret Cravens' suicide. Back in London beginning of Aug. Becomes Foreign Correspondent for Harriet Monroe's *Poetry* (Chicago)–till 1919.

1912–13 The moment of *Imagisme*—*Des Imagistes* first published Feb. 1914.

1913   In April via Paris to Sirmione. Meets Henri Gaudier-Brzeska in summer; also gets to know Wyndham Lewis. Begins association with Dora Marsden's *The New Freewoman: An Individualist Review*, later *The Egoist*. Receives Ernest Fenollosa's notebooks of Japanese *Noh* and Chinese poetry. 'Contemporania' and 'Lustra' series in *Poetry* in Nov. *Canzoni of*

Arnaut Daniel completed, but publication falls through. With Yeats at Stone Cottage Nov. to Jan. 1914.

1914 Feb.–April Gaudier sculpting 'hieratic head' of EP. 18 April, EP and Dorothy Shakespear marry—they move into 5 Holland Place Chambers, Kensington. *BLAST* no. 1, Wyndham Lewis's *Review of the Great English Vortex*, dated 'June 20th 1914'. Archduke Franz Ferdinand of Austria-Hungary assassinated in Sarajevo in July; August 1st Germany declares war on Russia, on the 3rd invades Belgium and declares war on France; on the 4th the British Empire declares war on Germany. Sept., T. S. Eliot introduced to EP, who sets about getting his poems published, in *Poetry*, *Others*, *BLAST*, and in EP's own *Catholic Anthology 1914–1915*.

1915 Jan.–Feb., EP and DP with Yeats at Stone Cottage. April, *Cathay* published. June, Gaudier-Brzeska killed—EP puts together *Gaudier-Brzeska: A Memoir* (1916). EP drafting early versions of cantos.

1916 End Dec. 1915 into Feb. 1916, EP and DP with Yeats at Stone Cottage. Sept., *Lustra* published.

1917 Jan., *'Noh', or Accomplishment* published. April, United States enters war. May, becomes Foreign Editor of Margaret Anderson's *Little Review*—till 1919. June, July, August, 'Three Cantos' in *Little Review*. Sept. 28, T. E. Hulme killed. Oct., The October Revolution in Russia—Lenin's Bolsheviks seize power. Nov., EP becomes *New Age*'s music critic, as 'William Aetheling', also its art critic, as 'B. H. Dias'. Dec., due to EP, Joyce's *Ulysses* begins to appear in instalments in *Little Review*.

1918 Composes *Homage to Sextus Propertius* (1919). *Pavannes and Divisions* published. Nov. 11, Armistice ends fighting.

1919 March, Mussolini organizes a small militant group called Fascisti dei Combattimenti. April–Sept., EP and DP in Southern France. June 28, Peace Treaty with Germany signed at Versailles. September, Adolf Hitler joins an insignificant nationalist group which names itself the National Socialist German Workers' Party, and is derisively nicknamed the 'Nazi' party. Oct., *Fourth Canto*, and *Quia Pauper Amavi* published—includes 'Three Cantos' and *Homage to Sextus Propertius*. Meets Major C. H. Douglas in *New Age* office—beginning of active concern for economic justice. Begins setting words of Villon to music.

1920 April, *Instigations* collects EP's important contributions to *Little Review* and *Egoist*, and adds 'The Chinese Written Character as a Medium for Poetry, by Ernest Fenollosa'. June, *Hugh Selwyn Mauberley* published; also *Umbra: The Early Poems of Ezra Pound / All that he now wishes to keep in circulation*. Becomes foreign agent for *The Dial*. May–July, EP and DP in Europe: Paris—Sirmione—back to Paris. First meeting with Joyce in Sirmione in June. End of Dec., Pounds leave London for Paris.

PART ONE : 1885–1911

For three years, out of key with his time,
He strove to resuscitate the dead art
Of poetry; to maintain 'the sublime'
In the old sense. Wrong from the start—

No, hardly, but seeing he had been born
In a half savage country, out of date;
Bent resolutely on wringing lilies from the acorn;
Capaneus; trout for factitious bait

'E. P. Ode Pour L'Election De Son
Sépulchre', [1919]

1 : Born in the USA

Four generations

Ezra Loomis Pound's father, Homer Loomis Pound, kept a scrapbook in which he pasted photographs and cuttings concerning his cherished only child. The earliest photograph, taken in the Fall of 1888 when Ezra was just 3, shows four generations of Pounds back to great-grandfather Elijah Pound III, born 1802. Elijah had moved his Quaker family from Pennsylvania to Chippewa Falls in the Territory of Wisconsin in 1847, there to farm in a small way, and he now looks very much the aged patriarch.

The child Ezra sits on the knee of his grandfather, Thaddeus C. Pound, with his head dropped comfortably on grandfather's chest. Thaddeus, born 1832, had risen from farm boy to Republican Congressman, representing his north-western district of Wisconsin from 1876 to 1884. He had raised himself by education; then by enterprise in the lumber business, in which he had made and lost a fortune, and in connection with which he had made and lost a railroad. Both the lumber business with its timber rights and the railroad fell to Weyerhauser, one of the powerful robber-barons of the age. Thaddeus had been regularly elected to the State Assembly from 1864 to 1869, was its Speaker in his last term, and was elected Lieutenant-Governor of Wisconsin in 1871. In 1888, all this, and his time in Washington, was behind him. He farmed unprofitably, was to discover and bottle Chippewa sparkling spring water but make no profit on it, and would die in 1914 with no money but with much honour in the State of Wisconsin. Ezra was not to see him again, but grandfather Thaddeus grew in his imagination into a legendary figure, a maker of America at once familial and heroic. That he was moved, in building a railway, or in labouring to get a measure through Congress to irrigate the desert, by other impulses than hope of riches was what most distinguished him for Pound, who wrote of him in 1920, 'And in his extreme old age when he no longer owned an inch of land ... he was still capable of being happy because the state's crops for the season were good'.

Standing very upright between Elijah III and Thaddeus is Homer, Ezra's father, now about 30, and at this moment with not much to show in the way of achievements, apart from his child. He had been offered a place at West Point, but had got off the train on the way there and returned to Chippewa Falls. He had worked for a time in his father's lumber business, then followed him to Washington where he mainly enjoyed the social life, though he did work for three months in 1881, and again in 1882, as an assistant assayer in the Mint in Philadelphia. That experience presumably qualified him to be sent out to Hailey, in the Territory of Idaho, in 1883, to open a Government Land Office there. He was to register mining claims and assay the silver ore. Thaddeus was behind this appointment, having acquired claims near Hailey and hoping Homer could protect his interests. Homer hadn't been able to do that, but he had held his own and done his job in the wild west mining town, and had done it without a gun and while, reportedly, drinking only lemonade in its saloons. One could underestimate Homer. If he didn't have his father's drive, it may have been because he never felt the need to prove himself. He followed his father by knowing his own mind, and if Thaddeus disapproved there is no record of it. Nor is there anything to suggest that Homer ever deviated from good sense, good will to all men, and absolute devotion to Ezra. Of Ezra, in 1888, there is little to record, beyond the great fact that he had been born in Hailey, Idaho, on October 30 1885; and had been carried from there a year or so later, his mother having found the far West rather too unlike New York.

The Westons

Though his mother, Isabel Weston Pound, and her mother, Mary Parker Weston, were present in Chippewa Falls on the occasion of the 1888 photograph, they don't figure in that all-male and Western context. The Westons were of New York. With the Pounds they could trace their line back through farmers in the north-eastern states to early seventeenth-century colonists; but about the time the Pounds moved out West the Westons were moving into New York. Mary Parker married Harding Weston in 1858, and their daughter Isabel was born in New York City in 1860. Harding then went on permanent leave from the family, and mother and daughter were taken into his brother Ezra's household, Uncle Ezra standing in as a father to Isabel.[1]

[1] 'Ezra' was a not uncommon name in America from the 17th into the 20th century, particularly among Presbyterians. It was associated with the Old Testament reformer Ezra the Scribe, author of

Ezra's was an hospitable nature. He had worked in banking in the financial district; then in 1870, with his wife Frances, 'Aunt Frank' to Isabel and later to young Ezra, he escaped from Wall Street and opened a hotel in Nyack-on-the-Hudson for 'artists, writers, and appreciators of The Beautiful'. There is a portrait of Isabel as a young girl which may have been painted by one of Uncle Ezra's artists. Sometime after 1877 an insufficiency of paying appreciators of The Beautiful forced the surrender of the Nyack property to the mortgagors, and drove Uncle Ezra and Aunt Frank back to New York City, where they started up and made a moderate financial success, and a lively though eccentric social success, of a boarding house on East 47th Street. That was where Homer, up from Washington at Aunt Frank's invitation, met Isabel, and where Isabel and Homer were married in December 1884; and it was to there that they returned from Idaho, with the infant Ezra, early in 1887. Uncle Ezra and Aunt Frank had no children of their own, and welcomed Isabel's Ezra like a grandchild. Much later Ezra recorded Uncle Ezra's lowering from a rear window a strawberry on a thread to the infant Ezra in his baby-carriage below, and this was to teach him 'to look about; to look "up" and to be ready for the benefits of the gods'.

Grandma Mary Weston, who by now was looking after a boarding house for young ladies on Lexington Avenue at 52nd Street, was another generous fountain of loving attention. It was a source of pride and romance to her that her mother had been a Wadsworth, and that the Wadsworths had a distinguished history, some serious wealth on the New York Stock Exchange, and a connection with Longfellow. She passed on to Isabel a perhaps rather vague air of superiority, or of aspiration to superior cultivation. And by his own account she poured out to her grandson, along with reading him Longfellow's *Hiawatha* and *Paul Revere's Ride* and the novels of Sir Walter Scott, a romanticized family history—a Captain Wadsworth saving the Connecticut Charter from the perfidious English by dousing the candles with a sweep of his cloak and riding off into the night to hide it in The Charter Oak. She wrote verse and prose to him— just as occasional verse, not as literature. She wanted him to write. When Uncle Ezra died in 1894 she gave up her establishment to help Aunt Frank run 24 E. 47th Street until her own death in 1897.

Those three, Uncle Ezra, Aunt Frank and 'Ma Weston were the loving guardians of young Ezra's ten most impressionable years. They stood

The Book of Ezra, a record of the return of the Jews to Jerusalem after the Babylonian captivity. Ezra lived in Babylon a century or more after that event, and went to Jerusalem to reorganize the returned Jews. (*Chambers Biographical Dictionary* 5th edn., 1990). 'Ezra' in Hebrew means 'help'.

for 'respect for tradition', balancing the rugged frontier individualism of Homer's family.

A small boy in Wyncote

The Homer Pounds stayed with the Westons in New York until Homer at last found a permanent position in the Philadelphia Mint in June 1889. They then made their home in the leafy suburb of Wyncote, ten miles north of the city on the Reading Railroad, at 166 Fernbrook Avenue. The estate agent described this, when they put it up for sale or rent upon Homer's retirement in 1927, as a three-story-and-attic dwelling on a 50 by 200 feet lot; first floor comprising hall, drawing room, library, dining room, kitchen and summer kitchen; second floor, four bedrooms and two baths; third floor, two bedrooms, bath and storeroom. That doesn't mention the flourish of a square tower at one corner. The top floor was Ezra's, the tower room his den.

In Homer's scrapbook there is a studio photograph of Ezra aged 8 or thereabouts. His face has a childish roundness, accentuated by round spectacles, but there is alert concentration in the eyes. There is no consciousness at all of the very wide lace cuffs and lace collar gracing his wrists and shoulders, nor of the great bow knot of cloth at his throat. His mother has dressed him up as a Little Lord, but he is not acting up to her idea.

A school photograph taken a year or so later shows the same poised and alert small boy in his ordinary clothes and setting. While his schoolmates are visibly suffering under the command to keep still and look at the camera, his gaze is level, serious and considering. Who can know the clear mind of a child? This was Miss Florence Ridpath's provisional Wyncote public school in spring 1895, with just seventeen pupils of all ages in the picture. Pound's previous schooling had been at an even smaller Quaker school run by a local family. Only his last two years before high school were at a formally established public school. No records survive from those schools; nor any anecdotes to suggest that he stood out particularly among his mixed ability schoolfellows. However, he did recall being called 'professor' at the Quaker school at age six: 'I wore glasses and used polysyllables, in the wake of my mother'. He was known as 'Ra' (pronounced Ray), a shortening of 'Ezraaa' or 'Ezray' initiated by Grandma Weston's friend Mrs P. T. Barnum.

On November 7 1896 the *Jenkintown Times-Chronicle* published a limerick by 'E.L. Pound, Wyncote, Aged 11 years', on the defeat of William Jennings Bryan. It is of no interest apart from the false measure in the second line: 'There was a young man from the West, / He did what he could for what he thought best'. Evidently young Ezra wanted to keep hold of his thought more than he wanted to keep in step.

Homer

A photo taken in Homer's office about 1897 or 1898 shows father and son together. Homer is seated and leaning back at ease, his head slightly turned as if drawn towards Ezra. Son is standing, leaning in slightly against Homer's shoulder, and his hand has found Homer's. Both have their eyes on the camera, while their hands are in undemonstrative private communion. There was to be always an unusual harmony between them.

Homer's skills were being able to assay the quality of silver simply by looking at it in solution, and to operate the gold balance which measures the fineness of gold by weight. That is all he did in the Mint, for forty years, rising over that time to second in command of the assaying department. It was a responsible but dull job, and not well paid. One is reminded of Hawthorne's Custom House. But Homer was not a dull man; he was just not ambitious to get on.

His cares were elsewhere. He provided for his family, whose comfortable style of life must have required great good management on both his and Isabel's parts. He was active in bringing about improvements in Wyncote, especially in promoting the provision of public education. He was most active in the Calvary Presbyterian Church at Wyncote, which he helped found. In making his profession of faith, in January 1891, 'Homer explained that he had not been brought up in a religious way and was now joining in the face of family opposition and ridicule', meaning his own Wisconsin family whose background had been Quaker. He was elected an elder in 1894; and became President of the Young People's Society of Christian Endeavour, 'a nationwide group that was zealously promoting a socially enlightened form of Christian action'. He worked in the Italian Settlement in the slums of South Philadelphia, and helped found the First Italian Presbyterian Church in the city and a College Settlement House for the poor. At home in Wyncote he grew vegetables for Isabel, and planted a row of fruit trees, pear, peach and cherry.

Ezra made his profession of faith in March 1897, and at least once attended a Christian Endeavour convention in Boston with his parents.

Isabel

The Westons in New York had been church-going Presbyterians, and Isabel arrived in Wyncote with her certificate of membership of the

Madison Square church. She served as vice-president of the Calvary Presbyterian Church's Women's Union, and helped train Sunday School children in the singing of Christmas carols. She worked with Homer in the Society of Christian Endeavour and in the Italian Settlement in South Philadelphia she played the piano to accompany the singing.

Wyncote thought Isabel's speaking voice 'high society'. She did flower painting on china. There is a studio photograph of Isabel and Ezra, taken possibly in 1897 when Ezra was about to begin high school. He is wearing his new dress uniform for Cheltenham Military Academy, and his hands are formally folded together on his knee. Isabel's hands are likewise formally folded in her lap. She sits upright in a dark silk dress, with a frill of lace at the cuffs, a full lace front and a high choker collar. Both mother and son are looking their formal best for the camera; no current can be detected flowing between them. Isabel's face is round, full-cheeked, good-looking in an inexpressive fashion. Ezra's face is round, chubby-cheeked, without expression. Both have eyes you would look twice at.

It was Isabel's habit to go every evening to Jenkintown Station, a five-minute walk downhill, to meet Homer as he returned from his day at the Mint. In their later years she would greet him at the door of their home, 'beautifully dressed'.

Cheltenham Military Academy

From just 12 until he was 15 Ezra attended the small, private Military Academy a mile from his home, sometimes as a dayboy, sometimes as a boarder. The boys wore Civil War style uniforms and were drilled in Civil War style exercises. A photograph in the Academy Catalogue shows cadets in a hollow square, down on their knees firing rifles (big puffs of smoke) from behind their prone bicycles. The cadets were to be 'schooled in self-restraint and self-mastery, in prompt obedience, in submission to law and authority, and in the exercise of authority under a consciousness of personal responsibility'. Ezra disliked the daily drill and the forming fours, preferred gymnasium exercises, and fenced well enough to be chosen in January 1899 to represent the Academy at a display in Philadelphia. He played tennis with enthusiasm, and chess. His main subject was Latin. There was at least one epiphany, though outside the classroom: 'it was old Spencer (,H) who first declaimed me the Odyssey', on a tennis court near some pine trees—'that was worth more than grammar when one was 13 years old'.

In the school photograph taken during Ezra's first year his is a very young face in the midst of the seventy or so cadets of all ages. He is looking straight back at the camera. While most of the other boys and young men have the usual self-conscious look of being looked at, he is intent on what the photographer is up to, absorbed in the object of his attention. That seems to isolate him, to set him apart as having an individual consciousness within the uniformed group.

Homer's caption to a photo of Ezra at home in his tower room, taken probably a year or two later, is 'E.P.s <u>Den</u>. (Photo by <u>himself</u>.)'. Here he is posed for the delayed shutter release, leaning back rather stiffly on a divan, wearing his Military Academy uniform and holding a large book. The interest is in what one can make out on his wall. There are crossed fencing foils, a framed picture of a young girl with a watering can (a Pears Soap advertisement?), several indistinct reproductions, a poster for '*Scribner's* for August', and another advertising *The Laurels of the Brave* by Marie Corelli, this illustrated by a woman wearing a sash and apparently standing at attention and saluting with her left hand.

The Grand Tour with Aunt Frank

Aunt Frank's regular habits included: dancing at each president's 'Inaugural' ball—Uncle Ezra had a house in Washington; attending the Madison Square Presbyterian Church to hear Dr Parkhurst's crusading sermons; and journeying to Europe in June. In the summer of 1898 she took Ezra and Isabel on a three-month grand tour. Ezra made a list of dates and places:

New York, USA—June 18
Southampton, England—June 28
Ryde, Isle of Wight—June 29
London, Eng.—July 4

Then it was Stratford-on-Avon, Kenilworth, Warwic (sic); across to Brussels on July 5, to Antwerp, down the Rhine from Cologne to Mainz, thence to Nuremburg, down via Constance to Zurich, Lucerne; through the Alps into Italy, and Milan, Genoa, Pisa—Pisa on July 16—on to Rome and Naples, back up to Florence, Venice, Como; via Lucerne on August 1 to Paris (two weeks in Paris); and finally back to London on August 22, and an excursion via Eton and Windsor to Oxford and Blenheim. Departed Southampton Sept. 6. And returned to Wyncote, and the local Military Academy, one imagines, with a much enlarged sense of the world and its possibilities.

Aunt Frank took Ezra on a second three-month tour in the summer of 1902, this time with both his parents. In London Homer took Ezra with him to visit His Majesty's Mint, where the official who received them 'seemed mainly concerned with his own lofty demeanour'. One gathers that Ezra, now 'a lanky whey-faced youth of 16', felt this as a slight to Homer, and also as offering an insight into the nature of the English as distinguished from the more genial American character represented by Homer. After 'doing Europe' even more rapidly than before, the party went on to Spain, Gibraltar, and Tangier. In Tangier Ezra regarded his great aunt's 'wide and white-bodiced figure...perched on a very narrow mule', and treasured the image as 'an object of pious memory as she herself is of gratitude'.

Suburban prejudice

Wyncote was WASPish. The *Jenkintown Times* reported April 18 1891, 'The new proprietors of Beechwood announce that hereafter no Jews will be taken to board there. In previous years the Hebrews have been plentiful'. May 30 1896 the *Jenkintown Times-Chronicle* called for 'Just no more Italians in Wyncote. Is our budding hope that this place will be entirely aristocratic squelched?'

If Homer and Isabel Pound shared that hope they appear not to have shared the prejudice. They let their home in the summer of 1902, while they were in Europe, and again in the summer of 1903, to Mr W. B. Hackenburg, President of the Jewish Hospital Association, and recorded the fact in the *Times-Chronicle*. May 8 1897 the *Times-Chronicle* reported 'H. L. Pound, secretary and treasurer of the Children's Institute...spoke on the work among the children in the Italian settlement in Philadelphia' during the prayer meeting in the Presbyterian church at Ambler. Evidently Homer and Isabel did not mind it's being known that they cared for Italians and would take Jews as tenants.

There is no record of its making any difference to their taking their turn at entertaining the Wyncote Musicale and the Round About Club, nor to their being active members of the Jenkintown Lyceum and the Wyncote Improvement Association, nor to Isabel's membership of the Wyncote Bird Club, nor to Homer's being elected director of the Wyncote public school around 1900. When he resigned in January 1903 from the Sessional Body of Calvary Presbyterian Church because he was moving into the city for a time in order be near his work in the Italian Settlement, the resolution unanimously adopted and recorded by his fellow elders could not have been more fulsome—a full printed page to the effect that 'none but a selfish interest can prompt us to retain him...feelings of heartfelt sadness...many years of faithful service...building up the church and creating feelings of Christian fellowship and goodwill...fervently wish for him a future of active usefulness in his chosen field of new interests'.

One must conclude that Homer and Isabel contrived to be approved and respected members of their suburban community without conforming to its prejudices. Isabel liked to play the fine lady, but was far from hardening her heart against others; and Homer was, as ever, simply too 'danged' independent to be swayed by what others might think.

XRa

The fond parents treasured young Ezra's letters to them. The earliest preserved in the archive at Yale is from Wyncote to his mother in New York, dated October 1, 1895: 'Dear Ma, I went to a ball game on Saturday between our school and Heacocks. the score was thirty-five to thirty-seven our favour, it was a hard fight in which wee were victorise.... As nobody has looked over this pleas excuse mistakes. Love from all / your loving son, E.L.Pound.' To his father from New York: '4/25/96—Dear Pa....With love, E.L.P.' In November '96 to his mother in New York: 'Dear Ma...Yesterday we went to the city and saw the minstrels which we enjoyed greatly; the description would fill ten sheets of paper and so I will not send it....Pleas excuse this writing as I sprained my little finger playing football—not when under a lot of fellows but when I tried to catch the ball which struck the finger with considerable force....I remain your loving son, and for the present your Ra.' To his father from New York in June '97: 'I remain your loving Ra / And ma your loving Dame'. There is nothing extraordinary about these letters. They show a bright 9-, 10-, and 11-year-old boy with a boy's interests, responsive to what he has been taught about spelling and writing, and playfully trying out styles of self-presentation. Just the occasional sentence, like that one about spraining his little finger, suggests a precocious ability to express things.

Something else emerges when Ezra is a cadet at the Cheltenham Military Academy. In January [1898 or 1899?] he writes home to his mother, about fencing—challenges from the Major and from Mr Doolittle, his Latin teacher; about having recited 'The bivouac of the dead' and 'got a pretty fair mark (I think)'; and then, 'I have tried to write a composition and have here inclosed the first coppy. I thought perhaps you would like to see it. [DO NOT PUBLISH IT] nor read it to anyone....E. L. Pound.' There is quite a flourish to the signature, and quite a consciousness to the presentation of his composition. One can tell that he wants his mother to see it; and the emphatic warning not to publish it nor even read it to anyone—meaning his father, her visitors?—is almost an invitation to do so. He might be remembering that his proud father had fixed the publication of the political limerick by 'E. L. Pound Aged 11 years'. But then if that could be an embarrassment to look back upon now, it would also be an encouragement to expect publication and to see himself as a poet.

In September of 1898, at sea on the return journey from Europe, he writes a really ambitious verse thank-you letter to someone who had given him a splendid knife. The verse is playful doggerel, but there is energy and enjoyment in the finding of words and stringing them together, and in the finding of rhymes. There is also a precocious sense of form. It is done in fun, but there is a feeling that beneath the fun the young author is thinking of himself as a maker of verse. He begins with the modest disclaimer, 'Though not among the famous bards / I send to you my kind regads / For knives galore'; and ends—after rhyming 'Naples' and 'the states of the Papals', and 'ice' and 'Aedelvice' [Edelweiss]—

> And now as the Muse will no
>   longer work
> I my duty will have to shirk.
> But when on land we once more be
> I'll think of you across the sea
>   In gay Paree
> And when we ride up in the handsome
> I'll think of you dear Madame Ransome.

He was now signing himself 'Xra'.

What he wanted to do

'Xra' did not graduate from Cheltenham Military Academy. He may not have completed even his fourth year there, but instead finished the year at a nearby high school. According to the Academy's Catalogue filed in the Library of Congress in June 1894, he would not have been expected to graduate until he had completed six years of study and was about 17. That would assume commencing at age 12, as Ezra did, and spending two years in the Lower School doing Penmanship, Spelling, Reading, Composition; Arithmetic; Descriptive Geography, Primary U.S. History and Natural History. However, if Ezra began Latin and Greek at the age of 12, as he implied in his essay on 'Early Translators of Homer' (1918)— 'well taught his Latin and very ill-taught his Greek'—then he must have gone straight into the Third Form, and then followed the Classical course designed to prepare the boys over the following three years 'for entering the best American Colleges'. The Third Form continued with the Lower School subjects, with the addition of beginner's Latin and Elocution. Greek was begun in the Fourth Form; German or French could be taken in the Fifth Form. A year and a half of algebra was followed by a half year of plane geometry. Grammar and Composition gave way to Rhetoric and Composition in the Fifth Form. English Literature was taught in the Sixth Form only. It is not clear why Ezra left half way through his fourth year. 'It was boring—boring—boring', he recalled in 1946, 'There was an awful book of Kipling'.

He already knew, apparently, pretty much what he wanted to do—that by the time he was 30 he 'would know more about poetry than any man living'. That at least is what he claimed in 'How I Began' in 1913. He had arrived at the conviction that while it is not within a man's control whether or not he is a great poet, 'It is his own fault if he does not become a good artist—even a flawless artist'. I doubt he would have expressed his ambition in quite those terms in 1901, but the fact remains that by some unaccountable process he had become possessed, at the age of 15, by the motive idea of his entire mature life: to be a good, even a flawless artist in words. His boyish way of expressing it to his parents had been 'I want to write before I die the greatest poems that have ever been written.' His father at least seems to have firmly believed that he would do just that.

2 : IN A WORLD OF BOOKS

College of Liberal Arts, University of Pennsylvania: 1901–1903

The record of Pound's background and childhood, being relatively well established and straightforward, could be presented as a series of snapshots, as if through the objective eye of the camera. Now the telling of his story becomes more complicated, as the materials become more various and more susceptible to subjectivities. We have to reckon with Pound's own deliberate fashioning of his image and history; and also with the differing viewpoints of those who observed him. Then there is what he was not revealing to his observers, the inner life where whatever was to be the real Ezra Pound was taking shape.

Pound's own account of how he began went like this:

Entered U. P. Penn at 15 with intention of studying comparative values in literature (poetry) and began doing so unbeknown to the faculty. 1902 enrolled as special student to avoid irrelevant subjects.

In this search I learned more or less of nine foreign languages, I read Oriental stuff in translations, I fought every University regulation and every professor who tried to make me learn anything except this, or who bothered me with 'requirements for degrees'.

Those statements would give us a dramatic image of youthful genius asserting itself against the tyranny of the old and dull—the perennially likely tale. And of course there was the other side to it. One of his professors dismissed his idea of comparative literature as a pose. The head of the English department, Dr Felix Schelling, was irritated into telling young Pound that he was either a humbug or a genius, leaving little doubt as to which he favoured. It would emerge that in his view the university was not there 'for the unusual man'. A young Latin professor, Walton Brooks McDaniel, was more tolerant and more generous. Pound regarded him as thorough 'in his own way', a way which was not Pound's but which he found useful as a 'counter irritant'. McDaniel noted how Pound would sit at the back of the class 'to be independent of excessive *ex cathedra* observation'; but he could still recall, at his 100th birthday in 1971, having been 'challenged by Pound's exuberance and brilliance'.

The brilliance didn't manifest itself in the regulation manner. His grades were mediocre, most of them mere passes. Even in Latin, his main subject, he failed to earn a single distinction, presumably because he insisted on going his own way, not McDaniel's. It would appear that, perversely, the deeper his interest in a subject the worse his academic showing. That he did interest himself in American history is attested by a dense sheaf of notes now in the Beinecke archive. Moreover, at least one of his teachers in this subject, the distinguished historian Herman Vandenberg Ames, allowed that even the 'cantankerous' young Pound 'might have a legitimate curiosity'. For that Pound remembered him with respect and 'strong personal affection'. Yet in the two courses he particularly appreciated, 'The Civil War and Reconstruction' and 'Foreign Relations of the United States', he achieved just a pass and a fail or 'incomplete'. It was probably just as well that as an undergraduate he chose to study not a single course in English poetry.

His trying to carry on a comparative study of foreign literatures went 'across the grain of American University conventions', and put him at risk of being perceived as arrogantly cross-grained. What he wanted to do—Comparative European Literature it might have been called had it existed—was simply not in the curriculum at the University of Pennsylvania at that time. And the problem was compounded by his resisting and rejecting the method of literary scholarship that was then dominant. He had been admitted to the university only on the strength of his Latin in the entrance examination. His Greek was not strong, and he avoided that option. But this meant that, beside Latin, he could take just one or the other of German or French but not both. He chose German, but found it difficult and 'stupid', and dropped it in his second year. That left him with Latin as his sole foreign literature, and with his options restricted to what was on offer in Latin. And it drove him to change in his second or sophomore year from a regular degree course to non-degree special student status, 'to avoid irrelevant subjects'. He was able then to choose some courses normally available only in junior or senior year. According to his transcript, in '02–'03 he took five courses in Latin (among them Catullus, Propertius, and Ovid), three in History, two in Philosophy (Logic and Ethics), and one in Political Science (Comparative Governments)—apart from the compulsory English Composition (for which he was given a B in each term), and a compulsory English literature course (Nineteenth Century Novelists, a pass).

When he complained that he could find no-one 'with a view of literature as a whole', or who had a 'coherent interest in literature as such (as distinct for example from philology)', he may have been thinking of his German teachers or of the way in which Layamon's *Brut* was studied in his first year, but he must also have been thinking of McDaniel's way with Latin. 'Philology' would become the catchword for all that Pound thought wrong with the university teaching of literature as he had experienced it. Properly, Philology is the scientific study of words and languages; applied to literature its inevitable tendency was to encourage attention to the language as such and to discourage attention to the further reaches of sense. This was done in an attempt to make literary scholarship as 'scientific' as possible by confining it to what could be objectively verified, to etymology, grammar and syntax, to textual variants, and to sources and analogues. It was at its best in editing ancient texts. But it allowed little scope for comparative valuations, critical responses, or discussion of whether one text was more or less pleasing, instructive or life-enhancing than another. And of course it did not cater for a bright spark of 16 or 17 who was secretly nursing the overweening ambition to know 'the dynamic content from the shell', and to discover 'what part of poetry was "indestructible", what part could *not be lost* by translation, and...what effects were obtainable in *one* language only and were utterly incapable of being translated'. The university which this wholly unusual young man wanted was indeed not there for him. And he, it must be said, was not really there for the university he found himself in.

He was leading a double life, attending classes and playing some part in student activities, while privately pursuing his own specialized studies of poetry. He played a great deal of chess, and was good enough to be a member of the university team. He kept up his fencing. He helped out as an usher at football games. In a celebrated production of Euripides' *Iphigenia among the Taurians*, performed by undergraduates 'under the direction of the Department of Greek', he was a member of the chorus whose gestures and dances, according to a reviewer, 'were gone through with care and some grace'. In class he was not above horseplay and acting the fool. He was, apparently, teased by the other students. There was the oft-related incident of his wearing socks of a colour forbidden to freshmen and being desocked and dumped in a lily pond, for which he was thereafter referred to as 'Lilly' Pound. (But, he would insist, he did defiantly sport the same red half-hose the following day.) We have to remember that he was two years younger than most of the members of his class, as well as more or less obnoxiously different. And if they could not take him seriously they were probably quite right not to, since his life among them was for the most part artificial. His real life was elsewhere.

'Artificial' was one term among many which his friend William Carlos Williams applied to Pound. His descriptions give us a better impression of Ezra in his youth than any photograph could, just because they are so multifaceted. They are coloured, naturally, by Williams's own temperament. He was fascinated by Pound, and felt a deep kinship with him—as Pound did with Williams. Like Pound his deepest commitment was to writing poetry, and to being free to write his own sort of poetry; yet he had always to be insisting on their differences and to be clearing a space for himself. He couldn't write Pound 'was often brilliant' without adding— 'but an ass'. Having told us of his own prowess at running and fencing, he says that Pound was not athletic—yet we know that Pound was a fair fencer and not bad at tennis. Again he is always putting down Pound's musical talent, telling us that he couldn't hold a tune, though it was just because he could 'hold a tune' in his head that later he was able to get his first opera written down by others who knew how to do it. In the matter of poetry, where they were most akin, Williams had always to set Pound over against himself. When they first met, at the beginning of Pound's second year and Williams's first year as a medical student, Pound was precociously (as Williams felt) reading contemporary poets such as Yeats, while he was doggedly sticking at Keats and writing his own 'Endymion'. In spite of that he maintained that while Pound was for 'caviare' he was for 'bread'. Pound would urge him to read Longinus' *On the Sublime* and he would choose to contemplate a particular brick wall in Philadelphia. Pound, he said, 'always had ideas of grandeur'; even at 17 he 'had to be the big guy. He had to tell everybody'—but he, Williams, knew better than to listen. So he goes on, always partial, often contrary, and quite invaluable as a witness because faithful to his own shifting impressions and reactions.

Looking back in 1927 at the Pound he had known at Penn, he saw him, as Pound had seen himself, successfully escaping the 'conspiracies of dullness against youth' which ' "Literature" . . . "art" . . . "the universities" ' largely are. Pound had seemed 'one of the few who have made out what life is about', and what his own life was to be about. 'He is really a brilliant talker and thinker', Williams had written to his mother in 1904; but, the letter went on, 'he delights in making himself exactly what he is not: a laughing boor'. Very few liked him and many detested him, 'Because he is so darned full of conceits and affectation'. And his friends 'must be all patience in order to find him out and even then you must not let him know it, for he will immediately put on some artificial mood and be really unbearable.' In his *Autobiography*, written nearly a half-century on, Williams declares that he could never tolerate Pound's ridiculous 'posturings as the poet' and his putting on 'side', as if it were not enough for him to be of the aristocracy of mind and spirit. Williams thought the poet should be content to be at his best in his work, and apart from that should 'live inconspicuously'. However, while he 'could never take [Pound] as a steady diet', he never 'tired of him, or ... ceased to love him'. 'He was the livest, most intelligent and unexplainable thing I'd ever seen, and the most fun'. He was 'at heart, much too gentle, much too good a friend' ever to kick you in the teeth. 'And he had, at bottom, an inexhaustible patience, an infinite depth of human imagination and sympathy'. Nevertheless he would joke, 'crudely, about anything'—except his writing. About that he was 'always cryptic, unwavering and serious'. For a time Pound 'was writing a daily sonnet'. 'He destroyed them all at the end of the year'— and without showing off any to Williams. One other quality Williams remarked in 1904: 'If he ever does get blue nobody knows it'.

Yet both suffered the woe there was in young desire a century ago: 'We talked frankly about sex and the desire for women which we were both agonizing over. We were both too refined to enjoy a woman if we could get her. Which was impossible. We were too timid to dare. We were in agony most of the time.' A main subject of Pound's poems in these early years would be desire for women redirected—painfully, joyfully, sceptically— toward the sublime.

Hamilton College, Class of '05

Towards the end of his second year at Penn the question would naturally have arisen as to what he was going to do in the following academic year. And it would have had to be faced that there was little purpose, and prob- ably no prospect, of his continuing in the College of Liberal Arts. For his own purposes he had pretty well exhausted its possibilities, having taken most if not all the Junior and Senior courses he would want to. From the College's point of view he had effectively disqualified himself, by opting out of the regular requirements, from graduating with a degree. And from his father's point of view there might have been a quite reasonable anxiety that there would be nothing to show for his having supported his son through college.

By June 11 1903 the situation had been resolved. 'Son', as he signed himself in a letter of that date to his father, had travelled up from New York on the Empire State Express—at 'about 54 miles per hr. on average', he tells him—to Clinton, a village (population around 1325) of Oneida county in upper New York State, principally noted as 'the seat of Hamilton College'. From there he reported, with evident relief, 'Saw Mr Stryker this p.m. and arranged my course. I should graduate with '05 OK.' 'Mr Stryker' was President of Hamilton College, and figured in its Register as 'Melancthon Woolsey Stryker, (A.B. 1872), D.D., LL.D., Walcott Professor (1892) of Theistic & Christian Evidences, & of Ethics; Pastor of the College Church'. Hamilton was a 'non-sectarian' but professedly Christian liberal arts college; and rather small, with (in 1903) fewer than 200 students and a faculty of eighteen professors.

How did young Ezra come to light on it? The likely link was Carlos Tracy Chester, himself a graduate of Hamilton (class of '74), and a close friend of the Pounds and of Ezra in particular. He had been pastor of the Calvary Church when Ezra made his profession of faith there in 1897. He would print Ezra's first published essays in 1906, in the Philadelphia *Book News Monthly* which he was then editing. And Pound would dedicate to him, 'in enduring friendship', *Exultations*, a volume of poems published in London in 1909. In 1903 Chester might well have known and sympathized with Pound's predicament, and he would have been in a position to recommend him to the President of Hamilton both as a professed Christian and as having a precocious if unorthodox desire to study as wide a range of poetry as possible.

Yet both Hamilton's taking him in, and his taking to Hamilton, are surprising, even mildly scandalous. For the College sternly disbelieved 'in the loose & indiscriminate modern scheme which abandons all the discipline of required courses to an unfledged caprice'. That should surely have warned Pound off, as a judgement not only on his record at Penn., but also on how he proposed to continue at Hamilton. But then Hamilton, as it turned out, was prepared to abandon its own discipline and let him do pretty much what he wanted. Some requirements it did insist on—daily attendance at chapel and Noon Rhetoricals (Declamation and Debate); a Bible course (with President Stryker) and one other compulsory 'irrelevant' course each term. Otherwise it was all 'foreign literatures'; and within them it was all poetry, so far as Pound was concerned. Even the fact that about one third of each 'literature and language' course was devoted to floundering, as it seemed to Pound, 'through the slough of philology', appears not to have brought him into conflict with the faculty. There must have been an unusual degree of appreciative seeing through appearances all round.

He was admitted to the Latin-Scientific Course 'for such as offer German and French in substitution for Greek', and would graduate Ph.B. (not A.B.). Yet he enjoyed the freedom accorded to Special Students who could obtain only a certificate, not a degree. The Professor of German, Herman Carl George Brandt who had studied at three German universities, was even pleased that he 'did *not* want to be bothered with German prose and skipped [him] to the poetry courses'. We may have Brandt to thank for the witty 'Translations from Heine' in *Canzoni* (1911). Italian and Spanish were taught in alternate years to the Seniors, but Pound was able to take Italian in his Junior year, and Spanish the next year. He doubled up his French, taking Sophomore and Junior French in one term, repeating Junior with Senior French in two other terms. The Professor of Romance Languages and Literature, William Pierce Shepard, gave him an extra-curricular course in Provençal, and that was counted towards his degree. In this way he reduced to the minimum the 'irrelevant subjects' he had to take. He may have simply avoided some, for his transcript appears to be short of the required total of credits. There is no record of his having done two required courses, 'Ethics' and 'Logic and Laws of Evidence'; and though he mentioned to his parents having to do an exam in Physics there is no record of that either.

So far as one can tell from the transcript, his grade average (which determined the quality of degree to be awarded), was arrived at in a spirit of forbearance and generosity. Instead of dividing the total of marks obtained by the total number of credits required, the marks were divided by the number of credits actually earned. By this method his average (when rounded up) was a bare 8—the minimum for a Credit and well below Honor, let alone High Honor (9.2 or over). His performance had been erratic: an A in Old English in one term and a C the next; an A in German followed by a D; a C in Junior French in the same term as a B in Senior French, then an A the term after. (That A secured him Second Prize in French.) His grades for Bible courses about sum it up: an A, three Bs, and a Fail in *Job* —the Bs win out, but only just.[1]

Some of those lower grades may be markers for where Pound was philologically challenged. Whatever the reason for them, the teachers of Language, Literature, and Philology seem not to have held against him his cavalier disregard of their hard-earned expertise. And he certainly

---

[1] Pound boasted to his mother in January 1905 that he had passed the examination in Analytic Geometry in spite of not knowing the necessary formulae and the inability of 'the faculty of mathematics in consultation' to fathom his method. He had done it 'on sheer intuition', he wrote when repeating the claim in *Gaudier-Brzeska* (p. 91). Yet the transcript records a mark of zero for the examination in Analytic Geometry, and a failing grade of E for that course. The faculty of mathematics consisted of just the elderly Professor and one Assistant. Since the Professor, Oren Root, also served as Registrar, he would have been responsible for the keeping of records and for the accuracy of the transcript. For Pound, the vivid experience of seeing 'where the line *had* to go' evidently left him feeling that he must have passed. The mathematicians must have been unimpressed by mere intuition.

discovered in them a readiness to recognize and respond to his special interests, and to give him an education adapted to his individual talent. Foremost among these was Dr Shepard. His Ph.D. (Heidelberg) was in Romance Philology. Next was the Professor of English Literature, Anglo-Saxon and Hebrew, Joseph Darling Ibbotson, who had studied at Berlin and Halle. Shepard was a high-powered scholar, notably of the old Provençal poets; and he had the reputation of not suffering students gladly. But he did suffer Pound gladly. In the preface to *The Spirit of Romance* (1910) Pound acknowledged his 'refined and sympathetic scholarship' which had 'first led [him] to some knowledge of French, Italian, Spanish and Provençal'. In fact that book is very much a product and a record of Pound's studies with Shepard.[2] The value of his teaching, especially on Dante and the troubadours of Provence—this was Pound's mature judgement, in 1942—was in enabling him, as a young serious writer, to learn his profession, 'i.e. to learn to know a masterpiece and to form his own critical standards'. 'Ibbotson's instruction in Anglo-Saxon' had the same value. And these studies were 'more important than any contemporary influences'—meaning, I take it, more important than the influence even of such then living poets as Yeats. Thus it was at Hamilton, with Shepard and Ibbotson opening the way, that he really began as a poet.

He formed the conviction that the study of European poetry must begin at its root in medieval Provence, following the example of Dante in his *De Vulgari Eloquentia*; and that it should be a study of technique or 'the modes of expression'. His own studies were practical, as if poetry could be learnt as painters and musicians learnt their arts, something undreamt of in university departments of literature. We glimpse him, through a letter to his mother, translating 'de Bornelh's Tenzon': 'It contains sixty-eight lines and only five rhyme sounds, and has been a stumbling block to several.' In May 1905 he sends her his translation of 'the Bilingual Alba or Dawn Song' which was about to appear in the *Hamilton Literary Magazine*. He was attempting, by translation and by imitation, to discover the specific achievements of past masters of his art and to find how to match them in his own language. With this went a strong interest in the stories told of the troubadours. These were generally based on their own poetry, and credited them with having really lived and loved what they sang. For Pound this way of reading the poems meant that his studies in technique were enlivened by the passionate tales the poets appeared to tell of their own loves. From these studies came a number of his early

[2] There is also, on p. 127, an application to Dante of what he had learnt in Analytic Geometry, though still with a shaky grasp of the formulae for triangles and circles.

'personae': 'Na Audiart', 'Marvoil', 'Piere Vidal Old'; and three based on the life and poetry of the troubadour Bertran de Born, 'Sestina: Altaforte', 'Planh for the Young English King', and later, in 1916, 'Near Perigord'. The culmination of this particular line of research was the sequence of translations published under the heading 'Langue d'Oc' in 1918. Then the matter of Provençe was carried into the *Cantos*, featuring strongly near the beginning in cantos 4, 5 and 6. Canto 5, first published in 1921, includes the story of Poicebot—Dr Shepard would bring out a few years later his perfected text of that troubadour's *Poésies*.

While his translations and imitations of the troubadours were of the first importance in Pound's training himself as a poet, it was Dante who was to be his main source of guidance throughout the *Cantos*. Dante entered into his consciousness very early. He read both his prose and his poetry with Shepard through his first year at Hamilton—by the end of June 1904 they had got up to half way through *Paradiso*. The course description indicates that while a philological knowledge of the language was required, a broader humanism did prevail: especial attention was paid to the relation of the literature of the Italians to European thought; and 'the "Inferno" of Dante [was] made the basis of a study of the whole culture of the Middle Ages'. Thus it was Dante who introduced him to the troubadours, through his criticism in *De Vulgari Eloquentia*, and in his encounters with some of them—notably Bertran de Born, Sordello, and Arnaut Daniel— in his *Inferno* and *Purgatorio*. Pound was less taken, at that time, with the 'European thought'. 'Got more mediaeval philosophy in one canto of Dante's Paradise than I ever expect to get again', he wrote to his mother in May or early June of 1904—

Bill [Shepard] spent most of the time elucidating. He told me if I wanted any more I could go to Thomas Aquinas & the other mediaeval latin writers. I said 'No thanks this is enough' so we go on to Canto X.

If it was the technical philosophy of canto IX that Shepard had been elucidating, then some markings in Pound's copy of the text might indicate that what had really excited him in that canto was the story of Cunizza. The notes told him that she was the sister of 'the hideous tyrant Ezzelino da Romano'; that 'her amours with Sordello were specially notorious'; and that she freed her slaves before her death. These were the details of her story which lodged in Pound's mind, to be worked into the *Cantos* twenty years and more later.

What Pound's marginal notes mainly reveal is that he was reading Dante comparatively. An image of the heart as a lake troubled by fear in the night is glossed with Heine's 'mein Herz gleist gang dem Meer'. In two places the mention of morning stars is connected with plate 14 in Blake's *Job*, 'When the morning Stars sang together, and all the Sons of God shouted for joy'. Condemned lovers blown hither and thither on the wind of hell make him think of Villon's thieves on the gibbet twisting in the wind; and then of his elegy for famous women, 'où sont les neiges d'antan'. The vision of Christ's cross in *Paradiso* XV is glossed with Caedmon's 'Dream of the Rood'. In these comparisons he is clearly making connections with the several literatures he was studying at Hamilton. Other connections are likely to have been Shepard's promptings. In *Paradiso* IX, beside Cunizza and Ezzelino da Romano, Browning's *Sordello* is noted—presumably as a suggestion to follow up their story in Browning's poem, something which Pound went on to do, finishing it in November. It would have been Shepard who could gloss 'there where the sun is silent' with St Augustine on the joys of paradise and the 'metamorphosis of sound and light'—just the sort of effect to intrigue Pound. And it would have been Shepard again who directed him to the two passages from Plato's *Phaedrus* neatly copied into the front of his copy of the *Paradiso*. In 1938 he would mock just those passages of ' "sublimity" about the heaven above the heavens', but in 1904 his appetite for the mystical sublime was eager and still growing.

One gets the impression that Dr Shepard was personally and socially rather reserved and formal. Pound dined occasionally at his home, and dined well, upon invitation. With Ibbotson, however, he felt free to drop in casually, even at late hours, 'knowing that he is still mostly college boy despite his family and professorship'. They would smoke and talk together by the fire, of the Anglo-Saxon poetry 'Bib' taught, or of what Pound had been reading. It was of Ossian once, when Pound had picked up an old German translation; or it might be of Blake's *Job*—'Bib' was Professor of Hebrew as well as of English. The conversation would have ranged over the poets Pound was passionate about—Rossetti, the translator of Dante's *Vita Nuova* and of other early Italian poets; William Morris and Swinburne and Yeats; Browning, of course; and Beddoes, the author of *Death's Jest Book* which Pound discovered in 1904. Chaucer and Shakespeare would have been in there too, and Malory's *King Arthur*. Ibbotson's teaching lies behind Pound's virtuoso translation of the Anglo-Saxon 'Seafarer', a version more firmly grounded in sound philology than some hostile critics have supposed. And the measures of that poem, and of *Beowulf*, stayed in his ear to contribute to the measures of the *Cantos*. But the great thing to come out of his talks with 'Bib' was the idea of his epic.

Out of their talking back and forth about 'The Seafarer' and *Beowulf*, and Dante's epic and his Bertran de Born and Cunizza, and Browning's

Sordello, and who knows what else—and given always Pound's urge to write his own great poem—out of it all there came, at a certain moment in 'Bib's' front room, the conception of a long poem in three parts, after Dante's. The first part, in *terze rime*, would have to do with *emotion*, 'or the state of man dominated by his passions'; the second, in pentameters, would have to do with *instruction*; and the third, in hexameters, would have to do with *contemplation*. Though little else survived of this first idea—not a word of it was ever written—that tripartite structure, a matrix for the mind in quest of its paradise, would hold as the major form of the *Cantos* all the way through to *Thrones* and the final *Drafts and Fragments*.

He thought his poem would be based on the life of Marozia, 'a one-woman Vortex' (in Hugh Kenner's apt phrase) in tenth-century Italy. Pound admired her as 'an example of genius in a woman'. She was reputed to have become the most powerful person in the Rome of her time through a combination of ungoverned passion, intelligence, and cunning. She instigated the death of one pope; placed her bastard son by another on the papal throne; married in succession three rulers or would-be rulers of Rome; and was stopped in her career only when her son by the first of those rulers revolted against the third of them and shut her up in a prison. One suspects that had she lived in Dante's time she would have figured in his *Inferno* with Ezzelino da Romano. Pound's admiring her is the first clear sign of his sharing Machiavelli's fascination with the kind of *virtu* that carries high ambition through to success—and which generally comes to a bad end. Sigismundo Malatesta would be one representative of such genius in the *Cantos*; and Benito Mussolini would be another in real life. But Pound intended, beyond the hell of passionate action, a purgatory of instruction; and beyond that again, a paradise of contemplation. With his admiration for Marozia went the more deeply felt need for a Beatrice. He had it from Dante—from his *La Vita Nuova* and *Divine Comedy*—that the genius of the sort of poetry he wanted to write began in *fine amor*. ' "Ingenium nobis ipsa puella facit", as Propertius put it'—our genius is down to a girl.

He was not, even at this early stage, simply the young aesthete that one might think from his first published poems and his taste for the Pre-Raphaelite sublime. In a long letter to his mother in February 1905 he told her in strong terms why 'Dante and the Hebrew prophets' were far superior to the Emerson she would have had him admire:

I beg you not to think I praise Messire Dante Alleghiere merely because he wrote a book most people are too lazy to read & nearly all the rest to understand. Ecce homo. He fought in battles where he probably encountered much more personal

Danger than Mr Roosevelt in Cuba. He also held chief office in his city & that for clean politics & good government. Also he was a preacher who will rank with Campbell Morgan in extent of his influence & some centuries before Luther dared put a pope in hell & a pagan without its gates & prophecy the fall of the temporal and evil powers of Rome.

'Of course if you don't want Dante you can use a Bible', he concluded, 'It's even better.' Even better, one must suppose, for putting down evil and promoting justice and goodness. If that was why he thought Dante supremely worth his studying then one must suppose that he already knew that in his own long poem he would have to attempt the work of prophecy.

Apart from what he gained from the teaching and conversation of Shepard and Ibbotson—that being quite enough to set him on his way to becoming a poet—his time at Hamilton was not idyllic. He had little in common with his fellow students and seems to have been close to none of them. One room-mate remembered Pound as often wanting to read his latest poem to him when he only wanted to sleep. He had told his father at the start that 'a fellow here must join a fraternity or be out in the cold', and then for reasons unknown remained out in the cold socially. He was in the chess team, and he played tennis. He introduced fencing into the College. But at times he was desperately lonely—

> homesick
> After mine own kind that know, and feel
> And have some breath for beauty and the arts.

The words are from 'In Durance' dated as of 1907, but he had felt that way at Hamilton. On April 29 1904 he wrote his father that he was not happy there and wanted to go back where he belonged. In August, however, on holiday in Port Jefferson, he wrote his mother that 'pleasant memories only remaining' he thought it best to return to Hamilton in the Fall. He would not be so much an outsider—and he would 'be more of a man at the end of it'. His signing off 'Cheer up. / Son' suggests he may have been telling her what she wanted to hear. He did get by better in his senior year, though he was perceived by his classmates as having little to do with them. For his birthday, 30 October 1904, he took himself to hear *Il Trovatore* in nearby Utica. In November he 'broke out' to take 'a little vacation' in Ithaca. He told his mother, 'I don't suppose anyone can live in books steadily & not get grouched occasionally'.

It is remarkable that he found no consolation in the natural beauty of the place. The College is on a hill, 'with extended views of vales & uplands, & high hills beyond'. The campus itself, the 1904 *Register* went on quite accurately, 'is a graceful park of . . . stately trees, broad lawns, rare vistas'.

Add the colours of autumn and the seasonal changes to the 'clean and tonic' air and one could well find 'The whole environment...ennobling'. Yet all that Pound had to say of it in his letters home was that it was a 'desolate mountain top' on which he felt bottled up—he sometimes gave his address as 'Buzzards Roost'.

He was living in a world of books and poetry, and it was mainly by way of books and poetry that he needed to connect with other people. In his Senior year he told his mother how he had butted in to help some freshmen with a rhetoric assignment. They were to dissect Emerson's 'Self-Reliance', and Pound could share with them the exhilaration he felt in detecting Emerson's sophistries. Upon this he built a 'prospect of a gathering of three or four sane people to read & kuss & discuss.' In a following letter he mentioned as about the only interruption of interesting work some 'necessary & healthy rough housing', and that 'a very decent gang of freshmen...have begun to meet here decently & in order on Tuesday evenings.'

Junius D. Meeker, who had liked and admired Pound, recalled fifty years later how he had joined a group of sophomores preparing rather desperately for an oral with Dr Shepard by spending the night before the exam reading through the four set texts. They started by taking turns, and soon saw they were not going to get through. But 'Ezra read along easily', so they asked him to go on as long as he could. 'He'd read for about an hour when we'd stick our heads out the window for fresh air and to cool off. Back we'd go and Ezra would read on. He read the rest of the night and at exactly 7:00 in the morning, he finished them all.' In the exam Junius surprised both Dr Shepard and himself by getting through 'the worst section of Cyrano' where he tells of 'the ways he had of going to the moon'. It was purely a matter of memory—'I could hear [Ezra's] voice translating every sentence'.

On one of his escapes from The Hill, at a church social in Utica, Pound met Miss Viola Baxter. She was 18, he was 19. They went dancing together; he was befriended by her family; and occasionally hired a horse and wagon to go driving in with her. He told Williams that she 'made hell homelike for me during my exile in upper new york'; and Williams, who knew her later in New York city, thought her 'beautiful and sympathetic'. In the '30s, now Mrs Viola Scott Baxter Jordan, divorced, she began writing to Pound again, in mothering, chatty, intimate letters. In one she addressed him as 'My very dearest first love Ezra Westinghouse Loomis Pound'. She also sent him stories she had written, among them 'The Kiss'. A girl of 18 goes to the Public Library for 'some interesting books that Prince Charming had told her of'—'his influence had settled upon her fancy like a rosy cloak, colouring and giving her a shadowy goal that was too far away and too delightful to inspect closely'. She comes away with the 'mysterious religion' of Swedenborg and 'The Sundering Flood of the romantic William Morris'—the heavy books balanced on her hip accentuating the slimness of her waist. The story then has her visit an elderly couple. The old man asks for a kiss, which she gives lightly, but then falls to brooding on what it might mean to him. It is as if the sexual charge generated by Prince Charming and his bookish influence had been first repressed in an innocent, unthinking gesture, and had then returned troublingly displaced and uncertain. It is a story of the arousal of love and hope, and of unacknowledged disappointment. 'Just a simple country girl', was how Pound introduced Viola to Williams, 'One of the few girls I have fallen in love with (and one of the rarer few, the unkissed)'.

What of that 'Ezra *Westinghouse*'? Viola was probably just misremembering. At Hamilton Ezra had become Ezra *Weston* Pound, or 'E. W. P.' on the end-papers of his books. 'Please don't part my name in the middle', he instructed his mother, 'It's EWL or Ezra W L or the whole thing is Ezra Weston Pound but not E.Weston or Loomis Pound'. In the search for identity he was favouring her side of the family, choosing to emphasize his kinship with Grandma Weston and Uncle Ezra and Aunt Frank. The frontier strengths of the Loomis side counted for less now than the worlds of American history, and of New York and of Europe opened to him by the Westons. Maybe Aunt Frank's donation counted the most.

Graduate School of Arts and Sciences: '05–'07

In the Hamilton College Commencement ceremonies at the end of June 1905 Ezra Weston Pound was graduated Bachelor of Philosophy. Then came as ever the inescapable What was he going to *do*? He knew what he wanted to *be*, but being a poet would not be counted as *doing* anything. His mother wondered if he might enter the U.S. Consular Service. He wondered if he might teach, say Latin at Cheltenham Military Academy, or do private tutoring. In the Fall he returned to the University of Pennsylvania to do the Masters course in Romance Languages.

Six of his seven MA courses continued the work he had most enjoyed at Hamilton. These—in Provençal, Old French, Italian, and Spanish— were all with a Spanish specialist, Dr Hugo A. Rennert, whose distinctive contribution to Pound's education shows in the chapters on *El Cid* and Lope de Vega in *The Spirit of Romance*. Pound remembered Rennert appreciatively in the *Cantos*, for his telling him that 'old Lévy' in Freiburg was the man to go to for Provençal, and for his remarking that in a university the faculty '*are* the plant'. And Rennert thought well of Pound, encouraging him to go on to do research towards a Ph.D., and securing for him a Harrison Foundation Fellowship worth $500 and tuition fees. He still felt kindly disposed towards him in 1911, when, responding to some request, he said it would always be a pleasure to do anything for Pound.

The seventh MA course was a 'Latin Pro-Seminary' on Catullus and Martial with Dr McDaniel. The Martial, having made him feel nausea and disgust at Roman life, was to prove useful in *Lustra* (1915), as a model for expressing nausea and disgust at British life. Catullus, in contrast, stayed with him into old age as a model for the definite presentation of desire. But McDaniel, when Pound proposed to use his Harrison Fellowship to do some original research on Renaissance Latin authors *not* included in the curriculum, tried to shackle him with the heavy 'yoke of the universities'. That is, he vetoed the proposal on the ground that 'We should have to do so much work ourselves to verify your results'.

So Pound decided on a thesis, under the direction of Dr Rennert, on the *gracioso* in the plays of Lope de Vega. The prospect of his Fellowship $500—to be paid in instalments over the following academic year—enabled him to set off just as soon as he had fulfilled the requirements for the MA to begin his research in the libraries of Madrid, Paris, and London. He sailed from New York on the *König Albert* on April 28 and landed at Gibraltar May 7. The next day he was in Cordova, where he ventured without a guide and was pelted with stale vegetables and chased by a pack of children offended by his foreign dress and behaviour. He fled to Alcazar, from where he wrote about that adventure to Viola Baxter on paper 'with a black border half an inch or more deep', as recorded in canto 81. He then spent three weeks in Madrid, and at first found the libraries closed, or if open unwilling to admit him, or unwilling when he did get in to yield the books that he wanted. He was rescued, as he told his parents, by Padre José Maria de Elizondo 'of the Capuchins' or Francisans, who 'ordered the University library to open up to' him and helped him find his way 'round the INCUNABULAE'. He had the American Consul arrange for him to be admitted to the library of the royal palace to see an unpublished manuscript. But it was the Velasquez paintings in the Prado which imprinted themselves most vividly upon his mind, so that he could recall them in detail thirty years later. He was in the crowd outside the palace for the royal wedding on May 31 and saw the attempted assassination of the King and his bride. Fearing to be mistaken for an anarchist he took the train to Burgos, 'the Burgos of Myo Cid Campeador', and spent some time there reliving his story in imagination. This time he had a guide, a boy of eleven, and the boy referred to him as a French, 'Franthes', and when he said no, he was 'Americano', the boy explained ' "It is all one. Here we know no other name for strangers save *franthes*." ' The Lope de Vega *incunabulae* and manuscripts yielded no such epiphanies. He 'was tempted to forget there were such prosaic things as doctors' theses to be writ.'

He went on, via Bordeaux and the Loire, to Paris—for two weeks of lectures at the Sorbonne, he told his mother. It was now mid-June, and he could sit at a pavement café table writing and reading, or loaf around old bookshops. In one he picked up Ghero's great collection of Renaissance Latin poets; in another his attention was caught by a new book on the mysteries of the troubadours. What he was writing at the time strongly suggests that his mind was much more on those poets than on Lope de Vega's plays. Nevertheless, in London at the beginning of July, he did obtain a ticket to the British Museum Reading Room to read for one week for his thesis. On July 8 he sailed from Boulogne for New York.

According to the doctoral degree requirements he now had to add a further dozen credits to the dozen earned for the MA. In the Fall he did six courses with Rennert, again all in the Romance literatures—Old Provençal, Old French, Early Italian Poets, Dante, Old Spanish, and Spanish Drama. For a course in French Phonetics with Rennert's assistant he received no credit, presumably because he did no work for it.

Then for some reason—possibly there were no more Romance courses available—he signed up for five courses in the English Department, and proceeded to spat 'with nearly everybody' in it. He objected to Josiah Penniman's teaching the history of literary criticism in 'drill manual' fashion, and was failed by him. Penniman, he wrote in 1920, would never forgive him 'for preferring the search for sound criteria to a parroting of dead men's opinion.' Of Dr Cornelius Weygandt's class on contemporary poetry he said, rather pointedly, that he had enjoyed the poetry. Dr Clarence Child who taught Chaucer was, in his view, the one man in the department 'with real love of letters & true flair'—a fine instance of the odious comparison.

But it was in Dr Schelling's Elizabethan Drama that he was at his most offensive. Maintaining that modern Shaw was better than ancient Shakespeare was the least of his provocations. Williams (who presumably had it from Pound himself) recounts how, as Schelling, the John Welsh Centennial Professor, lectured on Shakespeare's blank verse, Pound 'would be turning the pages of his own priceless manuscripts or . . . would take out an immense tin watch and wind it with elaborate deliberation'. Then there is the strange letter, dated 'Jan 15' ['07], in which Pound informs Schelling, rather than Rennert, 'I have already begun work on "Il Candelaio" which is eminently germain to my other Romance work and in which I have considerable interest'; and then goes on, in an apparent non-sequitur—

On the other hand, since the study of Martial there is nothing I approach with such nausea and disgust as Roman life (Das Privatleben). Of course if you consider the latter of more importance, I shall endeavour to make my hate do as good work as my interest.

Giordano Bruno's satiric comedy may have been germane to his work on Lope de Vega's plays, but what had either to do with Dr Schelling and Elizabethan Drama? And why bring in his hatred of 'Roman life'? Well there is a draft of an essay, likely to have been written for Schelling, in which Pound perhaps impertinently introduces *Il Candelaio* into a discussion of Ben Jonson's plays. The mention of 'Roman life' would be accounted for if Schelling had called instead for a discussion of Jonson's Roman tragedy *Sejanus*. In any case, Pound's letter is effectively telling Schelling that what Schelling wants him to write on is not worthy of his interest, and that his real work is elsewhere. Behind the apparent deference of the last sentence is insolent insult. This would have been rubbed in by the essay's concluding that two of Jonson's plays are not worth reading, as measured by Pound's high standard that 'The end of all art is this "That ye might have life and have it more abundantly"—

if a work of art does not leave you stirred and exalted with that extasse which is ever the result of beauty understood THEN has your reading or your beholding of that work of art been in vain.

Schelling detected humbug, and told Pound 'to waste no more of his time...with word or writing'. Even twenty years later, with the rancour and malice still keen, he would put down Pound 'as a remarkably idle student, absolutely evading all work'. Pound 'resigned' from his course, choosing not to take the examination. He earned no credits in English, and it seems likely that he refused altogether to submit himself to examination by the department.

Schelling was Head of the English department, Penniman was Dean of the Faculty—and Rennert was 'a poor thing without backbone'. Pound's fellowship was not renewed. Schelling told him he was wasting both his own time and that of his instructors by continuing at an institution of learning. It was the end of his doctorate, and of any prospect of a university career. Exactly when he abandoned the thesis is not known, but he may well have let it go with a sense of relief. The pages dealing with Lope de Vega in *The Spirit of Romance* suggest that his interest had been more dutiful than passionate. But surely it had all along been improbable that Pound would subordinate his ambition to be a poet to the requirements of a thesis, let alone to the requirements of professors whom he judged unequal to the literature they professed. It was a case of peg and hole being wonderfully mismatched.

Pound's answer to Schelling's later insinuation that he had taken no interest in his graduate work was that, on the contrary, he had taken 'sufficient interest in the system of instruction to protest against it with as much vigour as [he] was then able'. He did not say, as he well might have done, that he had put in a lot of serious work after his own fashion. As evidence he could have produced, along with much else, the typescript of his study of Lope de Vega's *Castevines y Monteses*, with its 'philological' transcription, translation, notes and critical discussion. But the fact was that his protest mattered more to him.

He had made it public in an essay, part invective and part defiant demonstration, published by Carlos Tracy Chester in the Philadelphia *Book News Monthly* in September 1906. The essay, on 'Raphaelite Latin', was introduced as by 'Mr Pound, who is Fellow in Romance languages for the University of Pennsylvania', and who is ready to defend the Latin literature of the Renaissance 'from the superficial charges of literary barrenness and inferiority of production that have been made against it.' It begins with what could only have been taken as a sustained attack on McDaniel:

The scholars of classic Latin, bound to the Germanic ideal of scholarship, are no longer able as of old to fill themselves with the beauty of the classics, and by the very force of that beauty inspire their students to read Latin widely and for pleasure; nor are they able to make students see clearly whereof classic beauty consists.

The scholar (singular) is then mocked for having 'to spend most of his time learning what his author wore and ate, and in endless pondering over some utterly unanswerable question of textual criticism'; he is further mocked for being grateful he need not read anything written after AD 400; and is finally exposed as reviling 'with the abject and utterly scornful "dilettante"' anyone who tries to build 'a comfortable house for his brain to live in'. 'No one knows the contempt and hatred that can be gathered into these few syllables until they have been hissed at him by one truly Germanized.' Evidently strong feelings had been aroused, on both sides. Pound goes on to demonstrate the neglected classic beauty by translating, into a diction of high old poesy, 'Castiglione's lines on the death of Raphael', and a night-song by Camillus Capilupus—this latter because it calls forth this new old truth: The old gods and tutelar deities are no mere machinery for the decoration of poetry, but the very spirits of the trees and meres. The nymph is . . . the very soul of the forest[.]

Pound's interest is wholly committed to this vision, and it is virtually a confession of faith when he declares 'the old gods are not really dead'. Evidently 'renaissance' meant to him, rather than the recovery of mere book-learning, that 'the old gods' should become real presences in the mind. One wonders what McDaniel had made of his related declaration, in an essay offering an otherwise 'Germanic' comparison of Martial X.v and Ovid's 'Ibis', that 'By the very force of his conception Ovid has recreated the old gods and given them back their power.' It becomes clear that Pound too wanted to revivify the perennial myths and to sing, after Metastasio, 'the Golden Age . . . still living in the hearts of the innocent.' And if this made him a 'misfit' in the university whose Fellow he was, then so much the worse for the university.

In June 1907, with no doctorate and no plans, he thought of making 'a little book' of satirical verses to be dedicated 'to my professors'. In these— they are mostly modelled on Kipling's 'Barrack Room Ballads'—he is 'the black sheep of the college' whom they had 'fired', 'slung out', 'expurgated'. They, meanwhile, 'sat tight as biler nuts on the eddicate machine', and by their '"germanic" system of graduate study & insane specialization in the INANITIES' made art 'bow down in homage / to scholarship's zinc-plated bull'. They had 'Tried to smother all the glory / of [his Balaam's] asininity'; they had bound and cramped him in their prison of philology; they had put him on the rack of their Ph.D. hell. But, like Farinata in Dante's hell, he would look down on them with 'royal scorn'; he would come forth to 'know each / Grass blade a special gift of God / And every wind his spirit'—'For the world is fair an' wide . . . For the black sheep'. So 'Cheer up! / Cheer up!'

Given that he could regard his being driven out of the university as a fortunate fall, it is puzzling that Pound persisted, for many years, in seeking academic recognition for his literary work. It may have been to please, or to appease, his parents. In 1920 he thought 'it might facilitate [his] getting a decent guarantee for a lecture tour'. But his main reason, he told his father, was that he wanted to test whether the university was genuinely committed to the advancement of learning. In 1910, according to Pound in 1920, Rennert had told him 'that he would accept *The Spirit of Romance*, [his] translations of Guido Cavalcanti and the work [he] then proposed to do on Arnaut Daniel in lieu of the usual Ph.D. thesis.' He had also said he would secure him a fellowship so that he could return to the university. But when it was objected that Pound was not intending to 'continue a professor' Rennert 'backed down'. That showed, in Pound's view, that 'the advancement of learning' had come to mean no more than 'continue a professor'—though he also believed 'there was the university's personal loathing of me behind that decision'. Then in 1920 Homer Pound, with Ezra's encouragement and possibly at his instigation, asked Dr Schelling if the university would award Pound the doctorate on the terms Rennert had thought acceptable. Schelling deviously and effectively made sure the university would not. 'Mr Pound...has done none of the work demanded' for the degree of Ph.D., he advised the Faculty. As Pound pointed out, at the very least the twelve units of his MA would be counted towards the Ph.D. He tried the university once more in 1931, this time offering as original philological research his *Guido Cavalcanti Rime* which was just about to be published. The 'proper University authorities' consulted, and decided that while the Cavalcanti edition could be submitted for examination as a thesis, Pound would first 'have to return to the University to fulfil the [outstanding] requirements for the degree', these being now accurately reported as 'six units'. Pound took this as proof that the university just did not want original research. Recalling Schelling's declaration that 'The University is not here for the exceptional man', he concluded 'the "university" is dead'.

But that is what he had thought all along—why go on proving it? The only point in doing so would be that he still held to an ideal of what the university ought to be. 'Dead' though it might be in Philadelphia, it still stood for something in his mind, for the authority and power there should be in the living universe of human knowledge. That its self-serving guardians, the professors, should react with personal animosity to his efforts to provoke them into living up to his ideal encouraged him to feel that it was he who was the true defender of live learning. They exercised the power, but he would assume the authority—the authority of alienated superiority. As an outsider he could have no power to reform the institution. He could only go on insisting, with scorn born of disappointment, that it was not what it ought to be. We will find the pattern repeated, but on a major and tragic scale, in Pound's later raging relations with the government of his country.

3 : First Poems: 1901–1908

Dryad

Pound thought he had found his Beatrice—she who should show the young poet his way to paradise—at a Hallowe'en party in Philadelphia in 1901. Her given name was Hilda Doolittle, and she was just 15, still two years from graduating from Friends Central High School. Pound was just 16, in his Freshman year at Penn. Hilda's mother, Helen Eugenia Wolle, belonged to a prominent family in the mystical Moravian brotherhood of Bethlehem, Pennsylvania; her father was Penn's Flower Professor of Astronomy and Director of the Flower Observatory; and the family— Hilda had five brothers—lived close to the Observatory in the semi-rural suburb of Upper Darby. In the woods and fields of Upper Darby, alone or with parties of friends, Hilda was in her element. A tree-sprite or wood nymph was what she wanted to be at that time. She became Pound's first muse, and his first love; but she was a muse with a mind of her own, and never a Beatrice.

Some years into their romance, between 1905 and 1907, Pound put together a little collection of poems in typescript which he bound in vellum and presented to her as 'Hilda's Book'. The first poem, as if approaching her on her own terms, addressed her as 'Child of the grass' and invoked 'All the old lore / Of the forests & woodways'. But then the most striking feature of the poems that followed is that they did not sustain the promised vision of the Golden Age with its pagan deities and elemental creatures. Instead the dominant language and sentiments are the clichés of romanticized Christianity, awash with vague longings for sublimation and transcendence. Several poems speak 'of mystic wings that whirr / Above me when within my soul do stir / Strange holy longings'. The fluttering benediction of her fingers laid on his—this is the unfortunate idiom of his ecstasies—lifts him above all terrene things. It is as if he had been led by his literary mentors, Dante and Dante Gabriel Rossetti, to look for a blessèd damozel beaming him up to heaven, and was unable to get that image out of his mind. In 'La Donzella Beata' he does try to

34

bring Rossetti's 'Blessèd Damozel' down to earth—he would have her 'Soul / Caught in the rose hued mesh / Of o'er fair earthly flesh' stoop down to be his light on earth, rather than cry from 'the gate / Of high heaven' for him to come to her there—but he can't escape the borrowed idiom and its decadent sentimentality.

There were other poems, not included in 'Hilda's Book', in the same idealizing and romanticizing vein, such as 'Sestina for Ysolt'. Frankly begun as an exercise to pass the time on a rainy day, this is a technically accomplished and wholly conventional set of variations upon 'eyes' and 'stars' and 'dreams'—'deep eyes like pools wherein the stars / Gleam out reflected in their loveliness', and so forth. Hilda, one gathers, was unimpressed by this sort of thing—it just wasn't her:

> "You lie to tell me that my eyes are fair
> The dreams you think you see lie mirrored there
> Are thine, I am but shadow in the play."

That was how Pound represented her protest, in an unpublished poem in which he went on to claim that his soul had eyes to see the truth of her—

> I found your inner childhood and the truth
> And will you mock me that the mirror shows
> But what the blind ones saw before I came?

If he had done that, Hilda might well have retorted, it was not in his poeticisings after the fashion of Rossetti.

In fact there were a few poems in which his imagination was more in accord with hers. 'She hath some tree-born spirit of the wood / About her', he wrote in one, 'The moss-grown kindly trees, meseems, she could / As kindred claim'. He called her 'Dryad', and she liked that and for the rest of her life would sign herself 'Dryad' when writing to him. She had wanted him, according to the highly stylized exercise in self-definition which she wrote many years later, 'to define and to make definable' her real being which was as yet 'a mirage, a reflection of some lost incarnation, a wood maniac, a tree demon, a neuropathic dendrophil'. Adolescent, living intensely in her imagination, she dreamt of getting free of the cocoon of the commonplace and the conventional by identifying with natural phenomena, especially with trees or with sea-coast flowers impervious to the battering of wind and storm.

Pound sympathized with her dream, but without making it his own. In 'The Tree', the one poem in 'Hilda's Book' not in the idiom of Pre-Raphaelite idealism, and the only one which he thought worth preserving in his collected poems, there is a kind of initiation into 'the old lore of forests and woodways'—

> Naetheless I have been a tree amid the wood
> And many new things understood
> That were rank folly to my head before.

The things newly understood are the contrasting myths of the metamorphoses into trees of Daphne and of Baucis and Philemon. Yet the poem is not so much about being changed from the human into the mythopoetic as it is about understanding how others may be changed. For the poet maintains his own identity and speaks as the observing, myth-conscious mind, not as one caught up in the immediate experience. The nearest he would come to the metamorphosis Hilda desired was in 'A Girl', first published in 1912. Here, with the simplicity if not the depth of one of Wordsworth's 'Lucy' poems, he first renders the experience directly—

> The tree has entered my hands,
> The sap has ascended my arms,
> The tree has grown in my breast—
> Downward,
> The branches grow out of me, like arms.

Then the poet separates himself out to affirm her imagined state of being—

> Tree you are,
> Moss you are,
> You are violets with wind above them.
> A child—*so* high—you are,
> And all this is folly to the world.

It seems that their youthful love for each other was sustained as much by their sharing this secret imagined world as by their passionate kisses. In her memoir of their relationship written late in her life Hilda remembered the ecstasy of their kissing, and how she had wanted to sustain 'the perfection of the fiery moment'. Their engagement in 1905 was a way of going on with the fiery kisses. (Her father, doing the right conventional thing, did not approve, seeing Pound as 'nothing but a nomad'.) But what bound them together in mind was the excitement and delight of being able to share their intense inner lives of thought and dream which very few others could relate to. And Hilda was caught up in Ezra's literary enthusiasms. They read 'the Iseult and Tristram story' together, and she became 'Ysolt'. They read Swinburne and William Morris—she remembered his reading

'The Haystack in the Floods' with 'passionate emotion'. They read Marcel Schwob's *The Childen's Crusade*, which for Pound was 'the great deep symbol of the pilgrimmage we all make each in the path of his own radius unto the great white unity which is the end and centre'. They read of course Rossetti's translation of *La Vita Nuova* and his 'The Blessèd Damozel'. Most of all they read Balzac's Swedenborgian romance *Séraphita*, about bringing the human soul fully alive by teaching it to see through earthly things to the divine goodness and beauty behind and beyond them. There may have been as much of Swedenborg as of Rossetti behind 'Hilda's Book'. For Hilda, Ezra was at that time the very image 'of adolescence in its Ariel, or Séraphita stage'.

When she wrote that in her memoir Hilda would have been aware that Shakespeare's Ariel—a tricksy spirit of air and fire whose great fear was of being shut up in a tree—would be the very opposite of herself as a dryad. Again, as Séraphita, Pound would not be content to have her define herself as an elemental tree spirit, but would want her to become an illuminated soul, a spirit of divine light. It is in effect as Séraphita that he was speaking in 'The Summons', when he wrote 'I can not bow to woo thee' as 'In that gay youth I had but yester-year'—

> But as I am ever swept upward
> To the centre of all truth
> So I must bear thee with me
> Rapt into this great involving flame,
> Calling ever from the midst thereof,
>   'Follow! Follow!'

But Hilda no more wanted to follow than to lead him into a Dantescan beatific vision.

Some such imperfect sympathies, amounting ultimately to profound differences, caused them to drift apart about the time Pound was dropping out of graduate school. In an unfinished draft towards a long poem, probably written in mid-1907, these lines appear to be placing Hilda 'at the gate of Childhood' rather than at 'the gate to Life':

> The Beatrice face.
> The illusion. The passionate kissing
> and return of dustiness of the way.

Then in January 1908, in a draft of a poem closely modelled on Dante's *Divine Comedy*, Pound had his poet encounter in the Earthly Paradise 'one whom in thy youth / thou calldst Hilda', and she tells him that they had missed each other because she had 'escaped through the flowers' of the field of pleasure while he was studying 'the cliff of knowledge'. He then had her say, like Dante's Matilda directing him on to Beatrice, 'there is one fairer / than I, being able / to speak unto all / whereas I am silent / & am not save with / thee'.

The idea that Hilda had no real existence save through him has its absurdity; yet it is what she might well have encouraged him to think in their time of psychic intimacy. Much later, in *Her*, she would so directly reject the notion as to imply that it had once been in the air between them. He could not have been 'her authentic intellectual progenitor', she would declare, for in the end only she could conceive her true self. The chapter ends with Her in this vein: 'I am the Tree of Life. Tree ... I am ... I am ... HER exactly. Her caught Her to herself.' Before this she has come to a realization of why she does not, can not love George, the Ezra figure. It was his always dragging in literature, and foreign literatures, that did it; and, at one particular moment, his dramatically intoning Longfellow in a funny voice—'This is the forest primeval!'. With that, 'George, so beautiful, healing her by his presence', became 'a hideous harlequin being funny on a woodpath'.

Pound might have been drawing on his own sense of the end of their romance in the third part of 'Near Perigord' (1915). There had been the Séraphitic ecstasy:

> And the great wings beat above us in the twilight
> And the great wheels in heaven
> Bore us together

Then the discovery of difference and estrangement:

> 'But I am like the grass, I can not love you.'
> Or, 'Love, and I love and love you,
> And hate your mind, not *you*, your soul, your hands.'

'There is no greater incomprehension', Pound would write in canto 29, 'Than between the young and the young'. Looking back at the two of them together from the distance of twenty years he would see H.D. as 'the mythological exterior' lying on the moss in the forest and questioning him about Darwin; and himself as a 'Lusty Juventus', aspiring 'To step in the tracks of his elders', and answering her with Dante's ' "Deh! nuvoletta ... " / So that she would regret his departure.' There had been more to it than that though—Dante was beseeching a lady not to distract him from his love of Beatrice in paradise.

So these two rarely gifted people fell out of love into their separate identities, 'each in the path of his own radius'. What Hilda was and wanted to be was not what Pound wanted of her; and what Ezra was and wanted to be was not what Hilda wanted of him. In the end it was their radical difference that defined them, not what they could share. Pound was striving, as yet ineptly, and by imitation, to realize a world or a paradise outside himself. Hilda was striving to be purely herself, uncontaminated by what was other and therefore alien to her. So far as Ezra could identify his mind with hers she felt the need of him and loved him—she wanted that to be absolute. But when he was on some other track she felt it as a falling off, a failure of the high seriousness she expected of him. And Ezra, who was no doubt at times 'a hectic, adolescent, blundering, untried, mischievous, and irreverent male youth', as Hilda described him when altogether out of sympathy with him, went his own way. It was not the end of their relationship—that would endure in one form and another to the end of their lives.

Katherine Ruth Heyman

The one fairer than herself whom Ezra had Hilda announce as his true Beatrice, because 'able to speak unto all', was a concert pianist and composer, Katherine Ruth Heyman. She would become a renowned interpreter of Scriabin; and she would be remembered by some of Pound's critics for her interests in Swedenborg, spiritualism, reincarnation and 'the occult' in general. Hilda, jealously sensing that Pound and this woman had 'a secret, a power' which she had not, lapsed into the WASPish prejudice she despised and tried to put her down as 'common . . . obviously Jew or German'. For the young poet himself she was 'the lady dwelling in his inmost soul', and he credited her with playing to him 'power at life's morn'. In an unpublished poem, 'To Baltasare Levy: Zionist', he portrayed her as 'thy sister dreamer / keen-souled, far-visioned'; then as 'mother of thy keen out dreaming / She whose very touch can set ones heart a teeming / with scorn of out worn selves / with dares of wonder'.

Ten years older than Pound, Katherine Ruth Heyman was already well launched into her musical career when they met in 1904. She performed in Utica in that year and Pound may have heard her there on one of his escapes from Hamilton. That summer he was hearing her play occasionally in New York. 'It's a comfort', he wrote home, 'to find a person with brains & sense'. At least once he took Hilda with him to hear her in Philadelphia—Hilda, in her later account, was in no mood to appreciate the concert. By July 1906, in 'Scriptor Ignotus', in the persona of one 'Bertold Lomax, English Dante scholar and mystic', dead in 1723 with his ' "great epic" ' unachieved, Pound was dedicating himself to honour

39

'K.R.H.', as Dante had Beatrice, in his own 'great forty-year epic / That you know of'. Inspired by the beauty of her music he would make 'A new thing / As hath not heretofore been writ'. One notes that whereas Dante had his Beatrice lead him to a vision of the divine order, Pound's preoccupation in this early poem is with the creation of his own 'new thing'.

In 'Blake's Rainbow' (1907), the earliest of his drafts towards an epic closely modelled on Dante's, 'K.R.H.' is identified with the power of Music, one of the 'three Powers in Man', according to Blake, 'of conversing with Paradise'. At a desperate moment in this draft the poet is discouraged by the mockery of the Sphinx, and the lady of his 1906 poem appears as a 'torch before life's gate'. This is Blake's 'gate of the resurrection of the body', which the soul passes through when the imagination perceives that truly all mortal things are immortal spirit. In another draft the lady is invoked as 'The Spirit of Power dark, by the Sphinx / bidding me be strong to go forward. / I am the gate to Life. my torch / ... and later calling in THE meeting of the Winds.' Again there is a suggestion of the Blakean cleansing of the doors of perception: 'Because of the light within us we began to see / in the perspective, all men as pearls upon the golden thread'.

'The Meeting of the Winds' is an unpublished poem in which two persons—the internal evidence would make them K.R.H. and E.P.—figure as two great winds meeting and tangling, blowing each other free of earth-dust and mounting to the stars, where they must disentangle and separate. 'It is well. We both blow to the gates of God', the poem closes, 'AVE atque VALE'. That this ideal spiritual relationship was all in the head, and possibly all in Pound's head, seems clear from that. And this is confirmed by a rare personal statement in an unpublished note concerning the soul's happiness:

comes a wonder woman that lifts him to the stars and makes him see visions of all heavens and sweeps him clear from earth . . For me some helter skelter dabs of calf love., and the Amor of the philosophers of Bologna, well regulated, psychic,. once half done for one that was not great enough to hold it (or me) once too great for my lesser selves to keep pace with.

That could refer, if I may speculate for once, to Viola; to Dante's third heaven, as explicated by Dr Shepard; to Hilda; and, not quite climactically, to K.R.H. This entry in an early notebook might be a record of the 'too great' experience:

First there was a vague sense of joy [...] the sense of music was never absent [...] / allowing our thoughts to be in harmony and unimpeded / I beheld our 'deus in nobis' / then spake commonly in us / the deep to which I called has answered me even in accordance with the promise of the older singer / Even as a preparation for a wider song

'These high moments are not with us alway', Pound added, 'Yet out of this dust are reared the petals of the 3rd kingdom'.

Katherine Ruth Heyman gave Ezra a diamond ring which had belonged to her mother in token of spiritual friendship—to 'keep till we are both very old'. Apart from that, strangely little is known of her sense of their relationship. In her memoirs there is only this barest mention: '1904 Pound'. What we have is altogether what Ezra made of it in an imagination eager for the sublime. I would guess that she could be his Beatrice or *donna ideale* just because she was not an insistently actual and other presence in Ezra's life as Hilda, the 'illusory' one, was. A year or two later, after some months of closer contact when Pound had been acting as a supernumerary promoter of her concerts in Venice and London—he styled himself her 'agent'—he would refer to K.R.H. as ''er bally 'Ighness' and 'her bally Ugliness', and complain of her high-handedness.

Aesthetics

Underlying Pound's quest for a Beatrice was his commitment to a most high-minded, ambitious and demanding conception of art. In a letter giving some account of himself to Viola Baxter in October 1907 he told her that his most real interest was in 'art and ecstasy', ecstasy being the 'the sensation of the soul in ascent', and art 'the sole means of transmitting, of passing on that ecstasy to others'. Further, since such ecstasy is 'the factive, potent, exalting' essence of religion, art is and does what religion only now and then rises to. He chooses therefore to interpret Swedenborg's 'angelic language' as 'artistic utterance'; he approves of Blake's holding that it is by music, poetry and painting that 'we ascend to meet God in the air'; and he brings in Coleridge's playing upon the Greek words Καλόν and Καλοῦν to make of the Beautiful 'a calling to the soul'.

The love of beauty, he wrote elsewhere, when it is a great passion, burns away 'our meaner qualities, our lesser selves', leaving the soul 'nothing save as a channel for truth, or beauty.' The passionate experience of music, such as of Isolde's 'Liebestod', 'can tear away the husks of a light way of looking at important things, which is the beginning and end of hell'. Again, a passionate experience of the natural world could be ecstatic, as of seeing 'the dawn's reflexion' in the West and 'feeling the flowing essences of beauty (here chiefly colour as I remember) until they gradually grouped themselves into form'. From such flashes of 'cosmic consciousness', he noted, rise the ancient myths of metamorphosis, of the origin of the demi-gods, and of Dionysus and Eleusis. That would make of his 'aube of the west dawn' a mystical revelation of the deathless source of all things in the living universe.

Finally, and above all, there is the ecstasy of poetry. In an essay dated July 31 '07, written partly in verse and partly in prose, and apparently provoked by Dr Schelling's telling him that he was wasting his time, and provoked also by the charge that he lacked originality, he asserted the rightness of his learning from and following Dante, or Browning. 'When one stumbles on a flaming blade that pierces him to extacy / is he to hide it . . . or to cry some greater truth higher and more keen.' He cited Browning's *Aristophanes' Apology* and *Balaustion's Adventure*, and placed himself as Browning had in the royal line of poets. Being 'continuously filled with burnings of admiration for the great past masters', he would 'at least strive upward *a rivider le stelle*'.

In all of this young Ezra could be seen as simply the pure product of his Presbyterian upbringing crossed with his reading in the then current lit-erature of 'the religion of beauty'. 'One read Fiona Macleod, and Dowson and Symons', he later recalled, 'One was guided by Mr Mosher . . . One was drunk with "Celticism"'. Thomas Bird Mosher of Portland, Maine, 'the celebrated aesthetic publisher and book pirate', specialized in writings by and of interest to the English 'aesthetic' movement. In his monthly chapbook, *The Bibelot*, and in finely produced limited editions, he offered his subscribers Fitzgerald's *Rubaiyyat* and Swinburne's versions of Vil-lon, Bédier's *Tristan and Iseult*, the *Pervigilium Veneris* and the idylls of Theocritus. He presented a thoroughly representative selection of the 'aesthetic' literature of the nineteenth century, from its honorary elders Blake and Shelley, through the Pre-Raphaelite Brotherhood and Pater to the Nineties and the Celtic Twilight, with Yeats somehow looming over it all at the end and Dante always somewhere in the background. This was the modern literature of its time. Mosher rejected Pound's 'Alba' in August 1905 as too 'old world', and advised him 'selections have to be modern to meet with much attention'.

It was a literature of visionariness and of dreams and of revolt against materialism. 'Fiona Macleod' (the pen-name of William Sharp (1855–1905)), declared that he wanted a poetry to make authentic 'the reveries of the imagining mind wandering in a world publicly foregone yet inwardly actual'—the 'otherworld' of Yeats's 'The Land of Heart's Desire'. He wrote of 'a visionary passion for beauty which is of immortal things, beyond the temporal beauty of what is unstable and mortal'. Pound was in that vein when he told Viola Baxter 'I give you [in my verse] that part of me which is most real...most nearly related to the things that [are] more permanent than this smoke wraith the earth'. Ernest Rhys wrote in *The Bibelot* of Macleod's 'mythopoeic faculty' in which 'the soul has to learn to become "one with the wind and the grass and with all that lives and moves"'—he might have been writing of Pound's 'The Tree' and 'La Fraisne'. 'The new mysticism', Rhys called this. Others saw the aesthetic movement as a whole as a new religion, one which found its revelation in the ecstatic apprehension of ideal beauty.

While Pound was clearly a confirmed devotee of this religion of beauty, in time he came to practise it with a measure of critical detachment. As in 'The Tree' or 'A Girl' he could give himself up to a state of mind and at the same time observe and understand its process, and thus attain an independent and original relation to it. He was decisively distancing himself from Fiona Macleod in the satirical judgement that 'The idealist too often misleads us to think of [beauty] as something found only in the "light that never shone" buried neath the snows of yesteryear or hidden in the purple land of dreams'. For himself he wanted rather to be a 'practical Idealist', or an 'ideal inspired realist'—one 'who would make the utmost of what the universe affords'. 'May I not be the rejector', he prayed.

That attitude is the basis of his critiques of Dowson and of what he called, parodying 'The Celtic Twilight', 'the crepuscular spirit in modern poetry'. Dowson's 'In Spring' had evoked the coming alive of nature in woods and flowers and birds etc., only to conclude 'But the spring of the soul, the spring of the soul / Cometh no more for you or for me.' Pound's riposte, in 'Autumnus (To Dowson–Antistave)', was to evoke the dreary world-weariness implicit in that conclusion, and then to turn it around in the assertion that 'the Spring of the Soul' might yet claim its own. He also wrote two versions of an 'Anti-stave' to Dowson's 'In Tempore Senectutis', to assert that love even in old age need not weary and go cold. 'When I read Dowson', he wrote in a note which hovers uncertainly between prose and verse,

> I am ashamed to call my
> halt lines verse, ashamed to dream I might be poet.
> Yet comes the answer, 'He hath no strong glad message to give
>   to men that be over weary.
>   It is only in the power of your optimism
> that you can succeed; in the strength that you
> have or must have. [...]
> This means the sacrifice of poignancy
> and thou must be strong in compensation therfor.'

Pound made a bold public statement of this position in 'Revolt—Against the Crepuscular Spirit in Modern Poetry', published in London in 1909:

> I would shake off the lethargy of this our time,
>   and give
> For shadows—shapes of power
> For dreams—men.

He questions whether 'It is better to dream than do', and answers 'Aye! If we dream great deeds, strong men, / Hearts hot, thoughts mighty'; but 'No! If we dream pale flowers, / Slow-moving pageantry of hours . . .'. But 'if we be damn'd to be not men but only dreams, / Then let us be such dreams the world shall tremble at / And know we be its rulers though but dreams'.

Pound's revolt amounted to a complete turning around of the religion of beauty and its sacred books of dreams and visions. He was directing it back to engage with the grey world it was meant to be an escape from. 'Make-strong old dreams lest this our world lose heart' would be the dominant motif of *A Lume Spento* (1908) and *Personae* (1909). 'Grace Before Song', at the start of *A Lume Spento*, would pray that his songs might be 'to this grey folk' as rain drops 'that dream and gleam and falling catch the sun', and so are 'bright white drops upon a leaden sea'. He told Viola Baxter, as he had told an unimpressed Dr Schelling, that it was his theory that 'The end of all art is that ye might have life and have it more abundantly'.

The 'ye' in 'that ye might have life' would be all-embracing, not restricted to aesthetes only. Pound's 'Dawn Song', published in *Munsey's Magazine* in December 1906, caroled, in the manner of Carman and Hovey's *Songs of the Open Road*,

> God hath put me here
> In earth's goodly sphere
>   To sing the joy of the day,
> A strong glad song,
> If the road be long
>   To my fellows in the way.

But such populist singing is in a strikingly different realm from his ecstatic 'blowing to the gates of God', and Pound felt the division. He did want to write his poem of heaven and hell for everyone. Thirty years later he still recalled as a shock that comes once in a lifetime a tough bloke's reproving him for hoarding learning. He was on a late night train from Philadelphia with his pile of books, and was told in 'a thick and heavy voice: "Huh! 'n yuh fellers! Wot got a lot of learnin' wouldn't GIVE any of that!"' He took his being 'envied...to the point of dislike' as a 'call to order'. Yet he acknowledged that it was an ideal difficult to maintain, 'this belief in the comprehension of others, this feeling that what shines before us with such effulgence can not but be visible to them'. 'Slowly and unwillingly', he conceded, we 'learn the rightness of Dante's *Voi Altri pochi* (*Ye other Few*)'—the equivalent of Milton's 'fit audience though few'. Hence the dedication of *A Lume Spento*, '*to such as love this same beauty that I love, somewhat after mine own fashion*'. And still it was not the love of beauty for beauty's sake that was driving him, but the determination to set a strong dream at the heart of the everyday world. That was to be the motive and the scandal of his yet unwritten epic.

False starts

Pound made at least three attempts to get his 'great forty-year epic' started between dedicating himself to the task in 'Scriptor Ignotus' and temporarily giving it up around January 1908. In 'Blake's Rainbow' he was seeking to assume the power of the prophetic imagination—the power which perceives the immortal spirit in everything—by 'gathering ore from every literature in the world and smelting it to fusion and to gold in that great flame himself'. He mines Blake and Yeats, Ezekiel, Job and Ibsen; is encouraged by 'KRH'; and finally has Dante 'Virgil' him among the 'high thundrous things' of Paradise. By entering into their 'Images in his Imagination', as Blake urged, he would find out the 'high mysteries' they had known and synthesize a new prophetic wisdom. The fragment breaks down, however, with the recognition that 'the scope of things...stretches out beyond my vision'.

The second attempt, taking up where the first broke down, was even bolder. It appears to have been written after Pound had abandoned his formal studies at Penn, and while he was feeling at once joyfully liberated from the prison-house of Philology and eager if not desperate to justify his existence as a poet with no prospects. 'ORBI CANTUM PRIMUM COS-MOPOLITI E TOLERENTIAE CANO' it begins with a flourish of the grandeur that was Rome, then shifts into the *afflatus* that was Whitman:

> The First Great Song Of All The World Cosmopolite Of Tolerence I Sing
> For I have stripped off the bands of custom
>   and the swaddling clouts of shame
> And my heart is free as the West wind
>
> . . . .
>
> Wherfor, I being of no set and land bound country
> But of that country of the spirit wherein I am at one

> with them of the spirit
> Whose word I am : being of myself nothing,
> A hollow reed thru whom is the song.
> I AM THE VOICE OF 'HOI POLLOI' CRYING IN THE SUN

This is after Whitman, but it is no 'song of myself' in Whitman's sense. The claim to be the voice of the people is directly contradicted by the declaration of allegiance, not to the American land and its people, but 'to them of the spirit / Whose word I am'. The contradiction can be resolved, but only by envisioning 'hoi polloi', the common multitude, as united in a spiritual state:

> For when man shall have put away the things of Tyre and Sidon
> of the flesh and of the mind,
> Then shall mankind be one spirit

This would wipe out Whitman's universe of densely marshalled particularities, all his diversity of things sensed, of persons glimpsed at, of lore and learning to stretch the mind. It would consume his democracy of the American Everyman in a sun symbolic of the realm of pure spirit, 'the great white unity that is the end and centre'.

That confident opening of 'The First Great Song Of All The World' is followed by several pages of fragments and notes in which 'the voice of "hoi polloi" speaks mainly in 'visionary' or 'prophetic' pastiche of the Bible and of Dante. Two images out of Pound's own experience make brief contact with the known world, one recalling seeing into the many avenues converging upon 'the Place de la Triumphe de l'etoile' in Paris, the other of 'coming from Toledo to Madrid / at the right hour of evening' and seeing 'the last sun on the water ditches / as of a myriad little fire of bivouac'. The one moment of significant surprise is when Dante appears to him in the setting of the entrance to his *Inferno* and says ' "Come and see the place where Hell lay" '.

Pound appears to have judged that in this draft he was 'seeking to sing the song of all wisdom before his time'. But 'out of the smoke of his failure came answering ... "Seek not the song of all wisdom but of all power, which is LOVE".' That marked the beginning of a profound reorientation. The third attempt to get his epic started is dated 'Jan 19 ['08]'. This time it is in the form of a medieval dream-vision, and begins at the broken gate of Hell with Dante explaining that 'high omnipotence by light hath pierced hell / & cast down the keepers thereof'. Our poet then comes upon 'the searchers for dogmas / that go not onward to the light, / nor think thereon', and who forbid 'that others go forward untill / they have accurately determined [the way] / delaying their own & others salvation'. After this first episode the draft breaks off, and is followed by notes giving the idea or schema of the intended poem. It is evident that Dante's *Divine Comedy* is now to be the direct model, and that Dante is to be the sole guide as Virgil was his. But Pound means to encounter figures of his own invention, and to judge them by his own scale of values. Thus where Dante's first encounter in Hell is with the trimmers, those who were neither true nor false, Pound's is with the 'dogmatics' who blind themselves to the light which is love and prevent others from finding their own ways to it. His concern, now that Hell is no more, is not with sin, damnation and redemption, but with degrees of enlightenment; and with the working of the divine light in this world and not in other or afterworlds.

This is the schema for the three divisions of the poem:

A   B   C

Hell in world / good in world / spirit

body   mind   soul

In A^1 the dogmatics were to be followed by the rich 'carrying worthless ore'; by anarchists, 'each... trying to dominate his neighbour'; by hypocrites awarded 'sham heaven'; by murderers unrepentant in a pit; by 'oppressors of the poor'; and by 'he that sold women's bodys ... some openly / some indirectly'. A^2 has only 'lines of hooded figures / hollow, having sold their souls'. A^3, suddenly topical and political, discovers beneath the surface of a drying mud pool the 'Czar– criminal / weakness / (Witte trying to draw him on)'. First in B^1 is 'Father—'(aiding Italians in foreign land)'; then 'Swinburne clinging to Greeks'; followed in the first light ('as the rising of a star / (Bethlehem)'), by 'Lincoln & the aiders / —charity, no malice'. B^2 gives notations for the 'field of pleasure / & cliff of study'; and B^3 for 'Sky / Elysium ... mirage of holy city / that thou mayst / know its verity'. The final notes, B^4, have 'one whom in thy youth / thou calldst Hilda' announcing 'one fairer than I'. There is nothing at all in this set of notes for C, the realm of spirit.

Pound appears to have made no further attempts at his epic for a number of years, possibly not until 1915. At this time, in 1907 and 1908, he still had everything to learn as to how he might achieve it. He knew it should progress from some sort of hell through some sort of purgatory to some sort of paradise. He had realized that love more than wisdom should be the motive. And he knew that he would not sing of himself, but be 'a hollow reed' through which the experience and the knowledge of others would sound. 'My own prejudices are not materia poetica', he told Williams, the student of *materia medica*, and that went for his own 'personality' as well. But what he had yet to discover, at least in these precocious attempts at his epic, was, firstly, his proper material, and then what to do with it.

He identified what may have seemed simply a technical problem. Though he had made his 'century of sonnets...striving for the cadences / of sweetest line that bow may draw / from out the viol of the soul', when it came to having 'some real thing to say' he would 'blurt it out bald as Browning...no pre raphaelite zitherns and citoles', and 'in a confounded hodge-podge' worse than Whitman's 'abomnible versifycation'. He knew now that rhyme would hobble the prophetic voice; and he knew that he had to break up 'Browning's dialect... the so-called iambic pentameter, or englische decasylab / movement'. His marking of the metre of one unpublished poem shows him working at 'bustin up' the iambic measure:

Ī ăm ă hŏllŏw rēed   Thĕ lēaf ŏf thĕ trēe thăt quĭvĕrs

Bŭt thĕ sōng ĭs blōwn thrŭ mē   Whĕn āll lēaves ĕlse ăre stīll

Ī ăm thĕ bēatĕn strĭngs ŏf thĕ lŭte   Ī ăm thĕ hōllŏw plăce ĭn thĕ rōck

Ănd thĕ lēaf ŏf thĕ Āspĕn tree.   Thăt wĭnd ŏf mў tīme shăll fīll.

Sometimes, he told Williams, speaking here of his shorter poems, he used 'rules of Spanish, Anglo-Saxon, and Greek metric'. But for 'the real thing' that he had to say, metric was not what was needed. 'We have had enough of metric...it is the inner thing that must be renewed'. When the spirit spoke in verse it should be 'Always the spirit within / Shaping the form without'. But this is to talk not of technique as such but of inspiration, of whatever it is that charges a poem's words with meaning.

And what exactly was this would-be shaping 'spirit'? 'Spirit' is a key word in Pound's early aesthetic, yet the more he invokes it the less definable it becomes. It is 'the inner thing', associated with 'the soul', with 'wisdom', then with 'love'. In Dante's time these terms could be invested with the precise and subtle senses of philosophizing theologians and could shape a canzone or a *comedia*. But in the time of 'the religion of beauty' they rather expressed the loss of any definite object and told more of pathos than of power. It is only when Pound connects 'the spirit' with having something real to say that we seem to be within reach of a clear idea. But then his problem was to know just what was it that he had to say. He appears to have favoured the notion that it was to be drawn from others' writings. Yet as the unsuccessful drafts show, simply to do that was to write shapeless pastiche. What was lacking was his own shaping spirit, operating as a detached critical intelligence understanding and judging his materials.

When he took 'Dante and Browning as best models if one has any thing to say', he was perhaps thinking only of Dante's allegory and Browning's thought, of what they 'had to say'. Before long though he would come to see that their more vital contribution was the form of dramatic *persona*, the main form of Browning's *Men and Women,* and the form also of Dante's most impressive encounters, as with Francesca da Rimini or Brunetto Latini in the *Inferno.* The special virtue of this *persona* form is that the inner meaning is not so much in what is said by the speaker as in how that is received and judged by the hearer. It is in that critical processing of what is said that we will find the shaping spirit of Pound's successful poetry.

'A Lume Spento'

In 1908 Pound put together for publication a collection of forty-five of his shorter poems. He hoped they would impress the 'aesthetic' publisher Thomas Bird Mosher, but Mosher was not interested in the unknown poet. In June he was in Venice and there he had the collection printed at his own expense in an edition of 150 copies, with the title *A Lume Spento.* The variety of verse forms and measures, with some real mastery of rhythm and rhyme, showed how effectively he had been studying the craft of putting words together to make music as well as sense.[1] What

---

[1] I make out the following arrangement—

A.	Grace Before Song	B.	Li Bel Chasteus
	La Fraisne		That Pass Between the False Dawn
	Cino		In Morte De
	In Epitaphium Eius		Threnos
	Na Audiart		Comraderie
			Ballad Rosalind
	Villonaud for this Yule		
	A Villonaud		Malrin
	Mesmerism		Masks
	Fifine Answers		On His Own Face
	Anima Sola		The Tree
	In Tempore Senectutis		Invern
			Plotinus
	Famam Librosque Cano		Prometheus
	The Cry of the Eyes		Aegupton
	Scriptor Ignotus		
	Donzella Beata		Ballad for Gloom
			For E. McC.
	Vana		Salve O Pontifex!
			To The Dawn: Defiance
			The Decadence
			Redivivus

C. Fistulae: 'To make her madrigal'—Song—Motif—La Regina Avrillouse—A Rouse— Nicotine – In Tempore Senectutis: An Anti-stave for Dowson—Oltre La Torre: Rolando—*Make strong old dreams lest this our world lose heart.*

49

did not draw attention to itself, and has passed unnoticed ever since, was the revolutionary intent and the bold ambition implicitly declared in certain poems but most of all in the arrangement of the collection as a whole. There is throughout a determination to challenge and drive out the 'crepuscular spirit' from modern poetry. In its place there is to be the life-affirming spirit of Villon and Browning and Dante, with Pound himself as their modern successor. This covert but ambitious plotting is of greater interest now than most of the poems in themselves. (Only a third of them would be preserved in the definitive collected poems of 1926.)

The opening poem, 'Grace Before Song', struck a keynote with its dedication to bringing the light of the sun in song to 'this grey folk'. Then came 'La Fraisne' ('The Ash Tree'), apparently in the place of honour. It was to have been the title-poem of the volume, according to the title-page; and it was introduced by a substantial 'Note Precedent'. Now this note is wholly in the vein of Fiona Macleod's 'new mysticism'; and it associates the poem explicitly with 'Mr Yeats in his "Celtic Twilight"'. It cites one 'Janus of Basel', apparently translating from his Latin, to the effect that 'When the soul is exhausted of fire, then doth the spirit return unto its primal nature...Then becometh it kin to the faun and the dryad, a woodland dweller amid rocks and streams/ "*consociis faunis dryadisque inter saxa sylvarum*"'. (There is a footnote to this, but instead of giving a reference for the citation it refers impishly 'for contrast' to another treatise, the '"Daemonalitas" of the Rev. Father Sinistrari of Ameno [1600 circ.]'.) The poet tells the reader that he made this poem when in a Celtic Twilight mood, 'feeling myself divided between myself corporal and a self aetherial "a dweller by streams and in woodland", eternal because simple in elements'. The poem itself is spoken by one who is, or who would be, a simple ash tree. He had been 'a gaunt, grave councilor', has been hurt in love, and is now withdrawn from the councils and ways of men to curl up 'mid the boles of the ash wood' with a woodland pool for his love. The speaker is bidding for our sympathetic understanding. But Pound, out of persona, briskly told Williams 'the man is half- or whole mad'. Take that view and 'La Fraisne' becomes a dismissive critique of 'the new mysticism' and the 'Celtic Twilight'. Possibly the 'note precedent', even as it draws us into the poem's mood, should have alerted us to its madness. How do we reconcile, unless with a smile, the farrago of book learning with the state of primal nature? Is it not mildly amazing or else amusing when 'a self aetherial' declares itself 'a dweller by streams and in woodland'? Our poet is being either very naïve or very knowing about his mood.

His detachment was signalled of course by the dissonance between the promise of the sun's light in song in 'Grace before Song', and the crepuscular state of the soul in 'La Fraisne'. The detachment is confirmed by the shift into a quite different state of mind in 'Cino', the poem which follows it. In fact the two personae make a pair in the way that Browning's 'Andrea del Sarto' and 'Fra Lippo Lippi' may be paired. Cino, the bold lover and singer of women and of the sun, is just the opposite of La Fraisne; and about as crazy in his own lively, syncopating fashion.[2] And if the poet can enter into the one mood and then the other, he is clearly not confined to either nor yet to be defined by either. Mood-shifter, he may know many moods and be subject to none. Pound thought of this as a process of shedding 'himself in completely self-conscious characters': 'to make a mood; slough it off . . . and then endow it with an individual life of its own'.

In the next poem, 'In Epitaphium Eius', it seems we have the poet himself speaking Cino's epitaph. This takes a flatteringly philosophical view of his libertine passion, presenting him as one who 'loved the essence tho each casement bore / A different semblance than the one before.' Then 'Na Audiart' has another troubadour, Bertran of Born, putting together his unique lady by taking a trait from each of several ladies of Langue d'Oc—a variation upon Cino's supposed loving the One in the many. Like Cino, Bertran evidently has an eye for the many rather than the one. Yet he is a kind of idealist to Cino's realist—and he is the subtler musician.

Thus the first three personae present a small set of related and contrasting states of the mind in and out of love. Theirs are the states of mind of men dominated by their passions, whose place, in Pound's version of the Dantescan scheme, would be in hell. That judgement is nowhere stated, but it becomes implicit as we read on through the next ten or so poems. There is a clear progression from La Fraisne's lapsing out of any kind of higher life up to the poet's promise, in 'Scriptor Ignotus', to do as much for his ideal lady as Dante had done for Beatrice. Pound was in effect blocking out through these shorter poems, and in miniature, the epic of judgement he meant to write.

We may notice that Cino and Bertran are poets, and then that so too are the personae or the subjects of the next set of six poems, and that in the following set of five the poet himself appears as a poet. So for the first third of the collection the states of mind being studied are those of poets in their poems. In one way or another then the protagonist is always the poet, and his action is always his struggle to shape his world in verbal music. And

[2] Dante wrote a sonnet to Cino da Pistoia rebuking him for his fickleness in love. Cino replied in a sonnet of his own, confessing that since he had been a wanderer in exile 'one pleasure ever binds and looses me; / That so, by one same Beauty lured, I still / Delight in many women here and there.' (D. G. Rossetti, *Works* [1911], p. 353.)

this holds on two levels, for what is going on within each poem, and then for what is going on in the composition of the whole run of poems. The essential concern here is with poetry as a mode of being in the world, and with establishing an appropriate scale of values for it. Thus Bertran's is a finer mode of being than Cino's, and La Fraisne's is the lowest.

To appreciate the two imitations of Villon, and of Swinburne's Villon, we must of course ignore the fustian diction and attend just to the strong rhythms and challenging sentiments. Here are Villon's low-life thieves and murderers boldly refusing to mourn dead loves, or to lose heart in the face of death. Above them comes Browning, celebrated in the virtuoso versification of 'Mesmerism' as 'Clear sight's elector', and then imitated in an imagined answer to his Fifine's question, 'Why is it that, disgraced, they seem to relish life the more?' Above that is the defiantly unconventional poet of 'Anima Sola', who might be Swinburne, flying 'on the wings of an unknown chord / That ye hear not'. 'In Tempore Senectutis' presents two lovers in old age, past passion and yet unwearied and refined into 'strange night-wonder . . . that grows not old'. It is as if they had become only mind and spirit, at a far remove from La Fraisne and Cino.

With 'Famam Librosque Cano' (that is, 'I sing of books and of fame'), Pound appears to bring his own poetry into question. While another's songs will be sung by mothers to their children in the evening and be laughed at by the children to each other the next day, his will be forgotten in a book, its only audience a ragged scholar who years later picks it from the secondhand bookstall and wonders at 'the strange rare name'. In 'The Cry of the Eyes' the poet's eyes tell him they are tired of reading print, and want the colours of the world and sight of one 'Whose smile more availeth / Than all the age-old knowledge of thy books'. However, behind the self-deprecation of both poems lurks a secret pride, that his poems are not for 'the little mothers' and their children, and that he has both book lore and eager eyes.

In 'Scriptor Ignotus' the pride of the poet in his power is unbounded. Certainly he makes some gestures towards humility: his epic is unwritten, it might be but a child's toy, it would be but words, his power is not equal to Dante's. But through all that sounds the confident boast that he will be the Dante of his time, and more. This is the culmination of the sequence of poems from 'La Fraisne'. If La Fraisne represented the lowest state of being, then in 'Scriptor Ignotus' we have the poet representing himself as aspiring to the most exalted state of his poetic soul. Evidently this does not mean achieving a beatific vision in heaven. 'Donzella Beata' praises his lady for descending from heaven to light his 'shadowy path' on earth. And in 'Scriptor Ignotus' it is her 'earthly glory' he promises to increase—her immortality will be in his poem. It is the poem itself, his 'forty-year epic', that is to be the high achievement of his 'greater soul-self'. And in writing it he is not only to be the lineal successor to Bertran de Born and Villon and Browning and Dante, the great poets by whom he has just been possessed, but he will 'smelt to fusion' in himself all their diverse powers to write of hell, humanity, and heaven.

After that the rest of *A Lume Spento* could not be anything but anti-climactic. There is an instant drop in 'Vana', with its 'Little grey elf words crying for a song', into the fey vein then very popular of Madison Cawein's lyrical fairyland. Yet what we have to reckon with is that this too, childish as it seems after the sophisticated intelligence and over-reaching ambition of the first part of the collection, is to be included in Pound's gamut. Nothing poetic is alien to him. But there are discriminations, and gradations. Above all there is always the difference between what makes for a more abundant life, and what does not.

The second part of the collection, as I make out its divisions, has twenty poems in three sets. The first set of six poems is dominated by recessions from life and love into dream and death. 'Threnos' is the one that stands out. All of them, though some are after William Morris rather than Dowson, exhibit a decadent taste for the passing away of things. The second set has eight poems forming a kind of ascending chain of poetic being: rising from uncertain or unresolved states in 'Masks' and 'On his own face in a glass'; entering into elemental nature in 'The Tree'; being brought out of that by reading Longinus in winter ('Invern'); then up through 'Plotinus' and 'Prometheus' to a transcendental state in 'Aegupton'. The scheme is of more interest than the poems. In the third set, again of six poems, the gloom and death of the decadence are confronted and overcome by the affirmative powers of poetry. Swinburne is hailed as the high priest of the life-principle in 'Salve O Pontifex!—an hemichaunt'. Pound would, in 1917, dismiss the poem as 'balderdash'. In 1964 he would dismiss the entire collection as 'stale creampuffs'. What he knew then made him see in it only 'the superficiality of non-perception—neither eye nor ear'.

But what he had possessed in 1907 and 1908 were the advantages of his untried youth: fresh energies and exuberant optimism. The spirit of youth in its springtime asserts itself in the final part of *A Lume Spento*, a group of nine songs under the heading '*Fistulae*'. The *fistula*, as he explained in an essay on one of his Renaissance Latin poets published in 1908, was the pastoral Pan pipe, the true instrument of the Golden Age 'still living in the hearts of the innocent'. His own songs for the Pan pipe do not conjure up the classical nymphs and shepherds. But they do sing of love and the love of dream; they hymn the Queen of the Spring, and rouse the young to spring revels. These motifs are combined in 'Oltre La Torre: Rolando', in which the anti-type of Browning's Childe Roland frees the lady in the dark tower and breaks 'my Lord Gloom's yoke'. This Rolando sees the world not as a waste land but as 'The good green-wood'—'Ol-la! Ol-la! ... The good green-wood is free!' After that there is the closing affirmation: *Make strong old dreams lest this our world lose heart.'* In that 1908 essay Pound observed that 'the Celtic beauty of sadness ... sets us a-following the wind of lost desire'. The distinguishing feature of his own strong dream is that in it desire is unconstrained, joyful and potent.

4 : HELL AND DELIVERANCE

The gadfly

The letter about 'art and ecstasy' which Pound sent to Viola Baxter in October 1907 was written from 'Milligan Place, Crawfordsville', and signed with the 'EP' drawn out into a flying gadfly. This was now Pound's usual signature. The gadfly was in imitation of Whistler's butterfly monogram, more particularly as he had deployed it in witty riposte to Ruskin's attack on his 'Nocturne in Black and Gold: The Falling Rocket'. Ruskin had said that picture flung 'a pot of paint in the public's face'. Whistler retorted that 'Art should be independent of all clap-trap', by which he meant independent of 'emotions entirely foreign to it, as devotion, pity, love, patriotism, and the like.' His butterfly represented the creative spirit of the artist flying free of the materialism of 'the public's' perceptions and pieties; and in his 'Ten O'Clock' lecture, and throughout *The Gentle Art of Making Enemies* (1890), he drew it in a hundred variations, mocking, defying and gleefully triumphing over his critics. It became a butterfly with a long tail armed with a sting; and Pound's long-tailed gadfly emphasized that gleeful arming of art against the uncomprehending public.

The fact that Whistler had been born in America gave his example a special significance for Pound. Whistler had left for Paris and London when he was 21 and by his success in Europe had proved 'that being born an American does not eternally damn a man or prevent him from the ultimate and highest achievement in the arts'. He had shown others 'Who bear the brunt of our America / And try to wrench her impulse into art' that 'there's chance at least of winning through.'

Another dimension to Pound's gadfly monogram is indicated by H.D.'s recording that it was suggested by Ethel Voynich's *The Gadfly* (1897), a novel set in Italy in which the hero is an idealistic young socialist who gives his life for the liberation and unification of his country. He publishes 'political verse-lampoons for the Republican movement under the pseudonym "The Gadfly"', and his signature is 'the sketch of a gadfly with spread wings'. Pound could identify with that as well as with Whistler, wanting 'the ultimate and highest achievement in the arts' not just for the art's sake but in order to advance the public good, and to advance the American republic in particular.

Wabash College, Crawfordsville, Indiana

In the Fall of 1907, however, the common round of American life seemed set to trap the winged dreamer. He was expected to get a job and to marry and generally to fall into the way of his world. He heard through Penn Graduate School that Wabash College of Crawfordsville in Indiana was seeking an Instructor in French and Spanish, to be Chairman and sole member of their newly formed Department of Romance Languages. Crawfordsville is south from Chicago, about 40 miles north-west of Indianapolis, and roughly 650 miles west of Philadelphia. Several major railways passed through it; it had a population of around 9,000; was famed as the home of the author of *Ben Hur*; boasted at least two theatres and a music hall; and called itself the Athens of the West, for no evident reason unless on account of its college. Wabash College had been founded in 1832, shortly after the town was laid out, by Presbyterian missionaries. In 1907 it had declared itself non-sectarian, had 345 students, 27 instructors, and a library of 43,000 books. Its new President was Dr George Lewes Mackintosh, a Nova Scotia-born doctor of divinity. He interviewed Pound in Philadelphia in early August, and appointed him at once. Term would begin September 16.

Pound was having a good summer. He was free to write and to spend time with friends and with Aunt Frank in New York. He was 'physically as fit a youth as youth ever turned out', in the words of someone who knew him then, and who recorded a striking image of Pound vaulting, in a graceful tour de force, into the old-fashioned rumble seat of a runabout car, 'without touching the back of the seat in front—gently as if wafted there'. And he had met Mary Moore of Trenton. He had been coaching one John

Scudder of Scudders Falls on the Delaware River near Trenton; Scudder knew Mary; and soon Pound was taking long walks with her, inviting her to lunch in Wanamakers in Philadelphia, canoeing and picnicking with her on the river, and calling on her at her home. One gets the impression of a young woman in bloom, between narcissus and rose: good-looking, good-hearted; liking to like and to be liked; lively and uninhibited in a well-brought-up fashion; socially assured by her family's solid wealth and standing; and with her life all exciting prospects and not yet a serious affair. It is unlikely that she and Pound were alone a great deal. On one especially enchanted night on or by the river 'Kitty' Heyman at least appears to have been with them. In spite of that Pound was moved to write after it to 'Mardhu', as he was now calling Mary, 'that when the very high gods will to do a thing perfectly they succeed rather well'. She had given him a green charm. He thought they were now in love. Mary had thought they were just 'warm loving friends', or so she told Carl Gatter when she was in her eighties. 'A kiss on the forehead was as far and as passionate' as their 'love-life' had gone.

By the time he reached Crawfordsville Pound was ready to do the expected thing. It was as if being married went with being a college professor. Not that either was altogether real to him. He would have '57 men to begin French, 30 in Spanish, 15 or 16 more in other French'; but all his classes would be over by 11 a.m., with none on Saturday. There was also the matter of sixty-one papers to look over four times a week, but it was 'perfectly ridiculous' to expect him to do that. All the time he was not in the classroom, he told his father, he was 'jamming out mss.' That was his reality, writing poems. But to Mary he wrote that when they were married and living 'à deux' in Crawfordsville he would have 'considerable time not to be allowed to get my work done and "just play with" you'. Or he imagined wanting to write a sonnet with her asleep on a divan preventing him. He was constructing the cynical domestic romance. When they walked the plank, he foresaw, she would arrive at the church door 'breathless, slightly bewildered mayhap, but happy'. There were the things they would need for setting up house, and what might they hope for from 'the nuptial hold-up'. He had been hemming his new green table cover which 'in all conscience' she should be there to do for him. Unable to find or to afford a suitable engagement ring he sent her, to serve until he could get one back East, the ring his 'Kitty-mama' had given him. All this within his first two or three weeks in Crawfordsville. By October 7 Mary had put an end to the fantasy by announcing that she was 'to marry Oscar' and returning the ring. Oscar, it appears, 'was paralyzed and in a wheelchair', and Mary Moore did not marry him.

Pound's reactions showed up his very odd state of mind. He had anticipated that his attitude on their wedding-day would be 'a graceful bending to the decrees of destiny, a certain untroubled passivity, as of one who sees the hodge-podge of life rather in the nature of little shadows, smoke wraiths from the pipe of the great Pan'. Now the most bitter thing he writes to Mary is, 'You see I trusted in a dream—having learnt to trust mine own dreams I trusted another's—presumed'. He asks her to return, not his letters, but his poems in which he has perhaps given away too much of himself to 'Oscar's fiancée'. Beyond that he is detached, philosophical, released. He tells 'Maridhu' that 'after the first pain' he is driven on 'from love of persons—dreaming with Plato—unto the love of the divine essences'. When Mary writes in tragic and pitying mood, seeming to Pound unable to decide between Oscar and himself, he replies that he is 'à vous' if she wants him, and that if not he won't be 'heartbroke'. When she writes that after all she loves him desperately, he distancingly remarks that 'it is a very proper state of mind, and I trust you will stay in it'; and then unkindly asks, 'Only how many people beside Oscar and I are you intermittently betrothed to—like a alternating current electric sign—"That's all", "Pears Soap", "Smoke Old Gold" etc.' Finally, assured that Oscar is the man, he regains his poise and takes control of the situation: 'Dear Funny Little Rabbit:—I do not love you at all except as I love all beautiful things that run around in the sun light and are happy.' He returns her green charm, and is sorry she does not like geniuses. But now that they 'are not bothered about mate-remony' he can see no reason why their 'friendship should not be as simple, as purely decorative & perhaps a shade more delightful than Oscar & J. S. fils [= John Scudder?] would approve.' The light-heartedness could be from having escaped the fatal destiny.

Other fates lay in wait for him. The better people of Crawfordsville and its college upheld a high moral code. It became clear to Pound that if he wanted to remain in town he would have to establish his respectability, and that his only way might be to get married. When that didn't work out, not only was he strangely relaxed about it, but he began to give outright offence and to write gleeful accounts of his misdeeds to Mary and other friends. Smoking was forbidden in the State of Indiana and by the college. Pound had 'cigarillos' sent to him from the East, and even smoked them in his college room just down the corridor from the outraged President's office. Some of his students went to the President 'to complain erbout me orful langwidge and the number of cigarillos I consume.' He got into trouble with his first landlord for having students talking in his room late into the night. Worse, he made over-frequent use of the parlour and music room to entertain the landlady's sister, a beautiful and sympathetic young widow, whose name happened to be Mary Moore Shipman Young. In his next lodging he contrived a genuine scandal.

Some details vary in Pound's several versions of this first of two scandalous happenings, but the main features are clear. The time was early November, before the 11th; and the place was a rooming house to which came 'all the traveling show folk'. A room across the hall from Pound's was occupied by 'a stranded variety actress'—an English 'lady male impersonator who is stalled here because she don't understand american and can therefore not make her monocled jokes appreciable to the "coster" audience'. She was broke and hungry and grateful for Pound's sharing with her his 'frugal meal' of 'coffee and salad'. It 'not being convenient to carry a dinner across the hall as I had done coffee and toast' he was 'caught in the act by two stewdents'—that is, 'Two stewdents found me sharing my meagre repast with the lady-gent impersonator in me privut apartments'. He expected to be damned for immorality 'when the she-faculty-wives git hold of that jewcy morsel'. However, he could 'prove an alibi from 8–12 p.m.', 'having spent the evening when supposed to have been in flagrante, with the widdy ole Mac was supposed to have wanted to espouse, / and what she wrut to the President, I have never known in detail'. The 'widdy' was Mary Moore Young, who must have dared the President to doubt her own respectability in order to save Pound's honour. She did reprove Pound, very kindly and gently, for his 'wild and erring ways'. But one can guess how free-thinking she was from her also saying to Pound, in tête-à-tête, 'if we (i.e. she and I) took an apartment here for mutual comfort and protection...Crawfordsville wouldn't understand'. There is the moral of the scandal, as Pound told it, 'Crawfordsville wouldn't understand'. It is a comic tale of the gadfly shocking smalltown prejudice, *épatant le bourgeois*, and getting away with it. Within that there is the sub-plot of the artiste/artist being not understood in Crawfordsville and needing to be saved from it. This is the aspect Pound brought out in a late version (of which the first statement at least was not the case): 'I was sacked from Wabash College, salary $750 per year, A.D. 1907, for paying a lady's fare to Chicago because I did NOT want her starving across the hall / SALVATION AND DELIVERANCE no romance involved'.

Crawfordsville, Pound told his correspondents, was the sixth circle of hell, the utmost pit of desolation. In the *Inferno* that is the city of Lucifer and the fallen angels, the lowest, darkest place and the farthest from Heaven. To Pound it seemed the farthest from London and Paris. But

59

everyone in it apart from Mary Moore Young and himself thought that the Athens of the West was the centre of the universe. There was also 'the town artist', Fred Vance, just returned from ten years abroad who had had an *atelier* at 72 rue Notre Dame des Champs—Pound relished the Paris address. When they were introduced Pound 'almost felt alive at his "au grand plaisir m'sieu"'. But Vance's was a sad story. His father, born on a farm, had wanted to be a painter but was made to stay on the farm. He had sent his son to art schools and to Paris—

> Ten years of life, his pictures in the salons,
> Name coming in the press;
>   and when I knew him:
> Back once again, in middle Indiana,
> Acting as usher in the theatre,
> Painting the local drug-shop and soda bars

In short, he had fallen back into the hell of Crawfordsville, offering an exemplum of the artist trapped in mediocrity to set against Whistler's exhilarating career. The two Vances, Fred and his father, were among the select few invited to Pound's late-night *soirées*. According to Wilhelm, Pound believed that Fred eventually 'made an Icarus-like escape to California'—an unfortunate image—but in fact he died near Crawfordsville in 1926 'from acute indigestion'.

Pound's 'great solace' in this 'most God-forsakenest area of the middle west' was the Carnegie Library. There he studied Dante's metre and discovered how his hendecasyllabic line was made up of combinations of rhythm units of various shapes and sizes. There he sought his 'kin of the spirit', 'homesick/After mine own kind that know, and feel/And have some breath for beauty and the arts.' And there he drafted new poems of his own, and sketched the great epic he dreamed of writing, and sought his escape.

Before winter set in Pound had moved to a room in the house of Misses Ida and Belle Hall at 412 South Grant Avenue directly across from the campus. The Misses Hall let rooms to bachelor professors and took a close interest in the life of the College. From mid-January to mid-February of 1908 there were severe snowstorms and blizzards. One bitterly cold night Pound met on a downtown street 'a girl from a stranded burlesque show, penniless and suffering from the cold'—thus begins the official version of his second and terminal scandal. Pound took her in, gave her his bed, and slept—'fully clothed...wrapped in his topcoat' another account assures us—on the floor of his study. In the morning he went out to an eight o'clock class, and the Misses Hall on going into his room to make the bed discovered the chorus girl in it. They telephoned Dr Mackintosh and one or two of the trustees. The predictable outcome followed, but only because Pound made sure that it did.

He was invited to resign; did resign; was offered his job back— and refused it. He was overjoyed to be free. 'Have had a bust up, but come out with enough to take me to Europe', he wrote to his father, 'Don't let mother get excited.' On the other side of the note he wrote this:

I guess something that one does not see but something very big and white back of the destinies has the turning & the leading of things & this thing & I breathe again.

He next wrote, 'Have been recalled but I think I should rather go to ze sunny Italia.' And then, 'Have had more fun out of the fracasso than there is in a dogfight'; and again, 'am having the time of my life'. The college paid him $200 on February 12, as 'balance of salary to February 29'. *The Crawfordsville Journal* of February 15 recorded his resignation and departure on the 14th for Philadelphia.

Had he himself given the destinies some help by deliberately courting the scandal? This second and worse offence against the morals of the place was so much a revised and improved version of the first that he must have expected that this time it would get him fired. Dr Mackintosh's accepting that his behaviour had been beyond reproach evidently missed the point. He had surely wanted to be fired because to him it meant his salvation and deliverance. Within a month of getting home he was on his way to Europe.

5 : OUTWARD AND AWAY

Via Gibraltar and Venice

Did young Ezra's poems warrant 'his being sent abroad for stimulus and study'? Homer put the question to the poetry editor of *McClure's Magazine*, Witter Bynner, perhaps not aware that Bynner was of about the same age as Ezra. The reply was encouraging, and a passage was booked through a Philadelphia travel agent on the Cunard Line Royal Mail Steamship *Slavonia*, sailing from New York on March 17. Legend has it that the young adventurer set forth for Europe on a cattle boat, but, alas for legend, that was not his, nor the family's, style.

Ezra urged Hilda to come away with him. In the buzz and hush of scandal over his leaving Wabash she had loyally reaffirmed their long-standing unofficial engagement, and the fiery kisses were renewed. Then Ezra brought the matter to its crisis by asking her father formally for his daughter's hand in marriage. This was the moment of his dismissal as 'nothing but a nomad'. The depth of the father's disapproval would appear in his later taking it upon himself to burn Ezra's letters to Hilda. Hilda was baffled, crushed—she had considered herself engaged, and now felt that even their private understanding was broken off. She would eventually follow Ezra to London, but not until 1911, and then she would learn that he was informally engaged to marry Dorothy Shakespear. It was Mary Moore who saw him off from New York on the 17th.

By the 23rd he was on shore in Gibraltar, and he made that his base for the next month or so. For part of that time he was earning $15 a day as guide, courier, and 'gard-enfants' to a wealthy American family on their tour of Tangier and Spain.[1] In *The Pisan Cantos* he would remember a

---

[1] Pound told Louis Untermeyer in 1930 that he 'landed in Gibralter with 80 dollars and lived on the interest for some time' (*EP to LU* 15). Since even 50 per cent p.a. for 3 months would have yielded only $10, one would like to know more. In any event, he was evidently being economical with the facts.

fakir's miracle in Tangier, and a ride over the hills 'near the villa of Perdi-caris'. There was still more 'stimulus and study' to be had in observing the human comedy under the direction of Yusuf Benamore, a Gibraltar tour guide, in his café, club, and synagogue—that would be vividly remembered for use in canto 22. He was experiencing these things with the eager intensity of a released prisoner.

But still, as he wrote to Katherine Ruth Heyman, 'America presents itself to my mind as rather a horrible nightmare, a dark blur behind me, or a jaws of Tartarus effect ready to devour me if I loose my grip on things present'. He was looking to Venice, where he would meet up with her, to secure his mind from such 'phantoms of the brain' and to restore his confidence in life's abundance.

It seems likely that it was as guide and courier to another American family that he travelled to Venice, going by sea to Genoa, then on by rail with visits to several of the cities of northern Italy on the way. By April 28 he was 'comfortably fixed' in Venice.

In Gibraltar he had prayed for the heart of all that was true in him to beat again, and for the love out of all that was true in him to rise again. Now, as he wrote it out in his poetry notebook through June and July, the sun of Venice was restoring him heart and soul. And at night, in its waters and silence, he felt the presence of God's Beauty moving him to tears and purifying his heart. 'Old powers risen have returned to me', he rejoiced, as he dedicated himself afresh to his mission as a poet. 'Lord Gloom' was again to be overcome, and dreams to be gathered to give ease to the people.

A new theme in these Venetian poems is the acceptance that his mission will entail loneliness and exile. One poem, 'For the Triumph of the Arts', declares that the world hates the arts and starves its artists because their truth that is beauty shames the world's littleness.[2] The Byronic figure of the artist as outcast seems to be taking shape here. In 'Purveyors General' the poet is one of the lonely ones wandering the world who 'through chaos have hurled / [Their] souls riven and burning'. In 'Lucifer Caditurus', Lucifer is about to fall because he chooses to bear his light beyond the bounds of heaven. However, this Lucifer is driven, not by pride, but by a desire to find others in sympathy with his will 'to break His bonds'. And the 'purveyors general' are driven into exile in order to bring back the things that make the ease of the home-stayers. These are Romantic

---

[2] This may account for the title *A Lume Spento (with tapers quenched)*, stated on the title page to be in memory of Pound's close friend in Philadelphia, William Brooke Smith, 'Painter, Dreamer of dreams'. 'A lume spento', from Dante's *Purgatorio* III, 132, indicates the burial rite of one who had been opposed and excommunicated by the Pope.

artists with a social mission, voluntary exiles claiming a vital role in the world they cannot rest in. It was probably too early for Pound to realize just how problematic his exile's mission to a difficult homeland could become.

He did suffer real loneliness, but did not let it get him down. It was cheering to reflect that, being alone with the beauty of his own great thoughts, he could not after all be lonely, since they were his 'paladins/Against all gloom and woe and every bitterness'. On the other hand, loneliness could be acceptable as the source of creativity. 'All art', he wrote, 'begins in the physical discontent (or torture) of loneliness and partiality'—

It was to fill this lack that man first spun shapes out of the void. And with the intensifying of this longing gradually came into him power, power over the essences of the dawn, over the filaments of light and the warp of melody.

So, he reasoned it out, loneliness might be the necessary condition of his art. In fact, marriage could mean 'art death', 'because there are so few sufficiently great to avoid the semi-stupor of satisfied passion—whence no art is.' One aches for the simple logic of youth!

He did not write in that fashion to his parents, especially not to Homer. Indeed, in his letters to his father he might be another person altogether. The poet entranced by the beauty of the West dawn is quite lost in a cynical commercial operator concerned only with money and publicity. He is sending his father short stories and travel pieces 'to sell and sell quickly'—

Try first on "Outlook". Then if not accepted Everybodies, McClure, Cosmopolitan, Book News in order. . . . Will try to get some more stuff off as soon as convenient.

Keep the advertising of "A Lume Spento" in full motion—advance orders to be desired and no vulgarity of publicity need be shunned. . . .

The Tangier . . . is worth $50 but don't suppose you will manage that.

With *A Lume Spento*, it is not money but publicity he is after. 'Whang—Boom—Boom—cast delicacy to the winds', he urges.

The American reprint has got to be worked by kicking up such a hell of a row with genuine and faked reviews that Scribner or somebody can be brought to see the sense of making a reprint. I shall write a few myself & get someone to sign 'em. [3]

[3] He sent Viola Baxter a notice of the success of *A Lume Spento*, signed 'John Vore', for her to submit to *McClure's* (letter from London, 1908, in Van Pelt collection). An unsigned notice of *A Lume Spento* in *Book News Monthly* does look like a piece of astute self-advertisement. It begins: 'Mr Pound

Before the book is even printed he is thinking of working up its rarity value by declaring only one hundred of the 150 copies. Again, his relations with Miss Heyman, which had been so spiritual, are made to appear merely commercial. 'You needn't worry about "affinities"', he tells his father, and goes on to mention possible commissions on organizing concert engagements for her, as if that is now his only connection. There is the further value that his 'position of secretary manager...has so far brought me into contact with a good many people whom I am glad to know and who will be of use to know later.' He is already thinking of doing a series of articles on the notable people he is meeting in Venice, such as the composer Wolf-Ferrari.

It all amounted in the end to very little in the way of either cash or publicity. The things written to make money were unsaleable—overblown, trumpery stuff, with no feeling for the market. There were few reviews of *A Lume Spento* and no U.S. edition. And as for his career as a concert promoter, the only certain products were two private concerts, a small puff in the Paris edition of the *New York Herald* and a report in the *Gazzetta di Venezia* of 28 July 1908, both certainly written by himself.[4] Possibly Pound's intention in all this commercial busyness was simply to show Homer that he meant to be financially independent.

He could be disarmingly insouciant when directly called to account by Homer.

As to ? ? ? what do I do   Somedays I don't other days it's scribbling of a most uncommercial variety.

You have my hearty sympathy for having possibility of genius in the family but I suppose it can't be helped.

It becomes clear that what he was really doing in Venice was saving his genius from a return to college teaching, and preparing to make his entry in London. To his parents' fond hope that he would apply for a position in Moscow, Idaho, he opposed a battery of objections—his application would be too late; it would need ten times any professorial salary to make

is talented, but he is very young'; and it ends by finding 'promise of simplicity to come—when Mr Pound has learned that simplicity and greatness are synonymous' (Homberger: 1972, 42). Pound also solicited a review from the popular versifier Ella Wheeler Wilcox, on the strength of Homer's having known her when they were young in Wisconsin. She published a genial salute, 'Success to you, young singer in Venice!' (Letter to Homer Pound, August 27 1908, Stock: 1970, 55; Homberger: 1972, 2–3 and 29 n. 2).

[4] In letters to his father in July and August 1908 EP wrote of having arranged 'two appearances' for KRH in Venice, one of them 'an affair at the Countess Morosini's'. The other will have been in 'the Liceo Benedetto Marcello Hall', for invited guests only, as reported in the *Gazzetta di Venezia*—for details see Stock: 1976, 76—and mentioned in a letter to Iris Barry in 1916 (*Letters* 147).

it worth his leaving Venice, 'the most beautiful face on earth'; he wanted to get to London to 'meet Bill Yeats (and one or two other humans)'. That this last was his great motive was apparent already in May, when he wrote of it much as he had written at the end from Wabash of 'something very big and white back of the destinies [having] the turning and leading of things':

Of course it was only a question of a year or so before I should have attempted to establish myself in London. And as events have always shaped themselves to hurry me along a bit faster than I should have moved myself, it may be that I am not to wait.

But he wanted to arrive as a poet, and for that he needed to have *A Lume Spento* in print. The book was finally ready at the end of July and he set off for London in early August. The charms of Venice may have held him in thrall for three months, but could not hold him back from his appointed destination.

It seems to have taken most of that three months to get the poems printed. The minister of the Scotch Presbyterian Kirk in Venice, Dr Robertson, whose tea parties he frequented, put him on to a printer soon after his arrival. Miss Norton, who let him stay through the summer in the San Trovaso apartment she had leased but was not using, was going about the bookshops of Venice as early as the end of May 'asking gently for "Il Lume Spento" and raising a row because they didn't have it'. In a moment of uncharacteristic discouragement, if *The Pisan Cantos* are to be believed, he wondered if he should chuck the bundle of proofs into a canal. But the book, in green paper wrappers, was 'Published by A. Antonini...In the City of Aldus' about July 20 1908.

Pound mailed twenty wrongly trimmed copies to his father to send out for review, plus five correct copies. His distribution list for the next thirty copies reads as an index to his life and hopes. The first four names were H. D., W. B. Yeats, W. C. W[illiams], A. C. Swinburne. Vance and Mrs Young are there from Crawfordsville; 'Bib' and 'Bill Shep' from Hamilton; only Child from Penn, with Whiteside, a Philadelphia painter whose work Pound admired; 'Bitter' for Witter Bynner, and C[arlos] T[racy] Chester, his literary patrons; Viola, as 'V.S.B.', and 'K.R.H.' surprisingly far down the list at no. 39; and Mosher, no doubt in hope that he would do a U.S. edition. Then there were some recent Venice acquaintances, Ferrari, Robertson, Miss Norton, and [Marco] Londonio who translated into Italian his poem for K.R.H 'after one of her Venetian concerts'. The initial listing accounted for seventy-five copies, and the rest Pound took with him for use in London.

His hard-headed calculation was that what would count was not sales but getting copies into the hands of the discerning few. He told his father that he wanted 'the copies of this first edition to go to the intelegant people who'll *understand*. The book is to be a rarity and I value one copy placed in the Norton family ... much more than several copies sold'. Miss Norton's father was Charles Eliot Norton, 'our foremost American Dante scholar', and her uncle was President of Harvard. But it was the intelligent people in London that he was really out to impress, foremost among them the poet William Butler Yeats.

6 : LONDON 1908–1910

A stiff white collar

'EP arrived in London in a stiff white collar', so Dorothy Pound recalled in 1951, 'and the floppy ones were made for him by Mr Wing.' He wore the collar—a 'butterfly collar'—for the portrait photographs he had taken in the Elliot and Fry studio in Baker Street not later than July 1909 when it adorned a write-up of Pound in *The Bookman*. It was the sort of collar worn by Henry James in most of his portraits, and worn at the time by such respected men of letters as Sir Arthur Quiller-Couch and Edward Garnett, men who had acceptable backgrounds and incomes and an entrée to the upper strata of society. The young American poet had none of those advantages.

He had £3 (worth about $15) in his pocket and expectations amounting to the $20 a month his father would contrive to remit. He had the entrée for the brief period that his credit lasted to Miss Withey's comfortable boarding house in Duchess Street, between Regent Street and Regent's Park in central London. Aunt Frank had stayed there in 1906. Then he raised 10 shillings from a pawnbroker and tasted for the few days he could stand it the 'unthinkable and unimaginable' foods and odours of a cheap Islington lodging-house with an out-of-order bath and no hot water. Finally, when his father's £4 arrived at the end of September, he found a clean room he could afford at 7 shillings a week, meals not included, in Mrs Joy's boarding house at 48 Langham Street, back near Duchess Street. He had one introduction, to the contralto Elizabeth Granger Kerr. The singer received him kindly, and lent him ten shillings. He gave her in return, as he had Miss Withey, a copy of *A Lume Spento*. And it was those two ladies whom he had to call on to endorse his application, in early October, for admission to the British Museum Reading Room. That would be his sole place of work, of self-appointed work with no money in it.

He would prove that it was possible to keep body and soul together and to write poetry on £1 a week—and to make a good impression where it mattered. Half-alien and alone—at once at home in the language and literary culture and yet socially a thorough outsider—he would somehow manage to keep his linen clean and his white collar starched in the fog and filth of London,[1] and he would gain entry to a number of affluent and cultured drawing rooms. But he was in need, he told Homer, of a two-piece suit, hat, socks, a vest and some new ties. And Homer had 'better send the two suits of winter underware'—they were new.

The stiff white collar stood for cultivation and for the old world culture he had been imagining in his poems and which he hoped to find alive in London. 'Mentaly', he noted, 'I am a Walt Whitman who has learned to wear a colar and a dress shirt (although at times inimical to both)'. It was his 'love of beauty' that differentiated him from Whitman; and from that came the intense feeling of his own need as an American, and of America's need, 'of all the lost or temporarily mislaid beauty, truth, valor, glory of Greece, Italy, England and all the rest of it'. The purpose of his exile, as he saw it now in harsher terms than in his Venetian 'Purveyors General', would be 'to scourge America with all the old beauty'. But that ardent love of the old beauty of course flattered and won him admission to cultivated English society. His invitations to dinner, he told his father whimsically, were earned 'by the pure charm of my lyric personality'.

Less agreeable to the English was his discovery that their world was in need of America's constructive energies. In London Pound realized as if for the first time his spiritual kinship with the open collared Whitman whose genius was the raw spirit of America's self-creation. He found him a nauseating dose for his cultured palate, and yet he now recognized that 'The vital part of my message, taken from the sap and fibre of America, is the same as his'. Along with meaning 'to be a strife for a renaissance in America' he felt a new impulse, to drive America's dynamic message into the old world—'to drive Whitman into the old world. I sledge—he drill'.

Pound's combining a love of beauty with American drive would later perplex his English hosts. His apparently inexhaustible energy was frequently remarked, and frequently put down as restless and tiresome. They would say that he broke the legs of chairs because he could not sit still,

---

[1] 'The fogs of London...apt to occur at all seasons, are common from September to February...Their principal cause is smoke from the general domestic use of coal' (*Encyclopaedia Britannica* 11th edn., 1911, vol. 16, p. 939). The smoke from the sulphur-rich coal not only thickened the fog but made it yellow, dirty and unhealthy. From the same source one learns that around 1908 the changeover from horse-power to the internal combustion engine had still some way to go in the streets of London—a further source of filth.

and that he played tennis 'like a galvanised, agile gibbon'. They wished he would put on his jacket in the drawing room after tennis. They would deprecate his dominating the conversation and holding forth to his elders on the mysteries of their art. He read his lyric poems rather loudly and in a Philadelphia accent which sounded barbarously of the Wild West in their English ears. In short, he broke what Ford Madox Hueffer had observed to be the 'general rule' of London society, the rule against animation. He did not practise the 'soothing personal effacement' which was all it asked of a man not in a position to give dinners or financial tips. He struck people as egregiously American; or, in the words of Hugh Selwyn Mauberley, Pound's later personification of the finest bloom of English taste in that era, he seemed someone 'born / In a half savage country' who put too much energy into trying 'to maintain "the sublime" / In the old sense'.

'London', in 1908 as now, was of course whatever one could make of it. To the *Encyclopaedia Britannica* (11th edition, published in New York in 1911) it was 'the capital of England and of the British Empire, and the greatest city in the world'. And the British Empire's glory was that upon it the sun never set. The British Navy ruled the waves. The City of London could think of itself as the financial heart of the world—and that made it, in Conrad's vision, the heart of the heart of darkness. It was, what the United States has become, the Rome of its day. But to Ezra Pound, in 1908, it was simply the metropolis of poetry. He was unaware of, or undaunted by, the warnings in such novels as Gissing's *New Grub Street* (1891) and James' *The Wings of the Dove* (1902) against the philistinism which could be the undoing of aspiring but unmoneyed young minds. His eye was on the London where the most poetry and the best poetry was published and where live poets might be met. It was there he hoped to find a publisher, and to find Yeats. It was, he then believed, the one right place in which to practise poetry.

That belief was about all he had to sustain him through a trying time from mid-August of 1908 to mid-January 1909. He had to keep assuring his parents, and himself, that he had an idea he was going to make good in London, 'a vague idea I am going to be a success', and that it would be worth his hanging on there through the winter. He would need one London season sometime, to get himself into a 'literary position that would take ten years at home', and it looked as if this were it. To go home, as he was being urged to do, would mean getting 'no recognition here at all'. Of course, if there were 'a definite salaried position' waiting for him back home that would be a different matter, he conceded—while doing nothing that might put him at risk of securing one. But if he were to be dependent on his father's charity then he might as well do it in London where he could put the dollars to better use than anywhere else. His appreciation of Homer's support was laced with encouragement: 'Being family to a wild poet aint no bed of roses but you stand the strain just fine.'

To Homer he bravely listed his possible sources of income. Smith, his Philadelphia travel agent, knew a man connected with Covent Garden Market who knew a man at the Regent Street 'Polytechnique', and thus he secured an engagement to give a short course of lectures there in January and February. Smith also thought he might get him another tour party in Spain next May. He could look for commissions from arranging concerts for Miss Heyman in London and America—though it seems most unlikely that Miss Heyman, who was in London 'between engagements' only in December, would have been looking to him for her arrangements. He even told Homer, as if there might be money to be made from them, that he was calling on publishers and magazine editors and showing them *A Lume Spento* and his new Venetian poems.

He did get 'Histrion' and 'For Katherine Ruth Heyman / (After one of her Venetian concerts)', into the *Evening Standard and St. James's Gazette*, the first at the end of October, the second in early December; and a brief notice of *A Lume Spento* appeared there at the end of November, unsigned, and sounding suspiciously like Pound himself. 'Wild and haunting stuff, absolutely poetic, original, imaginative, passionate and spiritual', the notice boomed; and having boomed some more, it banged, 'Coming after the trite and decorous verse of most of our decorous poets, this poet seems like a minstrel of Provence at a Suburban musical evening'. If this was indeed Pound's own puff, his intent would have been to use it on publishers. He tried John Lane without success, and left copies of *A Lume Spento* fruitlessly with Dent and Dutton. His one hope was Elkin Mathews, who seemed to be 'seriously considering a reprint from A.L.S.'. 'At least he says he wants to', Pound told his father in September. Yet he was reduced to having the Venetian poems printed at his own expense for publication in early December, as *A Quinzaine for This Yule*, before Elkin Mathews agreed to publish a further one hundred copies.

Mathews may have paid for the printing of his hundred copies, but nothing more. And any payment for the two poems in the *Evening Standard and St. James's Gazette* would have been cancelled out by the printing costs of the first hundred copies. In effect then, Pound earned nothing between August and January—indeed he had earned very little since departing from Crawfordsville in February. He appears to have expected some further payment from Wabash and to have experienced difficulty in cashing a cheque from Dr Mackintosh.

He was counting the pennies spent on bus fares—the difference between a penny ride to the British Museum and a threepenny one really mattered. His funds didn't run to a 'regular routine diet', and hadn't done so for 'ten or eleven months'. In Venice he had mostly eaten at cheap cook stalls, and in London he probably did the same. In the portrait photograph his face is fined down to the bone. He had a bout of shingles in November. Still he could write home at the end of that month, 'Had my Thanksgiving dinner solus at Pagani's which has the best feed in London & where the waiters hang round me for the sake of a few words of Italian'.

A Letter to his Mother

Pound's letters were generally full of his own concerns, taking it for granted that his parents wanted to know what he was up to and how he was getting on. In November 1908, however, his mother having sent him a photograph of herself, he for once showed some touching thoughtfulness towards her.

Well!

Looking more like a proud presbyterian peacock than ever. A la directoire with feathers & aa' that. having opened a recent package I so discover you. It has by the way occurred to me of late that for some years past I have been so over busied contemplating abstractions of the marvelous working of my mental internal workings that I have not taken time to regard you as an individual with a certain right to think, hold ideas etc. for yourself. & not necessisarily ideas in accord with my own. It seems to me that this action or rather lack of it on my part rather demands some sort of apology on my part which I here tender. It dawns upon me gently that perhaps the holding of a contrary opinion on your part is not a sin against the eternal order of things, and that however diversely we may regard life, society, etc. we may at least commence a polite acquaintance, or even broach some unexplosive intercourse. The necessity of reforming you, does not any longer seem imperative. Your opinions if egregiously incorrect & illogical may perhaps have some raison d'etre.

I suppose I might have granted these things before in a general way, but of late they have been borne in upon me more understandingly.

It seems to me that there have been times when no one has taken any particular trouble to consider what _you_ wanted, & why you had a certain right or reason to want it.

Lack of intellegent sympathy (I presume it is called) with your aims, views, etc.

I begin to perceive that there have been diverse and definite times when I might have displayed a little more horse sense to you ward without serious detriment to anything in particular.

Ebbene.
Manaña mejos.
   A rividerci.

Signed with a flamboyantly winged 'Epound'.

Elkin Mathews

In January 1909 things at last began to look up. Elkin Mathews agreed to publish *Personae*, a new selection of his poems, in April. There were fifty-five people, by his own account, at the first of his lectures at the Polytechnic. He began to meet some poets. And he began to be known as a poet, thanks to his and Mathews' distributing copies of *A Quinzaine for This Yule*. He was using that as a Christmas and calling card, to introduce himself as he wanted to be known.

He was lecturing for the money, though the pay was probably modest. Those attending the full course of six lectures were charged 7 shillings and 6 pence, which means that an audience of fifty, assuming the numbers held up, would have brought in only £18.15s. The lecturer would have been lucky to receive half of that. The lectures were billed as 'A Short Introductory Course...on The Development of Literature in Southern Europe...by Ezra Pound, M.A. (sometime Fellow in the University of Pennsylvania). Author of "A Lume Spento", "A Quinzaine for this Yule", etc. On Thursday afternoons at 5 o'clock. Commencing January 21st, 1909, in the Marlborough Room.' It was further stated that the course was 'designed as an introduction to a longer series to commence in October'. The Introductory Lecture, according to the 'Synopsis', would 'search for the essential qualities of literature' in the 'Dicta of the great critics', these being as one might expect of Pound, 'Plato, Aristotle, Longinus, Dante, Coleridge, De Quincey, Pater and Yeats'. This was no doubt his riposte to Dr Penniman's 'drill manual' course on the history of literary criticism. The second lecture was to be on 'The Rise of Song in Provence. The Troubadours'; the third would include 'The Childrens Crusade' under 'Medieval Religious Feeling', and the fourth would include Camoens under 'Trade with the East'; the fifth would deal with 'Latin Lyrists of the Renaissance'. So far, apart perhaps from the fourth lecture, Pound was following the interests he had cultivated at Hamilton and Penn. The final lecture, on the making of books from the earliest papyri up to Aldus and Caxton, drew on Putnam's *Books and Their Makers in the Middle Ages* which he had read at Hamilton, and was perhaps added to make a show, if not of philology, then at least of academic scholarship.

73

By all accounts Pound was an idiosyncratic but not a brilliant lecturer, though he performed well enough to be engaged to give the later longer series. The value of that would have been that it committed him to remaining at least a further year in London, and guaranteed a modest income to carry him through to the Spring of 1910.

Pound seems not to have minded what people thought of him as a lecturer, or in general. He wanted only to be taken seriously, by London, as a poet. He couldn't wait about for Elkin Mathews to make up his mind about publishing him. *A Quinzaine for This Yule* had to be out before Christmas, and before he appeared as a Polytechnic lecturer, so he had it 'published' by Pollock & Co., the printers used by the Polytechnic for their syllabuses, and thus forced Mathews's hand. But Mathews must have already recognized in Pound a poet after his own heart. His work was 'pure poetry', he told Harriet Monroe when she dropped into his bookshop in 1910, and with such conviction that she carried away two of Pound's books to read on her trans-Siberian journey to Peking.

Mathews was an expert antiquarian and general bookseller who also published poetry from his shop in Vigo Street 'between Regent Street and the Burlington Arcade'. 'Publisher and Vendor of Choice and Rare Editions in Belles Lettres' was his chosen description. Around 1908–1910 he was bringing out each year thirty to forty slim, elegantly produced volumes. He had been an enthusiastic publisher of the poets of the Aesthetic movement and of the Nineties, at first in partnership with John Lane as 'The Bodley Head', then from 1894 in his own name. Lionel Johnson and Dowson and Fiona Macleod were among his leading authors. He had published Yeats's *The Wind Among the Reeds* (1899); volumes by Carman and Hovey, whose *Vagabondia* Pound admired; and *Chamber Music* (1907), by the then unknown James Joyce. The young poet who had been guided by Mr Mosher 'the celebrated aesthetic publisher' might well have felt, when Mathews 'turned his shelves over to [him] to browse in', that here was the centre and source of the poetry of the age. And it would have come naturally to him there to present himself as the heir of 'Celticism' and the 'religion of beauty', and to play down his newly discovered kinship with Whitman.

'A Quinzaine for This Yule'

Pound created an alter ego, 'Weston St. Llewmys', perhaps an Anglo-Welsh aesthete, to preface *A Quinzaine for This Yule* with a poet's credo which would have hit exactly the right note for Mathews' 'modern' taste:

Beauty...is Marvel and Wonder, and in art we should find first these doors—Marvel and Wonder—and, coming through them, a slow understanding...as of a figure in a mist

That may have been part of 'the introductory matter' which Mathews had invited Pound to compile for the 'reprint from A.L.S.' he appeared to be considering in September. All fifteen poems 'selected from a Venetian sketch-book' are in that high-toned mood of 'art and ecstasy'. The 'prelude' takes up the theme, with the poet 'alone with beauty' in his room high over the Ognisanti. In 'Night Litany' his soul is purified in the beauty of God's Venice. In 'Purveyors General' he dedicates his art in exile to supplying such mysteries to 'the home-stayers'. In the fourth poem, 'Aube of the West Dawn: Venetian June', he makes out his *donna ideale*, his soul's bride, in the beauty of '"The dawn reflected in the west"'.

Pound told his father that whereas 'In A.L.S. the poems are fitted together, arranged, theoretically at least, so that one mood leads to the next, the "15" is separate poems without sequence.'[2] Yet already by the fourth poem it is apparent that there is a definite sequence and progression—prelude, purification, dedication, and beatific vision, these are the stages of a religious rite. Perhaps Pound simply did not want to have to explain this to Homer—'Beauty should never be presented explained', his Weston St Llewmys had warned. Another thing Pound told his father was that 'the Venetian stuff is as I should say painted on ivory where A.L.S. is on canvass'. He may well have heard in his course on Nineteenth Century Novelists at Penn that Jane Austen had said something like that about her writing—'the little bit (two Inches wide) of Ivory on which I work with so fine a Brush, as produces little effect after much labour'. She was of course too modest, and her novels prove how much may be effected 'on ivory'. If Austen's remark did lie behind Pound's

---

[2] I make out the arrangement of *QY* as follows:

Prelude: Over the Ognisanti	Fortunatus
Night Litany	Beddoesque
Purveyors General	Greek Epigram
Aube of the West Dawn	Christophori Columbi Tumulus
To La Contessa Bianzafior I & II	The Amphora (To T. H.)
Partenza di Venezia	Histrion
— — —	— — —
Lucifer Caditurus	Nel Biancheggiar
Sandalphon	
— — —	

then he was not being modest so much as asking for close attention to be paid to these seemingly slight and separate poems.

Certain developments do become apparent in the fine detail. There is a note to 'Aube of the West Dawn': 'I think from such perceptions as this arose the ancient myths of the demi-gods; as from that in 'The Tree'... the myths of metamorphosis'. But neither those 'ancient myths' nor 'The Tree' would ever yield a heavenly Lady. In these poems the elemental deities which H.D. claimed as her own have been wholly superseded by a vision of ideal beauty out of Dante and Swedenborg.

The fifth poem, 'To La Contessa Bianzafior', reveals another development. It begins, 'And all who read these lines shall love her then'. Reading on from 'The Aube of the West Dawn' one assumes that this refers back to the Lady of that poem, and that it is she who is now named as 'White Flower'. That would connect her with the final poem in the volume, 'Nel Bianchecheggiar' (in the whitening of the dawn), in which 'The flowers of the west's fore-dawn unclose'. And that in turn would give a connection with Katherine Ruth Heyman to whom that poem was dedicated—'(After one of her Venetian concerts)'—when it was first published. Given what she had meant to the poet in 'Scriptor Ignotus' and 'The Meeting of the Winds', and in those other notes honouring her as the inspiration of his poetic vision, one could readily assume that it is K.R.H. who is the Lady of the white dawn. And one would go on to assume, since the little book is dedicated 'To the Aube of the West Dawn', that it is all written in her honour. But here is a difficulty: the poet is justifying his leaving the Contessa Bianzafior. A singer's love, he would have her consider, should make him praise her in his songs and then move on, for his songs will bring a thousand souls to love her in his place. There is something of Cino in the conceit. And if 'White Flower' is to be understood as K.R.H. then she is being told, in effect, that she is no longer what she had been to him. Her place henceforth is in his song, not in his life. For all we know, Miss Heyman may have thought that all along. But Pound needed to find it out; and needed, apparently, to separate her out from the 'bride' she had empowered his soul to envision.[3]

That separation, added to his parting from the elemental demi-gods, would leave the poet with simply the idealised beauty of Venice and its dawns to be the inspiration of his art. This is confirmed in the following poem, 'Partenza di Venezia', which begins 'Ne'er felt I parting from a woman loved / As feel I now my going forth from thee'. It is

---

[3] The separation was effected before he reached Venice. Though the poem is written in the 'San Trovaso' notebook, it is there dated as 'Gibel-Taraj March 1908'. [*CEP* 298]

a poem of leave-taking after his three months in the city. No longer in his visionary ecstasy, he wants to be assured that his dream was real. He thinks of Venice as if it were Christ appearing upon the waves to reassure his disciples when they were afraid in the storm on the sea of Galilee, and has it say with Christ, '"I am no spirit. Fear not me"'. 'And thus thou, Venice', the poem concludes, 'Show'st thy mastery'. Remarkably, in contrast with the sense of communion in 'Night Litany' and 'Aube of the West Dawn', the poet places himself with the fearful disciples, having to learn to trust that 'mastery' while removed from the 'mystery'.

That closes the sequence of six Venetian poems. There is a sequence of six London poems to come, but first, between the two sequences, a pair of contrasting personae form a diptych. The first, Lucifer, God's light-bearer, would be a light-bringer, a Promethean 'purveyor general' to a realm which does not will the Mover's law. He is doomed to fall by that law. The second, Sandalphon, the angel of prayer in the Talmud (as a note tells us), fulfils his appointed task without any apparent will of his own. What he does is somewhat obscure—and Swedenborgian—but it amounts to transforming the angels' praisings of 'the Mover of Circles' into 'ever new flowers' of speech which are a new language for 'the earth-horde's age-lasting longing'. 'Marvel and wonder' are his watchwords—as they are Weston St. Llewmys's.

The strange diptych appears to be an allegory of art. What the artist wills, in Pound's idea, is to pass on to others the ecstasy of the soul in ascent, the ecstasies as it might be of 'Night Litany' and 'Aube of the West Dawn'. That motive informs 'Purveyors General'; it is the reason given in Cinoesque fashion for the poet's parting from his lady 'White Flower'. And it is, after his own fashion, Lucifer's motive. Sandalphon, however, does the work of the artist without apparent motive. He is unmoved as all the angels whose songs he gathers up and transforms burn themselves out in singing them. He is wholly caught up in 'Marvel and Wonder', the doors to the Beautiful. He is, one might think, prompted by 'Partenza di Venezia', mastered by the mystery. Lucifer, who would be his own master, represents the temptation of the artist to direct action—the temptation of a noble but self-willed spirit to try to carry the light of the beautiful to others by force of his will and by means other than art. That would be the great temptation of Pound's later life.

Here though, in the story line and argument of his *Quinzaine*, he is carried towards London, in 'Fortunatus', the first of the London sequence, 'Resistless, unresisting, as some swift spear upon the flood'. (He actually travelled by train, of course, but could not say that in his aesthetic diction.)

77

The first part of the poem insists, with much quibbling upon 'will', that he is being sped towards his triumph in London by a will that is not his will but which he will not oppose. It might be his destiny, it might be the life-force. (But it will be 'my triumph'!) The second part of the poem stages a wonderfully optimistic arrival. He is greeted by beauty 'through your London rain'—

> And though I seek all exile, yet my heart
> Doth find new friends and all strange lands
> Love me and grow my kin, and bid me speed.[4]

'All strange lands / Love me and grow my kin'—it is a huge and impersonal ambition that wants to be loved in that way.

The poems in this London sequence discover no beauty there to match that of Venice, and they afford no ecstasy. Their concern is rather with the art of poetry. 'Beddoesque' is a variation upon a few lines by Beddoes which had particularly impressed Pound and which would resurface in *The Pisan Cantos*. He had been 'greatly moved . . . at eighteen' by Beddoes' poetry, by its 'extensive and Elizabethan vocabulary full of odd and spectacular phrases', by its 'magnificent rhetoric'. Later, one gathers, he had come to feel that it would have been more effective 'if he had used a real speech instead of a language . . . which had no existence in the life of his era'. Yet along with his drawing on the hoard of archaic language Beddoes had a vision of great souls being 'Centuries hoarded' in order to endow a being who would leap into 'a mighty destiny'. Putting those two things together one arrives at the notion that the souls of his past masters can be drawn from the word-hoard to animate a living poet.

That is the claim which Pound enters for his poetry in 'Histrion', the conclusion of the sequence.[5] 'Histrion' resumes the argument of his 1907 essay in defence of his following Dante and Browning, and is at once a boast and his credo for this time:

> No man hath dared to write this thing as yet,
> And yet I know, how that the souls of all men great
> At times pass through us,
> And we are melted into them, and are not

---

[4] 'Weston St. Llewmys' added a curious note, about being 'Caught sometimes in the current of strange happiness borne upon such winds as Dante beheld whirling the passion-pale shapes in the nethergloom, so here in the inner sunlight, or above cool, dew-green pasture lands, and again in caves of the azure magic.' If that at first seems to locate its strange happiness in the gloom of a London railway terminal or the wind-tunnel Underground, it is quick to relocate to a conventional dream world—which is neither Pound's Venice nor his London.

[5] 'Histrion', from the Latin for an actor, was still in occasional journalistic use around 1890.

Save reflexions of their souls.
Thus am I Dante for a space and am
One François Villon, ballad-lord and thief. . . .

'Tis as in midmost us there glows a sphere
Translucent, molten gold, that is the "I"
And into this some form projects itself:
Christus, or John, or eke the Florentine;
And as the clear space is not if a form's
Imposed thereon,
So cease we from all being for the time,
And these, the Masters of the Soul, live on.

There is a boldness and vigour here that is not of the Nineties nor of the essentially recessive 'religion of beauty'. It could almost be a transposition of Whitman's 'Song of Myself'.

Along with its will to triumph as a poetry of the soul in love with Beauty, and as the voice of the Masters of the Soul, the *Quinzaine* gives an exhibition of technical virtuosity and craftsmanship. Each poem finds out its form from within, and no form is repeated. Most are in rhyme, but each has its own pattern, and these vary from the regular to the unpredictable. Lucifer seems to hit and miss his rhymes: *God* and *plod* and *sod*, *star* and *far*, *desire* and *fire*; but *soul* finds only *rule*, and his *light* finds no rhyme at all. Sandalphon seems not to care for his rhymes, letting them come or not of their own accord. *Singing* and *praising*, *wings* and *things* are words that his meditation quite naturally lights on, and *flowers* and *powers* make his only couplet; but he has a rich texture of internal rhyme and assonance. There are poems in sonnet form, but even such usually fixed forms are handled with an easy freedom. The metres too are at once controlled and free, with many natural shifts and breaks, and the iambic pentameter is as readily departed from as followed. A spirit of confident formal inventiveness prevails throughout. Occasionally though the language or the syntax, or both together, can be strained or contorted to serve the music or suit some artifice of style or thought.

The most remarkable effect is that although the poems exist in the rarefied realm which Keats dubbed 'poesy', they do have in spite of that a strikingly individual voice. It is not the voice of an individual personality; and it is not how anyone would naturally speak. Yet it has the assurance of someone speaking of shared experience in a common language. Its experience, though, and its language, are the experience and language of poetry. It is a voice of pure poetry. We know that the poetry has a real relation to Pound's actual experiences and aspirations in Venice, as well as in his reading and writing; but what was actual and personal is transmuted into something wholly poetical; that is, into a medium in which the words have little or no connection with any realm outside of poetry and its music. Paradoxically, it is just its being so confidently and boldly poetical that makes it individual. That, and the energy of its rhythms. Art that is so abstracted from the common world is usually world-weary, languorously in love with the dying fall. But Pound's aestheticism is alive with the desire to make its dream of beauty come true.

'People are interested'

A Quinzaine for This Yule was priced for sale at 1 shilling and 6 pence, but it is likely that the bulk of both editions was given away to poets and patrons of poetry. Miss Heyman took thirty of Pound's hundred, and another thirty went to Homer for distribution in America. Then it was six to 'Mrs Adams', copies to other hostesses, and of course copies to Yeats and to Arthur Symons, and to the poets he was now meeting. When Mathews announced his publication of it he added that it was for private circulation. There is no record of its receiving any review. Pound suggested to Mathews that he 'might send out 8 or 10 copies of the "Quinzaine"'—presumably from his own hundred—'where you think it will do the most good, Mr Windham or whosoever'. He received appreciative notes from Edward Dowden and Henry Newbolt, the one a Dublin professor and Shakespeare critic, the other a barrister better known for the immense success of 'Drake's Drum' and other songs of sea and Empire.

In mid-January Mathews introduced Pound to a young Australian poet who was then at Oxford preparing for a career at the English Bar and in politics, James Griffyth Fairfax. Mathews had published his precocious first poems, *The Gates of Sleep*, in 1906. Fairfax introduced him to another young Australian poet, Frederic Manning, whose father had been Lord Mayor of Sydney, who had independent means, and who now lived in rural Lincolnshire in the home of a scholarly vicar, the Revd Arthur Galton.[6] Pound and Manning took to each other. Pound enjoyed with Manning his first literary companionship in England, and declared that the two of them were 'the only significant writers under thirty'. They were both passionate about writing, and would disagree violently—Manning said they would 'rage against each other like bears'. Talent was the basis of their friendship, and disagreement was its mode. But they generously helped

---

[6] Frederic Manning (1882–1935), author of the *Scenes and Portraits* (1909), a prose work after the manner of Pater's imaginary portraits; *Poems* (1910); *Eidola* (1917) which included poems of the 1914–18 war; and the war novel *The Middle Parts of Fortune: Somme and Ancre, 1916* (1929).

each other too. Pound wrote an enthusiastic review of Manning's sixty-page poem *The Vigil of Brunhild* (1907) for the Philadelphia *Book News Monthly*. (He particularly approved the depiction of a soul striving 'against the boundaries of her time'.) Manning introduced Pound to Mrs Fowler's salon in Knightsbridge where he met Olivia Shakespear; and accompanied him a few days later to tea with Mrs Shakespear at 12 Brunswick Gardens, Kensington.

That was a crowded week. On Sunday dinner at the Adams. On Monday lunch with Mrs Fowler, and the afternoon with her doing the review of Manning's *Brunhild*.[7] Tuesday to Lady Russell's to see a parlour play, followed by invitations to dinner and the play 'when Miss Ward does Coriolanus', and again 'when the Forbes-Robertsons come as F–R wished to meet me'. Wednesday to lunch at Mrs Fowler's with Manning up from Lincolnshire and Fairfax down from Oxford. Thursday was his lecture, 'in smothering fog'. Friday to lunch with Miss Lowther 'at the house of a lady with wonderful sapphires' whose daughter and governess had been at his 'spiel on the Troubadours' the day before. Then tea with Manning and 'a certain Mrs Shakespear who is undoubtedly the most charming woman in London'. On Saturday lunch with Manning and Mrs Fowler at the Barkers 'who may want some private lecturing'. On at a run to the Portland Hotel to hear Henry Waller's new ballet music—Waller's opera had been staged in Berlin 'by special order of the Kaiser'. Then to dinner at the Birds, leaving afterwards with Sir Edward Sullivan who 'is going to send me his translation from Dante'. Sunday again—this must be January 31—and he is quite out of breath as he closes his account of all this to his mother with 'I have just come from a lecture by Gertrude Kingston (Sunday league lecture)'. He meant her to understand that he was now really on his way to being a success.

Manning and Mathews between them introduced him to a number of older and more established members of the London literary world, most of them connected in one way and another with Mathews's poetry publishing. He met Maurice Hewlett (1861–1923) who wrote historical novels and poems, had a house down in Wiltshire, and was a power in Edwardian literary society. He had been called to the Bar but hadn't practised, and had been Keeper of land revenue records until his novel

---

[7] Eva Fowler (1871–1921), U.S. citizen, daughter of Paul Neumann, a Prussian-born American who was Attorney-General in Hawaii and represented its Queen when Hawaii was annexed to the U.S.A. She was married to Alfred ('Taffy') Fowler, an engineer from Leeds whose business included manufacturing steam-ploughs, and who gets a mention in canto 18 (as 'Hamish'). Eva Fowler was deeply interested in psychic experience and the occult, and organized seances. Yeats experimented in automatic writing at 'Daisy Meadow', her house near Brasted in Kent.

The Forest Lovers (1898) brought him fame. Pound would recall him twice in *The Pisan Cantos*. He met Laurence Binyon (1869–1943), soon to be Keeper of Oriental Prints and Drawings in the British Museum and a poet in the tradition of Wordsworth and Arnold. He too would figure in *The Pisan Cantos*. Then there was Selwyn Image (1849–1930), an artist in stained glass and a religious versifier who had associated with Ruskin and the Pre-Raphaelites, been a founder of the Century Guild, and would be appointed Slade Professor of Fine Art at Oxford. He had been 'one of the gang with Dowson—Johnson—Symons—Yeats etc.', and was thought of as 'impartially imbued / With raptures for Bacchus, Terpsichore and the Church.' There was also Ernest Rhys (1859–1946), who as a young man had been a mining engineer in South Wales, and had then moved to London to lead the life of a writer and publisher's editor—he was the founding editor of Dent's Everyman's Library. Rhys at once befriended Pound, and was instrumental in securing a contract from Dent for the publication of his next full series of Polytechnic lectures as *The Spirit of Romance* (1910). At Rhys's house Pound met May Sinclair (1863–1946), the distinguished novelist, feminist and writer on philosophical idealism. She was to prove a most devoted friend and supporter, and she would shortly introduce him to Ford Madox Hueffer.

On February 23 Mathews took him to the Poets' Club dinner—Sturge Moore and Hilaire Belloc were to be 'the other attractions'. Hewlett was there, and so too was the great George Bernard Shaw. The Poets' Club was formed in 1908 and met once a month, in the United Arts Club in St James's Street, S.W., for the members and their guests to dine together, read their poems, and discuss papers 'on a subject connected with poetry'. T. E. Hulme was its secretary. The February meeting failed to impress Pound. Belloc 'sang to illustrate his points (most of which were unsound)'; Shaw, to his credit, 'expressed his habitual ignorance more entertainingly than anyone else'; but in general it was 'a bore'. 'The only poet [in the club] didn't show up'; and 'They discussed every thing under heaven except poetry'.

Pound may simply have been suffering from not being the centre of attention. At the same time it would have been true that on the whole the poets there, and the other poets he had been meeting, did not take poetry as seriously as he did and were not ambitious to do something new and on a grand scale. Beside his total dedication they were amateurs. Manning might be an exception; Yeats would certainly be the great exception. But the rest, with their careers at the Bar or the Civil Service or in politics, and with their lightweight novels and essays, were at best minor poets if not just talented versifiers working within the familiar conventions. The names of a few are kept alive by the odd poem in the anthologies of Victorian and early twentieth century verse. Most would never be mentioned now if it were not for their association with Yeats or Pound. Yet any natural and justifiable sense of superiority Pound might have felt towards them, setting aside mere arrogance of youth, would have been tempered by his need for the supporting company of poets, and by his need for their confirming recognition of his own claim to be a poet.

Hewlett's commendation of *A Quinzaine* counted for something; and 'May Sinclair's belief in my work ought also to be valuable'. As Pound told his mother, 'It is very pleasant to have people who have been more or less flooded with literature all their lives believe that you know your job.' It was also worth something that such people seemed inclined to treat him rather decently. 'Being in the gang & being known by the right people ought to mean a lot better introduction of "Personae"', and more and better reviews. 'I am not yet a celebrity', he confessed, evidently looking forward to being one, 'But it is indisputable that several very well known people are interested in what I am doing.'

'The Dawn' and Dorothy

The high point of his February would have been Thursday the 18th with the day after. 'I read "The Dawn" at the Shakespears after lunch. Then Lectured. Then the Adams automobiles took me to dinner & a show. Friday, they (the Schusters) gave me Ellen Terry [the great actress] to look after at the lunch party'; then—after calling in on Selwyn Image, who talked of 'when old Verlaine came over etc.'—to 'tea at Mrs Shakespears (they are quite the nicest people in London)'. In fact, 'I think the Shakespears & Selwyn Image are about the most worth while out of the lot I have come across'. 'The Shakespears' would have been Olivia Shakespear and her daughter Dorothy—Mr Shakespear, a solicitor, would have been at his office near Gray's Inn.[8]

---

[8] Olivia Shakespear (1863–1938), daughter of Major General Henry Tod Tucker, C.B., sometime Adjutant General of the Army in India; married (1885) Henry Hope Shakespear (1849–1923), born in India, son of a District Officer in the Bengal Civil Service; their daughter Dorothy born 14 September 1886. By all accounts theirs became a loveless marriage. Hope Shakespear was educated in England from the age of 6, went to Harrow, read law at Cambridge, became a solicitor and had his own legal practice in London. He painted landscapes in watercolour, and sometimes took Dorothy painting with him. Olivia wrote six novels, two plays, reviews etc. She and Yeats met in 1894, through Lionel Johnson her first cousin and his fellow poet; they became lovers for some time around 1895–97, until she realized that he could not forget Maud Gonne; she remained, according to Yeats himself, the centre of his life in London. Yeats married her step-niece, and Dorothy's closest friend, Georgie Hyde-Lees (1892–1968) in 1917, with Pound as best man—Pound being by then married to Dorothy.

The Shakespears' drawing room held a special interest and excitement for Pound: it was his nearest contact so far with Yeats, apart from a sighting across the theatre at a matinée of his *Deirdre* in November. Now he found himself sitting 'on the same hearth rugs that Willie Yeats sits on when he is in town'. And to add to the wonder, 'they tell me I read his poems very much as he does.' It may have been Dorothy who told him that.[9] She had studied him closely when he first sat on the hearthrug:

At first he was shy—he spoke quickly, (with a strong, odd, accent, half American, half Irish) he sat back in his chair; but afterwards, he suddenly dropped down, cross-legged, with his back to the fire: then he began to talk—He talked of Yeats, as one of the Twenty of the world who have added to the World's poetical matter—He read a short piece of Yeats, in a voice dropping with emotion, in a voice like Yeats's own[10]—He spoke of his interest in all the Arts, in that he might find things of use in them for his own—which is the Highest of them all.

While Pound was being excited by the thought of Yeats, Dorothy was being enraptured by Pound himself. 'Oh! Ezra!', she invoked him in her notebook, 'how beautiful you are! With your pale face and fair hair! I wonder—are you a genius? or are you only an artist in Life?' She wanted to remember his 'wonderful beautiful face'—

a high forehead, prominent over the eyes; a long, delicate nose, with little red, nostrils; a strange mouth, never still, & quite elusive; a square chin, slightly cleft in the middle—the whole face pale; the eyes gray-blue; the hair golden-brown, and curling in soft wavy crinkles. Large hands, with long, well-shaped, fingers, and beautiful nails.[11]

Some people have complained of untidy boots—how could they look at his boots, when there is his moving, beautiful face to watch?

His saying 'of one college, that it was only another tract of the barren waste he had lived in before', moved her to think 'he has ... suffered that which

---

[9] Dorothy Shakespear (1886–1973), only child of OS and HHS, educated at a girls' boarding school, with a year in Geneva; 'remained with her family in London after leaving school, tied closely to home in the Victorian manner, painting watercolours, doing needlework, reading, and attending concerts and lectures with her mother' (*EP/DS* xi).

[10] An Australian-born concert singer, Florence Wood (née Schmidt), who had known Pound around 1910, recalled how 'Ezra would "intone" his poems to us of an evening. I fear we used to think his recital of them unusual if not eccentric.' (Stock ed., *Perspectives* (Chicago: Henry Regnery, Company, 1965), p. 80)

[11] In 1971 Dorothy Pound added this note: 'On further acquaintance, I found that those eyes behind the glasses were green; and his nails were not so elegant!' (*Etruscan Gate* p. 1). How different from the young Dorothy's first impressions were those of Elkin Mathews' 11-year-old daughter: 'Mr E. Pound came to tea and supper', she wrote in her diary in March 1909, 'I think Mr Pound is a very sickly young man'. But she still recalled in her old age how nice he had been to her, and his 'high, copper-coloured hair' (Nelson 134).

is untellable'. There is nothing to suggest that Ezra was reciprocally struck by Dorothy.

Indeed, while we can see Dorothy beginning to fall in love with Ezra, we have to reckon with the likelihood that the work which he read after lunch on the 18th was devoted to turning desire away from the particular person and towards Ideal Beauty. We owe to Dorothy the only definite record of 'The Dawn'. It is known that it was a 'prose & verse sequence', and that some if not all the poems were early compositions. What appears to have been the only complete manuscript was lost in the post in 1910. Dorothy however had copied and preserved some 'Extracts from a set of M.S.S. verses entitled "*The Dawn*", *For it is a little book of her praises*'. There are ten 'extracts', and four of them are poems from 'Hilda's Book'. 'The Aube of the West Dawn' is there too, in a variant version, followed by 'Roundel', another poem from the 'San Trovaso Notebook'. Those are the last two 'extracts'. Now there exists in the Beinecke Pound Archive, on some loose sheets of manuscript in a folder of drafts associated with 'Hilda's Book', a prose setting for 'Aube of the West Dawn' and then for a final unnamed poem. 'Roundel', the last of Dorothy's 'extracts', would fit the context exactly. It is safe to conclude that these sheets formed part of a draft of the 'sequence of prose & verse'. And it seems reasonable to assume then that Pound's idea was to develop some or all of 'Hilda's Book', with some or all of his Venetian poems, into a book modelled on Dante's *La Vita Nuova*.

The first 'extract', a revised version of 'The Summons' from 'Hilda's Book'—see p. 37 above—begins 'I cannot bow to woo thee', and calls on the former lover to be rapt with him 'in that great involving flame' which would sweep them 'upward to the centre of all Truth'. The whirring wings are there in the second 'extract', raising 'my spirit from all Terren things'. The poems in the middle of the sequence effect a passage through darkness and separation. Then the Dawn's reflection comes to him, in the words of the prose setting, 'as the wraith of that eternal beauty, whereof is she the symbol'; and in the closing 'extract' he is following her 'unto that unbounded real of all the immages', as the prose setting has it, saying 'I come unto thee thru the hidden ways / Soul of my soul whose beauty quivereth / Within Her eyes . . .'. This is unmistakeably to follow after Dante's sublimation of his feelings for Beatrice—though there is no hint of Dante's theology.

Dorothy's notebook entries over the weeks and months following her first rapturous vision of Ezra show her struggling to understand and imitate him, and writing her own *Vita Nuova*.

26 February 1909 . . . I see him as a double person . . . His spirit walks beside him, outside him . . . He has conquered the needs of the flesh—He can starve; nay, is willing, to starve that his spirit may bring forth 'the highest of arts'—poetry. . . . 'It is worth starving for' he said one day. He has attained to peace in this world, it seems to me. To be working for the great art, to be living in, and for, Truth in her Greatness—He has found the Centre—TRUTH.

23 March 1909 . . . About three weeks ago I was living in the spirit—for some three days I went about in a dream, thinking, thinking, never ceasing to try & puzzle out the Truth—the Truth that Ezra has found. And I did not wish to find it *because Ezra* had found it—but because I knew that the Truth that I am searching for is the same that he has found. . . .

2 June 1909 It is not friendship & love that I am wanting—it is something beyond the horizon—friendship & love may help in the finding, but That Something is Life Eternal—my soul.

10 July 1909 'My soul'! It has not seemed to exist these last days . . . Nothing moves it, nothing even finds it. / Yes—One thing touched it, for an instant, and made it give a little cry—Ezra called me by a name that made me smile for joy—'You are Triste, Little Brother?' he asked three days ago. . . .

In July Dorothy wore a bunch of white poppies in her hat, and thought 'Each white poppy is a dream'. Pound wrote a 'plaint' for her beginning 'White Poppy, heavy with dreams'. It spoke of a deep hunger for the lips of 'the white folk of the forest'; and of 'sorrow, sorrow / When love dies-down in the heart'. It sought peace from the 'White Poppy, who art wiser than love'. Dorothy copied the poem into her notebook in October. In her mind she 'underlined so strongly the "I am come to thee for peace" . . . that [the poem] meant to me a friendship—rather cold & blue.'

31 October 1909 I might perchance find the other. I desire that a man should kiss me—I desire that a man should hold me with both hands, and read in my eyes such Things as cannot be spoken: That a man should make me shiver and be silent

That I may understand the chivalry and trust and joy of a great love.

Nevertheless I know that there be some souls who do not learn these matters by experience—but already know them by instinct—and that to such persons to touch hand with hand dims the vision rather than reveals.

Also Revelation comes to a man when he is alone; and until he has searched beyond others he will never be alone.

[no date—before 19 March 1910] . . . One can live as I have these last days, floating above the world, untouched—breathing only Peace; giving an exquisite delicate love, instead of the hot-coloured passion which dying leaves a blackness of Hell.

86

19 March 1910 Ezra! Ezra! . . . you are that which I desire—for you have given me understanding . . . enough to make me crave more, and more, until I shall have attained your dream land; until I shall live wrapt in the dream, touching the world no more.

Dorothy was approaching Pound's ideal of a wife. His mother, as mothers will, would bring up the marriage question; and Pound would dismiss it, on financial and practical grounds, but also on the ground of the general incompatibility of poets and women. But on one occasion in 1910 he made this concession to her: 'If the artist must marry let him find someone more interested in art, or his art, or the artist part of him, than in him. After which let them take tea together three times a week.'

When William Carlos Williams passed through London in 1910 he noticed that 'Ezra kept a candle on his mantel continually burning before the photograph of some girl'. It is not known whose was the image in the shrine, only that it was not Dorothy's.

'Personae of Ezra Pound'

In March 1909 Mary Moore asked Pound, was London fun? 'Six months ago it was decidedly not', he answered, but 'Today it has been. / I am being properly published. one book in the press, another finished, i.e. written. and more on the way.' These books would have been *Personae*, 'The Dawn', and the new poems which would go into *Exultations* in the autumn. About the same time Pound purred to Williams, 'Mathews is publishing my "Personae" & giving me the same terms he gives Maurice Hewlett'. In the event there would be little or nothing in the way of royalties, but he did have something to write home about:

Well mother mine: / We appear to be working out of the amateur class: Mathews is using the 'Personae' in his best series—a real live book with ornamentation & whiskers i.e. binding.

Set up by this prospect of professional status he felt able to tell Homer that 'No literature is made by people in other professions—except in the rarest of cases'. Poor Homer!

Personae of Ezra Pound—with the provoking *of* in place of the conventional *by*—made its (or their) appearance in mid-April, a neatly produced volume containing thirty-three poems, and rather cavalierly dedicated to 'Mary Moore of Trenton, if she wants it'. The epigraph was carried over from *A Lume Spento*, '*Make-strong old dreams lest this our world lose heart*'.

87

Half of the poems too were from *A Lume Spento*; the other half being now first published, though written at various dates going back as far as 1905. [12]

'Grace before Song' is again the prelude. [13] The first part is a sequence of twelve poems, reproducing in a tighter and more coherent form the first part of *A Lume Spento*. There is the same initial trio of 'La Fraisne' (but with the 'Note Precedent' removed to the end of the volume), 'Cino' (without 'In Epitaphium Eius'), and the de Born of 'Na Audiart': the disappointed lover, now in love with a woodland pool; the fickle lover of many; and the frustrated would-be lover of one. Then there is a small series of six poets as before, but without the Swinburnian 'Anima Sola'. Now the two poems after Villon and the two after Browning are followed by the anti-Dowson 'In Tempore Senectutis'—'we twain are never weary...For our wonder that grows not old'—and by the poet's downbeat fantasy of the likely fate of his own poems, 'Famam Librosque Cano'. 'Scriptor Ignotus' follows, but now it does not stand out as the climax of the sequence, but is rather the first of a group of three poems answering to the initial group of three. After the poet's promise to make for K.R.H. and for the beauty of her music 'A new

---

[12] *Personae*, plural of *persona* (Latin), from *per-sonare* 'to sound through': a stage mask, representing some particular character; thence a personage or character in a play; more generally, to sustain a part, to play a role. Cf. to impersonate. In the old ritual drama it was assumed that it was the gods or spirits themselves who possessed the actor and spoke through the mask.

[13] I make out this structural arrangement:

	Grace Before Song	II	Tally-O
	—		Ballad for Gloom
I	La Fraisne		For E. McC
	Cino		At the Heart o'Me
	Na Audiart		Xenia
	Villonaud for this Yule		Occidit
	A Villonaud: . . . of the Gibbet		Search
	Mesmerism		An Idyl for Glaucus
	Fifine Answers		In Durance
	In Tempore Senectutis		. . . A Vision of Italy
	Famam Librosqe Cano		
	Scriptor Ignotus		In the Old Age of the Soul
	Praise of Ysolt		Alba Belingalis
	Camaraderie		From Syria
	—		From the Saddle
	Masks		Marvoil
	—		Revolt
			And Thus in Nineveh
			The White Stag
			—
			Piccadilly

thing / As hath not heretofore been writ', comes 'Praise of Ysolt', then 'Camaraderie'.

'Praise of Ysolt' is an expansion and transformation of 'Vana' in such a way as to take both its place and that of 'Donzella Beata'. 'The little grey elf words crying for a song' are given new meaning and speak of an inspiration which seems to go beyond that of K.R.H. Three women come to him one after the other, and each moves him to song. The first, 'in the morn of my years', was as the moon and like the moon went from him, leaving him with no-one to sing when his soul called for a song. Then his soul sent 'a woman of the wonderfolk' crying for a song, and his song was ablaze with her until she too went from him. Last his soul sent 'a woman as the sun', who called forth song 'as the sun calleth to the seed', 'the song-drawer / She that holdeth the wonder words within her eyes'. And it is on account of her presence in his heart that his soul will sing now in spite of his telling it ' "There be many singers greater than thou" '. The psychology of this, with its distinctions of 'soul', 'heart' and speaking self, is in the manner of the Tuscan love poetry of Dante and his contemporaries, and even more opaque. One gathers that 'the woman of the sun' is his new *donzella beata* and ideal muse.

'Camaraderie'—in *A Lume Spento* it was 'Comraderie'—has a telling epigraph from the *Vita Nuova*. This comes from a passage in which Dante is travelling in a large company and must hide the anguish of going away from his blessed one lest he betray his love of her to the crowd. Love himself then tells him to seem to give his heart to another lady so that she shall be his defence. (Pound's naming 'Ysolt' in the previous poem could be such a defence against the discovery of his ideal love.) In this poem he summons up the delicate intimations of a beloved person which make him happily aware of her presence even when they are apart. That could be a retort to Dante. But the title makes it something else as well, by placing his relationship under the heading of comradeship or friendship rather than love. This places the person addressed at a remove from his heart—as Dorothy felt distanced by her 'white poppy' poem.

The three poems together—'Scriptor Ignotus', 'Praise of Ysolt', and 'Camaraderie'—declare what this poet loves and looks to for his inspiration. One might say that his genius is to be the idealization of beauty, not the actual presence of a woman. The relations and contrasts, both general and particular, with 'La Fraisne', 'Cino' and 'Na Audiart', hardly need to be spelt out. What is worth remarking though is that Pound has been concerned in this new book not so much to select the best or the strongest work from *A Lume Spento*, as to refine and develop and give a clearer formal arrangement to his thinking out the nature, scope and condition of his calling.

'Masks' acts as a pivot or hinge between the two parts of *Personae*. In *A Lume Spento* it introduced the set of poems which formed an ascending chain of poetic being, and there it seemed unremarkable enough. But here it not only links the two parts and helps our understanding of each, but also throws light on the title and intent of the book as a whole.

> These tales of old disguisings, are they not
> Strange myths of souls that found themselves among
> Unwonted folk that spake a hostile tongue,
> Some soul from all the rest who'd not forgot
> The star-span acres of a former lot
> Where boundless mid the clouds his course he swung

As a premise that resembles Wordsworth's 'trailing clouds of glory do we come / From God, who is our home', though Pound is not appealing to recollections of early childhood. He is prompting us rather to think of what he is doing in his *personae*, where he is himself putting on those 'old disguisings' and telling tales 'of souls that found themselves among / Unwonted folk that spake a hostile tongue'. In entering in imagination into their minds and moods he is of course, while feigning possession by their spirits, actually engaged in performing his interpretation of their states of soul and being. And the constant ground of his interpretation is the idea that the soul is native to heaven, that is, to the realm of the ideal. His La Fraisne, Cino, himself as the unknown poet, and the others still to come, are, each in their particular fashion and degree, souls moved by desire for the ideal beauty and truth which is their home. If they live imperfectly in this impermanent world, then all that they can be made to tell us of that other realm must be told in terms of their earthly experiences. But that means that the tales of their loves and deeds may be read as intimations or allegories of the soul's relations with its ideal. We will find 'In Durance', the poem of spiritual homesickness which he wrote in Crawfordsville, at the heart of the second part of *Personae*.

The most interesting of the new poems in this second part is 'An Idyl for Glaucus', a long dramatic monologue in which a lover laments the loss of her beloved who has been transformed into a sea-god. Ovid tells his story, and Dante alluded to it in attempting to give an account of how he was transformed into a state beyond the human as he looked on Beatrice in Paradise. Pound has invented the lover who witnesses Glaucus' transformation but does not know how to follow him, and who is left astray in the mortal world in which she can no longer be at home. In a letter to his father Pound wrote that 'the equation ought to hold good in any case where the man's further and subtler development of mind puts a barrier between him & a woman to whom he has become incomprehensible.'

The arrangement of the eighteen poems in this part amounts to an expansion and possible resolution of that problematic equation. The three big poems about spirits caught up in visions which alienate them from the ordinary life of earth are at the centre, with a sequence of six poems leading into that group, and another sequence of six following on from it. Within those sequences the poems come in pairs, and the first and second pair of each sequence are thematically related, giving an impression of ring-composition. Thus the initial pairs take up the sword against God, or Death, or in rising up from dreams to valiant deeds. The middle pairs tell of lovers separated from their ladies by their worldly occupations of wealth-seeking or war. That makes for a progression from the life of action, into the poems of longing for the visionary 'further and subtler development of mind', and then a return to more or less visionless warfare. But 'Marvoil' gives a turn to the condition of the lover separated from his lady by keeping his desire and his dream alive in his singing. Then 'Revolt: Against the crepuscular spirit in modern poetry' brings the whole series to a climax with its powerful resolution of the apparent dichotomy of dream and deed: let the poet in the world dream 'shapes of power . . . hearts hot, thoughts mighty'. This poet's business is not to escape 'this our world' but to put heart into it.

'And Thus in Nineveh', a wry coda, would have us believe that there poets were respected and honoured, and that maidens and men would scatter rose leaves on their tomb, because they 'drink of life / As lesser men drink wine'.

The final poem of part two declared that 'The White Stag' 'we're a-hunting' is '*Fame*'. The reviews brought Pound a foretaste of that. *Personae* was reviewed in *The Daily Telegraph, The Daily Chronicle, The Evening Standard and St. James Gazette*—newspapers noticed poetry in those days; in the weekly *Observer* and *Times Literary Supplement*; in *The New Age, The Nation* and *The Spectator*; in *The Bookman*, and in *The English Review*. There were more reviews, but that was more than enough to provide Elkin Mathews with glowing excerpts to fill out a publicity flier: 'Real poetry' (*The Observer*)—'full of human passion and natural magic' (*The Daily Chronicle*)—'No new book of poems for years past has had such a freshness of inspiration, such a strongly individual note, or been more alive with undoubtable promise' (*The Bookman*).

The reviewers mostly registered the shock of the revolt against convention, but were reassured to discover familiar beauties in the new measures. 'Beauty' was the vogue term. But the *TLS* found too much eccentricity and obscurity to leave room for beauty. F. S. Flint while giving high praise in *The New Age* to the 'craft and artistry, originality and imagination', expressed a well-wisher's hope that Pound's 'free form of verse' would not 'lead him into the wastes'. And he was sceptical about whether Mr Pound's strengthening his dreams with English verse would slay any dragons.

The most discerning criticism came from Edward Thomas in *The English Review*:

It is easier to enjoy than to praise Mr Pound, easier to find fault with him, easiest to ridicule. His *Personae* ... is strewn with signs of two battles not yet over, the battle with the world of a fresh soul who feels himself strong but alone, and the battle with words ...

He has no obvious grace, no sweetness, hardly any of the superficial good qualities of modern versifiers; not the smooth regularity of the Tennysonian tradition, nor the wavering, uncertain languor of the new, though there is more in his rhythms than is apparent at first through his carelessness of ordinary effects. He has not the current melancholy or resignation of unwillingness to live; nor the kind of feeling for nature that runs to minute description and decorative metaphor. He cannot be usefully compared with any living writers, though he has read Mr Yeats. Browning and Whitman he respects ... He is equally fond of strict stanzas of many rhymes, of blank verse with many unfinished lines, of rhymeless or almost rhymeless lyrics, of Pindarics with or without rhyme. But these forms are not striking in themselves, since all are subdued to his spirit; in each he is true in his strength and weakness to himself, full of personality and with such power to express it that from the first to the last lines of most of his poems he holds us steadily in his own pure, grave, passionate world.

Thomas was making an honourable effort to get the measure of a work that was quite out of the ordinary; and he was honestly if uncomfortably aware that there was something larger there that was eluding his grasp. But then none of the reviewers noticed the attempt at a major structure in the arrangement of the poems, or the will to organize them into a total statement of his poetics and his vision.

An anonymous reviewer in *The Nation* saw nothing except sedition. In a wonderfully reactionary laying down of the old law, he condemned *Personae* as the effort of an artistic malcontent to alter the poetic mode of expression, a thing which was not to be done. Mr Ezra Pound had defied 'the constituted, but extremely elastic, government of his state', i.e. the state of Poetry, and stood accused of 'rebellion and treason'. He would not, or could not, 'manage his thought according to the high and nameless, but rigorous...code of poetic law'. From Pound's point of view, as he remarked to his mother when sending her a copy, this review was as good as another for stirring up publicity.

Another revealing attack came from Rupert Brooke in *The Cambridge Review*. Betraying the provinciality of the intellectual élite, he was first amused at 'certain London papers' which had recently ' "discovered" ' Pound's poetry, and then amused at his name and his nationality. Could one be expected to take seriously as a poet someone named Ezra Pound, and an American—someone, besides, whom one had not oneself 'discovered' and patronized! Then came the incorrigible put-down. Mr Pound showed that he could be a good poet when he wrote 'in metre'; but he had 'fallen...under the dangerous influence of Whitman'—the metrically uncouth American. He wrote too many poems 'in unmetrical sprawling lengths' and so generally failed 'to express much beauty'. Someone should kindly hint to him, what anyone half-educated would know from Mr Saintsbury's codification of the laws of prosody, that poetry could only be written in metrical verse. 'Mr Pound has great talents', Brooke condescendingly allowed, and he deserved to be saved from going on stammering in prose.

This matter of metre was the crucial issue at the time. But F. S. Flint found an answer to Brooke, possibly having had a hint from Pound himself, in his second review of Pound's verse:

One thing is to be proved by these two little books of his, *Personae* and *Exultations*, and that is that the old devices of regular metrical beat and regular rhyming are worn out; the sonnet and the three-quatrain poem will probably always live; but for the larger music verse must be free from all the restraints of a regular return and a squared-up frame; the poet must forge his rhythm according to the impulse of the creative emotion working through him...

That was Pound's own belief and practice. 'Now as to my rhythmic principles', he would write in January 1911,

There is in every line a real form, or inner form, & an apparent. By the inner form ye shall know them. I, as often as I like, dispense with the other....

> Eyes, dreams, lips, and the night goes
>
> inner form
>
> Nel mezzo del camin di nostra vita

He had been following this principle, he wrote in the same letter,

Unconsciously from the time I was fifteen, falling in with my need for sincere rhythm.—I mean the thing that isn't the beat of the metronome. The thing that 'corresponds'...

He believed in fact in 'an exact correspondence between the cadence-form of the line & some highly specialized or particular emotion'. But these, the emotions and hence the cadence-forms, 'change with the seasons' and are specific, inimitable. As if in reply to Brooke's review, he named Whitman, 'the only American poet of his day who matters', as a major instance: 'He was sincere in his rythmic interpretation of his land & time.' He was also, however, 'too lazy to learn ... the arranging of his rhytmic interpretations into harmony'. There was another of Pound's rhythmic principles, all of them rather advanced for England around 1910. But Flint, Thomas, and some others, did sense the difference in his verse, and wonder what deeper developments it might signify.

In spite of his disturbing the established order, and also because of it, he was becoming known, even just a bit famous. There were reviews in New York, Philadelphia, Melbourne and Paris. He was accorded a celebratory lampoon in *Punch* as 'the new Montana (U.S.A.) poet, Mr Ezekiel Ton':

Mr Ton, who has left America to reside for a while in London and impress his personality on English editors, publishers and readers, is by far the newest poet going, whatever other advertisements may say. He has succeeded, where all others have failed, in evolving a blend of the imagery of the unfettered West, the vocabulary of Wardour Street, and the sinister abandon of Borgiac Italy.

Even better than that was having his name, Ezra Pound, mentioned in a letter to the *Saturday Review of Politics, Literature, Science and Art*, as one of 'our best writers' along with Conrad and Henry James. He was just 24 at that moment.

Yeats

No sooner was *Personae* published than Pound was thinking of his next move. 'I want to strike a double blow with two volumes published simultaneously about September (or before)', he wrote home at the end of April.

He was feeling good about the poems he had been writing in March and April. 'Ballad of the Goodly Fere' had come to him after he 'had been made very angry by a certain sort of cheap irreverence' in a Soho café. He wrote it at a sitting the next morning in the British Museum Reading Room, 'with scarcely any erasures', putting himself into the person of Simon Zelotes speaking of Christ after the Crucifixion.

No capon priest was the Goodly Fere
But a man o' men was he.

. . . . . .

A master of men was the Goodly Fere,
A mate of the wind and sea.
If they think they ha' slain our Goodly Fere
They are fools eternally.

I ha' seen him eat o' the honey-comb
Sin' they nailed him to the tree.

In the afternoon he 'peddled the poem about Fleet Street, for I began to realise that for the first time in my life I had written something that "everyone could understand", and I wanted it to go to the people.' He told Homer that it was 'probably about the strongest thing in english since "Reading Goal"'. But Fleet Street's popular press hardly looked at it and did not publish it.

About the same time, and again in the studious quiet of the Museum Reading Room, he wrote 'the bloody sestina', his war music for Bertran de Born as 'a stirrer-up of strife'. He had few books in his lodging in Langham Street and needed 'to make sure of the right order of permutations' behind 'the curious involution and recurrence of the Sestina'. He meant it to be 'blood curdling', 'to express the unadulterated lust for battle', and 'incidentally' to show 'Bertrand of Born in a peevish humour'. When he performed it with resonant fury and appropriate snarls and war-whoops in the Tour Eiffel restaurant to T. E. Hulme's group gathered there to dine and talk poetry, he so amazed and astounded all present that the management considerately screened off the poets' table from the other diners.

By June he had '30 odd' poems for the next book, but it was proving 'the devil to get them arranged in any sort of order'. He wanted 'Zelotes. & the Sestina tone to predominate.'

All this time Pound had been waiting to meet Yeats. Since the performance of his *Deirdre* the previous November Yeats had been in Paris and Dublin, caught up with Maud Gonne and with the problems of the Abbey Theatre, and with Synge's dying. Mrs Shakespear was expecting him in March, and had him 'nailed' for Pound to meet then. But it was not until the end of April that he at last arrived, and Pound at once 'had about five hours of him'. Yeats seemed inclined to be decent to him, that was all Pound had to say of that first conversation. Almost at once Yeats sent him a courtly invitation to the next one of his regular Monday evenings, and

95

from then on his week revolved around those Yeatsian evenings whenever the great man was in London.

He had other regular evenings, as he told Homer. 'I find one Victor Plarr of the old Rhymers club most congenial. He is in on Sunday supper-&-evenings.' Plarr would figure as 'Monsieur Verog' in *Hugh Selwyn Mauberley*, with his reveries over the manner of living of members of the old Rhymers' Club; and canto 16 would feature fragments of his memories of incidents in the Franco-Prussian war. Then there were 'Yeats Monday evenings', and 'a set from the Irish Lit. Soc. eats together on Wednesdays & a sort of new Rhymers gang on Thursdays.' This 'habit of dining once a week together, in the cheapest possible restaurant...regular Thursday, or other day, same spot', was one he was still recommending in his later years, 'to all who wish to live in their heads'. Writers, he would insist, need to have some sort of society in which to try out their work: 'If young men funk that sort of thing, I don't see what resonance they can expect; it is string without sounding board.'

The 'sort of new Rhymers gang' was T. E. Hulme's group of young poets who had just broken off from the Poets' Club's deathly 'tea-parties in suave South Audley Street' and who meant to be more lively in Soho. They read their poems to each other, and criticized them; and they discussed the state of poetry and how to reform it. Among other topics they talked of the image and of *vers libre*, with Hulme's voice generally dominating the rest.[14] Hulme was steeped in Bergson's philosophy, and followed him in thinking that the true life of the mind was in an intuitive consciousness of life-in-process, a consciousness not mediated by preconceived ideas. Wanting an intuitive poetry freed from cliché and from convention he called for the abolition of metre and regular forms of verse; and he called for a language of direct visual images 'which would hand over sensations bodily'. And 'the poet', he argued, 'must continually be creating new images', because the life force in images quickly dies out as they become received associations. But he was himself more of a philosopher than a poet. His 'Complete Poetical Works', as collected by Pound in 1912, consisted of just five short poems.

[14] T. E. Hulme (1883–1917): English philosopher, critic of literature, art and politics, and poet; especially interested in Bergson, translated his *An Introduction to Metaphysics* (1912) and published essays on his philosophy; around 1912 developed a theory of 'anti-Romanticism' founded on the doctrine of Original Sin, later approved of by T. S. Eliot; a soldier in the First World War, killed in battle 28 September 1917.

Much has been made of Pound's indebtedness to Hulme. F. S. Flint,[15] an original member of Hulme's group and then a rather malcontent member of Pound's, would claim in 1915 that Pound had contributed nothing to the Tour Eiffel debates, but had taken his whole Imagist programme from them. Later critics, eager to inflate Hulme's reputation or to deflate Pound's, have taken Flint's claim as gospel. But it was, at the least, an exaggeration. In the matter of freeing verse from metre and regular forms Pound was well ahead of Hulme and his group, and not just in theory but in practical achievement. After all, Flint himself had recognized by January 1910 that in *Personae* and *Exultations* the rhythms were free and forged 'according to the impulse of the creative emotion'. In the related matter of the charged image, however, Pound may well have learnt something from Hulme, and he acknowledged as much in his 'Prefatory Note' to Hulme's five poems. Those poems, he wrote, recalled 'certain evenings and meetings of two years gone, dull enough at the time, but rather pleasant to look back upon.' 'As for the future', he then declared, '*Les Imagistes*, the descendants of the forgotten school of 1909, have that in their keeping.' But this acknowledgment that his *Imagistes* derived from Hulme's 'School of Images' was significantly qualified by the remark that the latter 'may or may not have existed', and by some scepticism about 'its principles'. His meaning, if I understand him, was that Hulme's school existed mainly in theory but not convincingly in practice. The great difference between himself and Hulme, and between their two groups, was the difference between talking about 'the Image' and actually creating images. Pound would continue to have considerable respect and liking for Hulme, but he had no time for his Bergsonizing. To spend one's time calling for a direct intuitive poetry in the dead prose of abstract theory must have struck him as risibly oxymoronic.

There was friendship for a time between Pound and Frank Flint. The latter's superior knowledge of what was going on in French poetry may well have encouraged Pound to study it more closely. And Pound took Flint's poetry seriously enough to try to make an Imagist of him. Other members of 'the forgotten school of 1909' were of interest to Pound more for their lives and conversation than for their poetry, or because of their association with Yeats. He remembered Joseph Campbell, with his interest

---

[15] F. S. Flint (1885–1960): English poet, critic, translator, and civil servant. Joined Civil Service as typist in 1904 and rose to become Chief of Overseas Section, Statistics Division, of the Ministry of Labour. Published poetry, *In the Net of Stars* (1909), *Cadences* (1915) and *Otherworld: Cadences* (1920); included in *Des Imagistes* (1914) and the later Imagist anthologies. Mastered ten languages, and was an authority on modern French poetry.

in Irish folk poetry, telling him 'of meeting a man on a desolate waste of bogs, and he said to him, "It's rather dull here;" and the man said, "Faith, ye can sit on a middan and dream stars".' Francis Tancred, who was on the stock exchange and wrote epigrams, is remembered in the *Cantos* for his Dickensian conversation at Yeats's evenings; and Desmond Fitzgerald, who 'journalisms & poetizes somewhat', is remembered there as 'The live man, out of lands and prisons', and for having 'been at the Post Office' in the 1916 Easter rising in Dublin. Those are the things that stayed with him. Exceptionally, Padraic Colum, another Irishman who attended occasionally, is remembered for the uncharacteristic intensity of his poem beginning 'O woman, shapely as the swan, / On your account I shall not die'. Edward Storer, whom Flint thought deserved recognition as a proto-Imagist, remained unmentioned.

It is very likely that in 1909 Pound was concerned much more with the musical than with the imagistic powers of words, and with the auditory rather than with the visual imagination. That was the dimension in which his work had been thus far most inventive and advanced. He would have had on that account a strong common interest with Florence Farr who took him along to his first Tour Eiffel occasion—when he gave his memorable rendition of 'the bloody sestina'. Farr was an actress, an intimate friend and theatrical associate of Yeats, and close also to Olivia Shakespear—they had collaborated in writing and performing two 'Egyptian' plays in 1901–2. With Yeats she had developed a mode of chanting or intoning poetry to the accompaniment of the psaltery, a twelve-stringed instrument 'sympathetic to the speaking voice' which Arnold Dolmetsch had made specially for her. R. F. Foster records that George Bernard Shaw thought it created 'a nerve-destroying crooning like the maunderings of an idiot-banshee'. Yeats thought it exactly right for his spirit plays. In April 1909 Elkin Mathews had just published Farr's book, *The Music of Poetry*, in which she set out her method for bringing out the full music of words. This would have been of immediate interest to Pound—of greater interest at that time than Hulme's Image—and for a time that summer he was 'working at Psaltary settings' for some of his poems with Florence Farr. It involved a system of notation, and no doubt a great deal of Yeatsian keening and intoning. It was meant to give the sound of disembodied spirits, and would have seemed promising for certain of Pound's *personae*. Beyond that, working with her would have given him a start on the technique of discovering and realizing the music latent in vowels and consonants and their combinations, a technique which would be the basis of his mature verse, and of his first opera, *Le Testament de Villon*, composed and performed in the 1920s.

Yeats came to think that Pound had 'got closer to the right sort of music for poetry than [Florence Farr]—it is more definitely music with strongly marked time and yet it is effective speech'. That has its amusing side, since Pound's way of reading poetry was apparently very like Yeats's own. 'However', Yeats added, possibly clarifying what lay behind Williams's saying that Pound couldn't hold a tune, 'he can't sing as he has no voice. It's like something on a very bad phonograph.' Pound himself confessed at one time to being 'tone deaf' and having 'the organ of a tree toad'. Still, his ear for the music of words was evidently acute.

The long looked forward to acquaintance with Yeats brought no disillusionment or disappointment. Moreover, once Yeats was in London all the other poets he had been meeting there became merely a supporting cast. 'As Yeats is the greatest poet of our time I thought you might like [his] autograph', he wrote to his father in the summer of 1909, enclosing a note in Yeats's hand. He was even more convinced of Yeats's eminence when he wrote to his mother on New Year's Day 1910, 'Yeats left this morning for Dublin. He is the only living man whose work has more than a most temporary interest.' 'I shall survive', he added, as if in the mood of 'Famam Librosque Cano', 'as a curiosity'. But then he had the comfort of hearing from the Shakespears a few months later that Yeats had said of him in private conversation, 'There is no younger generation (of poets). E. P. is a solitary volcano.' The foundations were being laid for a life-long friendship based on reciprocal respect and affection deep enough to make light of their often profound differences.

From the first Yeats meant much more to Pound than the dreamer of *The Land of Heart's Desire,* or the poet of the Nineties' Rhymers' Club and the Celtic Twilight. When Yeats lectured at Penn in November 1903 Pound was at Hamilton, but he would surely have heard of his visit, and been aware that he was being noticed there not so much for his lyric poetry as for his part in the movement 'to reawaken a true national consciousness in Ireland', and for his efforts to create a theatre 'for the expression of the genius of the Irish race'. Such an awareness lay behind his referring to Yeats in 1907, in his 'Blake's Rainbow' fragment, as 'The celtic Eagle' who 'resang Oisin' and 'set a whole land singing'. He went on in that fragment to associate Yeats with Dante and Blake as an exemplar of the prophetic imagination to which he himself would aspire in his own 'Great Song Of All The World'. He would have had it in mind that in Biblical tradition and in Dante the eagle renews its vision by gazing into the divine sun; and in later referring familiarly to Yeats as 'the Eagle', as in corresponding with the Shakespears, he would have been paying affectionate homage to his superior powers. He had come to Yeats to learn what he could from the best living master of the art of creating the consciousness of his people.

As his relationship with Yeats developed Pound's letters to his parents became less assertive and more assured about what he was doing in London. 'Plans?', he began one letter to his father, who may well have asked when did he plan to return home, 'I am going to migrate into that part of London known as Hammersmith where a friend will lend me a garden & a hammock & where for several months it is to be presumed that there will be sunshine.' Who that friend was remains unknown—the address, when he found it out, would be 10 Rowan Road, Brook Green. The rent was only '3/6 per week but 3d bus [fare to British Museum] destroyed profit.' He meant to draw on Homer for not more than $250 over the next year—which was as much as to say that he had no intention of leaving London. What he did intend was simple enough:

1. To get myself sufficiently well known so that my next seasons lectures will have sufficient attendance to pay all my expenses for 5 months if possible.
2. To write as much good stuff as I can.

To his mother he wrote in mid-August 1909, 'You know I have never made any pretense of loving labour or believing in its dignity. I never voluntaraly do anything but write lyrics & talk to my friends.' Some time in the early part of 1910 he told her, 'Dear Mother...you cant expect me to seriously consider America as a permanent place of abode.'

Though it may have been unwillingly, he was doing rather more than writing lyrics and talking to his friends. Need drove him. At Easter he had been constructing the scenario of an opera for Henry Waller, an established musician, though nothing more was heard of that venture. He had been writing a novel, or two novels—'he has written and burned two novels and three hundred sonnets', according to a 'News Note' in *The Bookman* in July. At the end of July he heard that his full series of twenty-one lectures at the Polytechnic would be going ahead. 'It's a long road', he commented, as if tired by the mere prospect of them, 'but I suppose I'm getting over it quicker than most.' In September he signed a contract with Dent for a book based on the lectures to be called *The Spirit of Romance*, and had to get down to the grind of writing it. It would have to be done against his grain:

I should never think of prose as anything but a stop-gap · a means of procuring food. Exactly on the same plane with market-gardening. If a thing is not suf-ficiently interesting to be put into poetry, & sufficiently important to make the poetical form worth while, it is hardly worth saying anything at all.

By the time the labour was done, only six months later, he was more than ever convinced that prose was not for him:

My mind, such as I have, works by a sort of fusion, and sudden crystalization, and the effort to tie that kind of action to the dray work of prose is very exhausting. One should have a vegetable sort of mind for prose.

But the poetry did not pay. *Personae* had not covered its costs, and *Exultations* would not. The only financial return came from Ford Madox Hueffer's *English Review*, which published the 'Sestina: Altaforte' in June, and 'Ballad of the Goodly Fere' with two other poems in October, and paid £5 per poem.

Pound had found the arrangement for the poems in his next book by early August when he submitted the manuscript to Elkin Mathews. There is reason to deduce that he submitted with it the manuscript of 'The Dawn', hoping for his 'double blow'. The note in *The Bookman* in July stated that 'he has lately completed a new book, a prose and verse sequence, which he is calling *The Dawn*.' Mathews agreed in September to publish *Exultations*, but there was no mention at that time of this other book. However, he agreed the following April to 'take on "The Dawn" together with the poems you have ready for a new autumn volume on the same terms as "Exultations"'. But then Pound decided in May not to publish his 'earlier poetic attempts' and withdrew the collection. Mathews mailed the manuscript, unregistered, 'to Pound in Hammersmith'. That had been his address when he submitted the manuscript, but he had moved in September 1909 to what became his fixed address until 1914, 10 Church Walk in Kensington. Pound never received the manuscript of 'The Dawn'—apparently he had no other copy—and nothing more was seen or heard of it in his lifetime.

'Exultations of Ezra Pound'

Mathews agreed on 16 September 1909 to publish *Exultations* and 'to pay the Author', after the costs for production and publicity had been met, '10% up to 500 copies and 12½% afterwards counting 13 copies as 12 on all copies sold'. The Author was to pay for any corrections and alterations in the proofs; and to assign to Mathews 'the exclusive right during the legal term of copyright' to print and publish 'the work intended to be called "Exultations of Ezra Pound"'. The Author, feeling his newfound professional status upon him, asked for the same terms as Dent had just offered for *The Spirit of Romance*: 10 per cent on the first thousand, 12½ on the second, 15 on the third and 20 per cent on the fourth and any further thousands. That was taking the very long view, since only one thousand sets of sheets were printed, and of those only 350 were bound up for sale. When Mathews made up the account the following March, 203 copies had been sold, 74 free copies had gone out for review or as presentation copies, and he was still some way short of covering his costs. If all the bound up copies had been sold a royalty of perhaps six shillings would have been due to the Author, provided that no further costs or charges had been incurred. More likely to be fruitful was Pound's other request, that the copyright be assigned for only so long as Mathews personally remained in publishing. This was to avoid his being 'tangled up in business with some unknown third party in case [Mathews] died or withdrew'.

The book was published on 25 October, in dark red paper-covered boards with gold lettering on front cover and spine, at two shillings and sixpence a copy. On the verso of the title page it carried this epigraph:

> I am an eternal spirit and the things I
> make are but ephemera, yet I endure:
> Yea, and the little earth crumbles beneath
> our feet and we endure.

Thus the contracting Author transformed himself into the exulting poet 'Ezra Pound'.

'Exultation' is apt for the tone which Pound wanted to predominate, that of 'Sestina: Altaforte' and 'Ballad of the Goodly Fere'. The word has behind it associations of dancing with joy, of strong transports of delight, of triumphant rejoicing. It is a good word for the revolt against 'the crepuscular spirit'. In proclaiming that revolt Pound had called for poetry to bring forth 'shapes of power'; and if it must dream then to dream 'great deeds, strong, men, / Hearts hot, thoughts mighty'. That is a prescription for Bertran de Born's violent rejoicing in war, and for Simon Zelotes' quieter rejoicing in Christ's triumphing in the world. The tone of exultation is strong too in old Piere Vidal's celebration of the mad passion of his love for La Loba; and it sounds again, though with a difference, in de Born's powerful lament for 'the Young English King', and in the anonymous 'Alba'.

There are some poems, however, in which the note of exultation is not so readily caught, or is greatly modified. If 'Night Litany' and 'Sandalphon', both carried over from the Venetian work in *A Quinzaine for This Yule*, are exultant, then it is in a prayerful and contemplative fashion far removed from the energetically active living of de Born and Vidal and Christ. Again, the modes in which the love of beauty is celebrated in the sequence of poems from 'Hymn III' to 'Francesca' are surely of the Aesthetic movement, if they are not actually crepuscular. And in the rest of the collection, from 'Greek Epigram' through to 'Song of the Virgin Mother', the note of exultation is rather muted, except perhaps in 'Histrion'.

Of the latter sequence of eleven poems, nine were carried over from *A Lume Spento* or *A Quinzaine for This Yule*. Indeed, of the twenty-seven 'exultations', many had been written before Pound left America, and some (such as 'Sestina for Ysolt') date from as far as back as the period of 'Hilda's Book'. As few as ten were recent work written since his arrival in London—but among these were the most strikingly exultant. Some of the unevenness of the collection must be due to the putting together of poems from different stages of his development.

Of course he had his rationale for the collection. 'The collection as a whole should give a more or less proportioned presentation of life', he told Viola Baxter, adding that 'Each poem is in some extent the analysis of some element of life, set apart from the rest, examined by itself.' Moreover,

The position of the poem in a series of Exultations should be noted.

Thus. Night Litany—awe in the presence of beauty. Sandalphon—The joy of submission to an uncomprehended supreme power & wisdom.

Altaforte—*Strife* & love of strife for strife's sake & if you will love of Blood.

Vidal—sexual passion. ['Animal passion is very near—in its extreme form that is—to insanity'] The Goodly Fere—Love of strength.

The series, he recognized, was as yet incomplete—that is, he had yet to fulfil his ambition to give 'a more or less proportioned presentation of life'. 'In a man's complete work', he told his parents, 'there should be something for every mood and mental need.'

That gives a hint that he was thinking of the epic he meant one day to write even while putting together a modest miscellany of shorter lyrical and dramatic poems. There may have been another hint of that in his naming his collections the 'personae' or the 'exultations' *of Ezra Pound*, as we say *The Divine Comedy* **of** Dante Alighieri. Dante, he remarked in a 'tirade' on the epic aimed at his mother, while dipping into 'a multitude of traditions' had succeeded in unifying them 'by their connection with himself'. Was he hoping to unify the rather disparate and uneven poems in his *Exultations* by their connection with his poetic self?

If he was, then since he does not figure directly in his own person as Dante does, the unifying self would have to be looked for in the 'tone' of each poem and in the arrangement and total composition of the series.

There is in fact a definite structure to be made out,[16] one which is at once an arrangement of tonal effects and a working out of certain themes. The unifying concern appears to be the celebration of love in poetry, with the objects of desire ranging from de Born's 'blood', through a variety of beautiful women, up to the divine beauty of Venice. The epigraph to the volume point up its over-riding mood: the poet as 'an eternal spirit' is in love with what vanishes, yet his spirit endures.

One difference from *A Lume Spento* and *Personae* is that there is none of the gloom of decadence and death to be contended with. Another is that there is rather less of the soul's questing after unearthly beauty— it is now being schooled in the joy and the sorrow of loving mortal beauty. But the most significant difference is that the poet is here much less concerned to make claims for himself and for his art. There is no 'Scriptor Ignotus', and no 'Purveyors General'. True, the focus is on the poet and his dreams in that third group which has 'Histrion' at its centre, but those are all now familiar poems and the effect is of a well-known theme being revisited. The poet is more urgently engaged elsewhere.

In the poem which opens the collection, 'Guido Invites You Thus', he imagines what might have been Guido Cavalcanti's response to Dante's sonnet inviting him to join in a select boating party of poets and their ladies to talk of love. Pound's Guido would invite just his own lady, and want no other poet nor mere love talk. 'Lo, I would sail the seas with thee alone!', he writes, taking over Dante's image. He then makes the ship stand for his own poetry, with its merchandise 'thy heart and its desire' in which are fused 'Life, all of it, my sea, and all men's streams'. This is the

---

[16] These are the main groupings:

Ia	Guido Invites You Thus	III	Greek Epigram
	Night Litany		Columbus' Epitaph
	Sandalphon		Plotinus
	—		On His Own Face in a Glass
b	Sestina: Altaforte		Histrion
	Piere Vidal Old		The Eyes
	Ballad of the Goodly Fere		Defiance
	— — —		Song: 'Love thou thy dream'
II	Hymn III		— — —
	Sestina for Ysolt	IVa	Nel Biancheggiar
	Portrait (from 'La Mère Inconnue')		Nils Lykke
	Fair Helena		Song of the Virgin Mother
	Laudentes Decem I–X		
	Aux Belles de Londres	b	Planh for the Young English King
	Francesca		Alba Innominata
	— — —		Planh ('White Poppy')

enterprise to which the lady calls, and to which he also calls. She is no Beatrice figure, drawing the poet's soul heavenwards. His Guido's call is to what the heart desires, 'Life, all of it'.

That gives a different setting for 'Night Litany' than the Venetian 'Aube of the West Dawn', and it highlights the fact that it is God's beauty in an earthly city which purifies the heart. 'Sandalphon' is similarly set in a different light, with the emphasis falling more definitely upon 'the earth-horde's age-long crusading' and 'longing'. In his own sphere and fashion Sandalphon is transforming the heavenly angels' songs of God into words that speak of 'Life, all of it'.

The next three poems, 'Sestina: Altaforte', 'Piere Vidal Old', and 'Ballad of the Goodly Fere', all celebrate a love of life, each under a different aspect. They have in common strong rhythms and bold rhetoric. They have also this in common, that each is based on some objective source, the 'lives' of the two troubadours and the life of Christ. This was a poet who wished to 'make strong old dreams'; but it appears to be the case that his imagination is empowered by having something other than dream to work upon, something which purports at least to be a record of lived experience.

The seven poems from 'Hymn III' to 'Francesca' at first seem to regress into twilight dreams of over-refined beauty. The hymn 'From the Latin of Marc Antony Flaminius' gives the keynote: 'As a fragile and lovely flower unfolds . . . So doth my tender mind flourish, if it be fed with the sweet dew of the fostering spirit'. Thus in 'Sestina for Ysolt', 'There comes upon me will to speak in praise / Of things most fragile in their loveliness'. Thus in 'Portrait', 'Now I would weave her portrait out of all dim splendour.' And ' "Fair Helena" ' of the 'wistful loveliness' fades into the purple twilight 'Until she all forgets I am, / And knows of me / Naught but my dream's felicity.' These are artificial flowers fashioned out of Dowson and the Aesthetes generally. One might wonder, impatiently, why Pound was still imitating them.

An explanation can be found in a letter to Floyd Dell written in February 1911:

. . . I had a quarrel with you on the question of 'Dowson' a very sincere man & a very fine craftsman. I always wanted to contradict everything he said, & in some very early poems used his own forms to do so. . . .

The whole set of 'The Rhymers' did valuable work in knocking bombast, & rhetoric & victorian syrup out of our verse. And Dowson has epitomized a decade—exquisitely, unaffectedly . . . To me he holds a very interesting position, strategically, in the development of the art. . . . It is the 'Vale' of a number of spent force[s].

Pound's imitations are best taken as studies in craftsmanship, more especially in the craft of musical composition. The care over sound and syntax in 'Portrait' and '"Fair Helena"' is indeed exquisite. And it serves a desire to write of beauty unaffectedly. The significant achievement of the sequence is in its progression from the syrupy 'Sestina for Ysolt', to the simple directness of 'Francesca'—'You came in out of the night / And there were flowers in your hands'. 'Francesca' would outlast the rest of its sequence, and be the only one preserved in the definitive collected poems of 1926. It was the only one altogether free of those 'spent forces'—unless its last line, 'Alone', belongs to them.

'Laudantes Decem Pulchritudinis Johannae Templi', a set of ten poems in praise of the beauty of one Joanna or Joan Temple, follows '"Fair Helena"' in the sequence. This is so patently 'after' the Yeats of *The Rose* and *The Wind Among the Reeds* as to amount to an impersonation. Pound had evidently been studying Yeats even more closely than Dowson. The set begins with 'When your beauty is grown old in all men's songs', an obvious reworking of Yeats's 'When You are Old'—itself a reworking of Ronsard. That first poem had the title 'L'Envoi' in a manuscript fair copy, indicating that the sequence proper begins with 'I am torn, torn with thy beauty, / O Rose of the sharpest thorn!', a quite direct appropriation from Yeats's 'rose' poems. That is followed by the altogether Yeatsian lines, 'The unappeasable loveliness / is calling to me out of the wind'. Pound even goes so far as to give a Yeatsian heading, *'He speaks to the moonlight concerning the Beloved'*, to the section in which he reproduces the rhythm of 'The Lover Tells of the Rose in his Heart'. It is of course quite possible that while imitating Yeats's treatment of his relationship with Maud Gonne Pound was writing of an affair of his own. But the dominant effect is of his trying out Yeats's rhythms and idiom, and also of his trying on Yeats's emotion. He was trying to learn from Yeats, as from Dowson, how to write of the intensities of love naturally and without affectation. What he was particularly after, on the evidence of these imitations, was the quality of 'syntactical simplicity' which he found 'in the pages of *The Wind Among the Reeds*'. He was conscious also that the 'image' Hulme was talking about was already present 'in the early Yeats'. But these imitations are at best apprentice work and still far from rivalling even the master's early work.

The final group of three poems make for a strong close to the collection after the dozen relatively lightweight pages from 'Greek Epigram' to 'A Song for the Virgin Mother'. They end the series of analyses of life's elements upon the tone of lament, reminding us that the immortal spirit is in love with what must die.

'Planh for the Young English King', 'from the Provençal of Bertran de Born', is the complement and opposite to 'Sestina: Altaforte'. With equal rhetorical force it grieves over the death the other glories in. It cries out to be sung in the provençal mode just as the other does, though to vièle and organ drone rather than trumpets. And its language, if one must take it as speech rather than as a stately lament, is even further from any natural idiom. That it is artificial is probably the point: de Born had been in revolt against the English king and there was a suspicion that his grief was politically motivated. Nevertheless his lament does powerfully celebrate the dead king's nobility.

In 'Alba Innominata', a translation of the earliest complete Provençal dawn-song, the lady's celebration of the joy of making love with her lover is made the more intense by the pain of having to part at dawn lest her jealous husband discover them. Her song is framed by a sympathetic observer, her maid perhaps, who vouches for her beauty and truth in love. Pound will produce a much finer version in 'Langue d'Oc' (1918)—here the simplicity and directness he wants is overlaid in places by stilted turns of speech to suit the measure. But he is, one feels in spite of that, fully committed to the dramatic mood in which the lady even in the transports of ecstatic love is conscious of being at the mercy of time and worldly morality.

The last poem, the White Poppy 'Planh' written for Dorothy, makes for an unsettling end to the series of 'exultations'. Its note is of restless, unfulfilled desire; it vainly seeks peace in the White Poppy of dreams; and it closes upon the sad death of love in 'the Forest'—

> But oh, it is sorrow and sorrow
> When love dies-down in the heart.

I wonder if Pound had intended 'The Dawn' to be read as following on from that and providing a counter movement to it. It was uncharacteristic of him to order his work into a simple arc from joy to sorrow.

There were fewer reviews than for *Personae*, only about ten in all, but quite enough to give an idea of the state of the literary culture Pound was venturing into. The first, and worst, review was from Edward Thomas in *The Daily Chronicle* of 23 November:

Mr Pound's verses look so extraordinary, dappled with French, Provençal, Spanish, Italian, Latin and Old English, with proper names that we shirk pronouncing, with crudity, violence, and obscurity, with stiff rhythms and no rhythms at all, that we are tempted to think that they are the expression or at least the mask of an extraordinary man.... But having allowed the turbulent opacity of his peculiarities to sink down we believe that we see very nearly nothing at all.

There is a revealing little story behind this. Thomas's generous reviews of *Personae* in June had been not well received by the coterie of gentlemen poets who had taken him up—men such as Lascelles Abercrombie and Gordon Bottomley who would figure prominently in the *Georgian Anthology*. 'I shall never forget the meeting of the Square Club a few days after that monstrous action', Edgar Jepson was to write in his memoirs, 'the pale, shocked, contorted faces of the poet-makers.... Poor Edward Thomas! He did look so hot and bothered.... How *could* he have liked the verse of a man whom none of them had discovered, much less made?' Thomas recanted at once in a letter to Bottomley: 'Oh I do humble myself over Ezra Pound. He is not & cannot ever be very good. Certainly he is not what I mesmerized myself—out of pure love of praising the new poetry!—into saying he was & I am very much ashamed & only hope I shall never meet the man.... though of course I did indicate the chaos of the work.' As it happened he did meet Pound at a Square Club dinner in September. Pound, in a letter home, made nothing of it beyond mentioning that he had 'met Scott-James & Edward Thomas...(The fellows who have reviewed me to advantage...)'. But Thomas seems to have been confirmed in his taking against Pound. He wrote to Bottomley in December: 'Ezra Pound's second book was a miserable thing & I was guilty of a savage recantation after meeting the man at dinner. It was very treacherous & my severity was due to self-contempt as much as dislike of his work.' The abject contortions are of course all about assuring Bottomley and the coterie that they are the top dogs; and the savage review had behind it their disapproval of the unknown and upstart pretender. It was meant to nip in the bud the reputation he had helped to set on its way without their sanction.

An anonymous reviewer in the Birmingham *Daily Post*—could it have been Edward Thomas again?—took up the issue of metre and form and implied that Mr Pound was in danger of being misled by the unwise example of Mr Flint: 'Again we have the spectacle of a really sincere and vigorous artist driven by his revolt against the abuse of law and convention into mere chaos.' The one vital and notable poem was 'Laudantes Decem', and that succeeded because it conformed 'in general to a metrical scheme which has been built up on many generations of experience'. The anonymous reviewer in *The Nation* also thought well of that poem, and for the same reason. It showed that Mr Pound was learning 'to allow some outward form to his verses', where previously he had 'seemed to trust entirely to the formative powers inherent in his ideas', and to 'have been content with a savage and often ludicrous crudity of expression.' *The Nation* was willing to encourage the young poet where *The Daily*

Post could only give a warning. If only he would go on in this new way he might in time add something rich rather than merely curious to English poetry. And as evidence of Pound's becoming 'less derivative in matter' the review cited some of the most Yeatsian lines of 'Laudantes Decem'.

The Spectator was more perceptively encouraging. Feeling 'that this writer has in him the capacity for remarkable poetic achievement', it thought it only right just to hint at the danger of his being 'at present . . . a little too bookish and literary'. That was indeed putting it very mildly. Apart from that the review found a number of singularly clear merits. It concluded with the observation that while 'Mr Flint's *In the Net of Stars* has something of the same manner . . . the writer has not Mr Pound's richness or strength of thought.'

To Flint the comparison must have been invidious; and he may well have winced too at the irony of being supposed to be a misleader of Pound. He published two reviews of *Exultations*, one in *The English Review* in December, the second in *The New Age* in January. The first, a notice under 'Publications Received', was a firm put-down: ' . . . of our youngest poets he is the most alive as he is the most rugged, the most wrong-headed.' In the second he partly made up for that, but only after a certain amount of carping at Pound's 'hotchpotch' of diverse elements and tongues, which he attributed to his being an American. For 'a hotchpotch of picturesqueness', he declared, 'is the American idea of beauty.' That was a cultivated English sneer. The superior English would know of course that 'the picturesque' meant a proportioned harmony of diverse elements. But there may have been still more to the jibe. If Flint had heard Pound speak of giving 'a proportioned presentation of life' then he would have intended to strike covertly where it would hurt most. He went on to dismiss the 'Sestina: Altaforte' as 'rant', having suffered Pound's rendering of it, and possibly forgetting that it was a rant 'in character'. He was unimpressed by Pound's impersonations in general. Yet 'with all these reservations' he allowed 'that there is in Mr Pound's new book a rift of real, though vague, beauty, impalpable gold, as in the "Laudantes Decem . . ." and "Planh" '. Again, in spite of that, he allowed that Pound had freed himself from the outworn 'devices of regular metrical beat and regular rhyming', and proved that the poet's own creative emotion should give the rhythm.

Flint thought the language of 'Ballad of the Goodly Fere' a jargon. But many of the reviewers singled out that poem as the best thing in the book. Elkin Mathews had feared it would give offence. *The Observer* loved it: 'daring but beautiful . . . a magnificent picture of an often neglected side of the Christ-ideal.' *The Spectator* agreed: 'a wonderful presentation of Christ, haunts our memory'. Henry Baerlein in *The Bookman* asked for more: 'we should beg him to abandon his pursuit of knowledge and to make for us more "Ballads of the Goodly Fere" before it is too late.' Darrell Figgis in *The New Age* thought it was quite simply Pound 'at his best' And its success lasted. In October 1911, two years on, an undergraduate reviewer in Cambridge could find in *Canzoni* 'nothing so fine as the splendid "Ballad of the Goodly Fire [sic]", which to our mind, besides being Mr Pound's masterpiece, stands among the very best of modern religious poems.' Homberger notes that Edward Marsh wanted to include it in *Georgian Poetry*, and that T. E. Lawrence thought it 'by far his best thing'. *The English Review* had published the poem in October, shortly before *Exultations* appeared, and Pound reported to his parents almost at once that 'The Simon Zelotes ballad seems to have moved things. letters complimentary from one of the cabinet & Cunningham Graham & others & about 150 subscriptions stopped by the horrified.' That last was almost certainly wishful thinking. But Cunningham Graham—was it on account of 'Ballad of the Goodly Fere' that he named Pound among 'our best writers'?

Writing home at the end of December Pound mentioned some of the reviews of *Exultations*. 'Colourless notice in the observer. I am however past the point where the reviews make much difference.'

Ford Madox Hueffer [17]

The critical LIGHT during the years immediately pre-war in London shone not from Hulme but from Ford (Madox etc.) in so far as it fell on writing at all.... I used to see Ford in the afternoons and Yeats at his Monday evening...The EVENT of 1909–10 was Ford Madox (Hueffer) Ford's 'English Review'

The first number of the *English Review*, at nearly 300 pages as capacious as a full-length book, featured a poem by Thomas Hardy, Henry James's long story 'The Jolly Corner', Conrad's *Reminiscences*, the opening chapters of H. G. Wells's *Tono-Bungay*, and part of Constance Garnett's translation

---

[17] Ford Madox Hueffer / Ford (1873–1939): His father, Francis Hueffer, born in Germany, became music critic of *The Times*; his mother, born Catherine Madox Brown, was a daughter of the artist Ford Madox Brown, with whom she and her children lived after the death of her husband in 1889. Ford grew up in an atmosphere of European music and Pre-Raphaelite painting and poetry. In the 1890s he composed music, and began to publish children's tales, novels, and poems; in 1901 began a collaboration writing novels with Joseph Conrad; in the 1900s published novels, poems, art criticism, biography, and 'sociological impressionism'; founded *The English Review* and edited it from December 1908 to February 1910. Published about eighty books in his lifetime, most notably *The Good Soldier* (1915), and *Parade's End* (1924–28)—the latter based in part on his experiences in the 1914–18 war. After that war lived mainly in France and the USA. Changed his surname to Ford in 1919.

of Tolstoi's *The Raid*. This was the sort of company into which Pound was being introduced when his 'Sestina: Altaforte' appeared in June 1909, and 'The Goodly Fere' in October. Three of his 'canzoni' would appear in January 1910, and a further one in April. Two other new writers were making their first appearances in the review, Wyndham Lewis with a story in the May number, and D. H. Lawrence with poems in November and a story in February.

Hueffer's idea, as he set it out in an editorial contribution to the first number, was to promote 'a sober, sincere, conscientious, and scientific body of artists, crystallising, as it were, modern life in its several aspects'.

For, if the arts have any function at all, that function...is truly scientific. The artist today is the only man who is concerned with the values of life; he is the only man who, in a world grown very complicated through the limitless freedom of expression for all creeds and all moralities, can place before us how those creeds work out when applied to human contacts, and to what goal of human happiness those moralities will lead us.

The artist does this simply by making himself an instrument for the accurate recording of modern life:

this is his utilitarian function in the republic: his actual and first desire must be always the expression of himself—the expression of himself exactly as he is, not as he would like other people to think him, the expression of his view of life as it is, not as he would like it to be....

And what we so very much need today is a picture of the life we live. It is only the imaginative writer who can supply this...In England, the country of Accepted Ideas, the novelist who is content merely to register—to *constater*—is almost unknown. Yet it is England probably that most needs him, for England, less than any of the nations, knows where it stands, or to what it tends.

The nod, indeed a double nod, to Flaubert has this behind it: 'Nothing was more true than the words of Flaubert, when he said that, if France had read his *Education Sentimentale*, she would have been spared the horrors of the Franco-Prussian War.' Pound was impressed by that observation and would frequently repeat it; as he very soon incorporated into his own criticism Hueffer's general idea of the scientific function of the artist in the republic.

He learnt a lot from Hueffer, mainly from their afternoon conversations. 'One of the best minds then available in London', he said of him years later. The great lesson was 'that poetry should be written at least as well as prose'. But Hueffer's standard for prose was set by Flaubert with his concern for *le mot juste*, for the word that did justice to the thing. He 'held that French clarity and simplicity in the writing of English verse and prose were of immense importance as in contrast to the use of a stilted traditional dialect, a "language of verse" unused in the actual talk of the people ... for the expression of reality and emotion.' Pound's verse, in 1909 and 1910, was still stuck in that stilted language—'fly-papered, gummed and strapped down in a jejune provincial effort to learn' it—and Hueffer mocked him out of it and sent him back to his 'own proper effort, namely, toward using the living tongue'. As Pound told it, what actually saved him was Hueffer's feeling the errors of style in Pound's *Canzoni* (1911) to the point of falling over and rolling about on the floor. That gives a dramatic impression of the master making his point to the 'jejune provincial'; yet one just wonders, if the master felt the errors so strongly, why had he published four of those 'canzoni' in his review?

There is no doubt though that it was Hueffer, not Hulme, who showed Pound how to achieve what he was after. One difference was that he spoke as someone who was 'mad about writing' and not as a philosopher. Another was that he understood and sympathized with Pound's commitment to rendering things seen 'not with the bodily vision'. Hulme, for all his apparently related talk of intuition and the visual image, had no sense for the mystery of things. But above all Hueffer could give him confidence in writing of such things not as remote from life but objectively and in a natural language. If one put together Hueffer's idea of art as the science of the subjective experience of life, and his demand for the prose virtues of clarity and simplicity in the formulation of that experience, one might well arrive at the first principle of Pound's 1913 Imagist manifesto: 'Direct treatment of the "thing" whether subjective or objective'. Only it would take Pound some time to get there in practice. It seems he had to go by the way of Yeats and of his own 'canzoni'. Perhaps Hueffer published the latter because he could see that.

Hueffer maintained that the imaginative writer achieved his effect by exaggerating the impressions life made on him. His science did not deal in the literal truth, nor was it to be taken literally. Thus it was his way to tell stories about people and events that were simply not true so far as the facts were concerned. Lies, some would say; but to others they suggested the actual impressions of an extraordinarily sensitive mind. There would be an analogy with the French Impressionists, or with, say, Chagall.

His impressions of Pound should be read as 'characteristic exaggerations'—certainly they don't give us the literal facts. It was Hueffer (by then Ford) who stated that Ezra 'came over on a cattle boat'—'just after the Spanish-American War'—having been born in Butte, Montana, in a blizzard, and given kerosene for his first meal, which accounted for the glory of his auburn hair. And this was his sketch of a morning encounter with Ezra:

Ezra...would approach with the step of a dancer, making passes with a cane at an imaginary opponent. He would wear trousers made of green billiard cloth, a pink coat, a blue shirt, a tie hand-painted by a Japanese friend, an immense sombrero, a flaming beard cut to a point, and a single, large blue earring.

There was indeed a turquoise earring. That is, Stock records that as a matter of fact Arthur Symons's American friend Alice Tobin presented one to Pound on an occasion when they were at tea at the Shakespear's, and that Pound wore it for a short time in public 'as a joke'. That Ford cared for the overall impression and hardly at all for the facts can be judged by this variant version of the passage:

Ezra had a forked red beard, luxuriant chestnut hair...He wore a purple hat, a green shirt, a black velvet jacket, vermilion socks, openwork, brilliant tanned sandals, trousers of green billiard cloth, in addition to an immense flowing tie that had been hand-painted by a Japanese Futurist poet.

Those variations are a caution to the historian eager for the lowdown on Ezra. Ford's sketches should be taken simply as shining additions to the myth and the legend of Pound.

They differ from many of the anecdotes which make up the legend in two significant respects. Ford cheerfully declares his exaggeration; and he does not seek to get the advantage. In contrast there is the story of Pound's eating the floral decorations at dinner—this was one not embellished by Ford, and it was dismissed by Pound as 'apocryphal'—where the facts, whatever they were, are altogether lost in the various versions. But the story is always told as true, and the point is always how it looked to the shocked who knew better. And Pound's state of mind at the time is never enquired into, something which Ford, for all his impressionism, could somehow manage to convey.

Hueffer was living and editing the *English Review* at 84 Holland Park Avenue. He was living apart from his wife, who was thinking of divorcing but in the end would not, and beginning a passionate decade-long relationship with Violet Hunt. She lived not far away in Campden Hill Road, and her home, South Lodge, became the centre of their social world. Like Hueffer, she had a Pre-Raphaelite background; she wrote stories and novels; was a suffragette and a New Woman; and she 'had a way of knowing everyone in London belonging to the worlds of literature, art and the theatre and gathering mixed assortments of celebrities at her "At

Homes"'. Douglas Goldring, whom Hueffer had taken on to assist with the editing of the review, wrote that at South Lodge 'before the incursion of Ford and Ezra Pound' the society proprieties of wearing 'top hats and "London clothes" and [carrying] gloves and canes' were 'rigidly enforced'. It was Pound in particular who changed all that:

From his room in a lodging house in the little paved court behind St. Mary Abbott's, Kensington [i.e. 10 Church Walk], Ezra sallied forth in his sombrero with all the arrogance of a young, revolutionary poet who had complete confidence in his own genius. He not only subjugated Ford by his American exuberance, but quickly established himself at South Lodge as a kind of social master of the ceremonies. Opposite the house there was a communal garden containing tennis courts, which the Hunts and other local residents were accustomed to hire for their annual garden parties. Ezra immediately grasped its possibilities and having a liking for tennis which, with his long reach and lithe, wiry figure, he played excellently, insisted that the tennis courts should be made available. Ford and Violet, both of whom adored every form of entertaining and loved to be surrounded by crowds of friends, were delighted. The garden was taken over and every afternoon a motley collection of people, in the oddest costumes, invaded it at Ezra's instigation, and afterwards repaired to South Lodge—or to 84 Holland Park Avenue—to discuss *vers libres*, the prosody of Arnaut Daniel and, as Ford records, 'the villainy of contributors to the front page of *The Times Literary Supplement*'.

Pound, according to Ford, might 'read you a translation from Arnaut Daniel', and 'The only part of that *albade* that you would understand would be the refrain: 'Ah me, the darn, the darn it comes toe sune'.[18] Goldring had thought Pound 'a bit of a charlatan'—

But one day I happened to see round Ezra's pince-nez, and noticed that he had curiously kind, affectionate eyes. This chance discovery altered my whole conception of him. Perhaps it reveals part of the secret of his hold over Ford. Ezra could be a friend, and not merely a fair-weather one. By his insistence that poets should stick together, help one another, and present a united front to the Philistine world, Ezra taught literary London a lesson which, unfortunately, it refused to learn. . . . He was as free from petty jealousy as from the least trace of servility to the Established and, like Ford, he had a wholly disinterested love of good writing.

It was in that spirit that he wrote to Hueffer in November 1909, 'Manning has just written this quite beautiful "Persephone" which I can praise without reservation. I think you will thank me for getting it sent to you.' And Manning's 'Koré' appeared at once in the December *Review*.

[18] Cp. 'Ah God! Ah God! That dawn should come so soon!' ('Alba Innominata' in *Exultations*).

Pound first met D. H. Lawrence at Violet Hunt's 'at home' at the Reform Club in November 1909, and took him to supper at Pagani's and then back to Church Walk. Lawrence thought Pound 'rather remarkable—a good bit of a genius, and with not the least self consciousness'. They were the same age, 24, Lawrence remarked, 'but his god is beauty, mine, life.' They met and talked a number of times, though their being after different gods gradually put a distance between them. Pound continued to associate Lawrence with the *English Review* circle, so much so that when he reviewed Lawrence's *Love Poems and Others* in 1913—he reviewed it in both *Poetry* (Chicago) and the *New Freewoman*—it was as if Hueffer were speaking through him. The first review began with an equivalent of the rolling on the floor: 'the middling-sensual erotic verses in this collection, are a sort of pre-raphaelitish slush, disgusting or very nearly so'. But then there was unqualified praise for the 'realism' of his 'low-life narrative', with the final accolade, 'He has brought contemporary verse up to the level of contemporary prose'. And again, in the other review, 'Mr Lawrence, almost alone among the younger poets, has realized that contemporary poetry must be as good as contemporary prose if it is to justify its publication.'

In Pound's development Hueffer was the complement and corrective of Yeats, by confirming his instinct that even songs for the psaltery needed to have a prose ground under them. When he thought of them both in the *Pisan Cantos*, and compared their conversation, he reflected that

> Ford's conversation was better,
> consisting in *res* non *verba*,
>   despite William's anecdotes, in that Fordie
>   never dented an idea for a phrase's sake
> and had more humanitas

In the text 'humanitas' is glossed with the Chinese ideogram 'jen', which Pound read as 'Man in touch with both heaven and earth'. He was commending Ford for being in touch with the things of earth, as well as the dreams of heaven, and for using for both the natural language of lived experience. Hueffer needed to be persuaded by Pound that Yeats was worth taking seriously, but there was no meeting of their very different minds and worlds. Hueffer did not go to Yeats's Monday evenings, and Yeats did not go to South Lodge. They were 'NEVER', so far as Pound knew, 'at same dinner'. But they did come together, and most fruitfully, in his mind.

'The Spirit of Romance'

'Hueffer & Miss Hunt', Pound told his parents in October 1909, 'are trying to stir up the very very gilded to have me lecture privately'. Private lectures, such as the class Eva Fowler arranged for him to teach in her home in 1910, were much more lucrative than the Polytechnic lectures. And there was perhaps more kudos in the lecture he gave to the Poets Club in December of 1909. That was on Arnaut Daniel. He was elected an honorary member for the occasion; more than sixty came to hear him; the Irish poet Joseph Campbell, 'attired in bardic robes', declaimed 'The Ballad of the Goodly Fere'; and *The Book of the Poets' Club* for that Christmas included him among its twenty-six contributors. He enjoyed no such success at the Polytechnic.

Olivia and Dorothy Shakespear came to hear him there. But the attendance was disappointing, and Dorothy (near the end of her life) told Noel Stock that she thought Ezra had failed 'to get through to his very small audience because (she said) of his habit of over-estimating their intelligence.' Pound himself reported to his father in mid-November, 'fog is nothing short of murderous'. Ten days earlier he had assured his mother that he was 'imbibing cod liver oil & wearing a life belt like the rest of the inhabitants'. The awful weather may well have kept at home some who would have liked to be at the lectures.

It would have required real commitment, in any case, to attend the full course. The lectures were on Monday evenings at 8.30. There were to be twenty-one lectures, divided into a 'first term' from October 11 to December 13, and a 'second term' from January 17 to March 28—but the last lecture was cancelled because March 28 was Easter Monday and a Bank Holiday. The fees were slightly higher than for his short course earlier in the year—two shillings for a single lecture, fifteen shillings for ten, and twenty-five shillings for the full course. If the audience were around thirty persons—but it may have been as few as twenty—'Ezra Pound M.A. . . . Author of "Personae"' would have been lucky to receive a pound a week.

The lectures were billed as 'on Medieval Literature', a broad title designed perhaps to attract a wider audience. But the course was really a greatly expanded version of the 'introductory' six lectures on 'The Development of Literature in Southern Europe'. It began again with 'suggestions from the critics'. 'The Rise of Song in Provence' was developed into two lectures, preceded by a new lecture on 'The "Pervigilium Veneris": a link between Greece and Provence'. The third lecture of the original series on 'Medieval Religious Feeling' and 'The Childrens'

Crusade' disappeared. The fourth, largely on Camoens, and the fifth, on 'Latin Lyrists of The Renaissance', survived, with some revisions. But in the space between the troubadours of Provence and the Portugese epic there were thirteen altogether new lectures. There were three on the early literature of Spain and France, from the *Poema del Cid* and the *Chançon de Roland* to the *Tristan* romances and *Aucassin and Nicolette*. Then came the major group of six lectures, the heart of the course, the first introducing the Tuscan poetry of Cavalcanti and other contemporaries of Dante as deriving from Provence, and the rest dealing at length with Dante himself. The lecture on the *Paradiso* was followed by 'François Villon. Poet and Housebreaker. The End of Medievalism'. The other noteworthy new lecture was on 'The Drama in Spain. Lope de Vega'. There were to be lectures also on Lope's contemporaries, including Cervantes, and finally, after 'Latin Poetry in Renaissance Italy', on 'Metastasio and Leopardi'.

Those two last mentioned lectures aside, the full course corresponded exactly with the sequence of chapters in *The Spirit of Romance*.[19] Having started writing the chapters in August, Pound was able to keep the book ahead of the lectures. He had done the Arnaut Daniel and 'Proença' chapters in September; delivered 'the first half' to the publisher around January 20 1910; and completed the rest by February 23. By then he already had the proofs of the first half, and would receive the proofs for the remainder about the end of March. The book would be published on June 20, just four months from final delivery of the manuscript. And those were the days of hand-set type!

In a 'preface to the select reader' Pound declared at once, 'This book is not a philological work'. And indeed, as a contribution to scholarship, it would not amount to much. From that point of view one could only agree with the New York *Nation* that 'The book consists of a series of translations, some borrowed, some original, together with a few bits of information and some appreciative comment. The original translations, in prose arranged as verse, are intended to be "merely exegetic".' And that means that the book lacks even his own special form of criticism by translation and imitation. For that we must wait for his *Canzoni* and his versions of Arnaut Daniel and Guido Cavalcanti.

The interest of the book lies elsewhere, in what it reveals about Pound himself. As he noted in a postscript in 1929, it 'will have to stand as partial confession of where I was in the year 1910.' One can see where he had been in 1906 and in 1908 from his articles on 'Raphaelite Latin' and

---

[19] 'Psychology and Troubadours', first published in a journal in 1912, was incorporated into *The Spirit of Romance* (as chapter V) in 1932.

'M. Antonius Flaminius'; and the final chapter of the book, 'Poeti Latini', shows that there he was of the same mind still, if less combatively. He repeats that 'their myths and allusions are not a furniture or a conventional decoration, but an interpretation of nature'; and that 'In the poems of Mark Antony Flaminius we find signs of the scholar's sensitiveness to nature, both to natural things themselves and to those spiritual presences therein, which age after age finds it most fitting to write of in the symbolism of the old Greek mythology'. (In evidence he cites 'Hymn III', which he had included in *Exultations*.) What is new in *The Spirit of Romance* is his marshalling behind these Renaissance Latinists the cultural tradition which they had attempted to tap into and to resurrect. He might well have felt that his situation was much like theirs, minus a renaissance and the possibility of writing in Latin. But now he wanted much more than to recover the original Greek sense of nature. While that remained the enduring basis of the tradition he was constructing, there was also its flowering in Provence to be followed, and then its fulfilment in Tuscany.

The 'spirit' he was seeking in the poetic masterworks of the Romance languages could be traced, he believed, from the Greek rites of Spring into the celebration of the Roman festival of Venus Genetrix in the *Pervigilium Veneris*, and on to the dawn-songs of the troubadour lovers, and thence ultimately into what Dante has Picarda speak in his third heaven of love. Each step in this tradition is a fresh evolutionary development, rising from the cult of nature, to the cult of emotional refinement, and finally to the cult of intelligence in love with wisdom. All this is adumbrated in the book: a history; a myth of the live yeast of European culture; a programme.

As a history it was not altogether original. Scholars, especially French scholars, had been proposing a continuous Romance tradition from Greece through Rome into medieval Provence and France. But their tradition tended to lead into the Grail romances in the manner of Jessie L. Weston's *From Ritual to Romance*. Pound showed no interest in that lead, nor in the esotericism with which it became associated. Rather he departed from it quite radically in following instead the lead from Dante which had the poetry of twelfth-century Provence find its perfection in that of Cavalcanti and Dante himself. 'The art of the troubadours meets with philosophy at Bologna and a new era of lyric poetry is begun'. That philosophical poetic, which for Pound is the culmination of the spirit of romance, is at the furthest remove from the romance of the Grail.

As if to emphasize the difference, just at the point where he would have been expected to take up the Grail romances, in the chapter headed 'Geste and Romance', Pound refuses to take them seriously, excepting only 'the one immortal tale, the *Tristan*', and its 'antithesis ... the Picard comedy,

Aucassin and Nicolette'. His attention in that chapter is given mainly to
'the songs of deed' and action, and most positively to the *Poema del Cid*
which, he finds, is alive with 'the unquenchable spirit of that very glorious
bandit, Ruy Diaz', 'a practical fighting man' who 'came to be chosen the
national hero of Spain'. His story will be told in brief in canto 3. In a
parallel discrimination, the discussion of Camoens' *Os Lusiadas* finds that
'Modern interest in the poem centers in the stanzas of the third canto
which treat of Ignez da Castro', and this is because of the force of the
events themselves: 'the great poem "Ignez da Castro" was written in deeds
by King Pedro'. That story is given in a few lines in canto 30.

But how does this appreciation of narratives of live action relate to
the main argument—how does 'the unquenchable spirit' of El Cid go
with Dante's vision of the spirits of love in the third heaven? An answer
can be found in the chapter on Villon, another who had lived his story.
Pound's palpable enthusiasm for Villon is a response to his expressing
life exactly as he experienced it, without illusion, and without any higher
vision. In fact he sees Villon very much in the terms of Hueffer's idea
of the modern artist. And he places him in relation to Dante by saying
that 'He is a lurid canto of the *Inferno*, written too late to be included
in the original text.' Whereas Dante 'had gone living through Hell' and
'had gone on to sing of things more difficult', Villon 'lacked energy to
clamber out'. They 'are admirably in agreement', Pound writes, 'Dante
to the effect that there are supernormal pleasures, enjoyable by man
through the mind; Villon to the effect that the lower pleasures lead to
no satisfaction'. But this is an 'agreement' only in the philosophic mind.
In brute reality they are opposites, Dante an idealist living in the mind,
Villon the realist living the life of the gutter and knowing it. Moreover,
Dante is the medieval endpoint of the development of Pound's 'spirit of
Romance'; while Villon is the type of the modern artist cut off from that
tradition. Dante had 'sought to hang his song from the absolute, the center
and source of light; art since Dante has for the most part built from the
ground.'

That must have been a challenging observation for Pound himself. He
could not but be a modern poet, and yet he had been seeking to hang his
song from the centre and source of light. Did he realize that he too would
have to clamber out of hell and build his paradise from the ground up? It is
not evident in *The Spirit of Romance* that he was applying its implications
to himself. Indeed there is a sense of incongruity, of unresolved disparity,
between the myth of a continuous evolution of spirit from the Spring
rites of Greece to Dante's vision of paradise, and the lived actualities
of the real world of El Cid and Ignez and Villon. The book traces the

steps of an ascent to the paradisal vision; then drops abruptly into the inferno of heroic but hopeless action. Yet it is only necessary to regard this last situation not as an end but as where one is and from where one must begin, to rediscover Dante's scheme of things and his programme—and to come again upon the matrix of Pound's own long poem. For it appears that the modern poet like his medieval master must begin in the actual world he knows of unenlightened enterprise; from there the love of beauty or *fin amor* leads towards the light, as Dante observed in the troubadours he placed in the *Purgatorio*; and that love when perfected opens the intelligence to an apprehension of godly justice and wisdom.

Pound, putting on his scholar's gown, stated this in the terms of Dante's 'four senses'—'the literal, the allegorical, the anagogical, and the ethical'. Thus the *Commedia* is

1. 'a description of Dante's vision of a journey through the realms inhabited by the spirits of men after death';
2. 'the journey of Dante's intelligence through the states of mind wherein dwell all sorts and conditions of men before death';
3. 'a symbol of mankind's struggle upward out of ignorance into the clear light of philosophy';
4. 'an expression of the laws of eternal justice'.

That happens to give a formula that will fit *The Cantos* quite as well as the *Commedia*.

But that is in the future. In 1910 Pound was being most keenly attentive to the techniques appropriate to each stage in his spirit's progress. He notes that Ovid writes of the gods 'in a verse which has the clarity of French scientific prose'; and again, thinking rather of Crabbe now, that 'their annals are written as if copied from a parish register'. Thus 'The marvellous thing is made plausible, the gods are humanized'. Of the metric of the *Pervigilium Veneris* he remarks that it 'probably indicated as great a change of sensibility in its day as the change from Viennese waltzes to jazz may indicate in our own.' Having declared that 'the culture of Provence finds perhaps its finest expression in the works of Arnaut Daniel', and added that Dante took him as the type of those who sing well of love in their native tongue, he concentrates on his mastery of the music of rhyme and his skill in the 'language beyond metaphor'—as in his writing of his heart swelling with emotion like the Rhone in flood and yet *pooling itself* as the turbid Rhone cannot. When it comes to the Tuscan *canzone*, in which thought rather than emotion is predominant, he notes the combination of more complex grammatical structures with objective clarity of imaginative vision. He observes, as if in a laboratory notebook: 'An effect of one of Arnaut Daniel's canzoni is that of a chord struck repeatedly in crescendo. The sound-beauty of the Italian canzone depends on the variation of the rhymes.' Another observation: Dante's 'onomatopoeia is not a mere trick of imitating natural noises, but is a mastery in fitting the inarticulate sound of a passage to the mood or to the quality of voice which expresses that mood'. He must be listening there for the sound apart from the sense. There are purely technical notes, concerning 'the overtones and undertones of rhythm'; the 'government of speed' by 'the arrangement of quantity (*i.e.* the lengths of syllables) and accent'; and the 'question of vowel music as opposed to consonant music'. The analysis of Dante's 'swift perception of relations' distinguishes different sorts of adjectives, and epithets of primary, secondary and emotional apparition. On another plane, he writes that to Dante 'two blending thoughts give a music perceptible as two blending notes of a lute.' In all this he is being the apprentice poet eager to learn of the masters of his craft, and he is at his best. But if he put much of that sort of thing into his lectures he probably was talking over the heads of his audience.

A tirade on the epic

His mother set him off by quoting someone in Montana on The Epic of the West:

Epic to the West ?? My Gawd !!
What has the west done to deserve it—
    Whitman expressed America as Dante did mediaeval europe—& america is too stupid to see it—(—of course the result is somewhat appalling, but then—)

———

Kindly consider what an epic needs for a foundation—

1. a beautiful tradition.
2. a unity in the outline of that tradition
        vid. The Odyssey.
3. a Hero—mythical or historical.
4. a dam long time for the story to loose its gharish detail & get encrusted
        with a bunch of beautiful lies.

    Dante in a way escapes these necessities—in reality he dips into a multitude of traditions—and unifies them by their connection with himself. Poor Longfellow tried to hist up an amerikan epik.

———

Camoens is the only man who ever did a nearly contemporary subject with any degree of success & he had the line of Vasco de Gamas voyage for unity. & the mythical history of Portugal for back ground.

———

Mrs Columbia has no mysterious & shadowy past to make her interesting. & her present—oh ye gods!!

———

One needs figures to move on the epic stage & they have to be men who are more than men, with sight more than mansight. They have to be picturesque.

———

Bret Harte, Longfellow. (epic?)

Lo I behold a vision. Rockfellow marches in purple robes thru a cloud of coal smoke, Morgan is clothed in samite, and the spirits of the 3rd heaven foster their progress enthroned on trolley cars.

'J'ai lutte contre les empereurs de l'acier, contre les paladins du fer, contre les princes de la porcherie. Ils ont voulu me briser les reins, mais je les ai solides' says Tleethedore Rosenfeldt—as quoted by the satirist in the 'Journal de Paris'.

———

When business begets a religion of 'Chivalry in affairs of money, & when 3% per annum is metamorphorized into the clult of an ideal beauty.' & when america can produce any figure as suited to the epic as is Don Quixote, and when the would be litterati cease from turning anything that might in 500 years develop into a tradition, into copy at $4 per. col. within four hours of its occurrence

then there may begin to be the possibility of an american epic.

An epic in the real sense is the speech of a nation thru the mouth of one man.

———

Whitman let america speak through him.—The result is interesting as ethnology.

———

Just at present I can see america producing a Jonah, or a lamenting Jherimiah.

———

But the american who has any suspicion that he may write poetry, will walk very much alone, with his eyes on the beauty of the past of the old world, or on the glory of a spiritual kingdom, or on some earthly new Jerusalem—which might as well be upon Mr Shackletons antarctic ice fields as in Omaha for all the West has to do with it.—Canada, Australia, New Zeland, South Africa, set your hypothetical scene where you like.

Epic. of the West—it is [as] if I asked someone to write my biography—it is more as if I had asked them to do it 12 years ago.

———

It is truly American—, a promoters scheme, it is stock & mortgages on a projected line of R.R.,

———

which last sentence is the only one in the language of my native land.— surely we parley Euphues. . . .

After two more pages—largely on the commodification of fame—this lightening up: 'I hope the scrawl will amuse you. dont for heavens sake take it seriously.' And at the end, 'The tirade is to be read purely for "style".'

'Our renaissance in the egg'

Pound had gone to England to learn from Yeats, 'but from 1910 onwards that job was over'. That at least is how he told it to Denis Goacher in 1954. And if he had made any difference *to* Yeats, he added, it would have been under Ford's influence. In 1910 he took a new master, Guido Cavalcanti, as he declared in the final poem in *Provença* (1910) and again in *Canzoni* (1911):

> Dante and I are come to learn of thee,
> Ser Guido of Florence, master of us all,
> Love, who hath set his hand upon us three,
> Bidding us twain upon thy glory call.

In *The Spirit of Romance* Pound had credited Cavalcanti, along with Dante and Cino, with having brought the Italian *canzone* form to perfection. He placed him as Dante's equal for poignancy and intensity; then made this telling discrimination—he was 'less subtle than Dante' and 'less likely to give ear to sophistries'. That difference seems to have been what bound him to Cavalcanti, whose work he would intermittently but passionately study and translate and set to music over the next twenty-five years.

But he had, in February 1910, other and more mundane concerns. 'Please insert the following "ad" in some reputable daily', he wrote to his mother, 'POET / out of a Job . . . will do to travel, or stand unhitched while being fed.' The 'Specialities' on offer included 'ze grande manair (to order)'. His private class was proving lucrative, or so he told his father. And he was enjoying a 'Harmless variety of existance': 'Classes, lectures, scholarly prose works, proofs of Canzoni—regular routine plus a certain amount of tea & conversation.' At the same time he was intending to go to Italy for six weeks or so as soon as his Polytechnic lectures were over; and he could not put off much longer a return to America. He even applied to teach at Hobart College, Geneva, New York, having heard that a professor there was to be paid $1300 a year. He sounded out Rennert at Penn about a fellowship, but nothing came of that either. Nevertheless, he would go back to the United States in June.

Williams, who had been in Leipzig, stopped over with Pound for a few days in March. Pound wanted to show him the Turners at the Tate; Williams's delight was a visit to friends in the English countryside. Pound took him to dinner at the Shakespears', and then with Olivia and Dorothy they went on to Yeats's Monday Evening. Yeats was reading Dowson's 'Cynara' by candlelight to a small gathering of five or six—'in a beautiful voice', Williams conceded, only to add 'but it was not my dish'. He was underwhelmed too by the great poet's calling Pound back for a private word. But he allowed himself to be impressed by Pound's care and skill in making coffee.

The day before he left for Verona Pound lunched with Hueffer, who took him to Lady Low's for tea, after which they walked together. On the day itself he lunched with Violet Hunt, had tea with the Shakespears, and caught the boat train at 8.45 in the evening. 'Ezra has gone', Dorothy wrote in her notebook, '7 P.M. March 22nd 1910'. His American friend Walter Rummel was going to put him up overnight in Paris.

In fact he stayed two days with Rummel in his fashionable Passy apartment across the Seine from the Eiffel Tower.[20] Rummel introduced him to Margaret Lanier Cravens (1881–1912), from Madison, Indiana. An intensely idealistic student of the piano she had devoted much of her life and means to perfecting her musical abilities. She had studied in Boston and Florence and was now, at nearly 30, in Paris, where she worked with such noted musicians as Maurice Ravel and Harold Bauer.

Even though she had just met Pound, and before he went on to Verona, she spontaneously offered to place enough money at his disposal annually to free him to concentrate on his art. Her one condition was that he should tell no-one. It was 'all out of the Arabian Nights or some book of magic', that was his first thought; and the next was to accept it, impersonally, in the name of his art. 'You seem part of some larger beneficence that I have no right to interfere with', he told her, 'we both work together for the art which is bigger & outside of us.' He felt her gift as a consecration,

as a sort of sign from beyond that my work is accepted. It couldn't have come unless there was some real reason, behind us all, for the work to go on unfettered.

[20] Walter Morse Rummel (1887–1953): distinguished concert pianist and composer; a friend and foremost exponent of Debussy; studied early French music, with a particular concern for the relation of words and music, and worked with Pound in 1912 setting Troubadour poems to music; also set poems by Pound and words by Katherine Ruth Heyman; edited Vivaldi cello sonatas (1917); wrote incidental music for Yeats's *The Dreaming of the Bones* (1917); deeply interested in theosophy and the occult, and in the Troubadours' Provence; in the 1930s developed a theory that the Cathar stronghold at Montségur was the Temple of the Holy Grail. He is mentioned briefly in Pound's canto 80. (*EP/MC*, 151–8; *EP/DS*, 354–5)

From 'Hotel Eden' at Sirmione on Lake Garda he wrote that she had reversed the passage in the *Inferno* 'where Dante is leaving the classic elysium . . . for the wind driven spirits' of canto V: she had brought him instead out of the trembling air into the terrestrial paradise. The miles of sapphire lake under his window with Riva and the snow-capped mountains to the north made him think of how Catullus and Flaminius had seen their gods there. And to him too it seemed that in that sunlit blue 'Nature herself's turned metaphysical'. 'The gods have returned to Riva', he wrote to Miss Cravens as he contemplated the lake in the evening light, 'or to be more exact . . . they have never left it.' He wanted Miss Cravens to know what her money meant to him.

When he expressed concern at her drawing on her capital for his sake she replied that such details of their friendship were of no concern to either of them. He matched her with a 'Voilà! I have seen a beautiful thing beautifully done. . . . As one artist to another, my congratulations.' But he did ask her not to send money except when he let her know he needed it. And he told his father he would want no further remittances, letting him understand that he had enough from editors and publishers.

In the sapphire and azure of his Lake Garda paradise he was correcting the final proofs of *The Spirit of Romance,* and enjoying the freedom 'to attend to nothing but vowels and quantities, and the rest of the human part of the least known Technique of any of the arts'. He had 'a vague idea of distilling Garda into a Canzone'—and would do so in 'Blandula, Tenulla, Vagula' and 'The Flame'. And he was continuing his studies into the form of the canzone in Arnaut Daniel and Guido Cavalcanti by seeing what he could do in their style. In mid-April he wrote to Olivia Shakespear asking if someone—meaning Dorothy—could go to the British Museum and copy out certain stanzas of Daniel's to give him the rhyme schemes.

A collection of thirteen 'canzoniere / studies in form', with a dedication 'To Olivia and Dorothy Shakespear', would appear as the third part of *Provença* in Boston in November. Witter Bynner had recommended to his publishers, Small, Maynard, a selection from *Personae* and *Exultations* together with this new work. Writing to Bynner from Sirmione, Pound mentioned in passing that 'Two stanzas of the Canzon, The Yearly Slain, are tainted with Swinburne, but the form is very beautiful & has never before been used in English.' He was most concerned to defend his arrangement of the selection from *Personae*, which Bynner had apparently questioned, insisting that 'the sequence is practically one poem . . . if you break it you take my conviction from behind the words.' But his most striking claim is that 'we have here'—meaning, apparently, his studies in form—'our renaissance in the egg'.

That was an extravagant, hubristic claim, scarcely warranted by the work on show. Pound must have been in a state of highly energized exaltation. He had come through the testing time in London; but more than that, his ambition to bring about a renaissance in America by the force of poetry, his single-minded dedication to developing his talent to that end, and a sense of growing powers amounting to a conviction of genius, all this at that moment must have seemed to be sanctioned and favoured by the gods. He would not have known that Small, Maynard intended to publish an edition of only 200 copies. It might not have daunted him if he had known.

Towards the end of April Olivia and Dorothy joined him in the clean and sunlit Hotel Eden. Dorothy did some water-colour sketches of the lake, and remembered years later it 'was the first time I ever saw colour'. Ezra accompanied them to Venice in early May, and returned alone to Sirmione. On the 14th he was about 'to get drunk on Sirmione sun for the last time'. He then spent a week or more in Venice; was in Paris on 6 June, where he saw Margaret Cravens; and was back in London by the 11th.

D. H. Lawrence talked with him at Hueffer's, and wrote about him to Grace Crawford, a Paris-born American singer who was a good friend of Pound's. Pound had declared Sirmione 'the earthly paradise'; and Italy had improved his health, though not his temper—'he was irascible'.

He discussed, with much pursing up of lips and removing of frown-shaken eyeglasses, his projection of writing an account of the mystic cult of love—the dionysian rites, and so on—from earliest days to the present. The difficulty was that no damned publisher in London dare publish it.

Lawrence was provoked by this to impertinent sarcasm. Then Pound, it seems, had told him that he was returning to America to 'sell boots—there is nothing in that blown egg, literature'. Perhaps he had been provoked in his turn into putting on one of his artificial moods and making himself unbearable.

He was to sail on the 18th on the *Lusitania* for New York. About the 13th Dorothy wrote to him—

I take it that during your 'exile' you are forbidden to write to me? That being so—if you have promised—don't break your word—don't write to me . . . As yet, I have had no lecture—and have given no promise not to write to you—we pray I shall not be asked for the promise anyway.

It was the old problem—he was in no position to support a wife of her class. She beseeched him to remain a poet.

7 : PATRIA MIA

The exile's mission

Was all America except one drawing-room in Trenton going to be hell? Thus Pound to Mary Moore from Sirmione in 1910. 'All America except one drawing room *was* going to be hell in divers degrees'—thus Mary Moore Cross, annotating his letter some years later. In fact it seems not to have been as bad as he feared. A week after landing in New York he told Miss Cravens that 'The country seems strange to my eyes that have grown more European than I knew—strange but not so unpleasant as I expected.'

His parents were renting a house out at Swarthmore for the summer. They had let their Wyncote home and were living at 1834 Mt. Vernon Street, within reach of the Mint and the Settlement House. Pound joined them at Swarthmore on June 25 and spent the following six weeks with them. In early August he moved into Manhattan, 'first on Waverly Place near Washington Square, and then on Fourth Avenue (now Park Avenue South), with a view of the towers around Gramercy Park.'

As well as Mary Moore he was seeing Hilda and Williams and other old friends. Hilda it seems was disappointed that Pound did not resume their former intimacy, though he kept up their friendship and still encouraged her to get away to London. When Walter Rummel visited she was one of the party; and Ezra and Hilda went together to visit Williams in Rutherford. But when she followed him to New York in the Fall she felt out of things and soon returned to Upper Darby. In New York Pound was seeing Viola Baxter, now living in the city; and Kitty Heyman, back from her successful concert tour and engrossed with Prokofiev and Buddhism.

At Thanksgiving he was with the Williams family, and he and Williams were reading their poems. According to Williams, his father asked Pound what did he mean by 'six great sapphires hung along the wall' in his 'House of Splendour', and being told they were 'the backs of books as they stood on a man's shelf', exclaimed—much to Williams's satisfaction, one gathers—'But why in heaven's name don't you say so then?' Pound did not remember this at all. They 'did talk about "Und Drang" but there the sapphires are certainly NOT anything but sapphires'. Williams would repeat the story regardless of that, to the greater glory of his father's, and his own, plain sense.

He met Yeats's father, the painter J. B. Yeats, who introduced him to his patron the Irish-American attorney John Quinn, and was taken along in Quinn's party to Coney Island. He would remember its lights as seen from a distance, 'marvellous against the night'; and 'Yeats père on an elephant', and Quinn 'plugging away in the shooting gallery'. He also met up with Frank Bacon whom he knew from Aunt Frank's boarding-house, 'Baldy' Bacon of canto 12 whose only interest was in money business. Bacon evidently sold him a certainty—promising that the 'financial end of the game' was 'very straight and conservative'—but Pound's efforts to persuade Homer to invest met with a prudent refusal. He was no more successful with his two wealthy Wadsworth cousins, both of whom entertained him to dinner. William talked about his stocks. Charles talked about their relative Longfellow, and had him elected a member of the select Barnard Club of which he was treasurer.

He was calling on artists he knew, Frank Reed Whiteside and Hugh Henry Breckenridge in Philadelphia, and others in New York. He was taken to the theatre by the drama editor of the *New York Herald*, and went to the opera—once it was *Carmen*. He attended a meeting of the recently formed Poetry Society of America. He met the writers who hung out at Laurence Gomme's bookshop on 29th Street, though he may not have got on with them. J. B. Yeats told his son that the 'young literary men' he knew 'found him surly, supercilious and grumpy'. He and Quinn though had 'liked his look and air, and the few things he said, for though I was a good while in his company he said very little.'

Perhaps his success abroad was in the way with the young literary men, making for condescension on his part and resentment on theirs. Homer had managed all too well to have his acclaim worked up and rubbed in. 'An American Poet Discovered in England' ran a typical headline. A Philadelphia newspaper owned itself 'jealous of the fact that England should have discovered his genius rather than his own native America, but we are duly proud of him as a son of Pennsylvania'. The *Boston Herald*, copying from the *Philadelphia Bulletin*, wrote of his 'sudden fame' in England. And Small, Maynard described him on the cover of *Provença* as 'the American poet who has so significantly won his spurs in London'. All this booming of the young Pound provoked a resentful put-down from at least one reviewer, W. S. Braithwaite in the *Boston Evening Transcript*: 'We began the examination of this book of poems with great expectations and we lay it down with considerable contempt for the bulk of English criticism that has pretended to discover in these erratic utterances the voice of a poet.' Pound's 'English sponsors' were thus put in their place; and he was advised that he would do well to learn from the homegrown Longfellow.[1]

Provença was praised by H. L. Mencken and by Floyd Dell—neither was put off by Pound's having 'already received his critical accolade in England'. Dell, who was emerging in Chicago as an influential radical writer, recognized in *Provença* 'a very new kind of poet' whose work, if 'approached in some spirit of humility...is capable of giving a deep aesthetic satisfaction.' He made out that Pound always knew what he was doing and that even 'effects which are beyond one's immediate power of comprehension have been exquisitely designed and exactly carried out'. Pound was grateful for Dell's thoughtful attention, and told him he had found, since landing seven months ago, only one man to whom he could talk.

Who that one man was is not known. It might have been Walter Rummel. Pound later confirmed Dorothy's impression, formed when Rummel visited the Shakespears and played for them the following July,

---

[1] *Provença: Poems Selected from Personae, Exultations and Canzoniere of Ezra Pound* (Boston: Small, Maynard and Company, 1910) contained:

[I] *Personae*	[II] *Exultations*	[III] *Canzoniere: Studies in Form*
La Fraisne	Night Litany	Octave: 'Fine songs, fair songs'
Cino	Sestina: Altaforte	Sonnet in Tenzone
Na Audiart	The Goodly Fere	Sonnet: 'If on the tally-board'
Villonaud:...This Yule	Portrait	Canzon: The Yearly Slain
Villonaud:...The Gibbet	The Eyes	Manning's 'Korè'
Mesmerism	Nils Lykke	Canzon: The Spear
Famam Librosque	'Fair Helena'	Canzon: To be Sung...Window
In Tempore Senectutis	Greek Epigram	Canzon: Of Incense
Camaraderie	Histrion	Canzone: Of Angels
For E. McC.	Paracelsus*	Sonnet: Chi è questa?
Ballad for Gloom	Song...Virgin Mother	Of Grace
At the Heart 'o Me	'Love thou thy dream'	Canzon: The Vision
The Tree	Planh for the...King	To Our Lady of Vicarious Atonement
Idyll for Glaucus	Alba Innominata	Epilogue: To Guido Cavalcanti
Marvoil	Laudantes Decem	
In the Old Age of the Soul	Planh [White Poppy]	
Revolt		
And Thus in Nineveh		
The White Stag		
Piccadilly		

* 'Paracelsus in excelsis' was not in *Exultations* (1909)

that he had been helped by him. 'Walter & I had two weeks at Swarthmore that mattered', he told her. Those two weeks were in the first half of September 1910. Rummel for his part felt that Pound had encouraged an 'awakening' in him. In October he wrote from Paris, 'Swarthmore, that little nest which I often remember and cherish greatly. For we did have some beauty there and I did receive much strength.' One can only guess at what they talked of—Pound's *canzoni* and translations of Cavalcanti, the setting of words to music, his epic, Rummel's compositions, questions of technique, and a possible collaboration the next year in Paris. Also more esoteric matters, such as the mystic cult of love. There was music making too. Pound 'had a grand piano sent out from Philadelphia' for Walter, Hilda recalled, 'they said *Walter Rummel*—and anything was had for the asking'.

What Pound did for Rummel—bringing about an 'awakening' in him—he wanted to do for America. The pleasant suburban existence of Swarthmore was wearisome in its superficial sociableness and its culture of conventionality. In New York he missed the quality of conversation he had enjoyed in London—he could find no substitute for Yeats and Ford. 'Here people's deep seems to be so near their top', he reported to Miss Cravens. Finding the people he met wrapped in a sleep of complacency he looked instead to New York architecture for signs of America's 'possibilities':

I have found me an eyrie, with Gramercy park showing a block away, & a beautiful white double-towery sort of building on the far side. Our new campanile—the Manhattan Life building—is very beautiful.

There at least was evidence of the raw energy of America seeking a pleasing form. He wanted to see that taking place in all the arts. 'I want a "college of the Arts," *here*, & d—soon', he wrote to Miss Cravens, 'a sort of incubator for *risorgimenti*.' He wanted to 'turn America into a paradise of the arts'—a ludicrous ambition, he admitted. At times he more or less gave up the fight, 'deciding that the country wasn't worth saving.'

Still, that fight was what he was there for. If the somnolent people did not engage his genius, his country's need would. He had felt this in his first days with his parents at Swarthmore, as he confided at the end of June to Miss Cravens:

The events of a life like mine are of course fantasmagoria, but the events working inward—I mean the effects of events on whatever in genius takes the place of a 'self' in a human being are even harder to follow. . . . What I'm driving at is, with the new fight before me (mad enough tho' it seems), there has come a curious renewal of that kind of energy that I had before the first *battaglia*.

That first battle had been when he 'went up against London with a sheaf of verse'. At the end of his time there he had left for Italy with the sense of having 'lived out one life' or of rounding it out with Sirmione. Now he was 'come to another starting point', and 'The marvel to myself is that I have apparently the same absolutely unfettered puerile sort of feeling for the attack.'

He was given heart too by Yeats's 'new lyrics' in which 'he has come out of the shadows and declared for life . . . the movement of the '90'ies for drugs and shadows has worn itself out'. This meant

a tremendous uplift for me—for he and I are now as it were in one movement, with aims very nearly identical. . . . There has been no 'influence'. Yeats has found within himself spirit of the new air which I by accident had touched before him.

He was reading Swinburne 'with new eyes'—'The Ballad of Life', The Ballad of Death' and 'The Triumph of Time'. In that last he noted 'especially the stanza "I have put my days & dreams out of mind"'; and in 'The Ballad of Life', 'the tremendous significance of the *Acceptance*'— the acceptance of life in all its manifestations. There he found 'the *great* Swinburne, the high priest, the lifter of the hearts of men. His vision of our marvellous vitality, of our power for survival!' 'The unhappy', he concluded this letter, 'are only those who refuse to live.'

These thoughts, which perhaps he had been able to express only to Margaret Cravens while he was in America, he wrote out in two series of articles, 'Patria Mia' and 'America: Chances and Remedies', in *The New Age* in 1912 and 1913. He did believe, he insisted, 'in the imminence of an American Risorgimento. Of "Liberty" beautifully proportioned, of "Liberty" without that hideous nightgown wherein Bartoldi has arrayed her.'

A Risorgimento means an intellectual awakening. This will have its effect not only in the arts, but in life, in politics, in economics. . . . A Risorgimento implies a whole volley of liberations; liberations from ideas, from stupidities, from conditions and from tyrannies of wealth or of arms.

And America, at present enduring its Dark Ages, needed such an awakening. Yet for the artist there was the first light of dawn and the first sign of resurgence in the architecture of downtown New York. In the Pennsylvania Railroad Station and the Metropolitan Life tower 'the mire of commerce has fostered the beautiful leaf'. The attempt to fit form to purpose evident in them should bring on the search for beauty in the other arts. And thus America's renaissance should come about.

He knew this wouldn't happen of itself. 'We need conspirators, if the country is to be Guy Fawked into an artistic paradise', he had written to Miss Cravens. In more diplomatic terms, there should be a College of the Arts, to bring together and to subsidize as many as a hundred practising artists of all kinds—for 'you must gather such dynamic particles together; you must set them where they will interact, and stimulate each other.' Moreover, 'the best minds among the older men and the ready minds of the younger enthusiasts' should mingle and take fire one from another. He might have been writing there of his own experience in London; and he might have been calling in general for the Black Mountain experiment.

But for America then he could call up as exemplary masters of their art only the expatriates Henry James and Whistler. James was to be looked to for 'his continuing labour for individual freedom, his recurrent assaults upon cruelties and oppressions'; and for his understanding of 'all that is fine in American life, the uprights, or, so to speak, the piles that are driven deep, and through the sort of floating bog of our national confusion'. From Whistler's paintings he gathered 'more courage for living than . . . from any other manifestation of American energy whatsoever'. They were

the work of a man, born American, with all our forces of confusion within him, who has contrived to keep order in his work, who has attained the highest mastery, and this not by a natural facility, but by constant labour and searching . . . [H]ere was a man come from us. Within him were drawbacks and hindrances which no European can more than guess. . . . He is, with Abraham Lincoln, the beginning of our Great Tradition.

Whistler counted above all because he had shown that it was possible 'to wrench [America's] impulse into art'.

Whitman is notably not mentioned as an exemplar, in spite of Pound's judging him the only American poet of his day who mattered. He would not do because 'he was no artist, or a bad one'. That is, he was not, as James and Whistler were, 'in some degree master of the forces which beat upon him.' Behind that was the notion that Whitman had been too lazy to arrange his rhythmic interpretations of American energy into harmony. Pound's being dead wrong about that was no doubt due to his having never 'owned a copy of Whitman', and having 'to all purposes never read him'. But his exclusion of Whitman throws into relief the idea of art that he was then maintaining. It was the office tower built in the proportions of a belltower of the Italian Renaissance; or it was the song in the form of a Provençal or a Tuscan *canzone*. He had still to take Hueffer's point that poetry should be made of the actual life and talk of the people. He wanted New York City to be the slender maid of a pastoral lyric into whom he would breathe a soul, though he saw it as 'a million people surly with traffic'. Whitman's art of the people 'en masse' offended his aesthetic sense.

That sense made him feel foreign and culturally alien as he watched 'the surging crowd on Seventh Avenue'—

A crowd pagan as ever imperial Rome was, eager, careless, with an animal vigour unlike that of any European crowd that I have ever looked at.... One returns from Europe and one takes note of the size and vigour of this new strange people. They are not Anglo-Saxon; their gods are not the gods whom one was reared to reverence. And one wonders what they have to do with lyric measures and the nature of 'quantity'.

And one knows they are the dominant people and that they are against all delicate things. So much for the crowd, the future.

But that crowd, that future, could not be ignored. If he wanted to be America's poet his work would have to be *of* America, not merely *for* it. He would have to face his question in its proper form: what did lyric measures and the nature of 'quantity' have to do with the quality of American life? Would his studying them bring about the desired renaissance, that awakening for which he felt the need to use the foreign terms *Risorgimento* and *Risvegliaménto*? Were they really the right form for his renewed energies, and for the surge of America's vitality?

He had an idea that the finest poetry would free the populace from the tyranny of mass emotions and received ideas—that by the 'melody of words' it would draw the minds and wills of its hearers into harmony with the true nature of things. To this end the poet should master the techniques of sound quality and variation of stress and verse form, all the methods by which, in Dante's way of thinking, 'the soul is drawn unto itself'. So Pound studied, by translation and imitation, Arnaut Daniel's rhyme patterns and verbal effects in order to learn his technique of emotional refinement; and he studied in the same way Cavalcanti's *canzone* and sonnets in order to learn his technique for achieving a precise understanding of the nature and import of the feelings of being in love. He believed that 'the perfect rhythm joined to the perfect word' would energize the motor forces of emotion and will and illuminate the intelligence, and that the result would be more enlightened living. The perfect rhythm or cadence defines an emotion; the emotion charges the perceptive powers; and to alter the perceptions, as Blake taught, is to change the world. But only the best art, work in which the maximum of energy found its most efficient form, could lead the emotionally awakened intelligence toward the Light. And it was Pound's wholly serious intention to do just that for America.

Dorothy

Pound's *Canzoni*, his poems of love, had a more immediate and intimate meaning for Dorothy. When the volume was published by Elkin Mathews in July 1911 it carried a very proper dedication 'To Olivia and Dorothy Shakespear'. And indeed both Dorothy and her mother had been involved in the composition of the *canzons* and *canzone*, by copying the models for him and being an appreciative audience. But for Dorothy, cut off from Pound while he was in America by the ban on their writing to each other, the poems had a special poignancy. Pound was writing to her mother, and Olivia generally showed his letters to Dorothy, but that arrangement kept things impersonal and Dorothy was desperate for some real contact. She hoped to find out more from his new poems. When she received from the publisher a copy of *Canzoni* 'with the Author's compliments' Olivia had her do the correct thing and send a thank-you letter.

Dorothy wrote almost as if she were content to be in love with Pound at a distance, and to relate to him simply as a poet. Some of his poems she took personally, particularly two poems of separation, 'Excuses' which she puzzled over and then felt that it didn't matter that she could not make it out, and 'Abelard' from which she expected to 'get great calm'. 'Abelard' has the neutered philosopher calling on God to have his angels embrace Héloïse and bring her the peace that he no longer can. Dorothy told Pound that his prayer for her peace had been 'felt by the High Gods'—not the Chthonic, she specified. Her prayer for him was 'write well, & may the triune azure envelope you'. She was thinking of his earthly paradise of Lake Garda, as evoked in 'Blandula, Tenulla, Vagula'. She wanted him to believe that her soul would surely meet his there. Pound, replying from Garda, remarked matter-of-factly that 'the Abelard' was 'done two years ago'.

Dorothy's notebook entries over the previous months show her becoming more soulful, and more like Tennyson's Mariana waiting alone and weary in her moated grange for one who does not come. In August 1910 she thinks they must be together in the blue apart from common existence, having slipped one round the other and so found their own souls and 'tasted of the Truth & Life Eternal'. In November she almost makes up her mind 'to do a really serious thing. To ask you to come back next summer'. Olivia could still forbid their meeting, but surely she would be strong enough by then to say ' "I will have my own friends—I am old enough to choose my own friends" '. Then she sends him a brief note to say it is enough to have inspired him to write poems—'After all, that's as much as one ought to desire'. Let there be peace between them, 'the sort of peace one finds, at the moments when one is sure the world & other folk don't exist.' The following May, with Pound now in Paris or Sirmione, she has a feeling that he is 'about' and wonders 'Is it possible you are coming back to me?'—

And yet the news is bad—For Mercy's sake come back to me—I shall never rest until I have seen you again, & settled one thing in my own mind. How can I rest?

I have only lived by you; You have taught me all I care about—about poetry & Revelation—Inspiration. And you are exquisite, body & soul—that I swear. And troubled in both—And then I must love someone, soon—Life is no good for a girl, without love ... I think I have never been happy—really happy—all my life—except that one short time—which can never come again. And soon I shall be saying 'Oh! my lost youth!' ... Oh! my dear—come back to me—and let us spend our youth in dreaming dreams together. If only you would come back & fold away the veil between me & Life! Once I swore to serve Beauty always—but I have lost the Vision entirely, & the memory is faded—come back & give me the Vision again—because it was always yours, I saw.

In her thank-you letter in July she told him *Canzoni* had given her courage again. 'If you come to London you will come to see me, won't you?', she wrote. In Pound's allowed reply there was nothing Dorothy could not show to her mother.

'Canzoni'

What Pound told Dorothy in that reply was that *Canzoni* was supposed to be a sort of chronological history of emotions: 'Provence; Tuscany, the Renaissance, the XVIII, the XIX, centuries, external modernity (cut out) subjective modernity. finis.' The poems he had cut out at the last minute, '15 pages of 'em', had got on his nerves—a fit of 'hyper-aesthesia' was how he later explained it to Elkin Mathews. But everything in the book had been part of his 'criticism of emotion', and the whole thing had been a 'working out from emotion into the open'. It was 'a sort of Purgatorio with the connecting links left out'; and he felt, with the *Canzoni* done and with his Arnaut Daniel and Cavalcanti translations done, ' "sul monte" & out where I can breathe'.

The emotion he was primarily concerned to purge and purify was of course love. The book is in effect a version of what he had told Lawrence he was thinking of writing, an 'account of the mystic cult of love ... from earliest days to the present'. More exactly, it is an account of the mystic cult of love which, in Pound's mind at least, had its origins in the rites of Persephone at Eleusis; attained an ultimate realization in the work of Dante and Cavalcanti; enjoyed a kind of afterlife in the Renaissance; and lapsed into decay in the modern era. The book begins with lyric celebrations of *fin amor*, and ends with an ironic dismissal of what it had come to in certain poems of Rossetti and Yeats. It is an odd sort of 'Purgatorio' that starts out as if with Arnaut Daniel and Dante near the summit of its mountain and then descends by stages to the hell of unenlightened modernity. Its progress is certainly not towards any otherworldly paradise or beatific vision. The progress is instead towards an increasingly confident engagement with what we experience as the real world. There is no weakening of commitment to the visionary ideal; but nor is there any giving up on life as it is. What Pound was after was a viable modern form for the lost tradition of mystic love. [2]

In *The Spirit of Romance* he had distinguished two sorts of *canzoni* or love songs. In Provence they maintained 'that you must get the meaning

---

[2] I make out this arrangement of *Canzoni* (Elkin Mathews, 1911). Titles in italic were omitted at the proof stage; and a note after 'Era Mea', 'Finit Libellus' [here ends the little book], was deleted. Titles underlined are in *Personae* (1926) and *CSP*.

A		B	
Canzon: The Yearly Slain		Prayer for his Lady's Life	
Canzon: The Spear		Psyche of Eros	
Canzon: To be Sung...		'Blandula, Tenulla, Vagula'	
Canzon: Of Incense		Erat Hora	
Canzone: Of Angels		Epigrams	
		La Nuvoletta	
To Our Lady...		Rosa Sempiterna	
To Guido Cavalcanti		The Golden Sestina	
Sonnet in Tenzone		Rome (du Bellay)	
Sonnet: Chi è questa?		Her Monument (Leopardi)	
Ballata, Fragment			
		C Victorian Eclogues:	
Canzone: The Vision		I. Excuses	
		II. Satiemus	
Octave		III. Abelard	
Sonnet: The Tally-Board			
Ballatetta		A Prologue	
Madrigale		Maestro di Tocar	
Era Mea		Aria	
		[*Leviora I, II, IV*] [III] L'Art	
Threnos		[*To Hulme (T.E.) & Fitzgerald*]	
The Tree		Song in the Manner of Housman	
Paracelsus in Excelsis		[*Redondillas*]	
De Ægypto		Heine, Translations from: I - VII	
Li Bel Chasteus			
		Und Drang: I–XII (VII–XII)	

while the man sings it'. But in the songs of the Tuscan school the meaning was likely to be more subtle and not so readily grasped, and these 'make their revelations to those who are already expert'. This second sort is conceived and must be approached as 'ritual' with a ritual's 'purpose and effect'. Like 'a high mass', a sung mass, it 'calls for the presence of the god rather than calling upon him for some peculiar service'. The aim, we must assume, is to attain communion with the god. In the *canzoni* of course the desired divinity appears as a woman. She may be an actual person idealized; or she may be a figure of the natural life-wish, such as Persephone; or, as in Dante's Beatrice, a figure of the wish to know and be at one with the loving spirit which moves the universe. To Pound these distinctions marked the stages of a tradition which began in ancient Eleusis and culminated in Dante's *Paradiso*. They marked also the possible stages of an individual's progress in love. And of course those stages, amounting as they do to a hierarchy of value-judgements, establish criteria for a 'criticism of emotion'.

The opening poem in Pound's *Canzoni*, 'Canzon: The Yearly Slain', resumes in brief the whole tradition of the simpler sort of love lyric. The subtitle, 'Written in reply to Manning's "Korè"', relates it both to that poem and to his 'Canzone', which was dedicated 'To Dorothy Shakespear' and in which the beloved beauty again appears as Persephone. Pound then gives an epigraph which points up a relation with Dante's sestina 'Al poco giorno', and through that with Arnaut Daniel's 'Sols sui qui sai'. Pound has followed Dante and Daniel in his care for the melody and the musical qualities of his writing. But in the argument of his poem there is criticism of their poems as well as of Manning's.

But then each poem in the series stands in a critical relation to the others. Daniel's affirms that his entire love and desire is fixed upon his lady, and that nothing can exceed the joy he has in thinking of her. It could have been for this sentiment that Dante, when he meets Daniel's spirit near the summit of Purgatory, has him confess that he weeps for his past folly and sings now only for the joy he sees before him in paradise. Dante's 'Al poco giorno' laments that the lady who could make a summer of his love for her is in fact stony-hearted towards him and casts him into darkest winter. Reading the poem one wonders if he is addressing a young woman who is simply not moved to love for him; and then it might be the stone effigy of one still powerfully alive in his memory, a Beatrice remembered in her human form and not yet understood and envisioned in her spiritual glory. What is clear is that his desire is evergreen for a live woman, and that, in her present form at least, she is unobtainable. The remarkable thing is that in this poem Dante makes no move to sublimate desire. He remains in effect in the same realm as Daniel's poem, only without Daniel's joyfulness and vigour.

Manning's 'Canzone' is the song of one in love with a vision of bright Persephone as she passes with the leaves in the death of the year. He weeps for his wintry state; yet his soul is joyful remembering the splendour of her face. He is as it were in Dante's predicament but consoled by a memory—a memory of the sort Dante's Arnaut would have dismissed as foolish. In 'Korè' he again weeps for the passing of Persephone into the realm of Dis with the end of summer, but this time he concludes quite simply—

> Only I knew her for the yearly slain,
> And wept; and weep until she come again.

Manning's idiom is of the nineteenth century, out of Keats and Tennyson and Rossetti and William Morris—the same idiom that Pound started out with. It is an idiom in which it seems natural for the sensitive soul to find its joys and its griefs expressed in the beauty and the pathos of fragrant flowers and wintry woods. The tendency is to blend the self into the natural world, and to lose touch with the further possibilities of the world of the spirit, the world created by human vision and thought and action. That tendency Pound had long resisted and criticized, as in 'La Fraisne', and in *A Lume Spento* as a whole.

He had praised Manning's 'Korè' to his parents and to Hueffer as a beautiful poem, and had been responsible for its being published in *The English Review*. But in his 'reply' to it, in the next number, while adopting its idiom he effectively killed off its sentiment. His first three stanzas are a richly textured imitation of Manning's two poems, though with a more definite sense of Persephone's Eleusinian background in the first stanza:

> Ah! red-leafed time hath driven out the rose
> And crimson dew is fallen on the leaf
> Ere ever yet the cold white wheat be sown
> That hideth all earth's green and sere and red;
> The Moon-flower's fallen and the branch is bare,
> Holding no honey for the starry bees;
> The Maiden turns to her dark lord's demesne.

The fourth stanza introduces a new and critical point of view, one which is in the end irresistible but which the Daniel and Dante and Manning poems had all stopped short of. 'Love that is born of Time', it declares, is born and dies like any other product of time. That sounds close to Yeats's 'Man is in love and loves what vanishes'. However, Pound's next thought surprises: 'Korè my heart is'—not the expected 'Korè's my heart is', but a stark recognition that it is the natural loving heart itself which is the 'Yearly Slain'. The heart that loves what is born of time may have its season and then must die with it. This is more rigorous and more absolute than Manning's 'Korè', more so even than Dante's 'Al poco giorno', as it refuses any thought of another Spring and insists

> Barren the heart and dead the fires there,
> Blow! O ye ashes, where the winds shall please,
> But cry, 'Love also is the Yearly Slain.'

Pound said that his *canzoni* were written 'to serve that love of Beauty...which belongs to the permanent part of oneself', and evidently he really meant it. This poem, as a starting point for the collection, makes it apparent that the communion he was after was not with nature or with another person but with the deathless gods.

The 'spear' in Pound's second *canzon* is the shaft of light from heaven which both gives the wound of love and cures it. The conceit of the spear which can provide the cure for its wound is out of Ovid's *Amores* and *Remedium Amoris*, but here it is converted into a Neoplatonic metaphor of the light of life which quickens the heart and draws it back to itself. The shaft of that light's reflection upon earth's waters seems to give a way to pass beyond them; and as it shines within the eyes of his distant lady it gives a clear light of love to steer by. The meaning is lightly carried in the images and music of the lyric, which is 'rather to be sung than spoken', but it must amount to this, that the heart which fixes itself upon this deathless light will not be among those slain at the year's end.

The two songs which follow praise the lady for her graces and her gracious ways which draw the heart towards the light. Then 'Canzone: of Angels' closes the first suite in the Tuscan mode. The likely model is Dante's 'Voi che 'ntendo il terzo ciel movete', the first ode or *canzone* in *Il Convito*. Pound gave a careful translation of this in *the Spirit of Romance*, and explained that 'It tells how Dante is led out from his personal grief for the death of Beatrice into the sunlight of Philosophy; that is, becomes fit for his life's work, because of a deepened vision'. That fits Pound's own 'Canzone: of Angels' quite closely. It begins

> He that is Lord of all the realms of light
> Hath unto me from His magnificence
> Granted such vision as hath wrought my joy.

He sees the forms in which the angels manifest their 'lordly powers'—mainly in lights of various gem-like colours which, it must be said, don't much tax the intellect. But then the light enfolds and gives form and motion to one who seems to be the spirit of love, corresponding to the spirit who in Dante's ode descends from the heaven of Love upon the rays of Venus its ruling star. At its close the poem dedicates itself to this spirit, saying

> That since I looked upon such potencies
> And glories as are here inscribed in truth,
> New boldness hath o'erthrown my long delaying,
> And that thy words my new-born powers obeying—
> Voices at last to voice my heart's long mood—
> Are come to greet her in their amplitude.

The keeping to Dante's rhyme-scheme with the keeping up of a high-toned rhetoric do strain the grammar and syntax out of the natural, but one gathers that he is now prepared 'to serve that love . . . which belongs to the permanent part of oneself'.

In terms of Pound's chronological scheme, the first suite of five poems gives us 'Provence' caught up into 'Tuscany', and the second suite then gives us Guido Cavalcanti's 'Tuscany'. The distinctive emphasis here—it is this, in Pound's view, that most distinguishes Cavalcanti from Dante—is that the light from heaven is present and active in the living woman whom he loves. He does not require her to be dead in order to direct his desire towards that light.

'Canzone: The Vision' is possibly strictly for the expert. It is a prayer for union with an 'ivory woman' who with a falcon of light has caught his heron heart. She is a figure of Love whose touch brings peace exceeding that of the eucharist; and her 'caught sunlight' when cast over him outdoes 'God's light'. He is emboldened to declare, 'Were not the earth as vain, and dry, and old, / For thee, O Perfect Light, had I not sought thee?' The iconography is puzzling, being neither of Greek nor of Christian mythology. The 'ivory woman' is first seen ''neath the silver mist, / Ruling thy bark of painted sandal-wood'. That could be an image out of the Egyptian 'Book of the Dead'; and the heron and the falcon-headed sun-god are to be found there too. Could the ivory woman be Hathor, and the rite Egyptian? Hathor was the sky-goddess within whom Horus the sun-god was enclosed at night to be reborn in the morning. She was honoured as goddess of joy and love—the Greeks would identify her with their Aphrodite. She was also a Persephone figure as the light of the Westerners or the dead. If these are pertinent associations then Pound would here be going behind and beyond the usual origins of his tradition, to its even older sources in ancient Egypt. He would be putting off the later sense of sin and of the death of nature, and approaching the primal mystery of endlessly self-renewing light and life. Olivia Shakespear, co-author of a dramatization of the story of Hathor, may have been best-placed to understand this vision.[3]

The form of 'The Vision' is the same as that imitated in 'The Yearly Slain'. It is as though it were written over it to assert, against its statement of the death of living things and of the love of them, a vision of the enduring love of undying light. To those who know no better, Korè appears to pass away into the dark underworld; but to the initiate her light and life never cease their action. I take this poem to be the culmination and the major statement of that part of *Canzoni* which corresponds to the programme sketched out in *The Spirit of Romance*.

The next ten poems in two suites of five are of relatively minor interest—and some were included simply to fill out the scheme. Interest quickens again in the sequence from 'Prayer for his Lady's Life' to 'Her Monument, the Image Cut thereon'. This second part of *Canzoni* recapitulates Pound's 'chronological history of emotions' but within just the Italian peninsula. The light from Eleusis is rather faint in Propertius' prayer for his lady's life; stronger in the speech in which Apuleius' (and Pater's) Psyche recalls the lightness of Cupid's loving; stronger still in 'Blandula, Tenulla, Vagula', which chooses an earthly paradise at Catullus' Sirmione as against the emperor Hadrian's stoic sense of the afterlife, and against the Christian sense of heaven too. The notable omission from this sequence is 'Provence'. Where one would expect it, according to Pound's scheme, we have simply 'Erat Hora' and 'Epigrams'— two short pieces difficult to place in the historical sequence. With 'La Nuvoletta' we are already with the Dante who prays an attractive woman 'not to interrupt his cult of the dead Beatrice'; and 'Rosa Sempiterna' follows Dante's example, placing the red rose of love within his *Paradiso* where it turns to the yellow of the rose formed by Dante's 'souls in blissfulness'.

The high point of the sequence is 'The Golden Sestina—From the Italian of Pico della Mirandola'. This might be a Renaissance Neoplatonist's rewriting of Dante's 'Al poco giorno' in the recovered light of the pagan perception of the gods. It celebrates a *donna ideale* who is much like those of Pound's *canzone*. All 'intermingled ivory and gold', a 'mortal goddess and terrestrial sun', she is said to have been sent by Jove to show heaven's likeness in her face. The 'renaissance' style is somewhat over-ripe however, nearer to Spenser than to Chaucer, as if signalling that the vision was

---

[3] I confess that I can make nothing of the invocation of Calais in stanza VI.

no longer fresh and urgent and that its mystery had gone from it. After that comes du Bellay's much translated sonnet on the ruins of Rome as the grand instance of how Time batters all things down. Then Leopardi's Hamlet-like disillusion and cynicism confirm a total loss of the light from Eleusis. The image of his lady on her tomb only makes him think how all beauty, all delight, all lofty visions and the efforts to achieve them, but end in vilest dust. She is so far past praying for, or praying to, that her image ends the sequence with morbid finality.

With Leopardi's poem we are into the nineteenth century, and the third part of the volume, from 'Victorian Eclogues' on, carries Pound's history down to his modern age. The period appears to be given over to the analysis of subjective feelings. In the cadence and tones of 'Excuses' there is something of Matthew Arnold, though it is a dramatic monologue in the manner of Browning's 'Andrea del Sarto'. The speaker is addressing a woman he has loved and left for another, and his great concern seems to be to justify his having done so. One gets the impression that he is afraid of her strength and strangeness and has preferred someone who means much less to him. He is the weakly sensitive young man making speeches in a sentimental romance. 'Satiemus' is the speech of the more experienced cynic who will not fall in love with the lady because he fears, like Eliot's Prufrock, that he has 'known it all already, known it all'. In striking contrast, Pound's Abelard, although his loving really is all behind him, makes a passionate prayer for his lady's joy and peace.[4] It is not at all evident why this recapturing of the strong medieval vision of the great light of love should be regarded as 'Victorian'. Perhaps it is that there is no longer any question of communion with the lady, nor, through her, with the divine powers. But whatever the reason, Pound's Abelard, castrate yet still burning with desire for Héloïse, does show up the pathetic lack of passion and vision in the two *echt*-Victorian *personae*. Pound thought the 'Eclogues' 'overstrained & morbid but part of my criticism of emotion'.

'A Prologue', being a prologue for a Nativity play, seems an altogether odd inclusion. It was published in December 1910 in the Philadelphia *Sunday School Times*, and that would have been an appropriate resting place for it. However, it appeared there without the all-important closing

---

[4] Peter Abelard (*c*.1079–1142), a leading philosopher who lectured at the University of Paris. He fell in love with his pupil Héloïse, niece of the Canon Fulbert of Notre Dame: when their child was born they married in secret, but her brothers broke into his room at night and castrated him. Abelard became a monk, Héloïse a nun. Their story is told in Abelard's *Historia Calamitatum*. (*Concise Encyclopaedia of Western Philosophy and Philosophers*, ed. J. O. Urmson and Jonathan Rée (London: Unwin Hyman, 1989), p. 1.)

speech in which 'Diana in Ephesus', speaking as the goddess of childbirth, laments that she has just assisted at the birth of the Truth that shall eclipse her truth, the truth of the old gods. The full eclipse, we may gather, has come to pass in the nineteenth century. These lines from *Hugh Selwyn Mauberley*, come to mind—'Christ follows Dionysus, / Phallic and ambrosial / Made way for macerations'. That might reflect back on 'Abelard' as well. But we are having to dig deep for a rationale just here.

'Maestro di Tocar' and 'Aria' are perhaps showing how music can do what the Christian church is no longer good for. The first is a curious tribute to Walter Rummel, crediting the magic of his playing with melting away men's transient hearts and loves. 'Aria', one of three poems by Pound for which Rummel wrote a piano accompaniment in 1911, is a simple and most musical lyric which might on its own have the effect credited to his playing. It manages to catch in a few words and a clear image the essence of the earlier *canzoni*:

> My love is a deep flame
> > that hides beneath the waters.
> —My love is gay and kind,
> My love is hard to find
> > as the flame beneath the waters. . . .

But after this irony and satire take over, and an altogether new tone emerges.

Pound's Heine is one of his most original and successful *personae*. He has selected from the *Book of Songs* (composed in the 1820s) just the handful which strike a particular note of irony that smiles knowingly to itself; and thus he has invented a debonair Heine who has no sentimental illusions about himself or his world, whose polished wit is more than equal to 'Philistia's pomp and Art's pomposities', and whose careless heart has learnt not to look for true love. The other, better known Heine, the Romantic Heine, whose songs of the sorrows of youth are charged with plangent longings and who is overcome by the bitter pathos of life's disappointments, that Heine is deliberately left in the background. Pound has created a poet who can overcome heartbreak, or at least mask it with stylish ease—a prototype of Laforgue.

The importance of this creation is its achieving a measure of detachment from the unenlightened age, though at the cost of seeming to take nothing seriously. The air of superiority does depend on keeping quiet about the things not spoken of in good society, such things as 'the permanent part of oneself'. One may make light of them, however, as in this *jeu d'esprit*—

> I dreamt that I was God Himself
> Whom heavenly joy immerses,
> And all the angels sat about
> And praised my verses.

As for the light of love, we have 'The mutilated choir boys' singing

> of Love that's grown desirous,
> Of Love, and joy that is Love's inmost part,
> And all the ladies swim through tears
> Toward *such* a work of art.

The stress on *such*—italic here added to mark it—mimes the ladies' own inflection, adding another voice and another layer of irony to the comedy. And if the falsity of it all is breaking the poet's romantic heart he will not let it show.

In his Heine *persona* Pound had hit upon a way of getting clear of merely subjective emotion and of allowing greater scope for the free play of the poet's intelligence. That depended on his finding a language and a style that were more natural, closer to life and more objective than anything in his previous work. Making strong old dreams and recovering a bygone vision had required, it would seem, pastiche and reproduction, so that however fine the art there was always a sense of unreality about it. Now he was getting close to the objectifying technique of *Lustra* and of *Hugh Selwyn Mauberley*, but something—'hyperaesthesia' he would call it—held him back from carrying it further for another three years or so. Apparently he was too much in love with a vision of the sublime for which he had as yet no language of his own.

The 'Und Drang' sequence shows what he could do, in 1910, with 'subjective modernity'.[5] In the first six sections a *fin-de-siècle* world weariness and disillusion prevails. An anti-Nietzschean voice proclaims the advent of 'The great oblivions and the labouring night, / Inchoate truth and the sepulchral forces.' Against that an artist in his youth, gifted, too soon acclaimed, declares that life is good in all its ways, in what it takes

---

5 The sequence consisted of twelve sections—VII–XII are in *Personae* (1926) and *CSP*:

I 'I am worn faint'	VII The House of Splendour
II 'Confusion, clamour'	VIII The Flame
III 'The will to live goes from me'	IX (Horae Beatae Inscriptio)
IV Elegia	X (The Altar)
V 'How our modernity'	
	XI (Au Salon)
VI 'I thought I had put Love by'	XII (Au Jardin)
VI*b* 'I have gone seeking for you'	

1 (*above*). Four generations,
1888: Thaddeus C. Pound,
Ezra Pound, Homer Pound,
Elijah Pound III.

2 (*right*). Ezra aged about 8.

3 (*left*). Isabel and Ezra, *c*.1897.

4 (*below*). Homer and Ezra, *c*.1896

5 (*right, main picture*). 166 Fernbrook Avenue, Wyncote (*Photo: Dr J. L. Cotter*).

6 (*inset, left*). Cheltenham Military Academy, 1898 (*Ezra is top row, second from left*).

7 (*inset, right*). 'E. P.'s <u>Den</u> (Photo by <u>himself</u>)', (from Homer Pound's Scrapbook).

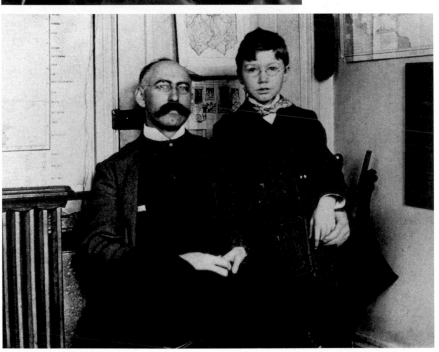

8 (*above left*). EP, 1908 (*Photo: Haessler*).

9 (*above right*). Hilda Doolittle.

10 (*left*). William Carlos Williams.

11 (*facing, above left*). Katherine Ruth Heyman.

12 (*facing, above right*). Mary Moore of Trenton.

13 (*facing, below*). San Trovaso, Venice—the boatyard EP looked down on in 1908.

With the affectionate regards
Katherine Ruth Heyman

Venezia - Squero S. Trovaso

14 (*left*). Dorothy Shakespear.

15 (*below*). EP in London, early 1909.

16 (*right*). Olivia Shakespear,
c. 1914.

17 (*below*). W. B. Yeats, *c.*1910
(*Photo: Lena Connell*).

18 (*left*). EP in Paris in 1910 (*Photo Henri Manuel*).

19 (*below*). Margaret Cravens.

away as much as in what it gives. The third voice, out of Dowson and Yeats, complains that love-sickness has taken his will to live, because 'she, the ever-living...would not go' from him. 'Elegia' begins with 'I have put my days and dreams out of mind', the line from Swinburne which Pound had especially remarked in writing to Margaret Cravens about the *acceptance* of life in all its manifestations. This is an elegy on the dark side of Pater's 'Conclusion' to *The Renaissance*, urging the living of life in the passing moment, but without hope of bettering it or fear of dying. The two positions of the dialectic that has been unfolding are set directly against each other in the fifth section:

> How our modernity,
> Nerve-wracked and broken, turns
> Against time's way and all the way of things,
> Crying with weak and egoistic cries!
>
> .   .   .   .
>
> All things are given over,
> Only the restless will
> Surges among the stars
> Seeking new moods of life,
> New permutations.

Even that will to live, however, discovers no certainty. A third stanza concludes: 'Bright threads leap forth, and hide, and leave no pattern.'

The sequence pivots upon sections VI and VI*b*. Here we are near to the decadent Nineties, with a love that had been put by, because too painful, being stirred by a glimpse of a face in the theatre; and that leading to a search for a face to mind him in the crowd on Fifth Avenue. Is this another of modernity's 'weak and egoistic cries'? 'The House of Splendour' then takes up from the bygone tradition the theme of the 'aureate light' in which the poet's Lady moves, and makes all the old claims for his love of her: there are powers in it 'Which, played on by the virtues of her soul, / Break down the four-square walls of standing time'. That's all very fine, says the modern spirit, but isn't this vision simply an outrageous pastiche of Rossetti and his Pre-Raphaelite paintings? Never mind whether the 'six great sapphires hung along the wall' are books or actual sapphires, the whole thing is out of the Victorian junk-shop. That may well have been Pound's critical point. He acknowledged that in the matters of translating Cavalcanti and getting to know Tuscan poetry Rossetti was his father and his mother; but he would also say in later years that in *Canzoni* he had 'succeeded in writing the *lingua morta*,' the dead language of the Pre-Raphaelites and the Nineties.

In 'The Flame' we have at last the poet in his own voice, spelling out directly where his heart is. It is the voice of 'In Durance' of 1907, only more assured now, not so self-consciously soulful. We have heard it before in *Canzoni*, notably in 'Blandula, Tenulla, Vagula', but here the election of an earthly paradise becomes a fully developed rite. First there is the renouncing of the world's marrying and giving in marriage, whether in the mating game or for material advantage. Even tender, seemingly unselfish love is dismissed as 'a sort of cunning'. Then there is the lesson of what 'Provence knew', in its cult of refined love; and beyond that there is the philosophic love which knows that through 'our immortal moments' we may become attuned to 'the subtler music, the clear light', and so be drawn out of time into the realm of 'the Ever-living'. The creed is based on what has been revealed on Lake Garda:

> We are not shut from all the thousand heavens;
> Lo, there are many gods whom we have seen,
> Folk of unearthly fashion, places splendid,
> Bulwarks of beryl and of chrysophrase.

> Sapphire Benacus, in thy mists and thee
> Nature herself's turned metaphysical,
> Who can look on that blue and not believe?

That leads on to the communion in which the soul loses its human identity and becomes 'translucent'. Its being utterly merged into the perfect light is confirmed, at the close, in the dismissal of one anxious to get through to the man she had thought she knew and loved: 'Search not my lips, O Love, let go my hands, / This thing that moves as man is no more mortal. . . . I have slipped / Your grasp, I have eluded.'

That is the final stage of the process of 'perfecting' love begun in 'Canzon: The Yearly Slain'; yet it is no way to treat a lady, not at least according to the conventions of Daniel and Dante. But then 'The Flame' has departed some way from those conventions. No goddess or *donna ideale* is invoked at all; and the woman, far from bringing light to the poet, becomes the one who by her possessive love would hold him back in the 'smoke and shadow of a darkling world'. This is a poet who will have no mediator between his soul and its light; and who would, moreover, become the light that is the light of the world.

The woman's allotted part—in 'Erat Hora', 'Horae Beatae' and 'The Altar'—is to share in the immortal moment, then to turn away asking nothing more, or to join in building upon it 'an exquisite friendship'. I cannot help thinking of the special meaning these poems associated with Sirmione had for Dorothy, and of how she asked Pound to build for her 'a little altar of stones down where your "perch" was'. Did she understand that his altar was to commemorate the victory of 'the flame' over 'the green rose'? We know that she resigned herself to not being able to make out where she stood in 'Excuses', but she must have wondered was she the new love, or the old, or neither?

'Au Salon' carries an epigraph taking pleasure in 'Her grave, sweet haughtiness', 'Her quiet ironies', and the fact that while 'Others are beautiful' none are more so. The appreciation is measured, and hardly passionate. The poem then shifts into the tone of light-hearted detachment of the Heine *persona*, though our poet is here more expansive and socially much more at his ease. He has adapted cleverly to the manners and ethos of the society drawing-room—he is, I suppose, what remains of Pound's 'external modernity'. He will talk so lightly of his religion that it seems of no importance at all as the talk goes round the tea table:

> I suppose, when poetry comes down to facts,
> When our souls are returned to the gods
>   and the spheres they belong in,
> Here in the every-day where our acts
> Rise up and judge us;
>
> I suppose there are a few dozen verities
> That no shift of mood can shake from us:
>
> One place where we'd rather have tea ...

And the lady of the sweet haughtiness and quiet ironies pours the tea and applauds his performance, or so I imagine it, for we are left to imagine for ourselves where she fits in. All that we are given is the poet's part in the social comedy. The unsympathetic might observe that society had brought out the egotistical in him, and that that would not be good for his work. The severe might say he was betraying his genius. Yet it could be that the assurance of his performance comes precisely from his having a life apart from all this. He is able to be so insouciant because really, as he looks down on it from his soul's high perch, it is simply not to be taken seriously. But then nor is the lady to be taken too seriously. Life in the every-day social world is after all just a game—a game to be played well and with style, and in the spirit of ironic detachment.

'Au Jardin' closes the sequence, and the book, with a jester-jongleur—he has something of Cino about him—making light of the clichés of romantic love. The poem is constructed around a line from Yeats's 'The Cap and Bells'—' "The jester walked in the garden" '. Yeats's jester sends up to his lady in her high window first his soul, then his heart, and finally—it means the death of him—his cap and bells; only then does the lady open her window and take them in. Pound's jester also addresses a lady 'away high there', but this one, leaning 'From amber lattices upon the cobalt night', might be Rossetti's Blessèd Damozel; and what is said to her is what no truly romantic lover should say to such a lady:

> Well, there's no use your loving me
> That way, lady;
> For I've nothing but songs to give you.

His declaration, altogether in the spirit of Pound's 1906 'Dawn Song', is that he is 'set wide upon the world's ways / To say that life is, some way, a gay thing'. As the conclusion to *Canzoni* this confirms, lightly but effectively, the displacement of the Lady as the ideal object of desire. Hilda Doolittle put herself into the picture by saying that it was she who had 'danced like a pink moth in the shrubbery' when the poet 'loved a love once, / Over beyond the moon there'. But the Lady for whom he has nothing but songs might as well be Dorothy, or any woman who would distract him from his calling.

Beyond that, in 'Au Jardin' Pound was distancing himself from the whole long tradition of romantic love poetry in which the poet's feelings are bound up with his lady's graces and favours, and in which the feelings become essentially self-regarding and egotistical. If *Canzoni* is a sort of *Purgatorio*, then it is because it has been progressively refining out those feelings and that sort of romantic love. And his sense of having come out at the end 'from emotion into the open' where he could breathe will have been because he felt he had got clear of the love of particular persons and become intent, like Arnaut Daniel at the summit of Purgatory, on the guiding light of paradise—in his case the light of the paradise of this world.

I noticed the puzzling absence of 'Provence' in the sequence from 'Prayer for his Lady's Life' to 'Her Monument'. We can see now that Pound's 'Provence' was in fact there in 'Blandula, Tenulla, Vagula' and 'Erat Hora', only translated into his Sirmione and combined with his 'Tuscany'. In those poems and in 'The Flame' he was reinventing the cult of love, making it over according to his own particular experience and thought. He inserted his new form of it into the tradition in that second sequence where the development from Provence into Tuscany is actually given as a progression from 'Blandula' through to 'Rosa Sempiterna'. Then 'The Flame' gathered up his whole tradition into a new rite for the perfecting of love in the modern world. He had told his mother that to attempt an epic you needed 'a beautiful tradition' and 'a unity in the outline of that tradition'. In *The Spirit of Romance* and in *Canzoni* he had been preparing the ground for his epic by defining and unifying his own special tradition. The essential dynamic which he had been clarifying and making his own is that love, which begins as a love of persons and things which live and die in time, is perfected by being refined into a love of the Perfect Light which is the undying source of all being.

In 1912 Pound wrote but did not publish an 'Epilogue' presenting to the American nation his 'five books containing mediaeval studies, experiments and translations'. The five would have been *The Spirit of Romance* (1910), 'the experiments and paradigms of form and metre—quantities, alliteration, polyphonic rimes' in *Canzoni* (1911) and *Ripostes* (1912), and the translations of *The Sonnets and Ballate of Guido Cavalcanti* (1912) and *The Canzoni of Arnaut Daniel* (then with a publisher). 'I bring you the spoils, my nation,' he began, 'I, who went out in exile, / Am returned to thee with gifts.' America was unmoved. *Canzoni* received no notice there at all. Critics in England said of it that Pound's 'strange fashions' dug up from the past were too bookish and too little related to life. Few if any noticed that in setting 'the flame' against 'the green rose of love' he was working out an attitude to life, and that though his materials were on the whole out of books he was intent on making something new and individual out of them. The simple fact was that *Canzoni* had no evident relation to American life, nor any apparent impact upon the nation.

'Redondillas, Or Something of That Sort', the two hundred and forty or so lines of 'external modernity' cut out at the last moment, would have made clear the nature and extent of Pound's personal alienation. It is a sort of *Time* profile of the poet, in which he says what he thinks of himself, his world and the universe. The manner is 'sententious, *dégagé*'. He sees himself at one instant as 'London's last foible in poets'; at another as a microcosm of the age—'Behold me my saeculum in parvo'; then again as 'that terrible thing, the product of American culture, / Or rather that product improved / by considerable care and attention.' He would 'sing the American people,' but 'God send them some civilization'. He would sing 'this, that, and the other'. But when he would sing of something that mattered, his mind turned to where his heart was, to Lake Garda, and to 'some power, some recognition / ... beyond the ordinary bonds / of passion and sentiment'. There is nothing to indicate any particular love for America or for anything specifically American. 'I'm not specifically local', he declared, 'I'm more or less Europe itself'. And his prescription for an American renaissance was in effect to import the old culture of Europe, though Whitman and Emerson before him had made that not the American way. He had far to go before he could connect constructively with America.

'Whatever I may seem to have done or left undone,' he wrote to his father from New York in February 1911, 'my time is still a time of preparation, not a time of accomplishment'. He was about to return to Europe, having found in America 'nothing so new or so different to build into the work'. To his mother, who was unreconciled to his going, he wrote 'I have my work to do and must choose my own way of getting it done.' He had just been in hospital with jaundice—he apologized to Margaret Cravens for the 'long dullness' it had brought on. Nevertheless on February 22 he sailed on the *Mauretania* for London. He spent just three days there, and wrote home that he had seen Yeats, Plarr, Hueffer, May Sinclair, and felt revivified. On the 3rd of March he was in Paris. His gross earnings during the eight months he had been in America amounted to 'exactly 70 dollars', the 'precise fare from Phila[delphia] to Paris, second class. And DAMMMMN well spent.' His next visit to the United States would be from Italy in April 1939.

PART TWO : 1911–1920, LONDON

8 : Prelude in Paris

As soon as he arrived in Paris Pound let Miss Cravens know he was there. He found a pension at 3 rue de l'Odéon in the Latin Quarter not far from the Jardin du Luxembourg, and he told her that he was expecting 'to work a couple of hours in the morning & study the leisure in the afternoons and perambulate aux jardins most of the rest of the time'. That, as it happens, had been more or less Hueffer's routine in London. Of course he would 'occasionally take tea with such of the elect as think it advisable'—and would she please let him 'come to tea when it's most convenient'.

It appears that they were often together while he was in Paris that spring and early summer of 1911. Margaret Cravens's Paris was musical, and there will have been concerts and recitals. There were the 'Concerts-Chaigneau' organized by three sisters, one of whom, Thérèse Chaigneau, would marry Walter Rummel in July 1912. Their chamber ensemble included Harold Bauer and Pablo Casals as well as Rummel and Thérèse, and they specialized in early music. The programme for their concert on March 16th, as Pound reported in the London *Monthly Musical Record* of 1 April 1911, included Rameau's *Orphée*, sonatas by Bach and Mozart, a quintette by Bocherini, and 'Airs from the sixteenth and seventeenth centuries harmonized and scored by Walter Morse Rummel'.

One great thing that Margaret did was to commission portraits of them both from the American painter Eugene Paul Ullman. In hers she seems at first a sort of Gwen John young woman, a thin vertical in a blank space looking out with still, sad eyes. But she is much more alive than that. She is turning as if to face a serious word or chord, and one hand has gone to her cheek as she ponders the meaning of it. The other arm, a strong pianist's forearm and wrist, extends down behind her back as if left trailing by the speed of her turn, or perhaps it is resting on some piece of furniture. There is arrested movement in her figure, in both the vertical and the horizontal planes. Her gaze is not so much sad as poignant, alive with feeling but not with joy or hope. A woman with much to give but doubtful of her own worth, unsure of her direction.

The image of Pound might be her antitype. A massive head and shoulders fills the frame; the face is serious, self-possessed, emotionless; the gaze is powerful, unquestioning and unyielding. This is not the youthful Pound of his contemporary photographs, but prophetic of an older, stronger Pound caught when his genius was upon him. Perhaps Ullman was giving Margaret Cravens the image she wanted of a godlike artist; and perhaps it is this image she is contemplating from her companion portrait, as the unworthy worshipper of what he represented to her.

When their friend Walter Rummel who had been away returned in mid-March Pound moved across Paris to stay with him in Passy. They were both at this time studying the relation of words and music in the songs of the troubadours as recorded in illuminated manuscripts in the Bibliothèque Nationale. There was the problem that the musical notation in the manuscripts indicated the pitch for each word or syllable but gave no indication of duration, leaving the would-be performer guessing as to the intended rhythmic structure. Pound and Rummel worked together on the hypothesis that the rhythm had therefore to be given in the weights and durations of the words themselves. Pound especially, going on from his work with Florence Farr in London, believed that the melody was in the words and that it was for the singer and instrumentalist to discover it there. Rummel agreed, and in March 1913 he brought out in collaboration with Pound 'Neuf Chansons de Troubadours des XIIième et XIIIième Siècles', a score for solo voice and piano which 'followed closely the rhythm of the text'—and which does have an authentic medieval feel to it, when sung *without* Rummel's piano accompaniment.

There is more of Pound's thinking about music and words in the introduction to his translation of Cavalcanti. Though this is dated 'November 15, 1910', which would mean that he wrote it in New York, he did later say that he had finished it in Margaret Cravens's apartment, and it is likely that the page or so about rhythm came out of his collaboration and conversations with Rummel and was added in Paris in the spring of 1911. His basic observation is that music is 'pure rhythm; rhythm and nothing else, for the variation of pitch is the variation in rhythms of the individual notes, and harmony the blending of these varied rhythms.' Evidently he is there equating 'rhythm' with frequency of vibration, and making out that the frequency of a note determines not only its pitch but also its natural tempo or duration.

So far so technical, but beyond this his argument is harder to follow. He declares a belief in the possibility of an exact and perfect correspondence between a thought expressed in a line of poetry, and the emotion given in the cadence or rhythm of the line: 'The perception of the intellect is given in the word, that of the emotions in the cadence'. Given that the rhythm arises from the weights and durations of the syllables this must mean that the corresponding emotion is latent in the very sounds, the vowels and consonants and tones, of the words which express the thought. He especially remarks the dependence of the melody in poetry on 'a variation of tone quality'. He does not go so far as to say that the sense of poetry is in the frequencies and vibrations of its words, but speaks of a 'double current' and of the emotion in the rhythm lighting up the perceptive powers.

It becomes apparent, however, not only that it is the 'rhythm' that is his primary concern as a poet and translator, but that his idea of rhythm is unusually far-reaching:

I have in my translations tried to bring over the qualities of Guido's rhythm, not line for line, but to embody in the whole of my English some trace of that power which implies the man. The science of the music of words and the knowledge of their magical powers has fallen away since men invoked Mithra by a sequence of pure vowel sounds.

Does Pound mean that there are magical powers in Guido's rhythm, that those powers *are* Guido, and that therefore to bring them over into English is to invoke and to embody the genius of the man?

In his introduction he wrote of Guido's power as his *virtu*, in the technical sense out of Aquinas and Aristotle of 'the potency, the efficient property of a substance or person'. In modern science, he explained, the *virtu* of radium would be its radiant energy; in the Neoplatonic metaphysics of the Tuscan poets the *virtu* of their lady was a spiritual power emanating from her eyes. 'Each thing or person was held to send forth magnetisms of certain effect.' We are led to conclude that Guido Cavalcanti sent forth the 'magnetisms' of his individual genius in the frequencies and vibrations of his poems; and that Pound, having 'lived with these sonnets and ballate daily month in and month out', and having been 'daily drawn deeper into them and daily into contemplation of things that are not of an hour', became so possessed by Guido's radiant energy as to aspire to communicate it as a living force. The germ of that idea was present in his July 1907 essay on Browning, and was more fully formed in 'Histrion'. But this was to carry it into the realms of metaphysics and natural religion. At the same time, however, Pound was seeking a technical, even a scientific basis for his practice, by locating the spiritual magnetisms in the measurable frequencies of sound and in the precise definitions of words.

As to how far he had succeeded in bringing over Cavalcanti's *virtu* in his 1910 translations, his own judgement may be implicit in his classing his 'Guido', in 1920, as an 'Étude' and not as a 'Major Persona'. But Shepard, his demanding teacher at Hamilton, cordially congratulated him on having done better than Rossetti, and on his getting back to what had been in Cavalcanti's mind.

Yeats was in Paris that May, working with Lady Gregory on stories of fairies in the West of Ireland. He was maintaining that 'what we call Fairy Belief is exactly the same thing as English and American spiritism except that fairy belief is very much more charming.' He and Pound dawdled together round Notre Dame and Pound observed him at the West front admiring the symbol of the rose-window with the stone Virgin appearing to stand inside it.

Yeats introduced him to Henri Davray, the influential literary editor of the English language section of *Mercure de France* who had reviewed *The Spirit of Romance* when it came out in 1910. He also introduced him to some French poets, but Pound was not ready to learn from them and thought them 'a gutless lot, given over to description'. He missed another opportunity when he met Arnold Bennett, who could have put him onto Corbière and Valéry and Remy de Gourmont, but Pound thought Bennett dull with a forced sense of humour. His mind was on Arnaut Daniel and ancient music and was evidently unreceptive to other influences. At the Salon des Indépendants he remarked 'two masterpieces by Dézire', a 'well-painted' canvas by Matisse, and 'Freaks in abundance'—among which he may or may not have included the Cubists. He mentioned to his parents that he had seen some Cézannes in a private gallery, but expressed no particular interest. There was a ferment of new work all around him in Paris—Braque and Picasso were doing Cubism, Diaghilev's Russian Ballet performed Stravinsky's *Petrushka* that year, the *Nouvelle Revue Française* was alive with new writing—but Pound seems to have been hardly aware of what was happening. The modern renaissance he wanted was well under way and he was not yet part of it.

The proofs of *Canzoni* came from Elkin Mathews and he cut out 'Redondillas' and other exceptions to his cult of Beauty. He left Paris about the end of May for Sirmione, and was still there when the book was published in July. William Carlos Williams's brother Edgar was in Italy studying its Renaissance architecture and Pound joined him to visit a number of northern towns. In Verona's San Zeno cathedral they particularly remarked the column which boasts the sculptor's inscription, 'Adam of San Giorgio made me'. On July 27 he wrote home that he had 'had a delightful morning' in the Biblioteca Ambrosiana in Milan and had 'found a mss. of Arnaut with musical notation which accords exactly with my theories of how his music should be written'. He sent a copy of the musical notation of the two poems to Rummel, and took another to show to the leading authority on the language and literature of Provence, Emil Levy, in Freiburg-im-Breisgau. He would work up that moment into a major episode in canto 20.

He was now on his way to spend some time with Hueffer in Giessen, a small German town north of Frankfurt-am-Main. Hueffer was putting in time there in the vain hope of obtaining German citizenship which might enable him to divorce his wife and so be free to marry Violet Hunt. He was rather bored and had invited Pound to act as his secretary, meaning someone stimulating to talk to and go about with. He took him about visiting spas and castles—the sort of thing he would have his characters do in *The Good Soldier*. But what Pound really got out of that visit was Hueffer's histrionic roll on the floor in dismay at the stilted language he had so earnestly crafted in *Canzoni*. That brought home to him at last the lesson Hueffer had been trying to teach him, that he must learn to use 'the living tongue'. It gave him the kick he needed to start modernizing his effort.

9 : 1911–1912 : SETTLING IN

Of heaven and the ground under it

Pound was back in London by 22 August 1911. 'It was time for me to get back here', he wrote to Margaret Cravens. His 'exile' had lasted well over a year. But his old room at 10 Church Walk, 'his own proper corner . . . where it is more cheap and more comfortable than any place in London', was taken until early November. In the meantime he was unsettled, having to rent a room for a month or so at 2a Granville Place, between Oxford Street and Portman Square, and then move in for another month or more with Walter Rummel, who was renting a house which came with a spinet and grand piano at 39 Addison Road near Holland Park.

A railways strike was raging that August. Essential supplies of coal and food were not getting through to London. According to *The New Age*, a socialist weekly, 'the world of labour' was 'seething with unrest', and in London the strikers were being 'heartily cheered by the public'. In its view the action of the Home Secretary, Winston Churchill, in calling out the troops against the strikers was likely to provoke a general strike if not civil war. It foresaw at the least 'a series of strikes of increasing intensity'—and indeed in time the coalminers and the dockers were to go on strike. *The New Age* was also picking up rumours of war—would Germany go to war with France over access to trade in Africa? Or would its urge to expand lead to war with Russia?

Pound was untouched by those rumours as by the railways strike. 'The strike carefully avoided the lines I wished to use', was his only comment on that state of affairs. He was intent on finding out who was in town, 'if anyone'. Yeats was in Ireland and about to go to the U.S. with the Irish Players. Hueffer was now in Paris with Violet Hunt, intending 'to be married . . . and go to the dentist', and would not be back until November. But he did see May Sinclair; and Elkin Mathews, who had just published *Canzoni*, had him out to dinner at his home at Chorley Wood in the country.

Apparently he saw Dorothy Shakespear, since he was able to report to Margaret Cravens that she had 'a horrible cough'; but within a very few days of his arrival Dorothy was away down in Dorset, at High Hall, Wimborne, and would go on from there to Fawley near Southampton, then back up to Southwold on the Suffolk coast. She would not be home again until October. Pound himself was down in Dorset, at Lady Low's country house not far from Wimborne, around 8–10 September; but there was no way they could meet, Dorothy told him, unless he were to present himself as Olivia's friend. In any event, on the 9th the Shakespears were passing through London on their way to Southwold.

In mid-September he spent a Sunday afternoon with G. R. S. Mead, a leading scholar of hermetic philosophy and an important figure in theo-sophical circles.[1] Mead invited him to give a lecture to his Quest Society, which he would afterwards publish in the society's quarterly review. The result was 'Psychology and Troubadours', later incorporated into *The Spirit of Romance*. Pound's interest appears to have been engaged by Mead's 'comparative study of religion, philosophy and science', as it had not been by the methods of communicating with spirits practised by Yeats and Olivia Shakespear and many of their friends. Pound also appreciated Mead's humourous good sense, as in his saying 'I know so many people who were Mary Queen of Scots, and when I consider what wonderful people they used to be in their earlier incarnations, I ask WHAT they can have been at in the interim to have arrived where they are.'

About the end of September Pound was taken out to a suburban garden to meet the son of the founder of the Baha'i religion, 'to find out whether I know more about heaven than he does'. 'At least, I went to conduct an inquisition', he told Margaret Cravens, '& came away feeling that questions would have been an impertinence'—

The whole point is that they have *done* instead of talking, and a persian movement for religious unity that claims the feminine soul equal to the male, & puts Christ above Buddha, to the horror of the Theosophists, is worth while.

'Its more important than Cézanne', he told her. In canto 46 Pound would recall his encounter with 'Abdul Baha', and relate his parable of the camel

[1] G. R. S. Mead (1863–1933). 1889–91 private secretary to Madame Blavatsky (d.1891); 1890–98 General Secretary of Theosophical Society which she had founded, and editor *Theosophical Review*. Resigned from the Society in 1908 in protest against charlatanism. In 1909 founded the Quest Society and edited its review *The Quest*, with the aims of promoting 'investigation and comparative study of religion, philosophy and science, on the basis of experience', and encouraging 'the expression of the ideal in beautiful forms'. He lectured and published prolifically on the pagan mysteries, Gnosticism, and early Christianity.

driver who would not talk with him about his religion but devoutly milked his camel, drank the milk, and danced.

It was probably in October that Pound was introduced to Alfred Orage, the editor of *The New Age*.[2] Orage was to prove a very necessary support through this London decade, by having him write a column at a guinea a week when he most needed the income. But beyond that he was to exert a major shaping influence on his thought and work. Orage had been in turn, and in his own way still was all at once, a Theosophist, a Nietzschean, and a Socialist. He believed that to achieve social justice it was necessary to bring about a 'new contemplative and imaginative order' which would 'co-operate with the purposes of life'. He must have seen Pound as someone who could contribute to that project, since he at once commissioned from him a series of articles on his 'new method' of poetic criticism—the first of 'I Gather the Limbs of Osiris' would appear in the *New Age* of 30 November. By the end of the decade, and more or less under Orage's tutelage, Pound would have transformed himself from the poet of 'the sublime' into one concerned, and concerned at the very heart of his long poem then at last getting under way, to expose and counter the economic causes of industrial strife and of war. One thing he learnt from Orage's example was that if you wanted to bring about heaven on earth you should have your feet on the ground.

A passive engagement

Something decisive must have happened between Dorothy and Ezra around 24 July 1911. Before that date Dorothy seemed to have accepted that it was simply out of the question for them to marry so long as Pound had no secure income; and she seemed to have resigned herself sadly to being his distant muse. She had known the happiness of love 'that one short time' at Sirmione in May 1910. Then her mother had intervened, taking her home and forbidding Pound to write to her. He was to keep away from her for over a year, time enough Olivia must have hoped for one or both to get involved with someone else. Olivia might have been reassured, when she received *Canzoni*, with its dedication to both mother and daughter and its associations with that time in Sirmione, that at least

---

[2] Alfred Richard Orage (1873–1934). Born Dacre, Nidderdale; 1893–1905, Primary School Teacher, Leeds; 1894 joined Independent Labour Party—wrote for Keir Hardie's *Labour Leader*, charismatic public speaker; 1896 joined Theosophical Society as led by Annie Besant, pioneering socialist and feminist; 1903 co-founder Leeds Arts Club, sought to animate Leeds with Nietzsche's thought; 1907 moved to London, edited *The New Age: a weekly review of politics, literature, and art*; 1923 gave up *New Age*, joined Gurdjeff's institute at Fontainebleau; 1924–31 in U.S. representing Gurdjeff; 1932 returned to England, founded *New English Weekly* to promote Social Credit.

the young man was sublimating his love and not looking to marry a mortal. 'The Flame', in particular, could have let her think the danger was past, with its 'Search not my lips, O Love, let go my hands...I have slipped / Your grasp, I have eluded'. But Dorothy did not let go, and Pound must have said he would marry her.

On 24 July she sent him this very brief note: 'Thank you—/ It is burnt. / Yours / D.' After that, from the time he was back in England, she was writing to him every two or three days, and in a manner that she would have felt to be highly improper were she not assured that there was now a firm understanding that they would marry. There is much play in her letters upon keeping the friends and relations she is staying with guessing as to whose handwriting it is on the envelopes that come for her, sometimes two by the same post. She tells him, 'Don't write too often: Letters are laid about here terribly—& I can't help it. You might send a line to [Olivia] if you are pining to write.' But then, a few days later, 'Yours came at glaring midday...I don't care, now. Everyone here has known for the last fifteen months, why I loved Garda.' Still, the proprieties had to be observed.

There is no knowing exactly what Pound said in that letter, evidently written in Sirmione or Verona, which Dorothy thanked him for and discreetly burnt. There may be a clue in 'Silet', a poem to which, quite exceptionally, he appended a dateline, 'Verona 1911'. That would mean it was written about the same time as the letter. The poem is in sonnet form, and begins by mocking the cliché that love may last forever in a sonnet's 'immortal ink'. Against that it repeats, as if now in a rondeau, 'It is enough that we once came together', seemingly letting love go with the passing of time and the turning of the seasons. But then comes the counter-assertion, 'Time has seen this, and will not turn again'. That would preserve something of their coming together in time, and make of it a moment to stop time. 'Silet', the Latin title, intimates that there is a mystery here which is being kept secret.

We are left to gather what we can from the surviving letters. 'I suppose you are now interviewing Madame ma mère?'—that was almost Dorothy's first word from Dorset. 'No ambiguities, are there?', she wanted to know. 'I hear that in [Sweden]', she went on, making clear what her mind was running on, 'if the girls are not married by 22—they are considered "terrible failures"'. (Dorothy was then nearing 25.) In her next she thanked him 'for two very welcome letters', and wrote of 'My Ezra' and of the moon having 'nothing to do with us'. She also wrote 'We are to be in Town 9th–11th—but I don't much see how we can meet'. Pound apparently had some brilliant ideas of how they might meet when he was himself down in Dorset. Dorothy chuckled over them, and crisply replied 'they won't work: chiefly this reason—that I would do nothing about you here except you came as O. S.'s friend & I think she had better have a holiday.' One does get the impression that her observance of the conventions and proprieties was stronger than her desire to see her Ezra.

Olivia had written to Pound about Dorothy after their interview. The first part of the letter is missing, probably because Dorothy destroyed it in her old age—but she preserved this:

What distresses me is that I see her becoming always more fundamentally selfish and self-absorbed. Of course this does not show on the surface, as her manners are too good—but I really don't believe she would stir a finger to help her dearest friend if it cost her a moment's trouble or inconvenience—she seems to have a perfect horror of being of any use to anybody.

'You will probably think all I say very brutal', Olivia conceded, but only 'because you are in love with her'. From that we may conclude that Pound, in their interview, had more or less formally declared an unaltered intention to marry Dorothy.

'You are very lovely & I am very stupid', was how he began his letter to her from Lady Low's 'Sea View' in Dorset on 10 September. But he had been possessed, as he went on to tell her, by a very different and much stronger state of feeling. The day before he had gone down to the sea-front—' "edge" (front?—whatever it properly is—at least in "Darset")'—

it was proper bleak & gray—& 'very odd' = very unpleasant, very poetic, & strong beyond anything. There is no place for senses in this scheme of things—only for feelings that last life out—deeper, more intense than all Italy, and silent. There are several of my family names about here—but that apart it is like getting back to the roots of things. / It is a place that would be very strong on one.

This must be the germ of 'Δώρια' (in transliteration, 'Doria')—

> Be in me as the eternal moods
>   of the bleak wind, and not
> As transient things are—
>   gaiety of flowers.
> Have me in the strong loneliness
>   of sunless cliffs
> And of grey waters.
>   Let the gods speak softly of us
> In days hereafter,
>   The shadowy flowers of Orcus
> Remember thee.

162

The Greek title, if it is connected with 'Dorian', as in 'the Dorian mode' of ancient music, would signify a mood of primitive simplicity and strength; and if it is connected with the word for 'gift' there would be an association with 'Dorothy' (which comes from 'gift of god'). The first certainly applies. But if the poem is to be read as invoking Dorothy, then she is being assimilated into the impersonal powers of the bleak wind and the grey waters, and is to be remembered as if she were Persephone in the underworld. Would Olivia have understood that this was his way of being in love, or would Dorothy?

Dorothy responded to Pound's letter with 'I am loving you for feeling all that about the cliffs & Darset'. (Had he sent her 'Δώρια' with his letter?) Then she went on, evidently referring to a part of the letter which she destroyed either then or later,

I should greatly distrust that £35 house! It probably has no drains (or few, which is worse) & no water-supply—but sounds nice with its gate-posts. Or else its horribly haunted.

She was attempting to sketch the church font at Southwold, and sent him a watercolour of a geranium.

'I go to London on Oct 2nd', she told Pound about a week in advance. That would be Monday—she would be 'busy' with one friend on the Tuesday—'occupied' with another on Wednesday—'& on Thursday Rummel is coming to us—& may bring you if it suits you both'. On second thoughts, in her next letter, 'you had better come early on [5]th & discuss the woman question with me upstairs'—she will have had her own sitting-room. By 'the woman question' she meant the question of her being able to afford hats, and her wanting 'a £1,000 a year for her clothes', but only if he could do it by verse alone. The following week on the 10th, 'Tuesday evening', she wrote Pound a plain, businesslike note: 'My dear: Yes: if we are to continue meeting, not à trois or à quatre, I think you should interview H.H.S.'.

That note was posted on Wednesday morning and Pound called the same day on Mr Shakespear at the offices of Shakespear and Parkyn, Solicitors. Mr Shakespear was taken quite by surprise and was unprepared 'to go at all fully into the statements you made to me as to your financial position & prospects'. He really needed to have in writing an account of what Pound had made in the past year, '& from what sources', together with an idea of what he could reasonably expect to make in the near future. He had understood Pound to say that from some source independent of his own exertions he could calculate on £200 a year, and if he could be satisfied that any such sum was or would be secured to him in any event that 'wd go far to meet the most obvious & glaring difficulty which presents itself'. Pound showed him his cheque counterfoils, and H.H.S. was 'glad to see you have a balance to your credit'. He also produced a letter from Macmillan the publishers, 'a pleasing recognition', as H.H.S. conceded, but meaning nothing in the way of income. Further, he had Homer write to Mr Shakespear to back him up, but Homer could only repeat what Ezra had told them both. Pound could muster nothing to move the father from the cautious solicitor's view that 'Literary work of the kind for which he is, no doubt, eminently suited is not likely for some years to furnish him with the means of supporting a Wife'. This reply to Homer's letter—it was now the end of November—concluded the matter:

We like him personally very much, & consider he has great abilities; but until he has some regular income in addition to a permanently secured £200 a year, it is obvious that he is not in a position to marry.

Pound had his own ideas about that. To Homer he had written, 'I am, as you may have surmized from my epistle of yesterday, attempting to marry the gentleman's daughter. I shall do so in any case but don't want to disturb the sepulchral calm of that english household more than need be.' To Margaret Cravens, his secret patronness, he now reported that 'the Shakespears are being quite amenable'. That is, it had been agreed that Pound and Dorothy might take tea together twice a week, with Olivia as reluctant chaperone.

Neither of them rebelled against this. In November Pound had suggested that Dorothy go with him to a lecture, but she had written back—

Dearest:
    No: I'm afraid I can't 'venture'! 'Until something is settled' as Olivia says ('settled', I ask you!) She would evidently so much rather we didn't do anything of that sort—anything for a quiet Life ... I'll be home by three ocl. tomorrow afternoon ...

The following May, while he was in Paris, Pound wrote that Margaret Cravens had offered to invite her there, and again her answer was 'No': 'No – of course, I can't manage Paris ... You see if we were officially engaged it might do – – – But as Father "won't recognize" our engagement – – –'. 'And don't talk to too many of your best friends about me', Dorothy added, 'I have had to suppress M. Moore'—that was his friend Mary Moore from Trenton, New Jersey, whom Pound had asked her to be kind to while she was over in London.

    In March 1912 Pound applied again to Mr Shakespear. He could now look to have 'about £400 per. year'. That 'would not go very far in

England', he conceded, 'but Dorothy seems to think she could live abroad for a year or so'. She might enjoy seeing things and places she would not be able to see if he were 'tied to an educational position'. 'At any rate', he moved quickly on, 'the idea seems to interest her more than the prospect of keeping house in one set locality.' There is no record of Mr Shakespear's response, if any. But, rather oddly, Dorothy wrote to Pound a week later that she had 'told H.H.S we won't bother him at present'. Perhaps the idea of living abroad on an uncertain £400 a year did not appeal to her after all.

So Dorothy went on with her life as before: the rounds of visits; the taking tea with friends and, with Olivia, receiving friends to tea; the going to lectures—Hulme on Bergson, Marinetti on Futurism; the going to the theatre and the ballet—Ibsen's *The Pretenders*, Nijinsky in the Diaghilev 'Prélude à l'après-midi d'un faune'; the going to concerts, or having Walter Rummel in to play Debussy and Schumann to them; the occasional sketching and the talking of books and of other persons' lives. To Olivia it seemed that she and Dorothy were living 'a feminine life practically *à deux*'. And Pound went on with his own busy London life. They might attend the same lecture of Hulme's, or be at the same dinner-party given by Mrs Fowler, but they might not be seen to be together. They kept telling each other what they were up to in chatty, affectionate letters. Once Pound invited Olivia and Dorothy to see Pavlova dance, and they went all three together, with Olivia insisting on paying.

After a year it got to be too much for Olivia—it got on her nerves, she told Ezra, the having to keep two days a week for him to come and see Dorothy. That 'was all very well whilst there was some chance of yr marrying her'—and if he had £500 a year she would be delighted for him to marry her—but as he hadn't, she was obliged to say that he 'ought to go away'. Dorothy '*must* marry', and 'any man who wanted to marry her wd be put off by the fact of yr friendship (or whatever you call it) with her'. Olivia didn't know if Dorothy still considered herself engaged to Ezra, but she wasn't the least likely—and couldn't 'in decency—"transfer her affections" to anyone else whilst you are always about'. Could Olivia trust him to tell Dorothy that they should see less of each other? 'I shouldn't mind your coming to see her once a week,' Olivia wound up, 'but she can't go about with you American fashion—not till she is 35 & has lost her looks.' Ezra, it appears, had already told Olivia that he was 'prepared to see less of Dorothy' in the coming winter.

'I'm to be let in *once* a week', he wrote to Dorothy on her 26th birthday. 'Once a week be hanged', she retorted. But that's more or less how it was to be, and in the event they seem not to have been too discontent. In their letters at least they give no sign of impatient passion insurgent against the restraints put upon young love by prudent elders. Dorothy, indeed, appears to act at the decisive moments as the upholder of the conventions which keep them apart. And Ezra appears to submit to them, and to the father and the mother and the daughter, with a disarming insouciance, quite as if he had more important matters on his mind.

There is no doubting the depth of Dorothy's attachment to Pound—it was the great fact of her life. She had nothing else to take her out of herself, or out of her mother's circle. She had no particular talent or training, apart from being a finished product of her class; she had no employable skill and no wish for employment of any kind; and she had had no preparation for any life except that of the socially presentable wife supported by a husband of means and by servants. She had the beauty and the cultivation for that. But she had also a will of her own, and a silent steely determination not to give up her Ezra. Only she did not want either to give up her comfortable, privileged way of life. She wanted to marry the bohemian poet, but on her father's terms, and there was her dilemma.

There is no doubting the genuineness of Pound's devotion to Dorothy. That would last a lifetime. But how was it that this 'young, revolutionary poet' who was liberating Violet Hunt's and Hueffer's South Lodge from the rigid proprieties of convention, and who was calling for a *Risorgimento* implying 'a whole volley of liberations'—how was it that he could so tamely submit to this oldest and most obvious of tyrannies?

One thinks back to his readiness to marry Mary Moore in the most conventional fashion and with the utmost detachment, with 'a graceful bending to the decrees of destiny, a certain untroubled passivity, as one who sees the hodge-podge of life rather in the nature of little shadows, smoke wraiths from the pipe of the great Pan'. He wrote something rather like that to Dorothy, near the end of October 1911 when things were still to be settled between them. 'As for the rest', the passage begins, apparently referring to some matter they had been discussing together,

I wonder if we can not look at the beginning of things as a sort of divine phantasmagoria or vision or what you will and the 'vagueness' etc as a sort of smoke—an incident in the much more difficult process of drawing down the light, of embodying it, of building it into the stiffer materia of actualities. The whole thing a process of art, of the more difficult art in which we are half media and half creators.

Was he thinking that their marrying was mere shadow-play, a more or less illusory 'incident' in the process of receiving and enacting the divine light? Was he again taking up that attitude of 'untroubled passivity' and giving himself up to 'the decrees of destiny', even though it meant letting himself be confined in sepulchral conventionality? It certainly appears to have been the case that he was reserving his active engagement for that 'much more difficult process' of building light.

The work of genius

In his letter telling Homer what to say to Mr Shakespear about his prospects Pound wrote, 'I have received orders to do my <u>own</u> work & not to worry about the immediate returns'. But to Margaret Cravens, who will have given him those orders, he expressed a willingness 'to earn at least part of my salt'. Her father had committed suicide in April and she had recently learnt that there was nothing to come to her from his estate. Pound wanted to reassure her that he would not need to call on her for more help than she was already giving him. That, he had told her in a previous letter, was simply 'the backbone of the whole show'. Now, at the end of November 1911, he gave her an account of the earnings that were coming his way.

He had received seven shillings and six pence for a short review of *The Dialogues of Saint Gregory* in the London *Daily News*. He would receive £12 for his translations of ten songs for Augener's *Selection from Collection Yvette Guilbert*. He was hoping for a guinea a week from the *New Age*. And Orage, its editor, had introduced him to his publisher, Charles Granville of Stephen Swift and Company, who was going to offer him £100 a year for ten years in return for publishing all Pound's new books. There would also be the fees from his lectures, the one to the Quest Society, and three on medieval poetry arranged by Lady Low and to be given in Lord and Lady Glenconner's private gallery. 'And none of these things seem to block or interfere', he told Margaret, meaning that they did not get in the way of his 'own work'.

But then, as he also told her, 'I don't any more need my time for study & practice'. If he meant that in all seriousness then he must have felt that he was now at the end of his apprenticeship. He had behind him his *Canzoni* and his studies in Guido Cavalcanti and Arnaut Daniel; and *Ripostes*, his next collection, would be ready for Stephen Swift in February. He was beginning to think about his long poem again, or at least *a* long poem, 'much more important than anything I've yet attempted'. It seems likely that he regarded 'Apparuit', a poem in the difficult sapphic measure which he had been working on throughout September, as his graduation exercise.

He described working on it, to Dorothy, as his 'one comfort', and to Margaret as his 'anchor'—'I'm keeping my head thru' the maelstrom because I *must* make a perfect sapphic ode before I pass on. That sort of anchor holds.' It was the difficulty of the exercise that was his stay, but it also taught him something of profound technical significance. Writing in 'quantity', the ancient Greek method of verse, was the only way, he now saw, to ensure that the words of a poem could not be knocked out of shape or obscured by a musician setting them to music, since it is the quantity or duration of syllables that give the true measure and rhythm of the spoken or sung word.

To observe the sapphic measure in reading 'Apparuit' is to find oneself compelled to chant it in the Yeatsian fashion, so strictly determined is the rhythm:

> Golden rose the house, in the portal I saw
> thee, a marvel, carven in subtle stuff, a
> portent. Life died down in the lamp and flickered
> caught at the wonder.

Technically the ode is not quite perfect. In one instance, where there should be a long syllable followed by a short one, we find 'with dew'; in another, where there should be a long syllable we find the '-ous' of 'glamorous'. To set against the few flaws of that kind are the places where the measure lengthens a syllable as one naturally would under the stress of the experience, as with the 'a' at the end of the second line, or the final syllable of 'the steely going'. Again the measure points up the meaning when we must read 'then shone thy oriel AND the stunned light / faded about thee'.[3] But beyond such detail is the sustained cantabile quality of the whole, with each strophe an unbroken rhythmic unit. This is writing that sings itself, a technical *tour de force*.

What it would sing into being is a vision—a vision which is itself a *tour de force*. The title is taken from Dante's *La Vita Nuova*, to recall the moment when the young Dante was first struck by the beauty of Beatrice and his spirit was moved to perceive her as a light of heaven. But the poem is charged with reminders and suggestions of the whole tradition of such epiphanies, from its immediate model, Sappho's ode to Aphrodite, through to Pound's own versions in *Canzoni*. There is a hint from Catullus, the only one out of all the imitators of Sappho, in Pound's judgement, to have imitated her successfully. Then one is reminded of Venus descending from heaven to speak with Aeneas in the first book of the *Aeneid*, and of her letting the glory of her divinity shine out only as she

---

[3] 'Oriel': here signifies the portal of the opening line. (Dorothy was sure he meant 'aureole', but that would not fit the measure.)

leaves him. One is reminded too of Persephone, the light of life coming forth from the dark earth in its Spring flowering. There is much to make one think of the story of Cupid and Psyche, as retold by Pater out of 'The Golden Book' of Apuleius. And Dante's, and Cavalcanti's, and Pound's own visions of the divine light of love are all in there too. The poem is a fusing together of those many apparitions of Love into a rapt celebration of its mystery, the fusion taking place under the pressure of the technical demands of the sapphic measure.

When Dorothy told Pound that Yeats was very pleased with 'The Return' and 'Apparuit', and 'read them to us with due music', it must have seemed the crowning of his years of study and practice. Yet 'Apparuit', for all his hard work on it, was the height of artifice, no more. The real thing would come in the latter half of canto 81, after a further forty-five years of study and practice. He knew perfectly well in 1911 and 1912 that 'The mastery of any art is the work of a lifetime'. As much as he could hope for then was to have got 'rid of the first froth of verse', and to have emerged 'decently clean after some reasonable purgation, not nearly a master, but licensed, an initiate'.

Even so, apparently he felt ready now to declare his genius. There was a bold, even over-reaching, assertion implicit in the title he gave to his first series of articles in the *New Age*. Any readers of the review who were keeping up with Frazer's *The Golden Bough*—the volumes entitled *Adonis, Attis, Osiris* had recently appeared—would have seen that to say 'I gather the limbs of Osiris' was as much as to claim, 'I am Isis gathering up and reanimating the buried fragments of a decaying civilization'. For Osiris had taught Egypt to grow grain and make bread; then to live in towns, to institute laws, and to worship gods. Afterwards he carried the gifts of civilization abroad into other nations. But his antagonists in Egypt murdered him, cut up his body and scattered the parts; whereupon Isis collected together the scattered parts and by her magical powers restored Osiris, to ensure that his genius would be always at work in the world. In a way, a very small way, that was what Pound had been doing in 'Apparuit', gathering some of the dispersed revelations of Love into a new whole. It was what he had been doing on a larger scale in *Canzoni*. But now he was declaring his ambition to recover and renew the vital principle of his civilization, to be its Isis.

The claim was far in excess of what he had to put on show in the series of twelve articles. 'It has been complained, with some justice', he acknowledged elsewhere about this time, 'that I dump my notebooks on the public'—and that to a considerable extent was what he was doing in the *New Age*. The series consisted of a version of the Anglo-Saxon 'Seafarer'; a selection of five of his translations of the sonnets and *ballate* of Guido Cavalcanti; translations of ten *canzoni* of Arnaut Daniel, these making up five of the twelve articles; and five prose articles, interspersed among the translations, devoted to expositions of his 'New Method in Scholarship'. In the penultimate article he felt the need to insist that there was 'a unity of intention, not only in these rambling discourses, but in the translations of Arnaut and of the other poets'; and this, if one stresses the hopeful 'intention' and notes the concessive 'rambling', is a fair statement of the case. The notes and translations do all hang together, but very loosely and disjointedly, and the reader has to do the work of making out how they might cohere.

Pound's unifying intent was to recover the force which makes for fuller and finer living from those rare poems in which it is present at its most innovative. To that end he proposed to do away with the kind of scholarship—he does not actually call it 'Philology' on this occasion—which seeks *all* the facts indiscriminately and stifles any vital interest in them. His new method would seek out just the 'luminous details', the few really significant facts which 'give one a sudden insight into circumjacent conditions, into their causes, their effects, into sequence, and law'. He had been reading Burckhardt's *The Civilization of the Renaissance*—it would have been for a prose book of his own on the Renaissance which he was thinking of undertaking but soon abandoned—and was struck by the passage in which Burckhardt singles out, as a decisive factor in the way the Venetians conducted their affairs, their keeping accurate statistical accounts of their resources and of their trading returns. These enabled them to calculate, as others then could not, that it would not be to their commercial advantage to join in a war against the Milanese. Here, Pound noted, 'we come upon a portent, the old order changes, one conception of war and of the State begins to decline'. He would deploy such 'luminous details' out of historical records as the staple material of his *Cantos*, though often pared down to minimal 'gists and piths'. But for now he was regarding certain entire poems and authors as 'luminous details'.

As he had sought to bring over the specific *virtu* of Cavalcanti, he now sought to isolate the specifically 'English' quality of 'The Seafarer', and to present Arnaut's work as marking a definite advance in perceptive intelligence. In his 'Seafarer' Pound consciously and deliberately stripped away the mentions of the Devil and angels and Almighty God, which appear to have been inserted by a monk intent on converting the pagan poem to a Christian vision of life. He wanted to recover the pre-Christian, 'heroic' mind of an individual working out his fate within a world defined only by the natural elements and by human society. And he did that by inventing a diction which kept as close as possible to the Anglo-Saxon, with a minimum of words from other sources; and by keeping as close as he could contrive to the actual sounds and rhythm of the original:

> No man at all going the earth's gait,
> But age fares against him, his face paleth,
> Grey-haired he groaneth, knows gone companions,
> Lordly men, are to earth o'ergiven

Pound's own bardic performance of the poem, in a recording he made in 1939, is a compelling demonstration of its 'Anglo-Saxon' power. He classed the poem, justly, as a 'major persona'.

His versions of Arnaut Daniel are utterly different, as Arnaut was of an utterly different world and time. Arnaut's distinction, Pound remarked, was to have discriminated more acutely than his fellows between one sound and another, and between one shade of experience and another. He perceived that the beauty of rhyming sounds depends 'not upon frequency' but 'upon their action the one upon the other'. And then the fineness of sense manifest in the artistry of his 'polyphonic' rhyming 'made him likewise accurate in his observation of nature'. Altogether, in Arnaut's powers of discrimination and precision, Pound detected 'some germ of the Renaissance, of the spirit which was to overthrow superstition and dogma, of the "scientific spirit"'.

The translations of Arnaut published in the *New Age* are strictly studies in technique, matchless for their sound, the way they reproduce the notes of the original, but not of the first importance as poetry. But then technique, as he argued in the *New Age* and elsewhere, really matters, insofar as it is the appropriate means of conveying precisely what the poet, 'at the very crux of a clarified conception', is able to say. Without a mastery of technique the aspirant will be able to do no more than approximate what others have said already—there will be no fresh creation, no exhilaration of new insight in his work. In short, Pound's investigations of such specialized questions as that of 'tone-leading'—'are there in words themselves tones that call for certain other notes, for a resolution or a close?'—were the steps by which he was making progress as a poet.

He believed that 'only after a long struggle'—such as his own struggle to 'master all known forms and systems of metric'—would poetry 'attain such a degree of development, of... modernity, that it will vitally concern people who are accustomed, in prose, to Henry James'. He thought it possible, no doubt having his own future development in view, 'that English verse of the future will be a sort of orchestration taking account of all these systems'. He knew that only by such developments of technique would the poetry of the immediate future be what it needed to be, 'harder and saner...."nearer the bone"'. At least for himself he wanted it to be 'austere, direct, free from emotional slither', to be 'as much like granite as it can be'.

At the same time he declared, in an apparent contradiction, that 'The artist discriminates...between one kind of indefinability and another'—

Our life is, insofar as it is worth living, made up in great part of things indefinite, impalpable; and it is precisely because the arts present us these things that we—humanity—cannot get on without the arts.

The function of art, then, would be to give exact definition to indefinabilities—or at least to things in our experience that matter to us but are as yet undefined or unrealised. 'Δώρια' would be an instance of the impalpable being made definite, 'as much like granite as it can be'. Pound would go on to argue, very much as Hueffer had, that the artist is the scientist of the human spirit. 'What the analytical geometer does for space and form', he wrote in 'The Wisdom of Poetry', 'the poet does for states of consciousness'; and again, 'As the abstract mathematician is to science so is the poet to the world's consciousness'. His permanent function in his world is to awaken minds to the mysteries latent in their experience.

That, in practical terms, is how the Isis–Osiris genius would work in Pound's modern times. By his art he would liberate the minds of his readers from false consciousness due to 'set moods, set ideas, conventions'; he would clear away from their perceptive faculties the obfuscating effects of passion; and he would delight the intellect and draw the emotions into accord with the truth of things by presenting his scientific observations, his 'luminous details', with that 'melody of words' which '"most doth draw the soul unto itself"'. That would be Pound's way of being the light of the world.

'Ripostes of Ezra Pound'

'The only man I ever met who had seen my stuff in *The New Age* was an admiral', so Pound recalled years later when he was living in Rapallo, and that was an admiral with whom he had conversed over 'Bath olivers' and claret on board a battleship of His Majesty's navy. His 'Osiris' articles could well have been passed over as rather lightweight alongside the serious political and topical commentaries in the paper. Even in their own sphere of the arts there were more obvious excitements in the issues for October and November 1911, such as a notice of the return of Diaghilev's

Ballet Russes to Covent Garden, T. E. Hulme writing on Bergson, Rupert Brooke's 'The Fish' with two other poems, or an illustrated article on Picasso as Cubist. There was also the intriguing announcement that 'on Thursday November 23rd Messrs. Stephen Swift., Ltd. will publish a new weekly feminist review, *The Freewoman*, which will be under the joint editorship of Miss Dora Marsden and Miss Mary Gawthorpe'. The world into which Pound was now venturing was full of its own busy and various doings, and not predisposed to comprehend him.

But then he was quite full of his own doings. He wrote to Margaret Cravens that Elkin Mathews was to ' "boom" ' *Canzoni* that autumn; and that he hoped that 'with the "Guido", and the "Arnaut" ' which Swift was to publish he would more than double his ' "position" '. And he was getting ready for Swift another book of his 'own things'—that was to be *Ripostes of Ezra Pound*. Though he would later describe this collection to Harriet Monroe as 'scarcely more than a notice that my translations and experiments have not entirely interrupted my compositions', modesty did not prevent him from congratulating Williams for perceiving that the book was a unified whole, nor from telling him that 'That of course is the artistic triumph'.

The artistry of the book was not appreciated, however, by the anonymous reviewer in the *Times Literary Supplement*. It would have the same effect on its readers, he suggested, as the Post-Impressionist exhibition at the Grafton Galleries was having on its viewers, making some dance with fury and others quake with laughter, some worship indiscriminately and a few use their brains coolly. For himself, he thought Mr Pound seemed rather too pleased with whatever he might casually 'chance to say'. Mr Pound might do well to consider John Keble's advice to the young men not to be satisfied with their occasional 'striking and clever patches'; and that it is only 'the great and earnest soul...which spares neither labour nor learning if only he may thus produce an adequate and beautiful representation of that in which his heart delights.'

It is galling to be thus told to strive for just what one thought one had achieved, and I suspect that we have Pound's retort, delivered indirectly, in Frank Flint's review in *Poetry and Drama*. The first half of the review at any rate reads as if it was drafted or else dictated by Pound:

[Mr Pound] is one of the few people in this country who do care for poetry as an art, and not merely as an accident, or the lazy pleasure of expressing one's twopenny-halfpenny personality in the easiest possible manner. Mr Pound has served a long apprenticeship in the technics of his craft, and with the sapphics of 'Apparuit', the 'free' rhythm of 'The Return' and 'Δώρια'...he has attained a skill in handling words that is astonishing to those who understand. The sapphics of 'Apparuit' and the alliterative verse translation from the Anglo-Saxon of 'The Seafarer'...complete his analysis of the development of the poetic art from the Middle Ages to the present which was begun in *The Spirit of Romance*, a prose work, and continued in the experiments in polyphonic rhyme of the *Canzoni* and in the translations from Arnaut Daniel....Mr Pound has earned the right to put his poetry into any form he pleases; he has given his *vers libres* a solid basis in tradition, and may laugh at the critics.

After some notes on particular poems which echo what Pound himself would have said of them, Flint asserted his independence by devoting the second half of the review to the 'Complete Poetical Works' of T. E. Hulme as appended by Pound to *Ripostes*, and to an account in his own style of the meetings of the Poets' Club. It is not apparent that he had appreciated the unity and wholeness of the book.

The notes on particular poems do give some helpful leads. 'Apparuit', 'Δώρια' and 'The Return' are singled out as 'the three best poems'—quite justly—and as 'Mr Pound's finest work'. 'Δώρια' is characterized as 'a perfect translation of pure emotion', and the other two as 'transcripts of emotional vision'. Certain other poems, 'Portrait d'une Femme', 'Sub Mare' and 'Plunge' among them, are said to be 'attempts at precise rendering of exact psychology'. This little complex of terms, 'pure emotion', 'emotional vision' and 'exact psychology', can be tied together with the key word of the collection, 'soul'. That word occurs in several of the poems, and is implicit or in question in most. One gathers that the soul is manifest and active in desire and vision; that it is constituted of what it loves and sees; and that it becomes fully itself and immortal when in love with the divine and disengaged from the local and temporal. It is the mind in its godly state, seeing what it loves as in a vision of its perfection. The opposite state is that of the loveless and visionless, as displayed in 'An Object'—'This thing that hath a code and not a core'—and in '"Phasellus Ille"'—'Come Beauty barefoot from the Cyclades, / She'd find a model for St Anthony / In this thing's sure *decorum* and behaviour.'

Following this lead, we might approach the collection as a series of slides, each exhibiting a specific state of mind or soul, and each prepared with the appropriate technique for displaying that particular state. The science, the critical study of mind, proceeds by discriminations, by observing likeness and difference, and by an effort to organize the findings into a qualitative classification. The quality or value, it must be said, is in the eye of the beholder, for while the relatively unenlightened states are presented with unsympathetic objectivity, the most illuminated states are realized with full clarity, immediacy, and intensity. The scale of value runs from relatively limited or defective states towards a pure or perfect 'emotional vision'. The arrangement of the poems, however, does not yield a simple progression from the lowest to the highest.[4]

'Silet' and 'In Exitum Cuiusdam' may be read as attempts to clear away false consciousness due to conventions and clichés, and due also perhaps to clinging on to past passion, to old loves or old friendships. 'Apparuit' then introduces the main theme of 'emotional vision', against which the states of soul in the following poems can be measured. The soul in 'The Tomb at Akr Çaar' remains bound to the body it once animated and will not go forth into the light of the living world. The woman of 'Portrait d'une Femme' presents nearly the reverse case. Her life is made up of all sorts of worldly things, but she has nothing quite her own. In one sense she is the soul of her society, while really she is all social surface—a Jamesian theme, before Eliot made it his also. 'N.Y.' then figures as the city without a soul into which the poet in his fit would breathe one, as if he were Pan and the city the nymph Syrinx. 'A Girl' presents the reverse case to that. Here a child is transformed out of her own being into a tree, like Daphne pursued by Apollo, or Wordsworth's dead Lucy. Her transformation is first given as she finds it happening to her, then observed with approving, godlike lucidity, as if by Apollo himself.

The contemptuous irony with which the hide-bound editor is observed in 'Phasellus Ille', and the cold detachment with which 'An Object' is defined, are expressed in verse of a hard, 'classical', formality. The effect is at once 'modern', and distancing. 'In Exitum Cuiusdam' is in the same style, and so too is 'Quies'. These poems engage with certain contemporaries only to damn them as lacking any life of the soul. There was some saving sympathy for the woman in 'Portrait', and some saving good

---

[4] These are the poems of *Ripostes* as originally published, in my analysis of the main groupings:

Silet	The Seafarer	Δώρια
In Exitum Cuiusdam		The Needle
	Echoes I*,	II Sub Mare
Apparuit	An Immorality*	Plunge
The Tomb at Akr Çaar	Dieu! Qu'il la fait	A Virginal
Portrait d'une Femme		
N.Y.	Salve Pontifex*	Pan is Dead
A Girl		The Picture
		Of Jacopo del Sellaio
'Phasellus Ille'		The Return
An Object		Effects of Music* I, II
Quies		

*Excluded from *Ripostes* as collected in *Personae* (1926).

humour when *Canzoni* touched 'modernity' in 'Au Salon', but in these cases the rejection is absolute.

That makes the case of 'The Seafarer' more challenging, for those three 'classical' epigrams point up the fact that in it too there is little or no spiritual vision. Pound might have been emphasizing this in his editing of the Anglo-Saxon text in such a way as to remove the accretions which gave it a turn towards a Christian vision. The protagonist's mind and heart are possessed by the hardships of seafaring. Life on land holds no delight for him, the lure of the sea is all, even though it brings only joyless suffering. It is remarkable that he never mentions the sun's light; that for him 'Cuckoo calleth with gloomy crying', boding sorrow in summer; and that he has no wish for wife, no love in his life. His only hope is of winning honour in death by enduring the hardship of his doom-gripped life. He is the heroic individual confronting a hostile world and an alien culture, whose vision of life is determined by what he feels himself to be up against. In the end, his is not so much a vision of life as of death, and his full heroism consists in his facing the reality of death without illusion and without flinching.

'The Seafarer' is one of the two central pillars supporting the structure of *Ripostes*. The other is 'Salve Pontifex'. There must have been strong reason for including the Swinburnian 'hemichaunt', since it was an old poem from *A Lume Spento* and, as Pound admitted to Williams, '"historicaly" [*sic*] out of place in this book'. It was there, he said, because it 'has rhythm', and 'solely for the rhythmic structure'. It is not clear whether he meant the rhythmic structure of the poem or that of the book, but it is the latter that makes sense to me. The celebration of Swinburne as 'High Priest of Iacchus' evokes the mysteries of Persephone and Dionysus and the vision of their perpetual renewing of the life of earthly things. This is the vision the heroic seafarer lacks. We will find the same conjunction and contrast in the difference between cantos 1 and 2, in the turn from seafaring Odysseus' looking to the sunless dead for guidance—and in the very measure of the Anglo-Saxon poem—into the sunlit vision of the Dionysiac world.

'Δώρια', with its evocation of 'the eternal moods', 'the gods' and 'The shadowy flowers of Orcus', might be a state of mind refined out of the noisy 'Salve Pontifex'. And it might be crystallizing a visionary awareness of the Seafarer's existence such as he himself has not the soul to comprehend. Then there is the further difference of its addressing another presence. In this it is picking up the motif of the four light love lyrics placed between 'The Seafarer' and 'Salve Pontifex', but with a shift from their known ways of loving to the strange intimacy of 'Be in me as the eternal moods / of the bleak wind', and the strange union implied in 'Let the gods speak softly of us / In days hereafter'. It must be a union of souls that is suggested here, of souls united in 'the eternal moods'.

That kind of union is what is being sought in the rest of this set of five poems. But the sequence moves away from the immediacy of 'Δώρια', into vain longing and alienation in 'Plunge', and finally a poesy-drenched dream of the fair lady in 'A Virginal'. This last is almost a parody of 'Apparuit', with the poet not after all rapt in his vision but merely wrapped up in his own precious subjectivities. There is irony in the title: it is he who is the spiritual virgin here.

It is not far from that irony to the ironies of 'Pan is Dead'. Behind this stands Elizabeth Barrett Browning's 'The Dead Pan', which celebrates the tradition that 'at the hour of the Saviour's agony, a cry of "Great Pan is dead"' was heard, and the pagan mysteries were no more.

Pound's poem sets up a dialogue with the maidens who think Pan dead, first bidding them 'weave ye him his coronal', and then, when they observe that they cannot do that since nature has died with Pan, he coolly leaves them to puzzle out why Death 'has taken our Lord away'. Our 'Lord' would seem to be Pan, but he, in pagan belief, is lord of life and not subject to death. On the other hand, Christians refer to Christ as 'Our Lord', and believe that he did die. At this point the poem seems to turn its Christian perspective back on itself, as if to say *Who* is dead? The effect is to question, not to endorse, the supposed death of the god of nature. But it does confirm that the maiden ladies have suffered a loss of vision.

'The Picture' and 'Of Jacopo del Sellaio', with their insistence that 'The eyes of this dead lady speak to me', give the riposte direct to those for whom Pan is dead. Only here what has been lost in nature is recovered in spirit. What the eyes speak is that the painter must have known out 'the secret ways of love'—meaning a love 'not to be drowned out' by sensual fulfilment. The painting referred to, in the National Gallery in London, has Venus looking for more while Mars lies exhausted, and would have invited, in its own time and place, a Neoplatonic interpretation. Pound's poem is not presenting the love vision, but simply asserting, almost didactically, that the art which it inspired bears lasting witness to it.

'The Return' is effectively the final poem in the series—Pound rightly discarded from his collected poems the subjective impressionism of 'Effects of Music'—and it is an excellent instance of his ability to give definition to something indefinable by precision of rhythm and image alone. The return of the exhausted, nearly extinguished, heroes or gods is seen in its full mystery, as a vision at once palpable and ungraspable. It might help to think of the retreat from Moscow of Napoleon's broken army. A stronger suggestion is that these might be Actaeon's hunting companions, shattered by the revelation of Artemis-Diana's terrifying divinity. Such a vision as theirs would be a glimpse into the nature of things, or more exactly, a revelation of the law of life.

That, however, is no more than a suggestion here. The clear understanding that right living depends directly upon seeing accurately into the natures of things will come later, as in canto 2. For the moment Pound's investigations have only served to establish the power of vision as the principle of the soul's life. But that is a distinct development beyond the concerns of *Canzoni* and the collections behind it. Now it is not the perfecting of love that is in question, so much as the perfecting of vision.

Love is of course understood to be the force that clarifies and intensifies and gives power to the soul in its seeing; but this is assumed as established fact, something that need only be stated, as in 'The Picture' and 'Of Jacopo del Sellaio'. It is no longer a matter for investigation. Williams apparently used the phrase 'sublimated to mere being together' in his letter to Pound about *Ripostes*. Pound replied that there might be 'various meanings' in that, but it would have been an astute observation, from Williams's un-Platonic point of view, of where Pound seemed to be at in his treatment of love. The phrase could yield the unspoken meaning of 'Silet'.

In his reply to Williams Pound coyly wondered 'what you'll say to my next book, which is *modern*—ehem! yes, *modern*'. That implicitly recognized that *Ripostes* was not yet modern, although, coming after *Canzoni*, it was definitely modern in its tending towards a contemporary idiom and a more natural syntax. We can let it rest as a work of transition, while noting that Pound thought so well of it that he kept it virtually intact in his later collected poems.

'This is where I belong'

Only a few of Pound's 'ripostes' were aimed directly at his contemporary world. '"Time's bitter flood"', in the first line of 'In Exitum Cuiusdam', pointed that poem at Yeats. 'Portrait d'une Femme' might have touched some particular Edwardian lady, and 'Phasellus Ille' would hit a type of late Victorian editor. There was disaffection from the modern city and its traffic in 'N.Y.' and 'The Plunge'. But otherwise, throughout the collection, the mind moves in the past, or in the timelessness of 'things that are familiars of the god'.

Yet Pound was of course all the while going about 'the beastly town' and making his way in it. 'I suppose this is where I belong', he told Margaret Cravens, '& one goes on finding delightful people'. Some old alliances were renewed and some new ones formed. He went up to see

Manning, and dined with Mead and with Hewlett. Hulme was now conducting a philosophical-aesthetical *salon* for the discussion of ideas on Tuesday evenings in a rather grand house in Frith Street, off Soho Square. The house belonged to his close friend Mrs Ethel Kibblewhite. It seems that almost anyone who was anybody in the intellectual and artistic life of London might be met there. Orage went, when he was not holding his own court at the Café Royal, and Pound may have been introduced to him there. Florence Farr, who went everywhere until she hid herself in Ceylon, would be there. Hueffer went, and D. H. Lawrence, and Wyndham Lewis, Jacob Epstein and, later, Gaudier-Breszka. Pound became a regular, until he set up his own Tuesday evenings in the autumn of 1912.

One evening he found himself seated on the floor next to Edward Marsh and Rupert Brooke who were then planning the first *Georgian Anthology*. He was invited to contribute, but they could not agree on a suitable poem. He met Harold Monro, who was to publish the *Georgian Anthologies*, and who was about to open his Poetry Bookshop and edit the *Poetry Review* in which Pound's 'Prologomena' and the first of his new 'modern' poems would appear, and in which he would review Hueffer's *High Germany*.

At Christmas 1911 he went down to Hewlett's place near Salisbury, the Old Rectory, Broad Chalke, or 'whats left of a nunnery built in 1487'. 'Going out from Southampton'—Hewlett would have picked him up from the train there—there was a sight of the old England that came back to him in Pisa—

> they passed the car by the dozen
> who would not have shown weight on a scale
> riding, riding
> for Noel the green holly...

More prosaically, during the visit Hewlett took him by car to see Henry Newbolt.

When Hueffer and Violet Hunt were back in London South Lodge came alive once more. Pound first saw Henry James there one day in February 1912. They 'glared at each other across the same carpet', in Pound's account. A short while later they were the only guests at a small luncheon party, and this time Pound thought James 'quite delightful'; he liked him 'still more' when they met again. It was his 'unforgettable' conversation that registered most deeply then and first won his affection, 'the long sentences piling themselves up in elaborate phrase after phrase, the lightning incision, the pauses, the slightly shaking admonitory gesture with its "wu-a-wait a little, wait a little, something will come" '; and his talk always enriched by 'so many years' careful, incessant labour of minute observation'. James would become in Pound's mind a companion spirit and guide as Sordello was for Dante in his *Purgatorio*, with the same *occhi honesta e tarda*, the eyes deliberately discriminating 'the tone of things'.

Another companion spirit met at South Lodge, though of a very different sort, was Brigit Patmore, a bright, beautiful Irish woman of about 30. Married to a descendant of the Victorian poet Coventry Patmore who was in insurance in the City, she preferred the milieu of Violet Hunt and Hueffer. She and Ezra became great friends, and he called her, romantically, 'Vail de Lencour', and would dedicate his next book to her under that name. Through Pound Brigit came to know Hilda Doolittle who was now in England, and then introduced them both to Richard Aldington, a wide-eyed young poet newly on the scene.[5] By her account the four of them 'would go around together most afternoons'.

Hilda had come over in May of 1911 with Frances Gregg, a Philadelphia friend who had taken Ezra's place in her love-life, and with Frances's mother, ostensibly to tour Europe. But when the Greggs returned to Philadelphia in September Hilda seized her chance to stay on in London. Pound introduced her to all his friends, and to May Sinclair and to Olivia and Dorothy in particular. Hilda and Aldington, who had been straightaway drawn to her strange beauty and intensity, became constant companions in poetry and fell into Pound's habit of working in the British Museum Reading Room and meeting up with like-minded readers in its tea room. In this way they became the nucleus of his very own movement, announced at the back of *Ripostes* as '*Les Imagistes*' who had 'the future...in their keeping'. In 1913, when Pound's *Imagisme* was having its moment, all three had rooms in Church Walk, with Pound at no. 10 and Hilda and Aldington across the court, one at no. 6 and the other at no. 8. Frank Flint, with whom Pound had met up again, was conscripted as a fourth member of the movement, and 'in return for being ressurrected' put him on to 'some very good contemporary French stuff, Remy de Gourmont, de Regnier etc.'

In March of 1912 he gave his three lectures, at 34 Queen Anne's Gate, S.W., 'by the kind permission of Lord and Lady Glenconner'. The lectures were at 3.30 in the afternoon, and admission was by ticket only, at half a guinea for the single lecture and a guinea (£1.1s.) for the course. Formal

[5] Richard Aldington (1892–1962): poet, translator, novelist, critic, editor. Studied for one year at University College London; shared H.D.'s Hellenism; one of the original *Imagistes*; asst.-editor *The Egoist* 1914–16. Married H.D. 1913; fought in World War I; separated from H.D. 1918. Liaison with Brigit Patmore 1928–38. Early publications: *Images, 1910–1915* (1915); *Images of War* (1919).

dress would have been *de rigeur* for the lecturer as for the audience. The first lecture, on Guido Cavalcanti—'Tuscany, A.D. 1290'—was chaired by Manning; the second was on Arnaut Daniel—'Provence, A.D. 1190'; and the third, with Yeats in the chair, was on Anglo-Saxon verse—'England, A. D. 790'. Pound had a note from Dorothy to come in to them on the morning of his third lecture, and to stay to lunch if he could. She was going that evening 'to hear Marinetti lecture in French, about les Futuristes'. Marinetti, also in evening dress, would have been demanding the violent tearing down of museums, the setting fire to libraries, a general smash-up of the idols of past literature and art.

In her memoir H.D. related a strange incident that must have occurred about this time. Frances Gregg had written to her from America that she was about to marry an 'English University Extension lecturer' who worked in Belgium, and that she was doing this in order to return to Europe and join H.D. Her idea was that they 'would all go to Belgium together'. Hilda agreed to this. She doesn't mention Aldington in this episode. It was Pound who appeared on the pavement as she was taking a taxi to the station and told her she was not to go with the newlyweds. 'There is a vague chance that the Egg...may be happy', he said, 'You will spoil everything'. So Hilda took back the cheque she had given the husband for her ticket, and Ezra, 'Glowering and savage', in her eyes, 'waited till the train pulled out'. For her Ezra's behaviour was that of the tyrannical patriarch, banging his stick of authority on the pavement, '*Pounding*' (as she insists), preventing her doing something she was in the course of doing. As she tells the story there is no room for reflecting on her own behaviour, nor for seeing Pound's in another light. But it is possible to see him as acting with an unexpected worldly wisdom, and with a sense of common decency. At the same time he may have been quite unaware of what Frances herself wanted. The honeymooning couple, bereft of Hilda, went off to Venice with Llewelyn and John Cowper Powys instead, and carried on there in a scandalous *ménage à quatre*, with Frances appearing in public dressed as a boy.

Hilda, went over to Paris early in May, where Margaret Cravens was kind to her, and Aldington followed her there soon after. It has been suggested that she was wanting to get away from Pound and to recover her equilibrium; but then it is odd that she should have gone to Paris, of all places, since he was already there, having taken the boat train on May 1st.

10 : IN THE STEPS OF THE TROUBADOURS

Pound was going to spend most of May 1912 in Paris, then head south to walk over a significant part of Provence in June and July. He stayed with Rummel in Rue Raynouard; saw a good deal of Margaret Cravens in the Rue du Colisée; and went about Paris with Hilda and Aldington. There was further work to be done with Rummel towards the *Neuf Chansons de Troubadours*. And there was material to be gathered concerning the lives of the troubadours from manuscripts in the Bibliothèque Nationale.

He hoped to glean from them information that might be of interest for his walking tour, and that would then go into the book he would be writing for Swift & Co. about the troubadours, their art and their way of life. One can guess, from the first half of an essay he published in 1913, what sort of notes he took—

Vidal was son of a furrier, and sang better than any man in the world; and Raimon de Miraval was a poor knight that had but part of a castle; and Uc Brunecs was a clerk and he had an understanding with a *borgesa* who had no mind to love him or to keep him, and who became mistress to the Count of Rodez.

Pound was wanting to document the conviction he had formed at Hamilton that those early medieval singers were real individuals who led 'a life like our own', and that they sang of real loves and deeds. The *vidas* or 'lives' written down by Miquel de la Tour were ideal for the purpose since they were written on just that assumption. Treating the songs as autobiographical, they made them yield tales of the 'real lives' of the troubadours. Some of these stories would be worked into the *Cantos*, such as those of Poicebot and Pieire de Maensac in canto 5; but the one that most interested Pound at that moment concerned Bertran de Born. That was a story he would be trying to trace out while walking over 'En Bertran's old layout'.

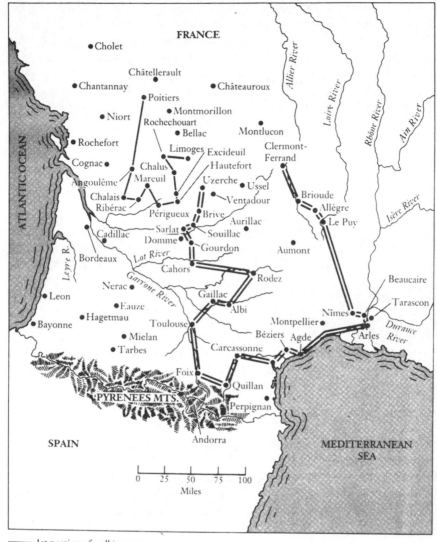

Map showing route of EP's 1912 walking tour in southern France. (*Courtesy of New Directions Publishing Corporation*)

With a card to show that he was a member of the Touring Club de France, a rucksack, Baedeker's *Southern France* and some large-scale maps, Pound took a night train to Poitiers on the 26th of May, arriving early on the 27th. He spent the day nosing about the town for traces of the earliest troubadours who had sung there 'at the court of the Plantagenet princes ... Daniel & De Born and Borneil and ... many another' whom the *vidas* say were of that region. He noted 'many rose bushes pleached against many walls' and made up his own *canso*, 'As the rose taketh no harm from trellis, so is my love unharmed by the strait bonds she puts upon me—and so on'. But he was disappointed and discouraged by the prevailing modernity of the place. The houses had *mansard* roofs, 'The people wore the clothing of Milan and Paris, the cathedral is too newly whitewashed', and the gardens had all the charm of Philadelphia's suburban Germantown.

Pound was aware—or perhaps Hueffer later made him aware—that he was 'violating all Hueffer's canons and principles of prose' with these 'irrational and emotional discriminations'. He was risking above all that nostalgic sentimentality which Hueffer had forbidden himself in his trilogy of books presenting England as it appeared to him. Pound agreed that 'sentiment is the father of lies', but claimed that it was something else to be 'a lover of strange & exquisite emotions', and, furthermore, that this was 'in no way incompatible with the "scientific spirit".' Yet as he walked through southern France and attempted to realize 'Provence' as it appeared to him his mood would keep shifting about between unwanted nostalgia, self-delighting fantasy, and objective observation.

On the night of the 27th he went on to Angoulême, just seventy miles south of Poitiers, but a journey of three and a quarter hours by slow train. He generally took night trains, perhaps because they were cheaper, and to save on hotels. There was nothing to interest him in Angoulême, since it had no troubadour associations that he knew of, but it was from here that he took to the road and began his thousand kilometer walk. He would average about twenty miles a day, in all weathers from drenching rain to blazing sun, and at the end, having walked thirty-three miles on his final day, would believe that 'with American boots & a little practice & a reasonably constructed pack a man might do 50 m. per day & enjoy it'.

His first fifty miles took two days, and brought him to Chalais by country lanes and trackways, and 'in the devil's own down-pour' for the last ten miles. He had to leave his clothing drying in the kitchen while he noted down his impressions upstairs. The country he had come through in the rain gets a brief mention, but what had drawn him on was that 'In this Chalais lived the viscountess of Bertran's Dompna Soisebuda', his 'borrowed' or ideal lady. According to Baedeker Chalais was 'a small decayed town ... with an old castle now a hospice.' The castle had been altogether transformed by Talleyrand in the eighteenth century, and in any case may not have been the one De Born knew; but all the same

Pound exercised his imagination to see it as if through the eyes of the 'stirrer-up of strife', as a fortress with a 'sense of crouch and spring in the masonry'.

The next day he went on to Ribérac where Arnaut Daniel was born; then to Vieux Mareuil which had its own Arnaut, the one impersonated in Pound's 'Marvoil'. Here Pound was the 'scientific' observer doing a Baedeker: 'At vieux Mareuil we have a church with thick walls, with battlements at the corners & what may have been the upper slant of a portcullis... This fortification seems to me in all likelihood the remains of the castle where Arnaut saw daylight. The transept was made very early XIII. The tower is new. The present mill stream may well have provided a moat.'

As he walked in rain down the long valley to Brantôme, going by back roads, he passed through the hamlet of Puychantu and there bought an umbrella. He came into Périgueux thinking that he was entering it as *jongleurs* must have done, on painful feet, weary and hungry. Then in front of the cathedral with its Byzantine domes and campanile—it was now June 2 and the *fête* of the Trinity—he came upon a fairground with 'fine immoral music', a whirl of dancing, 'showman's drums', and a merry-go-round all tinsel and crystal and thrones and howdahs 'lit by a flare of gasoline like a torch flare'. He passed on and over the bridge to see the reflected lamps in the river, and turned back to note that 'the faces in the crowd are gay, and simple, are primitive, approach deliria, and are for strangers suspicious, tending to be afraid'.

One is struck by how few people Pound seems to engage with, especially out in the country. There are more imagined troubadours and their ladies in his Provence than living people. Was the country really so deserted, or did he take its farmers and field-workers and shepherds for granted? Were there no other travellers? He will mention, later on, some gypsies on his road. In Bertran de Born's territory, to which he had now come, there are just two or three encounters. One made a lasting impression, though he gave it only an incidental mention in his notes. Having 'lost the road between Perigord and Excideuil' in the serpentine paths winding among the fields and scrub pine around the hamlet of Blis-et-Born, 'by the grace of god I came to a man at work who directed me to an inn without a sign', and thence he found the way into Born itself on the summit of the hill. From there, Pound observed, 'you have the valleys beneath you', with the implication that this was part of De Born's strategic network around his castle at Hautefort twenty kilometres or so to the east and north. He had De Born and his story so much on his mind that of the man himself he noted down only his pronunciation of 'Born'—'B*orrr*'. Yet he was 'a huge red-bearded peasant' who had been 'engaged in a job of amateur cobbling, mending one of his daughter's shoes', when Pound entered his cottage 'in search of an omelet'; and Pound was so surprised to find such 'gentleness and dignity' and such 'finished courtesy' in that hidden-away place that he would still be thinking of him twenty-five years later as an example of perfect manners.

From Excideuil he walked the ten miles or so south-east to Hautefort, which had been De Born's 'Altafort'. The castle had been long since completely rebuilt, as he knew, but from its situation he could imagine how it would have been for Bertran lording it there, how difficult it would have been for his foes to get at him, and how he 'might well have grown thoughts beyond his station, seeing so much land & nothing in it to withstand him'. Pound thought he would find in the lie of the land evidence of a political intent hidden in the seeming love-song, the 'Dompna Soisebuda'. Each of the ladies named by Bertran lived in a castle of strategic interest to him, or so Pound supposed, Maent herself at Montignac to the south, Anhes at Rochechouart to the north, the viscountess at Chalais to the west, Audiart at Malemort away to the east. When he came to write it all out in 'Near Perigord' in 1913, however, he would be content to shift his telling of the tale from fact into fiction and to leave unresolved the riddle of whether De Born's poem intended love or war or some combination of both.

From Hautefort he travelled to St Yrieix by a narrow-gauge tramway used mainly to carry wood to a factory to be made into 'tanner's essence', and while waiting for the tram he 'fell in with a comfortable man from Sarlat' who dealt in garments for the dead, and who told him that in his lifetime the chateau of Hautefort had been 'sold at a bargain to Armides who'd made his fortune in the Panama scandal'.

The next day he walked to Chalus where 'Richard Coeur de Lion got his death wound of an arrow' while besieging the castle in 1199. And that day his left shin became so painful that he took the train to go on to Rochechouart. There at last he found what De Born's *canzon* had had him seeking:

How sane he was, how strong in his comparisons to name in his poem such places, Chalais, Rochechouart, the pleached alley, & this pleasaunce, this high place of trees.
If ever god & man made a place to walk & sing in, to play viel, and lute—to pluck rings in, that place is Rochechouart, the uncaptured....
    Of Anhes, at Rochechouart, her hair golden as Ysolt's.
    Of Cembelins, her glances, of Aelis, her speech free running, of Audiar, of

the rest of them, this that & the other, to build the perfect beauty
    the peer for Montignac.

I might have done worse than choose that canzon as my guide to Aquitaine.

The brown hawk above the valley knows it.

Here in garden of trees came Sir Bertran, & spoke of any thing save what was in his mind & here many another.

Close high gowns of cendal, & long bliauts have had their day here, and after them many a fashion. It is a place for painted clothing, for vair & the rest of it.

And I am a fool to leave it—for Limoge, & new streets & clatter.

He had arranged for mail to be addressed to him *poste-restante* at Limoges. In the pile when he picked it up about the 7th or 8th of June there was a letter from Walter Rummel telling him that Margaret Cravens was dead. She had shot herself quite cleanly through the heart on June 1st, the Saturday after he had left Paris.

Pound returned to Paris at once, to Rue Raynouard, and there Rummel gave him the note Margaret had left for him:

Dear Ezra: I cannot leave without a word to you. I am entering into God's Kingdom not by this last act but before. The act believe me—one of extreme courage, as I could live also. I have reached a height and the call has come. . . . All the beauty of eternity is graven in my heart not given me to express but there and immortal.

She asked him, 'You who know how to express things in words', to write to her aunt Drusilla in Indiana, 'just from one who has seen me lately and knew that all was well with me at the last.' Her final wish, from 'your friend Margaret Cravens', 'to you both'—that is, to Ezra and Dorothy together—was 'all happiness and final attainment be yours'.

For Rummel she had left a much longer letter, 'just to say what it has meant to me to have met you, to have loved you as I have—to have seen someone the true symbol of all I have believed and *held to* in spirit always'. In a postscript she added, 'You have been the greatest influence in my life'. Rummel, who was about to marry Thérèse Chaigneau, appears to have been completely taken by surprise. 'Marguerite called on me several hours before her death', he told Pound, 'and seemed so quiet and so kind, that I don't understand a thing.'

Pound found his own way to understanding Margaret. His immediate reaction to the news of her death was to tell Dorothy that he could not write about it even to her, 'Sadness and nobility and so many things are in the web'. Then a week later he wrote this:

There is to be no funeral here, and what M. wrote of so blithely, in one of her last notes, as 'The remains' will be conveyed to the U.S.A. As M. is by now a small, fat, brown god sitting in a huge water-lily, splashing over the edge, the performance will probably amuse her. Said image may sound ridiculous, but it is a great comfort to one, and is so unanswerably true that I don't dare mention it to anyone else. It is however the solution of the whole affair, and we rest of us who are not yet ready for such damp white-petaled beatitude may as well continue with our *paradis terrestre*.

Pound published this image in June 1914 as 'His Vision of a Certain Lady Post Mortem', a poem of five lines in which three represent her as being 'glad and laughing / With a laughter not of this world'. He was seeing her as a newborn spirit, and therefore with joy rather than sorrow, which is perhaps how she had wanted to be seen.

Others of course reacted differently according to their diverse natures. There were those who wondered if they were to blame, and there were those who looked about for someone else to point the finger at. Among the latter some wanted to blame Pound. There was speculation that he had behaved unforgivably in some unspecified way to Margaret, that perhaps their relationship had become amorous and then when she wanted more from him he had rejected her. Nothing to support those speculations has come to light, and what is now known, in particular from her last letters to Pound and to Rummel, should quench them altogether.

Those who would keep up the suspicion that there was a romantic involvement seem to care little about how that reflects on Margaret herself. After all, she had known for some time of Pound's commitment to Dorothy; and she was giving him money, up to a thousand dollars a year. What sort of person do they think she was that she would then be wanting him to marry her? 'Hardly anyone has known my inner life', she wrote in her final letter to Rummel, and that seems to have been true. But her relationship with Pound was likely to have had more to do with that inner life than with the dark fantasies of some who claimed to have known her. At least he could see that 'She wanted a beauty that is more than the beauty of this world and ... went toward it'.

There is a question that seems not to have been asked, and that may be unanswerable: did Margaret leave a will, and did she make any provision in it for Pound? She had been supporting his work as a generous patron for over two years, and had evidently given him to understand that she intended to continue doing so. But with her death, so far as is known, that assured support vanished. He seems to have accepted the annulment by death of her patronage without comment of any kind. And it may have been not possible for her to leave anything to him, since her income had been from a trust. Yet one can wonder how it was that she could give no thought at the end to something so momentous for Pound, and surely of significance to her too. She had after all been making over to him up to two-thirds of her trust income. And in her last days she had considered the effect her death would have on others and had made careful arrangements to lessen the shock and distress to them. Did she say and do nothing to provide for Pound because she felt that such material concerns were beneath them then, at the moment of her passing to a higher plane of existence?

I am intrigued by a further possibility. Could she have been moved to be so generous to Pound by her feelings for Rummel? Her last letters are clear evidence that it was Rummel who was at the centre of her hidden inner life, and it was as Rummel's friend that she had met Pound and immediately offered to support him in his work. It seems to me likely that in doing that she was acting out an ideal of noble behaviour formed in her admiration of Rummel. She may have hoped that he would recognize her as a kindred spirit; and she may have been devastated by his suddenly marrying Thérèse Chaigneau. That at any rate seems to me a much more likely speculation than that it was Pound who had cruelly and tragically disappointed her. In fact Pound had 'tried more than the rest', Rummel told Dorothy, 'to help her and to develop her'.

Margaret's Aunt Drusilla, who had come over to do what needed to be done, enlisted Pound's assistance to decide what to do with her books. Her attitude towards him was at first 'doubtful', perhaps because of the rumours and gossip she would have heard. But then, on the eve of her returning to Madison with 'the mortal remains', she wrote to assure him 'that in reality I feel the deepest sincerity for the good and pleasure you were to our Margaret the loss of whom takes out all light for me.'

Pound stayed on in Paris until Friday June 27, in Rummel's apartment but with Rummel himself away in London from about the 15th. He corrected the proofs for *Ripostes* which Dorothy had forwarded to him from Church Walk. He also did some more research in the Bibliothèque Nationale for what he was currently calling 'the blooming opus', and wrote up the notes he had made for it between Poitiers and Limoges. He mailed 'Chap. I of "op 411"' to Dorothy on 24 June. The second chapter, taking him up to Chalus and possibly Rochechouart, was done by the 26th, and Pound was glad to find it 'more diverting' than he had expected. He had now written 'a little more than 1/4th of the opus' and was ready to resume his walking tour.

He took the train to Uzerche then followed the road southwards to Brive, and on to Souillac, finding the land 'not so thick with ghosts' as before, fewer troubadours having hailed from this part of Provence. On the third day he followed the Dordogne westwards for part of the way, then went across country to Sarlat, through wooded valleys where he felt that he had come into his 'proper land again', a land where there was the 'natural magic' of 'great trees, & a readiness for rain', and a system of ways by which 'the troubadours went & came'. Another day of heavy walking, southwards again then south-east by tracks where he went far off his way for a time before a postman directed him, brought him at last to Gourdon. It was July 1st, and there was a midsummer festival and a simple stage in the open with the players about 'with pikes & halbards'; and all the streets led up to the narrow peak of the town where the blue sky, 'the blue of the evening . . . clear, a little lavender, was drawn close to one, & close in at the sides', so that 'the sky was for once like a tent really, and not the plainsman's basin'. He had come 'once more over the border' into the timeless Provence he had been seeking.

That mood did not last. He was heading now for Toulouse, by train as far as Rodez, then on foot to Albi in three days, finishing off that stretch 'with a 30 mile sprint'. That was on 'such a day as makes a walking tour worth while, there was the smell of hay in the air, & everything was blue & green'. He had seen 'a lizard, a peacock, & some gypsies who were driving down the same route after the fair of St. John in Rodez, & who seemed well pleased that I could keep up with them'. But the town of Carmaux above Albi was 'nothing much to see—a brickish blotch full of smoke stacks'; and Albi was 'inhospitable—no good cafes meet one at entrance', the town seemed 'falling to pieces & half deserted', and the great brick cathedral was 'a new affair . . . 1277 they began it—when the gai savoir was dead'.

Another two days walking and a train for the last part brought him into Toulouse, with nothing much to remark save the full heat of the sun now in the real Midi, and a fresco in the church at Rabestens. The fresco he interpreted as if it were a medieval romance on the walls of the great hall of the Count of Limoges, taking the angels for 'Ladies in trailing white' and finding 'Tristan & Ysolt' among them, 'bar the halos'. In Toulouse, in the vast church of St Sernin he thought of Pierre Vidal; and in La Daurade by the Garonne, 'ruined as utterly as a church can be', he thought of Cavalcanti seeing his Mandetta there and felt that it was 'pleasant to be so near the scene of a perfectly constellated flirtation'. Outside the wind, which earlier in the day he had found 'so stiff as to be difficult to walk against', was blowing the greenish Garonne grey.

Although he was 'two days before schedule', having done ninety miles in the previous four days, he took the train that night down to Foix on the edge of the Pyrenees. He was 'heading for Carcassone with which Troubadours had little to do', and going, 'in sheer truancy', 'by a route that presumably no jongleur ever bothered to climb'. Even so, when he came to Roquefixade, 'along a ledge of rd. beneath towers & fangs of rock', he could see no reason why its ruined castle 'should not have been the hold of a certain little known Q de R'. He climbed the sheer face of rock to the castle, 'one of the maddest things I have done in my life & of the sanest', and lay there 'level with sunset' with 'the land below darkening to copper'. 'One may lie on the earth & possess it & feel the world below one', he noted that day.

That he was now in the heart of Cathar country seems not to have been of much interest to Pound at that time. He was within sight of Montségur, but passed it by; he rested in the noon heat in Puivert and took note of its ruined castle, apparently not knowing that Simon de Montfort had taken it in 1210 at the start of the Albigensian Crusade. In the late afternoon he reached Quillan, but 'My demons of energy & greed drove me thence straight on that night into Axat'. The road lay through the famously picturesque gorge of the Aude, 'flanked by sheer rocks, some hundreds of feet in height', as Baedeker put it. Pound was reminded of the buildings in Wall Street, though he also saw it as 'a mad stack of sheets & spires & obelisks', and at another moment was put in mind by the dwarf cedars clutching at crevices of a Ming landscape. He was wholeheartedly truant-ing into tourism, yet still he gave a thought, in a pine wood, to the hunting of mad Peire Vidal through such a wood in Cabaret. He had walked '47 k. since morning', very nearly thirty miles from Lavalenet to Axat.

Next day—it would have been now July 9—he left the Pyrenees behind, going north by train from Axat to Carcassonne and then on to Narbonne on the Mediterranean coast. Baedeker would have told him that the ancient *Cité* of Carcassonne was 'one of the most interesting spots in France', that it had 'suffered greatly in the Albigensian war', and that 'Anything more curious or unique in appearance than this town of the middle ages, with its double line of fortifications, furnished with fifty round towers and dominated by a citadel, can hardly be imagined'. Pound sniffily remarked, 'Carcassonne was as we all know overflowed by a mass of inertia which has preserved it as has the lava Pompeii.' What pleased him was to look out from the walls, over the newer town, 'to Pennautier which may have been Loba's'—he was thinking again of Peire Vidal who was of Carcassonne, and of his love for the lady of nearby Pennautier.

That evening he walked the ten miles or so from Narbonne north to Capestang, because there had lived the troubadour Guillem de Cabestaing who loved the lady Soremonde wife of Lord Raimon of Roussillon, and whose heart the jealous and fearsome Lord Raimon cooked and served to the lady, as it is related in the *vida* and in Pound's canto 4. What Pound thought was a castle with lights in its towers turned out to be 'only a ruined church that looked like a castle in the darkness', but he 'was too tired to mind the difference'. His comfort was 'veal stew with carrots & olives together ... a dish most excellent'.

He was now on the coastal plain and in the baking heat of midsummer it was 'too hot to move' during the day. A bus took him at 5 in the evening to Béziers, which he found 'irredeemably hideous', and so followed the Canal du Midi to Agde. There, on the quai by the water in the warm Mediterranean night, a strange mood came over him. 'Ah surely', he wrote in his notebook, 'when it comes to living I know my métier'. He was exalted with the feeling, brought on by the south and the water under his window and the complexion of the sky, that 'life, despite all its damnable tangles & circumformations is worth the candle', and that he was living it to the full. 'Can a man be bothered making poetry of nights like this!', he asked, making his grand denial, 'Fools, readers of books, go south & live there'.

The next five days he spent in Arles and Nîmes and Beaucaire and Tarascon, writing at his 'opus', reading Murger, de Maupassant and Turgenieff, attending 'a very amusing bloodless bull fight' in the Roman arena at Nîmes, noting 'the exquisite grey of Arles ... the grey in the cloister of S. Trophime', and generally wandering about like another tourist. He was resting up before tackling his last stretch between Le Puy and Clermont-Ferrand.

Once started he was eager to get on to the end. He went by train from Tarascon to Le Puy on July 16, then took to the road, doing it now 'for the sake of the open country rather than for that of auld acquaintances'— the troubadour associations could wait to be looked up in a library. He was in Allègre ('the joyous') by 2.15, and it was in a field near there that he experienced something so intensely that he made a note of the exact moment, 'July 16/4.04 P.M.'—it was apparently 'a field of larks' that made him think of some troubadour singing of nightingales, and which he would recall in the last fragments of his *Cantos*.

Two days later, with his mind 'already full of London & Paris', and having walked twenty-seven miles that day and with another six to go into Clermont, his trip reached what he felt to be its climax:

A rain storm . . . which displayed the full resources of the country had refreshed all my forces.

I was making at least 6 k. per hr. & about 9 in spurts & was already feeling in fair fettle but I nearly burst with RAGE when a strapping gipsy who was leading a monkey & an ape stopped & asked me if I had seen 'autres des camarades avec des ours et des singes'.

'That was the top of the walk' Pound affirmed when he wrote up the incident in 'The Gypsy' (1915). He worked in other details from his notebook, such as the 'mist clotted about the trees in the valley', and 'gray Arles', and the other gypsies he had seen on the road after Rodez 'Coming down from the fair of St. John'. But his rage does not appear in the poem. There it is only what he has seen, or not seen, that makes the occasion. The rage has evaporated leaving him to recover the objective facts of the experience, and the true value of it.

One might say that he has simply become more aware of the other fellow and of the world about him. But contrast that with the climax of the first part of his trip, the imagining himself back, at Rochechouart, into a fantasy of the time of Bertran de Born. The difference amounts to a radical adjustment of mind, or a moment of growth, such as one finds in many of Wordsworth's strange encounters on the roads. Pound was thrown into a rage, it would seem, because he had been in a world of his own and the gypsy's intervention had shattered his self-absorption. But at the same time he may have felt, and so set the incident down as 'the climax of the trip', that it was necessary and right for his fantasy to be broken. He had walked those roads trying to imagine himself a troubadour *jongleur*, though constantly reminded of mostly unwelcome modern actualities. But the gypsy, the *bohémien*, was the real thing, the modern performer who lived the life of the road and of the fairs. He had to be recognized in all his disturbing otherness and likeness as an objectively living presence, as (in Yeatsian terms) a challenging anti-self.

That gypsy seems to have brought to a crisis and helped resolve the conflict that had been more or less repressed throughout the walking tour. Pound had all the time been seeking his dream of Provence while inescapably immersed in the destructive element of ordinary, actual things. And in his poetry up to this time he had been able mainly to celebrate his ideal conceptions, though under increasing pressure, from Hueffer and from his own maturing, to attend to what could be directly experienced. He would emerge from these long weeks on the road more committed, as a poet, to contemporaneity and objectivity.

In Clermont Pound noted the times of trains to Paris, 9.45 p.m. arriving at 5.40 in the morning, 8.50 a.m. arriving at 5.45 p.m. Whichever he took he was back in Paris by Saturday the 19th of July. Rummel had married while he was away and he put up now in the Hotel de Londres on the Left Bank. Hilda Doolittle was still in Paris, Aldington was back in England. Pound was planning on returning to London about the end of the month.

He spent a week or so writing out the 'opus', which he was now calling 'Gironde', and going again to the library 'to crib some interpolative chapters'. He was finding it wearying hack work, and would become increasingly dissatisfied with his efforts, though he would persist with them through August and September when he was back in London. In mid-August he told Dorothy, 'This prose book is a dam'd nuisance'. In mid-September he went over the first eighty pages with Hueffer, who told him that it was as bad as Stevenson's *Travels with a Donkey in the Cévennes*—and that was 'very violent' for Hueffer. In spite of that he revised that part and counted up the rest of his material to conclude 'the book is about done in the rough'. A week later the word to Dorothy was 'I've hung about the 1st 1/3rd of 'Gironde' on my west wall as a sign that I'm dam'd if I bother much more with revising it'. By the 1st of October he had decided that his 'Patria Mia' articles in the *New Age* were going so well that he could 'stop Gironde about where it is', and put together the 'Patria Mia' and the 'Gironde' as two 'Studies in Mediaevalism Past & Present'. His last word on it, when he was asked in December if he had any prose that Seymour in Chicago might want to publish, was that he had 'a damn rotten prose thing, neither fish nor feather, a walk in the troubadour country, with notes on the troubadour lives etc.—awful hash.'

He could not make it cohere because he had been trying to write it out of a muddle of irreconcilable motives. The most damaging was probably that he was writing it for money while believing that 'Prose has a commercial value, increasing according to its worseness'. The work he had put in was not wholly wasted, however. Some of it went into essays, some into his cantos. But his best account of his walking tour was in 'Provincia Deserta' (1915).

In verse shaped by the free-running process of memory that poem traces the main features of the Provence he had walked over in imagination. Rochechouart with its 'place of trees' and Chalais with its 'pleached arbour' are there, and Mareuil, and the torches and laughter by the church in Perigord; Bertran de Born's Hautefort and his story are there, without emphasis; and a vision of the land around Foix and Rocafixade, followed by brief mention of Toulouse and Arles. The *vida* of Pieire de Maensac is given, so that Provence too may have its epic myth. And the end of all is,

> That age is gone;
> Pieire de Maensac is gone.
> I have walked over these roads;
> I have thought of them living.

The last word there is tense with equivocation. A first reading may make out the sense as 'I have thought of them *as they were when* living', or again as 'I have thought of them *as if they were* living *now*'. And yet it is only the thinker and walker over these roads who is actually living—whatever life there is here is his, in his walking and in his mind. Pound wanted to avoid the note of elegy, of melancholy over what was dead and gone; at the same time he wanted to make the *virtu* of the past a force in the present; and he wanted as well to engage with the modern world. The intention and will to do all that is a quiver in his 'living', but he had still to work out how to resolve past life and present living into a single vision.

11 : Stirring Things Up: 1912–1913

Embroidery and vortex

Pound was back in London and Church Walk by the beginning of August. He had been three months away. Dorothy had written that she would be delighted to see him back, though she would be away she supposed from the 3rd to the 6th and again from the 6th or 7th to the 14th. 'Don't bother to have me in until its convenient', had been his response. He had been closing his letters from France with such endearments as 'I kiss your eyes', and 'I kiss you—if you permit it'. Dorothy had been closing hers 'À Toi' or 'My love dear / Yours'. But their communion continued to be mostly by letter, though they lived within ten minutes walk of each other.

Dorothy was as usual away with her mother and Georgie Hyde-Lees for all of September and part of October—this year they were at Ilfracombe and Lynton on the north Devon coast. She told him what she was sketching—lots of rocks and clouds in the water. She included two sketches of the 'engaged and honeymooning couples' who were all over the place—'they walk about leaning towards each other'. She chatted about the people she was with and their cats and dogs, and the weather, and village cricket matches, and going once to 'the Kinema—most entertaining', and finding 'a whole heap of four- and five-leafed clovers' in a field. She was doing a deal of needlework and embroidery. Yeats was down with them *incognito* for a few days at the end of their stay. There was much easy conversation in her letters now, but no exaltation of desire or vision.

Pound's letters were meanwhile keeping her in touch with his affairs. Mary Moore of Trenton was now Mrs James Frederick Cross Jr. He had played tennis with Hueffer and seen Florence Farr. About the time Dorothy was finding four-leaf clovers he had become foreign correspondent 'for a Chicago "Poetry" magazine'. He had passed an idle Sunday with Aldington and Hilda, and had conversations and meals with them separately and together, and also with Brigit Patmore. He had invited a divorced countess to have tea with him having supposed from her letter that she was a male friend of Wyndham Lewis's. He had 'discussed the metaphysics of art' with Hulme until 11.30, and had had a meeting with Orage. He was writing 'damned prose' for his 'Patria Mia' series as well as for 'Gironde', his one consolation with the former being that he was 'making six enemies per paragraph'. *Madame Bovary* was 'the only oasis in this waste of ennui', though there was also Villon's verse which he was 'trying to memorize' in the British Museum. One night he had 'a most gorgeous dream about the marriage in Cana of Galilee—it began in symbolical patterns on a rug and ended in a wedding dance to exceed the Russians both in grace, splendour & legerity'. He wrote the dream up into a poem, a 'naive and oriental' exotic among the 'modern epigrams' he was otherwise composing, such as 'The Bath Tub' and 'The Tea Shop'.

On Dorothy's 26th birthday, 14 September 1912, he received Olivia's letter written from Devon telling him that since he could not marry Dorothy he ought to keep away from her, though he was 'to be let in *once* a week', as he reported to Dorothy, with the comment 'Sufficient unto the day is the damnability thereof'. His sardonic modern epigrams were spelling out the damnation. He observed that the girl in 'The Tea Shop' was not getting any younger, and was not so beautiful and so eager as before—'The August has worn against her'. A tepid 'bathtub lined with white porcelain' gave him an image for 'the slow cooling of our chivalrous passion'.

Through the rest of that year and through the whole of 1913 Dorothy and Ezra continued to lead separated lives. At Christmas she was down at High Hall, Wimborne in Dorset, while he was with Hueffer and Violet Hunt in what, he was told, had been John Milton's cottage near Slough. (Neither he nor Hueffer were impressed by that association.) Through April and half of May Dorothy was in Tivoli and Rome, while he was up in Sirmione and Venice. 'It is very stupid of you to be at the other end of the peninsula', he gallantly observed.

Towards the end of May, when they were both back in London, there was a bitter outburst from Dorothy which gave a glimpse of her suppressed feelings. She had mentioned in her last letter from Rome that her room at home had been newly papered, and that it 'will need some Jap prints perhaps'. Pound must have responded by asking, did her doing up her room mean that she intended to remain in it? and was she giving him his leave to depart? He may have been particularly provoked to ask that by her behaving in a bored fashion when he was allowed in to tea on Thursday 23rd. 'The boredom', she told him in a brief note the next morning, 'was of four square walls—not you. I am feeling better since I decided to have an Archaic Greek frock in sea-green.' But then she added, after her 'A toi', this teasing postscript: 'I have just been making love to Jim [Fairfax] in my dreams—Also a few night ago I dreamt of a really beautiful Mother & Child—statuesque, but warm & alive—nude & grouped Rodinesquely.' That revelation must have crossed with the questions from Pound which then provoked this bitter retort:

My dear.
I wonder if your congé is what *you* want? I wish I knew. If I gave it you, it would certainly be directement—or You can take it if you wish. As to my room, it is you who can give me an answer, as to whether there is any prospect of my being able to leave it within, say, the next six months? I feel you might have got a job if you had really wanted to, by now. . . . I think I have waited very quietly all this Spring for you to have time.

She ended by coolly telling him that she could not change her arrangements in order to see him sooner than the following Thursday, but still signed off 'My love / à toi'.

In June she told him off with all the cold condescension of the offended English lady speaking down to the uncouth foreigner. Walter Rummel was to play to Tagore at the Shakespear's, and Pound had apparently given Eva Fowler and Thérèse Rummel to understand that there would not be room for them in the not very large drawing room. 'Don't you know by this time', Dorothy wrote, 'that one of the things it is *pas permis* to do, is to interfere with other people's drawing rooms?' Then, to put him quite firmly in his place, 'On this occasion W[alter] & Tagore would be the important people—not yourself.'

In reply Pound sent her a poem beginning 'It is true that you said the gods are more use to you than fairies / But for all that I have seen you on a high, white noble horse'. 'It is odd', the poem mused, 'that you should be changing your face / and resembling some other woman to plague me'. Dorothy responded at once: 'Dearest. / I am afraid that I am troubling you. Will you come in nevertheless to see me on Thursday 19th?—It is an ungodly world.'

Ten days later she wrote: 'My very dear. / I cannot marry you. (I can but hope it's not mere cowardice, but a true instinct.) / I am sorry, sorry, sorry / and send my / Love.' To this Pound replied simply, 'you can not. / you can not. / you can not.'—thus returning her negative as a possible positive action. But there was no definite consequence, and formal relations were resumed. 'You might come in at teatime on Friday—if you care to. . . . As you will / Love D.' 'Bien. At what hour preciso? alle quattro? . . . Je t'aime.'

Dorothy spent the first two weeks of August up at Goathland in the heart of the North Yorkshire moors, with the heather getting to be 'a more lovely colour every minute'. She enclosed a purple sprig for Pound, busy about his literary affairs in hot and dusty London. Dorothy asked him to call in to see her on the 15th—she would be briefly in London before going down to Dorset. For September and some of October she and Olivia and the Hyde-Lees were at Coleman's Hatch in Sussex. Pound and Yeats would be spending the winter months, November to January 1914, in neighbouring Stone Cottage.

At one point Dorothy mentioned to Pound that she was 'doing some new early Vict[orian] wool work...half Italian & quite pretty'. That shocked him out of his usual reportage of his literary projects into telling her how she should live:

E.P.: I am not in the least sure that you ought to embroider. It kills time but it also draws off a lot of little particles of energy, that ought to be damned up until they bust out into painting.

D.S.: Doesn't energy to some extent generate itself, the more it is used?

E.P.: No! that is *preciso* the point. It is not as if embroidery *exercised* any faculty or required any specialized concentration. Its not much better than smoking. . . . Energy depends on ones ability to make a vortex—genius *même*. Chess, Tennis, fencing all help. They demand complete attention. . . . Anything that demands only partial attention is useless, for developing a vortex. . . . in time it would incapacitate one for serious creation of any sort.

Dorothy's response, if any, is not preserved. Apparently she detested games, and there is nothing to suggest that she aspired to 'serious creation of any sort'. Was Pound now fearful of her letting herself be, like the woman in his 'Portrait d'une Femme', a Sargasso Sea of her society? He counselled her to experiment in colour on days when she could not paint.

One thing and another

Pound, busy about his own vortex, was reinventing himself with a view to reforming his world. In his poems he was fashioning the persona of a thoroughly modern poet equipped to turn his art against the smug dullness of conventional society, especially as it was to be met with in London. At the same time he was creating out of a few promising poets his *Imagiste* gang with which to renovate poetry in English and advance the cause of intellectual liberty. Again, in articles in the *New Age*, while complaining of the deathly condition of England, he was prophesying a renaissance in America; and as foreign correspondent of *Poetry* (Chicago) he was doing what he could to bring on that renaissance.

Otherwise his London life continued much as before. One innovation was his setting up his own ' "Tuesday" evenings', as if in rivalry with or in secession from Hulme's. The first evening Florence Farr read 'from an unpublished english mss. translated from the Bengali of Ramanath Tagor'. For the second Marjorie Kennedy-Fraser sang Gaelic folk songs. That night Hilda, Aldington, and Brigit Patmore made up the company—Pound's small room would not have held many more. In time his Tuesdays seem to have become simply the evening he stayed in to receive friends and contacts.

Rabindranath Tagore also was new, in the sense that he was the latest sensation. His *Gitanjali* would go through a dozen printings in London in 1913 alone, the year in which he received the Nobel Prize for Literature. Yeats had taken him up, and written an introduction for the book—'these prose translations [of his lyrics] have stirred my blood as nothing has for years'. Pound too was much taken for a time by both his poetry and his philosophy of life. The measures, melodies and modulations of the songs in their original Bengali, which he had Tagore sing and explain to him, interested him as a seeker after 'fundamental laws in word music', and seemed to correspond to the sort of metric he was working for in English.

He went on to wax enthusiastic about the prospect of Bengali culture providing 'the balance and corrective' to a Western humanism which had lost touch with 'the whole and the flowing'. 'We have found our new Greece', he declared. 'In the midst of our clangour of mechanisms', Tagore's songs bring 'a quiet proclamation of the fellowship between man and the gods; between man and. nature'. In contrast with the Hellenic representation of 'man as the sport of the gods, the sworn foe of fate and the natural forces', and 'in sharp contrast with the Western mode, where man must be shown attempting to master nature if we are to have "great drama"', the Bengali musical ritual 'takes a man more quickly from the sense of himself, and brings him into the emotion of "the flowing", of harmonic nature, of orderly calm and sequence'. But Pound's enthusiasm soon waned. 'As a religious teacher he is superfluous', he told Harriet Monroe in April 1913, 'in a prose translation it is just "more theosophy"'. He remained eager, however, to find some 'new Greece'.

He may have been getting more than enough 'theosophy' from Yeats, who talked a good deal about the spirit world. At this time though Yeats was turning to Pound for criticism of his work. At least once he kept him with him till two in the morning, reading to him from his diary. One Tuesday evening at the start of 1913, when he was feeling there was something not right with his poetry, he had Pound in to go over 'The

Two Kings' line by line. Pound helped him to see where the trouble was, and that he needed to rid his work of its rhetoric and of 'Miltonic generalizations'. 'Ezra', he told Lady Gregory,

helps me to get back to the definite and the concrete away from modern abstractions. To talk over a poem with him is like getting you to put a sentence into dialect. All becomes clear and natural.

'I learned from him', he wrote some years later, 'how much further the movement against abstraction had gone than my generation had thought possible'.

Yet he did not learn all at once what Pound had absorbed from Hueffer. Later in 1913, when 'The Two Kings' had appeared in *Poetry* and was to be collected in *Responsibilities*, he had Pound go over it again, and Pound worked over the Cuala Press proof in much the way he would work over the drafts of Eliot's *The Waste Land* in 1922. He cut the opening seventeen lines down to seven; struck out four lines here, another four there, then several single lines; and condensed the last fifteen lines to eight. He also suggested the final ironic phrase, so that instead of ending upon a simple note of joyful return to an ancestral house, the poem now ends with a mature Yeatsian cadence, 'And bade all welcome, being ignorant'. One can see from the proof that Yeats not only accepted Pound's editing, but was prompted to further questionings and revisions of his own. And yet Pound dismissed the poem in the end as 'an old fashioned thing' of no interest—'one might as well read the *Idyls* of another', he wrote of it in *Poetry*, offensively putting it down as no better than Tennyson. He wanted more of the new 'prose directness' and the 'quality of hard light' evident elsewhere in *Responsibilities*.

While he was severe with Yeats's 'idyl' he was even more severe with a narrative poem of his own. He wrote home that he had done a 'huge wad of a monstrous long poem. about 1200 lines done. and 1800 more coming'—'which', he added just a week later, 'the public will be SPARED'. Comically though, he had to accept being dubbed 'Victorian' himself when Quiller-Couch, in 'a delightful old-world letter', asked if he might include two of his early and by then discarded poems, 'Portrait' and 'Ballad for Gloom', in his *Oxford Book of Victorian Verse*.

In October 1912 Pound's new publisher failed. Charles Granville, the genial manager who had undertaken to pay £100 a year for his work, ran off to Tangier with a woman and the firm's ready cash. Swift & Co. went into immediate liquidation. It had just published *Riposte*, and had brought out in May the English edition of *Sonnets and Ballate of Guido Cavalcanti*. Pound was able to arrange for Elkin Matthews to take over *Riposte* and

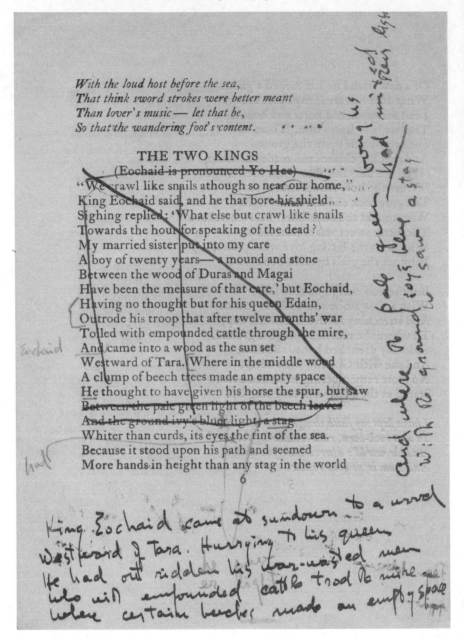

Two pages showing EP's revision in 1913 of Yeats's 'Two Kings' on proof of Cuala Press version. EP went through the poem first in pencil, bracketing many words and lines and suggesting some alterations; then he went through it in ink, this time striking through lines and whole passages, and drafting revisions. The reworking of lines 4–6 on p. 7 and in the

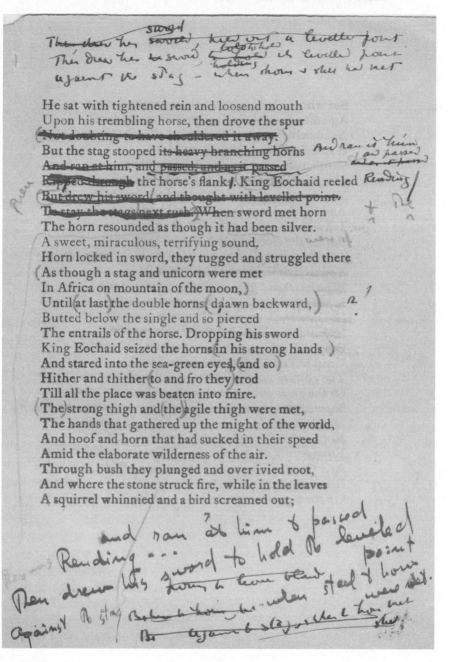

He sat with tightened rein and loosend mouth
Upon his trembling horse, then drove the spur
~~Not doubting to have shouldered it away.~~
But the stag stooped ~~its heavy branching horns~~
~~And ran at him, and passed, and as it passed~~
~~Ripped through~~ the horse's flanks. King Eochaid reeled
~~But drew his sword and thought with levelled point.~~
~~To stay the stag's next rush.~~ When sword met horn
The horn resounded as though it had been silver.
A sweet, miraculous, terrifying sound.
Horn locked in sword, they tugged and struggled there
(As though a stag and unicorn were met
In Africa on mountain of the moon,)
Until at last the double horns, dawn backward,
Butted below the single and so pierced
The entrails of the horse. Dropping his sword
King Eochaid seized the horns in his strong hands
And stared into the sea-green eyes, (and so)
Hither and thither to and fro they trod
Till all the place was beaten into mire.
(The) strong thigh and (the) agile thigh were met,
The hands that gathered up the might of the world,
And hoof and horn that had sucked in their speed
Amid the elaborate wilderness of the air.
Through bush they plunged and over ivied root,
And where the stone struck fire, while in the leaves
A squirrel whinnied and a bird screamed out;

right margin are in WBY's hand. (*Courtesy of A. P. Watt on behalf of Michael B. Yeats, and of the Yale Collection of American Literature, Beinecke Rare Book and Manuscript Library, Yale University*) to act as his agent for the *Cavalcanti*. Even better, the liquidator agreed in December that his contract should be honoured to the extent that he would receive £25 a quarter for one year and then a final payment of £65.

Coming after the death of his patron, Margaret Cravens, this might have been seriously discouraging. Yet Pound, while asking his father to 'stand to the guns' financially, told him that 'None of this bothers *me* much as I can by now look out for myself'. 'But', he went on, 'Dorothy's family is making a row and the whole brunt of the thing seems to fall on her'. He wondered if they might elope to Philadelphia, to save her from being 'sold off in the society fashion'. Only Dorothy would not think of it without a proper invitation from both his parents—'mother must sign'. Isabel did cable 'Come', but the Shakespear row subsided. 'So we procede as heretofore,' wrote Ezra to his father, 'with due placidity and decorum.'

His earnings, while not enough to marry a Shakespear, were enough to live on. In October he received £16.15*s*. from *The New Age*, *The English Review*, *Poetry*, and from Small, Maynard his Boston publishers. In November it was £4. 13*s*. 6*d*. from *The New Age*, Dent and *Poetry*. In December it was £20 from *The New Age* and Small, Maynard. That averaged out at just over £3 a week over the quarter, which was about what a clerk could expect to earn.

His occasional lectures brought in further small amounts. In the autumn of 1912 he read a paper to an undergraduate society at King's College, Cambridge—with Hulme and Edward Marsh in attendance. In January 1913 he gave a set of three afternoon lectures 'in Mrs Fowler's new chinese drawing room'—Eva Fowler had recently moved to Gilbert Street near Grosvenor Square. Tickets were 7/6 for the single lecture, and £1 for the three. The topics announced were 'The Normal Opportunity of the Provençal Troubadour', 'Rabindranath Tagore', and '"Vers Libre and Systems of Metric" with reading from the Lecturer's own work'. 'Eva', he told Dorothy, 'has ordered the cook on pain of death not [to] have anything for lunch that will pervade the celestial halls'.

In February he was invited to Oxford by T. E. Lawrence's brother Will, to present a paper on Cavalcanti to the St John's College Essay Society. He dined well with the dons in Hall beforehand, and one of them, 'the *very* aged Snow', capped Pound's praising Cavalcanti's *fa di clarità l'aer tremare* by declaiming Sappho's φαίνεταί μοι, thus creating 'considerable hilarity', as Pound would recall in his Pisan prison. In mid-March, 'by kind permission of Lady Low', he gave an afternoon lecture—ticket 7/6—at 23 De Vere Gardens, Kensington, on '"The Strophe" and the most recent developments in French Poetry'.

In early April he spent a week or so in Paris before going on to Sirmione. He saw Rummel, and was pleased with his setting of 'The Return'. Also he had the luck to go into the cellar of the 'Chatelet' one evening and to fall in with some of 'the younger energies' among the French poets Flint had been telling him about, 'Romains, Vildrac, Duhamel etc.'. 'The young party of intelligence in Paris', 'a vortex of twenty men', were holding a council of war to plot a glorious *blague*, a gigantic practical joke against the reign of general stupidity. They were electing to the grand title of *Prince des Penseurs* a certain M. Brisset 'Who held that man is descended from frogs'. Pound wrote to Flint to enlist him in the plot: 'You are secretary to the English Society of Ideologists & your one duty is to write to Vildrac ... the grave and serious document of congratulations to be read to Brisset at the banquet on Sunday. ... Speak of his works, "The Origins" & "Prophecies Fulfilled" & their influence on English Thought.' Remy de Gourmont was to send a telegram to be read out. Pound was excited and impressed by the insolent wit of the poets, and took it as evidence that in Paris at least the war against ignorance and stupidity was waged without mercy. He was even more impressed that de Gourmont, though of an older generation, could be looked to 'for comprehension, and even for discreet assistance'.

Though he was moving in these rarefied intellectual and social atmospheres, Pound was taking some notice of the world elsewhere. He took sides in the matter of the Turco-Bulgarian war, on the ground that Turkey was at one with 'the industrial tyrannies of Europe' in standing against 'the freedom of the individual ... equal opportunity for all ... [and] the conservation of human energy and dignity'. Again, in the coal strike of 1912, he was impressed by the spectacle of 'A million men going out of their work and keeping perfect order'. That was a luminous detail 'of far greater significance than this archaic row in the Balkans'—it showed that England still had some strength, and might after all have a future. And there were his 'Contemporania', his modern epigrams, such as 'The Garden', with its stark contrast of the overbred society lady and the teeming slum children:

> Like a skein of loose silk blown against a wall
> She walks by the railing of a path in Kensington Gardens
> And she is dying piece-meal
>   of a sort of emotional anaemia.
> And round about there is a rabble
> Of the filthy, sturdy, unkillable infants of the very poor.
> They shall inherit the earth.
> In her is the end of breeding. ...

He had seen that as he took his way through the Gardens, and felt it, and thought it through into a 'clear and natural' observation.

Then there is the story of Pound's dramatizing the offence given by the Georgian poet Lascelles Abercrombie when he called for a general return to Wordsworthian simplicity. 'Dear Mr Abercrombie', Pound wrote,

Stupidity carried beyond a certain point becomes a public menace. I hereby challenge you to a duel . . . My seconds will wait upon you in due course.

The challenged poet, having the choice of weapon, proposed that they pelt each other with unsold copies of their books. Pound enjoyed the comic riposte and the affair ended in laughter. All the same, he really did mean to give no quarter to public stupidity.

Taking on the contemporary

In his 'Contemporania' and 'Lustra', as they appeared in Harriet Monroe's *Poetry* in April and November 1913,[1] the poet, while still declaring his love of the beautiful, assumes the new role of sardonic critic of his society's way of life. And it is remarkable how he takes his stand simply on his own unconventional tastes and desires, and on the authority of his art. This is a poet with all the easy-mannered assurance of the individual who answers to nobody but himself. He has learnt to say 'I', as he would have the 'bound and entwined' woman of 'Ortus' do; that is, he has brought his 'soul into separation' from everything that would make claims on his inner being. To the artists discouraged and thwarted in America, those few 'who can know at first hand' but who are 'Broken against false knowledge', he offers the encouraging thought, 'I have weathered the storm, / I have beaten out my exile'. To critics who would have him relate to an audience, he boasts 'I mate with my free kind upon the crags'—implicitly imaging himself as a centaur, a figure of unconfined energy and intelligence, and explicitly setting himself against people whose 'virgin stupidity' will not 'be touched with the truth' and who would seek to shut him up.

His truth is what one knows at first hand. So, if he were the poet in the conventional garret, being the sort of poet he is there would be none of the

[1] The April sequence consisted of: 'Tenzone'—'The Condolence'—'The Garret'—'The Garden'—'Ortus'—'Dance Figure'—'Salutation'—'Salutation the Second'—'Pax Saturni'—'Commission'—'A Pact'—'In a Station of the Metro'. The November sequence consisted of: 'Ancora'—'Surgit Fama'—'The Choice' [= 'Preference']—'April'—'Gentildonna'—'Lustra' I - III [= 'The Rest'—'Les Millwin'—'Further Instructions']—'Xenia' I–VII [included 'A Song of the Degrees'—'Ité'—'Dum Capitolium Scandet']. 'Pax Saturni' and 'Xenia' I–II were not reprinted by Pound. The rest were collected in *Lustra* (1916).

conventional pathos; instead he would look down in pity upon the better off, because for him

> Dawn enters with little feet
>   like a gilded Pavlova,
> And I am near my desire.
> Nor has life in it aught better
> Than this hour of clear coolness,
>   the hour of waking together.

Those are instances of what he values, and he makes them the measure of others' behaviours. At least he assumes that others too desire such states, and that if they do not honour them it is because they are unfortunate or in bad faith. 'O generation of the thoroughly smug / and thoroughly uncomfortable', he salutes those who would not be happy 'picnicking in the sun' in the company of fishermen with their untidy families and their ungainly laughter. He would have those who are buttoned up with respectability reflect that 'the fish swim in the lake / and do not even own clothing'; and he would have them perceive that spontaneity and naturalness are superior to propriety and convention.

He commissions his poems to speak out against all forms of oppression, in particular against enslavement-by-convention, against 'the tyranny of the unimaginative', and against the bondage there can be in marriage and in families. 'Go to the bourgeoise who is dying of her ennuis', he bids them, 'Go to those whose delicate desires are thwarted, ... Bring confidence upon the algae and the tentacles of the soul.' In comic mood, as in 'Salutation the Second', he would have his songs be little lords of misrule, 'naked and impudent'—

> Go and dance shamelessly!
> Go with an impertinent frolic!
> Greet the grave and the stodgy,
> Salute them with your thumbs at your noses.
>
>   .   .   .   .   .   .
>
> Go! rejuvenate things!
> Rejuvenate even 'The Spectator'.
>   Go! and make cat calls!
> Dance and make people blush,
> Dance the dance of the phallus
>   and tell anecdotes of Cybele!
> Speak of the indecorous conduct of the Gods!
>   (Tell it to Mr Strachey.)
> Ruffle the skirts of prudes,
>   Speak of their knees and ankles.

> But, above all, go to practical people—
>   go! jangle their door-bells!
> Say that you do no work
>   and that you will live forever.

Harriet Monroe felt such poems might shock even her readers' modern sensibilities.

The songs have outlived their own century at least, and they have done so because their bright youthful energies are being celebrated in verse that is itself freed from all conventional constraints. Each song finds and follows at every move its own inner form. It also helps that they are straight-talking—not 'poetical'. The words and the word-order are such as anyone might naturally use. All the same, only someone who had developed a fine ear for the natural music of words could put them together in such exactly measured and cadenced shapes. There is a crisply sculpted, lapidary quality about them, only this is carving that dances and sings.

The poet's confidence in his own powers must come from this modernizing of his work. So too must his sense of being so superior to his readers, for while he has outgrown his apprentice work, the *Personae* and *Canzoni* in which he was assimilating the lessons of his masters, their taste is still for more of the same. To his new poems, 'with nothing archaic about them', they would say, '"his first work was the best." / "Poor Dear! He has lost his illusions."' He mocks them for that, and elects his ideal audience—

> Go, my songs, seek your praises from the young and from the intolerant,
> Move among the lovers of perfection alone.
> Seek ever to stand in the hard Sophoclean light
> And take your wounds from it gladly.

One notes the ambitious, perhaps overreaching, progression; and wonders, did Pound already identify with Sophocles' Herakles whose death agony is illuminated by an Apollonian understanding of his fate?

The time for his variant of the Herakles story to be played out would come thirty and more years later. In 1913 his election of 'the hard Sophoclean light' was simply an arrogant gesture in one of his *xenia*, so called after Martial's little epigrams for giving to guests. The slight poem then became one of his *lustra*, a word for what went on in the brothels and moral morass of the city's life; and also for the offering made by the Censors in expiation of the sins of the people and to purify the city. Pound, in 1913, was only doing for contemporary London what Martial had done for Rome, and he knew well enough that it was a low sort of job for a poet—

Irritation with the general asininity is a passion common enough in great minds, and sufficiently pardonable to the intelligent, but it is not, after all, the highest of human emotions. And even scorn, which is a very fine thing indeed, is not the one thing essential.

There spoke the sober artist, after enjoying the exhilarating fun of flushing out the asinine.

There were just two poems among the 'Contemporania' which express his higher emotions, 'Dance Figure', his dream of a dancing woman, and 'In a Station of the Metro'. In the latter, at the close of the sequence, the crowd of other people, previously viewed with antipathy, become ghostly faces in the dim light of the underground, and thus simplified are seen in imagination as Whitman might have seen them, not as the dead but as if reborn in the next year's almond or olive blossom:

> The apparition   of these faces   in the crowd:
> Petals   on a wet, black   bough.

This is the vision, not of the superior critic seeing only the failings and follies of his society, but of a mind inwardly intent, as in '$\Delta\omega\rho\iota\alpha$' and 'The Return', on deeper, more ultimate things—on those things the smugly self-satisfied will not see. It had taken the poet over a year to refine an experience in the Paris Metro into that nineteen-syllable *haiku*.

Making enemies in 'The New Age'

The polished epigrams, with their arrogant stylishness, their good humour and high spirits, their strong sympathy for the oppressed and their readiness to love and delight as much as to hate, were calculated to amuse and flatter those who were of a mind with the poet and to draw them into a conspiracy of enlightened resistance to dullness. In his public prose, in stark contrast, Pound seemed now to be intent on making as many enemies as possible, and on standing alone against them all. 'For the welfare of things at large', he declared in *The New Age*, 'We need the old feud between the artist and the smugger portions of the community revived with some virulence'.

He was most virulent in *The New Age* against the smugness of the English. He chose to live in England, he explained, because it was a comfortable if rather musty place for an artist, and because London, while not 'the Paradiso Terrestre', was 'at least some centuries nearer it' than St Louis. But he knew that he was 'perched on the rotten shell of a crumbling empire', and that the country, like Rome in its decadence, had lost its impulse and energy. It was as dead as a heap of iron filings with no magnet to create the rose pattern. As for its social arrangements, its hedging them about with conventions and proprieties, though strange to an American, was quite in order, he could appreciate, given its anaemic state. And then there was the peculiar English sense for what was right, which, so far as he could make out, was wholly bound up with its sense of property. Whereas in America 'those things are right which give the greatest freedom, the greatest opportunity for individual development', in England 'A thing is right if it tends to conserve an estate, or to maintain a succession, no matter what servitude or oppression this inflict.' The violence with which otherwise quiet persons would claim *their* possessions, with a '*my* house' or an '*our* empire', left him, as an American, unfailingly astonished. 'You have squandered human resources for the material resources', he told his hosts.

As if that wasn't offensive enough, he told them that their finest authors—naming Yeats, James, Hudson, and Conrad—were all foreigners; that the 'powers' in their world of letters were *papier maché*; that the art of verse was more advanced in Paris than in London; also that one must go to the cafés of Paris in order to find free intelligence plotting the revolution against general stupidity.

Best of all, he told them that their women were inferior to the American woman. 'Heaven knows', he granted,

your Society women have, at times, humour and understanding and all the graces, but their minds are preponderantly derivative. They may have gathered from one man or from many, but their individuality, when they have any, is only a sort of guide to their eclectic processes. They are more than likely to accept an idea because they like the person who has it.

He was reflecting, freely and frankly, on the women he was accustomed to meeting in London, including, one must suppose, his intended and her mother. Then came his partisan contrast. 'Our women in civil life', he boasted, were women acquainted with life at first hand, as probation officers, tenement inspectors, 'and in various offices of the national and municipal housekeeping'; they had minds of their own, 'unconditioned by sex or caste'; were 'usually of generous humour'; 'and their opinions on many matters of detail are held in utmost respect.' In short, 'our women' were 'of considerable use in the conduct of our American affairs.'

Orage did not much care for his columnist's contempt for the English and their way of life, nor for his boosting America and Paris at England's expense. He put up with it through the 'Patria Mia' series of eleven articles in September and November 1912, and the abbreviated series of just four articles under the telling title 'Through Alien Eyes' in January and February 1913, and still through the six articles in May and June 1913 on 'America: Chances and Remedies'. But he began to mount a counter-attack in September 1913 when Pound declared, in the first article of his series on French Poetry, that there were just two great and interesting phenomena in the world, 'the intellectual life of Paris and the curious teething promise of my own vast occidental nation'. Writing as 'R. H. C.' in his 'Readers and Writers' column, Orage dismissed Pound's 'two great and interesting phenomena', saying he could see in them 'little either of promise or of performance'. When Pound challenged him 'to show that our modern English writers are as good or that our classic English writers have anticipated [the French] modern verse forms and wave-lengths', Orage, leaning on Samuel Johnson's 'Life of Cowley', simply charged him with 'Pindarism'. At the same time he published 'The Way Back to America' by T. K. L[ister], a parody designed to ridicule Pound's 'Through Alien Eyes'; and he tied a further mocking parody by 'T. K. L.' to the tail of each of the remaining four articles on French poets.

Pound, with his last words in that series, added deliberate insult to the injury already done to English *amour-propre*:

for the most part both writers and critics in England are so ignorant that if a man attempt these finer accords and simplicities [such as he had pointed out in the work of de Gourmont, De Regnier, and other French poets] there is hardly anyone who can tell what he is up to.

Pound was partly getting his own back there for a review of *Ripostes* which had appeared in the *New Age* in April, and which had dealt roughly with the finer accords and simplicities of 'Apparuit'. 'Complex rubbish', it had called 'carven in subtle stuff, a / portent'; and had then made nonsense of it, 'In plain English, how can a man fitted to make songs like "The Seafarer" stuff a portent?'

Orage now went for Pound in a way that was clearly meant to wound. He first disposed of Pound's preferring the poets of Paris to those of London—T. K. L.'s 'brilliant' parodies had shown each successive French star to be 'little more than a candle or a bog-light', and had left him with no respect at all for Pound's judgement. Then he condemned Pound as ignorant of English writing, and ignorant even of how to write English. The final offence was Pound's thinking nothing of Milton and admiring 'Mr Yeats and Mr Tagore'. In a later issue Orage put solid ground under his objection to Pound's kind of poetry. 'Every part of the *New Age* hangs together', he wrote; 'the literature we despise is associated with the economics we hate and the literature we love is associated with the form of society we would assist in creating.' And therefore, 'Mr Pound—I say it with all respect—is an enemy of the *New Age*.'

In time Orage's economics and Pound's poetics would converge. But Pound accepted his being cast out for a while from the pages of the *New Age* patiently and without rancour. It rather confirmed his identity as a poet and an American to be declared an enemy in that way. 'The editor is a good fellow', he told his mother, though 'his literary taste . . . is unfortunate'.

Making a renaissance in 'Poetry'

' "England" is dead as mutton'—'There just is nothing alive here except W. B. Y. and Les Imagistes'. In such terms Pound encouraged the American editors of *Poetry: A Magazine of Verse* to seize their chance to become the nucleus of a new world order. He spelt out for their readers the provinciality of London as it appeared to him, an American seeking art that was up to world standard. Yeats was 'the only poet worthy of serious study'; Hueffer was good for talking poetry with; but then 'The important work of the last twenty-five years has been done in Paris'. Of course one could find in London any number of writers contributing to its 'charm' and 'atmosphere', he allowed, 'but it is one thing to take pleasure in a man's work and another to respect him as a great artist'.

He would not have it thought that things were better in the United States. There simply was 'no man now living in America whose work is of the slightest interest to any serious artist.' No 'living and effective style' was to be found in its contemporary literature. And worst of all was 'the appalling fungus of our "better magazines".' What made them so deadly was that their editors neither knew 'good work from bad', nor cared for poetry as a living and changing art.

Harriet Monroe's Chicago-based *Poetry* promised to be different.[2] She was founding it on the conviction that poetry was 'the highest, most complete human expression of truth and beauty', and with the public-spirited intention of encouraging the production of poetry of the highest quality to meet the need of the people of America for a truly interpretive modern poetry. She saw that 'In the United States today the poet is rarely able to devote his best energies to his art because, unlike his fellow artists in painting, sculpture and architecture, he cannot make it yield him even a bread-and-water-living.' There was the further difficulty that America had

---

[2] Harriet Monroe (1860–1936) of Chicago, poet—commissioned to write the 'Columbian Ode' for the Chicago World's Columbian Exposition of 1893—and founding editor (1912–36) of *Poetry: A Magazine of Verse*.

no centre of literary taste and authority of its own. She wanted to provide such a centre; and she meant to pay poets for their work. To be sure of doing that she had persuaded over one hundred citizens to pledge at least fifty dollars annually for five years. There was great wealth in Chicago, which had grown to be the second city of the United States as 'hog butcher to the world' and the hub of the mid-West. Some of that wealth was going into its new 'skyscraper' architecture and into its Art Institute and its symphony orchestra, and now, thanks to Monroe and her supporters there would be a very modest share for poetry. She was moved to hope that 'the poetic Renaissance' might be on its way.

In August and September 1912 she sent a circular letter to the poets whose work she thought good, asking them to submit their best work for a magazine devoted to showing the public 'the best that can be done today in English verse'. She was especially eager to secure Pound as a contributor. He was interested but wary. What she was promising was virtually what he had just been calling for in his 'Patria Mia' articles, but could she deliver? Could she 'teach the American poet that poetry *is* an *art*'? Was she for American poetry only, or for poetry?—the former having its importance, but the latter mattering more. He agreed, on condition she 'conceive verse as a living medium' and really meant not to insult the serious artist, to give her exclusive publication of his work in America. And he offered to keep her 'in touch with whatever is most dynamic in artistic thought' in London and Paris. He sent her at once his 'To Whistler: American', as 'not out of place at the threshold of what I hope is an endeavour to carry into our American poetry the same sort of life and intensity which [Whistler] infused into modern painting'. By the end of his first letter he had come round to the idea that *Poetry* would bring closer 'our American Risorgimento'. In early October he was writing home that his connection with the magazine 'gives me the over-grip for the future'—evidently he intended to make it serve his own projects.

Harriet Monroe named Pound *Poetry*'s 'Foreign Correspondent', and so began a collaboration in which shared purposes were often crossed by profoundly different notions of how to carry them out, and in which her calm determination to maintain her editorial control had to coexist with his storm and stress. He was frustrated when she wouldn't follow his advice, and was unsparing in castigating what he saw as her shortcomings. And she, while coolly maintaining her independence, valued his criticism and his contributions as the best, the most stimulating and educative that she could have hoped for. 'Controversy is good for the soul', she reflected.

Pound at once laid down his idea of what they needed to do. The United States already had the makings of its renaissance, the necessary force and impulse; but it had yet to achieve 'the guiding sense, the discrimination in applying the force'. Now was the 'time for carving', as he wrote in his pact with Whitman. He meant it was the time for developing *the art of poetry*; and that meant seeking out *master-work* and being intolerant of mediocrity. 'My idea of our policy is this', he told Miss Monroe in his second letter,

We support American poets—preferably the young ones who have a serious determination to produce master-work. We *import* only such stuff as is better than that produced at home. The *best* foreign stuff, the stuff well above mediocrity, or the experiments that seem serious, and seriously and sanely directed towards the broadening and development of the Art of Poetry.

They must aim at 'an international standard', he insisted, 'a universal standard which pays no attention to time or country—a Weltlitteratur standard'. Otherwise there was no hope, as there was no hope for England because it did not accept such a standard. 'The worst betrayal you could make', he warned Miss Monroe, 'is to pretend for a moment that you are content with a parochial standard.'

They could be the best, he assured Alice Corbin Henderson, Harriet Monroe's very bright assistant editor, and they could become so authoritative that every other periodical would have to follow them, because they had his judgement to rely on. From his twelve-year 'study of the laws of the art, the fundamental, eternal etc. in ten languages', he knew 'more about poetry of every time and place than any man living'. He mentioned his 'nine months on Arnaut for polyphonic rime' as one instance of how he had gone at things, '6 months on Sapphics' as another, or '400 sonnets destroyed'. He wanted them to know that with him as their leading light 'we can afford the utmost strictness, we can and must take risks, and we can quite well afford to insult anyone we like'.

He himself was ready to insult anyone who might be content with less than the best. In his 'To Whistler, American', which appeared in the first number of *Poetry*, he dismissed Whistler's and Abe Lincoln's contemporaries as 'that mass of dolts'. When 'wrathful correspondents and indignant critics objected to such a wholesale slamming of our fellow countrymen', as Harriet Monroe put it, he refined the insult with a wonderfully double-edged discrimination. He explained that the insult was 'leveled more at the pseudo-artists than at that helpless stupid cow the bloomin' vulgus.' It was 'these dam charlatans who go about professing to be artists' while having no 'care for the master-work' and 'no intention of producing it' that he really hated. As for the public, 'one knows they're a set of asses' with 'no natural preference for either the bad or the good.'

Miss Monroe was more concerned to seek out and to encourage promising poets than to persecute mediocrity; and she had demonstrated a more hopeful view of the American public by nailing to her masthead Whitman's 'To have great poets there must be great audiences too'. Her instincts were democratic and inclusive, where Pound's were all for an exclusive élite of superior individuals like himself. Yet she found a way of defending her foreign correspondent from the indignant critics, while both keeping her distance from his braggadoccio, and shrewdly inviting sympathy for him as a young poet who had suffered neglect. In his situation, she suggested in an editorial, he might be entitled to view Americans as 'a mass of dolts'—

Mr Pound is not the first American poet to have stood with his back to the wall, and struck out blindly with clenched fists in a fierce impulse to fight. Nor is he the first whom we, by this same stolid and indifferent rejection [of our own art], have forced into exile and rebellion.

'What has become of our boasted sense of humour if we cannot let our young poets rail', she asked, putting him kindly in his place; 'or our sense of justice', she went on, willing to give him a hearing after all, 'if we cannot cease smiling and weigh their words?'

She did weigh the young poet's advice and criticism and smiled at it sometimes, and sometimes heeded it. He told her what was wrong with her own verse. She was rather pleased with her long poem on an electric turbine, and thought it very modern. Pound wrote quite mercilessly that it was no such thing. The modern subject only made its faults more glaring, he said, pointing to the lack of 'direct presentation', 'the lack of economy of phrase', the excess of decorative adjectives—'have you ever let a noun out unchaperoned???'—the unreal and unspeakable 'literary dialect', and the old pentameter 'full of traditional cadences'. Harriet Monroe did not take offence, perhaps because she was used to writing just such astringent criticism to her contributors. But there was more to it than that. She came to believe that Pound 'was the best critic living, at least in our speciality, and his acid touch on weak spots was as fearsomely enlightening as a clinic.'

She also appreciated his bringing in good work for *Poetry*, especially in its first years. His first coup was to secure two groups of poems from Yeats, including 'To a Shade' and others in the new harsh mood of *Responsibilities*. His next move was to launch the 'Imagistes', H. D. and Aldington and himself. The terms in which he introduced H. D.'s first poems make it clear that he wanted his new school or movement to set the standard for modern American poetry. 'This is the sort of American stuff I can show here and in Paris without its being ridiculed', he enthused to Harriet Monroe as he pointedly laid out its distinctive qualities, 'Objective—no slither; direct—no excessive use of adjectives... straight talk, straight as the Greek'. In early 1913 he sent in his 'A Few Don'ts by an Imagiste', offering it as an 'Ars Poetica' or 'instructions to neophytes' and suggesting that copies of it should be inserted in all 'returned msss. for the next decade'. He hoped it would stimulate or accelerate 'the younger American poets to a higher efficiency.'

He also introduced a number of coming poets not of his own school, among them the Frenchman Charles Vildrac, and D. H. Lawrence—'he learned the proper treatment of modern subjects before I did'—and some serious Americans he had come across in Paris and London, John Gould Fletcher, Skipwith Cannell, and Robert Frost. It took him six months argument to persuade Miss Monroe to publish the 'VURRY Amur'k'n' Frost's 'The Code'.

He approved of some, but not many, of the American poets Miss Monroe found for herself. He was glad when she published William Carlos Williams, whom he had been promoting in London. He had reservations about Carl Sandburg and Vachel Lindsay, two of her major finds, but allowed that *Poetry* certainly ought to be publishing their work. He thought well of Orrick Johns' 'Songs of Deliverance'. For the rest, in these early days, he had hardly a good word. Even the occasional more promising poem would reveal to him a 'howling need of training'. When Miss Monroe was left feeling that it was impossible to put together a number that would please him, he assured her that it was 'a possible feat, tho' I'd probably have to choose the contents myself.'

He itemized for Alice Henderson the poetry he would have in the magazine. 'All the Yeats and all the me it can get, and when it gets us I think it should fill in with people whom I can take seriously'. The latter, 'under rather strict surveillance', would be mainly Aldington, H.D., Lawrence, 'Williams (very severely chosen), A. Lowell (ditto), Flint (now and again), Translations three or four times a year... And that dull beast Frost, whom I continue to believe in'. 'That lot', in his very exclusive view, 'would make an interesting review.'

Harriet Monroe was never going to be so restrictive as that, and she cared much less for international prestige than for raising the standard of American poetry. After a year and more of trying in vain to get her to do as he wanted, Pound made a show of resigning in terminal exasperation. That is, he asked Hueffer to 'please take over the foreign correspondence of *Poetry* & communicate with them to the effect that I have turned it over to you.' Hueffer then wrote most diplomatically to Miss Monroe, saying he couldn't do the job half so well as Pound, and 'Besides, if I tried to help you that energetic poet would sit on my head and hammer me till I did exactly what he wanted and the result would be exactly the same except that I should be like the green baize door that every one kicks going in or out.' Pound agreed to stay on, while grumbling to Miss Monroe 'I don't think you have yet tried to see the magazine from my viewpoint.' Then, at his most formal, 'I am willing to reconsider my resignation pending a general improvement of the magazine, and I will not have my name associated with it unless it does improve.'

It was a kind of lovers' quarrel, a quarrel of two people in love with poetry and committed to putting it at the heart of things, but two people with such very different tastes, talents, and temperaments. Their collaboration in *Poetry*, and their quarrelling, or at least Pound's making a war of it, would continue for several years. 'Harriet's *Home Gazette*', he would call it in 1938.

Individualism in 'The New Freewoman'

In the summer of 1913 Pound was offered the opportunity, or so he thought, to get an 'over-grip' on things in England. Rebecca West, who was assisting Dora Marsden edit her *The New Freewoman: An Individualist Review*, wanted to develop a literary side to it, and asked Pound whom she knew through Hueffer and Violet Hunt to help her do that. Pound offered to fill a page per fortnightly number, alternating verse with criticism of current poetry. He stipulated that he must do the selecting. 'If I am to make the page efficient, I must follow my own scheme', he insisted to Miss Marsden, 'I can't work it if "diluted" with chance stuff of a different sort'—'I have certain standards and the work printed would have to come up to them.' Already in his first letter he informed her that he had secured some cash from an 'anonymous donor'—now known to have been John Gould Fletcher—so that he could pay the poets something for their verse and thus spare them 'the disgrace of printing creative stuff without being paid'. However, because he thought so well of her periodical, he would give his own verse free, something he wouldn't do for anyone else. He also informed her that he had already succeeded in getting for her 'a translation of Remy de Gourmont's *Chevaux de Diomède*'—that would run as a serial from August through to the following March.

He wrote home that three columns had been turned over to him—out of the regular thirty-six columns of print—'Which means to say I can amuse myself drawing invidious comparisons between the intellegence of my friends and the utter imbecility of my enemies'. But to Harriet Monroe he wrote that he had 'taken charge of the literature dept.' as 'our left wing'; and to Alice Henderson he wrote, more frankly, that it was 'as our, or at least my organ on this side the drink'. He was taking it on 'as the official organ of Imagism'. That was in August. By mid-October he was 'more or less running' the review—not all of it, not the 'bilge'—'but I'm somewhat a guiding star and I choose about a third ... of the contents'. 'The advantage of a woman's paper', he explained to Milton Bronner, was that 'a male editor often wants to run his own'—by which he meant, presumably, his own 'lit. dept.'. But he wasn't going to continue unless he could 'run about half the paper to suit myself'.

Miss Marsden had no intention of allowing him to do that. When Rebecca West resigned in October she quickly appointed Richard Aldington to her place, and thereafter Pound had no direct control over the contents of *The New Freewoman*. He had 'run its literature department' for just about three months. Miss Marsden had been put on her guard by Rebecca West against Pound's looking to take over her review, and was quite justifiably suspicious of his intentions. And Pound, who may not have met this particular female editor at that time—she was running the review from her mother's home at Ainsdale, near Southport just north of Liverpool—had quite the wrong idea if he thought she would let him have his over-reaching male way. He probably had no idea at all of what had gone into the making of this extraordinary English woman.

Dora Marsden B.A., as she declared herself on the masthead of *The New Freewoman*, was born in March 1882 in the village of Marsden, on the northern edge of the Peak District moors and in sight of smoky Huddersfield with its immense industrial wool-working mills. Her father dealt in shoddy, the waste wool from the mills, until he abandoned his family and went off to America in 1890; her mother was a seamstress. At 13 she was made pupil-teacher in the village infant school, qualifying as a teacher at 18. Three years later, in 1903, she graduated B.A. from Owens College in Manchester, joining the small but growing number of English women with university degrees. She taught for five years, as she was bound to do by her government scholarship, and in 1908 was appointed Head Mistress of Altrincham Pupil-Teacher Centre. In 1909 she resigned to become a full-time organizer in the Pankhursts' Women's Suffrage Movement, and quickly emerged as a star militant. She was arrested and jailed for a month for assaulting a police officer, she being all of 4′ 6″ tall. Her finest exploit was sensationally ambushing the Home Secretary Winston Churchill as he was addressing a meeting in Southport, by demanding votes for women from the lantern in the roof where her small band of

Suffragettes had concealed themselves overnight. She resigned from the Pankhursts' organization in 1910, finding them too autocratic and their single-issue feminism too restrictive.

She was in fact beginning to think her way beyond feminism too. She founded *The Freewoman* in November 1911, with support from Orage and some of his *New Age* contributors and from Granville of Swift & Co. Its first subtitle was 'A Weekly Feminist Review', and the declared aim was to free women to be masters of their own fate, to be responsible for themselves as individuals. However, the subtitle was soon changed to 'A Weekly Humanist Review', because 'the two causes, men's and women's, are one'. Publication ceased after a year, but in June 1913 there appeared *The New Freewoman*, now 'An Individualist Review'; and that became, from January 1st 1914, *The Egoist: An Individualist Review, Formerly The New Freewoman*. Dora Marsden herself generally wrote the leading article and also the 'Views and Comments' section—altogether a quarter to a third of each issue. From 1913 she had the financial backing as well as the moral support of Harriet Shaw Weaver, another remarkable English woman, who in time would relieve her of the editorial role and allow her to concentrate exclusively on her philosophical work and to figure as the review's 'Contributing Editor'.[3]

Dora Marsden's only guide in working out her ideas may have been Max Stirner's *The Ego and His Own*, a work which maintained that 'the Ego is the only reality, the only ideal.' She had no training as a philosopher and was not in touch with any school or group of philosophers. Indeed her philosophical convictions required her to do her own thinking as an autonomous individual free from all received thought. Nevertheless her preoccupations were very much of her time. She began from three axiomatic perceptions: that our reality or truth is necessarily individual;

[3] Harriet Shaw Weaver (1876–1961), born Frodsham, Cheshire; her father a wealthy doctor; the family religion Evangelical Church of England. Educated by governesses; moved with family to 'Cedar Lawn', Hampstead, London in 1892; discouraged by parents from attending university ('what would be the use?'); lived at home until *c*.1914. From 1895 to 1905 voluntary social worker in London's East End. 1905–06 lived in Settlement House in Bethnal Green in the East End; continued her social work there, helping school-leavers into apprenticeships, until 1912. In 1905 started formal study of problems of social justice and the economic basis of social relations. Became financially independent upon the death of her mother in 1909. Gave financial backing to Dora Marsden's *New Freewoman* and *Egoist*, and took over editing of the latter from July 1914. Had T. S. Eliot as assistant editor 1917–19. Set up Egoist Press and published Eliot's *Prufrock and Other Observations* (1917), Wyndham Lewis's *Tarr* (1918), Pound's *Quia Pauper Amavi* (1919), and Joyce's *Ulysses* (1922). Suspended *Egoist* December 1919 to concentrate on getting *Ulysses* into print, and continued thereafter to support Joyce financially. Published Dora Marsden's *The Definition of the Godhead* (1928) and *The Mystery of Christianity* (1930). T. S. Eliot dedicated his *Selected Essays: 1917–1932*: 'To HARRIET SHAW WEAVER in gratitude and in recognition of her services to English letters'.

that our reality is made up in the mind, that it is mental reality; and that, insofar as it is made up in language, it is verbal reality. She then concerned herself with the inevitable tension or conflict in the mind between the specific truth of the individual's experience, and the generalizing nature of a common language. In the latter, as she saw it, the individual truth was always being filtered out by received ideas and by abstraction and cliché.

The consequence was a loss of individuality and the prevalence of false consciousness and bad faith. The false consciousness infected all relationships, personal, social, economic, and political. The 'Woman' question and the Suffragette 'Cause' had between them enslaved the progressive energies of large numbers of individual women by a mere trick of rhetoric, since 'Woman' did not exist and any abstract 'Cause' was a delusion. 'Democracy' by a similar trick subjected each individual to the tyranny of the non-existent 'All'. Any statement whatsoever that was not governed by the singular 'I' must be false and contrary to the interests of the individual.

The individual must learn to say '*I* am', '*I* desire', '*I* feel', '*I* think' in order to be free, for the only freedom is in freeing one's potential Self from the bonds of convention. For the few authentic *I*ndividuals the only goal in life is the intensive satisfaction of their own needs and desires—they know they are 'Ends-in-themselves'. That is, they are 'Egoists'. The Egoist has the courage to measure the intrinsic value of things purely by their value to his or her own self. The Egoist accepts, moreover, that it is up to the 'I' to make its own reality and its own world; and, beyond that, to create its own god—meaning not some mere thought of an Abstract Absolute, but 'the utmost emotional reach of himself'. 'Our existence is not dependent upon the will of the gods', Marsden wrote rather bravely in 1913 in still Christian England, 'the existence of the gods is dependent upon *our* will'. And again, 'If we have no purposes of our own', and no force of our own, 'we are lost'. But given the will and the force we 'can create gods, attain to them, and project more powerful.'

There was a real affinity between Marsden's philosophizing and what Pound was bringing to her review. He too was a thorough-going individualist, though in his own proper way, since he was a poet and not a philosopher. Where she invoked the all-creating Ego, he would speak of the unique *virtu* of the serious artist. Believing that 'the life of the race is concentrated in a few individuals', those rare truly original makers of reality, he was as opposed as she was to the democratic idea which would subject individual genius to a species of mob-rule. He too would have the young learn to say 'I', and to go in fear of conventions and abstractions and clichés. He was very close to Marsden's thinking when he declared in *The New Freewoman* in October that a god was a state of mind—'an eternal state of mind'; that the god is manifest when the state of mind takes form; and that a man becomes a god 'When he enters one of these states of mind'. As specific instances he might have mentioned 'Δώρια' and 'The Return', or 'In a Station of the Metro' which had appeared in the review in August with half-a-dozen of his 'Contemporania'. That had been his first appearance in *The New Freewoman*, and the poems might have been deliberately selected to reveal the affinities between his *imagisme* and Marsden's concern for each mind to realize its own world in words.

Yet there was no meeting of these like minds, for neither seemed able to appreciate the other's particular mode of Individualism. The one had no time for poetry, the other no time for philosophy. Marsden associated a 'literary intellect' with 'cultural brain-rot', that is with the disease of unthinking rhetoric. Though she printed Pound's 'Contemporania' she didn't read them; and nor did she read Joyce's *A Portrait of the Artist* when that was running as *The Egoist*'s serial for over a year and a half in 1914 and 1915. Pound, from his side, as good as told her that in her prose she was doing what he as an artist would not descend to, 'gassing about art'. From his point of view it was simply absurd to develop a general theory of the uniqueness of each individual's knowing and being.

The wonderful, and comical, thing here is that in securing de Gourmont's *The Horses of Diomedes* and Joyce's *A Portrait of the Artist as a Young Man* for *The New Freewoman*, Pound was bringing in work which did exactly what Dora Marsden was calling for. Joyce's novel is after all a thinking through of the whole complex process of individuation by which his own young mind, as it becomes more aware of its world, progressively frees itself from the layers of imposed false consciousness, and grows towards the artist's god-like state of originality. Again, the terms in which Pound later wrote of de Gourmont's work might have been refined out of Marsden's editorials. Recognizing 'the right of individuals to *feel* differently', de Gourmont 'differentiates his characters by the modes of their sensibility', that is, by their 'modalities of apperception'. Moreover, 'He had passed the point where people take abstract statement of dogma for "enlightenment"'—he knew that 'an "idea" has little value apart from the modality of the mind which receives it.' More generally, Pound observed, de Gourmont, a supremely civilized intelligence, enforces the recognition that 'Civilization is individual', that 'the truth is the individual'. *The Horses of Diomedes*, regarded by Pound as 'the most complete expression of his *façon d'appercevoir*', is a very strange piece of writing, and its strangeness is that of a genuinely individualist mind going about its business. It is an excellent instance of what Dora Marsden's theory could lead to in practice.

Could it have been by sheer luck of the *zeitgeist* that it appeared in her 'Individualist Review'?

The Imagiste vortex

The surprising affinity between Pound's *Imagisme* and Dora Marsden's thinking was such that each could provide an illuminating commentary upon the other. But the comic ironies of their relationship have again to be allowed for. It is as Miss Marsden reacts against *Imagisme* and pursues her own line at a tangent to it that she throws most light upon it. And the comedy is improved by the fact that her *Egoist* did after all become the organ of Imagism, though only after the school had been taken over by its scholars, and was no longer, given Pound's judgement that they had given up on the principles of *Imagisme*, truly in accord with Marsden's thinking.

Imagisme, Pound recorded, 'began certainly in Church Walk with H.D., Richard, and myself.' It was first announced in his note to Hulme's poems as appended to *Ripostes* in October 1912; and its first poems appeared in *Poetry*, Aldington's in November 1912 and H.D.'s in January 1913. Both were introduced as '*Imagistes*', and the *Imagistes* were said to be 'a group of ardent Hellenists who are pursuing interesting experiments in *vers libre*'. Pound protested that 'Hellenism & vers libre have nothing to do with it'—*Imagisme*, he insisted, 'is concerned solely with *language and presentation.*' A statement of the guiding principles, as dictated by Pound to Flint, followed in *Poetry* in March 1913. Economy of language and directness of presentation were fundamental, and also, as to rhythm and metre, 'to compose in the sequence of the musical phrase'. Then there were Pound's forty things *not* to be done, and a grand definition: 'An "Image" is that which presents an intellectual and emotional complex in an instant of time', thereby giving 'that sense of sudden liberation...that sense of sudden growth, which we experience in the presence of the greatest works of art.' That was an indication that there might be rather more to Pound's *Imagisme* than a concern with technique alone.

Imagisme made its appearance in *The New Freewoman* in mid-August 1913, with six of Pound's 'Contemporania', 'written since he became an *imagiste*', prefaced by Rebecca West's condensed version of the propaganda in *Poetry*. In the following issue there were poems by Aldington, H.D., Amy Lowell, Flint, and others, under the heading 'The Newer School'.

Pound was now thinking of putting together an anthology to present his *Imagistes* as a force in the world. The difficulty was that the 'movement' consisted of just the three founders, plus Flint whom they had co-opted, and the very wealthy and forceful Amy Lowell who was attaching herself to them in the conviction, which Pound did not share, that she too was an *Imagiste*. To make up a slim volume of sixty-four pages he had to include some other poets whose work had at best an accidental connection with his principles. He put in Williams's 'Postlude' though Williams would never wear his label; and Allen Upward's invented Chinese prose poems; and, oddest of all, Hueffer's 'In the Little Old Market Place', Hueffer being a prosing 'Impressionist' by his own account, and not a creator of short, sharp psychic images. At the last minute he included, on Yeats's recommendation, James Joyce's very Yeatsian 'I hear an army' from *Chamber Music* (1907).

He managed to get *Des Imagistes* into print by having it appear first as an issue of *Glebe*, a little magazine edited by Alfred Kreymborg in New York, in February 1914, and then, from the same setting of type, as a book under the imprints of Albert and Charles Boni in New York and of Harold Monro's Poetry Bookshop in London. It did not make much of a splash at the time, receiving little notice outside its own circles in *Poetry* and *The New Freewoman*. Its influence and its significance have been magnified over the years, with some reason, though probably excessively.

When the anthology appeared the movement was already mutating into what Pound would disparage as 'Amygism'. There were personal disaffections and power-plays and a breaking away from the briefly binding principles. Already in October of 1913 Aldington and H.D.—who married that month—were wanting to dissociate themselves from 'the affectation of "Imagiste"'. They may well have resented Pound's declaration that 'Hellenism & vers libre' had nothing to do with *Imagisme*, since most of their poems were just that, Hellenism in vers libre. The rest of the *Imagiste* imperatives which were supposedly driving the movement were all Pound's idea, and its members were beginning to resist being driven by him. Flint too 'was really in opposition to my constant hammering on vortex, concentration, condensation, hardness.' The fact was that Pound had managed, 'by slightly overbearing arrogance', as he claimed in a letter to Flint in 1921, to coerce a few individuals 'into a semblance of unity for a few weeks or months in [1912], and to hold together till 1913.' But by early 1914 his vortex of *Imagistes* was breaking up. Pound was allying himself with Wyndham Lewis's more energetic Vorticism, and the others were re-grouping around Amy Lowell.

Amy Lowell (1874–1925) was a Boston Lowell, a poet and a woman of letters. Having discovered *Imagisme* in *Poetry* she at once took herself to London to join the movement. She invited Pound to call on her in her hotel suite overlooking Piccadilly and Green Park, took him in her hired automobile to visit Oxford, and allowed him to think that she might put money into one or another of his projects. He included one of her poems, 'In a Garden', in *Des Imagistes*, but he got nothing more out of her. Instead she made common cause with the dissidents and financed their anthologies of 1915, 1916, and 1917. It was as if she had put in a bid to take over the movement Pound had created and had had it gratefully accepted. Pound of course had to go, and went quite readily, only asking that they not appropriate the title he had invented, the more especially that some of them had objected to being labelled with it, and that they probably would not maintain the standard of clarity and intensity that it was meant to stand for. But the dissidents disputed his claim that the movement had been of his making, and made the title their own by Anglicizing it.

In the preface to *Some Imagist Poets* (1915) they openly celebrated their release from Pound's efforts to organize and direct them. They had constituted themselves into a democratic committee 'consisting of more than half the authors'. Moreover, 'instead of an arbitrary selection by an editor', they declared, 'each poet has been permitted to represent himself by the work he considers his best'. As for the three firm principles of *Imagisme*, these were 'explained' into six rather woolly 'essentials', the last of which laid down that 'most of us believe that concentration is of the very essence of poetry'. That compromising 'most of us' was exactly what Pound had expected. He had turned down Miss Lowell's first offer to find a publisher for an annual anthology because of her condition that he work within a 'democratized committee'. He wasn't going to waste his time, he told her, pretending that 'a certain number of people' were his 'critical and creative equals'. That would only lead to 'dilutation' of the essential principles, 'floppy degeneration', the end of *Imagisme*. On that account, if he could not control the group he did not want to be part of it. Of course, from the other side of the battle to own Imagism, Pound's intransigence was seen to be the real problem. 'You had the energy, you had the talents', Flint told him in 1915, 'you might have been generalissimo in a compact onslaught: and you spoiled everything by some native incapacity for walking square with your fellows. You have not been a good comrade, voilà!'

In July 1914 Pound declared *Imagisme* dead with a *blague* at Amy Lowell's expense. She was back in London and was giving a grand dinner at the Dieudonné restaurant in St James's, ostensibly to celebrate *Des Imagistes*, but more to position herself to displace Pound. After the 'Bombe Moka' and 'Friandises' she called on her guests to say what they meant by 'imagism'. Hueffer and Upward each said they had no idea what it was, they were there only because Ezra had declared them to be *Imagistes*. Upward spoke of Miss Lowell's 'In a Garden', and drew attention—with all eyes on its somewhat spherical author—to its final image, 'Night and the water, and you in your whiteness, bathing!' At which point 'Pound carried in from an adjoining salon, where it had been placed under a leak, a circular [tin] tub, clearly large enough for Miss Lowell to bathe in.' *Les Imagistes*, he announced, were about to be succeeded by a new school, *Les Nagistes*, and this bathtub might be taken as their symbol. So all ended in uncomfortable laughter. But Amy Lowell did carry off with her the committee of equals, Aldington, who as assistant editor of *The Egoist* could exhibit their work there, and H.D., now Hilda Aldington and more confused than ever in her relations with Pound, and Frank Flint who would write the official history and make it appear that Pound had been neither the inventor nor the dynamic intelligence of the movement.

Imagisme as such was short-lived, but what Pound intended by it would be of lasting significance for his work. He didn't much care for theorizing, and would throw out a remark here and a statement there without concerning himself with constructing a full account of it. Yet a coherent and cogent theory can be put together from those occasional remarks.

One might begin from his assertion that 'the natural object' is 'the proper and perfect symbol'. A hawk, for example, must be always a hawk and not any other thing, whatever further 'symbolic' sense, as in heraldry or heroic poetry, might be attached to it. This looks like a call for objectivity, for seeing things always as they are in themselves. Yet it is evident that 'the natural object' here, the hawk let us say, is a hawk-in-the-mind. It is already, as we think of it, a subjective mental object. It follows that when Pound wrote of recording 'the precise instant when a thing outward and objective transforms itself... into a thing inward and subjective' he must have been thinking of the transformation of a thing already in the mind. That would be a change then in its state or in its meaning, as through its being more intensely felt and more deeply understood. Such a change occurs when the faces seen in the underground station become 'petals on a wet, black bough'. The faces are faces in the mind, the petals are petals in the mind, and then under the pressure of attention they become identified the one with the other in a further apprehension charged with unexpected significance.

That would be a particular instance of what he had spoken of in one of the most striking passages in 'Psychology and Troubadours'. There is a sort of mind, he explained there, which inwardly experiences the living universe about us, 'the universe of fluid force... the germinal universe of wood alive, of stone alive', a mind which 'is ever at the interpretation of this vital universe'. Something of that kind is going on in at least two of his *Imagiste* poems, 'The Return' and 'Δώρια'. But it was probably H.D.'s poems that he was mainly thinking of, since he would say in retrospect that 'imagism was formulated to give emphasis to certain qualities that she possessed to the maximum degree: a mytho-poetic sense which was deep, true and of nature'. In 1914, in *BLAST*, he cited as the exemplary *Imagiste* poem H.D.'s 'Oread', in which she assumed the consciousness of a mountain-nymph:

> Whirl up sea —
> Whirl your pointed pines,
> Splash your great pines
> On our rocks,
> Hurl your green over us,
> Cover us with your pools of fir.

There the imperative verbs will a psychic experience of the energies of the mountain nymph's world. But that means that the apparently outward and objective world of pine forest and rock becomes a wholly subjective state of mind. So to be 'ever at the interpretation of this vital universe' is to be realizing one's individual nature in its terms. 'Image REFERS ultimately to emotional condition', as Pound explained to a correspondent in the 1930s, 'Inside expressable BY outside.'

So far we have discerned a two-stage process whereby 'the outward and objective' is first transformed into 'the inward and subjective', and then emerges again as the 'objective' expression of the inner 'condition'. Now 'The real' for Pound was not the thing in its outward and objective form but the subjective condition as objectified in the Image. ' "Know thyself" ', as he told Dorothy, 'is about the only way to find out about any thing or any body else.' He was being true to Egoistic Individualism there—'the truth is the individual'. But Dora Marsden did not believe that the artist could deliver individual truth and reality and challenged Pound to make his case for poetry in her 'Individualist Review'. His new *Defence of Poesy*, 'The Serious Artist', appeared there in three instalments in October and November 1913. It did not so much answer her scepticism about poetry as raise the ante by claiming that the only proper basis for the outer world of public affairs was the inner world of individuals as discovered and defined by the artist.

He was proposing, in all seriousness, to found the ideal state upon the Image. Poetry, he argued, was the necessary basis of the just society, because to attain the good of the greatest number we must first establish accurately and precisely of what nature individuals are and what it is they desire. That is the scientific work of the serious artist. His task is to present the true 'image of his desire, of his hate, of his indifference'; to define and bear witness to 'the inner nature and conditions of man'; to give 'lasting and unassailable data regarding the nature of man, of immaterial man, of man considered as a thinking and sentient' individual. Thus the arts, and poetry in particular, provide the essential data for ethics and civics—and by extension for the proper government of the state.

Dora Marsden took issue with Pound in her editorial articles. She was 'having spasms' over the first instalment, or so he reported to Dorothy, adding 'N. A. [*New Age*] ditto' over the 'Approach to Paris'. In fact beneath her spiky disputatiousness Miss Marsden was often so close to Pound's thinking as to be virtually paraphrasing him, as in her telling him that poetry, 'the highest manifestation' of the self's consciousness of itself, should be a true delineation of the individual soul in all its movements. Where she disagreed was that she simply couldn't see any art that was doing what art should do. Compared to the progress being made in experimental science, she argued, artists were still at the primitive stage of playing with fancy ideas about the natures of things which they didn't know how to observe. So far as she could see, the poets, far from delivering unassailable data concerning the states of the individual soul, were recycling worn-out words and images which did not connect to the reality of living beings.

This very pertinent critique drove Pound back to the matter of technique. He had to show just how his poetry was going to effect his outrageously ambitious project. They both knew in their different fashions that the challenge was to connect knowing and being; or, to put it another way, to convert experience into energy, into the power to be in one's real world. And for the poet the job had to be do-able in the medium of words.

The pre-requisite is intense emotion. The trouble with young Aldington's poems, Pound explained to Alice Henderson, was that they fell apart for lack of it. 'There must be intense emotion before language simplifies itself to the point of Imagism'. The greater the emotional energy, the greater the compression and 'the austerity or economy of the speech'. Emotion is 'the fusing, arranging, unifying force'. It is the primary energy; it 'causes pattern to arise in the mind'; it is an organizer of form in the poem; it creates that 'vortex or cluster of fused ideas...endowed with energy' which is what Pound meant by 'the Image'.

Another way of putting that was to call it 'an intellectual and emotional complex'. There he was using 'the term "complex" rather in the technical sense employed by the newer psychologists, such as Hart'. Bernard Hart,

'Fellow of University College, London; Physician in Psychological Medicine', contributed to the *New Age* in 1912 and 1913 and published *The Psychology of Insanity* in the 'Cambridge Manuals of Science and Literature' series in 1912. In a chapter on 'Complexes', following acknowledgments to the recent researches of 'Prof. Freud of Vienna and Dr Jung of Zürich', Hart declared his aim to be 'ascertaining the causes determining the flow of our consciousness', and 'the elucidation of the real springs of action'. He then found 'complexes' to be 'at any rate partially responsible for the direction of our thoughts and actions'; and so defined 'a complex' as 'a system of connected ideas, with a strong emotional tone, and a tendency to produce actions of a certain definite character'. As a clinician he was most interested in the extreme forms which lead to abnormally obsessive behaviour; but his starting point was the observation that even our 'normal' everyday living is governed by the forces of unconscious complexes.

Evidently Pound, in defining his Image as 'an intellectual and emotional complex', was intending that it should shape and give a definite direction to thought and action. 'The strength of the arts', he had written, is that 'Their statement is a statement of motor forces'—of what motivates action. He was thinking of inner, instinctive motives, of the aroused and focused desires and hates that are the natural springs of action. And he was thinking that these, in the form of image-complexes, or *Gestalten*, would be 'germinal', would be 'thought-seed' and 'the seed of civilization'. There are some minds, he wrote in 'Psychology and Troubadours', whose 'thoughts are in them as the thought of the tree is in the seed . . . and these minds are the more poetic, and they affect mind about them, and transmute it as the seed the earth.'

And this sort of mind, he added, 'is close on the vital universe' and is its interpreter. Elsewhere he remarked that the 'order-giving vibrations' which the good artist can produce may be merely his giving a specific form or mode to 'such part of the life force as flows through him'. The shaping power then would be the life force itself, what we term 'nature'. That would be directing the individual to act out his own nature. Beyond that, it would be working through individuals to bring about a social order based, as we loosely say, on 'the nature of things'.

The technique of *Imagisme*—'direct presentation of the "thing" whether subjective or objective', 'absolutely no word that does not contribute to the presentation', find the natural 'musical phrase'—was a technique for the precise, scientific, expression of that process of the life force in and through the individual mind. It was designed to serve and to be the agent of the process whereby the human mind can be the intelligence of its sphere of existence, by discovering the natures of the things which concern it and thus coming to act in accord with them.

The 'sense of sudden liberation' and of 'sudden growth' comes with the discovery of the true nature of things. The liberation is from clichés and conventions which prevent fresh thought and obstruct the free action of intelligence; it is liberation from false consciousness and acting in bad faith; and it is liberation from the rhetoric and cant of poor poets and of conformist teachers and preachers and politicians. The growth is the becoming aware of and coming alive in one's real mode of existence, a consciousness which is empowering and energizing. And the liberation and the growth together bring a joyous confidence in the sustaining and directing life force.

'Go in fear of abstractions', Pound warned the neophyte. The general theory I have been constructing opens up a beguiling prospect, but the proof of it must be in particular poems. And it would not be put fully to the proof until Pound was well into the *Cantos*. His strictly *Imagiste* poems, such as those he selected 'to fit the formula' of the 1914 anthology, were no more than very small-scale experiments in the scientific presentation of psychic phenomena. But at least they were particular and they were practising what the theory called for.[4]

Dora Marsden also issued frequent warnings against the lure of generalizations and abstractions, and yet all her thinking remained generalized and abstract. She wanted thinking to be 'a definite process to liberate not *thoughts* but living impulses . . . to liberate life ready for action, not to bind it up to construct a system'. Yet she would give up her life to developing her Egoism into a philosophical system. She called for 'Images . . . which can magnetize the vital power, first to Attention and thereafter to Action'. Yet she could neither create nor appreciate such images. She argued that the individual must construct its own self and world in words, anticipating Wallace Stevens and such a poem as his 'Idea of Order at Key West', but she had not the words for the creative act.

She was driven rather to deconstruct and even, if it were possible, to destroy the common language. She declared war on words 'in their every aspect: grammar, accidence, syntax: body, blood and bone', because by their centuries-acquired meanings they had become the powerful instruments whereby Authority stupefied and beat down Individuality. She could be 'at home only in that aura of images which is thrown off from the living "I"'. But all the time she was driving herself deeper into a solipsistic

---

[4] Pound's six poems were: 'Δώρια', 'The Return', 'After Ch'u Yuan', 'Liu Ch'e', 'Fan-Piece for Her Imperial Lord', 'Ts'ai Chi'h'—two after the Greek, four after the Chinese.

isolation. As she had no use for the common language, so she had no use for the cultural heritage. Nor did she have any time for the existing social order. Those things which were for Pound the great resources of his art, and the world in which and for which to practise it, held nothing of value to her.

In 1920 when *The Egoist* ceased publication Dora Marsden retired on her own to write in a former miner's cottage in 'Seldom Seen', a row of ten small dwellings standing alone on the fellside in a hidden valley above Ullswater in the Lake District. The scenery is magnificent there and it is grand country for walking, but she did not walk and took no interest in her surroundings. She produced two volumes (of a projected seven) of her great philosophical work, and Miss Weaver revived the Egoist Press to publish them in 1928 and 1930. A reviewer in the *TLS* of *The Definition of the Godhead* (1928) observed that it depended on 'a belief in the vision of immediate truth bestowed on the primitive "mythopoeic" mind which many may hesitate to accept'. When there was in effect no acceptance at all of her work she broke down, and for twenty-five years, from 1935 until her death in 1960, she was a patient in Crichton Royal Hospital for the mentally ill, in Dumfries, Scotland. It was a terrible decline for a brave and brilliant spirit.

'The image', Pound wrote when he was converting *Imagisme* into Vorticism, 'is a radiant node or cluster; it is...a VORTEX, from which, and through which, and into which, ideas are constantly rushing.' His *Imagiste* moment had been just such a vortex of ideas and inspirations. His very early thinking about the symbolic imagination in Dante and Blake and Yeats is in there, together with the 'mythopoetic' mind of the Celtic Twilight and of H.D. The idea of the 'luminous detail' is in there, expanded now to encompass 'great works of art' as 'lords over fact, over race-long recurrent moods, and over to-morrow'. The idea of the artist as Osiris is in there, of the artist as the agent of the organizing, civilizing intelligence at work in the world. Altogether, *Imagisme* was a crystallization of everything he had thought and learnt about the art and use of poetry up to the year 1912 or 1913.

Also in there were Hulme's talk of the image, and perhaps even some contamination from his lectures on Bergson and the *élan vital*. Certainly Hueffer's talk of the scientific virtue of prose was a basic component. There would have been some reaction to Flint's redefining French *Symbolisme* as 'an attempt to evoke the subconscious element of life, to set vibrating the infinity within us, by the exquisite iuxtaposition of images.' Kandinsky on painting was drawn in. Pound mentioned his *Ueber das Geistige in der*

Kunst in the first number of *BLAST*, and one finds this formulation in a selection from it earlier in the same number: 'The development of art ... is a progressive expression of the eternally objective within the temporarily subjective.' Hart, as a representative of 'the newer psychology', was drawn in. Philosophical provocations from Dora Marsden played their part. The theory, so far as there was a theory, drew in many and various ideas that were in the air of the time.

Yet for all that it was not a complete theory of art. Its attention is all on the precise imaging of psychic or spiritual realities, with little apparent concern for or connection with the actualities of the common world. Pound's modern epigrams were deliberately excluded from *Des Imagistes* on that account. But on all other occasions his epigrams and his strictly *imagiste* poems appeared together, as if in symbiosis, each requiring the other. 'The cult of beauty and the delineation of ugliness are not in mutual opposition', he declared in 'The Serious Artist', they are as necessary to each other as diagnosis and cure. The cure is 'sun, air and the sea and the rain and the lake bathing'; it is 'a swift moving thought in Plato' or 'a fine line in a statue'; it is even 'this pother about gods'. And for diagnosis there is the satire and naturalistic realism of, for example, Villon, Corbière, Flaubert—and, he might have added, of Ford Madox Hueffer.

Whatever he meant by the inclusion in *Des Imagistes* of Hueffer's 'In the Little Old Market-Place', its effect was to provide something in the way of a complement to the rest, but also to throw them into critical relief. In an appendix Pound included a glib parody by Aldington of Hueffer's mannerisms, as if to remark how his conversational method disobeyed the rule of absolute economy of language. But then he followed it with Hueffer's devastating retort. This was a parody of Aldington's 'Au Vieux Jardin', a poem printed in the anthology. Hueffer transliterated his own English words letter by letter, schoolboy fashion, into pseudo-Greek, and added some genuine Greek interjections out of Sappho and Xenophon. He was making fun of Aldington's Hellenism, insinuating that his imitation Greek lyrics were the weak products of an immature mind. The point was sharpened and driven home by his citing Xenophon's *Anabasis* in such a way as to imply that grown-ups would prefer to imitate him, Xenophon having been a historian who registered the events of his own time, and the characters of those who shaped them, in the living speech of the time.

Hueffer had called for contemporary poets to do that, to register their own times in terms of their own time, in the preface to his *Collected Poems* (1914) which appeared in 1913 in both *Poetry* and *The New Freewoman*. As a personal instance of what for him was 'the real stuff of the poetry

231

of our day' he described how he went one night to the Shepherd's Bush exhibition in London,

and came out on a great square of white buildings all outlined with lights. There was such a lot of light—and I think that what I hope for in Heaven is an infinite clear radiance of pure light! There were crowds and crowds of people—or no, there was, spread out beneath the lights, an infinite moving mass of black, with white faces turned up to the light, moving slowly, quickly, not moving at all, being obscured, reappearing.

This surely is intended to recall Pound's account of how he came to write 'In a Station of the Metro': 'I got out of a train at, I think, La Concorde, and in the jostle I saw a beautiful face, and then, turning suddenly, another and another, and then a beautiful child's face, and then another beautiful face'. And the eventual outcome of that apparition was 'Petals on a wet black bough'. Hueffer's response to the faces in his crowd is the reverse of Pound's. Instead of condensing and refining them to 'petals' he looks for their individual characters and stories, as if they were Japanese paper flowers which would open themselves up in his imagination. He notes 'the larking of the anaemic girls', and 'the idealism of a pickpocket slanting through a shadow and imagining himself a hero whose end will be wealth and permanent apartments in the Savoy Hotel.' And he reflects that 'the anaemic shop-girl at the Exhibition, with her bad teeth and her cheap black frock, is [a safer card for the poet to play] than Isolde. She is more down to the ground and much more touching.'

One might be tempted to say that Hueffer had the novelist's approach, and that the poet's mind works in a different fashion. Pound did not take that line. He knew that to be the sort of poet he meant to become, and to write his 'poem containing history', he would have to find his own way of doing what Hueffer recommended. He too would have to follow the example of Xenophon, and of Flaubert. *Imagisme* was an emphasis only, not the whole art.

Odd ends

By the time the slim 64-page *Des Imagistes* was issued in London in 1914 the much more substantial *Georgian Poetry 1911–1912*, also published by The Poetry Bookshop, was into its ninth printing. Edward Marsh's poets—Lascelles Abercrombie, Gordon Bottomley, Rupert Brooke, and a dozen more of the poetical establishment—were the talk of the town. Marsh presented them as heralding a great new age of English poetry. Pound was sarcastic: 'Those who have read the *Lyric Year*—[a hundred poems by a hundred American poets]—with interest will peruse this anthology with deepest admiration'. When he told Harriet Monroe's readers that English poetry was dead it was the 'Georgians' in particular he was burying. But the power for the time was with them, and naturally they looked down on *Imagisme* with uncomprehending derision.

Pound reviewed Frost's *A Boy's Will* (1913) enthusiastically, both in *Poetry* and *The New Freewoman*. But Frost, although it was the first recognition his work received, was ungrateful. He feared Pound's recommendation would do him no good with his Georgian contacts in London, nor with American editors and publishers. He felt misunderstood and patronized, even bullied by Pound's advice that 'his North of Boston series was the next thing for him to do'. He supposed Pound 'meant to be generous', but on the whole he was aggrieved at being 'discovered' by him. William Carlos Williams, on the other hand, appears not to have resented Pound's introducing his work in *The Poetry Review*, encouraging Elkin Mathews to publish *The Tempers*, his first collection, and then promoting it with a 'tactful' review in *The New Freewoman*.

A 'College of the Arts' was still high on Pound's wish-list. In his *New Age* articles he proposed that it should respect the individuality of its artists and require nothing of them save to present the thing as they saw it; that it should be 'guided by an almost blind hatred of mediocrity'; that therefore there should be no professors; and that it should be funded by persuading millionaires to invest in a renaissance.

In 1913 someone, possibly Allen Upward, announced in *The New Free-woman* the setting up of 'An Order of Individualists' to be known as 'The Angel Club'—'Angels' in this case meaning 'Overmen'—to foster genius for the general good. The order was to be somewhat monastic—its members, to find freedom of mind, would retire from the 'territories of the Moneylenders trading as Christiandom (*alias* the Concert of Europe, *alias* the British Empire, *alias* the American People, etc., etc.)'. Pound responded that he could not afford to retire, and that, besides, 'My natural cruelty permits me to take some pleasure in the antics of a capital'. But, he asked, could not an order of secular lay persons be attached to the monastic order, an 'Order of the Brothers Minor', consisting of 'poor men who must for food's sake, as well as for art's sake, remain scattered abroad in the world'? The artists should of course be subsidized; and they might be regarded as 'the church of *Genius in Crucem*'.

That last flourish looks like an in-joke, since Upward had written that it is the fate of genius—that is, of the man who is a vortex of the vital universe—to be crucified rather than honoured by his fellow citizens. Pound's own idea of the fate of the artist in the modern world was pitched at a less exalted level, seeing the artist as heretic rather than Christ. As 'the only modern heresy is an uncontrollable propensity for telling the truth', he wrote, the artist must suffer the modern penalty, not the stake, but 'starvation, or at least forced and irregular fasting, which doth little good to the soul'. That has the ring of personal experience to it. He felt good being a heretic, but could have done without the poverty.

In October 1913 he had another bout of jaundice. There is a photograph taken at the time by Alvin Langdon Coburn, showing him in his dressing-gown. Both his landlady and Frederic Manning noted a likeness to 'the good man of Nazareth'. Dorothy's father thought it a portrait of 'a sinister but very brilliant Italian'. Pound himself thought it a suitable frontispiece for his *Lustra* (1916).

Ralph Fletcher Seymour, who published *Poetry*, was seeking manuscripts and agreed to publish Pound's translations of Arnaut Daniel, and also his *New Age* articles on America. In March 1913 he issued a handsome 'Announcement' calling for 150 subscriptions for '*The Canzoni of Arnaut Daniel*, Translated by Ezra Pound, with original music transcribed by Walter Morse Rummell'. The limited edition 'of three hundred copies on hand-made paper and ten copies on Japan Vellum' would be 'designed and printed . . . in the style of the fifteenth century printers', and the size would be 8 x 11 inches. It would have been a very fine book, but, due to insufficient interest, the project was cancelled. The revised version of 'Patria Mia' and 'America: Chances and Remedies' did not appear either, due to Seymour's entering into a new partnership.

Also in this year, 1913, Pound sent so much as he had ready of his 'Lustra' to a publisher, but with no immediate result. Since he was later to explain the title with reference to '*Lustrum*: an offering for the sins of the whole people, made by the censors at the expiration of their five years of office', he may well have been thinking that his five years of censuring the English were up, counting from his arrival in 1908.

John Cournos, a Russian-born poet and journalist from Philadelphia, observed Pound in London about this time:

If you saw Ezra in the street for the first time, you'd notice him . . . this tall distinguished looking young man with a shock of red hair flaming backward and his sharp red beard poised at a forward-downward angle and well-shaped features and deep-set blue eyes . . .

His salient impression as he watched him in a pub on the occasion of their first meeting was

234

of almost exuberant kindliness. And Ezra, as I had cause later to find out, was one of the kindest men that ever lived. . . . He likewise revealed a keen interest in any stranger he met, casting upon him an appraising eye, taking prompt stock of the furnishings of his mind, annexing him if he proved worthwhile with a frank eagerness I never met in anyone else.

Cournos himself, as Charles Norman remarked, was promptly 'annexed'. Pound introduced him into the circles he moved in, included him in *Des Imagistes*, and gave him practical assistance as a writer. When he moved out of Church Walk Cournos 'inherited' the room.

He could be violent in a good cause. Yeats casually complained about the India Society being mean with complimentary copies of Tagore's *Gitanjali*, and then had to write an apology because Pound had passed on the complaint rather forcefully:

I assumed that he had done it in the way that is customary among the faint energies of our dying European civilization . . . He is a headlong ragged nature, is always hurting people's feelings, but he has I think some genius and great good will . . . Hercules cannot help seeming a little more than life size in our European Garden of the Hesperides. His voice is too loud, his stride too resounding.

Yeats had his own view of the poetry Pound was writing. *Poetry* awarded him its £50 prize for the best poem published in the magazine in 1913, and he agreed to accept £10, but suggested that the greater part be given to Pound. His recommendation was strong, certainly strong enough to be accepted by the editors, but there were strong reservations also:

although I do not really like with my whole soul the metrical experiments he has made for you, I think those experiments show a vigorous creative mind. He is certainly a creative personality of some sort, though it is too soon yet to say of what sort. His experiments are perhaps errors, I am not certain; but I would always sooner give the laurel to vigorous errors than to any orthodoxy not inspired.

Pound spent his £40 on a new typewriter and on two small sculptures by his newly discovered friend Henri Gaudier-Brzeska.

12 : GOING TO WAR: 1913–1915

One day in the summer of 1913 Pound was looking round an art show in the Albert Hall with Olivia Shakespear—it was acceptable for him to be seen with her—and was (by his own account) playing the fool with 'the appalling assemblage of consonants' in 'Brzeska', when the sculptor himself darted from behind his 'Wrestler' and told him, 'with the gentlest fury in the world', it is 'Jaersh-ka'. He seemed to Pound 'a well-made young wolf or some soft-moving, bright-eyed wild thing', who declared 'C'est moi qui les ai sculptés', and 'disappeared like a Greek god in a vision'. Pound tracked him down to his studio, half of a mud-floored railway arch in Putney, and found a 21-year-old Frenchman who was alarmingly intelligent and possessed by such a 'daemon of energy' that even 'his stillness seemed an action'. To impress the young artist Pound did his 'Altaforte' and 'Pierre Vidal', and it was his impersonation of de Born's furious lusting after war that 'convinced him that I would do to be sculpted'. Over the next year and a half Pound would delight in his fierce energy and intelligence, in the stimulus of their 'long, gay, electrified arguments', in Gaudier's eye for 'the dominant line in objects', and in his marvellous powers of drawing and sculpting. He was '*the* coming sculptor', likely to equal Epstein. 'The most absolute case of genius' Pound ever ran into. A year into the war Henri Gaudier-Brzeska would be killed in action, *mort pour la patrie* at 23.[1]

---

[1] Henri Gaudier-Brzeska (1891–1915), b. Henri Gaudier in St Jean de Braye, near Orléans, son of a carpenter. In 1907, on a French Government scholarship, studied business methods at a College in Bristol; in 1908 worked for a firm of coal exporters in Cardiff—in both places was always sketching and drawing. April 1909 to Nuremberg then Munich, where he drew figures and faces in the ghetto for 'a Rembrandt factory'. In Paris early 1910 met Sophie Brzeska, a Polish woman; when they moved to London together in January 1911 he added her name to his. Henri, now determined to be a sculptor, had no money and found work as a typist and foreign correspondent in the City, starting at thirty shillings a week. In 1912 began to get small commissions, and to meet writers and artists; though still poor gave up his City job in mid-1913 to sculpt full time; by 1914, now one of the Vorticists, was being

Pound was finding more *virtu* in certain sculptors and painters than in his fellow *Imagistes*. Along with young Gaudier there was Epstein whom Pound had met at Hulme's gatherings, already notorious for his monumental Oscar Wilde tomb in Paris, and now bringing a new kind of art into England. In February 1914 Pound admired, without precisely knowing why, his 'green granite, female, apparently pregnant monster with one eye going around a square corner.' It was undeniably 'a new beauty'. And it was evidently the work of an artist aroused to the fact that the war between art and the unbearable stupidity of humanity 'is a war without truce' and that 'his only remedy is slaughter'. After further consideration, in March, Pound was beginning to comprehend the work in his own terms: 'The green flenite woman expresses all the tragedy and enigma of the germinal universe', he wrote; and it was like 'the gods of the Epicureans' in its unrelenting representation of 'the immutable, the calm thoroughness of unchanging relations'. It would therefore infuriate minds attuned to *The Times* and its notion of news. There was no mention on that occasion of recourse to war and slaughter.

Pound remarked to Epstein that he found his and Gaudier's sculpture more interesting than Wyndham Lewis's painting, and Epstein said 'But Lewis's drawing has the qualities of sculpture'. That set Pound off looking at Lewis's work.[2] He had known Lewis for years without getting on terms with him, and now he found in the drawing and design of his *Timon* (1913) an expression of his own inner state and what he took to be that of his generation—'the sullen fury of intelligence baffled, shut in by the entrenched forces of stupidity'. He saw Lewis then as 'a man at war', a man engaged as he himself was in the everlasting, 'traditional struggle...of driving the shaft of intelligence into the dull mass of mankind'. Theirs was the war of 'the intelligent god...incarnate in the universe, in struggle with the endless inertia.' 'And we', Pound declared, 'will sweep out the past century as surely as Attila swept across Europe.' He acknowledged Lewis as his generation's 'most articulate voice'; gave the name 'Vorticism' to his

---

compared to Epstein. Returned to France to enlist at the outbreak of the war and was killed by a bullet in the forehead at Neuville St Vaast near Arras 5 June 1915.

[2] Wyndham Lewis (1882–1957), English artist and writer. Studied at the Slade 1898–1901, then moved about Spain, Holland, Germany, and France until 1909. Published first stories in Hueffer's *English Review*; exhibited in group shows in London from 1911; joined Roger Fry's Omega Workshops July–October 1913; formed his own Rebel Art Centre March 1914; edited and wrote much of the Vorticist *BLAST No. 1* (June 1914) and *BLAST No. 2* (July 1915). *Tarr*, his first novel, serialized in *Egoist* in 1916–17. Joined army as gunner 1916; seconded as war artist December 1917. First one-man show February 1919. Thereafter continued painting until blindness stopped him in 1951; and wrote prolifically in many forms. Described himself, Pound, Joyce, and Eliot as 'the men of 1914'.

effort; and became his ally in *BLAST: Review of the Great English Vortex* in 1914 and 1915.

Another important addition to Pound's inner circle about this time was Allen Upward, a thinker rather than an artist, but nonetheless a combatant in the revolt of intelligence 'against the crushing dominion of the stupid classes'.[3] Pound associated him with 'the forces of intelligence', both for his original perceptions of the slow advance of those forces in modern as much as primal societies, and because he saw his work as itself a force for liberation from ingrained superstitions and ignorance. He particularly noticed in *The Divine Mystery* (1913) Upward's connecting individual genius or intelligence with sensitivity to the vital universe, and his looking for a civilization founded upon that order of intelligence. There he would have been finding confirmation of his own thinking. But Upward started him off in a new direction by putting him on to the Chinese classics. He had him reading Confucius and Mencius in French in October 1913, and he would have shown him his own selection of *The Sayings of Confucius* (1904). That was one of the 'Wisdom of the East' books brought out by a small press he had set up in Fleet Street with a friend, as an act of resistance to the stupidities of its newspapers.

In a short while Pound would be writing that 'China has replaced Greece in the intellectual life of so many occidentals'. He had found his 'new Greece' at last, not in Bengal but in the moralized history, the philosophy and the poetry of Confucian China. In time, if not immediately, he would follow Upward in reading the Confucian classics as a record and an illustrious example of good government. Confucius 'was first and foremost a practical statesman', Upward wrote, and his real monument

is not the literary canon associated with his name, but the Chinese Empire itself, the greatest and most enduring of human societies, under whose shelter nearly a third of the human race have lived in comparative civilisation and happiness from an age far antedating the foundation of Troy or the Exodus of the Hebrews, down to the present day, and which, during that vast period, has been known to those who inhabit it as the Heavenly Kingdom.

Confucius, by his own exemplary life and by editing the classic anthology of ancient Chinese poetry, had placed before his countrymen the ideal of

---

[3] Allen Upward (1863–1926), English barrister, writer, scholar; political activist while practising in Cardiff 1890–96; 1897 volunteer soldier in Greek army when it invaded Turkey; 1901 appointed Resident administering two provinces in Nigeria—back in England by 1908. Contributed to *New Age* and *New Freewoman*; wrote plays, romantic novels, poems; his two serious and original contributions to thinking about the origins and developments of religions and cultures, *The New Word* (1907), and *The Divine Mystery* (1913), went unnoticed by the institutions of scholarship. Took up school-teaching, Head Master of Inverness College 1916. Committed suicide 1926.

'an empire governed by the wise, under the shield of a sacred dynasty, in the interest, and for the happiness, of the humble'; and, averred Upward, to the realization of this ideal 'the efforts of Chinese statesmen have been directed ever since'. Pound would find, however, when he came to make his digest of the official histories of that empire, in cantos 52–61, that the ideal was rarely realized, and that the drama was all in the efforts to overcome the damage done by unenlightened emperors. Even in the Heavenly Kingdom there was war against 'the unbearable stupidity of humanity'.

'I seem to be getting orient from all quarters', Pound exclaimed to Dorothy in October 1913. Beside Upward's Confucius, and 'real Japanese prints' at Harriet Shaw Weaver's house in Hampstead, he had just been introduced by a Bengali poet to the widow of a very distinguished scholar of the traditional arts of Japan, Ernest Fenollosa.[4] Mary McNeil Fenollosa had prepared the manuscript of his *Epochs of Chinese and Japanese Art* (1912) for publication. Now she was looking for a suitable person to entrust with the notebooks containing her late husband's studies in the Noh plays of Japan and the poetry of ancient China. It had to be someone who 'cared about the poetry not about the philology', and Pound, she decided almost at once, was the only person who could finish 'a book on the Japanese drama & an anthology of chinese poets' in the way Fenollosa would have wanted. She gave him the notebooks and other manuscripts unconditionally, while hoping 'that you will become really interested in the material, absorb it in your own way, and then make practically new translations'. Coming to him at just the moment when his interest in 'the orient' had been aroused this was a windfall to wonder at. 'It is a very great opportunity', Pound wrote home, and 'Like everything worth having it has come out of a clear sky without any effort on my part.' Mrs Fenollosa even 'got £40 out of someone so that I might have a little spare time to get started'; and 'said I was to have all I could make out

---

[4] Ernest Fenollosa (1853–1908): b. Salem, Massachusetts; graduated Harvard 1874; appointed Professor of Political Economy and Philosophy, University of Tokyo, 1878. Drawn to study traditional art of Japan and China, instigated its preservation; 1882 began study of Noh drama; 1885 recommended re-introduction into schools of purely Japanese art techniques, and drew up plans for national Art Museum; confirmed in *Tendai* Sect of esoteric Buddhism; 1886 appointed Commissioner of Fine Arts, responsible both for the teaching of art in schools and registering and conserving all the art treasures of Japan; formally honoured by Emperor and accorded Court rank. 1890 accepted appointment as Curator of Oriental Art, Boston Museum of Fine Arts; told by the Emperor: 'You have taught my people to know their own art; in going back to your great country, I charge you, teach them also.' Instigated a new system of art education in America, assisted by Arthur Wesley Dow. 1896–1900 returned to Japan, intensified studies in Buddhism, renewed research into Noh and Chinese poetry. 1900–08 mainly in USA, lecturing, writing *Epochs of Chinese and Japanese Art* (1912). Died London 1908. 1909 his ashes re-interred in the temple grounds of Miidera, Lake Biwa.

of it'. In fact the financial return would not have paid for a typist and most of the work was done at his own cost. But the real value of what he had been given was immeasurable. Thanks to Upward and Mrs Fenollosa he now had the makings of his new Greece, his China, which would be a lifelong resource in the struggle to remain sane while fighting the world.

Spirits at Stone Cottage

Yeats retired into the country to write in tranquillity from early November 1913 through to mid-January 1914. He took Pound with him, to act as secretary, taking dictation and looking after his business correspondence; to read to him after dark so as to save his chronically troubled eyes; and for conversation and companionship. The two poets would spend the ten weeks or so in a hum of creativity, composing, writing, reading; listening to and discussing each other's work; walking and talking in the woods and lanes; fencing for exercise when the weather was bad. The cottage Yeats was renting faced a heath of scattered birch trees and bracken—'wild moorland' it seemed to Pound in its winter state, 'with curious dark colours'. At its back were the ancient pine woods of Ashdown Forest. Four of the six rooms were theirs; and they had their cooking and housekeeping done for them by Alice and Ellen Wellfare, sisters who lived in the other two rooms. There was a Post Office within walking distance at Coleman's Hatch, and an inn for cider. The station was Forest Row, two miles further on, and Yeats reckoned the journey to London at an hour and a half. He went up every week, for a session with his current Soho medium whose voices and automatic writing he was eagerly investigating, and to keep his Monday Evenings going. Pound also went up most weeks, to keep up with the London Vortex and to see Dorothy if her arrangements permitted. He had expected to be disgusted with the country and bored to death by Yeats carrying on about his psychical research. Yeats too must have had his apprehensions about being shut up for days at a time with his young Hercules. But as it turned out he found him 'a learned companion and a pleasant one', and was able to tell Lady Gregory that it was 'the best winter I have had in years'. For his part Pound found Yeats 'much finer *intime* than seen spasmodically in the midst of the whirl.' The two of them were 'very contented', he informed Williams in mid-December. He was 'very placid and happy and busy'.

He was reading Confucius, and deciphering Fenollosa's notes on Noh plays. That would have had him moving between two very different worlds. The 'Confucius' would have been Pauthier's *Doctrine de Confucius:*

Les Quatre Livres de philosophie morale et politique de la Chine (Paris, 1841), containing *The Analects* and the two books which Pound would translate as *The Great Digest* and *The Unwobbling Pivot*. We can get a good idea of what he made of this reading from the way he condensed it into canto 13. There his Confucius is concerned for the proper ordering of the family and of the state, and finds the basis of order in being true to one's own individual nature: 'If a man have not order within him / He cannot spread order about him'. 'And Kung', Pound emphasizes, 'said nothing of the "life after death"'.

The Noh plays, in absolute contrast, can appear to be concerned with little else. They feature encounters with spirits of the dead troubled by what they have done or left undone while they were among the living. The first play Pound put into a finished form from Fenollosa's very rough crib was *Nishikigi*—he sent it to *Poetry* before the end of January 1914. A wandering priest comes upon a man and a woman whom he takes to be man and wife. In fact they are 'the ghosts of two lovers who died unmarried a hundred years before'. He had courted her for three years, night after night placing at her door the *nishikigi*, the crimson wands declaring his love; but she had gone on with her weaving, so that night after night for response he heard only the click-click of her loom through the window. He died of despair, and she, then regretting her cruelty, died too. But in death they have been as in life, together and apart like the warp and weft of a coarse cloth. It needs the priest's prayer for their union to bring it about, and the play ends with the spirits' marriage dance, followed by the fading of the vision.

In these plays, Fenollosa had written, 'we see great characters operating under the conditions of spirit-life', and it was this that had made them 'a storehouse of history, and a great moral force for the whole social order of the Samurai.' That would have been enough to interest Yeats in what Pound was doing, since it was close to what he and Lady Gregory were looking for in the folk-tales of the Irish peasantry. He could think of an Arran legend, recorded in Lady Gregory's *Visions and Beliefs in the West of Ireland*, similar to that of the ghost lovers. Beyond that he was to find a new inspiration for his own plays for the Irish Theatre—*At the Hawk's Well* (1917) and *The Dreaming of the Bones* (1919) would be closely modelled on the Noh, the latter drawing directly on *Nishikigi*. But his first response was to exclaim, 'Nearly all that my fat old woman in Soho'—meaning his medium—'learns from her familiars is there in an unsurpassed lyric poetry and in strange and poignant fables once danced or sung in the houses of nobles.' The plays brought more grist to his ghost mill.

Much of what he had Pound read to him that winter was concerned with ghosts and spirits and their communications. A favourite was Joseph Ennemoser's *The History of Magic*, with its appendix 'of the Most Remarkable and Best Authenticated Stories of Apparitions, Dreams, Second Sight, Somnanbulism, Predictions, Divination, Witchcraft, Vampires, Fairies, Table-Turning, and Spirit-Rapping'. Pound would recall Yeats 'hearing nearly all Wordsworth / for the sake of his conscience but / preferring Ennemoser on Witches'.

Did Pound share Yeats's fascination with what is loosely called 'the occult', as some have argued? His close association with Yeats and Olivia Shakespear and with others in their circle, with Mead and his circle, even with Orage, certainly meant that he was in the thick of it. Then there's the fact that he owned a copy of *De Daemonalitate, et Incubis et Succubis*, 'a nineteenth-century occult tract' pretending to be the work of 'the Rev. Father Sinistrari of Ameno (1600 circ.)'. He seems to have interested Yeats in the book, for he told his father that Yeats wanted it and asked for it to be sent over. Furthermore, in his youth in America, he had been under the spell of Katherine Ruth Heyman, who is known to have been deep into spiritualism and all that. There can be no denying that he was exposed to 'the occult'. But did it 'take'?

As soon as we give some definition to the term by restricting it to what it meant for Yeats at this time it becomes clear that Pound kept his distance from his occultism. So too, for that matter, did Mead and Orage who had no time for mediums and their false mysteries. What Yeats was after was evidence that the human spirit survived the body and lived on at least in its memories. The still passionate memory of the dead, he believed or wanted to believe, would be caught up into the collective Great Mcmory which animated the world of the living. So he sought communications from the passionate dead, even through shilling mediums in Soho frequented by shop-girls, and through séances and table-rapping and automatic writing. He was to attribute to what his spirits told him through his wife's automatic writing the gain in substance and power in his later poetry. To Pound though, Yeats's carrying on with ghosts seemed rather a loss of intelligence. 'He will be quite sensible', he told John Quinn in 1918, 'till some question of ghosts or occultism comes up, then he is subject to a curious excitement, twists everything to his theory, usual quality of mind goes.'

Pound did not take part in séances, consult mediums, or enter the Hermetic Order of the Golden Dawn. When he wanted access to the collective memory he went to the great library in the British Museum and read the communications of the dead in their writings. As he saw it, the way in which their thought would animate the world was by poets new-minting it—refining the tradition, he called it. And this was not a matter for mystification. 'As the abstract mathematician is to science so is the poet to the world's consciousness', he declared in 'The Wisdom of Poetry'; and 'neither of them is superhuman or arrives at his utility through occult and inexplicable ways.'

He very likely thought that his own powers of mental vision were superior to those of Yeats's 'fat old woman in Soho'. When Dorothy asked at their first meeting 'Have you ever seen things in a crystal?' he answered 'I see things without a crystal'. Blake might have given such an answer. The real difficulty about seeing the truth of things, for Pound as for Blake, was not that the truth is concealed from us in occult mystery, but that we must look for it with the mind's eye, with the eye which sees not only outward appearances but can penetrate them with insight. So a tree, to take an instance from Upward, is a fountain of energy. Blake would have said it was a fountain of divine life. Pound too cultivated those states of mind in which the universe came alive to him, as to Acoetes in his vision of the Dionysiac sea in canto 2. But then he wanted to see with the same clarity into the making and unmaking of societies and civilizations. And for this he went after the luminous details to be won from the intelligent reading of historical documents. He wanted the revealing facts, as he wanted the natural image that had the life-force in it. He had no use for Yeats's ghosts. '"Intellectual vision" is, acc. Wm. Blake & others, the surest cure for ghosts', or so he told Dorothy, writing from Stone Cottage in November 1913.

He was not a rationalist dismissing psychic experience as a disorder of the brain. He knew the value and the use of seeing things 'not with the bodily vision'. But he also knew that such vision should extend the reach of intelligence, and satisfy reason, not flout it. After a lecture by Mead on '"The Book of the Hidden Mysteries" by Hierotheos'—a Neoplatonic meditation on the state of the spirits in the heaven of heavens—Pound advised his mother 'before embarking on these affairs . . . fortify your mind with the simplicities of Aristotle & Aquinas.'

As for what he thought of Yeats's Rosicrucianism, we can make a fair guess from his summing up of the Nineties, in effect Yeats's Nineties, as a 'period of funny symboliste trappings, "sin", satanism, rosy cross, heavy lilies, Jersey Lilies, etc.', in short yet another in the sequence of 'periods [which] had mislaid the light of the eighteenth century'. Like the dead souls in Dante's hell they had lost the clear light of, let us say Voltaire's or Johnson's, critical intelligence: 'hanno perduto il ben dell'intelletto'.

When Yeats had worked out in full the system derived from his wife's automatic writing between 1917 and 1920 and had written it up as *A*

Vision, he prefaced it with 'A Packet for Ezra Pound'. 'You will hate these generalities, Ezra', he wrote, having acknowledged that Pound's art was the opposite of his own, and that Pound's criticism commended what he most condemned. He was a man with whom Yeats 'should quarrel more than with anyone else—if we were not united by affection'.

Towards the end of their first winter at Stone Cottage Pound organized an event designed 'to gather from the air a live tradition'. Perhaps he intended to show Yeats how to do that. On Sunday January 18 a party of poets met at Woburn Buildings to go down in a hired motor to honour Wilfred Scawen Blunt at his home, 'a sixteenth-century defensible grange in Sussex'.[5] Each of them brought one hand-written and signed poem to be placed in a small coffer 'carved in Pentelican marble by the brilliant young sculptor Gaudier Brzeska, ornamented with a female nude recumbent and an inscription, "Homage to Wilfred Blunt"'. There is a photograph of the occasion, with a bewhiskered Blunt in the middle, Yeats, Sturge Moore, and Plarr on his right, and the younger generation of Pound, Aldington, and Flint on his left. Waistcoats were worn, and stiff collars, except that Pound's was one of his 'floppy ones', and Yeats—he was about to do a lecture tour in the United States—sported a bow tie. They dined on roast peacock, at Yeats's request it was said. Whether he meant it as an emblem of nobility or of pride and vanity is not recorded. The poets read their poems—Pound's was 'The Return'. The coffer was presented, with Pound praising Blunt for going his own way, making mock of the world and its institutions, writing fine verses, and upholding Mazzini. There were speeches. Yeats was autobiographical. Blunt, in reply, said he had only written poetry when he had nothing better to do or was down on his luck; that what he had been admired for was taking up the cause of the Indian or the Egyptian, and for his horse-breeding; that he appreciated the verses just read to him, if they were verse—he had waited for a rhyme that seemed not to come. The next day he wrote in his diary:

Somehow or another the poets' visit has left me out of conceit with poetry. The modern poetry represented by these young men is too entirely unlike anything I can recognize as good verse that I feel there is something absurd in their expressing admiration for mine.

[5] Wilfred Scawen Blunt (1840–1922) b. Sussex; diplomatic service 1858–69; travelled Egypt, Arabia, Persia; strong supporter of Home Rule for Ireland, imprisoned there for two months 1887 in connection with agitations; Little Englander opposed to British Imperialism. Published *Love Sonnets of Proteus* (1880), *In Vinculis* (1889), *Complete Poetical Works* (1914), *My Diaries* (1919–20).

He also noted that Pound 'had confused my political *adventures* in Egypt with those of an earlier generation in Italy where I had played no part.' In fact Pound probably knew very little about Blunt, beyond the double sonnet 'With Esther' which he steadfastly admired, and what he would have gathered from Yeats's conversation. It is said that Yeats, who knew him well, would have made much of Blunt's aristocratic airs and connections.

Pound visited Blunt again towards the end of March, and this time it was Pound he found absurd:

Pound it turns out is an American born in Idaho and Europeanized at Paris, where he has contracted all the absurdities of the day, and is now a cubist. Here he makes himself a sort of understudy of Yeats, repeating Yeats' voice with Yeats' brogue, an odd nervous little man with a mop of reddish hair looking as if dyed and a jerky manner as if afflicted with St. Vitus' dance.

Pound either did not register Blunt's dislike or did not allow it to disturb his homage. He visited again with Dorothy in July, and again Blunt was dismissive:

Though I do not see much intellectually in Pound, I find his wife a pleasant little woman, refined and sensible and of a delicate paste which has already humanized and deodorised him (and he needed deodorising).

Another dinner guest, Reginald, had been 'distinctly of use in the small change of our weekend party conversation, helping to cope with Pound's eccentricities'.

Not the least of Pound's eccentricities was his being able to make of the ludicrously mismatched event an enduring image of what he had wanted to honour:

To have, with decency, knocked
That a Blunt should open
    To have gathered from the air a live tradition
or from a fine old eye the unconquered flame
This is not vanity.

Another image from that winter at Stone Cottage was of Yeats sounding to Pound in the room upstairs like the wind in the chimney as he composed 'a great peacock aere perennius', a 'perdurable' peacock. And Yeats 'would not eat ham for dinner / because peasants eat ham for dinner'.

A marriage

On the 21st of January 1914 Pound, now back in Kensington, wrote to Dorothy: 'I think you'd better perhaps marry me and live in one room more than the dryad.' Dorothy that morning was up at the British Museum reading a book on Chinese literature. Next day she let him know that she couldn't say 'which day you had better come in next week'—she was 'waiting to hear from Nancy'. But by Friday 13th February it had been decided that they would be married; though it remained for Olivia, who thought it would be more diplomatic for her to speak to him first, to secure the reluctant consent of H.H.S. The Banns were read. *Mr and Mrs Hope Shakespear were At Home on the occasion of the marriage of their daughter Dorothy to Ezra Pound on Saturday April 18th 3.30–6.30.* And on April 20 it was entered in the marriage registry of the Parish Church, Kensington, that on that day 'Ezra Pound, 28, Bachelor, MA, Poet, of 5 Holland Park Chambers, [Son of] Homer Loomis Pound, Assayer, and Dorothy Shakespear, 27, Spinster, of 12 Brunswick Gardens W.8, [Daughter of] Henry Hope Shakespear, Solicitor', had been joined in Holy Matrimony 'according to the Rites and Ceremonies of the Established Church.' Present were just half a dozen persons, all apparently members of the bride's family.

Five years had passed since Dorothy's raptures at her first meeting Ezra; and two and a half since the first of his two formal requests for her hand in marriage. That had been preceded by his year and more of exile from her. Since the refusal of his second request, two years ago now, and Olivia's telling him he should go away for good, things between them had seemed to be at a calm impasse. They were corresponding, so far as we know, as intimate friends, no more; they were meeting, so far as we know, about once a week and always in the company of others.

They seem not to have been planning to marry just then. In October 1913, in a letter to his mother, Pound had written 'it is settled that you come over ... in April ... to be here for May and June.' Moreover, 'I shall go to a Welsh lake later in the season instead of going to Garda in the spring. having been in the country through the winter I shall probably not need Spring cleaning.' Dorothy too had other plans. She was due to spend the whole of March in Rome with Olivia and Georgie Hyde-Lees, and did indeed do that.

In any case, the great impediment to their marriage had not been overcome. Pound was as dependent as ever on his uncertain earnings from little magazines, mainly *Poetry* and the *New Freewoman / Egoist* at this time. He could tell John Quinn in 1922 that he had 'never had £300/ in any one year', and in 1914 his income was probably far below that. Dorothy had £50 a year of her own, made up to £200 by her family, just enough to 'pay her own expenses'. What then had happened suddenly to enable them to marry?

Olivia's finally agreeing to it, and her intervention with Hope, must have been crucial. But what changed her mind? She would have seen that as things were Dorothy was on the verge of becoming an 'old maid' and of being left 'on the shelf' and on her hands. I wonder too if there might have been some prompting from *Nishikigi*'s tale of a lover who left it too late. And might Yeats have put in a word for Pound, playing the part of the priest? I do not know. It appears that Olivia went bail for their flat.

Ezra had scruples, on religious grounds, against being married in church. It was the lack of religion in the Church that bothered him, he declared to Mr Shakespear in a formal, typed, letter making the point that he 'should much rather go through the simple and dignified service at the Registry':

I think, seriously, that the spiritual powers are affronted when a person who takes his religion seriously complies with a ceremony which has fallen into decay.... I should find myself much more in the presence of the aerial and divine powers in taking a formal legal oath with a spirit of reverence than in complying with rites of that religion "which the Nazarene has been accused of having founded".

I should no more give up my faith in Christ than I should give up my faith in Helios or my respect for the teachings of Confucius, but I think this superficial conformity, an act which would amount, practically, to an outrageous lie at what should be one of [the] most serious moments of a man's life, interferes.

On the other hand I shouldn't mind any ceremony if it were performed by someone who was really a priest, I mean some man who did actually and fervently believe in some sort of divinity. The whole sanity of classic religion was in their recognition that different men have different gods and that there are many sorts of orthodox piety.

H.H.S. drafted his reply at the office of Shakespear & Parkyn, Solicitors, after a couple of days of 'anxious consideration'. What he wanted to say was utterly reasonable, unanswerable, and had no patience with what Pound was on about. He saw the contradiction in Pound's straining to apply his personal credo to the public aspect of marriage and thought of showing it up:

I don't really know whether you write seriously for I thought it a matter of common agreemt. that the validity of any ceremony perpetuated by a duly constituted official was not affected by any personal disqualification of the official–do you mean that you propose to satisfy yourself that the Registrar who is to officiate at the 'simple & dignified service' is a man of irreproachable character.

247

'But let that pass', he then thought, and deleted that paragraph. His own position was, he believed, simply the normal and expected one. He thought of putting it first in this way:

When my consent was asked to Dorothy being married nothing was said as to her wishing to be married otherwise than in the manner in which people in her station in life are usually married & it came as a shock to me much later to learn that she contemplated being married other than in Church.

That was deleted, and instead he stated his reasons as a sequence of logical propositions:

1. That as an English Woman [Dorothy] is entitled to be married in the National Church.
2. That as she does not profess to belong to any other defined Religion there is no procedure other than a marriage in Church by which she can show that she enters into the solemn obligations of marriage with the conviction that she does so in the sight of & seeking the assistance of the Divine Powers.
3. That the one thing definitely indicated by a merely Civil marriage is the precise negation of this.

He concluded by countering Pound's going for the moral high ground with some emotional blackmail:

However I shall in no way try to force my views upon her, & if she conscientiously believes it is not right for her to take her vows in a Church I shall say no more of it tho' it will be more distressing to me than perhaps you can understand.

I am a man of few words & keep my views on religious matters between myself & God and it pains me to have to write on such matters.

This episode gives in a nutshell the whole drama of Pound's challenging the established, not-to-be-questioned, social and religious conventions which officially governed life in England. His future father-in-law was writing as the guardian of its morals and *mores*, while he was championing the right of the would-be-free individual to live by his own more authentic religious vision. But there was to be no showdown. H.H.S. was able to add a note before sending off his letter: 'Since writing the above I hear from D. that you have both decided to defer to my wishes & I heartily thank you.' Convention and the quiet life had prevailed once again. A month later, when he was about to give notice for the Banns to be read in church, H. Hope Shakespear enquired, without apparent triumph or irony, if Ezra had any other Christian name 'as we must get that right'.

He intimated in the same note that he would be in that evening 'if you care to come in & smoke a cigarette'. It might have been their first real conversation, for Dorothy, writing from Rome, was glad they had spent an evening together and wondered 'what you talked of, & what he makes of you'.

While Dorothy was in Rome Ezra was busy preparing the flat that was to be their home until 1920. This was 5 Holland Place Chambers, virtually round the corner from Church Walk. The Aldington's, Richard and Hilda, were in the flat next door. The Pound's flat, as described by Wyndham Lewis, 'was designed by an imbecile or an Eskimo'. There was 'a large, gaunt and very dark room...lighted only by one window in the extreme corner, opening on to the central air-hole.' In that room Pound would do the cooking, on a gas range, by artificial light. 'A minute water-closet nestled indelicately in the small hall, the first thing to confront the visitor.' There was no bathroom. The first thing Pound had to do was put in gas and install a geyser for hot water. Then he bought an enormous table which furnished the cavernous room. 'I shall be lord of that room & you shall govern the other two', he wrote to Dorothy, 'I can keep all my much there, & work there.' In the event the need for light drove him to work and receive visitors in the eccentrically shaped sitting-room. 'At least the tiny quintangle...had all the light London ever gives', he recalled when looking back from St Elizabeths to his Kensington days. He acquired a triangular oak table which fitted into a corner to type at. 'I must bind the ends of the carpet', he mentioned to Dorothy, but he knew better now than to say she should be there to do it for him. And, 'There've got to be enough dishes & implements to last the day & they'll only get washed once per diem.' He was to be lord indeed of the kitchen domain. Dorothy had made it clear that she did not cook and would not cook. 'Remember, I can't do a thing myself', was her last word on that subject. Pound asked his mother to send recipes 'for pan-cakes, waffles, fried chicken *à la Lucy*...cream-soups, tomato and potato, and any other of the simple pleasures of the poor that you think I can cope with.' He was also wanting 'an American ice cream freezer'. He could and did cook, 'excellently', according to Lewis and others.

There were wedding presents. Six 'High Wycombe' small chairs from Hueffer; two early Picasso circus drawings from the bride's parents; a necklace and some coral from the groom's—they had 'mumbled indistinctly about table-silver', but had then apparently been put right as to what would be acceptable. An old friend of the family gave Dorothy a cheque for £20—'much too much', Ezra decided, 'to spend on anything but a magnificent work of art'. He wanted her to consider Epstein's new 'Bird pluming itself' which was being exhibited at the Goupil Gallery. 'It's the proper quattro-cento thing to patronize living artists', he told her. With Yeats's present Pound commissioned a clavichord from Arnold Dolmetsch, and told him they hoped his cheque would 'flower into deathless music—at least into an image of more gracious & stately times.'

Pound had his moments, in the interval between the season at Stone Cottage and the wedding, of imagining that he was living in the Quattrocento. He had bought a half-ton block of marble for Gaudier who was transforming it into what came to be called the *Hieratic Head of Ezra Pound*. As he sat for it, on a cheap wooden chair with the trains rushing overhead, and Gaudier bobbing about cutting the stone with the chisels he forged himself from old steel spindles, it came over him that this was a renaissance moment, and that he could have none finer, 'and no better craftsman to fill it'. 'And it is not a common thing to know that one is drinking the cream of the ages.'

Gaudier began work on the block at the end of February. In early March Pound thought the bust was beginning 'to look like father Tiber'. Then it was getting 'more gravely beautiful & more phallic each week'. In its final state he saw 'a great calm', and 'infinitely more of strength and dignity than my face will ever possess'. It did not look like him, and was not meant to. 'It will be the expression of certain emotions I get from your character', Gaudier had told him. And Pound mused in his memoir that Gaudier had stiffened up his character quite a lot; and remembered how they had joked of selling the bust 'to the "Metropolitan" for $5000' and living 'at ease for a year...some two or three decades hence'. The phallic head, Gaudier's largest and most important work, was exhibited in May at the Whitechapel Art Gallery, in a show called 'Twentieth Century Art: A Review of Modern Movements'. It was bought by Hueffer for £2.10s., the cost of the marble.

After the wedding Ezra and Dorothy Pound went down to Stone Cottage for a time. They were agreed, it seems, on not having children. When the question of adopting a French refugee family came up, in 1917, Dorothy wrote, 'I hereby declare that, refusing a family of my own, I won't adopt one!' And there is evidence that Pound thought it wrong to bring a child into the world without financial security. It was suspected that they slept apart. Hilda Aldington, not always a reliable witness, is said to have said that Dorothy appeared to be sexually unawakened. Another not wholly reliable source reported that Pound said to him in the 1930s, 'I fell in love with a beautiful picture that never came alive'.

Yet he had married, as Yeats remarked at the time, 'a beautiful and clever wife, and that is what few men get'. And it was a marriage that endured. It is possible that Pound had really meant it when he wrote in 1912 that there are things more important than sex. At least for Americans, he had declared, 'perhaps because we are a young and inexperienced people', there remains a belief in the Artemis type—'and likewise a belief in affection; in a sort of intimate sympathy which is not sexual'. He had seen something like that in one of Cavalcanti's poems, where 'Exhausted by a love born of fate and of the emotions, Guido turns to an intellectual sympathy... and in this new force he is remade'. He is drawn by 'the spirit of the eternal beauty made flesh... in her'; and this drawing is as a magnet giving direction to his *virtu*, 'the noble spiritual powers, the invigorating forces of life and beauty'. Pound's invocation of Artemis would put that in rather different terms. The virgin huntress 'chaste and fair', Apollo's twin, has like the moon a dark aspect: to those she favours she is a bringer of light and abundance; but to those who offend her she deals death. She represents the powers of nature which are to be honoured, and must not be violated. It is not easy to combine Cavalcanti's idealized lady and the Artemis type into a single image, but that perhaps is what Pound was after. It is perhaps what he saw in Dorothy.

'Love-Song to Eunoë', a poem which he published in an American magazine in 1915 and never reprinted, might be the prayer to his bride of one who cherished such images. 'Eunoë' would invoke the Artemis type in her kindly aspect:

> Be wise:
> Give me to the world,
> Send me to seek adventure.
>
> I have seen the married,
> I have seen the respectably married
> Sitting at their hearths:
> It is very disgusting.
>
> I have seen them stodged and swathed in contentments.
> They purr with their thick stupidities.
>
> O Love, Love,
> Your eyes are too beautiful for such enactment!
> Let us contrive a better fashion.
>
> O Love, your face is too perfect,
> Too capable of bearing inspection;
> O Love,
> Launch out your ships,
> Give me once more to the tempest.

It was of course the semi-divine Helen's face that launched a thousand ships to wage war at Troy, disastrously.

In their everyday lives things must have been more prosaic. That metaphorical tempest might have been, objectively speaking, *BLAST* number two. And the love song might have been written about the same time as this note to Wyndham Lewis: 'My invaluable helpmeet suggests that the Thursday dinners [to discuss *BLAST*] would maintain an higher intellectual attitude if there were a complete & uncontaminated absence of women. She offers to contribute her own absence to that total & desirable effect. / Offer duly accepted.' In this light Dorothy was taking her place as one of the 'literary men's wives' whom the men themselves, Yeats among them, liked to escape.

But it wasn't always like that. Lewis took an interest in and encouraged her art. And Yeats was pleased to have her company as well as Pound's at Stone Cottage in the winter of 1915. He told Mabel Beardsley that they were obviously devoted to each other although so unlike. Dorothy 'looks as if her face was made out of Dresden china. I look at her in perpetual wonder. It is hard to believe she is real; yet she spends all her daylight hours drawing the most monstrous cubist pictures.' Yeats thought she was 'merely playing up to [Ezra's] revolutionary energy'. But Lewis included one of the designs she had made at Stone Cottage, 'Snow Scene', in *BLAST* 2. There it faced the notice of Gaudier-Brzeska's death in action.

As an artist Dorothy had been a landscape watercolourist, taking after her father. Her drawings around 1913 and 1914 show the influence of her studying Japanese prints in the British Museum, and possibly some influence also from Gaudier's drawings. Once married to Pound she began to frequent Lewis's Rebel Art Centre, and soon developed her own style of Vorticist abstraction. In that style she designed striking covers for the 1915 re-issue of *Ripostes* and for *Catholic Anthology*. When she signed her work it was as 'D.S.', but though she continued to paint and draw impressively, at least into the early' 1940s, she never exhibited.

Now that they were married Ezra and Dorothy could go about together, do things together, be seen together, and that must have been a great liberation. There is a notebook bought in the British Museum shop and used in the North Room of its Library by Dorothy, in which the first entry is her question, 'Can we leave the books while we have lunch?' There was another great change, the effect of which may only have struck her during the war when she was informed by the police that she had no right to be in the 'restricted area' where Stone Cottage happened to be. In marrying Pound she had automatically and perhaps unknowingly assumed his U.S. citizenship and become an alien in her own country.

The 'BLAST' vortex

On the 22nd of January 1914, at a meeting sponsored by the Quest Society in Kensington Town Hall, T. E. Hulme spoke on 'The New Art and its Philosophy'. His delivery, according to Kate Lechmere, was mumbled and indistinct. Wyndham Lewis spoke after him, inaudibly, with his head buried in his notes. Then Pound read some of his own and Hulme's poems, snarling or clowning them in a mid-American nasal twang. But he was, in his velvet jacket and red tie, completely self-possessed, witty, urbane and fluent, and so saved the occasion.

Miss Lechmere, who would shortly give Lewis the money for his Rebel Art Centre and for *BLAST*, would also cause him to fall out with Hulme. At the time of the Quest Society meeting she was attached to Lewis, who there introduced her to Hulme, to whom in the course of the following months she transferred her attachment. Lewis, in proprietorial mode, went to find Hulme at Mrs Kibblewhite's to have it out with him, and abruptly found himself suspended by his trouser-cuffs from the iron railings in Soho Square. He could never afterwards 'see the summer house in its centre without remembering how [he] saw it upside down'.

Pound, in his account in the *Egoist* of the Quest Society meeting, said that all three speakers were 'almost wholly unintelligible', but he attributed this to the difficulty of 'fighting through the obscurities of a new convention'. Hulme had wanted to separate *geometric* art from *vital* art. The third speaker, evidently Pound himself, had expressed the same idea, that is that 'you could believe in something beyond man', the realm of cubes, triangles and circles apparently, or of Epstein's 'pregnant monster with one eye going around a square corner'; or you could, on the contrary, 'believe that man was the . . . lord of the universe or what you will, and that there was no beauty to surpass the beauty of man or of man as conceived by the late Sir Lawrence Alma-Tadema'. *Vital* art then would be 'from the life', though with the living treated as in historical charades or *tableaux vivants*. That sort of humanistic art, in Pound's view, is for the stupid mass of humanity, among them the 'cultured' and the 'educated', who are incapable of sharing the true artist's delights and pleasures among the universal forms of things.

His article amounted to a call for all true artists to rise up in rebellion against the oppression of the majority and their clichéd realism. The artist 'knows he is born to rule'—and he is at last done with the folly of democracy. 'We artists who have been so long the despised are about to take over'. Art rules! Pound believed in revolution by propaganda.

Hulme hadn't put it quite like that. But he did say that the new *geometric* art would change the general outlook on the world. He was thinking of Cubism with which Lewis and his Rebel Art Centre collaborators were associating themselves in early 1914. He saw it as an art which took no pleasure in nature and people as we ordinarily see them, but instead sought their abstract and inorganic forms. It found in a face its planes and cylinders and quadrilaterals, as Picasso had recently been doing. Or there were Lewis's designs and paintings where human beings were seen as mechanical constructions, the arm a lever, the rest 'a few abstract mechanical relations'. There was Epstein's pregnant woman in green granite, where the very essence of organic life had been transformed by abstraction into 'something as hard and durable as a geometrical figure'. He might have seen the same process, though in a more restrained form, in Gaudier's *Hieratic Head of Ezra Pound*; or in Dorothy Shakespear's 'Snow Scene'. To see things in this way, he argued, was to take them out of nature and set them in the realm of the gods—to do what Byzantium had done for its royal persons in its mosaics. Yeats would make that particular theme his own in his two 'Byzantium' poems (1927 and 1930).

Hulme's thinking stimulated Pound's, as did Lewis's conversation and Gaudier's. He felt himself to be at last among equals, and began to speak his own mind in their terms. In place of the *image* it was now *form* that preoccupied him. He gave Epstein credit for having been 'the first person who came talking about "form, not the *form of anything*"'. More, in his sculpture Epstein had shown 'form-understanding': he 'has worked with the sphere and with the cylinder'—and consequently 'a contemplation of [his] work would instil a sense of form in the beholder'. Of Vorticist art in general Pound wrote—this was after Lewis's 'Cubists' had agreed to be known as Vorticists—that it was more interested in the arrangement, or the organization, of forms, 'than in the dead matter arranged'. It was interested also in discovering forms previously unperceived, or in creating new forms. There is 'the understanding that you can use form as a musician uses sound, that you can select motives of form from the forms before you, and that you can recombine and re-colour and "organise" them into new form'—and 'this state of mental activity brings with it a great joy and refreshment'.

But where is the poet in all these abstractions about the beauties of abstract form? What was there in Vorticism for Pound? In his poetry he was of course in his own way a musician, so that connection holds, though it is a connection with music not with Vorticist art. But that apart, where is his *geometric* poetry of spheres and cylinders, a poetry altogether removed from human life and from nature? Pound tried something of the sort just once, with 'The Game of Chess' which he published in *BLAST* in 1915, but it did not answer to his motive concerns. They were better served by 'Provincia Deserta', or by the satirical 'Salutation the Third' in the first *BLAST*. His poetry simply did not allow for the extreme abstraction and the counter-humanism practised by Epstein, and by Lewis above all. Strictly speaking, in his poetry he was not a Vorticist, not if the term is to be defined primarily by their art at this time. Lewis himself observed that Pound's 'fire-eating propagandist utterances were not accompanied by any very experimental efforts in his particular medium'.

What allied him to Lewis and Gaudier and Epstein was that they were seriously revolutionary artists, and the only ones around with whom he could plot an English revolution. Yeats and Hueffer meant a great deal to him, but they were not good for brazenly overturning the old order. And while the Vorticist's art was not his art, he could make common cause with them in the war on the great powers of malevolent mediocrity and petrifying conventionality. His part was precisely to be the propagandist for their art. In his own, and in particular in the art of the long poem, he was still finding his way.

Vorticism, as Pound always insisted, was Lewis's movement; or, if it was a movement of individuals working separately who, having found an underlying agreement, decided to stand together, still without him 'there would have been no movement'. Lewis, with his originating genius, 'supplied the volcanic force' that made it happen. First there was his Rebel Art Centre in Bloomsbury, set up in dissidence from Roger Fry's Omega Workshops, and also in rivalrous reaction to Futurism. At the Omega post-impressionism had become an art of genteel decoration. Marinetti's Futurism, on the other hand, 'accelerated impressionism' as Pound called it, was an art of frontal assault on the accepted ways of seeing and doing things; it was dedicated to the ever-increasing speed of machines, to the world-shattering energy of the high-explosive shell, and to making nonsense of common sense. Lewis, and Pound in his propaganda, had a similar taste for destructive violence; but they could distance themselves from Marinetti by charging him with rubbishing tradition and with being willing to destroy indiscriminately much that they had a use for. They certainly wanted to get rid of what was dead and rotten in England and its Empire, but in order that it might live more intelligently, and thus more fully.

Lewis conceived of *BLAST* as a follow-up to the 'Cubist Room' which he had infiltrated into the Camden Town Group exhibition in Brighton in the winter of 1913–14. Pound was mentioning it in his letters early in 1914. It was to be a 'revue cubiste', then a 'Futurist, Cubist, Imagiste Quarterly'. A full-page advertisement in the *Egoist* of April 1st announced that *BLAST* would be ready that month and would discuss 'Cubism, Futurism, Imagisme and all Vital Forms of Modern Art'. It would contain 'MANIFESTO'; would feature 'THE CUBE' and 'THE PYRAMID'; it would be the 'END OF THE CHRISTIAN ERA'. That last was Pound's particular proclamation. When it appeared as for 'June 20th, 1914'—a week before the assassination in Sarajevo which triggered the Great War—the title had become *BLAST*: *Review of the Great English Vortex.*

Pound contributed a dozen 'nice blasty poems', most of them squibs—'Chinese crackers', Lewis called them—expressing his lesser loves and hates; and a two-page statement, 'Vortex, Pound'. Gaudier contributed his personal 'Vortex', a brilliantly original and thoroughly Vorticist history and theory of sculpture in just four and a half pages. There was a story by Rebecca West, and the first instalment of Hueffer's wonderful novel, *The Good Soldier* – neither of them in Vorticist mode. There were twenty pages of variously Vorticist 'illustrations', by Lewis and his associates. All the rest, about two-thirds of the whole, was Lewis's own work. He put together the thirty-three pages of 'MANIFESTO', which blasted and blessed and asserted itself in combative black type and aggressive capitals half an inch high. He contributed over thirty pages of miscellaneous prose 'Vortices and Notes'. And he contributed the one truly innovative piece of writing, 'Enemy of the Stars', which reads now as if he were already able to stand outside his characters and see the mechanical workings of their minds in language in the way Samuel Beckett would be doing twenty years and more on. Without question, *BLAST* was most of all a manifestation of Lewis's complex and disturbing genius, as Vorticism was his movement.

Imagisme was not mentioned in *BLAST* except in Pound's brief 'Vortex' note, and there he placed it among the ancestors of Vorticism, with Pater and Whistler. Yet his personal idea of Vorticism as defined in that note was really *Imagisme* by another name, if in a more developed state. He said nothing of geometric form. His key word now was *energy*. 'The vortex is the point of maximum energy', he began; then, under the heading 'THE TURBINE', this main statement:

All experience rushes into this vortex. All the energized past, all the past that is living and worthy to live. All MOMENTUM, which is the past bearing upon us, RACE, RACE-MEMORY, instinct charging the PLACID, NON-ENERGIZED FUTURE.

The DESIGN of the future in the grip of the human vortex. All the past that is vital, all the past that is capable of living into the future, is pregnant in the vortex, NOW.

This is the 'intellectual and emotional complex' again, only emphatically energized. But there is a significant new development. In the theory of *Imagisme* the sources of energy had been intense emotion and the life-force. Here, evidently, the energy is not the raw energy of the vital universe or of primal feelings, but rather what has been distilled from living into instinct and tradition.

Pound was now thinking of human culture in biological terms, as if it were a life-form with its genetic inheritance, its life-advancing instincts and traditions, concentrated in and transmitted by the creative intelligence of its artists. He invoked 'the theory of the dominant cell, a slightly Nietzschean biology', as appropriate to Vorticism. By that, I take it, he meant that the Dionysiac genius of the race worked through the few individuals of genius to advance and shape the life of the race. The artist, he insisted, was not a mere receiver of sensations and impressions, not merely a seismograph, but could be a power in his world: 'think of him as DIRECTING a certain fluid force against circumstance, as CON-CEIVING instead of merely observing and reflecting'. That 'fluid force' would be at once the life-force and the force of intelligence—the life-force as intelligence, and intelligence as the life-force in a civilization.

That idea of the artist as Dionysiac intelligence penetrating and fecundating the passive mass of ordinary citizens found its perfect expression in Gaudier's phallic, and hieratic, *Head of Ezra Pound*.

Against that there is Lewis's image of Pound as at first 'an unassimilable and aggressive stranger' among the English, who had become 'with his Imagism...aesthetically a troublesome rebel'. But then Pound saw Lewis as 'a restless, turbulent intelligence...full of sudden, illuminating antipathies...[and] bound to be always crashing and opposing and breaking.' Rebellious intelligence was their common factor.

And 'the English', as they fully expected, resented them for it. Orage dismissed *BLAST* as 'not unintelligible...but not worthy the understanding'. The editor of the *Quarterly Review*, G. W. Prothero, who had been pleased to accept Pound's long article on the *Noh* before *BLAST* appeared, let him know that henceforth his pages would have to be closed to Pound because to be 'associated publicly with such a publication as *BLAST*...stamps a man too disadvantageously'. At least Orage readmitted Pound to the pages of the *New Age* in 1915.

The coming of war

Pound hadn't allowed for a real war. When it came, seemingly very suddenly, at the beginning of August 1914, it quite overshadowed all

his furious propaganda for art to go to war. His artists, Gaudier and
Lewis, Hueffer and Hulme too, became infantrymen and artillerymen,
killing and being killed with actual bullets and shells. He had called for
slaughter in a war without truce, meaning it metaphorically. The real thing
seemed to him the final stupidity of the world he had wanted to destroy,
a mindless murdering contest between detestable 'teutonic atavism' and
'unsatisfactory Democracy', the latter characterized by 'the loathsome
spirit of mediocrity cloaked in graft'. But there was evidently more force
in that loathsome spirit than in the art he had opposed to it. His *Imagiste*
movement and the Vorticist movement would be swept away in the general
mobilization for war.

Hueffer had seen it coming from as far back as 1910. He had remarked
in the *English Review* that Germany was building battleships with intent,
and that England was doing the same. But Pound's poets and painters
had their minds on other things. Unaware that a war was two weeks
away the Vorticists celebrated the publication of *BLAST* with a dinner
at Dieudonné's; and Miss Lowell celebrated *Des Imagistes* with another
two days later. Pound had his parents over from Philadelphia, and though
Homer had to return to his work in the Mint about the end of July,
Isabel stayed on into October by which time German submarines were
sinking shipping in the Atlantic. Lewis went up to a house-party in southern Scotland after the *BLAST* dinner, and there everyone was agreeing,
except Hueffer, that Britain would *not* go to war, even as the papers
were carrying in scare headlines the news of the British ULTIMATUM to
Germany.[6]

The war seriously complicated life for the rebel artists. It was not their
war, yet they could not keep out of it. Back in London Lewis noticed a
general enthusiasm for going to war among its crowds. The spectacle of
individuals giving themselves up to the mass emotion, roaring approval at
the declaration of war, at once interested and alienated him. His artist's
instinct made him take in the crowd-spirit and yet resist it by analysing
the experience. He was saving himself from the mob by understanding it;
and that 'was a triumph (as [he] saw it then) of the individualist principle.'
Once in the war he would have to save himself in that way through all
its disciplines designed deliberately to beat down the individual into the

---

[6] Austria-Hungary, following the assassination of the Archduke Franz Ferdinand in Sarajevo, had
declared war on Serbia on 28 July 1914; Russia mobilized along the Austrian and German frontiers
the next day; Germany declared war on Russia on 1 August, then invaded Belgium on 3 August
and declared war on France which was committed, with Britain, to the defence of Belgium; Britain
declared war on Germany on 4 August, on behalf of its entire Empire. The U.S.A. would stay out
until April 1917.

mass. Four years on, when he had come to know all there was to know about war, he could still regard it from his own point of view, and conclude that war, modern war, was not 'good or bad—only supremely stupid'. Or, 'if we must deal in moral values', 'the greatest wickedness of all . . . is the perpetuation of foolishness which these carnivals of mass-murder involve'. Yet he, and his fellow artists, had been forced to serve in the mass folly.

The Egoist of February 1, 1915 gave official statistics for French (and only French) casualties in the first five months of the war: 217,000 dead; 400,000–500,000 wounded; 119,000 taken prisoner.

'There is no other news' than war news, Pound told his father in early September 1914. He was 'finishing up another batch of Fenollosa notes and translations'. In October Gaudier had written from within shell range of the front, and May Sinclair was with the Red Cross in Belgium— and he had 'found a new good poet named Eliot'. Later that month he mentioned—among other things such as 'Walter [Rummel] over for a concert' and 'Yeats back in town'—'London not yet dynamited by the Deutschers'. To his mother, after she was safely home, he mentioned 'Bulletins announce Cracow in flames'. In November or December he was being kept going by some fine stuff in Fenollosa's Chinese notes and getting 'a good little book' out of them. 'War losing interest', he wrote, 'have stopped taking in the paper'. His 'topics of the moment', as he went through them in a long letter to Harriet Monroe in November, did include Gaudier's news from the trenches and May Sinclair 'pulling wounded off the field', but were mostly about artists and current exhibitions. He was not letting the war distract him from his work.

Gaudier was writing regularly to Pound and to Mrs Shakespear and to other English friends, giving detailed and bloodthirsty accounts of the fighting. 'Ezra's "Altaforte"' was much on his mind. Before the end of September he had been in a bayonet attack, 'a hell from which few escaped'; but he found the night-patrols great fun. As it turned out he was rather good at the desperate business of trench warfare, and quite proud of his exploits. At the same time he was viewing his experience with the detachment of the artist. Probably in November he wrote from the trenches 'a short essay' for the next *BLAST*:

HUMAN MASSES teem and move, are destroyed and crop up again.

. . . .

THE BURSTING SHELLS, the volleys, wire entanglements, projectiles, motors, the chaos of battle DO NOT ALTER IN THE LEAST the outlines of the hill we are besieging. A company of PARTRIDGES scuttle along before our very trench.

. . . .

MY VIEWS ON SCULPTURE REMAIN ABSOLUTELY THE SAME,
IT IS THE VORTEX OF WILL, OF DECISION THAT BEGINS.
I SHALL DERIVE MY EMOTIONS SOLELY FROM THE ARRANGEMENT OF SURFACES, I shall present my emotions by the ARRANGEMENT OF MY SURFACES, THE PLANES AND LINES BY WHICH THEY ARE DEFINED.

. . . .

I have made an experiment. Two days ago I pinched from an enemy a mauser rifle. Its heavy unwieldy shape swamped me with a powerful IMAGE of brutality.
I was in doubt for a long time whether it pleased or displeased me.
I found that I did not like it.
I broke the butt off and with my knife I carved in it a design, through which I tried to express a gentler order of feeling, which I preferred.
BUT I WILL EMPHASIZE that MY DESIGN got its effect (just as the gun had) FROM A VERY SIMPLE COMPOSITION OF LINES AND PLANES.

'The thoughts of an artist . . . under fire', was Hueffer's admiring comment, 'an artist who had a mystical and beautiful mind and who had been long under fire.'

Through the hard winter of 1914–15 Gaudier wrote of life in the trenches in the spirit of ironic detachment:

I again indulged in the luxury of 'mud-baths', very good for rheumatism, arthritis, lumbago and other evils. But nowadays I am a trench veteran. I have experienced all sorts of weather in these hellish places, so that I can stand a night under heavy rain without sneezing the next day, and sleep beautifully a whole day on hard frozen ground without any ill result to the 'abdomenalia'.

Pound had sent him his translations of a couple of war poems from ancient China, 'Song of the Bowmen of Shu' and 'Lament of the Frontier Guard'. 'They depict our situation in a wonderful way', Gaudier told him. After about eight months, however, the strain was starting to show: 'It is a gruesome place all strewn with dead, and there's not a day without half a dozen fellows in the company crossing the Styx. . . . Hope all this nasty nightmare will soon come to an end.' In the same letter, missing news of 'artistic London', missing poetry and books, he reflected 'a desert in the head a very inviting place for a boche bullet or shell'.

One got him there a day or two later. It was as if his mind had been bullet-proof so long as it could be creating. 'A great spirit has been among us, and a great artist is gone', Pound wrote. 'It is part of the war waste'.

Pound did not get into the 'stupid' war. He did volunteer for it, but as a foreigner was not eligible. Being out of it made him feel that it wasn't for him to write about it. 'Those who aren't carrying rifles ought to keep quiet', he objected when *Poetry* and some newspapers were staging 'war poem' competitions. 'Be still, give the soldiers their turn', he advised the 'two-penny poets', 'And do not be trying to scrape your two-penny glory / From the ruins of Louvain'. His only poem dealing directly with the war was actually 'abbreviated from the conversation of Mr T. E. H[ulme]' in 1915. It is a strong poem, partly because it articulates the experience of someone who had been in the front line, and partly because Pound knew how to condense the detail into a timeless image of men at war, one to match 'Song of the Bowmen of Shu'.

> Over the flat slope of St Eloi
> A wide wall of sandbags.
> Night,
> In the silence desultory men
> Pottering over small fires, cleaning their mess-tins:
> To and fro, from the lines,
> Men walk as on Piccadilly,
> Making paths in the dark,
> Through scattered dead horses,
> Over a dead Belgian's belly.
>
> The Germans have rockets. The English have no rockets.
> Behind the lines, cannon, hidden, lying back miles.
> Before the line, chaos:
>
> My mind is a corridor. The minds about me are corridors.
> Nothing suggests itself. There is nothing to do but keep on.

That was a poem, like much of the poetry of that war, in which the mind is the merely passive register of an experience that is too much for it. It was not the kind of poetry Pound wanted to write. Rather than accepting the war as the fittest subject for poetry just then he soon came to see it as the enemy of art, crushing the civilizing intelligence of the artist as it killed off the artists themselves. He saw it as the triumphant manifestation of what the arts were up against. In 'Salutation the Third', in the first *BLAST*, he had set about *The Times* as representing what stood in the way 'of free speech and good letters'. 'You slut-bellied obstructionist', he had sounded off, 'You fungus, you continuous gangrene'. There he had been trying, as 'the really vigorous mind might', to 'erect *The Times*, which is of no importance, into a symbol of the state of mind which *The Times* represents, which is a loathsome state of mind, a malebolge of obtuseness.' Now that what *The Times* represented was making war, it was the war itself that had to be seen as 'a malebolge of obtuseness'. In February 1915, in some verse he never published, he spoke up for the arts rather in the spirit of his *BLAST* 'Salutation', or (taking a hint from Lewis) in a rage like Shakespeare's *Timon*:

> This war is not our war,
> Neither side is on our side:
> A vicious mediaevalism,
> A belly-fat commerce,
> Neither is on our side:
> Whores, apes, rhetoricians,
> Flagellants! in a year
> Black as the *dies irae*.

That was invective and lament, not poetry. But it declared in unmistakable terms what Pound felt, as a poet, about the war in the Spring of 1915. Though he would shortly change his mind and come to see the war as one that had to be fought against 'teutonic atavism', that first fury would endure and would emerge as a major theme in the *Cantos*.

Poets in a world at war: 'Cathay'

In January 1915, at the end of an 'affirmation' of Arnold Dolmetsch in the *New Age*, Pound mused on what it took 'to make a great age'. Did 'the quattrocento shine out because the vortices of power coincided with the vortices of creative intelligence?' And when those vortices do not coincide does it mean 'an age of "art in strange corners" and great dullness among the quite rich?' But were they now 'on the brink of another really great awakening, when the creative or art vortices shall be strong enough, when the people who care will be well enough organised to set the fine fashion, to impose it, to make the great age?'

It was not clear who 'the people who care' might be—persons in power, the rich, the aristocracy? Or the patrons of artists, if they existed? Or were the artists themselves, the individual creative intelligences, to organize the vortex of power and be themselves the ruling aristocracy? The thinking was vague on that crucial point because Pound was uncertain of the answer. How could you accomplish in his London and New York what had been possible in fifteenth-century Florence and Milan? Lorenzo de' Medici had gathered around him and heeded the leading minds of his time; the Council of Florence had employed the talents of Michelangelo and Leonardo da Vinci; the latter was employed also by the Sforza in Milan and by the French king, Francis I. Wyndham Lewis, as a leading artist of his day, was sometimes in Society drawing rooms with the then Prime Minister, Mr Asquith who had 'plunged England into an unprecedentedly destructive and unsuccessful war', and he was always politely questioned by him; but Mr Asquith, later Lord Oxford, could make nothing of his 'Great London Vortex', except that it must be suspect politically. That was how it was in London in 1914 and 1915: even when they were on speaking terms, the politician could not see the point of the artist, while the artist had to declare in mere politeness that he had no interest in power.

Pound's particular vortex of creative intelligence was not in meaningful communication with the vortices of power. But that only made the issue of the 'relation of the state to the individual' the more acute. It was right and proper that the Vorticist movement should be 'a movement of individuals, for individuals, for the protection of individuality.' But then for Pound, unlike Dora Marsden, the individual exists and acts as a cell in the social body. To be a dominant cell, creative intelligence needs to be sharing in and shaping the life of the world. So the artist who would be the intelligence of his world must be in touch with the powers of his world. To be cut off is to be impotent—a condition which 'the mere aesthete' may rejoice in, but which 'the serious artist' will rage against, uncreatively.

Pound himself had very little power of any kind in these years. Even in his own wedding the dead hand of custom had prevailed over his idea of an appropriate rite. He was at the mercy of editors such as Prothero of the *Quarterly*. He was writing for the *New Age* again, for the sake of the shillings it paid, but had to submit to Orage's refusing to print his affirmation of the free verse of Edgar Lee Masters' *Spoon River*. His efforts to bring on a renaissance seemed everywhere to come up against incomprehension, inertia, and outright hostility. And now he was up against the war.

In November 1914 he announced the creation of 'The College of Arts' which would 'aim at an intellectual status no lower than that attained by the courts of the Italian Renaissance'. It would offer 'contact with artists of established position, creative minds, men who for the most part have already suffered in the cause of their art'. The list of prospective faculty included:

Atelier of Sculpture	GAUDIER-BRZESKA
Atelier of Painting	WYNDHAM LEWIS
Atelier of Design	EDWARD WADSWORTH [& EDMUND DULAC]
Portaiture, & History of Art	REGINALD WILENSKI
Ancient Music	ARNOLD DOLMETSCH
Music: 'Cello	FELIX SALMOND
" Piano	K. R. HEYMAN
Comparative Poetry	EZRA POUND
Photography: studio	ALVIN LANGDON COBURN

Other fields of painting, music, letters, and crafts were to be provided for. 'Communications should be addressed to the Secretarial Offices, 5, Holland Place Chambers, Kensington, London, to Vaughn Baron, Sec.' 'Vaugn Baron, Sec.' was presumably a Pound alias. This was to have been the realization of his long-projected super-college, his answer to 'Philology' and the sterile, professorial, academic system; but the Prospectus was as far as it got. The war blew it away.

Through January and February of 1915 Yeats and Pound with Dorothy were in their winter retreat at Stone Cottage. There were now troops training for war on the heath in front of the cottage. One week the military came by and ordered 'that no light should be shown after 5 o clock'. They were reading Norse sagas, in William Morris's versions; Doughty's *Travels in Arabia Deserta*; and the occultist Eliphas Levi, in whom Pound 'found a few sane paragraphs'. Yeats was dictating to Pound his autobiography, *Reveries over Childhood and Youth* (1916). 'We are having a great gale of wind', Pound mentioned to his father in mid-January. Both poets, the one Irish, the other American, felt out of the war. Asked for a war poem Yeats replied 'We poets...have no gift to set a statesman right', and took his stand on the personal and private life, content to 'please / A young girl in the indolence of her youth / Or an old man upon a winter's night'. He would later, in 'Meditations in Time of Civil War' (1923), mock the inadequacy of that sort of response. The poet shut in on himself in a time of violent action would then feel his powerlessness, and feel also the need to reassert the constructive power of art.

Quite apart from the war Pound was not having a good year as a poet. Apart from a small number of *Imagiste* poems—'Heather', 'Ione dead the long year', 'The Spring', and 'The Coming of War: Actaeon'—he was mainly producing small, smart epigrams, 'sketches' as he would call them, which looked down their elegant classical noses at the oddities and absurdities of other people's behaviours. The emotions in these poems, as 'Epilogue' frankly admitted, were 'those of a *maître-de-café*'—that is, I suppose, of someone inwardly scornful of the crowd he serves. Not that Pound's epigrams were at all restrained in their expressions of contempt and amusement. The middle reaches of *Lustra* (1916), say from 'The New Cake of Soap' (from *BLAST* no. 1) through to 'Our Contemporaries' (from *BLAST* no. 2), give the impression that the world was fuelling his hates far more than his intellectual vision. And this was not what the public wanted, or at least it was not what publishers wanted to give the public. Back in February 1914, at the Blunt presentation, Yeats had alluded to this. 'Ezra Pound has a desire personally to insult the world', he had said, 'He has a volume of manuscript at present in which his insults to the world are so deadly that it is rather a complicated publishing problem.'

The difficulty in getting even the earlier 'Lustra' poems collected fed Pound's general paranoia about the way editors and publishers, and print-ers and reviewers too, all ganged up to obstruct original creation. And it was not only his own work that was being censored and kept from the public. There was the history of how publishers in both London and Dublin had tried to censor Joyce's *Dubliners*, and of how the Dublin printer had burnt the entire print-run rather than let it come out. There was the battle he was having with Harriet Monroe to get her to publish Eliot's 'Prufrock' uncut—'the best poem I have yet had or seen from an American', and she apparently wanted it bucked up for her American readers. Then again there was the iniquitous tariff on books imported into the U.S. under a law which 'forms the excuse for a lot of swindling and a restriction on the circulation of contemporary and even modern books'. See 'my attack not yet written', he urged Alice Henderson as he tried to set a campaign going, 'A la guerre'.

Through all this Pound was developing the image of himself as the embattled poet standing alone against the enemies of 'free speech and good letters'. 'Salutation the Third' declared his refusal to 'die at thirty'—he would turn 30 that year—to flatter those who 'do away with true poets'. He would 'stick it out' and mock them as 'fools, detesters of Beauty'. In the second number of *BLAST*, in July 1915, he was seeing himself as the Anglo-Saxon seafarer braving a wintry climate:

> I cling to the spar,
> Washed with cold salt ice
> I cling to the spar—

Insidious modern waves, civilization, civilized hidden snares.
Cowardly editors threaten: 'If I dare'
Say this or that, or speak my open mind,
Say that I hate my hates,
Say that I love my friends

          .   .   .   .   .   .

              Then they will have my guts;
They will cut down my wage, force me to sing their cant,
Uphold the press, and be before all a model of literary decorum.
                                      Merde!
Cowardly editors threaten,
Friends fall off at the pinch, the loveliest die.
This is the path of life, this is my forest.

That last phrase, with its implicit identification with Dante in his dark wood at the start of his epic journey, just hints at a commitment beyond all this warring in the little world of London letters. But the main sense is simply that as that world is against him so he is against the world.

That sense of negative reciprocities showed at its most raw in a defiant note rather gratuitously tacked on to *Cathay*. Ostensibly an apology for presenting so few poems and for not providing notes and commentary, this revealed fear and hatred of those who feared and hated him:

if I give [the poems], with the necessary breaks for explanation, and a tedium of notes, it is quite certain that the personal hatred in which I am held by many, and the *invidia* which is directed against me because I have dared openly to declare my belief in certain young artists, will be brought to bear first on the flaws of such translation, and will then be merged into depreciation of the whole book of translations. Therefore I give only these unquestionable poems.

The little book in fact needed neither the defence nor the offence.

Pound read the proofs for *Cathay* at Stone Cottage in early February, and it was published by Elkin Mathews in an edition of 1,000 copies on 6 April 1915. *Cathay* mirrors an empire in which the vortices of power and those of creative intelligence are both of them weak and ineffectual. The best poet of the day has no wish to serve the state, and the state does not care for his work. The state itself is at war with the barbarians on its borders; while in its heart, at court, it is in a condition of high decadence. Its energies, such as they are, are concentrated in its soldiers dying and forgotten far from the court and from their homes. Separation and sorrow are the keynotes, set against brilliant but enervated display and self-indulgence.

The fourteen poems, selected from about 150 in Fenollosa's notebooks, make up a single, multifaceted image of a great empire in a dysfunctional phase. And this image is for the most part the work of one poet, Rihaku (the Japanese form of Li Po). It is then Rihaku's imperial China that we are being given. Pound makes him out to be the poet of his age in every sense except the crucial one. He is the outstanding poet of his time; and he is a mirror to it; but he registers it passively and makes no effort to shape it. Poet and empire are well matched. That may be why Pound labelled the age of Li Po 'Petrarchan'. He associated the 'Petrarchan' with absence of *virtu*, and with decadence and over-elaboration; and he once included Petrarch, along with Virgil, among those who are mere registers of their milieu and time.

As the image of eighth century China is Rihaku's, so of course Rihaku is here Pound's Rihaku. When he listed ' "Exile's Letter" and *Cathay* in general' as a 'major persona', along with 'The Seafarer' and 'Homage to Sextus Propertius' (1917), he was signalling that it should be read not so much as a translation as a dramatic interpretation. His relation to Rihaku is, as with his other *personae*, at once close and critical. He is faithful to the poems, in his fashion; but at the same time he is intent on bringing out what kind of poems they are, and on showing Rihaku's quality as a poet. He is intent, moreover, on implicating the condition of the empire in the condition of this individual poet. There may be then a further relation, between Rihaku's China and the British Empire in 1914. In both there were barbarians to be fought off, by soldiers having a hard time at the front; in both there was a lack of enlightened direction from the ruling class at home; and in both the arts, including the art of government, were in their usual decadent state. Pound's situation as a poet was after all quite like Rihaku's, but with the essential difference that while he wanted to put things in order, Rihaku, a Taoist, had been content to drift with the flow.

It is probably significant that the first poem in *Cathay* is not by Rihaku, and comes from the earliest era of Chinese literature. It is found in the classic anthology reputedly established by Confucius in the fifth century BC. 'Song of the Bowmen of Shu' is a soldiers' chorus, mixing complaint at the hardships of a war far from home with grim resolve to fight on: 'Our sorrow is bitter, but we would not return to our country'. The second poem, 'The Beautiful Toilet', is also not by Rihaku, and is from the second century BC. Its theme is the waste of young beauty that is not well loved. The grass by the river is green and 'the willows have overfilled the close garden', but the mistress of the house 'has married a sot' who 'leaves her too much alone'. There is pathos in the contrast of the neglected young woman and the fertile growth around her; and there is toughness of mind in the straightforward explanation: she was a courtesan and made a bad marriage. In style these two poems work by direct observation and statement. Emotion is generated through attention to the telling detail: the bowmen must pick the first fern-shoots for food, and as the year goes on there are only the old fern-stalks for them to grub up; the lonely woman shut up in the house just 'puts forth a slender hand' as she passes the door. We trust such 'objective' writing to give us things as they are, to tell what is true to experience.

Rihaku's 'The River Song', the third poem, cultivates a very different order of experience. The poet presents both himself and the emperor as pleasure-loving aesthetes. For himself he creates a world of ornately decorated fantasy, a wine-induced dream of 'musicians with jewelled flutes' and singing girls, of exquisite effects of water and willows and nightingales. He looks at the dragon-pond in the emperor's garden 'with its willow-coloured water / Just reflecting the sky's tinge', and hears 'the five-score nightingales aimlessly singing'. Things blur into each other, wilfully, as in an opium-eater's pleasurably deranged vision. In the midst of this there is one moment of plain realism: 'King So's terraced palace / is now but barren hill'. Rihaku's response is to turn away at once to some illusory effect: 'I draw pen on this barge / Causing the five peaks to tremble'. The emperor, meanwhile, has gone out in his jewelled car, accompanied by the imperial guards 'with their armour a-gleaming', to inspect, not his troops, but his flowers, and 'to hear the new nightingales'. Rihaku has moped in his garden 'awaiting an order-to-write' which won't come, the irony being that the emperor is quite as idle and out-of-office as he is. In any case Rihaku, with his wonderfully drunk and disorderly mind, is not the poet to show him how to order his empire.

As if in clear contrast to that splendid rendering of decadence at court, the next poem, 'The River-Merchant's Wife: A Letter', is intimate, direct, and without pretension or illusion. This also is by Rihaku—but it is about someone not himself. And it works by the same method as the first two poems in the little book, by direct presentation of meaningful detail and straight statement of the fact of the matter:

> The paired butterflies are already yellow with August
> Over the grass in the West garden;
> They hurt me. I grow older.

That has a power of truth quite lacking from Rihaku's letting his mind drift in the emperor's garden. If it has something in common with the study of the neglected wife in 'The Beautiful Toilet', that sense again of young life being wasted, it has also a quality of a maturing love which is missing from the earlier poem. It has more in common with the first poem, 'The Song of the Bowmen', in its loyal enduring of separation. Indeed the two poems correspond with each other like the panels of a diptych, the one showing how things are at war on the frontier, the other showing how things are at home.

When one glances ahead to the following three poems a clear design now emerges:

a. Song of the Bowmen of Shu — *of the sorrow of war*
b. The Beautiful Toilet — *a neglected ex-courtesan*
c. The River Song — *decadence at court*
d. The River-Merchant's Wife — *a love letter*
c. Poem by the Bridge at Ten-Shin — *decadence at court*
b. Jewel Stairs' Grievance — *a neglected court lady*
a. Lament of the Frontier Guard — *of the sorrow of war*

These seven poems, arranged into a closed or 'ring' sequence, thus make up the first part of *Cathay*. 'The River-Merchant's Wife: A Letter' is at the centre structurally, and also ethically; and the war poems on the circumference give another, complementary, ethic. Between them they establish a basis in common human values by which the conduct of the court and the state of the empire may be measured.

The discriminations may be made in the subtle modulations of an image. The river in 'The River Song' is 'drifting water'; in 'The River-Merchants Wife' it is a 'river of swirling eddies', energetic and going somewhere; in 'Poem by the Bridge at Ten-Shin', its 'back-swirling eddies' are seen by the watchers hanging over the bridge-rail as carrying away their lives like petals 'on the gone waters and on the going'. In 'Separation on the River Kiang' the mind's eye is drawn out of this world: 'His lone sail blots the far sky. / And now I see only the river, / The long Kiang, reaching heaven.'

'Poem by the Bridge at Ten-Shin' as a whole takes up the theme of 'The River Song' in an altered mood. Now there is regret for the old days when there were men of power, and a detached view of the hollow ceremonial and effete pleasures of the court. The emperor is absent, and the poet is withdrawn in disillusion. He would identify if he could with 'Han-rei / Who departed alone with his mistress' when his time in office was up, she 'with her hair unbound, and he his own skiffsman'. That is an image of two people putting off court dress and court ways, and energetically making their own way on the river. And it is an image to set against the following poem in which the no doubt effete aristocrat has disappointed the lady, leaving her to contemplate the moon alone.

The bowmen of Shu would not return to their country because their war was ongoing. 'Lament of the Frontier Guard' gives the aftermath: it is really a lament for the frontier guard who are now high heaps of bones 'covered with trees and grass'. The speaker must be the ghost of a guardsman haunting the empty desolation at the North Gate. Does that mean that the empire, rotten at the heart as it is, is now vulnerable to the barbarian hordes? (In time the Mongols of Ghengis and Kublai Khan would break in and reconstruct the empire, but Rihaku wasn't to know that.)

The second part of *Cathay* is made up of poems of exile and departure. The dominant tones are nostalgic and elegiac. 'Exile's Letter', the major poem of the book—Pound said it gave 'not just the whole man, and his whole life-course, but the age'—is Rihaku's sustained complaint of the hardships on the way to his pleasures and of pleasure coming always to an end. He is again the subjective poet of 'The River Song', an aesthete happiest when drunk and rapt in strange effects—

> And the vermilioned girls getting drunk about sunset,
> And the water, a hundred feet deep, reflecting green eyebrows
> —Eyebrows painted green are a fine sight in young moonlight,
> Gracefully painted—

He looks back to times when 'we were drunk for month on month, forgetting the kings and princes', and 'Intelligent men came drifting in' to be of that fellowship; and to one special occasion when they had met up again after a separation, and what with Sennin music and wine his spirit was 'so high it was all over the heavens'. But the best of such times ends in parting and regret—'like the flowers falling at Spring's end / Confused, whirled in a tangle'.

Rihaku, like one of Browning's *Men and Women*, would have us see him as he sees himself, and his closing reflection, 'There is no end of things in the heart', would surely have us feeling the sadness of things with him. Yet one might be moved to ask, what did his 'ancient friend, Chancellor of Gen', think of him when he had to get back to his official duties? And what did his ancient friend's father think, the governor who had 'put down the barbarian rabble'? Might he have been for them the drunken guest who insists the party go on although the host must go to work in the morning? Perish the cold thought, of course. But then who's keeping the bridge, or the border? Are all the 'intelligent men' at the party? If the empire is to be kept running then sooner or later Rihaku must be let go on his way. Or at least that ought to be the view of the forgotten kings and princes and of the men of intelligence while in office. Perhaps, after all, it should be held to the court's credit that when he put himself up for examination Rihaku 'got no promotion'.

Pound inserted 'The Seafarer' into *Cathay* at this point, before the 'Four Poems of Departure'. His stated reason was that it was written down at about the same time as 'Exile's Letter', in the eighth century of the Christian era, but that is not much of a connection. He must have had more in mind. The obvious thing Rihaku and the Seafarer have in common is that each is outside his social order and yet its representative figure. Rihaku gives us a view of eighth century China, as the Seafarer gives us a view of Anglo-Saxon England. But when they are set side by side it is the difference of ethos that is most striking. Through all his hardship and pain the Seafarer, as Pound noted, is active and 'doom-eager', eager to work out his fate, 'eager for the glory of it, ready to pay the price'. In ancient China, one would imagine, he would have been with the bowmen of Shu, or the river-merchant. What he represents is the heroism of his time and place. What Rihaku represents is the decadence of his era, and the pitiful waste of its wars.

Cathay, in its first form, was rounded out by 'Four Poems of Departure' and a third war poem. The four poems are variations on the theme of the passing away of friends and cities and dynasties: they offer the consolations of sad reverie. 'South-Folk in Cold Country' returns to the hardship and heroism and waste of war. It closes the book on the note of 'the pity of war', but what it shows is far from the 'passive suffering' Yeats would object to in war poetry. In spite of the endless hard fighting, and the lice 'like ants over our accoutrements', still 'Mind and spirit drive on the feathery banners'. Such 'Loyalty is hard to explain'—indeed it is inexplicable in the light of the court's way of life, or the poet's.

Finding himself

Gaudier, in the trenches, immediately identified his situation with that of the Bowmen of Shu. Pound must have intended the broader parallels between the emperor and court of Rihaku's China, and the king, aristocracy and government of the British Empire. And we know that he had the relations of state power and the potential power of poetry very much on his mind.

Yet these dimensions of *Cathay* appear to have gone largely unremarked at the time. Hueffer was full of praise for the 'supreme beauty' of the poems and for their technique. He did draw a lesson from Pound's skilful

271

'handling of words' to express emotion 'intact and exactly': 'I daresay that if words direct enough could have been found, the fiend who sanctioned the use of poisonous gases in the present war could have been so touched to the heart that he would never have signed that order'. It is a good lesson, but it did not touch on the way *Cathay* might be a mirror for the present state of the world. Hueffer concluded that 'this is much the best work [Pound] has yet done', yet it was not apparent that he had seen just what it was that Pound had done. Orage too judged *Cathay* 'the best and only good work Mr Ezra Pound has yet done'—though he deprecated the childlike simplicity of mind in the poems, and the absence of regular rhythm and rhyme. So even the social and political commentator missed the social and political implications.

Pound himself showed no desire to point up the topicality of *Cathay*. Wyndham Lewis's colonel had wanted to know what 'Imagisme' was, interrupting some gunnery instruction on his officers' training course to put the question, but had then confessed that he could never be made to understand such things. Pound offered to send the colonel a copy of *Cathay* so that he 'may be able to understand what is imagisme'. He hoped this might help Lewis keep on good terms with the colonel and so get his commission. But he did not suggest that *Cathay* might have any bearing on the colonel's, or Lewis's, then occupation. He was apparently content again when Eliot, in 1917, in writing a brochure to publicize Pound's poetry in America, simply incorporated much of Hueffer's review without even mentioning the war. And for Eliot in 1928, when he was introducing his selection of Pound's poetry, the interesting question about *Cathay* was simply to what extent was it translation or paraphrase, and to what extent original? That feline phrase, 'Pound is the inventor of Chinese poetry for our time', has stuck, and for good reason; but it has also helped to keep attention off the more critical relation to the time.

There is much to be said about *Cathay* as translation, and about its technique, and a great deal has been written on those matters. It has also to be said though that there is little point in holding Pound to account as a translator on this occasion. He could not read the Chinese characters— he could not even sound them out. Dorothy, with some money given her as a wedding and birthday present, had just bought from a second-hand bookshop in the Charing Cross Road Morrison's great seven-volume *Dictionary of the Chinese Language*. She at least was making a start on the language, trying to teach herself. But Pound was absolutely dependent on Fenollosa's simple crib with its halting one-English-word-for-one-Chinese-character, followed by a paraphrase of the line. Fenollosa in his turn, even though he was seriously studying the language, had been dependent on the 'decipherings' of his Japanese tutors. The sort of thing Pound had to work from were lines of ideograms which meant nothing to him, with this underneath them:

crimson or   paint   want to   drink   had better   incline   sun
vermilion   (on face)

The red painted girls about to be drunk, are appropriate to the inclining sun (look beautiful with glow of sun very fine in colour) the red here refers to all 3, all girls red—also drink, also sun—

hundred   feet   prove   deep   copy   green   eyebrow
                                            reflect

Where the hundred feet deep clear water are reflected their green eyebrows . . .

green   eyebrow   beautiful   early   moon   shine
                (of lady's face)

The green eyebrows are graceful and beautiful (and like) the new moon shines shining

It was a triumph not of translation but of inventive imagination and technique to make from such raw materials such finished and authoritative poems.

Just about all that need be said about the technique is that it does its work so well that one is hardly aware of it. Directness, economy, phrase that leads on to phrase—all of that has gone into writing that has an unforced simplicity and naturalness. Its characteristic is not so much the sudden illumination of the single Image—though there is that too, as in 'Separation on the River Kiang'—but rather a continuous insight into things, as if what is there for the eye to see is being contemplated steadily with the mind's eye and inwardly felt and understood. In this way it creates its human world—that is, an objective reality known personally, individually. But the beauty of it is that we are not getting the individual personality of Ezra Pound, nor indeed of Li Po. What we are given is impersonal in the sense that it belongs to no one person, and may be common to all. That is Pound's great technical achievement in *Cathay*, to have found a voice that can speak quite naturally of a common humanity in war and love and other relations, and of himself not at all.

Eliot accurately observed that 'good translation like this is not merely translation, for the translator is giving the original through himself, and finding himself through the original'. But the poetic self found in *Cathay* is far removed from the Pound of the aggressively insulting 'Lustra' and 'Xenia' and *BLAST* poems. In those he is the irritated individual exulting over the common herd, all too full of himself and determined to speak his own mind. In *Cathay*, in compete contrast, he is wholly absorbed in representing Rihaku, and yet in doing so he finds a voice which can speak with authority of timeless things exceeding the momentary rages and hates of Ezra Pound.

So the poet finds himself in losing himself, that at least would be Eliot's idea. But in Pound's case there was a real and abiding contradiction between his poetic genius and his urge to wage instant war against folly and stupidity. He wanted poetry, and the arts generally, to be 'the acknowledged guide and lamp of civilization', and he liked to pretend that his 'aristocracy of the creative arts' would bring about a better world if only the government was in their hands. But when Shelley proclaimed poets 'the unacknowledged legislators of the world' he knew well enough that poets do not legislate as politicians do, and that their power is not to make and enforce customary laws but to reveal the unchanging laws that we learn from long experience are in the immutable nature of things. He knew that poetry changes the world only by changing the way we perceive it. Pound knew that too, but still he would be making war against the imbeciles actually running the world, as if he could triumph over them by satire and abuse; and still he would be engaging in propaganda as if that might somehow do the work of poetry.

Yet in the particular matter of the folly and stupidity of the Great War he did not publish his invective against the 'Whores, apes, rhetoricians' he blamed for it. Instead he found his properly poetic way of dealing with it through *Cathay*. And he did create, in 'The Coming of War: Actæon', one image with the power to alter perceptions of the ongoing tragedy:

> An image of Lethe,
>   and the fields
> Full of faint light
>   but golden,
> Gray cliffs,
>   and beneath them
> A sea
> Harsher than granite,
>   unstill, never ceasing;
> High forms
>   with the movement of gods,
> Perilous aspect;
>   And one said:
> 'This is Actæon.'
>   Actæon of golden greaves!
> Over fair meadows,

> Over the fair face of that field,
> Unstill, ever moving
> Hosts of an ancient people,
> The silent cortège.

The first four lines locate the poem in the classical Elysian fields, where the heroes of ancient wars might be met; but then the more sombre 'eternal moods' of 'Δώρια' are evoked. In this setting Actæon is named, Actæon the hunter hunted down by his own hounds for violating the divinity of nature. The final section begins as a recapitulation, only to lose Actæon in that never resting dead march which belongs more to Dante's hell than to the classical underworld. Only the title connects this with the war begun in 1914. There is no explicit protest or condemnation, no hint of anti-war propaganda. Yet it is a complex image to move the mind to contemplate certain immutable realities of wars whether ancient or modern.

13 : Shaping an Intelligence Unit: 1915–1916

There were Zeppelins over London, dropping bombs, in September 1915. Dorothy's uncle Herbert saw one of the airships and said 'it was a fine sight, silver grey and very graceful'. Mrs Langley who had been Pound's landlady in nearby Church Walk said they had been right over the church steeple there, and the portress at Holland Park Chambers had seen them over Kensington Gardens. Pound himself had 'only heard some gunshots'. He had been having a 'peaceable evening playing draughts with Sauter', and 'we were so busy talking art...that we didn't go out to look at the night birds'. By the time he did come out 'everything was over...Merely people standing about in the streets'. Lewis had seen the old Rebel Arts Centre building burn to the ground. And Dorothy, who was down in Worcestershire at 'The Myrtles, West Malvern', had heard that 'Several offices close to H.H.S. are blown out'. 'Mind you write about Zepps!', she wrote to Pound, 'I feel all away from life here!'

She was enjoying 'wonderful weather' and 'doing a chessboard of an agricultural hill, using more amusing colours than the natural two shades of green.' Pound was being as busy as ever in London. On July 21 he had sent Dorothy an account of his day. He had been in the British Museum Reading Room in the morning; then found Hulme out and Monro out; had a conversation with Elkin Mathews about *Catholic Anthology*; lunched at the Vienna Café; conferred there with Etchells, then with Lewis who had been discussing a book on Vorticism with a publisher; had a conference with Orage who would use his 'political note' in the *New Age* and take two further articles; he had seen Chaplin 'on cinema', and been bored by 'Mother Roses'; he had been in conversation with Hulme and had dinner with him at the 'new Italian restaurant' which was 'not so pleasing as Bellotti'. 'Thence home', to find '6 bloody great boxes in hall, for british prisoners.' The next day he spent three hours on the clavichord, and Dolmetsch came, and then Eliot who was about to sail for America, 'so I shall get no more tennis'. The final instalment of Joyce's

A Portrait of the Artist as a Young Man was just out in the *Egoist*, and was 'very fine'.

The three 'political' notes which appeared in the *New Age* were attacks on America's neutrality. Pound no longer saw the war as 'not our war', that is as not his Vorticist war of individual intelligence against mass stupidity. 'The struggle at Ypres', he had told Harriet Monroe, 'is the struggle for free life and free thought'; and again, 'it is civilization against barbarism'. The great issue of the war, he now declared in an unpublished article and in the *New Age*, was between 'those who believe that the state exists *for* the sake of the individual...and those who believe that the individual's function is to be of use to the state.' Germany with its militarism, its State 'Kultur', its State-education (of which Philology was a product), stood for the subjection of the individual; while ' "the Allies" believe that the individual has certain inalienable rights which it is the duty of the State to preserve to him'. Democratic America should therefore be 'unquestionably an ally', and should join in the war on the side of 'civilization'. This was a remarkable turn in Pound's view of England and its empire, and indeed of America too. But it quite resolved the problem of his relation to the war. If that could be understood as, ultimately, an affair of free individual intelligence standing up against the brute tyranny of the Prussian state, then the Allies' cause was his cause, both as a Vorticist and as an American.

The surprising reason for America's remaining neutral, in Pound's analysis, was that England and America lacked both self-knowledge and knowledge of each other; and this was due to there having been in neither country 'any sufficient sense of the value of realism in literature, of the value of writing words that conform precisely with fact, of free speech without evasions and circumlocutions.' Indeed there was such a 'hatred of realist letters in both countries [that] nearly all that is finest in either is hopelessly obscured from the other'. There was the stifling of 'American thought with "the genteel tone"—i.e. with the habit of mental evasion'. And there was the Englishman's habit of lying, 'unconsciously, because he wants to be considered as holding "sound opinions"'. The consequence was that for want of honest writing neither country knew 'where it was at'. Unenlightened about themselves and about each other, they could find no better basis for their relations in this time of war than commercial self-interest. And that meant that England was not clear that it was in its interest to have America as an ally, while America could not see why it should ally itself with England. They were unable to articulate what, in Pound's view, should have been their common and bonding interest: the inalienable value of the individual person.

The promotion of realist writing became Pound's war effort. He believed with Flaubert that *le mot juste*, the word that did justice to the thing, was the only cure for war. (Evidently he also believed, for war propaganda purposes, in the sort of loose rhetoric which would set up 'British civilization' against 'Prussian barbarism'.) His chosen realist allies were Joyce, Lewis, and Eliot; and he drove himself hard to ensure that those three were kept in funds, and that their work got written, published, and noticed. He developed the vein of realism in his own verse, and in some prose experiments. Privately, he declared that he was 'temporarily off mediævalism', and that the sort of poems he had written in *Canzoni* were as 'moribund' as 'a review in the *Times*'. He was off the *Noh* plays too because they were on the whole 'too damn soft' and 'celtic', too like Fiona Macleod and *Peter Pan*. And when he revised his Arnaut Daniel translations, that was an exceptional five weeks taken off for 'idealism'. For most of the time he gave himself up to mobilizing and maintaining 'a party of intelligence', by which he meant in those years a party of realists of contemporary mentalities. The formidable list of works which Pound in one way and another helped into print would have at its head Joyce's *A Portrait of the Artist as a Young Man*, and *Ulysses*; then Lewis's *Tarr* and 'Cantleman's Spring Mate'; and Eliot's poems from *Prufrock* to *The Waste Land*; along with his own *Lustra* and *Homage to Sextus Propertius*.

He was able to achieve so much, and more, because he had found his Renaissance-style patron. In an aside in his affirmation of Epstein in the *New Age* in January 1915 Pound had been dismissive of 'American collectors buying autograph MSS. of William Morris, faked Rembrandts and faked Vandykes'. He wished they would learn that 'keeping up the arts means keeping up living artists'. John Quinn in New York, with Morris manuscripts in his collection, had taken this personally and been hurt by it— hurt all the more because he knew and admired Pound's work, and because in that article Pound the journalist was at his flamboyantly brilliant best. Firmly but without rancour Quinn informed Pound that as a matter of fact he had already bought half a dozen Epsteins, and had probably been doing as much for contemporary artists as any man of moderate means. Indeed he was willing to buy at once some of the work by Gaudier-Brzeska which Pound had mentioned.[1] Pound apologized unreservedly— 'If there were more like you we should get on with our renaissance', he told

[1] John Quinn (1870–1924) b. Dublin, went to New York 1895, practised there as a very busy and highly successful financial lawyer. Used his wealth to collect first editions, literary manuscripts and works of art, and to support artists and writers—described as 'the twentieth century's most important patron of living literature and art', even though he had only about half a million dollars to spend in

Quinn—and wrote at once to Gaudier, then at the front in France, to see what he had and how much he wanted for it. That was how Pound's career as an impresario of modernist art and letters took off. It was a career made possible by Quinn's generously and energetically backing his projects with practical as well as financial assistance. Quinn became not only Pound's patron but also his agent in New York. And Pound became Quinn's agent in London, though a free agent enabled by Quinn to pursue his own ends.

He wanted Quinn's money to go into the production of new work, art that would not otherwise exist. He wanted artists who had good work in them to be given simply what they needed to get on with it, 'money to buy tools, time and food'. He wanted to create an economy directed exclusively to the making of art, and having nothing to do with collecting and with making money out of art. Yet in practice he would make the best of far from ideal actualities.

He sent Quinn photographs of two of Gaudier's works that were available, and described one of them, the red stone dancer, as a good example of extreme Vorticist work, 'the face a triangle, and the two nipples a circle and ellipse'. Then Gaudier was killed, and Pound observed that there was nothing more to be done for him and nothing more to come from him. His concern now was that 'Decent publicity for his work *might* do some good to young sculptors'—he hoped to bring out 'a well-illustrated memoir', and suggested an exhibition in New York. Then it emerged that no-one knew who now had title to Gaudier's estate, so that a year later Pound was still rushing about between the French Embassy and Sophie Brzeska attempting to negotiate on Quinn's behalf; and by the time it was established that Miss Brzeska could sell the sculptures she had put Gaudier's prices up, because she wanted his work to have as good a market value as Epstein's. In the end though his work was seen in New York; and Pound's 'well illustrated memoir' did do some good to one young sculptor, Henry Moore, who came across a copy in 1922 and was greatly impressed and encouraged by Gaudier's life and work.

Caring for Wyndham Lewis and James Joyce

With Gaudier gone the number of living artists whom Pound really cared about came down to 'the two men of genius', Joyce and Lewis, along with Eliot who 'has a quaint mind full of intelligence', and John Rodker[2]

his lifetime. Helped organize the Armory Show of international modern art in New York in 1913, in which he was both the biggest single lender of paintings and the biggest buyer.

[2] John Rodker (1894–1955), poet, dramatist, novelist, translator, critic, editor, and publisher. Born in Manchester; grew up in the Jewish community of the East End of London. Began to publish in

who 'has a small vein, but his own'. Hueffer he regarded as an impressionist, not a realist, and besides he was rather out of it because although over age he had gallantly got himself a commission in the regular army. And Yeats, now the respected elder, was 'getting too flighty, too subject to chimaeras to be of much use in a compact fighting' unit.

As for the Imagists or 'Amygists', Aldington and H.D. and Flint who now had the run of the *Egoist*, he washed his hands 'of the lot of 'em.' They were pointedly excluded from his *Catholic Anthology 1914–1915*, which appeared in November 1915 with a striking Vorticist cover by D[orothy] S[hakespear]. Pound led off with Eliot's 'Prufrock' and 'Portrait of a Lady', then first published in England and 'the only advance since the first imagist stuff'; and he included Williams's 'The Wanderer', his 'first "long" poem', which in turn led to *Paterson*. The rest of the collection was devoted mainly to American poets associated with *Poetry*, with Edgar Lee Masters and Sandburg the most prominent. Yeats's 'The Scholars'—'Bald heads, forgetful of their sins'—was printed in italic at the front, as a point of departure; and the volume closed with four of Rodker's pieces for silent theatre which seem now to have been pointing ahead to some of Beckett's late plays. One of them, 'Fear', would be absorbed into 'A Game of Chess' in *The Waste Land*. But to a contemporary reviewer the anthology appeared to be 'the work of "literary Cubists" who threatened "anarchy" and "red ruin"', and Eliot's poems in particular were likened to the foolish gesticulations of a drunken slave imitating his masters. Another attack came from Francis Meynell, a leading Roman Catholic, who thought the title blasphemous and warned the publisher, Elkin Mathews, that it would not sell. It seems likely that the rival *Some Imagist Poets 1915* did indeed have better sales.

Pound's 'two men of genius' were forever in need of money and other assistance. Joyce was forced to leave Trieste in June 1915 when Italy declared war on Austria-Hungary, and took his wife and two children to Zurich where he had no work and no income. Pound at once moved Yeats to persuade Edmund Gosse, as an Englishman and an official of the Royal Literary Fund, to recommend that a grant should be made to Joyce. Gosse was concerned that neither Yeats nor Joyce, Irishmen both, 'had given

The New Age, The Egoist, and *Poetry* in 1912–14. Conscientious objector in 1914–18 war—wrote about his experiences in *Memoirs of Other Fronts* (1932). Succeeded Pound as London editor of *Little Review* in 1919. Founded Ovid Press (with Mary Butts) in 1919: published *20 Drawings from the Notebooks of Gaudier-Brzeska* (1919), Pound's *Fourth Canto* (1919) and *Hugh Selwyn Mauberley* (1920), T. S. Eliot's *Ara Vus Prec* (1920), Wyndham Lewis's *Fifteen Drawings* (1920), and Pound's *A Draft of Cantos 17–27* (1927); also organized the publication in Paris of the Egoist Press edition of *Ulysses* (1922). Took an early, deep and lasting interest in Freud and psychoanalysis. Pound serialized his novel, *Adolphe 1920*, in *The Exile* in 1927–28.

any statement of loyalty to the Allies in the war', and had to be assured by Yeats that he himself certainly wished them victory, and that Joyce, whom he had never known to agree with his neighbours, would surely be out of sympathy with the Austrians. Pound sent in a characteristically uninhibited letter of support, writing 'as a foreigner, viewing as a spectator the glories and shames of your country', and hoping that his being 'persona non grata to most of my elders ... might be overlooked for the moment in a matter so intimately concerning the welfare of English letters'. He wished to state that he considered Joyce '*without exception* the best of the younger prose writers', that his style had 'the hard clarity of a Stendhal or a Flaubert', and that Joyce had 'lived for ten years in obscurity and poverty, that he might perfect his writing and be uninfluenced by commercial demands and standards'. A grant of £75 was made to Joyce in July and helped him, Ellmann suggests, to settle to work on the Bloom episodes in *Ulysses*. Pound also arranged for J. B. Pinker to become Joyce's literary agent.

In August Lewis was asking Pound for an advance against the possible sale of his work to Quinn. He had two children in the care of his mother to support. Pound, already in debt himself, borrowed a further £20 and sent Lewis £5 out of it. In October another advance was sought, and this time Pound said he couldn't help, his gross income having averaged just £2 2s. and 4d. a month for the past three months, which put him in about as bad a hole as Lewis. His income for the entire year had amounted to just £42 10s. However, in December he was able to send Lewis £15 from Quinn for some of his drawings, and he urged Quinn to buy more—'THIS IS the time to buy a big picture or a collection of drawings by Mr W. L.' At the same time he was trying to find a publisher for *Tarr*, and in order to get Lewis an immediate £50 for it he arranged for Miss Weaver to take it on, first as a serial in the *Egoist* then as a book, the £50 being dependent on Pound himself 'raising £20 of it to lend them'.

He was also trying with Pinker to find a commercial publisher to bring out Joyce's *Portrait* in book form, but six publishers, one after another, turned it down as not what their readers wanted. Then Miss Weaver said The Egoist Ltd. would publish it, and now seven printers refused to set it up for fear of being prosecuted for 'indecency'. The recent prosecution and burning of Lawrence's *The Rainbow* had turned them into the frightened censors of literature. Pound thought of having Miss Weaver 'print it with blank spaces and then have the deleted passages done in typewriter and pasted in', even if he had to do it himself. He told Joyce that 'Judging from Lewis's troubles and yours ... none of the commercial houses will *ever* be any use'. But he was 'much pleased with Miss Weaver ... for being ready to start publishing good literature, at her own risk, with no chance of profit & a certain steady loss on the paper'. There was to be the same arrangement as for *Tarr*, '£50 to Joyce...part of which I have got lent to them'. As part of the arrangement he 'would send [the *Egoist*] a series of twelve articles free', and his twelve 'Dialogues of Fontenelle'. But there was still the problem of getting the novel printed. Pound persuaded John Marshall, a New York publisher who had agreed to bring out a collection of his journalism and essays under the title 'This Generation', to bring out Joyce's *Portrait* instead, but Marshall's wife developed TB and he took her off to Canada, and both that chance and the manuscript of Pound's 'This Generation' were lost. Finally, in July 1916, B. W. Huebsch of New York agreed to publish *A Portrait of the Artist as a Young Man*, and actually did so in December. Miss Weaver then imported sheets of the New York printing and The Egoist Ltd. issued its English edition in February 1917. Pound celebrated in *The Egoist* with a review headlined 'At Last The Novel Appears'.

He had been busy about Joyce's affairs, and Lewis's, in other ways throughout 1916. There was Joyce's play *Exiles* which he had been hawking about theatre agents for months, even though he was sure it wouldn't do for the stage because it required too much thought. Just reading it had left him with 'a tired head'. But then he spent the best part of one fine day typing an article to promote it. In January 1916 he was telling Joyce that he was worried that, apart from enlisting Miss Weaver, he couldn't see what else he could do in the way of helping him to money and a publisher. Quite possibly he was beginning to weary of Joyce's always crying poor, and to think he might do more to help himself. Writing from Stone Cottage he told him that he was down in the country with Yeats because he could not afford London, could not afford even the fare to go up. And yet a few days later there he was up in London cabling Quinn that he could have Lewis's big 'Kermesse' for £80 and five drawings at £10 each, or £120 the lot.

Lewis, about to become Gunner Lewis and then Bombardier, was writing to Pound every few days from his training camps, after moneys from Quinn for his drawings, and about his troubles with the army. He was regretting having joined up in the ranks, but Pound was unsympathetic about that, telling him that he didn't see that the future of the arts demanded 'that you should be covered with military distinctions'. 'Endure your present ills with equanimity', he counselled, and 'don't be more irritating to your "superior" officers than you find absolutely necessary to your peace of mind'. He invited him to reflect that 'Nothing exists without efficient cause', and sent him £25 of Quinn's money.

About the same time Pound was applying for a grant to be made to Joyce from The War Emergency Fund of the Incorporated Society of Authors, Playwrights & Composers, and in June 1916 he was able to tell him that a grant of £2 a week had been made to him, initially for thirteen weeks but probably renewable. He could also expect cheques of £10 each from Marshall, possibly as an advance on *Portrait*, and from Quinn, this at Pound's suggestion; and in July there was another £20 'from an anonymous donor' who may have been Lady Cunard, and again it would have been thanks to Pound. Then in August, at Pound's instigation, Lady Cunard spoke to Edward Marsh who was 'in some way in charge of these grants', and after due enquiries Prime Minister Asquith granted a Civil List award of £100 to Joyce. Altogether Pound had raised £200 or thereabouts for Joyce in the summer of 1916, apart from what was due to him for the book publication of *Portrait*.

In the course of seeking details of his needs from Joyce Pound had raised the possibility of his practising certain economies:

I do a good deal of my own cooking, and I suppose you and your wife can manage that sort of thing. Would it be an advantage if you could take an unfurnished place and furnish it (I have made most bits of furniture save beds, one MUST buy beds)....

Could you go to a village in the country, where life would be cheaper, IF you had guarantee of supplies for the next year and didn't feel obliged to look for work that you can't find? Various young writers here have done so.

Joyce, who was often on the move in Zurich in search of a better apartment, and whose habit was to stay late in convivial cafes and restaurants, must have laughed at that. His way of life and Pound's were cultures apart. While Pound was living according to his bare needs and directing Quinn's and Lady Cunard's bounty away from himself to the artists he believed in, Joyce was living at the rate of Pound's and others' generosity, and caring only for his own genius.

Lewis complained of being treated by a particular non-commissioned officer 'with the most absolute and unwavering unfairness'. Pound told him '*No one* has the least sympathy with your present troubles'. Mrs Bonham-Carter, whom he had approached with the idea that she might use her influence to secure an officer-cadetship for Lewis, and who had four brothers in uniform, had declared that he was lucky not to be mutilated or dead. 'Descend with me, Poet, to my miniature personal, military hell for a second', Lewis then wrote, 'If Quinn's consent to your transference of some funds you have of his to me does not arrive in a week or so, I shall be penniless...If you could advance me (without entering into unnecessary details) £5 at once...' Pound did send the £5 at once, and an assurance that Quinn, from whom Lewis was receiving the £120 for 'the Kermess' and the drawings, almost certainly intended to take more of his work. But he was finding his own position, Pound remarked, 'a little embarrassing as I have constantly to approach you in the paternal, admonitory, cautionary, epicierish bloodguttily INartistic angle.' He could see no way out of Lewis's 'impasse', nor of several of his own. How should such 'particles hostile to the current' as himself and Lewis not 'feel the pinch' at such a time?

Still, his efforts on Lewis's behalf did bring in at least another £100 from Quinn in 1916. The proposed showing of Gaudier's work in New York had become a Vorticist show, with Pound doing all the organizing and despatching, and Quinn managing it in New York and doing most of the buying. There were cheques not only for Lewis but for Wadsworth, Etchells, Roberts, and others, 'so they are no longer on my mind either', Pound told Joyce when he had just received the news of his Civil List award.

At the beginning of September 1916 he could tell Quinn, 'I no longer feel responsible for the welfare or upkeep of Joyce or Lewis, and Eliot seems to be getting on all right (though he is producing very little, practically nothing)'. To another correspondent he wrote, 'At the present moment I feel I have no one to look after but myself. Which is odd after four years of propaganda.' And to Joyce he declared, 'I shall devote the next six months entirely to my own interests. (Which will do them no good whatever.) All life's blessings except loose change seem to have been showered upon me, it behooves me to remedy that deficiency AT ONCE.' When he reckoned up his 'income for year ending Oct 31' it amounted to just £48. He had taken none of Quinn's money for himself, and had taken no commission from either Quinn or the Vorticists on the sales in which he had played an agent's part. He was translating the libretto of Massenet's *Cendrillon* for Beecham—the 40 guineas would be due to others as soon as he received it. He told Alice Corbin Henderson that he was sweating at the translation to pay the rent, and that might imply that it was Dorothy he was in debt to. He was also 'Cadging for penny a line reviewing', though with little success. Nevertheless he was able to clear his debts at the beginning of 1917.

'Lustra of Ezra Pound': the censor censored

While he was battling to get *A Portrait of the Artist as a Young Man* into print as a book Pound was having difficulties of his own with a commercial printer and with his publisher Elkin Mathews. Mathews had agreed to publish his new collection of poems, and sent the typescript in April or early May of 1916 to William Clowes and Sons, where 'the entire text was set up in print and page proofs were run off'. The proofs were seen by a managing director, who showed them to the senior director, W. C. K. Clowes, an eminent and eminently respectable member of his profession, and he let Mathews know that they didn't at all like what he had asked them to print. In late May Pound heard by way of Yeats that Mathews had been alarmed and horrified by what Clowes had pointed out to him in the proofs, and that he was now refusing to publish a number of the poems and wanted cuts and verbal changes in others. Pound then received a set of proofs with twenty-one poems violently slashed through by Mathews' thick blue pencil. It was, he remarked, 'like the Greek statues in the Vatican with tin fig leaves wired onto them'.

Among the blue-pencilled poems were 'Salutation the Second' and 'Commission' which had appeared in *Poetry* in 1913 in Pound's 'Contemporania'. Yeats would have had them in mind, along with others, when he said in early 1914 that Pound's 'insults to the world' were so deadly that it was a problem getting them published. Since then Pound had composed further mocking observations of contemporary manners and morals, many of them in the style of classical epigrams, as if he were writing about Martial's Rome. One, if not two, distinguished authors known to him were portrayed in that way in 'The Temperaments':

> Nine adulteries, 12 liaisons, 64 fornications and something approaching
>   a rape
> Rest nightly upon the soul of our delicate friend Florialis,
> And yet the man is so quiet and reserved in demeanour
> That he passes for both bloodless and sexless.
> Bastidides, on the contrary, who both talks and writes of nothing save
>   copulation,
> Has become the father of twins,
> But he accomplished the feat at some cost;
> He had to be four times cuckold.

While such cold, hard epigrams dominated one part of the collection, there were now also a good number of poems in other registers. Several cultivated a naturalistic realism to dismiss poetical fantasies and illusions, notably 'The Lake Isle', an anti-pastoral parody of Yeats's 'Innisfree'; and 'To a Friend Writing of Cabaret Dancers', which observed the dancers, as Pound explained to Mathews, not with false glamour or sensational moralizing but simply as 'human beings like anyone else'. There was a different, more subjective realism in 'Villanelle: The Psychological Hour', and in 'Dans un Omnibus de Londres'. Then there were the *Imagiste* poems, with 'The Coming of War: Actaeon'; and the reverie of 'Provincia Deserta'. 'Near Perigord', an extended study of the story of Bertrand de Born, added a further dimension, as a poem investigating history. And *Cathay*, with four new translations from the Chinese, was now incorporated into *Lustra*.

Altogether the new collection was something of a miscellany, a bringing together of different kinds of work done since *Ripostes*, with no very clear pattern beyond some groupings of like-toned poems and some ringing the changes from one tone to another; and with, overall, a sense of a loosely chronological progression, the most recently written poems being placed at the end. Yet Pound did want the book to be seen as a whole. 'Even certain smaller poems, unimportant in themselves have a function in the book-as-a-whole', he insisted to Mathews when resisting his demand for certain poems to be deleted, 'This shaping up a book... is almost as important as the construction of a play or a novel.' He must have been thinking, as with his earlier collections, of making up a whole by giving 'a more or less proportioned presentation of life', with 'something for every mood and mental need'. There should be harsh moods as well as gentle, biting satire as well as moments of vision, gaiety as well as justice. *Canzoni* had suffered, he told Mathews, from his having cut out 'the rougher poems'. He was perhaps hoping that, like a performance of 'Noh' plays, his *Lustra of Ezra Pound* would be read as 'a complete service of life', that is, as 'a sort of musical construction' in which the several dimensions of a human life were represented—divine states of mind or gods, battles against evil forces, occasions of peace and love, also the inner dramas of the human spirit, and the comedies of ethics in action.

Clowes and Mathews were never going to see *Lustra* whole in that way. Clowes sent Mathews a post card of impatient jibes: 'Tenzone' and 'Condolence'—'Sorry stuff to begin with'; 'Salutation the Second'—'An impudent piece'; 'Commission'—'D[itt]o'; 'Les Millwin'—'Silly nonsense'; 'Further Instructions'—'Better keep his *baser passions* to himself. No one else wants them'; 'The Temperaments'—'<u>Beastly</u>'; 'The Seeing Eye' ['The small dogs look at the big dogs']—'Smelly like its subject'; 'Ancient Music' ['Winter is icummen in, / Lhude sing Goddamm']—'Pitiful parody of beautiful verse'; 'The Lake Isle'—'Profane and flippant'. Clowes concluded that 'the only poems worth reading are the translations', and that 'the only redeeming feature of most of the others, which with a few exceptions are more fitted for the Waste Paper Basket than for the literary public', was 'the splendid self conceit... of the author.' These and the other comments on the post card are Podsnappish objections, intended to get rid of what was considered unsuitable for the innocent Young Person and the right-thinking Family. They take offence on the grounds of taste and social decorum, but not, it should be noticed, of morality.

Nevertheless Mathews appears to have taken fright, as if Pound's poems might turn out to be another *Rainbow* and get him prosecuted for publishing work of an immoral tendency. Pound denied that there was any immoral tone or tendency whatsoever in *Lustra*, and boldly declared that as a serious writer he recognized no-one's 'right to interfere with the freedom of letters'. However, he would be 'willing to sacrifice a few of the shorter poems on the altar of bigotry, and also to make a few verbal deletions', upon condition that his note objecting to the deletions be printed in the book. He wanted to cite the defence of realism which Edmond and Jules de Goncourt had prefixed to their novel *Germinie Lacerteux* in 1864, and which he had recently cited in connection with the difficulties of getting *Tarr* and *A Portrait of the Artist* 'published "through the ordinary channels"':

Now that the novel...begins to be the serious, passionate, living great form of literary study and of social research, now that it has become, by analysis and psychological inquiry, the history of contemporary ethics-in-action ['l'Histoire morale contemporaine'], now that the novel has imposed upon itself the studies and duties of science, one may again make a stand for its liberties and its privileges.

'Poetry', Pound wanted then to assert, 'is as serious and as grave a form of expression as is the prose of a novel'. He was hoping thus to appeal to 'the best part' of Mathews's mind, but it didn't work.

He tried other, less high-toned angles. Mathews had said to Yeats, 'not only men come into this shop, *but ladies*', so Pound told him that 'four perfectly well bred women', Mrs Shakespear among them, had read the whole of the manuscript and not been shocked. He reminded him that most of the poems Clowes and he were objecting to had already appeared in both England and America without causing any disturbance, and that 'YOU CAN'T POSSIBLY BE PROSECUTED FOR POEMS THAT HAVE ALREADY APPEARED and created no scandal'. To put his 'mind at rest on the subject of prosecutions' he consulted J. B. Pinker, the literary agent, and Augustine Birrell who could speak for the Home Office. He was told, he reported to Mathews, that 'No prosecution is of any effect unless the Home Office takes it up', and he had been assured that 'the Home Office will not make a fool of itself over my book'. In the case of *The Rainbow*, Pinker had said, 'The Home Office had inspected the book...and decided they would do nothing.' It had been seized by the police upon the order of a magistrate to whom someone had complained that it was immoral, but the magistrate was acting beyond his powers. If only Methuen, the publisher, had defended the book, or refused to hand it over to the police, 'NOTHING could have been done'. Pinker 'put the whole blame on' the publisher, for agreeing that the book was immoral and for co-operating in its suppression. Birrell confirmed to Mathews that in his view it was 'simply out of the question that any of the poems [in *Lustra*] are exposed to the risk of prosecution for indecency'. But to that Mathews replied, 'are not there other considerations for a publisher besides the mere avoidance of prosecution?'

Mathews now drew up, no doubt in the light of those 'other considerations', 'a list of the minimum number of emendations and omissions which must be made before I can consent to publish the work'. His list included most of the poems jibbed at by Clowes, and added one or two on his own account. He wanted all but the opening lines of 'Salutation the Second' to be cut, and ten lines of 'Commission', apparently disapproving of the naked impudence of the one and its mocking 'the grave and the stodgy' with 'the dance of the phallus'; and disapproving in the other of its speaking of 'the hideously wedded' and of 'the adolescent . . . smothered in family'. Pound refused to make the cuts and both poems were suppressed. Also suppressed was 'The New Cake of Soap', because it named G. K. Chesterton; but 'Further Instructions' and 'Salvationists' were not suppressed, although Mathews had blue-pencilled them in the first proofs. 'Epitaph' had to go, 'because the meaning is dubious'. (What *could* Mathews have been reading into 'Leucis, who intended a grand Passion, / Ends with a willingness-to-oblige'?) Then there were half a dozen 'nasty' or otherwise offensive epigrams that 'must be deleted': 'The Temperaments', 'Phyllidula' and 'The Patterns', '$I\mu\acute{\epsilon}\rho\rho\omega$' ('The poem to Atthis—anything but "delicate"'), and the doggy poems 'Meditatio' and 'The Seeing Eye'. Mathews was of one mind with Clowes about 'Ancient Music': 'Blasted blasphemy & a damn'd parody—must be omitted'. He also called for 'O God' to be changed to 'O Jupiter' in the 'profane and flippant' (according to Cowes) 'The Lake Isle', and when Pound refused on the ground that 'O Jupiter' was 'not living speech' that poem too was suppressed. Mathews didn't like the mention of 'whores' in it either; and 'Pagani's, November 8' was banned, presumably because of its 'very beautiful Normande cocotte'. And yet 'To a Friend Writing on Cabaret Dancers', which also mentioned whores—and which Harriet Monroe had refused to publish in *Poetry*—did get by. Mathews had suggested that 'some of the very "delicate" allusions might with advantage be toned down', and had asked was 'it necessary to describe that *particular* intaglio?', that is, 'my fat great-uncle's heirloom: / Cupid astride a phallus with two wings, / Swinging a cat-o'-nine-tails'. Pound refused to tone it down, and the poem was printed intact.

If Mathews, and Clowes, could allow that, then what exactly was bothering them in those other poems? They wouldn't stand for naming 'God' in jest, that at least is clear. Then they appear to have been reacting against what the genteel family didn't talk about or like to admit. More seriously, in wanting to stop him saying the things one didn't say they were defending just those social institutions and conventions and pieties which Pound meant to subvert. Their objections countered his attack quite exactly.

Pound, from his own point of view, quite understood this. A couple of months later, in July, when John Quinn had had to tell him that he could not persuade the American branch of Macmillan & Co. to become his publishers there, he wrote back,

The minute people begin to realize a few simple facts which my work reveals they cease to swallow a lot of victorian slosh. That cessation will be very bad for certain ancient publishing houses . . . It is their bread and butter to prevent innovation and wider knowledge.

It is all perfectly 'rational'. If I didn't stir their opposition I wouldn't be worth my salt.

Again, what they don't understand they fear, and turpitude springs out of terror.

'I don't think I have a persecution mania', he had written in May. He could see that it was only natural that those whom he upset should want to suppress him.

Yet in practice it didn't quite come to that. At the end of May there were some feverish days of letters and consultations and 'final terms', but by June 10 a settlement was negotiated in which all the parties got down off their high horses. Pound had to accept the deletion of the thirteen poems Mathews would not publish, and this without the inclusion of his note of protest. But Clowes would print, at Mathews's expense, and Mathews would sell to those who asked for it, a 'private edition' of 200 copies to include nine of those thirteen poems. Clowes absolutely would not print, even in the 'unexpurgated' edition, 'The Temperaments', 'Ancient Music', 'The Lake Isle' and 'Pagani's: November 8'. Pound had written to Mathews, 'This much you can be certain of, whatever you take out of this book posterity will put back into it, and they will do so ridiculing an age and a bad taste that removed it.' He was quite right, except that it was not left to posterity to put them back. The New York edition of *Lustra* which Quinn saw through the press in 1917 contained all the expurgated poems except 'The Temperaments', and that too was included in the 1926 collected poems in the United States, and in the 1928 *Selected Poems* edited by the 'reverend' T. S. Eliot in England.

It seems in retrospect to have been a tempest in a teapot, one man wanting 'to write poems a grown man could read', and the other saying 'but not in front of the ladies'. It was a fully serious case, on both sides, of 'ethics-in-action', yet the ethical argument was left undecided. Mathews won on the day because, as Pound allowed, he had 'some right to decide how he'll spend his money'. It was simply that, and neither a better argument nor any special legal or moral standing, that gave him the power to censor what he published. And still the title page as he published it carried the implicit claim that it was the poet who was the censor here. 'Lustrum', it copied from a school dictionary, 'an offering for the sins of the whole people, made by the censors at the expiration of their five years of office'. It was five years since Pound had settled in England, and what else was his book if not an attempt to reform it? He could be confident that the book would outlast its publisher.

Dialogues at Stone Cottage

Pound spent the winter months of 1916 with Yeats in Stone Cottage. It was the third and last time they would winter together in this way. Dorothy was with them again, doing the housekeeping, according to Yeats, though it seems improbable that Dorothy, with the Misses Welfare on hand, would have 'done' for them. Pound was secretarying for Yeats, taking letters at his dictation and typing them for him. They both kept up an energetic correspondence, and the walk to the post office, a mile away, was a daily ritual. Then they would be writing, Pound in one of their four rooms with Yeats 'brrring in the next room, re-doing a lyric'. They walked in Ashdown Forest, or exercised with the foils. In the evenings Pound read aloud from Herbert of Cherbury's autobiography, and Landor's *Imaginary Conversations*.

Lord Herbert presents himself as a sort of Cavalier Tom Jones, his life a series of picaresque adventures through the courts and countries of Europe. His writings on Natural Religion, which were noticed by Locke and Descartes in his own time, and which earned him a mention among the philosophers in Pound's late cantos, come in only as an afterthought on his final page. He preferred to write of himself as a man who knew his world and had played his part in it, and who could tell over its incidents and anecdotes in a lively, direct and amusing manner. In temper and tone the book is closer to Fielding's and Sterne's rational and sentimental eighteenth century than to his brother George Herbert's 'metaphysical' seventeenth century. Pound would have been enjoying it for its sophistication and its realism—for its Odysseus-like familiarity with 'many men's manners'.

He found a similar enlightenment in the more artful *Imaginary Conversations*. In these Landor invented exchanges between a great gallery of historical persons from both ancient and modern times, and also between fictional characters or gods and heros of myth. Pound admired these conversations as the work of a truly civilized mind interpreting not only its own but other and 'different eras with sureness and thoroughness'. That's what he was wanting to do in the long poem which he had begun to work at again in the latter half of 1915. But while pursuing that interest of his own he might also have been making a point to Yeats, about how the dead might better be made to speak through the medium of a learned imagination than through a fat old woman in Soho.

Yeats was just then writing both sides of a correspondence with Leo Africanus, a much travelled Moor who flourished in the sixteenth century and who had been speaking to him in séances since 1909. But was he, Yeats was asking himself, in communication with the real Leo, or did it all come from his own imagination? He wanted to believe that his Leo Africanus was the still living spirit of a dead person who had sought him out as his anti-self or opposite in order that each might make the other more complete. It might well have been this wanting the projections of his imagination, his phantasmagoria, to be more than that—to be actual disembodied spirits—that exasperated Pound and made him confess to Alice Corbin Henderson that after this time with Yeats in the country he was 'so tired of a lot of dead ideas', evidently meaning that it was Yeats's preoccupations he was tired of.

Pound had never entertained the temptation to confuse the dead he made speak in his poems with the real Vidal or Villon or Bertran de Born. And his idea of a complete poetic self was very different from Yeats's. 'In the "search for oneself"', he had written in 1914,

one gropes, one finds some seeming verity. One says "I am" this, that, or the other, and with the words scarcely uttered one ceases to be that thing.

I began this search for the real in a book called *Personae*, casting off, as it were, complete masks of the self in each poem. I continued in a long series of translations, which were but more elaborate masks.

This is very different from Yeats's idea of the Mask, which would have Leo Africanus be an other self, an *alter ego*. Pound neither wished to communicate with spirits nor to perfect his own self. To put it simply, he just wanted to make real poems—to make images that would come alive in the mind, ultimately to make a poem containing a various enough history to form a new mentality. That the reality (or *virtu*) he was after could be carried over from one written text to another shows how far he was from attending to disembodied spirits. While Yeats was engaged in his dialogue with Leo Africanus, Pound was translating a selection of Bernard de Fontenelle's *Nouveaux dialogues des morts* (1683).

What was new about Fontenelle's dialogues of the dead was that he had his historical persons talk as if they were all at the brilliant court of Louis XIV. His Alexander, his Dido, his Homer and Aesop, his Paracelsus and Molière, might be at Versailles or on the stage of a Paris theatre, conversing on the questions Fontenelle's contemporaries would want to put to them with the elegant wit and sophisticated intelligence those contemporaries would demand. The dialogues are exercises in historical imagination in which the viewpoints of honoured Ancients and of critical Moderns challenge each other, and in which the rationality or cynical realism of the French Enlightenment always prevails. In the last of the twelve Pound translated, Bombastes Paracelsus speaks for the study of the sublime mysteries of the invisible genii, and dismisses Molière's preoccupation with the low comedy of human follies as unworthy of serious attention. But Fontenelle gives Molière the last word: 'although I have never worked upon subjects save those which lie before all men's eyes, I can predict that my comedies will outlast your exalted productions...for he who would paint for immortality must paint fools.' One can imagine Pound being specially amused by that dialogue as he translated it with Yeats communing with his invisible genius in the next room.

They still had some shared ground in the Japanese *Noh* plays, but these also brought out their differences. Pound was finishing off his big edition which Macmillan would send to the printers in August and publish in early January 1917. In the meantime four of the plays were to be published by Yeats's sister at her Cuala Press in Ireland, as *Certain Noble Plays of Japan* 'with an introduction by William Butler Yeats'. The certain plays were *Nishikigi*, the spirit play; *Hagoromo*, a 'god dance'; and two heroic plays, *Kumasaka* and *Kagekiyo*. In his introduction Yeats was enthusiastic about a new, non-naturalistic form of drama which he had developed with the help of the *Noh*, 'an aristocratic form', 'indirect and symbolic and having no need of mob or press to pay its way'. Naturalism and realism, he declared, were for common minds 'educated...by schoolmasters and newspapers' and lacking 'the memory of beauty and emotional subtlety'. He looked back rather to the time when the *Noh* had become the court drama of Japan and young nobles, 'forbidden to attend the popular theatre...a place of mimicry and naturalism, were encouraged to witness and to perform in spectacles where speech, music, song and dance created an image of nobility and strange beauty.' He was just then 'elaborating', as he put it, *At the Hawk's Well*, a noble play of his own set in 'the Irish Heroic Age'.

His play was to be performed in April in Lady Cunard's London drawing room before a 'very noble & exclusive' audience, as Pound told Quinn, mimicking Yeats; or, more cynically, 'before an audience composed exclusively of crowned heads and divorcées'. Pound also had written a play modelled on the *Noh* which he expected to be performed on the same occasion. As a matter of fact he had been writing it in his room at Stone Cottage while Yeats next door was 'brrring' away at his. Pound's play was supposed to be the *kyogen* to Yeats's *noh*, that is, an interlude in which one or two actors represent the action in a simplified form. But it turned out to be more like a comic dialogue for the contemporary popular theatre, a thoroughly naturalistic imitation of risible Irish peasant behaviour and just the sort of thing Yeats would not want in his noble theatre.

At the Hawk's Well celebrates the doomed heroism of those who would give up a comfortable life for the chance of drinking at the well of the superhuman. The characters, an old man and young Cuchulain, and the hawk-woman who guards the well and distracts them when it flows, are masked, hieratic. And there are musicians who double as chorus, and, as in the *Noh*, place the action in a realm of imagination estranged from commonplace reality. In Pound's *The Consolations of Matrimony* there is no such intensified and heightened consciousness. The scene is a far from heroic 'warty' Irish village where nothing ever happens. Two men sit at a cottage table debating whether it is a better thing to have known many women or to be dully married for life to just one, with the married man enviously recalling the other's conquests and wishing he were as free. For dénouement a boy brings a message that his wife has run off to America with another man, thus giving him a chance for the sort of life he wanted, but still some reflex makes him chase after them. If this were performed with *At the Hawk's Well* it would seem a cynical parody, bringing down memory and desire and imagination to the level of impoverished banalities. Pound's idea must have been to counter the soft lyricism of Yeats's 'celtic noh' with some hard realism, and Yeats appears to have gone along with the idea, at least until the rehearsals were under way. But there were only three weeks between their getting back to London and the performance on April 2 and it was decided that there was not time to prepare both pieces, so Pound's farce was dropped from the programme, and thereafter forgotten.

Pound and Dorothy had been involved in an interlude of their own in early February, one of those wartime experiences which was serious enough for them and yet farcical to those not directly concerned. They were discovered to be, according to war regulations, aliens in a prohibited area; and worse, they had failed to register with the local police. Three times the police called on them at Stone Cottage, then Pound was summoned to be questioned by a magistrate at East Grinstead on suspicion of being a foreign spy. He asked Mrs Masterman to get her husband who was a cabinet minister to use his influence with the authorities; and Yeats asked Robert Bridges, the Poet Laureate, to vouch for Pound's identity. Bridges replied as one entering into the spirit of a Conan Doyle mystery: what evidence was there in Yeats's letter to prove that any of them were who they claimed to be? Pound settled that question by going up to London and obtaining from the American Embassy, on a folio sheet of parchment paper with a large red seal, a passport which declared him to be 5′ 10$^1/_2$″ in height, with green eyes, a straight nose, an imperial chin, fair hair and an oval face. (His next passport, issued in Paris in 1919, would say that he had grey eyes and light brown hair.) Dorothy's identity too was established by a passport declaring her to be a citizen of the United States, 5′7″ in height, with medium brown hair, a medium forehead, blue eyes, a small nose, a round chin, and an oval face. The summons was withdrawn, thanks probably to Masterman's intervention with the Home Office.

Works and days

Back in London Pound was 'glued to [his] mattress', or so he told Lewis, 'not paralysis but sciatica = depression of last Saturday logically explained'. Only a day or so later he was typing a long letter to Kate Buss about his 'immediate activity': *Gaudier-Brzeska: A Memoir* would be published in April by John Lane; he was trying to put a little life back into the *Egoist* with Lewis's *Tarr*, and being 'much pleased with their sporting intention of publishing Joyce's novel in despite of all fools, printers, censors, etc.'; he was expecting 'proofs any day' from the Cuala Press for *Certain Noble Plays of Japan*; then—

My occupations this week consist in finally (let us hope) dealing with Brzeska's estate; 2, getting a vorticist show packed up and started for New York; 3, making a selection from old father Yeats' letters, some of which are very fine (I suppose this will lap over into next week), small vol. to appear soon; 4, bother a good deal about the production of Yeats' new play.

His 'Editor's Note' to *Passages from the Letters of John Butler Yeats*, published by the Cuala Press in 1917, is dated 'May 20th, 1916', so that task
may have overlapped into the next month or two. A remarkable detail in
that account of his activities is the absence of any mention of *Lustra*, and
his saying resignedly 'I shan't publish again here until after the war'.

In mid-March Pound told Joyce that he had 'never been so hurried
in my life, as during these weeks after return to town, with all sorts of
accumulations.' In May it was still 'nothing but letters letters letters all
day', to Quinn, Lewis, Joyce, Elkin Mathews, Harriet Monroe and the
rest, and now and again Dorothy 'raging *for me* to *come forth* to supper'
at Bellotti's. Yet through that spring and summer he found time for a
series of sometimes long letters to Iris Barry, a young woman who had
had some poems published in Harold Monro's *Poetry and Drama*.[3] There
was a clinical lack of respect for conventional pieties in her poems, such as
the author of *Lustra* might have found promising, and he had asked to see
more with a view to selecting a group for Harriet Monroe's *Poetry*.

When she asked for criticism and advice he at once set out to pass on
to her what he had learnt through his own apprenticeship, giving her
in effect a correspondence course in the art of poetry. His first question
was, did she mean to go on with it, to master the medium? Then he
got down to detail. 'In "Impression", I don't think "dissolved" is just
the right word'—'because it really means a solid going into liquid, and
when you compare that to pear-petals falling, you blur your image'. 'In
"The Fledgling", "emancipated from the home" seems to me a definitely
Fabian Society or cliché phrase', and to be besides out of key with what
is otherwise an effective poem with 'all its words in one tone ... save this
one Latin, doctrinaire term'. ' "Too tender to have become grimed" is a
weak line ... let the grime *do* something to the leaves.' (That with a nod
to Fenollosa's 'a thing only is what it *does*'—'a very good [theory] for
poets to go by'.) 'A new line or a new word may demand the rewriting
of half a poem', he advised, 'get the trick of throwing the whole back
into the melting pot and recasting all in one piece' rather than patching.
'I can't read ["Persian Desert"] so as to make the final cadence really a
close or ending ... The last line seems to me to be a tripping little line,
gaily running tatatati, four very short little vowels, the soft "owl" and
then the long *ie*.' 'So many of your pentameter lines seem all in one

---

[3] Iris Barry (1895–1969), born Iris Crump, was a correspondence clerk in the General Post Office
in Birmingham in 1916, then found a wartime job with the Ministry of Munitions in Whitehall and
moved to London in 1917. Wyndham Lewis's 'Praxitella' is his portrait of her. After the war she became
a film critic and formed the London Film Society in 1925; moved to New York and from the 1930s was
film curator at the Museum of Modern Art.

jog whereas the metre skilfully used *can* display a deal of variety.' 'With some of the things…there is nothing to distinguish you from a lot of neo-imagists, and there are too d'd many neo-imagistes just at present.' 'No, hang it all, the stuff in *Poetry and Drama* (Dec. 1914) seems to me to have more passion and considerably more individuality than anything you have sent me in this sheaf.' 'Ah well,' he concluded the first lesson, 'you may have got a worse overhauling than you wanted, but one can't criticize and be tactful all at once.' He sent a group of her poems to *Poetry*, and another group to Williams for *Others*, and Iris Barry was published in both.

In July she travelled to London and they arranged to meet on a Sunday on Wimbledon station—he was to be identified by his 'perfectly plain ebony staff… *without* any tin bands, etc.' They talked as they walked on the Common, in a gale that carried his words away 'across the landscape'. What she heard was a voice packed 'with undertones and allusions', 'the base of American mingled with a dozen assorted "English society" and Cockney accents inserted in mockery; French, Spanish and Greek exclamations, strange cries and catcalls, the whole very oddly inflected, with dramatic pauses and *diminuendos*.' She 'knew as little as a dog he might have been taking for a walk of…the sort of thing he was talking about.' But in retrospect she saw 'the whole incident [as] typical of Pound, of his friendly attitude and his impulse to impart and instruct in case instruction might fall sometimes on good ground.'

The next stage in her course of instruction was an outline of what she should read in order to attain 'KOMPLEAT KULTURE'. These letters amount to a rough sketch towards 'How to Read' (1929) and *ABC of Reading* (1934). 'The main thing', he began, is 'to have enmagazined some mass of fine literature which hasn't been mauled over and vulgarized and preached as a virtue', and which will save one 'from getting swamped in contemporaneousness' AND 'serve as a model of style, or suggest possibilities of various sorts of perfection or maximum attainment'. First, Greek as 'a storehouse of wonderful rhythms, possibly impracticable rhythms'. In Latin 'Catullus, Propertius, Horace and Ovid are the people who matter.' 'There was poetry in Egypt', that is, he had seen 'a small book of interesting translations and forgotten the name.' '*Cathay* will give you a hint of China, and the "Seafarer" on the Anglo-Saxon stuff. Then…nothing matters till Provence. / After Provence, Dante and Guido Cavalcanti in Italy.…you should have a copy of Villon…'. At which point Pound broke off 'to shave, out of respect to the Chinese Minister' he was about to meet, and Iris Barry was able to interject that she had read Villon at least and had most of him by heart.

His next letter, just a week after the first, continued the syllabus. After Villon 'skip everything down to Heine'. 'Burns is worth study as technique in song rhythms'. 'Théophile Gautier is, I suppose, the next man who can write. Perfectly plain statements like his "Carmen est maigre" should teach one a number of things.' After that 'you'd do yourself more good reading French prose', Flaubert and Stendhal—Flaubert writes better and yet Stendhal has the more solid basis, 'A trust in the thing more than the word'. (That was an interesting discrimination.) Pound then threw in some recent enthusiasms and some prejudices. 'Perhaps you should read all of [Voltaire's] *Dictionnaire Philosophique*. Presumably no other living woman will have done so.' But Landor, 'a whole culture', had better be kept till later. 'Your first job is to get the tools for your work'. 'And English poetry???? Ugh. Perhaps one shouldn't read it at all. Chaucer has in him all that has ever got into English'—Wordsworth 'a dull sheep'— 'Byron's technique is rotten'—Crabbe's *The Borough* 'at least shows a gleam of sense, the man *was* trying to put down things as they were'. 'What about Browning?...Is it possible to read him after you've been reading Russian novels?...The hell is that one catches Browning's manner and mannerisms.' By way of a general theory there was simply this:

The whole art is divided into:
   a. concision, or style, or saying what you mean in the fewest and clearest words.
   b. the actual necessity for creating or constructing something; of presenting an image, or enough images of concrete things arranged to stir the reader.
   Beyond these concrete objects named, one can make simple emotional statements of fact, such as 'I am tired', or simple credos like 'After death there comes no other calamity'.
   I think there must be more, predominantly more, objects than statements and conclusions, which latter are purely optional, not essential, often superfluous and therefore bad.
   Also one must have emotion or one's cadence and rhythms will be vapid and without interest.

There was probably no better teaching to be found in any world or time, if you happened to be the right neophyte for this new master of the art. Iris Barry was fascinated, and willing to be instructed, but she was never going to be another Ezra Pound.

She moved to London in January 1917 and became better acquainted with Pound and his circle. When she looked back on that time from New York a dozen or so years later she saw Pound always in rapid motion and conversation, striding across Wimbledon Common instructing her; 'striding about the streets with his head thrown back, seeing everything, meeting everybody, as full of the latest gossip as he was of excitement about the pictorial quality of Chinese radicals or a line of Rimbaud's'; coming into 'the restaurant with his clothes always seeming to fly round him'—this would be for his weekly dinner group—'clearing his throat, making strange sounds and cries in his talking, but otherwise always quite formal and extremely polite.'

Dorothy would be with him at those dinners, 'carrying herself delicately with the air, always, of a young Victorian lady out skating, and a profile as clear and lovely as that of a porcelain Kuan-yin.' Violet Hunt was usually there, and Hueffer might be; and May Sinclair, and T. S. Eliot, 'generally silent', and H.D. 'looking, somehow, haunted', and Richard Aldington if he was home on leave from France. Lewis too might be there, 'back from the Front, ghastly pale under his black hair and ... full of inimitable conversation, riotous song, and an unequalled play of humour'. Miss Harriet Weaver, who would be 'sitting up so very straight with her severe hat and nervous air—she might have been a bishop's daughter', 'was never known to speak of herself or of anything to do with [her] remarkable publishing activity' save 'under extreme pressure'. Edmond Dulac was a regular; Yeats appeared now and then; and there were other more vaguely connected figures, Edgar Jepson who collected jade, and Arthur Waley the Oriental expert from the British Museum, and Mary Butts who married John Rodker.

Nearly fifty years later Arthur Waley would say that Pound was the ruling spirit at these gatherings, that they took place 'every Monday evening ... in a restaurant in Frith Street', Soho, and that 'what [Pound] said about poetry and this business of making poetry is much the best that I've ever heard said in the course of my life'.

The weekly dinners, 'cheap enough for the poorest members of the ever-changing group', were important to Pound because he had a 'passion for communication and continuity, for the verbal tradition and personal contact'. So, Iris Barry would recall, 'To the accompaniment of air-raids without, we younger ones heard for the first time of Proust and the Baroness Elsa von Freytag Loringhoven, of Negro music and Chinese poetry, of the Oedipus complex and Rousseau the Douanier and Gertrude Stein'. And 'The effect, all too little realized at the time,'

was as though something that mattered very much had somehow and rather miraculously been preserved round that table when so much else was being scattered, smashed up, killed, imprisoned or forgotten. It was as though someone kept reminding us that the war was not perpetual (as it certainly seemed by then) and that it was in the long run more important that there should be new music and new and fresh writing and creative desire and passionate execution than that one should believe angels descended at Mons... It was, for the hours the gathering lasted, less important that so many were being killed and more that something lived: possible to recall that for every Blenheim there is a Voltaire and that the things that endure are not stupidity and fear.

Thinking not only of those dinner conversations, but of all that Pound was doing, for young hopeful writers like herself, for Joyce and Lewis and Eliot, for *Poetry* and the *Egoist*, and in all the rest of his activities, Iris Barry reflected that 'It has never been sufficiently recognized what heavy and important work he did for letters at that time'.

There were of course things that young Miss Barry missed. For instance, she doesn't mention seeing him 'on a free front seat at the opera between Balfour [the Foreign Secretary] and a duchess'. He had his free seats for a season or two from Thomas Beecham, the opera conductor and impresario, as a bonus for translating the Massenet libretto. That commission probably came his way thanks to his having been taken up along with Yeats by Lady Cunard, who was then *en liaison* with Beecham. Pound made the most of rubbing shoulders with government ministers and the titled aristocracy to lobby for his artistic causes, to solicit subscriptions to the *Little Review* or say a word in the right ear. Yet he could exercise discretion, as when he told Lewis that he was waiting 'for a fitting moment' to press his, Lewis's, case for advancement, since 'Balfour between the second and third acts did not... present a favourable target—it is not his dept. and he would have been distinctly annoyed.' There would have been more urgent talk going round, as Pound recorded in canto 16:

> So we used to hear it at the opera,
> That they wouldn't be under Haig;
>   and that the advance was beginning;
> That it was going to begin in a week.

Another thing Iris Barry may not have registered is that for all his busyness and gaiety Pound wasn't finding it easy to pay the rent or to get on with his own poetry. He had his agent in London and Quinn in New York trying to interest publishers in a number of proposals: a book on Wyndham Lewis in the style of his *Gaudier-Brzeska*; a 'Chinese Poetry' to follow *Noh, or Accomplishment*, to contain *Cathay* and new translations, 'Fenollosa's profound essay on the Chinese Written Character as a medium for poetry', and essays by Pound himself on early Chinese poets; also 'a monograph on Greek sculpture before Phidias'. 'One makes a number of shots', he remarked to Quinn, 'and some hit the target.' But none of these did.

As for his poetry, there the problem went deeper than his difficulties with editors and publishers. Quinn had been startled to read in his *Gaudier-Brzeska* that he felt that 'any man whose youth has been worth anything, any man who has lived his life at all in the sun, knows that he has seen the best of it when he finds thirty approaching.' Pound reassured him that feeling middle-aged did not mean 'that life ceased to be worth living'. However, he went on,

I do think the artist loses something both from his life and his art which it takes the whole skill of a lifetime to restore.... It is perhaps only that at the start certain things come of themselves, without will, or half consciously, and that after a certain date they require a definite act or act of volition.

He had realized that 'a renaissance is a thing made—a thing made by conscious propaganda'. His weekly dinners were a conscious effort to keep up the communications which are the lifeblood of a civilization. Now he was finding that his poetry required the same kind of deliberate effort, and that the poems were not coming to him as readily as before. He had published nearly 200 original poems between 1908 and 1912, but then only half as many between 1913 and 1916. Moreover, recently there had been fewer each year, dropping from about thirty-five in both 1913 and 1914 to twenty in 1915 and just twelve in 1916. But by then he was trying to get his long poem going.

Poems of 1915–16, and the measure of realism

In May 1916 Pound was 'trying to decide how much of my first three or four books ought to be scrapped before another edition'. *Ripostes* he thought hadn't 'much waste matter in it'; but the others, *Personae, Exultations, Canzoni,* 'are only good enough to be taken one at a time—bound into one they are too dull for bearing'. He was of course no longer the poet who had written those masks, and his disaffection was due to his having moved on. Moreover, he had left behind not only his early preoccupation with the perfecting of the soul in its visions, but also, for the time being at least, the *Imagiste* preoccupation with the inner world of the individual mind. The emphasis now, in his reviews and letters, was mostly on the concrete thing and the objective fact, and on writing that tells things as they are. 'Realism' had become his keyword.

'My preference is for realism, for a straight statement of life, of whatever period you will', he declared in the course of recommending Edgar Lee Masters for writing 'quite directly and simply of the life of "Spoon River"', 'without circumlocution, without resonant meaningless phrases'. And he went on to offer it as an axiom that 'The lasting enjoyment of a work of art is that it leaves you confronted with life, with the objective fact.' 'Objectivity and again objectivity,' he instructed Harriet Monroe, 'and expression ... nothing that you couldn't, in some circumstance, in the stress of some emotion, actually say.'

He approved of Joyce's *Dubliners* because while dealing with 'subjective things'—such as the 'vivid waiting' of 'Araby'—'he presents them with such clarity of outline that he might be dealing with locomotives or with builders' specifications.' He praised Eliot's *Prufrock and Other Observations* for (among other things) its realistic treatment of 'our contemporary condition'—'his "lonely men in shirt-sleeves leaning out of windows" are as real as his ladies who "come and go / Talking of Michelangelo"'. 'All good art', he added, 'is realism of one sort or another'. When Quinn disliked Lewis's drab reds Pound put it to him that 'Lewis with his fundamental realism has been trying to show the beauty of the colour one actually sees in a modern brick, iron, sooty, railroad yarded smoked modern city'.

One gathers that Pound's older friends, Yeats and Hueffer, weren't measuring up to his new standard. He wrote two reviews of Yeats's *Responsibilities*, one of the Cuala Press edition in May 1914, the other of the Macmillan edition in December 1916. In the first he hopefully predicted a new development in Yeats's poetry, on the basis of its 'becoming gaunter, seeking greater hardness of outline', and being 'no longer romantically Celtic' but 'at a *prise* with things as they are'. He would say nothing against 'the glamour' of his early poems, and yet 'one is about ready for hard light'. In the later review, while there is still high praise, there is no longer any hope of the hard light of realism: 'despite ... occasional bits of realism, the tone of the new book is romantic—Mr Yeats is a romanticist, symbolist, occultist, for better or worse, now and for always.' Pound wasn't writing him off, but he was writing him out of his special force of realists.

In both those reviews the comparison with Joyce is left implicit, but in the case of Hueffer there is no mistaking Pound's judgement that he had been left behind by Joyce. Hueffer, as a follower of Stendhal and Flaubert, had always talked of exact presentation, of the importance of 'clarity and precision'; but then in his own expansively 'impressionist' writing he would 'neglect intensity, selection, and concentration' and end 'by putting one out of conceit with his narrative'. Joyce excelled him by his 'more rigorous selection of the presented detail', and was on that account at once closer to Stendhal and Flaubert and more modern. It marked him, Pound wrote, 'as belonging to my own generation, that is to the "nineteen-tens"', while Hueffer was back in the decade after ' "the 'nineties" '.

Pound's preference for realism led to another telling discrimination. In his reading list for Iris Barry he did not recommend the Japanese *Noh* plays, even though they were shortly to appear. And when they did appear he wrote a curiously qualified notice of them for the *Little Review*, saying they were 'infinitely better than Tagore and the back-wash from India', but 'not so important as the Chinese work left by Fenollosa'. One can make out that he was comparing 'Song of the Bow men of Shu' and 'South Folk in Cold Country', in which 'you find a man telling the truth about warfare' and showing 'a sort of rugged endurance', with *Kumasaka* in which the heroism is presented as 'a fine point of punctilio'. That made the Japanese dramatist ' "romanticist" against the "classical" *and* poetic matter-of-factness of the Chinese writer'. The latter has 'solidity' and 'body', while the other is preoccupied with 'nuances'. (Pound had remarked that Yeats, though a 'romanticist', could yet give the satirist's bite if he would 'but turn from ladies with excessive chevelure appearing in pearl-pale nuances'.)

'It is very important that there should be clear, unexaggerated, realistic literature', Pound insisted as he welcomed the book publication of *A Portrait of the Artist as a Young Man*, 'It is very important that there should be good prose.' He blamed 'the hell of contemporary Europe' on 'the lack of representative government in Germany *and* ... the non-existence of decent prose in the German language'; he connected the decline and fall of the Roman Empire with the decadent rhetoric of its latter days; and he suggested that 'If more people had read *The Portrait* and certain stories in Mr Joyce's *Dubliners* there might have been less recent trouble in Ireland'. He laid it down that

Clear thought and sanity depend on clear prose. They cannot live apart. The former produces the latter. The latter conserves and transmits the former. . . . .

A nation that cannot write clearly cannot be trusted to govern, nor yet to think. . . .

Clear, hard prose is the safeguard [of civilization] and should be valued as such. The mind accustomed to it will not be cheated or stampeded by national phrases and public emotionalities.

And Pound wholeheartedly agreed with Hueffer that poetry had to be at least as well written as prose, that it should be measured by the same standard.

There was precision and clarity in the writing throughout *Lustra*, and realism both objective and subjective, mainly objective. But was it a book to save the nation from the hell of the war? One reads through the volume as through an album of sketches or snapshots, remarking a whole range of clarifications of manners and motives and emotions; but even in its entirety it has nothing like the irresistible cogency and power of *Dubliners* and *A Portrait*. 'The Garden' and 'Commission' and 'The Coming of War' and 'The Lake Isle' and 'Cabaret Dancers' are all fine and good in their several ways; and 'Near Perigord' has its importance; and 'Provincia Deserta', and the 'Impressions' of Voltaire at the end, are excellent modern poems. This is certainly 'realistic literature', yet it lacks the 'solidity' and the coherent grip on 'things as they are' that Pound was demanding. In fact *Cathay*, although physically contained within *Lustra*, is poetically the larger work with a far deeper and more comprehensive grasp on life.

Pound held that it is not enough for the realist simply to present life as he sees it. There is always the further challenge to connect the life of the individual with the common experience of life, as Joyce and Eliot and the early Chinese poets do. He commended *Dubliners* because Joyce 'gives us things as they are, not only for Dublin, but for every city'—'he is capable of getting at the universal element beneath them'. He said much the same of Eliot's poems: 'they are the stuff of our modern world, and true of more countries than one'; and this time he gave it as an axiom that 'Art does not avoid universals, it strikes at them all the harder in that its strikes through particulars'. In the case of the Chinese poet he put it another way: 'One cannot consider Rihaku as a foreigner, one can only consider him human'.

It is that depth of humanity, that getting at something universal, which distinguishes *Cathay* from the body of original poems in the *Lustra* collection. The original poems mostly present the observations and point of view of a superior artist who is too amused or too alienated by what goes on on the surface of his society to want to engage more deeply with it. His I-saying poems are inevitably superficial, acute but superficial. Moreover, they present refractions of himself, not an image of the society; they reveal his attitude, not its ethos.

They also mark the awkward situation Pound was in as a poet. He was the poet of *Lustra*, but he meant to be more than that. He wanted to write the long poem which would bring into focus the whole ethos of his world and time; or at any rate he wanted to measure up to the early Chinese poets and to Joyce and to Eliot. And that meant that the poet he was in *Lustra* had to be another mask to be cast off in its turn. But how to become the impersonal and objective realist he wanted to be?

He was working at this problem from as early as 1915, in drafts for his long poem, and in some of the later poems in *Lustra*, most directly in 'Provincia Deserta' and 'Near Perigord'. Those two poems frame *Cathay* in that volume, the one coming immediately before it and the other immediately after, and the collocation prompts the thought that they are attempts to capture the ethos of ancient Provence as *Cathay* captured that of ancient China. But then one finds them setting about their work so consciously and deliberately that they don't so much catch the ethos as dramatise the attempt to do so.

'Provincia Deserta' may be read as one way of attempting to bring the past to life in the present. Pound had read the books of the troubadours' lives and poems; he had walked the roads they had walked, and exercised his imagination in recreating their stories; now he is going over the whole experience again in memory. The writing has the clarity and vividness of direct experience directly expressed; and the whole reverie is a sustained composition 'in the sequence of the musical phrase', with a rhythmic construction that runs without a false or an awkward turn from beginning to end. That was about 'as far as you could go in free verse'. But what comes alive in this process of memory is not the lives and the ethos of the troubadours, but simply Pound's effort to rediscover them. It remains a poem about himself and his Provence, not theirs. As the title declares, the troubadours he was seeking are not to be found there.

'Near Perigord' tries three different methods of getting at historical truth, all of which would claim to be objective: first that of the historian, then that of the historical novelist, and finally that of a poet. The historian finds his leading facts in Bertrans de Born's poems, particularly in 'Dompna pois de me no'us cal', the one in which he put together a composite 'borrowed lady'. He is set to questioning the poem by the love of war in some of Bertrans' other poems, and by his reputation as a 'stirrer-up of strife': 'Is it a love poem?', he wants to know, or 'Did he sing of war?' How to unriddle his secret heart? He goes about and about the story and its background, (incidentally getting most of the historical details wrong according to twentieth century historians); he calls in Dante's condemnation of Bertrans in his *Inferno*; constructs a political scenario on the basis of the lie of the land around his castle; imagines what he might have meant if he did send his *jongleur* to sing the poem to the lady; and ends up still questioning. His 'facts' have dissolved in speculation, and the speculation yields no clear insight.

Then the novelist tells the story over in his own way, much as Maurice Hewlett did in *The Life and Death of Richard Yea-and-Nay* (1900). He creates a scene in which Bertrans writes his poem, giving him 'a red straggling beard' and 'a green cats'-eye' after Pound himself; in a second scene the jongleur is sent out to sing the song, he meanwhile having an affair of his own at heart; in the third scene one of the lords at the lady's court sees the supposed political stratagem behind the song and sets Bertrans' enemies upon him—'de Born smoked out, trees

(right). Walter Rummel
d EP, Swarthmore, 1910.

(below). EP, 1913 (Photo:
vin Langdon Coburn).

(below right). Dorothy
akespear and EP, c.1913.

23 (*above*). 10 Church Walk, Kensington W8, where EP lived from September 1909 to June 1910, and from November 1911 to April 1914—his room had the furthest two first-floor windows. EP wrote on the back of this photo in 1958 that Imagisme was born there in 1912.

24 (*left*). Elkin Mathews, publisher.

25 (*above left*). Harriet Shaw Weaver of *The Egoist*.

26 (*above right*). Harriet Monroe of *Poetry*.

27 (*left*). Dora Marsden of *The New Freewoman* and *The Egoist*.

(*facing above*). Blunt pre-
sentation, January 1914: Victor
Carr, Sturge Moore, W. B.
Yeats, Wilfred Scawen Blunt,
EP, Richard Aldington, Frank
Flint.

(*facing below*). Stone
Cottage.

(*right*). John Quinn, W. B.
Yeats (*Photo: Arnold Genthe*).

(*below left*). EP in London,
1912 (*Photo: Swaine, New
Bond Street*).

(*below right*). Wyndham
Lewis, 1914.

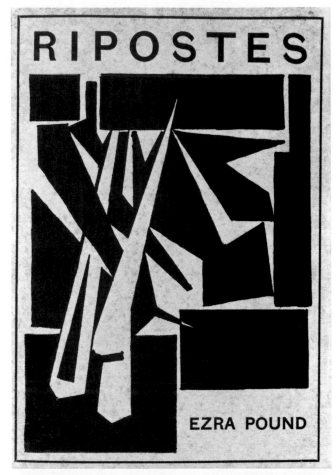

33. Dorothy Shakespear, cover design for EP's *Ripostes*, 1915.

34. T. S. Eliot (*centre*) at Merton College, Oxford, October 1914.

Wyndham Lewis, cover design for BLAST, *War Number*, July 1915.

36 (*left*). Henri Gaudier-Brzeska, self-portrait, 1912.

37 (*below*). E.P.

38 (*facing*). Henri Gaudier-Brzeska, Hieratic Head of Ezra Pound (1914) (*Photo: David Finn*).

39 (*left*). T. E. Hulme.

40 (*below*). Ford Madox Hueffer (*Photo* E. O. *Hoppé*).

41 (*left*). A. R. Orage of the *The New Age*
(*Photo: Anselm Adams*).

42 (*below*). EP, 1918 (*Camera Portrait by E. O.
Hoppé, London*), frontispiece to *Pavannes and
Divisions*—homage to Whistler's portrait of
Carlyle.

43. Wyndham Lewis, portrait of EP, 1919. It was lost
apparently when Lewis left it in a taxi.

felled / About his castle, cattle driven out!' But at that moment of high drama there is this sudden turn, 'Or no one sees it, and En Bertrans prospered?', and it hardly seems to matter which was the case, for this after all is a fiction, to be told as you like it. Cut to a later time, and another scene as sumptuously established as in J. H. Smith's romantic fantasy *The Troubadours at Home* (1899), and now Richard Coeur-de-Lion and Arnaut Daniel talk of de Born in the night before the battle in which Richard will be killed. Each knew de Born, as man and poet, and still they can reach no conclusion as to whether he wrote his poem for love of the lady or for a covert political end. The novelist appears content to leave it at that, an unresolved riddle serving his story-telling quite as well as an answer might.

Now the poet of 'Near Perigord' takes over the poem himself—so far he has intervened only to set the historian going at the very beginning and then to manage the transition from 'fact' to 'fiction'. First he creates a condensed image out of Dante's description of de Born in hell:

> Surely I saw, and still before my eyes
> Goes on that headless trunk, that bears for light
> Its own head swinging, gripped by the dead hair,
> And like a swinging lamp that says, 'Ah me!
> I severed men, my head and heart
> Ye see here severed, my life's counterpart.'

That has all the immediacy and force of objective fact and quite eclipses the riddling and the romancing of our historian and our novelist. It gives a real Bertrans de Born, not of course the man as he lived and died, but one who is real in the mind reading those lines. Finally the poet has Bertrans speak for himself, following Dante's method, though not his moral judgement. He speaks rather as William Morris or Browning might have him speak, as a lover parted from the woman he loved and estranged and who was shattered by her marriage to another. Implicitly he lays the pathos and the tragedy on her, on her not having a mind to respond to his, on her being 'a shifting change, / A broken bundle of mirrors'. Perhaps he would have us understand that that was what drove him to love making war. However, as with Browning's men and women, it is what he does not say that most gives him away: was not the mind that she hated in him a mind for war, and was it not that which divided them and destroyed her? We are brought, at any rate, to the method of Browning's dramatic monologues, a method which goes on from Dante's by preferring psychological analysis to moral judgement. The objective facts, in this final part of 'Near Perigord', are the strong images in which an imagined mind is dramatizing itself, telling its story, and, naturally, figuring in it to advantage.

Read in this way the poem proves to be a thoroughly Browningesque study in ways of doing history, and one designed to show how the dramatic monologue outdoes both 'fact' and 'fiction'. So far as its versification is close to blank verse it is virtually a homage to Browning, though it is more sensitive than he usually was to quantity and the musical phrase. It is most sensitive and departs most from his 'hippety-hop' blank verse where it is closest to his dramatic method, in de Born's direct speech at the end. That speech is also more natural and has less of the fustian unreality of the other two parts. All in all, I take it that Pound's poet is quite committed to Browning's method. And Pound himself did say, when praising Eliot's 'Prufrock', that the form of Browning's *Men and Women* was 'the most vital' in Victorian English.

But then hadn't he already done what he could with that form and method in his early *personae*? Why would he be reverting to it now? And why, when he had studied so hard and so successfully to free his verse from the iambic pentameter, would he fall back into it? In short, what was he doing writing so Victorian a poem in 1915? It would seem that as he was setting himself once more to begin on his 'poem containing history' he felt a need to go to school again with Browning.

'Three Cantos': finding his form

It becomes apparent, however, that he was going back to his old master not so much to learn as to argue with him and assert his independence. He was taking Browning's *Sordello* as a point of departure for his cantos, as 'the thing to go on from'. He had to start there because he thought it 'the best long poem in English since Chaucer', and the only one with a 'live form'. But that form was not right for what he had to do, and he would be finding his own in breaking free from Browning's.

He first began to mention being at work on his long poem in the summer of 1915. 'It is a huge, I was going to say, gamble, but shan't', he told Alice Corbin Henderson in early August; and in September he told Milton Bronner that it was 'a cryselephantine poem of immeasurable length which will occupy me for the next four decades unless it becomes a bore.' His Scriptor Ignotus, back in 1906, had likewise predicted that the great epic would take just so long to write. He told his father in mid-December that his mind was then 'in the Vth canto', but the surviving drafts show that he was still casting about for a form at that date, and it was a full year before he had the first three trial cantos in any sort of shape. He sent them off to Alice Henderson for *Poetry* in January 1917, but immediately began revising them again for the New York edition of *Lustra*. On May 24 he wrote, 'revised and condensed my long poem, i.e. the first three cantos of it, between Saturday 11.15 p.m. and Sunday 8.a.m.' And still in or after 1919 he was striking out line after line of the third of the trial cantos until he had reduced it very nearly to what became 'Canto I'.

His materials could be endless, immeasurable, but he hardly knew how to put them in order. He had any amount of the past and the present to sort through, and, since he chose to examine it without preconception, it presented itself to him as a vast heap of random records and anecdotes. The best he could do at first was to set about abbreviating some of those, and he produced a litter of fragmentary drafts, some of them in typescript. In one of these, headed 'Fragment / Modern World', the valet of Ser D'Alviano gossips about what his master was saying about writers and their books in 1520. In another, numbered '[page] 102' and headed 'Foot-Note. A toss-up', Pound's visit to the great Provençal scholar Emil Levy in Freiburg is woven into the tale of de Maensac. A sequence of six or seven pages tries out ways to envision paradise, as by seeing points of colour, making stars of them and then making each star 'a nest of noble voices'. Bits of all those drafts, and of others, will turn up in 'Canto V', though the visit to 'old Levy' will go into 'Canto XX'. Two un-numbered pages, one with the date 'Aug. 9 1915' added to it, touch on wars in general before evoking the tangled jungle of the *Mahabharata*'s dark wood of life. Three other pages take up that image of a wood, shift to an English forest, and to the killing of King Cynewulf, an episode from the Anglo-Saxon chronicle included in Sweet's *Anglo-Saxon Reader*. A draft headed 'III' begins, 'What do I mean by all this resonant rumble? / Bewildered reader, what is the poet's business?', and answers by presenting some further envisioning of paradise as the way to 'pass beyond humanity' and see things as the gods do. Another four-page typescript begins 'But what's all this to us?', then brings in 'the modern world' via an allusion to Napoleon and the opening chapters of Stendhal's *La Chartreuse de Parme*; and follows that with 'a bullet headed fellow's' account of how he was settled in Germany when the war began, escaped, enlisted, was six months in the trenches, and now was in the secret service, in intelligence, and could not make head or tail of any of it. 'What am I at ?', is asked again, and given the answer that all these things are life and that none of us make head or tail of it.

Pound would observe that Dante had had an 'Aquinas map' to help him sort out his world into all the ascending degrees of damnation, purgation, and blessedness; and that even Browning, with his modern scepticism about human certainties, still 'had some basis, some set belief'. But as for himself, he would subscribe to no single belief and value system. Indeed he believed that the only measure of truth is the individual's own perception of it, and that what is most intensely perceived and realized is most true. Yet at the same time he believed that there is an objective truth to be perceived, that is, what is permanent in the tradition. He allowed that truth so defined may be perceptible only by genius and seem nonsense to common sense. In any case such permanent truth can be communicated in its integrity only through myth and through the patterns and forms of art. It cannot be given as 'meaning' in paraphrase; and the felt experience of it can be felt again only in fully formed dance or music or poetry.

When Pound asked himself, as he started on his trial cantos, did his fragmented modern world need 'such a rag-bag' as *Sordello* 'to stuff all its thought in', it was a real question but one which surely expected an answer in the negative. He knew perfectly well that while Browning may have patched together his *Sordello* out of his own thought and emotion and 'intensest life', still his motive had been to render 'the incidents in the development of a soul'. He had 'Watched "the soul", Sordello's soul, / And saw it lap up life, and swell and burst—/ "Into the empyrean?"' The scepticism about 'the empyrean', Browning's and his own, didn't make it any the less the object of the soul's, and the poem's, desire. Pound's early drafts provide clear evidence that he too was after 'the empyrean', though he would put it in terms of an earthly paradise of light. He also wrote of making a cosmos of his fragmented world, of somehow putting it all together into an ordered whole. The mere 'rag-bag' was the last thing he needed.

He had not after all given up his early idealism. He was still the *scriptor ignotus* determined to write a new epic, one which would be directed towards a beatific vision or paradise of this world. It would begin, as he had first conceived it in college, in its own hell of passionate action—the sort of hell in which de Born the divider would be a hero—and it would proceed through a purgatory of instruction towards its paradise. The poet himself would figure in it, even as he had in those false starts at Wabash, as one bringing the words of his dead masters into the living world, and so as a bringer of light into its darkness. And the light would be that of the tradition of the intellectual love of the vital universe which he had worked out in *The Spirit of Romance*. Dante and Browning would still be his guides, though adapted to the realities of Pound's modern world.

What he needed to discover was the right form in which to be the idealist in and of his real world, and the first thing he had to work out was exactly how he should figure in his modern epic. Dante's way was inimitable, being specific to his medieval Catholic world-view. And Browning's 'new form, the meditative, / Semi-dramatic, semi-epic story' was specific to himself. He was the showman who would steal the show, getting in the way of the story he is telling by constantly commenting on it. And why must he pretend that what he has to show is Sordello when it is really *'our* life, your life, my life, extended'? Pound would exclude from his poem both the person of the poet and the feigned hero; and he would present his 'intensest life' quite directly, as directly and as objectively as in his *Imagiste* poems. He would be purely and simply the intelligence at work in the poem. That of course was what Dante and Browning had been in their poems, but they had covered up their real work by disguising themselves as characters in a story. Pound would strip away the illusions of character and story, and let his poetic genius be the protagonist—a protagonist everywhere in action and manifest only in its acting.

In the mythical terms he had invoked in 1911, he would be Isis gathering up the scattered fragments of his world and making it whole. Or he would be like the primal god in a creation myth, forming chaos into cosmos. Or in the terms of Porphyry's mystical philosophy as cited in these drafts, he would be pure intelligence able to assume any and every form, '*"Omniformis omnis intellectus est"*'. Or again, in more immediate terms, he would be the poet who could be Bertran de Born in the final part of 'Near Perigord', only on an epic scale. His breakthrough was to conceive of the poet's intelligence as operating independently of a particular self or soul, and as wholly engaged in comprehending its objects. One can see him actually breaking through to that as he cuts away everything in that third trial canto to leave, as the proper beginning of *The Cantos of Ezra Pound*, just his performance of Odysseus' account of sailing to consult dead Tiresias.

Those who take Odysseus as he sails after knowledge to be the implicit hero of *The Cantos* are nearly right: he is, in that aspect, indeed a type of the poet. He has left behind the heroic action of the Trojan war, and is now in the poetic realm of myth and vision. On top of that he has the poet's skill to make his extra-ordinary adventures appear as immediate and as real as any other human experience. But this is all the poets' doing, Homer's and then Pound's after Homer; and the deeper reality of 'Canto I' is that it is the poet who is the true protagonist. The action is, on the face of it, what Odysseus does; but the real action is in the poet's editing, performing and interpreting Odysseus' story.

Throughout *The Cantos* the continuing action will be the struggle of the poetic intelligence to inform, to present and to relate all the fragments of its world in its effort to make a unified whole of it. Its method will be to sort things into categories according to their natures, and then to arrange them by likenesses and differences. Along with that there will be a searching out of their relations and interactions. 'The theme', Pound indicated in one unpublished note, was to be 'roughly the theme of *Takasago*', a Noh play which celebrates the interrelatedness of all things in the cosmos. And the main structure, the great formal principle, will be the opposing of the light of active intelligence to the dullness and darkness of unenlightened living.

In the first of the three trial cantos the poetic intelligence reveals itself in just forty or fifty lines. The rest of this 'sort of prologue', the baldly Browningesque debate with Browning, is simply rhetoric. But in the summoning up of the earthly paradise of Lake Garda, more realistically than in 'The Flame' and more effectively, the poet's mind is alive to and alive with the action of light in the world. The passage begins in the street, with his seeing 'the small cobbles flare with the poppy spoil'—even on the ground here the light is colour and energy, aflame. On the lake

> the sunlight
> Glints on the shaken waters, and the rain
> Comes forth with delicate tread, walking from Isola Garda—
> *Lo soleils plovil* [....]
> The very sun rains and a spatter of fire
> Darts from the 'Lydian' ripples

In the air the olive leaves glare like owls' eyes, or the eyes of Athene, as they catch the light; and 'The air is solid sunlight'. Later, 'Gods float in the azure air. / Bright gods, and Tuscan'. Beyond that would lie ' "the empyrean" ', the highest heaven of fire, as of the sun itself, the source of life-giving light, and (in Dante's scheme) the realm of God and the angelic intelligences. But Pound stays with the light alive in nature, in the photosynthesis of poppy flowers and oak trees, or in the face of a young girl seen in Venice—'there were not "those girls", there was one flare, one face'. He would affirm with Metastasio that the world revealed in the myths of pagan gods is always about us, and that here is our paradise if we can but see it.

Now it becomes apparent that everything in the canto has to do with *seeing* in one way or another, and that its diverse materials, far from being grabbed at random to be stuffed into a rag-bag, have been selected to compose a unified force-field. Nearly everything here is visual, with different kinds of vision set off against each other. In the opening lines there is the direct observation of a catch of 'shiny and silvery /...fresh sardines flapping and slipping on the marginal cobbles'. Against that there is an obviously manufactured description of a castle in which the author, (after Browning or Hewlett?), is freely associating elements from various castles and eras. And against that there is the sustained seeing of paradise around Lake Garda, ending with 'And the water is full of silvery almond-white swimmers, / The silvery water glazes the up-turned nipple'. In the last quarter of the poem a series of visual images is built up in rapid succession, each one a specific way of perceiving divine energies at work in nature. In Shang art 'The sea-monster / Bulges the squarish bronzes'—should we exult with it in 'squatness'?; or should we follow Egypt and 'Daub out in blue of scarabs?' Should it be rather Confucian China that we follow, with its temple art, and 'Kwannon / Footing a boat that's but one lotus petal'. At the close Botticelli's Birth of Venus is evoked—'Brings her ashore on that great cockle-shell...And Spring and Aufidus fill all the air'. But a line from Shakespeare's *Pericles* that seems to go with that, 'she comes / "Apparelled like the spring, Graces her subjects"', conceals a warning to look for the truth of the matter and not to trust mere words.

The whole canto has been a carefully composed presentation and discrimination of different ways of seeing and painting the world we live in. More exactly, it appears to be looking for ways of envisioning its ever-active energies. There can be no doubt that there is a shaping intelligence at work here, though it is being rather distracted and obstructed by the self-assertive figure of the poet who keeps intruding into the poem to carry on his argument with Browning.

The second trial canto contrasts in nearly every respect with the first— except for the officious poet, who is best ignored. There is no sunlight— only the distant stars are alluded to—and no vision of the sustaining energies around us. Instead of things directly seen, this canto is made up from writings concerning matters of love and war, and in these there is much darkness and nothing lasting. Loss, sorrow and violent death predominate. What was the mythopoetic imagination has become in Camoens a 'resonant bombast' so out of touch with reality as to elide the difference between the 'dug-up corpse' of a murdered woman and Proserpine returning from Hades in the spring. This is the hell on earth of those who have lost the paradisal vision that is the light of the intellect. To perceive that is to make out the 'single moral conviction' which orders and unifies the otherwise heterogeneous material. In terms of the analogy Pound had already hit on, the power of the intelligence to so understand its material is like that of a magnet energizing a pile of iron filings on a tray and causing them to spring into an orderly pattern.

The first part of the canto deals with unilluminated love. In an ancient Chinese poem from the Fenollosa collection a woman is heard singing in the dark on an autumn night, of how she was formerly beautiful and accomplished, ' "And then one year I faded out and married".' 'We heard her weeping', the poem ends. Then Catullus' story is sketched in. At first his love for Lesbia was a blinding passion such as Sappho sang; a year on it was ' "I love her as a father" '; and in less than a year after that, ' "Lesbia ... is now the drab of every lousy Roman".' Next comes a romance about a troubadour who by his song (which Pound probably made up) wooed and won a lady, ' "And they were taken with love beyond all measure" '; he then went off to war and was reported dead, and she had candles lit for his soul and masses said; but he turned up alive, and ' "At this news she had great grief" ', and sent him away; and ' "Thus was there more than one in deep distress" '. There is a happy ending, for another lady heard the song and took him in. This burlesque of courtly love marks the death of its ethos, and the putting out of the 'light from Eleusis'.

The canto now turns to the dark 'gestes of war'. First there is the story of El Cid, with its end in 'Dismantled castles ... piled men and bloody rivers'; and a sea-fight, told in just two telling images: the portent before the engagement of ' "sombre light upon reflecting armour" '; and the aftermath, 'Full many a fathomed sea-change in the eyes / That sought with him the salt sea victories'. Then, from the *Noh*, there is 'Kumasaka's ghost come back to tell / The honour of the youth who'd slain him'. Not so heroic is the king 'come in an unjust cause' to lay siege to a city, and who, being fired with love for a woman in armour on its battlements, and being told by El Cid that it is his own sister, cries out for a like ill flame to be kindled in her. As climax there is the horror of the tragic story of Ignez and Prince Pedro of Portugal. She was murdered to prevent their marrying, and when he came to the throne, years later, he had her corpse brought into his court for a wedding ceremony and coronation, and 'Who winked at murder kisses the dead hand, / Does leal homage'. That is a tale of infernal justice.

Apparently tacked on to the canto, and yet an integral part of its conception, is a modern instance of a living hell. This is the sad story of Fred Vance, the frustrated artist Pound had known in Crawfordsville, who had had his vision 'Adoring Puvis' in Paris, but was then stuck back 'in middle Indiana', 'Painting the local drug-shop and soda bars', or painting sheep. Pound had thought that the last pit of hell, a real hell.

The third trial canto is the *purgatorio* to the *paradiso* and *inferno* of the other two, that is, it is concerned with learning how to get through the world's hell and to find the way back to the earthly paradise. Its predicament is error, and its response is errantry in quest of valid instruction.

The way of the occult is first considered, as it is to be found in the *Holy Guide* (1662) of one John Heydon, a seventeenth-century English dealer in late varieties of Neoplatonism. Yeats had a copy of his *Holy Guide* with him at Stone Cottage, and Dorothy had copied extracts from it in her British Museum notebook in 1915. The canto presents Heydon's 'pretty visions' as decorative fantasy, 'lacking the vigor of gods'. The spirit who 'promised him the way of holy wisdom', he reveals, wore a dress with 'sleeves of yellow silk / Slit to the elbow, slashed with various purples', and 'Her eyes were green as glass, her foot was leaf-like'. What Heydon has to say of wisdom after that is treated as no more than the 'deep platitudes' of Ficino's Renaissance 'hotch-potch' of 'Christian and Pagan mysticism, allegory, occultism, demonology, Trismegistus, Psellus, Porphyry' and so forth. None of that, which so fascinated Yeats, is found to be of use.

Lorenzo Valla, a Renaissance humanist, is then preferred to Heydon and Ficino, for reasons more clearly set out by Pound in the prose of an article in the *New Age* in February 1915. Valla's *virtu* was his 'great passion for exactness', and from that came 'the finest force' of the Renaissance, the 'revival of the sense of realism'. Valla established by exact attention to language that the Donation of Constantine, by which the Papacy had claimed temporal power over Rome and Italy, had to be a forgery. He helped in the revival of Roman Law, and the writing of Latin. And his exactness contributed to the clarity of Machiavelli's prose and to his realism.

But then, Pound observed, 'in the midst of these awakenings Italy went to rot, destroyed by rhetoric',

For when words cease to cling close to things, kingdoms fall, empires wane and diminish. Rome went because it was no longer the fashion to hit the nail on the head.

And Italy too, in mid-Renaissance, had gone in for 'rhetoric and floridity', as can be seen in 'the Hymns to the Gods appended to Divus' translation of the Odyssey into Latin'—an example is given at the end of the canto. The same symptoms of rot, floridity, and the rhetorical 'habit of defining things always "in terms of something else"', were noted in England's Heydon at the start.

The putting down of Heydon's fey occultism, and the affirming of Valla's passion for the precise word, was by way of introduction to the realism of Homer which, as Pound believed, had been behind Valla's and Machiavelli's. It was to Homer, and in particular to his Odysseus, that he turned now for instruction at the outset of his epic effort to get through hell and to make cosmos.

In Book XI of the *Odyssey* the hero, following the instructions of Circe, the bewitching daughter of the sun, sails to the dark side of earth where the sun never shines and even the stars are hidden, and there in a primitive ritual he sacrifices to the deathless powers, Pluto and Proserpine, and calls up the ghosts of dead brides, of 'souls stained with recent tears', and of 'men mauled with bronze lance-heads...bearing yet dreary arms'. This is an ancient vision of the hell of the second trial canto; and the first ghost to speak, Elpenor, a friend witlessly dead in Circe's house, a man of ill fortune and no renown, is of the type of Fred Vance. But Odysseus is there to learn what is to be his own fate from Tiresias, the Seer 'Who even dead, yet hath his mind entire' because he sees by the light of Persephone, the life-principle of the vital universe. And Tiresias can see that Odysseus will reach his Ithaca, though all his companions will be lost on the way, because he alone has the wit to understand the powers in play in his universe. He will get through by force of intelligence, while the others will fail in their efforts to do it by force of arms alone.

That's a lesson that has not lost its relevance. But Pound was not simply summoning up Odysseus to tell his story once more. It was the poem itself, the *Odyssey* rather than Odysseus, that he needed to be instructed by. He needed to learn from it how to make such a story come alive and stay alive—he wanted to be able to do in his own time and language what Homer had done in his.

What he had to start from was Andreas Divus' Renaissance Latin version, as published in Paris in 1538, in a volume which he had picked up for a few francs from a bookseller on one of the *quais* by the Seine during one of his early visits to Paris. Divus had done a word for word crib in 'very simple Latin', and for Pound, with his good Latin and little Greek, that made 'just the difference of permitting [him] to read fast enough to get the swing and mood of the subject, instead of losing both in a dictionary'.

The first two lines of Divus' Book XI transpose Homer's Greek directly into Latin:

> 'At postquam ad nauem descendimus, et mare,
> Nauem quidem primum deduximus in mare diuum.'

Literally, ' "And then to the ship we went down, and to the sea, / The ship then first of all we dragged down into the godlike sea" '. Pound's rendering avoids the repetitions of 'ship' and 'sea' and condenses the two lines into three emphatically shaped phrases:

'And then went down to the ship, set keel to breakers,
Forth on the godly sea'

That emphasizes the action, gets things moving; and it also, in the very free 'set keel to breakers', gets closer to 'the thing'. Pound will go on in that way through the entire passage: editing to achieve concentration; finding words to create a world of material objects and physical actions; and through the strongly marked rhythm sustaining 'the swing and mood of the subject'.

Now Odysseus' world is for the most part created and characterized by matter-of-fact directness and simplicity, by direct action and simple fact expressed in plain Anglo-Saxon words and clear syntax. Indeed much of the language, like the alliteration, recalls Pound's 'The Seafarer' and its comparable ethos. The exceptions are significant. There is some indirect syntax, as in 'Sheep bore we aboard her, and our bodies also', and that serves to throw the emphasis from the subject to the verb, and so to keep the action in focus. Then there are the occasional special effects out of Latin or Greek: *Circe* and *Kimmerian*; *libation*, *sacrifice* and *pyre*; *Pluto* and *Proserpine*; the *cadaverous*, *impetuous*, and *impotent* dead; *Avernus* and *Tiresias, Theban*. The peculiar feature of these words is that they distinguish what they name or describe without giving any immediate sense of the thing itself. With *Pluto* and *Proserpine* in particular, Odysseus knows their names, but does not *see* them as powers. It was the same at the beginning, when he gave the sea its epithet 'godly', without fully realizing its divine power. Pound will cut Tiresias' long speech down to his forewarning of the sea's power to hinder Odysseus' return.

It is in such details as his keeping 'godly' unaltered at the beginning, then picking out 'shalt / Return through spiteful Neptune, over dark seas' as the gist of what Tiresias has to reveal, that we find Pound's poetic intelligence in action. He is able to see that while Odysseus is the outstanding representative of his heroic world, because the most knowing and resourceful of its men of action, he is as yet still in the dark as to the radiant universe of divine energies. He sees everything in material terms, as instrumental to his own purposes; but he lacks the mythopoetic vision. In *The Cantos of Ezra Pound* his canto will be followed by one which does open the mind's eye to the divinity of the sea.

The *Cantos* will start, when they get properly under way, at a great turning point in human culture, the moment of turning away from the darkness of the heroic world of valiant killing and being killed—the world of the *Iliad*, and of Europe in 1914–18—and of turning towards the light of the living universe, which is the light of intelligence.

14 : INTO ACTION: 1917–1918

Editor, male, seeks magazine (1912–16)

Pound received $100 for the 'Three Cantos' when they appeared in three separate numbers of *Poetry* in mid-1917, and had little or no positive response to them. Harriet Monroe had thought it would be 'suicidal' to do them in one number, and had wondered, 'Is he petering out, that he must meander so among dead and foreign poets? has he nothing more of his own to say?' Robert Nichols, in 1920, would be likewise unable to see the design for the detail, and would dismiss the revised version of 'Three Cantos' as 'merely a ragbag [of erudite allusions] without synthesis'. Eliot was apparently 'the only person who proffered criticism instead of general objection'; that is, he had 'said it was worth doing', and Pound had 'got some very valuable objections to various details' out of him, though only 'after standing over him with a club'.

He had thought, or hoped, that there existed at least a 'few hundred people...capable of recognizing what I am about'. But then he believed that 'Great Art is NEVER popular to start with'. Indeed, when it came to the judging of art he had no faith at all in the 'public', as he declared to John Quinn. Of 'liberty, equality, fraternity, democracy...there ought to be as much...as possible. BUT art exists in spite of them—Any art that matters'. There had to be an aristocracy to defend it, an 'aristocracy of culture, brains, society etc.'; and 'this aristocracy, composed of a few artists, a few people who know, a small amount of money, has to subjugate a certain milieu', a milieu composed, apparently, of 'snobs, people who want to be thought part of the aristocracy', and whose 'aspirations' and 'asininity' make their subjection possible. 'The rest', presumably the indifferent public at large, 'are a herd of sheep.'

The milieu he was aiming to subjugate at this time must have been the one he encountered at Lady Cunard's and Lady Low's or at the opera, one in which you might meet the powerful and the influential and those who ministered to them: Arthur Balfour and Edward Marsh and Mrs

Masterman, for example. Pound was intending to subjugate this milieu with a magazine 'that would concede nothing to the general stupidity', and would have for its subscribers none of the 'unintelligent sheep' but only the 'few hundreds or [the] very few thousands of people capable of doing anything of *any* sort, or of getting anything done'. The force behind his magazine would be his chosen few artists, Lewis, Joyce, Eliot, and himself; Quinn would put up the necessary 'small amount of money'.

Pound had been angling to get a magazine of his own, or at least to get control of one, since his first connections with *Poetry* and the *New Freewoman* back in 1912 and 1913. He had tried without success in 1914 to persuade Amy Lowell to finance 'an international review...on the lines of the *Mercure de France*'. In May 1915 he had glimpsed 'the faint nuance of a chance' of getting, with Quinn's backing, an ancient and dormant weekly to edit. 'I should make it London, Paris, America', he told Quinn, and 'should give the two continents a chance to converse with each other'. When that chance was missed he had overwhelmed Quinn with a flood of ideas and plans for a new monthly magazine. He had drawn up a prospectus, commissioned printers' estimates 'based on 112 pages at 300 words per page', and had calculated that with £500 a year from Quinn there would be £8 a month for himself as editor, £5 a month for an assistant editor, and enough to pay contributors at the rate of £1 per 1000 words.

It was to have been 'a male review', on the ground that 'active America is getting fed up on gynocracy'. Pound wondered 'if it would be possible to make a really bold plunge and hoist the banner "No woman shall be allowed to write for this magazine".' He knew 'It would cause outcry, boycott, etc.', 'but the ultimate gain...in vigour.—in everything—might be worth it.' He wanted to exclude 'the ills of American magazines' which were due to 'young women, old women (male and female)—both those who write & those who are catered for—sugar-teat optimism etc. etc.' For 'etc. etc.' one might read 'lack of realism'. He expected that 'a few very intelligent people (women & men) would be pleased'; and he knew that 'We would start with fifty sworn vendettas against us.' He ended this letter with the prediction that 'IF THIS DOCUMENT GETS OUT OF YOUR HANDS INTO THOSE OF MINE ENEMIES I SHALL STARVE OR BE HUNG AT ONCE.'

The 'male review' did not materialize, and he continued to suffer and to work with his gynocrats. He had to put up with Harriet Monroe's rejecting his 'Cabaret Dancers'—he accused her of wanting it 'bundled up into slop, sugar and sentimentality'—and with her deleting a line from Eliot's 'Mr Apollinax' because it contained the word 'foetus'. 'The better the stuff I send in, by me or by anybody else', he complained to her co-editress, 'the more God damn worry, fuss, bother to get it printed.' Then there was Dora Marsden on the *Egoist*, 'another trial' when he took up with it again in early 1916, for the sake of having Miss Weaver publish Joyce's *Portrait* as a book and Lewis's *Tarr* as a serial: 'She don't interfere but . . . there is her four pages of slosh on the forehead of every number'. It was to her credit though that 'she hasn't H's mania for genteelness, & she believes in individual differences.'

Pound had thought, for a month or so in early 1916, that with '£120, or so per year guaranteed for a year' to pay himself and contributors, he might even take over the *Egoist*. 'I think they would let me run all the paper except Dora Marsden's contributions', he told Quinn; and with Lewis's novel running, and Eliot, Joyce, and himself contributing regularly, he would renew it and gather the available forces about it. Miss Weaver had been 'all for it right and hearty', but Miss Marsden had been unwilling, had wanted 'to consult some phantom directors', so Pound had withdrawn. Eliot would be disappointed, he wrote, without explaining why, but could 'wait for the "Male Review".'

'I've no connection with the *Egoist*', he told Miss Henderson in August of 1916, and 'no monthly or weekly "organ" at present.' He didn't know that he had need of one, being just then at ease about Joyce's and Lewis's welfare; and all quiet for the moment on the propaganda front. *Lustra* was about to appear, the big *Noh* book was in the press; and he was busy about nothing more than translating Wang Wei from the Fenollosa material, and writing 'a story with a nice thick nauseous indian atmosphere . . . mostly cribbed from the Kamasutra'.

As a diversion he invented with the photographer Alvin Langdon Coburn the 'Vortoscope', an arrangement of three mirrors which produced kaleidoscopic or 'Cubist' photographs; only it was 'a dam'd sight more interesting than photography' because it freed 'the camera from reality and let one take Picassos direct from nature'. Coburn's first 'vortographs' experimented with refracted or superimposed images of Pound's face, the refractions rather Vorticist in effect, the superimposition somewhat Cubist. At the opening of Coburn's exhibition at the Camera Club in February 1917 Pound 'was surprised to see how many of the aged had got to the point of "admitting" the non-representational'.

The Vorticists and his other usual associates were scattered. 'That about cleans out our gang', he had observed in June when Wadsworth was sent on a naval job to the Eastern Mediterranean and Rodker had got himself arrested as a conscientious objector. Hueffer had been reported shell-shocked but 'safe in a field hospital'. Lewis was about to be at last 'delivered from the ranks and sent . . . to be trained as an officer'. Yeats was 'buying the remains of a castle' in Ireland. Roberts, the Vorticist painter, was 'still at the front' in December, and 'young Aldington went out with the Xmas draft'—leaving H.D. to stand in for him at the *Egoist* as assistant editor. Joyce was safe in Zurich, but now the condition of his eyes was worrying Pound. And there was Eliot to worry about. He has 'chucked school-teaching', Pound told Miss Henderson in January 1917, 'and steps forth with only his writing to protect him. (result: lumbago or something of that sort.)'

Thomas S. Eliot (1914–16)

Thomas S. Eliot, as he then styled himself, had arrived in England shortly after the outbreak of war in August 1914. He held a Travelling Fellowship from Harvard and would spend the coming academic year as a highly promising graduate student of philosophy at Merton College, Oxford. He had published some youthful verses in the *Harvard Advocate*, the latest in 1910, but his more recent work, 'Portrait of a Lady' and 'The Love Song of J. Alfred Prufrock', had been meeting only rejections. With an introduction from Conrad Aiken, a Harvard classmate, he called on Pound on September 22, and Pound at once welcomed his intelligence and his poetry. 'Prufrock', he told Harriet Monroe just a week later, 'is the best poem I have yet seen or had from an American'. He was especially impressed and delighted by Eliot's having adequately prepared and trained himself to write poetry, and by his having 'modernized himself *on his own*'. Pound knew all too well the difficulties of setting a *persona* 'in modern life, with the discouragingly "unpoetic" modern surroundings'. It was 'such a comfort', he rejoiced, not to 'have to tell him to wash his face, wipe his feet, and remember the date (1914) on the calendar'.

Eliot had not been so enthusiastic about Pound. He reported back to Aiken that Pound was 'rather intelligent as a talker'—'his remarks are sometimes good'—and that 'his verse is well-meaning but touchingly incompetent'. The important thing was that he was 'going to print "Prufrock" in *Poetry* and pay me for it'. In the same letter he mentioned 'a possibility of dining at a Chinese restaurant Monday with Yeats—and the Pounds'. That was an interesting way of putting it, given the likelihood that he had been invited by Pound and been told that Yeats might be there. One thinks of the guest who, as he is introduced to one person, is already looking away for someone more important.

Pound had been quick to introduce his new find to his fellow artists. Wyndham Lewis wrote an amusing account of meeting the author of

'Prufrock', who might have been mistaken for Prufrock himself, in Pound's small odd-angled front room, with Dorothy 'hieratically rigid as she moved delicately to observe the Kensington Tea ritual'. On 2 February 1915 Eliot wrote to Pound from Oxford, sending 'Portrait of a Lady' for him to get published, and thanking him for his 'introduction to the Dolmetsch family' with whom he had 'passed one of the most delightful afternoons I have ever spent'. On 4 April, in a letter to Isabella Stewart Gardiner, the wealthy Boston collector of art, he wrote that he had 'been seeing a good deal of some of the modern artists whom the war has so far spared', naming Gaudier, Hulme, Lewis, Epstein and Wadsworth, mentioning *Blast* 'because it promises to contain a few things of my own', and also that he had met Yeats. In the long letter there was no mention of Pound.

Pound had sent 'Prufrock' to *Poetry* straight away in early October, and when Harriet Monroe objected to it as too much a portrait of futility he insisted that she print it unaltered, and then gave it his vote to receive *Poetry*'s $200 prize as the best poem it had published in 1915. (The prize went to another.) He sent 'Portrait of a Lady' to *Others* because she had delayed publishing 'Prufrock', and had Lewis include 'Preludes' and 'Rhapsody of a Windy Night' in *Blast 2*. He printed all of the poems Eliot had ready in 1915 in *Catholic Anthology* although, as he told his father, he himself would get nothing out of it 'except the satisfaction of getting Eliot's poems into print. between covers'. The next thing would be to help him bring out a volume of his own.

'Eliot has suddenly married a very charming young woman', Pound reported to his father in the summer of 1915. He had married Vivienne Haigh-Wood at Hampstead Registry Office on June 26, in the presence only of a close friend of Vivienne's and one of her aunts, and without any forewarning to his family or to his friends. Moreover, he had taken the desperate decision to give up philosophy as a profession in favour of poetry, and to stay on in England in order to do that. He had Pound write at once to his, Eliot's, father to offer on his behalf 'some sort of apologia for the literary life in general, and for London literary life in particular'. It was as if he wanted Pound to assume responsibility for his decision to go against his family's expectations and hopes that he was to have a brilliant career as a philosopher. In a very long letter Pound assured Henry Ware Eliot that his son was a poet of quite unusual talent and promise; that he had the advantage of having Pound as his energetic agent and publicist; that he needed to be in London to get on as a poet; and that, as Pound's own case proved, it was quite possible to exist there as a man of letters, especially if he were to be allowed $500 to begin on. It would have been about this time also that Eliot gave into Pound's keeping, 'so'z not to 'ave it in the 'ome', as Pound later put it in music hall vernacular, 'his earlier EPOS on King Bolo', together with various other 'ithyphallique' or bawdy poems.

Eliot crossed to America for three weeks in August to explain himself to his parents. At the end of September his father, having heard nothing from him after his return to London, cabled Pound for reassurance. Eliot then wrote to his father, 'I am sorry that you cabled to him, because he is not the sort of person whom I wish to be intimate with my affairs. He has shown a keen interest in my career; and has been and will be useful; but my acquaintance with him is primarily professional.'

In early October he discussed his prospects with Bertrand Russell who had taken the newlyweds under his wing, and Russell reported the discussion to Eliot's mother, possibly at Eliot's request. He wanted to reassure her about 'the financial outlook for him if he stays in England', and about the hope of his 'considerable literary gifts' bringing him 'reputation'. He also wanted to present Vivienne as a good wife for Eliot. 'The chief sign of her influence', he reported, 'is that he is no longer attracted by the people who call themselves "vorticists".'

Actually Eliot was being attracted by Russell's influential Cambridge and Garsington and Bloomsbury friends, while continuing to maintain useful relations with Pound and Lewis. The difficulty was that the two groups were on the whole hostile to each other, not least because Lewis's Vorticists had fallen out with Roger Fry's Omega Workshops. Yet Eliot managed to move in both circles without making the mistake of introducing Pound to his new friends. In July 1916 Pound wrote to Lewis:

just returned from a dam'd week by the seawaves. Eliot present. Eliot in local society. Fry, Canon [Gilbert Cannan], Lowes-Dickenson [Dickinson], Hope Johnson [Hope-Johnston]. (None of whom I met.)

Eliot did offer Pound (and Lewis) the sop of allowing that Fry was ' "an ass" '.

Thanks to introductions and recommendations from Bertrand Russell Eliot was doing a good deal of paid book reviewing in 1916, some for serious philosophical journals, some for the more intellectual press, and some which were in effect just advertising copy. But he was not writing any new poetry. His poems in *Catholic Anthology* had been singled out in the *Nation* as 'far and away the best'—because, Russell thought, the editor had probably had them called to his attention by his friend Lady Ottoline Morrell at Garsington. 'The Love Song of J. Alfred Prufrock' had been called 'brilliant', but Eliot feared that it was 'a swan song' and that his poetic mind had shut down. That was precisely what Pound hoped was not the case. 'Pray God it be not a single and unique success', he had exclaimed upon first reading it.

Eliot did have a lot on his mind. He was anxious about money, and about being a success in order to justify himself to his parents; Vivienne was in constant ill-health; and he himself gave the impression of being always in a state of exhaustion. He was teaching at Highgate Junior School throughout 1916; and in the autumn he began giving a three-year course of weekly tutorial classes in Modern English Literature in Southall, for the University of London Joint Committee for the Promotion of the Higher Education of Working People. That was a two-hour class every Monday evening. On another day he travelled up to Ilkley in Yorkshire to give 'a Course of Six Lectures on Modern French Literature' as an Oxford University Extension Lecturer. When he gave up school teaching he thought he might be able to live on what he could earn from the reviewing and extension lecturing. But then he was glad to be introduced to Lloyds Bank by a friend of Vivienne's family, and to be appointed in March 1917 to its Colonial and Foreign Department at a salary of £120 a year. Working from 9.15 to 5.00 gave him security and left his mind free outside banking hours.

Pound hoped that this would enable him to start writing poems again. To clear the way for new work he helped him arrange his poems to make up a first slim volume, *Prufrock and Other Observations*, then subsidized its publication by The Egoist Ltd., and promoted it in strong reviews in the *Egoist* and in *Poetry*. In the event Eliot did make a new start in 1917, at first with some poems in French, then with a series of poems in quatrains, these in part at least stimulated by his agreeing with Pound that *vers libre* had gone slack in the work of the 'Amygists' and that a return to the rigour of rhyme was called for. Pound also hoped to engage Eliot's critical intelligence in his 'compact fighting sheet', when he could get hold of one. But Eliot was not a willing volunteer and would join up with Pound only on his own circumspect terms. He needed to be financially secure and to be respected and esteemed by respectable and influential people, and for those purposes Pound was of no use at all.

'The Little Review' and the Great War: arrival of new force

Pound began to take the *Little Review* seriously when its editor, Margaret Anderson,[1] rather than publish writing that was less than outstanding,

[1] Margaret C. Anderson (1886–1973), b. Columbus, Indiana; editor, writer, radical. Founded *Little Review* in Chicago 1914, moved to New York 1916, continued to edit it with Jane Heap (jh) until 1929. The *Little Review*, she wrote, 'believes in Life for Art's sake ... [and is] written for Intelligent

and as a form of 'Want Ad.', left blank a dozen pages of the September 1916 number. Might he come to her assistance, he asked her, could she use a foreign correspondent? She had made it clear from the first that she wanted her review to be internationalist in outlook, and open-minded and radical in its criticism 'of books, music, art, drama and life'. Pound could be sure that she would welcome, as Harriet Monroe had not, his wanting to import 'French individualism, french realism' as a 'first step toward better art conditions in america'; and he saw in her refusal to compromise her ideal of a 'magazine of Art' a possible basis for building up 'a stronger party of intelligence in America'. Could he do with the *Little Review* what he had not been able to do with *Poetry*?

He set out his idea of what he might make of her review in a long letter to Anderson in January 1917. He first secured some leverage by mentioning that he had just been offered regular space in the *Egoist*—that would be, as he told Quinn, 'four pages a month, and eight pages any time I care to put up £3 for the printing of the four extra'. He was playing hard to get, but then he let her know that he would rather like to be got: 'ON THE OTHERHAND, the *Little Review* is perhaps temperamentally closer to what I want done ????????' He 'DEFINITELY' wanted 'an "official organ" (vile phrase)'—

a place where I and T. S. Eliot can appear once a month (or once an 'issue') and where James Joyce can appear when he likes, and where Wyndham Lewis can appear if he comes back from the war. / Definitely a place for our regular appearance and where our friends and readers (what few of 'em there are) can look with assurance of finding us.

'A magazine is made with FOUR writers', he would later say, thinking of the *Little Review*. He had a 'prospective guarantor'—who would want his support kept secret—ready to give '£120 or £150 [$600–$750] per year to pay a few contributors and myself'. Pound's 'name to appear on the magazine', perhaps as 'Contributing London Editor'.

As to what he would contribute, there would be his own 'best stuff'— apart, that is, from his 'original poetry, which still must go to *Poetry*'. He had by him 'a simple tale of indian life ("Jodindranath's Occupation")'. He would 'count on Eliot a good deal for ... criticism and appreciation' of any interesting books that might appear in London and Paris—'save when he has something original'. Joyce was working on another novel— he didn't know how much he would send in—and little could be expected

[Individuals]...whose philosophy is Applied Anarchism, whose policy is a Will to Splendour of Life...' MCA told its story and her own in *My Thirty Years War: beginnings and battles to 1930* (1930, 1969).

from Lewis while he was on active service. In the event Lewis would contribute quite a lot, some of it explosive; Joyce would in time send in instalments of *Ulysses*; and Eliot would contribute just a prose sketch, an essay on Henry James, and two groups of poems. Pound would take care of the current criticism himself; continue a series of 'Imaginary Letters' begun by Lewis; put in several tales, dialogues and translations, these to be collected as 'pavannes'; contribute his satirical poem, 'L'Homme Moyen Sensuel' and the pair of sequences of poems, 'Moeurs Contemporaines' and 'Langue d'Oc'; and he would edit besides an entire special issue of French Poetry (an anthology with commentary), another special issue on Henry James, and a part of one on de Gourmont. Altogether, with these, with some substantial contributions of poems from Yeats and of prose from Hueffer, and with occasional things from Rodker and others, Pound would be responsible for from half to the whole of most issues from May 1917 through to April 1919 when he ceased to be Foreign Editor.

One other thing he specified in his January 1917 letter, he 'should want to feel free to say' that 'The Tariff on books is an INFAMY'. That may have been because he believed that a magazine needed to stir up controversy to stay alive. But the tariff of 25 per cent on books imported into the United States had long concerned him as an obstruction 'to the free circulation of thought'. It was, he would say, 'most deleterious to the mental health of that country . . . and to America's relations with foreign countries'. A little later he would have occasion to connect the tariff on imported books with the censorship of literature within the United States, and to write of 'the war for internal freedom, and for the arteries and capillaries of freedom, the mail-routes and presses'. Censorship would become a live issue for the *Little Review*.

One can get some idea of the kind of thought he meant to import into the United States from the terms in which he rejected a story submitted by his friend Edgar Jepson. 'The damblasted trouble is that it *is* a magazine story', he told him, and he wanted to 'use nothing which is not definitely an insult to the public-library, the general-reader, the weekly press'. He would not have the '"women's dresses, music, champagne"' kind of writing. He was looking for bitter satire charged with 'contempt for contemporary mentality, for the reading public, for the way the "world of letters" goes on'. If sugary sentimentality was unavoidable he wanted it laced with venom. He wanted to subvert the self-preserving complacencies of small minds and small worlds, to unsettle established pieties and proprieties, to explode every kind of cliché and conformist conventionality.

His 'corner' of the *Little Review* was to be '*BLAST*, but *BLAST* covered with ice, with a literary and reserved camouflage'. It was to be for 'the current prose writings' of Joyce, Lewis, Eliot, and himself; and 'Most good prose', as he saw it from his poet's point of view, arises 'from an instinct of negation; is the detailed, convincing analysis of something detestable; of something which one wants to eliminate'. He knew that Lewis's stories were impelled by that 'instinct of negation'; he had observed in *Tarr* 'a highly energised mind performing a huge act of scavenging; cleaning up a great lot of rubbish, cultural, Bohemian, romantico-Tennysonish, arty, societish, gutterish'; and *Ulysses* would prove to be 'a great work of Katharsis', a purge for the contemporary mind.

When Margaret Anderson, with effusive enthusiasm, appointed Pound to be 'Foreign Editor' of the *Little Review* starting with the May 1917 number, he used his first editorial to declare that he intended to make it 'the instrument' of his 'radicalism' in a way that *Poetry* had never been. It had been too genteel to tell 'fools and fogies', 'public nuisances' and literary mediocrities 'to go to hell'; and it had clung on to its notion that American poetry had to be democratic. At his instigation the *Little Review* would alter its masthead to declare itself 'A Magazine of the Arts / Making No Compromise with the Public Taste'. 'There is no misanthropy in a thorough contempt for the mob', he asserted, 'There is no respect for mankind save in respect for detached individuals'. His strained relations with *Poetry* were just about finished off by his taking up with the *Little Review*, though he would continue to contribute poems of his own and to be named as its Foreign Editor through into 1919.

At the same time he was reviving his alliance with the *Egoist*. In the course of his editorial he expressed the wish that the *Little Review* should 'aid and abet *The Egoist* in its work'. Miss Anderson was wholly in agreement. 'By getting the *Little Review* and the *Egoist*', she advised her readers, 'you will be in touch with the two most important radical organs of contemporary literature'. Of course, for Pound at least, the work of the *Egoist* was represented not by Dora Marsden's 'slosh', but by its publishing *A Portrait of the Artist as a Young Man*, and *Tarr*, and '*Mr Prufrock and Observations*'. He could confidently associate the two magazines just then because Eliot, at his suggestion, and with Quinn's money paying a third of the salary, was about to take over from H.D. as assistant editor of the *Egoist*. He would recover it from the Amygists and 'keep the writing as much as possible in Male hands'. 'So there'll be a buttress for L. Review there', Pound told Quinn.

The whole venture depended on Quinn's money, but Pound wanted to use it 'to call up stuff that wouldn't get done unless the L. R. was ready for it', and he would take no more than he needed:

The point is that if I accept more than I <u>need</u> I at once become a sponger, and I at once lose my integrity. By doing the job for the absolute minimum I remain respectable and when I see something I want I can ax for it. I mean to say, as things stand I can ask for money when Joyce finishes his next novel, or if Hueffer ever gets his <u>real</u> book finished.... My whole position and the whole backing up of my statement that the artist is 'almost' independent [of patron and public] goes with doing the thing as nearly as possible without 'money'.

He would take for himself while he was Foreign Editor just enough to pay his rent, 'not food and clothing'; and the rest of the $750 a year assured the regular and prompt printing of the writing he wanted to appear in the *Little Review*, and in the *Egoist*.

In February 1917 Pound told Anderson that he wanted 'to start off the new order of things with a bang.... BOMM! Simultaneous arrival of new force in pages of *Little Review*'. On April 6 the United States declared war on Germany, forced out of its neutrality by Germany's submarines sinking American ships in the Atlantic. 2/^{LT} P. Wyndham Lewis's Siege Battery of six inch guns was sent into France at the end of May as reinforcements, and almost immediately he was in the firing line 'in the midst of an unusually noisy battle'. He had left behind with Pound a number of writings, among them 'Cantleman's Spring-Mate', a savagely naturalistic story about a soldier about to be sent to fight in France which would cause the October issue of the *Little Review* to be seized and destroyed by the U.S. Post Office.

Communications between the front line and London were rather good—letters, Lewis found, took about three days to get through, and he kept up a regular correspondence with Pound and other friends. He was 'particularly lucky', he wrote in his first week at the front, 'in dropping into the midst of a very big attack'. He wanted to have the experience of the war, to see it directly and intimately, not for vain glory but in order to bring his intelligence to bear on it; and already he was able to edit his impressions into a sequence of clear and objective pictures, as if he were making a film. First he gave the distant view: 'From [an Observation Post on the top of a hill] I saw an immense and smoky struggle for a village:

saw tanks advancing, cavalry etc.: tanks hit, air fights—panorama of war.'
Then the near view:

in late afternoon walked up with my Battery commander to the line gained a
few hours before: through the desolation of the Bosche concrete dugouts in a
wilderness of charred spikes that was formerly a wood, everything not trenches
pits and gashes: dead Germans lying about like bloody waxworks.

Only then did he become personal, though still with perfect detachment:
'We passed through a field Battery that was being shelled, though quies-
cent itself, and there I came nearest to a black shell-burst: about twenty
yards, twice. They were coming over every few seconds.'

After three weeks he went down with trench fever and spent six weeks
in hospital, where he did an amount of writing and drawing. He also
appointed Pound as his literary executor, and asked him to pull whatever
strings he could to get him transferred into Intelligence. He had had just
about enough of the war experience to reach certain conclusions about
it. In August he was sent back to the Ypres salient where General Haig
was testing his grand strategy to the point of nearly destroying his own
army in the mud of Passchendaele. In a crowded dugout under constant
bombardment Lewis decided that what he most disliked about the military
life was 'the too frightful incompatibility of my companions', on account of
their disgusting banality. 'Nature & my training have made me curiously
sensitive to ugly & stupid influences', he told Pound in October, 'The
whole point of <u>Me</u> is that'. And then 'the futility, trickery, the element
in fact of despicable inhuman swindle in all this dreary & rotten business
is borne in upon me more sharply than upon most people.' At the same
time he had discovered something interesting about himself, that he was
'truly <u>not</u> sanguinary except when confronted by an imbecile'. He had
been directing his Battery's fire on a church, and been 'glad that it was
a presumably <u>empty</u> ruin'.

Lewis escaped from his circle of that hell in November when he was
given London leave because his mother was ill, and Pound and Lady
Cunard and other friends contrived to have him transferred to Lord
Beaverbrook's Canadian War Records project, so that he could spend
the rest of the war creating images of Batteries for posterity rather than
directing their high explosives at ruins. In January 1918 he was back in
France locating a gun-pit fit to paint, and reported to Pound that the
Americans were all over Paris.

When the United States declared war it had a navy but no army it
could send against the enemy in France, and it would take it months

to conscript, train, and arm one. What its coming in meant at first was simply increased bank loans to the Allies, to be repaid after the war. Pound sent his name in to the American Embassy in London and was informed that volunteers were not wanted. On April 19 he told Quinn that London was 'in much gayer mood than since the beginning of war—the advance has cheered everyone'.[2] There was apparently a feeling in the air that the war would be won even before the Americans could get into the fighting. The best thing they might do, so far as Pound could judge, was to organize transport, 'some system of *direct supply* . . . straight from the factory to the particular section of the front where stuff is wanted'. He suggested Quinn mention this to ex-President Theodore Roosevelt when he next lunched with him. In June he filled in a form for foreigners to volunteer for National Service in a coal-mine or agriculture, and asked if his knowledge of foreign languages—French, Italian and Spanish, some German—could be of use. But the Board 'shook its head' over his account of himself, having 'never had anything like it before', and decided he had neither the 'manual' nor the 'clerical' skills that were needed.

From a letter to his father

In August 1917 Pound wrote a long letter to Homer about the war and the *Little Review*:

Dear Dad : I don't quite know what 'feelings' you want me to run up. It is of course pleasing to see the stars and stripes and the union jack amorously entwined on the same flag pole at the British Museum. As you know an Anglo-Franco-American alliance has been in my eyes a desirable thing for a long time. America had sunk lower than the mud, and everything I had written on the subject had been suppressed. I don't know how much impressed I can now be at the sight of America doing what England has been doing all along. I don't know (now that one can scarcely read the communiques from the front for boredom with the same phrases repeated year after year) I don't know what waves of emotion a Billion dollars is expected to raise. Simply, America is doing what she damn well ought to do, and what so far as I can see, she ought to have begun doing sooner. . . .

    I do not favour conscription, but I indubitably benefit (personally) by the present American system of it. / It is ironical that both Homer and David [his cousins] should go, and that I who care something for civilization should be left

---

[2] There was no advance worth cheering. On April 9 1917 the British and Empire Army set off the Allied Spring offensive with the battle of Arras, in which the Canadians took Vimy Ridge; apart from that the net gain after a week was 142,000 British and Empire casualties, with 85,000 on the German side. On the 16th the French attacked on the Aisne and secured an advance of 600 yards, after which their army was ground down over weeks and months to the point of mutiny. April 16th was the day on which Lenin arrived in Petrograd to seize control of the Russian Revolution.

at my typewriter. It must be especially bitter for Florence who certainly dont give a curse whether London and Paris and all that they mean, are destroyed or not. / An intelligent government would of course preserve people like Lewis and myself. Lewis is however in the thick of it.

I don't think Wilson tried to make America understand the war, before he came in, and I don't much believe America knows what the conflict means. However I am thankful she is in. (On the other hand, she never would have recovered if she hadn't come in.)

As I am for the present definitely left out, through no act of my own, or through no neglect of my own, I think it would ill become me to go about shouting magniloquently about the glory of war. Just as it is not Mr Rockfellow's business to do so. / America is fighting on my side, probably for reasons not in the least my own. That is about as far as I can get with it. . . .

Certainly the bosche must be beaten. That proposition is of more importance to me than what America now does. The greater part she takes in it, the better for her. / I see nothing to do but keep quiet. I would have had America in two or three years ago with a volunteer army. And I suppose I should now be taking less interest in mundane affairs, unless I had been rejected for eyesight or given some job where my brains instead of my hide were of use. (It is not however the habit of democracies to use my sort of intelligence.)

I shall not write against conscription, or do anything to impede the executive in the least. Besides I should have done it months ago if I had been going to. / So long as I am myself 'too old tew fight' I can't see that it is decent for me to flag-wave. Neither can the acts of America to date, fill me with any feeling in excess of what one feels for the French and English troops that have been in the field since the start. That is to say I care for america merely as I care for Australia or any other part of 'The Allies' who are 'my country'. I am glad that America is now part of it. So is Siam.

I have never taken any stock in Russia. I can only hope she wont make too hellish a mess of her front. They are and always have been a stupid and uninteresting people. Coming from one barbarism I can not be expected to take interest in another.

Re / the Review. I do not expect to 'get' anything 'out of it', apart from my stipend. It is not the business of literature to exploit or 'get things out of' people. / One's job consists in putting down what one thinks clearly and with no regard to the local prejudices or temporal prejudices of the proletariat or public or whatever it is called.

If there can be printed in America a paper that can be read in Paris or London without boredom one might have a sensation of gratification. Up to now America has produced local gazettes. . . . *Poetry* has escaped in a small corner. and this was NOT due to the Chicago board.

As Lewis has said (July number) 'Matter which has not sufficient mind to permeate it grows . . . gangrenous and rotten'. / That is the American 'world (or rather

329

village) of letters'. / The shock of hearing that ideas, not current in Omaha, exist is probably too much for America ... infant industries ... infant mentalities. / There is no need of people 'adopting' other ideas. I don't see how I can be much clearer than I am in the end of my Poggio dialogue [July number]. . . .

The blight of ... American dulness, once of *Century, Harper*, now of *New Republic, Dial*, (creeping over Harriet's part of *Poetry*). One wants relief from this stifling. / Fortunately I am over here. Otherwise I should get entoiled in endless controversy over things that do not matter. And get nothing done. / Look at the correspondence in the L. R. . . . yelling that we give them 'invention instead of interpretation', i.e. creation instead of gas. . . . It was perhaps a mistake to join up with an American paper at all. Nothing can be done except in London or Paris. One can not turn a province into a capital, and the province is always a series of impotent and diminishing ecchoes.

One can not stop however merely because people have not yet read De Gourmont ... / One would also like to give people something better than the Shaw, Wells, Bennet, generation, daft on abstract ideas, and the last two, sunk in vulgarity.

As for American literature, the odour of decayed thought is almost tangible in the Seven Arts and New Republic. . . . / Lewis, Joyce, Eliot, Romains ... do think. This active chemical in the mind is the thing worth preserving. It must have its court yard. These men do not perpetually go on pawing over other-peoples cast off thoughts. / The long prose of Hueffers to begin in Jan. is also active, in a rather gentler way, but still, living. / Yeats again made his own place. He didn't simply produce to supply a market demand.

There is no earthly need of agreeing with what people think. But there is a need that some people should be capable of thinking, not merely of pawing over thought already formed. AND they should have space and licence to do it.

Of course all intellectual freedom is loathed in America. . . .

'The Little Review' and the Great War: the enemy

'I have been in action, mental moral and physical uninterruptedly for some days', Pound told Lewis some time in July 1917. At the end of August he said he had been 'turning out an article a day for weeks', and was now 'doing "Studies in Contemporary Mentality" in *New Age*'. He had become a regular contributor to the weekly *New Age* again, as well as to the *Little Review* and the *Egoist*, and he was also contributing articles on his special interests such as Beddoes and Landor to Charles Granville's new monthly, *Future*. It did not amount to an article a day, though at times it must have felt that way; but he was averaging about two articles a week, since he published over sixty items in periodicals between May and December 1917. Add in all his correspondence and one can understand his telling Lewis, in a letter mainly concerned with Lewis's writings, 'My present existence is that of a highly mechanized typing volcano'.

He may well have felt that Lewis was his only active ally on the magazine front, which meant that he had to find and fire all the ammunition himself. Joyce declared himself unfit for journalism, indeed doubly unfit on account of his eye troubles, though those did not prevent him from getting on with *Ulysses*. Through the spring and summer of 1917 Pound and Quinn engaged in a busy correspondence with Joyce about the worsening condition of his eyes and his need of an operation, and of money to pay for it. Pound showed some sound knowledge of optics based on his own experience of having worn glasses from the age of 5 and having one oculist discover, when he was about 20, that an 'inharmonic astigmatism' was twisting his spine. He had 'suddenly felt "a weight lifted"' when the appropriate adjustment was made, and he looked into the possibility of his oculist putting right Joyce's eyes. In August he asked Quinn to raise money for Joyce's operation by selling two autograph letters of King Ferdinand and Queen Isabella of Spain dated 1492 which he had picked up 'in Las Americas', the old bazaar in Madrid, and left in his father's safe-keeping. Quinn's response was to mail Joyce a cheque for $125. They were probably unaware that Miss Weaver had instructed her solicitors in February to pay Joyce £50 quarterly, quite independently of Pound's efforts, and anonymously.

For the May *Little Review* Eliot had produced the first of what Pound expected would be a series of 'Eeeldrop and Appleplex' sketches. 'His two queer chaps are quite real', Pound told Quinn, 'and I think they will be an excellent pair of pincers wherewith to pick up and display certain present day types and characters'. They reminded him of Flaubert's Bouvard and Pécuchet; but now they make readers think rather of Eliot and Pound themselves, though there is much more of Eliot in Eeldrop's point of view and observations than of Pound in Appleplex. It took Pound three months to drag the second and only other instalment out of Eliot. 'Mrs Eliot has just been in', he told Margaret Anderson shortly before extracting the second part, 'says T.S.E. has done <u>no work</u> for weeks, that he returns from the bank, falls into a leaden slumber and remains there until bedtime.' 'However don't despair, something will get itself done about it', he added. One of the things he did was to take Eliot to meet a certain Prima Ballerina, 'with the firm intuito that a poem wd. result & intention that it should', and thus evoked Grishkin of 'Whispers of Immortality'. His detailed work on that poem amounted to virtual co-authorship. At the same time he suggested Gautier's *Émaux et Camées* as a model, and thus called forth the series of poems in quatrains collected in Eliot's *Poems* (1920).

331

Pound was not publishing much poetry himself in 1917 and 1918. Apart from the 'Three Cantos', which had been composed in 1915–16, his only new verse of any significance was 'Moeurs Contemporains' and 'Langue d'Oc' in the *Little Review* of May 1918. (They appeared there because Harriet Monroe had rejected them as too unprintably frank for *Poetry*.) He did devote five weeks around December 1917 and January 1918 to retranslating Arnaut Daniel, in order further to refine his ear for the music of words; and he was working after that on *Homage to Sextus Propertius*, which would appear in 1919. But most of his energies at this time were going into his attacking prose.

He was fighting as ever for his idea of a civilization based on individual genius and individual difference. And the enemy, as he defined it in a series of articles in the *New Age*, was provincial ignorance, 'ignorance of the manners, customs and nature of people living outside one's own village, parish, or nation'; or rather, it was that ignorance when combined with the lust 'to coerce others into uniformity'. 'The whole fight of modern enlightenment is against this', he asserted. He named Henry James both as a defender of the individual against the oppressions and tyrannies of family and society, and as a crusader for an internationalism which would open England, America, and France to each others' manners and customs. He also praised Confucius for his 'constant emphasis . . . on a man's right to preserve the outlines of his personality, and his duty not to interfere with the personalities of others.' Against that enlightenment he saw ranged any clergy seeking to impose a religious dogma; those who would cry up nationality, or race; and above all those who would subject the individual to the State or nation. Evidently the German state was the current enemy of enlightenment. But another incarnation of 'the ever damned spirit of provincialism' was Napoleon, with his idiotic imperial ambition to impose a uniform code by force of arms upon not only France but the whole of Europe.

The stories, dialogues, and imaginary letters which Pound wrote for the *Little Review* were all directed against the spirit of provincialism. 'Jodindranath Mawhor's Occupation' is an account, rather in the manner of Voltaire or de Gourmont, of a mode of life which shows a shocking disregard for the conventions and values of decent, hard-working, church-going middle America, the occupation in question being the cultivation of refined and entirely selfish pleasures. In 'An Anachronism at Chinon', Pound, in the guise of an American student in conversation with Rabelais, was getting off his chest a 'set of basic propositions': that is, he was sounding off against a stew of oppressions that bothered him personally, such as Germanic Philology; 'states where a man's tobacco is not safe from invasion'; censorship by ignorant printers and prudes; the everlasting ringing of damned church bells over his head in Kensington; and perennial follies, such as that which caused 'the shores of Gallipoli' to show red 'to the airmen flying thousands of feet above them'. 'As for personal morals', he has Rabelais conclude, 'there can be no permanent boundaries.' It is a high-spirited dialogue between men of quick-witted intelligence, each complaining of the follies and vices of their own age and eager to find advantages in the other's. 'Aux Étuves de Wiesbaden. A.D. 1451', another dialogue, is less personal, and more focused in its exploration of varieties of sexual morals and customs. 'Men have a curious desire for uniformity', Poggio observes, but 'What dignity have we over the beasts, save to be once, and to be irreplaceable!' He counts himself lucky to live in an age when 'men are prized for being unique'. The dialogue closes with Pound's familiar reflection that Roman rhetoricians, with their passion for making others think with them, ruined the empire.

He called some of these imaginary dialogues 'pavannes', and it is an apt word for most of his contributions to the *Little Review*. It is from the Latin for *peacock*, and named a stately court dance in which the performers dressed up in the most elaborate fashion. Pound was indeed strutting his stuff in these pieces, displaying the outlines of his personality in highly stylized and idealized performances of the views and opinions which were the staple of his conversation and his journalism. The most brilliant display is the 'divagation' from Jules Laforgue's 'Salomé', 'Our Tetrarchal Précieuse'.

The displays were of course meant to be improving, to be freeing the minds of his readers from cramping prejudices and deadening orthodoxies and blank ignorance of the varieties of human experience. 'Our Tetrarchal Précieuse', he informed Margaret Anderson, 'indicates a state of sophistication which the denizens of Oshkosh might well be reminded of' – it would 'serve to stir up the rural population'. However, while there is no doubting the sophistication of both Laforgue's and Pound's coruscating word-play, one might question its bearing upon the lives of the denizens of Oshkosh. One might think that Willa Cather was more closely in touch with them than was Pound, and that her application of the classics to small-town Nebraska was possibly more relevant.

About as strange as his thinking that his imaginary conversations would open the mind of Oshkosh to the wider world was his thinking they might liberate the mind of Mayfair. In a letter bearing the date '11/11/17' he sent to Margaret Anderson a list of new subscribers to the *Little Review*, among them Lady Leslie, the Duchess of Rutland, the Duchess of Marlborough, Lady Howard de Walden, the Rt. Hon. Mrs Montagu, and Mrs John Astor. He had caught them all together at Lady Cunard's, apparently, organizing a charity bazaar to benefit wounded soldiers. These were people who did things and got them done, and he asked for ninety copies to be sent immediately to be put on the book stall at the bazaar, in the hope that many more in their spheres of influence would be moved to subscribe. It must have been a surreal juxtaposition: Mayfair Society doing its bit for the tens and hundreds of thousands of war wounded being brought back from the front; and Pound's propaganda to make it see that the real enemy was provincial ignorance, and that the real struggle was for the survival of the individual, more especially of the individual artist.

The enemy was not mortally wounded by Pound's 'pavannes and divagations'. 'Look! he's throwing pebbles at our skyscrapers', mocked one reviewer. But 'the ever damned spirit of provincialism' could muster powerful support when it perceived a serious threat to its sense of propriety. There was a New York Society for the Suppression of Vice, founded by Anthony Comstock and headed at this time by John S. Sumner. In 1916 it had all but succeeded in having Theodore Dreiser's novel *The "Genius"* banned as blasphemous and obscene. Pound, in signing the letter of protest, had declared that the attempt to suppress 'Dreiser's fearless and unexaggerated realism' was an attack, ultimately, upon personal freedom in the United States. 'Christianity has become a sort of Prussianism', he wrote to Mencken, 'and will have to go'. But of course it did not.

Moreover this 'Prussianism' had the law on its side. When subscribers to the *Little Review* complained that they had not received the October 1917 issue the editors enquired at the Post Office and learnt that it had been seized under Section 211 of the U.S. Criminal Code, otherwise known as the Comstock Law. This was a law which, as Pound put it, lumped 'literature and instruments for abortion into one clause': *'Every obscene, lewd, or lascivious, and every filthy book, pamphlet, picture, letter, writing, print, or other publication of an indecent character and every article or thing designed, adapted or intended for preventing conception or producing abortion, or for any indecent or immoral use ... is hereby declared to be non-mailable matter and shall not be conveyed in the mails'.* The offending article in the *Little Review* was Wyndham Lewis's indecorous and indelicate volcano—Pound's words—'Cantleman's Spring-mate'. Cantleman's predicament could be thought of in Christian terms, as that of an intelligent soul in rebellion against being trapped in an animal body and thus immersed in the brute processes of nature and warfare. His rebellion takes the form of acting the amoral animal that he is, while his mind stands aloof thinking that this is the way to get back at Nature. 'He had no adequate realization', the story concludes, 'of the extent to which... [this] was to the advantage of the animal world'. It is a deeply ironic tale calculated to make one think. But the trouble was that Lewis's analysis is conducted in practical rather than abstract terms:

At their third meeting he brought her a ring. Her melting gratitude was immediately ligotted with long arms, full of the contradictory and offending fire of the spring. On the warm earth consent flowed up into her body from all the veins of the landscape.... He felt that he was raiding the bowels of Nature: not fecundating the Aspasias of our flimsy flesh... Cantleman was proud that he could remain deliberate and aloof

Evidently this was not an honest and deeply thoughtful report on experience but an incitement to indecency and immorality, in the view not only of the Postmaster General but also of Judge Augustus N. Hand who rejected John Quinn's appeal against the seizure and burning of that issue of the magazine. Judge Hand did allow that the classics, 'because they have the sanction of age and fame and usually appeal to a comparatively limited number of readers', might at times escape the ban. But that meant, Pound commented, that 'no living man is to contribute or to attempt to contribute to the classics'. 'No more damning indictment of American civilization has been written than that contained in Judge Hand's "opinion"', he concluded.

The Comstock Law would stand nonetheless, to be deployed again by the New York Society for the Suppression of Vice against *Ulysses* when it was appearing in the *Little Review*.

His several fronts: chronicle

T. E. Hulme was killed by a German shell in Flanders on 28 September 1917. On October 20 Yeats married Georgie Hyde-Lees, Dorothy's step-cousin and close friend, with Ezra as his best man. They would not winter together again at Stone Cottage. As for Dorothy, we get only rare glimpses of her in Pound's letters in these years. 'My wife don't care much about late hours', he told Joyce as part of an explanation of why he did not 'go to the theatre'. He told Quinn that Dorothy would meet most of his, Quinn's, specifications for a wife, 'save possibly the "concentration"... at least I cant guarantee sustained concentration'. In any case she wouldn't do because 'Three days in an office like yours would end her'—she didn't have the 'vitality' for that. Dorothy's own view of 'vitality' might be gathered from her letting him know that 'the *energy* in Joyce, W. L. & myself is what

335

upsets people'. Even so, she was among Joyce's 'constant readers' and had 'a growing affection for Bloom'. She apparently read a great deal. Pound notes something—a pension for Walter de la Mare—'in the paper that D is reading'. When Lewis recommends Henri Barbusse's war novel, *Le Feu*, it is Dorothy that has read it and has 'quoted chunks of it' to him. In the summer of 1917, in her letters to Pound, she mentions reading Pierre Bayle 'in English, 1733'—Ezra had bought the 'four huge folios' of Bayle's *Dictionnaire historique et critique* 5th edition (1740) for a guinea in Tottenham Court Road in May—also Voltaire's *Traité sur la Tolérance* (1763), and Wace's history of King Arthur's Britain. She found those books in the country gentleman's library of Leweston Manor, near Sherborne in Dorset, where she was visiting with Olivia and relations according to their usual summer routine. She mentions strawberries, cows and crops, haymaking, and hoeing up thistles. In a later letter, in October, she notes that 'The Austrians seem to have been really routed over the Piave.'

In November 1917 it occurred to Pound that 'the less I think myself dowered with a mission to EDUCATE untutored America, the BETTER. If I had ANY sense whatever I should confine myself exclusively to writing for the ten or dozen intelligent people I know, or have heard of'. He had a correlative thought: 'God knows I have to work hard enough to escape, not propagande, but getting centred in propagande'. But in spite of these salutary reflections he published eleven articles in five different periodicals within that month, all of them educative propaganda of one sort or another.

He wanted to administer Laforgue to America as 'a purge and a critic'. 'Comstocks, societies for the prevention of all human activities are impossible in the wake of Laforgue', he advised *Poetry*'s audience, 'And he is therefore an exquisite poet, a deliverer of the nations'. He recommended Landor's collected works, in Granville's *Future,* as 'the best substitute for a University education that can be offered to any man in a hurry'. In the *Egoist* he wrote about the humanizing influence of the Greek and Latin classics, if only they could be saved from Philology. In the *New Age* each week he was casting a withering eye on the magazines of the day, in a series of 'Studies in Contemporary Mentality'.

There he was doing what would be invented in universities in the 1930s and 1940s as the sociology of literature, that is, he was searching for the psychology of the nation in its popular magazines. His method, of course, was not that of the scientist but simply that of a highly individualized intelligence applying itself to the reading matter of the masses. He remarks in the *Quiver* 'a mother's' words: 'I want my girls to marry. The wise

Creator did not intend man or woman to live alone. I am old-fashioned enough, etc.', and comments:

Note possessive 'my' before girls; 'wise' before Creator. Tribal possessive. Primitive, folk or peasant pessimism as to bitterness of life, overlaid with unhellenic belief in wisdom of Creator. Stand made for the 'old-fashioned' wifehood and motherhood. Note the association of 'virtue' with old custom.

When 'a mother' declares her belief that 'The nation must have mothers', Pound notes 'The need of the State tending to coerce the act of the individual'. After working through 'four pages double column' of motherly common sense he concludes that such writing is by and for people who take 'no count of the divergence of personalities and of temperaments'. 'Are the people for whom this stuff is poured out', he asks, 'so devitalised that question of individual passion, individual drive, is not a factor in their existence?' 'Good customs and enlightenment must...be surreptitious', he reflected after looking into the *Church Times*, 'what terrible cunning is required for any man to exist with intelligence'.

While he was still investigating popular culture Pound set up as the *New Age*'s critic of high Art and Music, contributing either 'Art Notes' or 'Music Notes' each week from November 1917 until January 1921, under the noms-de-guerre of 'B. H. Dias' and 'William Atheling'. He had done art criticism before, largely in the Vorticist cause; but the music criticism was a new departure, and more nearly allied to his own art. Writing 'art and music critiques under pseudonyms' was a queer thing to be doing, he told his father, but it paid the rent and was rather entertaining. As 'Atheling' he had to attend 'an irreducible minimum of about three concerts a week', but did not have to sit through any that proved unbearable: 'Three minutes scraping are enough to demonstrate that a given concertist is an ass, a duffer, a card-board imitation, a stuffed shirt, a pupil of promise, a pupil of no promise, a performer with possibilities, *or* a musician.' He made it his business to encourage 'the best performers to present their best work...without making any concession whatsoever to ignorance and bad taste'. 'Atheling's' own taste was for early music: 'he sympathised with Arnold Dolmetsch' opinions, he might very well have thought that music ended with Bach' and that 'British music ended effectively with Lawes, Campion, and John Jenkins'. In particular he shared Pound's great interest in the fitting of words to music and in the drawing out of the music that is in words. On that account he probably did not mind at all that the *New Age* could only get its critic free tickets for recitals at the Bechstein [later

Wigmore], Steinway and Æolian halls, and not for full orchestra concerts in the larger halls.

In December 1917 Pound was 'doing ten and twelve hours a day' on a new version of Arnaut Daniel's *canzoni* which the Reverend C. C. Bubb of Cleveland, Ohio, had asked to print on his private press. (The only copy of the manuscript would be lost on its way to Cleveland, presumed sunk by enemy action in the Atlantic.) Also in December Pound received the first episode of *Ulysses*, which was to appear in both the *Little Review* and the *Egoist*. After reading it he had mixed feelings about whether it might get the *Little Review* suppressed again. Yeats had said that the suppression of the October number for 'Cantleman' was 'great luck, and ought to be the making of the magazine'. In any case, Pound considered *Ulysses* well worth being suppressed for; though it was an open question whether the law would consider the mention of urination 'lascivious' and likely to 'lead to copulation by the reader'. In the event thirteen episodes and part of the fourteenth were published in the *Little Review*, from March 1918 to December 1919, and only then was *Ulysses* banned. In England, however, Miss Weaver could find no printer who would agree to set up the unexpurgated text, and the *Egoist* was able to publish only 'a series of extracts', and even those not until 1919.

In January 1918 'Atheling' became very excited by a performance of old French folk-songs by a young soprano, Raymonde Collignon. She sang the words exactly as he would have them sung, with perfect articulation and accurate expression, while striking each note with an exact ear for pitch and a true sense of rhythm. Her voice was small, 'a clavichord among singers', yet with the greatest variety of emotional effect within the slender sound. 'Her art', he wrote, was 'as delicate as the art of the cutter of intaglios, and as firm'. She was just the singer needed for the reconstructions of troubadour music which he and Rummel had worked on in Paris in 1911 and 1912, and he immediately persuaded her to perform them. 'It means a new start on the whole thing (Provencal XII century music)', he told Quinn, 'and probably the resurrection of as much of it as is worth while'.

'Anyhow', he went on, 'it is more important than trying to save America from itself'. His interest in early music was being nourished again, and in February he told Margaret Anderson that he was 'at the moment interested in Henry Lawes, "who knew how to do it"', and that Dolmetsch was going to play Bach properly on his clavichord, and that he was

for the time being, bored to death with being any kind of an editor. I desire to go on with my long poem; and like the Duke of Chang, I desire to hear the music of a lost dynasty. (have managed to hear it, in fact.) And I desire also to resurrect the art of the lyric, I mean words to be sung, for... there is scarcely anything since the time of Waller and Campion. AND a mere imitation of them won't do.

Just two days later, however, he was telling Quinn, 'Feel I must pull myself together and "edit" it [i.e. the *Little Review*] a bit more'. He had been depressed by the suppression of the October number, by 'general feeling of hopelessness of doing anything with or in U.S.A. so far as literature is concerned', by 'Hueffer's petering out', by 'Eliot's exhaustion, and Lewis' desoeuvrement', and also by 'the newest variation of "flu" on top of [doing] French number and "Arnaut Daniel" in rapid succession'. 'Damn, damn, DAMN I must pull myself together and DO something', he told Margaret Anderson the same day. In another letter, his third to her that day, he wrote, 'I have spent this whole bloody day writing letters, bar [short] interruption for tea to discuss music with La Belle Collignon'. He was an ass to be exhausting himself in clerical work a typist or secretary could perfectly well do, and as it happened he had the chance of one, if only the *Little Review* could raise him from £60 to £104 a year so that he could pay the typist £2 a week. Then he could give more time (unpaid) to editing AND have a lot more energy for composition: it would be a 'perfectly sane economy, ALL round'.

There was more to this than he was letting on. The 'typist or secretary' in view was Iseult Gonne, Maud Gonne's delicately beautiful and intelligent daughter who was then 23. Yeats had proposed to her in 1917 after finally despairing of marrying her mother, and though she refused him they remained close. He had secured work for her as an assistant librarian in the London School of Oriental Studies, but there was an idea it might be better for her if she could work as a typist, and Pound was trying to arrange that. Although he did not get the raise he had asked for from the *Little Review*, he still told Yeats that he proposed to turn over to Iseult the £5 a month it paid him 'in order to get more time for actual composition'. Iseult should not be referred to as 'his secretary', however, his poems being 'too Ithyphallic for any secretary of her years to be officially in my possession'. It is said that she became his mistress; it has even been said that he said he would leave Dorothy for her. Her maid Josephine sent scandalized reports to Yeats, according to Foster, and Yeats then wrote her reproving letters about Pound. But there is no deposit of definite evidence in the record. There was talk enough in a general way to lead Conrad to remark to Quinn, 'he has many women at his feet; which must be immensely comforting'. It is a fact that about the time of her death in 1953 Pound did memorialize 'Yseult' in a canto, along with Rummel and

Ford, as '*familiaris*', one of the family. It is also a fact that in July 1918 he told his father that he had 'a typist three days a week so that I . . . can use my lofty intelligence for more intelligent matters than swatting a Corona.'

He had been kept on by Orage when wartime newsprint rationing forced the *New Age* to cut down to sixteen pages, and he was indeed the only regular (via his aliases) to be retained. This was in spite of his old conviction that Orage's 'political mind [was] bound to fall out with the artist and with literature, tolerating them only up to a point, and as "addenda".' Yet rather than being at odds with the social and political agenda of the paper, Pound was beginning to be drawn into active sympathy with it. In the last of his 'Studies in Contemporary Mentality', having found that the popular magazines he had been examining endeavoured mainly 'to prevent thought, or at least to deaden it', he concluded that the chief thing they covered up was the 'economic situation'. This was a new and startling idea in his writings. And indeed it appeared to him to be a new matter for discussion altogether—presumably he had not yet discovered Marx. He was already persuaded though that for intelligent people 'the future struggle' would be to sort out the complications of 'the economic reality'. In the previous article he had declared—

International Capital is under the present state of things, very nearly irresponsible. I am by no means sure that during the period when Capital shall be internationalised and before Labour has been so internationalised, international capital might not very well focus the force of the world's arms upon any section of the planet which too daringly attempted to interfere with, tax, or restrict the action of Capital.

He admitted, with no way of knowing just how prescient those words were, that these were 'the thoughts of an amateur in these matters, of one who has turned from the, to him, far more serious matter, that of making poetry'. Even so, it must have been dawning on him that to be wholly serious his long poem would have to participate in the investigation of economic reality.

In April he looked back over his year's effort in the *Little Review*, saw much to be pleased with, but did not see how he could keep it up much longer. There was the rather stupid burden of office work, tying up stray copies for posting and 'answering queries as to why last month's number hasn't arrived'; there was the necessary burden of editorial work dealing with manuscripts and their authors; and then there was his own production of critical and creative writing for the review. And because the *Little Review* paid him so little he was compelled in addition to 'write six sorts of journalism four days a week' in order to pay board and rent, all of which left him with no leisure for his own creative processes. 'I have been pouring out journalism', he informed Margaret Anderson, 'I am smothered in the Henry James . . . But I get no poetries written. I simply cant run the triple ring circus forever'.

He sent her the material for the Henry James special number in May. In that month he published: in the *Little Review*, an 'Imaginary Letter' and the two sequences of poems, 'Homage à la langue d'Oc' and 'Moeurs contemporains'; five articles on art and music in the *New Age*; the second part of 'Chinese Poetry' in *Today*; and a review of Joyce and others in *Future*. In this last he remarked that the Egoist Ltd. edition of *A Portrait of the Artist as a Young Man* had ' "reached its fourth thousand" ', and that this marked 'the beginning of a new phase of English publishing':

The old houses, even those, or even *more* those, which once had a literary tradition, or at least literary pretensions, having ceased to care a damn about literature, the lovers of good writing have 'struck'; have sufficiently banded themselves together to get a few good books into print, and even into circulation.

At that moment all of Joyce's work was in print, largely thanks to Pound and John Quinn, Mathews having re-issued *Chamber Music*, and Grant Richards having published *Exiles*. On the 23rd of the month, in the course of a long letter to Margaret Anderson about *Little Review* matters, Pound noted, 'Am in state of complete physical exhaustion, and will probably collapse into chronic and total aphasia'.

In June, however, he felt 'ten years younger now that the weight of the James is off my back', and was rejoicing in maintaining the momentum of the *Little Review*, 'the active motion of Joyce, Lewis, and now thank god some more T.S.E.' He had just received four 'cameos' from Eliot, including 'Sweeney among the Nightingales' and 'Whispers of Immortality'. In this month Pound's *Pavannes and Divisions* was published in New York, with a dedication to John Quinn, and a 'camera portrait by E. O Hoppé' showing Pound in the attitude of Carlyle in the Whistler painting. The book collected the recent prose that had been appearing in the *Little Review* and the *Egoist* and a few markers from the past, the *Imagiste* 'Retrospect', 'Hueffer and the Prose Tradition in Verse' and 'Troubadours: Their Sorts and Conditions'.

'MUST STOP writing so much prose', he grumbled on 9 July 1918, 'Time I quit fussing about other men's work and attended to my own.' A week later he wrote to Joyce: 'Am flat on my back with some crotchety variant of the chill-cum-flu-cum-spew'. That may have been the 'Spanish influenza' which carried off about twenty million in a worldwide epidemic in 1918–19. However Pound reported 'Faint animation reviving', and that he was hoping to start a new quarterly, 'on lines of L. R. with rubbish left out & more serious matter inserted.' In the same letter there was the first mention of 'my Propertius', with an intimation that he was likely to have trouble getting it printed.

In August there were military manoeuvres of a sort. It seemed likely that Eliot was to be called up for the U.S. Army, and Pound went along to the Embassy 'to point out that if it was a war for civilization (not merely for democracy) it was folly to shoot, or have shot one of the six or seven Americans capable of contributing to civilization or understanding the word.' In fact Eliot by this time was trying to get into the U.S. Navy with 'a non-combatant commission either in Quartermasters' or Interpreters' Corps', though in the end, as he said, 'everything turned to red tape in my hands'. Back at the Embassy, Pound had felt that 'as a sop' he should put his own services at the disposal of his country, and was sent along to the propaganda department where he was given 'pamphlets written in Oshkosh for the denizens of Spokane' to place with London papers. The next morning he had a note from the Embassy, would he 'go to Persia by Wednesday', it being then Friday and Monday a Bank Holiday. On Tuesday his going had still to be approved by the head of the commission, a commission as he now learnt 'to feed the starving Persian'. Days passed. He was asked to call his man at Claridge's, missed him there, was asked to call him at the Embassy 'at six'. By this time he had 'blown £12/12 or so on stray bits of wardrobe' for the Persian expedition; and had 'finished up the Hellenist series for the Egoist . . . arranged most of "Instigations" . . . marked out two or three months work for a copyist . . . [and] got ahead with N. Age regular stuff so as not to leave Orage in the lurch'. Then at 4.30 he wired the Embassy: 'unavoidably detained, and unlikely to go to Persia'. That was as near as he came to military service.

The war was in any case dragging to an end. When the Armistice was declared on November 11 he wandered 'about for hours mostly in drizzle to observe effect . . . on the populace'. Crowds were cheering in front of Buckingham Palace; the King drove 'through the drizzle in an open carriage'—Pound was just two feet from him in the cheering crowd in Piccadilly; and there was singing in the streets, good singing that made him think 'the sense of rhythm is not dead in this island'. 'Thank god the war is mostly over', he wrote in his letters, and that he was looking forward to the lifting of paper restrictions, and to being able to travel again. 'I want to see the Lago di Garda sometime', he told Joyce.

A range of Pound's writings filled over forty pages, that was two-thirds, of the November *Little Review*. There was a little miscellany of 'Nine Poems';

four 'Imaginary Letters'; an article on H.D.'s 'Choruses from Euripides', another on 'Tariff and Copyright'; 'Memorabilia' on the levels of national consciousness in America and France, to the end that 'The intelligent man must fight the dominant imbecilities of his time'; and, in demonstration of that principle, a translation of Voltaire on 'Genesis, or the first book in the Bible'. Contributions from Pound's select group had filled most of the previous ten issues, sometimes squeezing out even the editors themselves, and this November issue gives the impression that they were having a clear-out of his work—an impression confirmed by there being not a line of Pound in the December issue. After that he gradually withdrew from the magazine, apart from putting together a De Gourmont number in February 1919. His name stayed on the masthead as 'Foreign Editor' to the end of his second full year in April, and then he handed over to Rodker.

One reason he gave for this withdrawal was that he had spent all that Quinn had made over to him for the *Little Review*, and 'without that meagre allowance for self and contributors' could not afford to give time to it. But his not asking Quinn to renew the subsidy suggests that he had had enough anyway, having done all that he wanted to do or could do with it. He had his idea of starting a new quarterly in London. The conviction had come over him again that there was no hope for literature or civilization in the U.S. And with the war over he could turn again to France, as well as to Lake Garda.

It was a moment for consolidation in order to be ready for something new. In January 1919 he collected into a volume of essays to be called *Instigations* the most important work he had done for the *Little Review* through 1918. Unlike the fairly miscellaneous gathering in *Pavannes and Divisions*, this volume brought Pound's seemingly various interests together in a clear and coherent structure. First there were the immediate predecessors: the French poets he had searched 'for *maestria* and for discoveries not yet revealed' in English poetry; Henry James, as an exemplary defender of the individual against all sorts of bondage, and as a great internationalist labouring to make America and Europe more intelligible to each other; and De Gourmont, who 'prepared our era'. Then a gathering of his pieces on Eliot, Joyce, and Lewis under the heading 'In the Vortex', that is, where the action is now, the present moment. Part Second opened up communications with the more remote past, seeking a live tradition: Laforgue in the nineteenth century, Voltaire in the eighteenth, Arnaut Daniel in the medieval era (as translated by Pound into the twentieth century), and the ancient Greek poets as translated in the Renaissance and after. Finally, tapping into that other cultural deposit, there was Fenollosa's essay on 'The Chinese Written Character as a Medium for Poetry'.

The book was printed by Boni and Liveright in New York in 1920 in an edition of eight hundred copies; there was no London edition, and no reprint. Yet *Instigations* was as original and groundbreaking a collection of essays as Eliot's far more noticed and celebrated *The Sacred Wood* (1920); and one which, besides, carried out a whole series of practical investigations of the theory of tradition and the individual talent. At least two American reviewers, Van Wyck Brooks and James Sibley Watson of the *Dial*, appreciated Pound's instigations. The one wrote that he had done American literature a great service by the profound seriousness with which he upheld the 'vocation of letters'; the other asked, 'Is nobody aware that a contemporary writer is actually giving a course on the Comparative Literature of the Present, that a first rate literary man, with the rarest gift for translation is bothering to teach school?'

Pound had hoped to discover a promising young writer or two to bring on in the *Little Review*, but Iris Barry had dropped out—into the arms, apparently, of Wyndham Lewis—and in the end he had told Margaret Anderson that Rodker 'is all *les jeunes* that there are'. Then Marianne Moore sent in some poems and the talent spotter in him was roused again to offer enthusiastic criticism and practical support. He wrote to her that he thought 'the poems too good to print without paying for them', and since he had no more money for the *Little Review* could he hold them over for the new quarterly he was hoping to start. Could he help her get a book together and into print, as he had done for Eliot and Joyce and Lewis? The next day he wrote to Miss Weaver not to go to the expense of publishing his Hellenist series in a booklet, and that he would rather the money 'go to printing a book like *Prufrock*, by some new poet'—he believed he had one in sight.

Miss Moore replied after a thoughtful pause, welcoming his criticism and responding to it positively, but telling him also that she had little enthusiasm for publication nor for embalming her poems in a book. She set the tone for what would prove a lasting literary friendship by telling him, 'merely to be honest', that while she had 'taken great pleasure in both your prose and your verse', and while she liked a fight, 'I admit that I have at times objected to your promptness with the cudgels'. Pound was stimulated by this to write, in verse that imitated her own way of putting things, a defence of his 'taking up cudgels'. He put it down in part to being male and demanding wider and more varied contacts than the female, to having a public existence as against the secluded private life she had professed herself content with. 'The female is a chaos', he began, 'the male / is a fixed point of stupidity'; but they were different—

> You, my dear correspondent,
> are a stabilized female,
> I am a male who has attained the chaotic fluidities . . .

In a further intriguing contrast he declared himself a 'Manichean' and Miss Moore 'a Malthusian of the intellect', by which he meant, I take it, that while she was for restricting the propagation of the light he would have it penetrate everywhere.

It was the dullness and benightedness of his fellows that provoked Pound to combat, though he knew that being combative did his prospects no good, and did his poetry no good. He was forever trying to drive intelligence into the unthinking, though Orage warned him that he 'should go to the National Liberal Club and learn how ONE intelligent remark can blast a man's whole career'. He knew that getting 'drawn into controversy . . . is the death of all good writing'. Years before, in 1916, he had advised Alice Corbin Henderson,

Think of your own work. Nothing else matters, we have been mad with crusading. Nothing matters save the occasional good poem. Nothing else lasts out ten years. The bad stuff will go. Our own follies will be forgotten. We can live 'em down with a few decent poems.

Now, at the end of 1918, he pondered whether he was not 'perhaps better at digging up corpses of let us say Li Po, or more lately Sextus Propertius, than in preserving'—as it were in formaldehyde? – 'this bitched mess of modernity'.

'Langue d'Oc' and 'Homage to Sextus Propertius'

For all his groaning in 1918 that he had no time to write his own poetry Pound did produce two 'decent poems', one of which he classed as an 'étude' and the other as a 'major persona'.

'Langue d'Oc'—'Homage à la Langue d'Oc' was its title in the *Little Review* in May 1918—is a sequence of five Troubadour songs (initially six) translated with varying degrees of freedom from the Provençal. It opens with an apparently slight and conventional *alba* or dawn song which in fact contains the germ of the whole sequence in one finely wrought musical statement:

> *When the nightingale to his mate*
> *Sings day-long and night-late*
> *My love and I keep state*
> > *In bower,*
> > *In flower,*
> > *'Till the watchman on the tower*
> *Cry:*
> > > *'Up! Thou rascal, Rise,*
> > *I see the white*
> > > *Light*
> > > *And the night*
> > > > *Flies.'*

A whole world of love and its drama is there in little: the nightingale acts in the realm of natural instinct; the lovers are in the realm of cultured and refined instinct; and the watchman looks away to the Light which all desire and sometimes fear. His cry rhymes a set of discriminations and tensions which remain to be resolved.

In the first numbered song, humorously subtitled 'Compleynt of a gentleman who has been waiting outside for some time', the watchman calls upon the 'true celestial light' which shapes this world to aid his friend who is within. Either he must be blasphemously calling upon God to assist an adulterous lover, or his god is not that of Christian morality. In any case he is not himself enlivened by that light. Through five stanzas, each repeating the same rhythmic form, he is all faithful anxiety for the lover within, and has no evident desire of his own, unless to be taken notice of. All the energy is in the lover's 'Bass voice from within', confident and unafraid,

> For such joy I take
> With her venust and noblest to my make
> To hold embracèd, and will not her forsake
> For yammer of the cuckold,
> > Though day break.

If the might of the 'Plasmatour and true celestial light' is anywhere in the poem then it is within this lover and his mate.

'Avril' is a springtime song of William of Poitiers, the earliest of the troubadours, and, on this showing, the least refined. His desire is as natural and straightforward as his verse, with no time to make music or visions out of it. His one strong and simple virtue is that his love is fixed, no matter who comes between them, upon the 'charmer' who has given her love to him. Cerclamon, in Pound's comic descant on a theme of

346

his—the third numbered song—would be as constant a lover, and more, if only his love would care for him. But his is the wintry plaint, all wailing and sighing, of someone made witless by love's fever. His rhymes are feeble; his verse formless, with no sustaining rhythm; he speaks in cliché, and his statements drop from pathos into bathos. Altogether his is the sorry state fit only to be laughed at of the ideal courtly lover of the convention in its late decadence. The force that drives the world is not in him, as it is in William of Poitier's song.

In 'Vergier' we are again in the situation of the 'Alba' and the watchman's 'compleynt': the lovers are together, the watchman is on his tower, the refrain is his ('And day comes on'), and the prayer is 'O Plasmatour'. But here it is the lovers who speak, not the watchman. They are outside, 'In orchard under the hawthorne'. The watchman in his tower will cry the dawn, but not yet; indeed he is forgotten by the close. And it is the woman who prays to 'Plasmatour', that time might stop and their loving have no end. This is a singing of fulfilled desire, though subtly nuanced through several voicings. The first, that of an observer, unless the woman speaks of herself in the third person, begins 'In the orchard . . . / She has her lover till morn'. She speaks then, only in silent prayer, 'end not the night, / Nor take my beloved from my sight'. After that she speaks aloud to her lover, in full awareness of their adulterous situation and the danger of discovery by daylight, but with unaffected love of him and unquenched desire. Next he speaks aloud, but of her, not to her, as if realising in words what she has given him; and finally he sets down as if in formal speech or writing the nature of their love:

> Venust the lady, and none lovelier,
> For her great beauty, many men look on her,
> Out of my love will her heart not stir.
> By God, how swift the night.
> > And day comes on.

The rhythm is firm and confident, less assertive than the earlier 'bass voice', and more possessed by an assured mutual and conscious love than by his own pleasure and delight. There has been a progression through the song from frank desire, through love-making, to this clear realisation in the mind that theirs is a love that will now endure in each of them even in the daylight with all that it may bring.

It will bring the jealous husband, of course, and the condemnations of church law and property law and of the social order they maintain. But the writing of the song and its strongly flowing rhythm are unequivocally on the side of this growing and fulfilling love. The sequence has been a concise study in an ethos in which the erotic motive is all-important; and this song closes the sequence with a demonstration of the power of love at its full to set aside the social attitudes which would repress it.

In 'Psychology and Troubadours' Pound had speculated about how far the cult of Amor in Provence might have gone in the direction of divinity. He assumed that it had this at least in common with ecstatic religion, that it would 'stimulate a sort of confidence in the life-force'. But did it lead to visions of the divine order? 'Langue d'Oc' gives no such lead, or none beyond twice calling the lady 'Venust'. That sees her as having her divinity upon her as a lover. The further development, whereby Dante or a younger Pound, in quest of their own perfection, would pass beyond the individual woman to the all-embracing Light, is just not there. These lovers are fulfilled in loving and contemplating each other. This was confirmed in the sixth poem in the sequence as it was originally published, Arnaut Daniel's 'Sols sui qui sai'—in Pound's version, 'I only, and who elrische pain support'. Daniel sings his unchanging desire for his adored lady however far he may be from her: 'In her alone, I see, move, / Wonder ... For in my thought my lust hath touched his aim'. This is the Daniel who does not yet weep for having so loved, as Dante will have him do at the summit of Purgatory as heaven dawns ahead.

Always attached to 'Langue d'Oc' is 'Moeurs Contemporains', a set of 'sketches' in the manner of *Lustra*'s modern epigrams. These deal very sketchily and partially with the manners and morals of the superior class of English society as Pound himself has observed them. There is this unifying insight: that here the erotic motive is so repressed as to be scarcely discernible. When the large-muscled landowner, Mr Hecatomb Styrax, marries, his ineptitudes drive his wife 'from one religious excess to another'. And here is 'Clara', whose name would promise a clear light, but whose 'life is obscure and troubled':

> At sixteen she was a potential celebrity
> With a distaste for caresses.
> She now writes to me from a convent;
>
> .   .   .   .   .   .
>
> Her second husband will not divorce her;
> Her mind is, as ever, uncultivated,
> And no issue presents itself.
>
> .   .   .   .   .
>
> She will neither stay in, nor come out.

That lack of energy and direction appears to be a general affliction. There is culture and refinement—of cleverness. The lady novelist speaks to the young American pilgrim 'of the monarch, / And of the purity of her soul'. One of the male gender breaks out—'After years of continence / he hurled himself into a sea of six women'—but only to drown himself in that sea. Only among the old is there any clear definition of individual personality, and some memories of passionate living. The very old lady remembers that Browning had once 'stomped' into her bedroom and demanded to know did he 'Care too much for society dinners?', and she 'wouldn't say that he didn't'. The contrast with the ethos of ancient Provence tells entirely against this sampling of the modern world.

One can gauge from 'Moeurs Contemporains' the degree of irony in Pound's saying, to account for 'the archaic language' in 'Langue d'Oc', that 'the Provençal feeling is archaic, we are ages away from it'. There was the same irony in his then saying, to explain his treating ancient Rome's Sextus Propertius as a near contemporary, that 'We are just getting back to a Roman state of civilization'. Ancient Rome and contemporary England seemed to him to have much in common.

Homage to Sextus Propertius came out in 1919. *Poetry* printed four of its twelve sections in March—just 'the left foot, knee, thigh and right ear of my portrait', Pound remarked when Harriet Monroe would not have the rest in her magazine. The *New Age* printed six sections separately through the summer. It first appeared whole, along with 'Langue d'Oc', 'Moeurs Contemporains' and 'Three Cantos', in *Quia Pauper Amavi* in October. Pound would attach the date '1917' to it, but that is almost certainly not the date of its composition. He had told Iris Barry in July 1916, 'if you CAN'T find *any* decent translations of Catullus and Propertius, I suppose I shall have to rig up something'. But the next mention of his Propertius is in a letter to Joyce in July 1918; and in November he described it to his father as 'a new *oeuvre*'. In December he was telling Marianne Moore that it was his 'last and best work', and that two publishers had just balked at it.

The *Oxford Classical Dictionary* (3rd edition, 1996) in its account of the historical Sextus Propertius, along with recording that he lived and wrote under Augustus Caesar in the latter part of the last century BC, particularly remarks his 'irreverence towards the government', and his claim to have done his military service as a lover rather than in the imperial army. It also speaks of 'the poet's wit'. The irreverence and the wit were not noticed by J. W. Mackail in his *Latin Literature*, a standard 'university manual' when Pound was a student. That they now are commonly recognized is largely due to his poem, though this notable service to classical literature does not rate a mention under either 'Commentary' or 'Criticism' in the *Oxford Classical Dictionary*.

Homage to Sextus Propertius is certainly not a translation in any usual sense—Pound was explicit about that—and it is inadvisable to approach it by way of the Latin texts he was working from. For those who can read Latin well enough to attempt that approach the originals seem only to obfuscate what Pound was doing. It leads them to look for what isn't there and to miss what is, rather as if one were to look for a photographic likeness in a Picasso portrait. Pound's *Sextus Propertius* is a thoroughly modern, Vorticist 'portrait'; the refraction of the ancient poet through a modern intelligence, or the superimposition of the one upon the other. He is at once a Roman writing in his own terms of his life and times, and a critical consciousness that could only have been forged by Ezra Pound in English in the year 1918 or thereabouts. He is best taken for what he is, a selection of poems and fragments from the four books of Sextus Propertius, rearranged and transposed to create a new work, and a new kind of poetry.

Pound would insist on his poem's 'relation to life', by which he meant a relation to 'the infinite and ineffable imbecility of the British Empire' in 1917, that being much the same as Propertius' relation to 'the infinite and ineffable imbecility of the Roman Empire' of his day. That directs us to the key to the whole sequence: that Propertius was a poet who wanted to celebrate his love for Cynthia in a state mainly concerned to maintain and to expand its empire by war. 'My genius is no more than a girl', he declares, in a phrase Pound had associated with the refining love of the troubadours and of Dante, the love he had celebrated in his *Canzoni*. Yet that quality of love is nowhere to be found in the *Homage*. The evident cause of the genius in the poem is rather the complicated and over-stimulated state of the poet's intelligence, brought on by the uncertainties of a love which has its ecstatic moments, but which will never be constant nor clear of cynicism and disillusion; and behind that there is the poet's alienation from the Rome that he must resist, the Rome which would have him serve the warring state rather than his love. The genius manifests itself in the irreverent wit, the sardonic parodies of imperial rhetoric, the brilliant 'dance of the intellect among words' and meanings, the mercurial shifts of mood and tone, the manic energy of a mind like Hamlet's that seems able to play everyone's verbal game and to make a game of everything. But the bright energy of this mind comes from its disintegrating, splintering under the pressure of baffling conditions it can do nothing about; and beneath the bold mockery, and the self-mocking comedy and farce, and at the heart even of the celebration of love, there is a persistent undertone of defeat in love and by Rome. Death will be the common factor to resolve this conflict of personal love and a public world given over to war.

In the first two sections the tonal shifts dramatize the tensions between the lyric poetry Propertius would take his stand on and the heroic rhetoric of empire. But the underlying tone is one of irony towards both. Though great fun is had with the inflated imperial style, and though the modesty of his claims for his own 'dance tunes' may be mock-modesty, still he is on the defensive and speaks of his love poetry as those would who dismiss it as light reading for girls. He does begin with a confident invocation of his lyric measure; but once he engages with the martial mode his tone is destabilized and the writing becomes a wildfire of wit. He settles into seriousness again only when he speaks solemnly of inevitable death, and of his own immortality: 'Stands genius a deathless adornment, / a name not to be worn out with the years.' He will take his stand at the end of the poem not in the dance of life but among the dead elegists.

The third and fourth sections present the Roman lovers in comic, even ridiculous circumstances. Summoned to his mistress at midnight, Propertius is overcome with fears of what might happen to him on the way, and imagines his funeral, even, improbably, that 'She would sit like an ornament on my pyre'. With all this reflecting on what could be his fate as a lover out late he fails to go to her. Then he prompts his servant to speak of her being desolated by his not going, and of her being bitter with jealousy of 'the other woman', and of her asking '"Will he say nasty things at my funeral?"'—and he knows perfectly well, 'after twelve months of discomfort' at her hands, that none of this is in the least likely. Cynthia, after all, is not 'his' Cynthia but 'an educated freedwoman and a courtesan'.

The fifth and sixth sections further develop the themes of the first two. Propertius responds to a demand for an imperial poem, and attempts a suitably 'loud-mouthed product', only to give it up, saying 'my ventricles do not palpitate to Caesarial *ore rotundos*'. He 'will sing war when this matter of a girl is exhausted'; and meanwhile, 'if she plays with me with her shirt off, / We shall construct many Iliads'. That is followed by thoughts of those who die in war and of his own funeral, and again seriousness breaks through. He would have his *stele* inscribed, '"He who is now vacant dust / Was once the slave of one passion"'. 'Slave', though a worn cliché by now, was not a word to use lightly in the imperial circle in which Propertius moved.

His passion has its moment of celebration in the seventh section. This begins in sensual playfulness and delight, but there is no development beyond sensuality. 'Eyes are the guides of love', urges Cynthia, and thinks how 'Paris took Helen naked coming from the bed of Menelaus'. In Propertius' mind love-longing finds strangely negative images. 'Let the gods lay chains upon us / so that no day shall unbind them', he prays.

'Love's madness' is what he is into, and for a few lines the natural order of things goes mad:

> The flood shall move toward the fountain
> Ere love know moderations,
> The fish shall swim in dry streams.

The thought of death brings his most intense declaration: 'To-day we take the great breath of lovers, / to-morrow fate shuts us in'. At the end of the section he does reach to this sense of ecstasy, 'If she give me many [such nights], / God am I for the time'. Even so, the stress falls on his 'I', leaving Cynthia instrumental to his exaltation. It is all so very different from the 'archaic' Provençal 'Vergier'.

The following sections of the *Homage* confirm the main impression, that Propertius can no more glorify his love for Cynthia than he can glorify the empire. There is only irony in his writing 'Light, light of my eyes' when everything goes to show that he is not on the whole guided by any light of love. The truth is that he feels enslaved by desire that none can escape: 'Amor stands upon you, Love drives upon lovers, / a heavy mass on free necks'. Love is selfish, divisive, it 'interferes with fidelities', causes duels and wars—all this Propertius discovers when his friend Lynceus sleeps with Cynthia and passes on to him 'a swig of [venereal] poison'. But the ethos requires him to deal with that by affecting a tone of high civility: 'in one bed, in one bed alone, my dear Lynceus / I deprecate your attendance; / I would ask a like boon of Jove'.

In the end Propertius can be wholly serious, or most nearly serious and undivided in mind and tone, only when he contemplates death. And the irony of that is in the fact that the empire too makes much of its dead heroes. When he speaks of death he speaks their common language, implicitly subscribing himself a citizen of the empire after all. And when he puts himself down as a slave of love, however ironically he means it, he puts love in the place allotted to it in Rome.

For Pound the *Homage* was a mirror to the ethos which honoured service to the empire or the state, but had no culture of the emotions, no cult for the refinement of sexual desire. But few if any have looked into his poem and seen their own society. Its relation to modern life has been ignored while debate rages about its relation to Propertius' Latin.

That deflection began even before the poem was published. Harriet Monroe, apparently taking it for a translation, sent it to be looked over by the very distinguished Professor of Latin at the University of Chicago; and he, apparently going through it in red ink as if it were an exercise by one of his students, found 'about three-score' elementary mistakes, crass blunders and monstrous howlers. 'Mr Pound is incredibly ignorant of Latin', was Professor Hale's expert conclusion. 'Of one peculiarly unpleasant passage in Mr Pound's translation', he said, 'there is no suggestion in the original', and about that he was quite correct philologically. Pound had Propertius say, 'in the meantime my songs will travel, / And the devirginated young ladies will enjoy them'. But the Latin text had this:

Carminis interea nostri redeamus in orbem
Of songs meanwhile ours / let us return into the orbit
   gaudeat in solito tacta puella sono.
   may [she] take pleasure / in [my] usual / the girl being touched / noise.

Or in English order, 'Let us return meanwhile into the orbit of our songs / and may the girl, being touched [by it], delight in [my] usual noise'. Hale's version was more genteel:

Meanwhile let me resume the wonted round of my singing;
   let my lady, touched [by my words], find pleasure in the familiar music.

Pound's play upon *tacta puella* was grammatically impossible, Hale pointed out, so there was 'no hint of the decadent meaning'. Quite so, if no play is permitted. But to the seriously playful mind, in the general context of the libertine and explicitly decadent world of Propertius' love poems, *tacta puella* might well bring an echo of *virgo* **intacta**, an **un**touched maid, and so lead to the faux-decorous 'devirginated'. Orage came to Pound's defence, arguing that 'the mind behind the text of Propertius was a mind which the Latin Professor of the Chicago University would call decadent, if only it expressed itself in English'. Then Robert Nichols objected in the London *Observer* to the 'ignorance and bad taste' of Pound's decadent phrase, and offered his own affecting version: 'Let the girl, much moved, take delight in this music of mine she knows by heart'. Pound dismisssed that as 'Victorian sentimentality'; but his main line of defence was that he had never intended an '*ad verbum* translation', that in fact he had 'paid no conscious attention to the grammar of the latin text', and that all his 'revisions were made *away* from and not *toward* literal rendering'. This only confirmed the classical scholars in their outrage, even into the 1950s. More recently most if not all the interested parties have 'got to the point of "admitting" the non-representational', and even of admitting that it can be more faithful to the essence of the original.

The fuss in *Poetry* was the last straw in Pound's strained relations with Harriet Monroe's magazine. She sent him a copy of Hale's attack shortly before publishing the more decorous parts, and his terse reply began,

'Cat-piss and porcupines!! The thing is no more a translation than my "Altaforte" is a translation, or than Fitzgerald's Omar is a translation'. His letter closed, 'In final commiseration', and six months later, having heard nothing further from him, Miss Monroe let him know that she took that 'as a resignation from the staff of *Poetry*'. Her dignified letter expressed resigned regret, grateful goodwill, and cordial admiration.

T. S. Eliot had by now come round to a thoroughly positive appreciation of Pound's poetry. His 1917 pamphlet, written to accompany the New York *Lustra*, had cagily mined the reviews without giving away much beyond generalities of what he himself thought of the work. His review of *Quia Pauper Amavi* in the *Athenæum* in October 1919 provoked Pound to write, in a letter to the editor, that while 'struggling beneath the enormous weight of granite laurels . . . so generously' loaded on to his book, he was 'still puzzled to know . . . whether T.S.E. has or has not found my "Homage to Propertius" enjoyable'. In fact, although he was careful not to show too much enthusiasm in the intellectually superior *Athenæum*, Eliot was telling at least one of his friends privately that he did very much like Pound's poems. And back in March 1918 he had told John Quinn, having just given high praise to 'Langue d'Oc' and 'Moeurs Contemporains', 'I value his verse far higher than that of any other living poet'. Just the same, he would exclude *Homage to Sextus Propertius* from his otherwise nearly complete 1928 *Selected Poems* of Ezra Pound, on the dubious ground that if the reader were not a classical scholar he would make nothing of it, and that if he were he would think it all wrong.

It remained for Basil Bunting to declare unequivocally, 'So far as American poetry is concerned, that poem is (though the poets rarely recognize the fact) the foundation document.'

15 : GOODBYE TO ENGLAND: 1919–1920

The smell of French asphalt

Had the war killed off art, or made it redundant? More particularly, had it killed Vorticism? Those questions were in the air in 1919, and on Pound's mind. The war had certainly killed Gaudier, he acknowledged, or accused. But then wasn't it also the case that Vorticism had proved its utility in war, as when Wadsworth had been able to improve naval camouflage by virtue of his advanced 'knowledge of *how the human eye is affected by colours and patterns in relation*'. That was all very well, but it could not answer his anxiety about what the war might have done to Lewis's genius.

When Pound, once as 'B. H. Dias' and once as himself, reviewed a showing of Lewis's 'war paintings' in February, he looked for the former 'revolutionary inventor of forms' and of abstract ' "forms in combination" ', and saw instead a 'narrative painter' of the realities of war. He looked for the savage and violent satirist of 'smugness and hypocrisy and stupidity' but found studies of men and machines of war charged with tragic emotion. And this was quite in order, he decided, given that the war was tragedy. Still, he insisted, in Lewis's drawings there was, 'from the purely aesthetic point of view, a calm pleasure to be derived from clear tones, the cold air, the desolation of the Ypres Salient, with the pyramidal arrangement of three men in the wilderness'. That showed that Lewis was still the artist, that his paintings had not simply 'come out of the war', but had 'come a good deal more out of art; out of art's resistance to war'.

Pound was seeking reassurance that the artist had survived the war as well as the man. He was concerned for the survival of all his select band of artists in the exhausted and shaken up post-war world, and concerned for his own survival as a poet. Lewis was all right, being furious at having had four years of his creative life taken from him, and being intent on making up for the lost time. Hueffer too had come through, though it would take him some years to turn his war into *Parades End* (1924–28), the best novel to come out of that particular hell. In the meantime he was recuperating in rural Sussex, enjoying love in a cottage with Stella Bowen, a young

Australian painter, raising pigs and reconstructing himself as a writer. In June 1919 he would be reborn as 'Ford Madox Ford'.

Joyce was getting on with *Ulysses* in Zurich, with the steady support now of Miss Weaver, and the occasional support of other benefactors. In May 1919 Miss Weaver settled upon him, in place of her monthly transfers, an outright £5000 in 5 per cent War Loan bonds, thus guaranteeing him £250 a year. He was also in receipt, from March 1918 until September 1919, of 1,000 Swiss francs each month from Mrs Edith Rockefeller McCormick, who was reputed to be the richest woman in Zurich. Royalties and other gifts apart, that meant that his income at this time was at least £720 a year. Pound meanwhile was struggling to get together the payments due to Joyce for the instalments of *Ulysses* as they appeared in the *Little Review*. Joyce did tell him in November about his windfall from Miss Weaver, but added that the first lot of interest would not arrive until January 1920 and that he was broke until then. Pound felt he may have mentioned a windfall 'just to take himself off my mind'. His enthusiasm for *Ulysses* grew chapter by chapter, though he did cavill, to Joyce's displeasure, at what seemed to him the excessively detailed account of Bloom's morning defecation, and again at the conclusion of 'Sirens'—'fahrt yes, but not as climax of chapter=not really the final resolution of fugue'. He had still to take it in that for Joyce nothing was sacred, nothing at all save his own art.

Eliot, in 1919, was very deliberately establishing a reputation and a position of power in the London literary world, and he was using Pound as an example of how not to do it. He had kept his distance from the *Little Review*, while recognizing the value of such things as Pound's French number and its publishing *Ulysses*, because he was wary of its offensive aggressiveness. When Middleton Murry invited him to become his assistant editor on the *Athenæum*, he gave as one reason for keeping on in the bank a wish to stay 'out of the intrigues and personal hatreds of journalism'. He was doing well in the bank, and had just been put in charge of a new department dealing with the problems of post-war international settlements. That meant more responsibility, more respectability, and the prospect of a salary exceeding £500 per annum. It also meant that he could continue to write only what he wanted to, and by doing that, he told his mother, he would 'influence London opinion and English literature in a better way'. His strategy was 'to write very little' and to print just two or three poems in a year, making sure that each one should be perfect in its kind and 'an event'. Then, to attract attention and receive good reviews, it was 'essential... [to] establish solid connections with at least one important paper', as he had done with the *Athenæum*, and as Pound had altogether failed to do. He already felt confident of 'a small and

356

select public which regards me as the best living critic, as well as the best living poet, in England'. When he wrote in that way he had published only *Prufrock* and a scattering of reviews, essays and poems in various periodicals. Yet he declared, in the simple present and not the prophetic tense, 'I really think that I have far more *influence* on English letters than any other American has ever had, unless it be Henry James'. As for Pound's effort to be a force for the revival of intelligence, he had lost out through making too many enemies.

In fact, according to Vivienne Eliot, Pound was now 'ruined'. 'See what he has become', she wrote to Mary Hutchinson, a Bloomsbury friend, 'A laughing stock. And his work all bad'. Still, they went dancing together at the Elysée Rooms, the Eliots and Mary Hutchinson and Brigit Patmore and Pound. Eliot wanted to learn 'the new dances and steps'; or, as Pound put it in a letter to Dorothy who was visiting at Bexhill-on-Sea, he was 'experimenting in milieux'. What Pound himself most wanted just then was to get out of England into France and Italy. He was suffering from having been 'boxed in one city' by the war—

> Four springs, five springs gone over
> And no stink of block coal in my nostrils,
> No smell of french asphalt,
> No waits at Milan station . . .

He wanted his 'chocolate at the Café de la Paix', his 'café at Florians'. In April he and Dorothy would take off for France and stay there into September.

He was not 'ruined', though there were plenty in London who rejoiced in that thought. New cantos were on the way, and at the end of the year he would show London what he thought of it in the supremely accomplished *Hugh Selwyn Mauberley*. But it was a difficult time for him journalistically and financially. When he broke off his connection with *Poetry* he lost a small but regular income; he was at the end of Quinn's money for his part in the *Little Review*, and had to give that up; and the *Egoist*, because of the problems involved in printing *Ulysses*, was appearing irregularly and would soon cease altogether. Nothing would come of his post-war plans to start a new quarterly of his own. And he had made too many influential enemies for the 'important papers' to take him on. His only assured source of income in 1919 was from appearing as three distinct persons in the *New Age*. The expenses of the months in France would be paid for by an extended series of articles for Orage written as it were on the run.

357

Dorothy and Ezra crossed to France from Southampton on 22 April 1919. In Paris they called on Natalie Barney, Gourmont's 'Amazone', in the rue Jacob on the Left Bank, and Pound carried away a memory of her garden and a sheaf of poems on which she wanted his advice. On the 24th they were in Toulouse which they would make their base for the next three months. The father of their friend Edmund Dulac found them a room at 13 rue Ste Ursule and gave them, as Dorothy recalled, many hospitable meals.

On this visit Toulouse steeped Pound in 'the sensation of provincial desolation'. He was shocked to find its Place Capitole empty of life after 9.30 p.m., and failed to discover evidence of intelligence anywhere in the city. After three weeks he went across to the Rhone for ten days, so that he might recuperate and 'renew [his] retina with certain outlines' in a round tour of Nîmes, Beaucaire, Tarascon, Avignon, St. Rémy, Les Baux, Arles and Carcassonne. But here too his views were disenchanted. Arles seemed to him, with its carefully preserved Roman remains, just a dead historical monument with a population employing 'the highest possible number of mental, emotional and inherited clichés'. In Nîmes he noticed 'the clock in the rose-window of the new church', and reflected that it showed 'its architecture coquetting with the utilitarians'. In Avignon he saw religion paying homage to science by putting 'a lightning-rod up the back of the "disastrously gilded" parody of the Virgin ... thus shielding the image from the devirginating bolts of Zeus πατηρ'. He was not even looking for the glamour and the romantic associations which had meant so much to him on his 1912 walking tour.

Instead he was rather deliberately looking, at least in the first articles he sent back to the *New Age*, for evidences of the damned spirit of provincialism, though he was soon bored with that undertaking. There is only so much interest in observing 'an American officer ... combing his hair at table, between the soup and the fish ... in a rather good hotel'; or in remarking, more generally, that Toulouse appeared to export its best brains and its best cocottes to the metropolis along with its cloth and its cheeses, while receiving in exchange an abundance of cheap railway novels. It was a town crying out for its Flaubert, he wrote, and that about said it all.

There was more nutriment to be had in the country to the south and south-west of Toulouse. They took the train more than once to stay at Montréjeau at the mouth of the valley through which the Garonne flows out from the Pyrenees, and walked from there the few miles across to Saint Bertrand-de-Comminges and the further few miles up to Mauléon-Barousse. Savairac de Mauléon is mentioned in canto 5, in the anti-romantic tale of the troubadour Gaubertz Poicebot, and both are mentioned again in canto 48 in association with Saint Bertrand. Baedeker declared the latter's cathedral on its high rock 'one of the most interesting in the S. of France and particularly worth seeing', not least for the superb Northern Renaissance wood-carving of the Choir. But what Pound recalled were some traces down on the plain of the much earlier, pre-Christian history: a Roman pavement buried six feet beneath a wheat field, and an ancient milestone, 'an altar to Terminus, with arms crossed/back of the stone'; and he remembered that there the sun's light at evening 'shaves grass into emerald'. Dorothy painted a number of watercolours in the vicinity of Montréjeau.

At midsummer they were at Montségur, some miles to the south of Lavelanet where the branch line ended. Montségur is not mentioned in Baedeker's 1907 *Southern France*, which might suggest that it was not yet on the tourist map. It was of course well known that the Albigenses or Cathars had made their last stand there and been treacherously massacred in 1244. Their stronghold, Pound was told, was destroyed centuries later 'by order of Louis XIV'. 'If that statement is accurate', he wrote, 'the gratitude for the gilded chaise-percé should be diminished, seeing that a Cantabrian sun-temple with a Roman superstructure is worth a good deal of gilt furniture'. Aside from the witty playing off of the Sun King and his gilded commode against the primitive sun-temple, there are two noteworthy points here. One is Pound's associating the sun-temple of Montségur not directly with the Cathars but with the wild pre-Christian Cantabri of the western Pyrenees who were subdued by the Romans only after sustained resistance. The second point is that he expresses dismay at the destruction of the sun-temple rather than of the Cathars. His mind now was not simply preoccupied with the religion and culture of the troubadours' Provence but was reaching for a larger conception of history in which their story would be just one of many 'luminous details'. He put with it the burning of Beziers after Simon de Montfort attacked it; the destruction of Beaucaire by Richelieu; the ruin of Rocafixade; the turning of the Palais des Papes in Avignon into a barracks after the Revolution; and the pulling down of the cloister of La Daurade in Toulouse 'to put up a tobacco factory'. In his way of thinking, apparently unrelated 'Snippets of this kind build up our concept of wrong, of right, of history'. Indeed, 'Any historical concept and any sociological deduction from history must assemble a great number of such violently contrasted facts, if it is to be valid'. Those particular facts had to do with religion turning to violence in its determination to coerce those who did not believe its dogma; with the Church's violence then serving the growing power and centralization of the French monarchy; and then with the violence inherent in the exercise of centralized state power. 'And every one of these vandalisms, and ten thousand other examples as vivid, lay as open to the inspection of the last destroyers in 1914 as they do in 1919'. 'Out of the welter', Pound wrote, 'I get perhaps only an increasing hatred of violence, an increasing contempt for destruction'. He called this an 'underlying conviction-plus-passion'— not a theory, not a general idea, but, in other words, 'an intellectual and emotional complex', a motive for action. Did he know, as he dashed off that article back in Toulouse, that he had just sketched out the basic formula for his *Cantos*, for his 'poem containing history'?

From Montségur Ezra and Dorothy walked by way of Rocafixade to Foix. They were there on 22 June, and returned again on the 28th, to find, as they walked in, 'flags flying' for the Peace that had just been signed at Versailles. In mid-July they were at Montréjeau again for a few days. Then on the 21st they left Toulouse and moved north to spend a month in and around Brive and Excideuil. They rather favoured the latter on account of Madame Pujol's excellent cooking and the pleasant room in her Hôtel Pujol. Though they did some walking this was not a repeat of Pound's 1912 walking tour. They got about by train and steam-tram as well as on foot, going as far as Ussel and Clermont-Ferrand to the north-east, and from Excideuil southwards to Hautefort, Montignac, and Rocamadour. Dorothy's post-cards mention Bertrand de Born but Pound appears to have lost interest in all that. What caught his attention at Maent's Montignac was a 'complete guide [to etiquette] for bourgeois families'.

In mid-August Pound went into Périgueux to meet 'a rucksacked Eliot' who was taking a three-week vacation in the Dordogne and would spend a few days walking with Ezra while Dorothy remained in Excideuil. Eliot was run down, kept falling ill and having to take to his bed, and Pound hoped 'to put him through course of sun, air & sulphur bath & return him to London intact'. The two of them set out on the 17th and got as far as Thiviers, then went on to Brantôme on the 18th. 'T. has 7 blisters', Pound reported by post-card to Dorothy; and so, as he recalled when thinking back to that time after Eliot's death, 'le papier Fayard was then the burning topic' of their conversation. 'Will probably proceed by train tomorrow', he told Dorothy, but 'le papier Fayard' must have eased the blisters since it seems they walked on to Bourdeilles. From there Eliot went on alone to view what he would shortly refer to as 'the rock drawing of the Magdalenian draughtsmen' in the 'Cro-Magnon caves' at Les Eyzies, while Pound returned to Excideuil.

While they were looking over what was left of the castle of Excideuil Eliot had said to Pound, '"I am afraid of the life after death"', and then,

' "Now, at last, I have shocked him" '. The remark would have brought up their profound difference in religious sensibility and belief. Eliot believed in the immortality of the individual soul, and was schooling himself 'not to expect more from *life* than it can give . . . [and] to look to *death* for what life cannot give'. 'What faith in life may be I know not,' he would write, 'for the Christian, faith in death is what matters'. Pound rather took his stand with Confucius who 'said nothing of the "life after death" '. His youthful idealism had matured into a conviction that 'paradise' was a state of mind one might hope to achieve from time to time in the here and now, and that 'hell' also was a state of mind the living could lapse into. His delayed response to Eliot's remark, delivered two years later by the arena in Verona, where Christian martyrs had embraced death in the Roman era, was to confess ' "But this beats me, / Beats me, I mean that I do not understand it; / This love of death that is in them" '. When he wrote these episodes into a canto concerned with the varieties and confusions of love and desire and the life-process, he set them off against 'the wave pattern cut in the stone', and against a celebration of the rising sun. The stone with the wave-pattern cut into it by some medieval craftsman is an odd fragment from the ruined castle of Excideuil enjoying an afterlife in a later wall there, whenever an intelligent eye lights on it. The celebration of the sun also recycles and gives new life to an ancient and for long unknown *alba*, one fashioned about the tenth century in both late Latin and the just emerging Provençal language. The wave-patterned stone and the lyrical invocation of Light may be read as intimations of a total life process in which human creativity honours and keeps faith with primal energies, and in which what survives of us is what will light up the intelligence of the living.

An inescapable part of the process, for Pound in the spring and autumn of 1919, was contending with the obtuseness and stupidity of junior officials in his country's consulates. In order to get to France in April he had had to work around the obstructions put in his way in the London consulate: 'Pie faced Y. M. C. A. clerk threatening to stop passport unless I went home and "took up duties of citizenship" '. This clerk also told him he was not allowed to go to France unless he had business there; that Dorothy could not go with him 'unless she were ill'; that he must go to one place and not move about. Someone he had met in the propaganda department had to swear 'to several contradictory statements' on his behalf before he was given what he needed. In Toulouse they did things very differently. 'The clerk of the 1st Police arrondissement' had the wit to constitute Pound 'a law-abiding member of the French public for five months', and assured him he was free to go where he wished. He had no trouble until he got back to Paris in September and came up against 'the brute stupidity of the gentleman behind the partition' in the U.S. Consulate where he applied for the visa to get back to London. He was told that they wanted all Americans to return to America, and was categorically forbidden to return to London. He said that he lived there, that his means of livelihood and all his possessions were there. He suggested someone higher up be involved, after which 'a nasty little whining voice was heard saying "We waaant 'em all to go back"'. In the end he went round to the Embassy, and the Ambassador who happened to have known his father in Hailey, 'in the Rocky Mountains', 'sent a chit back to the Consulate'. Even then, in order to be approved by the American consular mind, Pound had to declare as his occupation, not poet, but 'journalistic work'.

Ezra and Dorothy were in Paris for the first ten days of September, staying at the Hôtel Elysée in rue de Beaune on the Left Bank, between Natalie Barney's old garden in the rue Jacob and the Gare d'Orsay. In an interval from looking up the poets and painters he knew Pound visited Margaret Cravens' old apartment, 'seeking for buried beauty' now seven years gone, and 'a strange concierge' showed an empty room divided by an ugly brown paper partition. Yet 'the passion endures', he would assert when he incorporated that 'ghostly visit' into canto 7.

Back in London Pound was grateful for Orage's readiness to let him go on earning his rent by writing up to two pages a week of the *New Age*. He soon began a new series of combative articles under the heading 'The Revolt of Intelligence', and resumed his busy reviewing of art and music. 'I perceive', 'Atheling' wrote after one concert, 'that this season my capacity for being bored is going to be vastly inferior to what it has been during preceding autumns'. After another concert he uttered the timeless protest that 'it is rank bad art to use . . . German music with foreign words which have no relation to the melody . . . of the originals'. As 'B. H. Dias' he went to 'London's first important exhibit of Matisse's work', and registered how his 'renewal of colour sense' made one 'see the surrounding pictures painted in mud'. In December 'Dias' declared that 'Wyndham Lewis' portrait of Ezra Pound rises with the dignity of a classic *stele* to the god of gardens amid the bundles of market-garden produce at the Goupil Gallery "salon"'.

In a third persona, 'Marius David Adkins', he enjoyed 'two opulent weeks as dramatic critic on *The Outlook*', but then was 'fired in most caddish possible manner'. His first review had begun, '*Daddies*, at the Haymarket, is a bad show'; his second had ended, 'the chief cruelty of the author is in giving his actors Corneillian passages with nothing but *Daily Mirror* [cheap journalism] to speak them on'. One can quite see how he might have failed to give satisfaction to a number of interested parties. But he was not best pleased. 'Have had my work turned down by about every editor in England and America, but have never before felt a desire for vengeance', he wrote to Quinn, 'but if you do see a chance for doing that rotten paper, its editor or owners, an ill turn I hope you will do so, in memoriam.'

In amongst the journalism quickly written for cash he had some permanent work coming out that October. The Egoist Ltd. published *Quia Pauper Amavi* containing 'Homage to Sextus Propertius' and the trial 'Three Cantos'. He had read the proofs for that elegant slim volume in Toulouse. Then *The Fourth Canto*, the first of the *Cantos* to be fully achieved, was printed by John Rodker at his Ovid Press, in an edition of 'forty copies *privately* printed, for author's convenience'. And now 'The Chinese Written Character as a Medium for Poetry', Pound's version of an essay by Fenollosa which he regarded as 'basic for all aesthetics', and which he had been struggling to get into print since 1915, was at last appearing in instalments in the *Little Review*.

'The Fourth Canto', and a new poetic

In *The Fourth Canto* Pound had finally found the method he had been long seeking for his epic. Indeed, as it turned out, he had invented a wholly new kind of poetry in English. This canto had begun in the same welter of materials as the three trial cantos; but it had advanced beyond them after much drafting and redrafting by eliminating the Browningesque presenter/narrator, and by then doing away altogether with any evident mediating and interpreting consciousness. All the props to the reader's common sense of reality and identity are gone: there is no character or authorial point of view to relate to, and no story or argument to follow. Altogether, there appears to be little or nothing to give moral or emotional or intellectual bearings, and so no readily discernable 'meaning'. The reader is likely to feel rather challenged as to what to make of it all.

Yet whatever is there to be experienced is already known or inherited in the tradition; and it is made immediately present in vivid image and clear-cut rhythm, just as *Imagisme* would have it. The familiar world of sense is brilliantly realized, as in 'Dawn, to our waking, drifts in the green cool light'; in 'The water whirls up the bright pale sand in the spring's mouth'; and again in 'This wind is held in gauze curtains'. Light, moving air, and water pervade the canto and constitute its elemental world— earth is noticed only at the very end—and those three come together in the evening as 'The peach-trees shed bright leaves in the water'. Then there are the readily accessible materials drawn from history and myth and art: the classic tales out of Ovid, of Philomela and of Actaeon, and the Provençal tales of Cabestan and Vidal; Catullus' hymn for the marriage of Aurunculeia; a Chinese poem of the wind, the king, and his courtiers; the tale of Danae, again out of Ovid; a religious procession Pound had witnessed in Toulouse; and a painting seen in Verona. Taken each in itself these components become perfectly clear in the mind; the only question is this, how does one thing connect with another, and what does it all add up to?

That challenge is felt especially acutely in the opening lines:

> Palace in smoky light,
> Troy but a heap of smouldering boundary stones,
> ANAXIFORMINGES!   Aurunculeia!
> Hear me.   Cadmus of Golden Prows!

The second line at least is clear: Troy has been taken and burnt to the ground, having been under attack by the Greeks for ten years for holding Helen, daughter of Zeus, wife of Menelaus, a Greek, and lover of Paris, a Trojan. I like to think the palace in the first line is Agamemnon's back in Argos, where his wife Clytemnæstra waits to kill him in revenge for his sacrificing their daughter Iphigeneia at the outset of the Greek expedition to Troy. She will also kill the Trojan priestess of Apollo, Cassandra, whom Agamemnon is bringing back as spoils of war to be his concubine. The big mouthful of Greek is Pindar getting his audience's attention in his second Olympian ode by crying out, 'O LORDS OF THE LYRE', meaning, in a word, his songs. But it is how Pindar goes on that seems to the point here: 'which of the gods', he asks, 'what hero, what mortal shall we sing?' One might think of Zeus or of the other divinities who were behind what happened at Troy; or of such heroes as Achilles and Hector. The naming of Aurunculeia proposes instead a mortal bride, brought to her man in a Roman ceremony invoking Hymen, their god of marriage. And Cadmus? He put to sea to recover his sister Europa when she was carried off by Zeus in the shape of a bull; unable to find her, Cadmus went on to found Thebes, the walls of which, it was said, were raised by the power of Amphion's lyre. Connections, interactions, begin to appear. A city destroyed, another built; but most of all running through the allusions and in their background there are women, brides, ravished by Zeus; seized, carried off, held by men; or, one of them, given in marriage. Violent death and destruction come of those violated by men. Thebes rises, to music, when Cadmus has given up his mission to get back Europa.

So a reader might pick apart the seemingly random allusions and discover an inner coherence and pattern. Pound had found a theoretical basis for this practice in 'The Chinese Written Character as a Medium for Poetry'. Fenollosa had observed that certain of the characters in Chinese script were formed by combining two or more distinct ideographs, and that the meaning of the character was generated by the interaction of its components. An eye over running legs, read as the eye moving in space, meant the act of seeing; the mouth with words and a flame coming out of it meant the act of speaking; the sign of a man between heaven and earth, as it were binding the three planes together, meant ruling or governing; and a man standing by his word meant just that. This method of generating meaning through the interactive relations of quite separate elements was deeply interesting to Fenollosa, and to Pound, because it provided a way of freeing the mind from Western conventions and habits of thought. 'Relations', Fenollosa wrote, meaning dynamic interactions, 'are more real and more important than the things which they relate'. Pound endorsed that: 'Swift perception of relations, hallmark of genius', he noted out of Aristotle's *Poetics*. Hence his own Vorticist ideogram of 'planes in relation': Troy down—Aurunculeia—Cadmus of Golden Prows—plus, perhaps, the palace in Argos.

It is a special kind of meaning that is generated in this way in the spaces between the things that are said. Being unstated, it is generated only in the mind of the reader, and is therefore necessarily individual. Moreover, the canto does not lay down what is to be thought, but simply what is to be experienced and then thought about or contemplated. With luck it will generate new meaning free from received ideas and conventional sentiments. Perhaps it should not be thought of as 'meaning' at all, but rather as an energizing of the mind to see things in relation to each other and so to develop an original way of conceiving the ready-made world. Fenollosa and Pound would maintain that it is a way of bringing the mind's creative process closer to nature where everything is interrelated and interactive.

Those opening lines of canto 4 turn out to be both an introduction to all that follows, and a template for its method. First there is a lovers' dawn song, a song rather in the mood of the Renaissance revival of innocent paganism than of 'Langue d'Oc'. For a moment it seems the Golden Age might have returned. As the lovers wake, nymphs and satyrs are seen and heard dancing to primitive music in the grass under apple-trees. After just a few lines, however, the vision is broken by a discordant image: 'A black cock crows in the sea-foam'. Pound wanted the cock, the bird of dawn and warning, to be 'purely apparitional' and to give a 'hypernatural atmosphere'. Part of the estranging effect is that, after the Botticelli-like scene, the black cock is where radiant Aphrodite might have been seen taking shape in the sea-foam. The discordant image effects a necessary transition to the contrasting episodes of violent passion which follow.

The scene-setting is ominous: 'And by the curved carved foot of the couch, / claw-foot and lion head, an old man seated / Speaking in the low drone'. We are out of the living world, in a realm of artifacts and old men's tales. Yet the tale, a double tale in fact, is vividly enacted. '"Ityn, Ityn"', heard as 'eaten', evokes the myth in which Tereus rapes Philomela; and Procne, to revenge her sister, kills, cooks and serves up their son for him to eat. When Tereus makes to kill the sisters all of them are transformed into birds, Procne into a swallow crying her son's name. That myth becomes the frame for the Provençal story of Soremonda, whose jealous husband killed her lover, the troubadour Cabestan, and served up his heart to her. '"No other taste shall change this"', she retorts, and casts herself down from a high window of the castle. As the tale is told here, 'the wind out of Rhodez / Caught in the full of her sleeve', and we lose sight of her among the swallows, as if she too had been transformed. Such metamorphoses seem merciful, but, as in Ovid, they are a form of justice. They occur when there has been some outrageous violation of the human order; and if they bring a resolution it is by removing both the perpetrators and the victims of ungovernable passions into some non-human realm.

The next episode has also to be resolved by metamorphosis. The troubadour Peire Vidal, as the legend and Pound's early poem have it, was hunted with dogs when he 'ran mad, as a wolf, because of his love for Loba of Penautier'. Here Pound has Vidal play out Actaeon's fate. In his folly, like a driven voyeur intent on seeing the goddess of the wild wood naked rather than in her manifestations, he forces his imagination to conjure up Diana, shutting out the sunlight, seeing the skin of her naked nymphs as unliving ivory and silver, courting her anger. So the dogs leap on Vidal-Actaeon, now a 'spotted stag of the wood'; and what Vidal had seen as 'the pale hair of the goddess' also changes, from 'gold' to a 'sheaf... / Thick like a wheat swath', to then 'Blaze, blaze in the sun'. There is of course a moral implicit in the tale, that the powers of nature, as figured in Diana, are not to be possessed and confined, even in a man's furious imagination.

Those episodes are closed and a transition is effected with an image out of Ovid: 'The empty armour shakes as the cygnet moves'. Cygnus, son of Neptune, fought with the Trojans against the Greeks, and was invulnerable even to Achilles' fiercest blows. In his frustration Achilles crushed him in his armour; but even then the semi-divine Cygnus eluded his violence, shedding the armour and flying off as a young swan. 'Thus the light rains, thus pours' goes on from that, leading into a passage in which the energies of light and water flow freely from the heavens and through springs, streams, trees, and, at least in myth and a Noh play, through a faithful couple immortalized in two ancient pine-trees. The marriage song for Aurunculeia also invokes the powers of nature though with a Roman difference, since this bride is for breeding: 'One scarlet flower is cast on the blanch-white stone'. The Chinese wind poem, as Pound adapts it, returns to an ideally non-possessive attitude to nature. The king, told by a courtier that the wind within the palace is his wind, won't have it: ' "No wind is the king's" ', he insists.

Against that, and against the free outpouring and unpossessive enjoy-ment of heavenly light and rain, there is the tale of Danae. Her father, told by an oracle that Danae's son would kill him, shut her up in a tower to keep her from men. Pound has conflated her story with that of the young woman exposed on a tower as a fertility offering, to draw down rain. So Danae becomes 'the god's bride ... waiting the golden rain'. In her story Zeus does indeed come to her as a golden shower, and she conceives Perseus ... who does kill her father. But Pound does not go into that. In his treatment the god's bride laid 'Upon the gilded tower in Ecbatan / ... lay ever, waiting the golden rain'. She is sacrificed in vain. What her father did to Danae is associated with how two husbands, Polhonac and Gyges, exposed their wives to the attentions of others; and associated also with the violence against woman and nature committed by Tereus and by Soremonda's husband, and by Vidal. Another 'god's bride' comes in at the end with the contemporary procession by the Garonne hailing a virgin believed to have conceived the Christian God's son, and to have been taken up bodily into heaven. In response to that Stefano's 'thin film of images', as seen by Cavalcanti on a church wall in Verona, brings the Madonna back down to earth: 'My Lady's face it is they worship there', was Guido's claim.

Nearly every episode and detail in the canto connects with the main theme: how men, in a variety of ways, seek to possess and to exploit women and the freely given energies of nature, generally with disastrous consequences. Against that runs the counter-statement: there is delight and peace to be found in living in accord with nature, contemplating its manifestations, not seeking to possess or to control them. The lovers' dawn vision, the raining of light in the fullness of day, and the evening scene with the peach leaves on the stream, these three passages in which light prevails underpin the canto with a natural rhythm. But the whole thing is held together by the relations and interactions of the disparate materials. The canto is in the end one great ideogram, generating not so much a paraphrasable meaning as a certain 'underlying conviction-plus-passion'.

In writing about musical composition and performance Pound had stressed the importance of what he called 'main form' or 'major form'. He meant that there should be 'a central, main concept' governing the whole composition and determining both its overall structure and the proportions of the materials with which the 'main concept' was filled out. That analogy from music would be another and very appropriate way of understanding his new method.

Pound allowed for considerable 'freedom of detail' in this kind of composition. This freedom, as we find in canto 4, makes it possible for him to range over the whole of human history and tradition from ancient Troy to contemporary Toulouse, and from Homer through Ovid to medieval Provence; and then to bring in as well the alternative cultures of China and Japan. It is as if the individual poet is free to bring relevant materials from the entire past into focus, for the moment of the canto, to reveal some 'permanent basis in humanity' for his convictions.

This is where Pound was being truly revolutionary. His new method liberated the individual intelligence from the authority of the established historical and cultural narratives, determined, most of them, by the interests and imperatives of church, state, and property or capital. In his cantos he could now reconceive and reorganize history and tradition on the basis of the vital interests of the individual person. If he succeeded he would bring about a radical revaluation and reorientation, by putting the individual at the centre of things in place of any and all external powers and authorities. It would mean the end of consulate clerks telling a poet he must drop everything and do his duty by the republic. It would mean the end of husbands having property rights over wives and fathers over daughters. It would change religion, and challenge the discipline the capitalist state imposed on its workers. It would free minds by leading them to know themselves and to comprehend their world from their own point of view. Of course this is the perennial revolution many have worked for throughout recorded history, from Socrates and Confucius down. Pound's was not a new revolution, just a new effort and a new method specific to his time.

Canto 4 was a culmination of his early *personae* and idealism; of his studies directed to constructing a tradition of his own and acquiring the *virtu* of his chosen masters; of *Imagisme* and Vorticism and the conviction that intelligence is individual; of his critical interpretations of ancient

China and Augustan Rome; and not least of his sustained determination to produce an epic poem. But still it lacked realism, lacked the direct engagement with the conditions of contemporary living which he had been calling for in his criticism and celebrating in the works of Joyce and Eliot and Lewis. The canto's method was modern, but its bearing on the modern world was oblique. Composed as it was out of myth and legend and poetry, it was not grounded in ordinary reality. As if in recognition of this the 1919 version ended—after all the imagery of light and air and 'the liquid and rushing crystal'—with this affirmation, 'The Centaur's heel / Plants in the earth-loam'.

Public affairs

'The man of letters . . . must have some concern for public affairs', Pound declared in November 1919, but he must also recognize 'the impossibility of his works having any immediate effect'. After all, 'for five centuries a series of intelligent men have written intelligently, have collected the fragments of earlier civilisation for reinforcement, and [yet] the few people who still live, write, read, cogitate, do so, as it were, in a small globe lit by Bunsens, and surrounded by incredible stupidity'. A concerned intelligence could only try 'to conserve at least a free corner, a "lighted spot", a "sound core", somewhere in the gehenna'; though with the assurance that amid wars and revolutions the enlightenment he worked for would be 'the only stabilising element'.

In his articles in the *New Age* in the autumn of 1919 and on into the spring of 1920 Pound continued his war on the enemies of enlightenment, concentrating his fire now on organized religions, on nationalisms, and on the Capitalist economic system. All three, as he regarded them from the viewpoint of a free intelligence, offended against the rights and liberties of the human person and were destructive of peace and civilization.

He began one of the articles in his series 'The Revolt of Intelligence' with the assertion that 'Two great obstacles to human fraternity are religion and nationality', and of these, he added, 'religion is probably the worse'. 'All religions are evil', he had written,

because all religions try to enforce a certain number of fairly sound or fairly accurate or "beneficial" propositions . . . regardless of the temperament or nature of others. Every religion is a "kultur" . . . an attempt to impose a thought-mould upon others.

Religions were at their worst when they sought to impose their ideas by violence, as by putting to death blasphemers and heretics and infidels,

369

something to which those who believed that their god was the only god seemed to be given. The curse of monotheism and its associated intolerance had descended, Pound observed, from Judaism into both Mohametanism and Christianity. 'We write', he wrote, 'in the fifth century of the Struggle for Deliverance from these religions'.

But then he went on to make a point about 'the futility of violence' in a passage that now, after Hitler's attempt to exterminate all Jews just twenty years later, reads more as an unenlightened expression of an antisemitic thought-mould:

We note … that since the lions of the Tribe of Judah gave up the sword, 'beat it' metaphorically into the pawn-shop, their power has steadily increased; no such suave and uninterrupted extension of power is to be attributed to any 'world-conquering' bellicose nation.

Those of us who live in immaterial things, in art, in literature, 'owe more' to Greece and Rome; the rest of the world 'owes', or is alleged to owe, to the Jew.

That 'antithesis', he insisted in the following article, 'sprang from no antisemitism':

I point out simply the practicality of avoiding needless coercions, strifes, and combustions. Inasmuch as the Jew has conducted no holy war for nearly two millenia he is preferable to the Christian and the Mahomedan.

One can take that point without being so naive as to suppose that in 1919 remarks associating 'the Jew' with 'the pawn-shop' on the one hand and with supra-national 'power' on the other would not register as prejudicial stereotypes. Such remarks were fairly commonplace in the *New Age* in those years, and so too were objections to them. Pound, being engaged in a war against clichés and stereotypes and false generalizations, should surely have been among the objectors.

What are we to make of his sliding from monotheistic Judaism to 'the Jew', that is, from the religion to the race; and then sliding from 'the futility of violence' to the implication that Jewish non-violence was a devious and more effective way of imposing a materialist ideology upon the world? Why this messy contamination of his thinking about the curse of monotheism, a subject he did know something about, with the quite unrelated, undemonstrated and prejudicial line of thought about the alleged hidden power and influence of Jewish financiers? Here it would be very easy to short-circuit our search for understanding by simply writing Pound down as antisemitic and so being done with the vexing problem; but the fact is that there is too little evidence in his writings up to 1920 to support such a heavy judgement at this stage. Just half-a-dozen prejudicial remarks such as the above scattered through the hundreds of pages of his journalism don't make a case. And there is nothing of that sort in his letters in these years. Those remarks do show him lapsing on a very few occasions into the endemic antisemitism of the time; and they do indicate a flaw that was to grow, in the 1930s and after, into a most grave failing. We will come to that in its proper time and place. The troubling questions won't go away.

Pound in 1919 and 1920 suspected any and every organized group with power over the lives of others, whether it was a church, a state, or a network of bankers, of being a conspiracy against the rights and values of the individual citizen. He was against the assertion of nationalities and nationalisms because that led to the subordination of the individual to an actual state or to an idea of one. He regretted that Ireland had sought its freedom on the basis of Irish nationalism. He regarded D'Annunzio's seizure of Fiume as the victory of an individual intelligence over the statist mentality, while deprecating his doing it in the name of 'Italia'. He should have done it, in Pound's view, on the basis of Italy's being more civilized than Jugo-Slavia, as attested, for example, by its agricultural guilds. As for the then proposed 'league of *nations*', that appeared to him 'about as safe and as inviting for the individual as does a combine of large companies for the employee'. It would mean power being removed even further from the people and being put in the hands of 'a small committee appointed by Governmental inner cliques in each nation'. Pound really did believe in democracy, even in a pure and absolute democracy in which every individual should have the opportunity to be true to his or her own nature without let or hindrance. He believed that in a democracy the state should obey and serve its people rather than the other way round. His position was complicated though by his dividing 'the people' into the few and the rest—the few self-determining individuals and the mass of sheep.

What he really wanted was a society of and for the genuine individuals, a civilization which would transcend nations and collective cults and corporations, and from which enlightenment would spread and prevail. 'The function of civilization', he declared, 'is to depreciate material values and to build up values of intelligence'. Rather than a League of Nations let there be 'a centre of civilization', what we would now call a transnational research institute, to bring together creative thinkers imbued with a profound understanding of what made life worth living; and let them concentrate on solving the pressing problems of the post-war situation, starting with the dysfunctional economic system. He probably did not expect that such a centre would be set up; but he did find what he was looking for in one odd individual, Major C. H. Douglas.[1]

Pound met Douglas in the *New Age* office and was powerfully impressed by his thinking, as Orage had been. The 'Einstein of economics' Orage would dub him. Paul Selver, a lightweight member of the *New Age* circle who did not take to Douglas, recorded that 'He was squat and bald, with a foghorn voice', and that 'when he was present there was little chance for anyone else to get a word in', nor was there 'the remotest likelihood that anything else but Social Credit would be discussed, or rather expounded'. However, Pound seems to have got his word in on at least one occasion. Douglas was vigorously stating something he had learned in India, and it suddenly struck Pound with the force of a blinding revelation that 'In that case any government worth a damn could pay dividends instead of collecting taxes?', and 'The major chewed it a bit and sez: "Y—es"'. If it weren't for Douglas, Pound later wrote, 'I should have remained ignorant'—ignorant about the root cause of wars and of the obstruction of civilization.

Douglas had a diagnosis for the phenomenon of industries being unable to sell their products at home in spite of there being millions in dire need of them; and their being driven to compete for markets abroad when that led as in the recent hecatomb to international wars. The problem, he said, with the devastating simplicity of the child who knew no better than to say that the emperor had no clothes on, the real problem was that people did not have the money to buy the goods and services which they needed and which industry could supply in abundance. Scarcity of supply was an illusion; over-production was an illusion; lack of capital for investment was an illusion; poverty and its associated ills could be done away with. The solution was obvious: give the people the purchasing power to buy the things which industry needed to sell and which they needed for a decent life. That is what any enlightened government would do: distribute credit, not take it away in taxes.

In a system in which banks not governments created the public credit that was unthinkable, mad, a crank's economics. Yet gradually, over the course of the century, what Douglas had called for came to pass, though

[1] Clifford Hugh Douglas (1879–1952), English engineer, economist, founder of Social Credit movement. Chief Reconstruction Engineer for British Westinghouse Company in India; Deputy Chief Engineer for Buenos Aires and Pacific Railway Company; Railway Engineer for London Post Office underground railway. In 1914–18 war commissioned major in Royal Flying Corps and served as Assistant Director Royal Aircraft Works at Farnborough. On basis of his experience there formulated theory of Social Credit; his first book, *Economic Democracy* (1920), serialized by Orage in the *New Age* in 1919; *Credit-Power and Democracy* (1920) included a 70-page commentary by Orage; *Social Credit* (1924).

in a form he would have seen as a perversion of his idea. Instead of Social Credit created by the state there was consumer credit created by banks and finance houses, first in the form of hire-purchase or 'on the never never', then in the form of credit cards. Consumer credit means that banks are investing in consumption rather than in production, and thus helping to correct the imbalance between production and purchasing power. But this form of credit does not increase the sum of purchasing power, since what is borrowed must be repaid. Moreover, so far as interest charges are incurred—and these can be as high as 20 and 30 per cent—it actually decreases the sum of purchasing power by taking as interest what could otherwise be spent on goods and services. Consumer credit then is not a solution to Douglas's problem, but simply a way of managing the problem; and one which rather than creating credit to sustain production and consumption constantly draws money off from production and consumption into bank profits. Douglas would see it as a system for creating debt rather than credit. Orthodox economists have no problem with that, since as they see it the system runs on that sort of debt. What would trouble Douglas though is that for individuals, and indeed for whole societies, interest-bearing debt is an obstruction to 'the inalienable right of man to life, liberty and the pursuit of happiness'.

The crankiest, most revolutionary aspect of Douglas's thinking was that he viewed economics from the viewpoint of the individual and not of the system. He took as the first principle of any human endeavour the above 'majestic words of the American Declaration of Independence', words which 'are an assertion of the supremacy of the individual considered collectively, over any external interest'. 'We must build up from the individual', he wrote, 'not down from the State.' This is where Pound started to cheer for Douglas in April 1920 in two reviews of his *Economic Democracy*, one in the *Little Review* and one in the *Athenæum*. He welcomed Douglas as 'a Don Quixote desiring to "*Make democracy safe for the individual*"'; and again as a humanist driven by his implicit 'protest against the wastage of human beings' 'under the present system of wage-tyranny, and his instinctive revolt against any system of ratiocination which treats man as a "unit"'. He went on to declare that Douglas's 'fundamental denial that man with his moods and hypostases is or can decently ever become a "unit"' gave his work a 'philosophic value' over and above most economic treatises which, 'in the main, neglect human values'. The basic human value, Pound implied, was 'a free exercise of the will'; and Douglas's 'paragraphs arouse and rearouse one to a sense of how far we have given up our individual wills in all matters of economics'. Pound would make the free exercise of the individual will the foundation of his own 'Volitionist Economics' in the 1930s.

It becomes clear that Pound finds Douglas's economic doctrine convincing 'on the basis of ethics or equity' and is content to leave open the question of whether it would work in practice. Moreover, he hardly bothers with the technical and strictly economic arguments. So far as he is concerned this 'new declaration of independence' can be condensed into a few summary statements, such as 'Real credit is a measure of the reserve of energy belonging to a community', and 'the state should lend, not borrow . . . in this respect as in others the Capitalist usurps the function of the state'. He did say, without further explanation, that Douglas's doctrine was a 'profound attack upon usury', and that usury, along with taxation, was 'the counterforce, the destroyer of civilizations'. That would become a major preoccupation in the 1930s.

'Don't imagine that I think economics interesting—not as Botticelli or Picasso is interesting', thus Pound, in the summer of 1921, qualified a note on *Credit Power and Democracy* in a little magazine edited by Williams and Robert McAlmon in New York. The economic system, that is, the present 'reality under political camouflage', concerned him much as 'a gun muzzle aimed at one's own head' would concern him. It concentrated the mind on the threat to civilization and on what might be done about it. That was what Douglas's diagnosis was good for: helping one to understand how it was that power was not with the people but with those who owned and controlled the people's credit and who were capable of exercising it against the common interest. If only that were more widely understood it might 'prevent those who now hold the credit power from flagrant use of it—war making etc.'.

In an effort to promote Douglas's ideas Pound arranged for him to meet Wickham Steed, the editor of *The Times*, and John Maynard Keynes who had recently published *The Economic Consequences of the Peace* (1919), a 'fairly courageous' critique of the Treaty of Versailles. Steed is 'intelligent', he told Quinn, but Keynes he now considered 'an ass'. Douglas, 'the real mind', had asked Keynes what was the cause of the high cost of living, and Keynes, 'The economist consulted of nations, said: "Lack of labour"', and since 'there were two millions of men out of work' Douglas gave up. But Pound 'went on plaguing' Keynes, 'Who said finally: "I am an orthodox / Economist"'. In fact, in Pound's view, Keynes had 'invented a whole new Roman and Apostolic church of economics: "Orthodox Economics"', which before long would be bamboozling 'young minds from various endowed "chairs" and settees' and helping to keep from them the real nature of the economic system.

374

If there were to be any hope for England economically, Pound concluded, it would not be from its economists or its politicians or its financial interests. It would have to be from 'the national heritage', that is, from 'the dogged belief that power resides in the people':

what has long since become an instinctive attitude toward 'political' rights must ultimately become operative toward economic rights...The right to credit-control is implicit in English custom, in the English attitude toward life.

That Jeffersonian belief was as much the American heritage, and the only hope for America.

But as for contemporary political leaders with the 'lucidity or honesty or sense of justice' to carry that wise belief into action, Pound in 1920 seems to have been willing to endorse only one, and then largely on the basis of a recently published essay. In *The New Europe. (The Slav Standpoint)* (1918), Tómaš Masaryk (1850–1937), the philosopher-statesman who had just become the first president of the new independent Czech-Slovak republic, had taken his stand on the principle that 'The recognition accorded to the value of human personality is what establishes the civic value and the right to exist of . . . states, churches, nations'.

Pound believed passionately in that principle as the natural and necessary basis of a good society. And he saw it as the motive cause in a permanent revolution. It was the cause of the protestant revolt, carried on over the centuries from the Cathars to Luther, against the Papal theocracy; it was the cause of the series of revolutions, in England, America, and France, against the assumption of absolute powers by kings and nobles; and it was the cause now requiring the revolt of intelligence against the hegemony of international capital. The contemporary revolt, Pound maintained, must be based upon clear and honest thought such as he found in Masaryk.

Yet he could be made angry and be driven to extremes when he considered how 'A bloated usury, a cowardly and snivelling politics, a disgusting financial system, [and] the saddistic curse of Christianity' all worked together to degrade humanity and destroy nature. Taking off from W. H. Hudson's protest against the destruction of the most splendid wild animals for 'game' and of fine feathered birds for the fashion trade, he wrote that ' "Their strangeness and their beauty" may well go unheeded into desuetude if there be nothing to preserve them but usurers and the slaves of usury and an alleged religion which has taught the supreme lie that the splendour of the world is not a true splendour'. 'Where is the basis', he demanded, 'of a glory in the colour sense without which the birds-wings are unapprehended', so long as ' "Christendom" is permeated with the superstition that the human body is tainted and that the senses are not noble avenues of "illumination" '. Moreover, men kept 'at starvation level' could not be expected to care about the destruction of the splendours of nature and of art. 'Medieval Christianity had one merit', he allowed, 'it taught that usury was an evil',

But in our day Rockefeller and the churches eat from one manger, and the church has so far fallen into vacuity that it does not oppose 'finance', which is nothing but a concatenation of usuries, hardly subtle, but subtle enough to gull the sheep and cow humans.

For the 'milkable human cows' and the 'shearable human sheep' who allowed themselves to be exploited Pound showed little sympathy. 'The only part of humanity worth saving' from the attack of the combined forces of destruction and degradation, he wrote, was 'the bright plumed and fine voiced species of the genus anthropos, [those] favoured of the gods'. Again we are brought up against the paradox, if it is not a real contradiction, of Pound's being concerned to bring about a truly democratic civilization, and yet caring apparently only for the artists and individuals of genius who would compose it. Prose simplifies for the argument's sake, and in his prose, when overcome with impatient rage against usury, Pound could lose touch with his democratic conviction that in the republic the common good should be the good of all. But then, as he saw it, the common good depends absolutely upon 'the creative, the intellectually-inventive-creative spirit in man', and if that spirit fails then civilization fails and all is given over to Moloch, to the powers that feed on their own subjects.

'Hugh Selwyn Mauberley'

It is characteristic of Pound, in his hasty prose, to speak his mind with firm, unequivocal, even aggressive conviction. He leaves as little room as possible for uncertainty as to where he stands, or as to the rightness of his stand. In his poetry, however, and in *Hugh Selwyn Mauberley* especially, there are few simple certainties of that sort. In *Mauberley* we have always more than one voice or point of view to reckon with; and usually there are layered ironies in the undertones and overtones of the words and allusions. This is writing in which anything that is said may be unsaid in the saying; in which statements may be turned against themselves; in which nearly everything becomes equivocal, and meanings are hard to pin down. Readers anxious for certainty may turn to Pound's prose for fixes upon what he must have meant, and apparently find them there, only to discover that the poem won't conform, or else must be greatly simplified

376

to make it fit what Pound or 'Aetheling' had plainly said. The fact is that prose is one thing and poetry quite another, and that poetry into prose just won't go. It is the wrong way round, as would be changing wine into water. In his prose Pound called imperatively for 'individual intelligence' to be supreme; but it is only in his poetry that we find his intelligence doing the sort of advanced creative thinking that would justify that demand.

A major source of perplexity has been, who or what is Mauberley? As a *persona* he is unlike all the others in Pound's gallery in that there is no objective backing to him, no attested historical character such as de Born and Vidal, no actual poet such as Li Po and Propertius, no poem such as 'The Seafarer'. He is entirely 'made up' then. Moreover, to complicate the fiction he is to a very considerable extent made up of experiences and attitudes that are very near to Pound's own. Yet 'I'm no more Mauberley than Eliot is Prufrock', he protested—a protest which could be leaving unsaid, 'and no less'.

Pound told one correspondent in the 1930s that Mauberley was ' "ANY" non producer in the stink of London 1919'. He had done him, he explained, 'When even tolerably half intelligent people couldnt understand' that his Propertius 'related to ANY empire declining onto the shit pile'. In a letter to Basil Bunting he wrote,

Mauberley / sure / the picture of ANY young man in Eng / even EP eviscerate / VOID of ALL creative impulse // EP/ done a picture of what ANY young educated bloke wd / have SEEN, and all he wd/ have done about it IF he had no guts, balls, viscera.

To Scofield Thayer, whom he hoped would publish the poem in *The Dial*, he gave this outline: 'first Mauberley's probable contacts with the world, and then Mauberley, enfant de son siècle'. These indications all point away from Pound himself and direct attention upon Mauberley as the object of interest. Pound even pretended to have written himself out of the poem in the well-known statement that 'Mauberley buries E.P. in the opening poem; gets rid of all his troublesome energies'.

As for Mauberley's contacts, apart one assumes from E.P. himself— that is, Monsieur Verog, Brennbaum, Mr Nixon and the rest—these, Pound insisted, were not to be identified with particular people known to him, with, let us say, Victor Plarr, Max Beerbohm, Arnold Bennett or his 'stylist' friend now called Ford Madox Ford. He had 'in each case', he declared, 'synthesised a type and a situation'. For example, as he told Agnes Bedford, the 'starting point' of the 'Conservatrix' was a married woman known to him—'I have eaten her dinners (long ago)'—'a person fulfilling exactly the specifications set down in the verses', which

377

were 'equally applicable to *all* the bloody denizens of all suburbs'. He had called that, in his review of Eliot's *Prufrock,* striking at universals through particulars; and the universals, doubtless, are what should concern the reader looking for enlightenment. Still, when we can't help knowing, if only because the critical tradition keeps passing on the received identifications, exactly who was 'the starting point' behind each 'contact', along with where and how Pound knew that person and what he thought of them, then that knowledge must complicate our perception of Mauberley.

It can be an enriching complication, on condition that we don't simply translate the universal back into the particular. To think that the singer in 'Envoi' and 'Medallion' *is* Raymonde Collignon would be to do that. Collignon may well have been Pound's starting point, but the singer *in the poem* is not Collignon. Just the same, to detect Pound's particular friends and acquaintances behind Mauberley's universal types—and to make out Pound's interests and opinions behind many if not most of Mauberley's—is a necessary corrective to those hints and indications to his correspondents which would lead us to overlook the fact that, in certain telling respects, Mauberley *is* Pound. Or let us say that the starting point of Mauberley is Pound himself. If Mauberley is also the child of his time, as Pound maintained, then he is presumably Pound as a child of that same aesthetic culture of the Pre-Raphaelites and the Nineties. It would follow that any criticism to be levelled at Mauberley must be intended not only as a critique of his milieu but equally as Pound's critique of his younger self.

We must not leave out after all the overriding reality here, that, as the title-page of the first edition stated, the whole work is *Hugh Selwyn Mauberley* 'BY E.P.'[2] There are then these four factors in play: (1) E.P. as the declared author of the work; (2) Mauberley, as E.P.'s fictive author; (3) the fictive E.P. as represented by Mauberley; and (4) the modern milieu or mind out of which both fictive characters come. That makes the poem a rather complex set of interacting discriminations, much like Joyce's *A Portrait of the Artist as a Young Man*, or his treatment of Stephen Daedalus in *Ulysses*.

---

[2] *Hugh Selwyn Mauberley* by E. P. (London: John Rodker, The Ovid Press, June 1920)—an edition of 200 copies. Reprinted in *Poems 1918–21* (New York: Boni & Liveright, 1921), as one of 'Three Portraits', the others being *Homage to Sextus Propertius* and 'Langue d'Oc' (with 'Moeurs Contemporains'). Both editions indicate the division of the work into 'Part I', containing [I]–XII and 'Envoi (1919)', and 'Part II. 1920 (Mauberley)', containing I–[V] 'Medallion'. In 1918–21 the subtitle '(Life and Contacts)' was added, though the actual order, as Pound would later remark, is 'Contacts and Life'.

In the first poem it appears that Mauberley is writing an obituary for young Ezra Pound. I take the first two quatrains to be an account of Pound in the years 1905–08:

> For three years, out of key with his time,
> He strove to resuscitate the dead art
> Of poetry; to maintain 'the sublime'
> In the old sense. Wrong from the start—
>
> No, hardly, but seeing he had been born
> In a half savage country, out of date;
> Bent resolutely on wringing lilies from the acorn;
> Capaneus; trout for factitious bait;

That would be the intensely independent and idealistic youth who urged Williams to read Longinus *On the Sublime*, who meant to celebrate in poetry the ecstasy of the soul's ascent to the divine, and who followed Swedenborg and Dante in sublimating his adolescent sexuality: in retrospect a young trout rising to an artificial fly, getting hooked on the unreal ideal. The third and fourth quatrains then would correspond to his sailing, a latter-day Odysseus led on by the siren-song of his unwritten epic, to Gibraltar and on via Venice to London, where his pursuit of a literary career had its parallels—always in Mauberley's clever conceits—to Odysseus' encounters with Circe and the 'obstinate' Wandering Rocks as he tried to get home to 'His true Penelope ... Flaubert'. In the final stanza, in his thirty-first year—that would be 1916, the year *Lustra* appeared— young Pound faded out, apparently, and 'passed from men's memory' to the satisfaction no doubt of the enemies he had defied in 'Salutation the Third'.

The joke is that Mauberley's obituary fails to notice that E.P. had emerged from the chrysalis of his early poems in *Lustra* and had gone on to publish his first cantos, and *Homage to Sextus Propertius*. What's more, E.P., *in propria persona*, had anticipated the critique of his 'sublime' phase, notably in 'Salutation the Second':

> You were praised my books,
>   because I had just come from the country;
> I was twenty years behind the times
>   so you found an audience ready.
> I do not disown you,
>   do not you disown your progeny.

Beside the lightness and nimbleness of such verses Mauberley's wit seems laboured and humourless. He just doesn't get what was happening in

Lustra, the joyful liberations, the glad realism, the moments of vision in among the mocking satires, and the general shedding of both sublimations and repressions. He wouldn't know either that Pound had just shown how he regarded his early idealizing aesthetic by preserving in *Umbra*—a collection published in the same month as *Mauberley*, and containing all 'the early poems of Ezra Pound...that he now wishes to keep in circulation'—just one poem from *Canzoni*, 'Au Jardin', the one in which he light-heartedly detached himself from that aesthetic.

Even on his own terms Mauberley may be missing something. His conceits register as put-downs, but need not be. 'His true Penelope was Flaubert' suggests that E.P. was straying from life into art for its own sake; yet it might be no bad thing for a young poet to want to get back to Flaubert, if that meant that his verse would be precisely faithful to its object. Again, to observe 'the elegance of Circe's hair / Rather than the mottoes on sun-dials' might be sensibly to imitate wily Odysseus rather than his men who rued rashly seizing the day. (Not, it must be said, that Pound was not, at least in reputation, gathering rosebuds in his later London years.) As for his being 'Unaffected by "the march of events"'—a fine cliché touching nothing in particular—one could think *that* the case only if one missed the bearing of *Cathay* and *Homage to Sextus Propertius* upon the world of 1914–18.

Mauberley's animadversions upon the age in the following two poems show him to be at once alienated from it and trapped in it—much like Propertius in his Rome. He is no doubt meaning to reflect, and to deflect with an ironic inflection, the philistine attitude of the age to art when he speaks of it as 'the obscure reveries / Of the inward gaze'. And yet he offers no more promising idea of art than that. Perhaps after all he really is still rhyming and dreaming of classic Beauty in the Celtic Twilight—in which case those words would have been the *mots justes* for his kind of art. His trouble, or it may be our trouble with him, is that he can see only what his age lacks, not any way to recover what has been lost. In fact his telling over of the culture's losses seems to take more pleasure in his own wit than to care for how something might yet be saved:

> Faun's flesh is not to us,
> Nor the saint's vision.
> We have the press for wafer;
> Franchise for circumcision.

That is ever so clever—but nothing follows from it, only that 'a tawdry cheapness / Shall outlast our days'. The notion of making it new, of *renaissance now!* never disturbs Mauberley's complacent gloom and conviction of his own effortless superiority.

It takes the wastage of beauty in war and the overwhelming sense of death to rouse him to passion, and to serious poetry—in this too he is much like Propertius. His image for the trenches, 'walked eye-deep in hell', outdoes all his witty conceits and is a true 'intellectual and emotional complex'. In this fourth poem pity and anger break down the constraining artifice of his quatrains to speak out with oratorical eloquence. There is fellow-feeling here, and even a movement towards political engagement:

> Died some, pro patria,
> > non 'dulce' non 'et decor'...
> walked eye-deep in hell
> believing in old men's lies, then unbelieving
> came home, home to a lie,
> home to many deceits,
> home to old lies and new infamy;
> usury age-old and age-thick
> and liars in public places.

This compassionate and angry elegy is Mauberley's finest achievement. But it is followed by disillusionment, not reconstruction: all he can see is that the myriad dead died 'For a botched civilization ... For a few thousand battered books.' He can only look back, it appears, not think forward with the living to new creation, as Pound had done when Gaudier was killed.

The rest of Part I of *Mauberley* consists of anecdotal sketches of Mauberley's background—the Pre-Raphaelite movement and the Nineties—and of a selection of his contemporaries, these leading up to his own portrait of the artist in society. (There are of course some notable absences—no Browning or Henry James, no Gaudier or Lewis or Joyce.) Taken together those sketches amount to an indictment of the aesthetic culture of which Mauberley is to be taken as the typical product—an indictment of it for failing both art and life which will be hammered home in Part II.

Mauberley's self-portrait is charged with wry irony at finding himself, a 'soul / "Which the highest cultures have nourished"', waiting upon 'The Lady Valentine's commands'. In his fantasy she might have been Daphne to his Apollo. In reality she will put his poems, his preciously cultivated 'Pierian roses', to uses he perhaps rather despises—as 'A hook to catch the Lady Jane's attention', for example. He can only think that there is no demand in the popular press for what he writes—he is stuck with serving the self-serving Lady Valentine.

His book, the first part of the work, is closed by 'Envoi (1919)'. The question always comes up, whose poem is this? In the anthology he compiled with Marcella Spann, *Confucius to Cummings* (1964), Pound claimed it as his own, and evidently judged it worthy to represent his art. But that does not settle the question. Obviously Pound wrote it, but the real question is, what did he write? And the answer to that must be that in 'Envoi' he wrote the choicest of Mauberley's 'Pierian roses', his prize exhibit. Or to put it another way, he beautifully embalmed Mauberley's dead art.

> Tell her that's young,
> And shuns to have her Graces spy'd,
> That hadst thou sprung
> In Desarts, where no men abide,
> Thou must have uncommended dy'd.

That is from Waller's song, 'Go lovely Rose', which would have his young beauty 'Suffer her self to be desired' and not 'waste her time and me'. But this is the variation which the 'Envoi' would address to a young singer of Henry Lawes's setting of that song in Mauberley's day:

> *Tell her that sheds*
> *Such treasure in the air,*
> *Recking naught else but that her graces give*
> *Life to the moment,*
> *I would bid them live*
> *As roses might, in magic amber laid,*
> *Red overwrought with orange and all made*
> *One substance and one colour*
> *Braving time.*

The verse takes off from Waller's cadence and develops it skilfully through phrase after musical phrase of the well-wrought sentence. And the image of roses laid up in amber is delightful to contemplate. Simple, sensuous, and passionate; making new the old conceit of immortality in art—is this not how poetry is meant to be? But consider what is being done here: living beauty is being consigned to timeless art, to be enjoyed not as Waller's song urges but as unchanging, breathless Beauty. In the final strophe the singer is told that her song may still be sung and *'gain her worshippers, / When our two dusts with Waller's shall be laid'*, as if that's how she should wish to be worshipped. But the song itself is saying even as she sings it, live and be loved now—only our poet is not attending. All he wants is 'Beauty alone', the ideal beauty of art. Pound, in December 1919, must have written the 'Envoi' in the same spirit as the rest of Part I, that is, in the spirit of detached presentation of Mauberley the modern aesthete. Mauberley has

382

all Pound's mastery of the art of composing words and images into music, but he is his opposite when it comes to the relations of life and art. Not life for art's sake, but art for life's sake had always been Pound's cry.

Detachment is not the word for the way E.P. sets about Mauberley in Part II, '1920'. The dissection of his limitations, his inadequacies, his ineffectualness—his having 'no guts, balls, viscera'—is carried out at length, with merciless explicitness, and with great art. E.P. is most determinedly burying Mauberley, getting rid of his troubling combination of refinement and *abuleia*, his strange ability to love beauty and see the ugliness of his world yet have no will to bring beauty alive in it again.

In the first of the four poems dealing with Mauberley the mention of 'the strait head / Of Messalina' is probably an allusion to Beardsley's 1895 design, 'Messalina returning home'. Messalina, wife of the Roman emperor Claudius, figured in Juvenal's satires as a woman of such insatiable sexual appetite that she picked up men in the street and offered herself through long nights in Rome's brothels. The design is a fascinated image of decadence done in stark black and white and with Beardsley's usual precision and grace of line. It is a striking picture and yet quite emotionless, quite amoral, wholly without any 'reforming sense'. That, in short, is the charge Pound lays against Mauberley's art, that it lacks 'the skill / To forge Achaia'—lacks the moral energy to create the 'Attic grace' he longs for. Pound would have him be like Pisanello, whose iconic medallions of such rulers as Lionello d'Este of Ferrara, Francesco Sforza of Milan, Sigismondo Malatesta of Rimini and the Gonzagas of Mantua, helped create the Italian Renaissance.

Since Pound, even while still an idealizing young lover of Beauty, had always wanted his art to make for more and better life and to promote a renaissance, there is no way he could be identified with the Mauberley he is attacking there. One wonders why he spent so much of his energy and art disposing of him through the third and fourth poems of Part II; and one is forced to conclude that he must have been profoundly offended by 'cultured' and privileged 'non producers'.

> The glow of porcelain
> Brought no reforming sense
> To his perception
> Of the social inconsequence.
> Thus, if her colour
> Came against his gaze,
> Tempered as if
> It were through a perfect glaze

>He made no immediate application
>Of this to relation of the state
>To the individual . . .

—whence the fading out of Mauberley's art into hedonistic impressionism. The account of his decline is detailed, and specifies along the way his failure to meet Pound's artistic standards in respect of conserving 'the better tradition', refining the medium, 'elimination of superfluities' (in plain speech, 'use no unnecessary word'), and above all 'concentration'. For his end Pound casts Mauberley away on a colourful tropical beach where his consciousness blurs out 'in the cobalt of oblivions'—not the worst of hells, perhaps, but a fitting punishment for losing 'the good of the intellect' in his fashion.

There is a related yet distinct analysis of Mauberley in the second poem of Part II, and this does implicate the young E.P. who had been 'Bent resolutely on wringing lilies from the acorn'. 'For three years, diabolus in the scale', is a variant way of saying 'out of key with his time', but here the dissonance is attributed to his having been in Arcadia—until the need to make a start in the world drove him out, to Wabash as it were. What follows would have had as its starting point the romantic relationships of his youth, especially his Arcadian engagement to H.D. The desperate adolescent state of being in the dark about the other sex and longing for the sublime is presented in 'Attic' terms, as if it were a mythic tale told on a Greek vase, though all the time with an under-sense of the old comedy of inexperienced 'Lusty Juventus'. It leads up to this:

>He had passed, inconscient, full gaze,
>The wide-banded irides
>And botticellian sprays implied
>In their diastasis;
>
>Which anæsthesis, noted a year late,
>And weighed, revealed his great affect,
>(Orchid), mandate
>Of Eros, a retrospect.

There are simpler and more direct ways of saying that it was too late when he realised that with his eyes wide open but his mind on divine beauty he had failed to respond to the life-force in her eyes. That leaves him, in the vivid image, a mouth 'biting empty air'—or a 'trout for factitious bait'. But such a paraphrase would change the register and invite a different response in the reader. The effect of Pound's putting it as it were in Greek is to distance and objectify the tragedy of excessive idealism and missed opportunity, to give it the hardness and coldness of marble, so that it may be contemplated with perfect detachment. It makes it a matter not for pity or anger but purely and simply for the intelligence to observe. And it is of course E.P. coldly portraying with extreme prejudice the young artist that he was and no longer is.

The connection with Mauberley would be in the implication that his socially inconsequent response to beauty was due to there being no sexual charge in it to energize his aesthetics. The life-force is not in him nor in his art. 'Medallion', the final poem of Part II, makes the point. Again the question is raised, whose poem is this? And again the answer must be that it is E.P.'s treatment of Mauberley's art. The medallion in question appears to be one in which Mauberley has succeeded in catching his singer beneath a perfect glaze, as if 'in magic amber laid'. He has made of her a 'Luini in porcelain'. In Salomon Reinach's *Apollo*, which E.P. has evidently been looking into, we read that Luini

translated the ideal of Leonardo into simple terms, a process which he carried out not altogether without vulgarity, for his elegance is superficial, his drawing uncertain, and his power of invention limited. His most characteristic trait is a certain honeyed softness that delights the multitude.

Against the medallion's Luini effect is set 'a profane protest' from 'the grand piano' and the singer's 'clear soprano'; and there is set also the image of the singer herself, as 'Atheling' might have seen her live in the Wigmore Hall:

> The sleek head emerges
> From the gold-yellow frock
> As Anadyomene in the opening
> Pages of Reinach.

The reference would appear to be to the head of Aphrodite of which Reinach gives a photograph (in profile), and this description:

in Lord Leconfield's London house there is a head of Aphrodite, so marvellously supple in execution and so exquisitely suave in expression that we may fairly accept it as the work, if not of Praxiteles himself, then of one of his immediate pupils. The characteristics of the feminine ideal as conceived by this great and fascinating genius are all clearly defined in this head. The form of the face, hitherto round, has become oval; the eyes, instead of being fully opened, are half closed, and have that particular expression which the ancients described as 'liquid' ... The hair ... is freely modelled; and finally, the whole reveals a preoccupation with the effects of chiaroscuro, of a subdued play of light and shadow which precludes any lingering vestiges of harshness and angularity.

The marble virtually comes alive in that account, so that the comparison graces the living singer. The poem then turns back to the medallion, and remarks the elegance of the hair:

> Honey-red, closing the face-oval,
> A basket-work of braids which seem as if they were
> Spun in King Minos' hall
> From metal, or intractable amber . . .

The effect of that is rather inhuman, or at least of the human having been transposed into some artifice. But then at the close there is colour in the eyes, 'as, / Beneath half-watt rays, / The eyes turn topaz'. The half-watt lamp, invented in 1913, gave a strong light which was good for colour discrimination because it had more yellow in it than the then usual bleachingly white electric light—it was a more 'natural' artificial light. Under that light the eyes in the medallion appear to come alive—to E.P.

It is a complex irony. Eyes have been a major motif throughout the poem. The war meant 'Quick eyes gone under earth's lid'. In 'Yeux Glauques' the eyes of the woman used by the Pre-Raphaelites as a model and mistress are said to be 'preserved' in Burne-Jones's 'King Cophetua and the Beggar Maid': her 'vacant gaze' there is related to the indifferent treatment and neglect she has endured. Mauberley did not particularly remark the singer's eyes in his 'Envoi'; and young E.P. missed the 'botticellian sprays implied' in the eyes he had looked into. Only now, when examining the medallion under a special light, do the eyes appear alive to him, as if to bring home, definitively and mockingly, the vital revelation that has been missed in the world of *Hugh Selwyn Mauberley*.

In the 1926 definitive collection of his poems apart from the *Cantos* Pound added a note on the separate title-page for *Mauberley*, declaring it 'distinctly a farewell to London'. He also placed it, out of chronological sequence, before *Homage to Sextus Propertius (1917)*, which made the latter the final work in the collection. That was quite right since there is far more substance and resonance in the Rome of the *Propertius* than in the London of *Mauberley*; the *Propertius*, moreover, leads on to the *Cantos*, the 'poem containing history', whereas *Mauberley* is the real culmination and the end of his work in shorter lyric and satiric poems.

The 'London' comprehended in *Hugh Selwyn Mauberley* is primarily what London had meant to the idealizing young poet Pound had been in

America and in his first years there. It was for him then the metropolis of poetry and the only place in which to master his craft and to make his name—an 'aesthetic' London compounded of the religion of Beauty and the Celtic Twilight and brought into some sort of focus by Yeats. This was the London he was bidding a final farewell to in *Mauberley*, along with the young poetic self it had nurtured. He had been detaching himself from it of course throughout most of his time there, as he developed his art and extended his connections through *Ripostes* and *Imagisme*, Vorticism and *Lustra*; and in this, an intensified and accelerated *Lustra*, he was doing his Oedipal turn and killing it off.

The lethal instrument was brilliantly polished satire which at once created its object and revealed it as void of creative energy. But what does Mauberley, even with his aesthetic background and his modern contacts, actually represent? 'The Mauberley is thin', Pound admitted to Hardy early in 1921, and certainly it is thin as a representation of even the cultural life of London in 1919 and 1920. It doesn't touch on the circles Pound was then moving in, that of the *New Age* for one, and the Lewis–Joyce–Eliot nexus for another. Again, Hardy published *Moments of Vision* in 1919; Yeats's *The Wild Swans at Coole* came out that year, and *Michael Robartes and the Dancer* in 1920; and Lawrence's *Women in Love* also appeared in 1920. Whatever of the Nineties still lingered on was minor and marginal. If he meant to target the Georgians, the aim was hardly accurate, since one is reminded only of Rupert Brooke towards the end, and then only on account of an association set up by 'Our Contemporaries' in *Lustra*. The War Poets, Owen and Sassoon and others, were being published in those years, and their criticism of the war is synthesized in Mauberley's best work. But otherwise his London is too limited to bring out its driving forces and dominant ethos. It is very far from being the dark beating heart of the British Empire.

In the end Mauberley remains the type of poet who begins in the decadence of romantic idealism and does not grow up to take on the empire of money. He is the anti-type of the poet Pound had always meant to be, even in his time of youthful idealism, and which he was at last becoming.

A pair of old shoes

Mauberley 'was done in Dec. and Jan.' In those months Pound was also drafting cantos. 'Have done 5=6=7', he informed his father in mid-December 1919, an 'episode' which would appear in the *Dial* the following August. He now had enough material to make up a volume for publication in New York, to be called *Poems 1918–21: including Three Portraits and Four Cantos*. This, he told Quinn, 'contains the Imperium Romanum (Propertius) / The Middle Ages (Provence) / Mauberley (today) / and cantos IV–VII'—

It is all I have done since 1916, and my most important book, I at any rate think canto VII the best thing I have done;

If America won't have it, then Tant Pisssss as the French say. I have my answer, and it means twenty more years of Europe, perhaps permanent stay here. / Thayer tells me the A. Lowell poems … are what America wants. Patria mia (I hardly conclude).

At any rate the three portraits, falling into a Trois Contes scheme, plus the Cantos, which come out of the middle of me and are not a mask, are what I have to say, and the first formed book of poem[s] I have made.

He had instructed Homer to ask Liveright for a royalty of 15 per cent *and* an advance.

He was also, in December 1919, beginning to draw out the music within the sounds of poems. He was collaborating with Agnes Bedford, a pianist whose performance as a recital accompanist 'Atheling' had approved of, in her arrangements for voice and piano of *Five Troubadour Songs* (1920). Pound found the original melodies for some of the songs, and supplied 'the original Provençal words and English words adapted from Chaucer' for all five. The English words, 'for singers who do not wish to sing the Provençal', were not a translation of the Provençal, but poems by Chaucer—among them 'Hyd, Absolon, thy gilte tresses clere', and 'Your yën two wol slee me sodenly' from 'Merciless Beauté'—these freely adapted to fit the music. A 'Proem' over the names of both Ezra Pound and William Atheling stated that 'In the main, the tempo, accent and duration of the notes are indicated by the words'.

Implicit in that was Pound's desire, as strong as in 1911 when he had worked with Rummel in Paris, for an 'exact concord of *motz el son* (word and tune)', with the words determining the tune, and even somehow giving rise to it. Now, at the end of 1919, he was trying to give external form to the music latent in the words of certain poems. 'Chère Agnes', he wrote, 'serieusement, there are two of the Villon poems for which I think the melody is about made, and could be set rather quickly'. He needed her help to get them down on paper in standard notation. There was also 'The "Frères Humaines" [which] I had never thought of setting until yesterday'. Out of this would grow over the next few years his opera *Le Testament* (also referred to as his *Villon*), which Bedford would take down 'from Ezra's singing and performances on the piano'. That would be his *carte de visite* in Paris in the 20s. In the same letter he wrote, 'There is a Cavalcanti sonnet full of music, and . . . the music is made, absolutely made, by the words'. From that would come, a decade later, his second opera, *Cavalcanti*.

A concern for the 'concord of *motz el son*' informed a good many of 'Atheling's' reviews. In his music column in the *New Age* of 15 April 1920 he noticed six recent concerts, among them recitals by his most admired singers, Raymonde Collignon, who specialized in French folk songs, the Kennedy Frasers who were reviving Hebridean folk music, and Vladimir Rosing the Russian tenor. He was struck on this occasion by the way Miss Collignon became, for so long as she was on the stage, non-human, 'a china image', a 'Ming porcelain'. This recalls what Mauberley would make of his singer, but to the opposite effect. Pound was seeing the singer wholly absorbed in the interpretation of the song, alive for the moment only in her art, and so making the song come alive. Mauberley, however, cares more for the porcelain image than for the living song. Pound didn't often go in for aesthetic appreciation of his singers and their songs, being more interested in matters of technique. He listened and analysed as a fellow-artist or a composer. One of his concerts in that fortnight featured 'the traditional music of Morocco' sung by Madame Thérèse de Lens, and he noted especially 'the "extraordinary" length of the rhythm pattern units, comparable to the mediæval rhyme-scheme of Provençal canzos', and how 'the effect of the subtler repetitions only becomes apparent in the third or fourth strophe, and then culminates in the fifth or sixth, as a sort of horizontal instead of perpendicular chord'. Pound would exploit that effect in his setting of Villon's 'Frères Humaines'.

At the beginning of March 1920 Pound had become a theatre critic once more, while continuing to write music and art criticism in the *New Age*. The editor of the *Athenæum*, Middleton Murry, prompted in all probability by Eliot, had taken him on at £10 a month to review two or three West End shows each week. Pound, disguised this time as 'T.J.V.', could not repress his 'general dislike of the modern English theatre', and when he was not savage he would be sarcastic. Of one unfortunate play, *Mumsée* by Edward Knoblock, he wrote, 'It is doubtful . . . if even the hardened theatre-goer knows quite how much of the nondescript spate of tears and sentimentality is to be thrust upon him at a sitting'—

The language is one's chief diversion: 'Over there under those Southern skies . . the stars . . seemed closer than ever.' Alas! the critic, innocent of shorthand, has lost this and many another pearl of precious speech. 'He took me out to that cursed Casino.' Immortal words like these, mighty lines that Marlowe never penned, a splendour of imagery such as is known only to the faithful readers of 'Sexton Blake' and 'Forget-me-not'....

In another review he wondered what Gogol's *The Government Inspector* 'would be like if acted as a scathing realist satire'; and then, thinking on the leading lady, he added, 'not of course that it would be possible for Mary Grey to act anything'. A fortnight later the *Athenæum* expressed its regret for anything in that review 'which might be construed as imputing to Miss Mary Grey want of ability in her profession.' Pound could not subdue himself to the ethos of theatre reviewing, in which, as *Mauberley's* 'Mr Nixon' would have told him, such bare-knuckle frankness is not the best way to get on. He was not fired exactly, but when he returned after a three months absence abroad Murry coolly let him know that the temporary replacement for 'T.J.V.' would be staying on as the *Athenæum's* theatre critic.

While he was having some mordant fun as a theatre critic Pound was engaged in the serious business of becoming a salaried foreign agent for the *Dial*. In 1919 the *Dial*, then a failing 'fortnightly review of literature of increasingly radical social and political thought', had been bought by Scofield Thayer and James Sibley Watson, two wealthy young Harvard alumni, who intended to transform it into 'a cosmopolitan monthly magazine of literature and the arts'. Thayer and Pound had met in 1915—it was in Thayer's rooms at Oxford that Eliot had been introduced to Vivienne Haigh-Wood—and had discussed Pound's ideas for such a magazine. Now Thayer was rather guardedly sounding out Pound about a possible collaboration.

He wanted him to know that he was one of a number of writers—along with Eliot, Joyce, Lewis, Lawrence, Beerbohm...and Mrs Meynell— whose work they would always be most willing to consider; and he mentioned that Yeats and Quinn had suggested that Pound 'might not be bored at being asked to give us a hand'—'More exactly, would you be willing to give some of your time to picking up good things and sending them over here?' Quinn had suggested 'a monthly payment at the rate of $750 per year'—would that be 'all right'? Thayer made it very clear that Pound was to be an 'agent' merely, and that all editorial and policy decisions would rest with the editors in New York. There was no way he was going to let the *Dial* go the way of the *Little Review*. It would be hospitable to authors such as the nonchalant Beerbohm and delightful Mrs Meynell whom Pound would want kept out. 'As to C. H. Douglas, we should be interested in anything not too political, i.e. revolutionary.' And as to Pound's own work, while agreeing to print the 'Fourth Canto' Thayer initially rejected Cantos 5=6=7 as too 'unconventional'. Moreover, Pound must 'remember the Post Office in whose sinister shadow we live and move and have our being'—they could not afford 'honourable martyrization' for publishing such offensive matter as *Ulysses*.

Pound agreed to Thayer's terms, probably with much silent gritting and grinding of his critical teeth. He would 'use [his] best efforts to make the Dial a live periodical', guided by the 'understanding that America is NOT a free country' and 'Thus, that "Ulysses" would be impossible'. He showed willing to act as agent for whomever the editors should desire, only remarking that he did not know what rates Beerbohm and Mrs Meynell commanded. He went so far as to say that he had no quarrel with certain uncreative time-servers who never did a stroke towards the advancement of art and who *invariably* boosted the second-rate and crabbed 'the few men who really create'. He didn't even care whether what he sent in were accepted or not, 'BUT you must realize that it will probably be impossible to get a second mss. from any author worth printing if the first is rejected *save on definite grounds*, i.e. that it would cause suppression, or that it is too technical'. Finally, he agreed to Thayer's stipulation, conveyed to him through Quinn, that his name would not appear in the *Dial* as its agent; indeed the letterheads for the London Agency would print his address but not his name. Thayer could not prevent him from signing his own letters, but he was doing everything short of that to ensure that the *Dial* should not be seen to be associating with that dangerously modern and dubiously American character Ezra Pound.

Unconcerned, Pound poured out a flood of lengthy letters to Thayer, just as he had done when it was *Poetry* or the *Little Review* he was committing himself to, offering advice, throwing in ideas, and at the same time being coolly hard-headed about the practicalities. All he asked for himself was that the 'Arrangement wd. have to be for a year, with three months notice to quit from either side'. He told Joyce, in the course of inviting him to contribute to the *Dial*, that he was 'trying without much hope to mode a new Civitatem Dei, shall have stodge...to contend with'. To T. E. Lawrence he wrote that he was hoping, 'rather rashly, to ginger [it] up to something approaching the frenetic wildness of *The Athenæum*'. Was his irony masking an unwonted spirit of compromise with the American public, or a new realism? That it was 'a convenient way of getting [his] rent' had something to do with his playing at being a tamed tiger; but still he must have thought the *Dial* really could be brought to publish the best international literature and art. When Thayer proposed 'printing anything unconventional—either verse, prose, or pictures—in a department of the magazine devoted entirely to what we shall call "Modern Forms"', and asked for the three cantos to be sent back for inclusion in it, Pound was himself again. He would send back the three cantos, 'if you think they won't wreck the paper'. And, observing that 'The vendetta of imbeciles is endless', he prophesied that

if you and Watson have any trace of intelligence you will in spite of all efforts at moderation, all circumspectious cautions, all heedings of sage council, find yourselves stoned, and ultimately driven into taking sides quite definitely with the few really intelligent authors . . .

In the meantime, 'a segregation of . . . the more active elements' would have the advantage of letting 'both the dead & the breathing sections of yr. readers . . . know which part of the magazine to look at'. Rather than compromising, he was working on the editors as well as with them to see how far they would go.

He told Thayer that on May 1st he would be setting out for 'Paris, Milan, Venice, Trieste (pass ports etc. permitting)', and asked if he should look about for 'continental contributors'. By the end of July he had secured the agreement of a score of mainly French writers to collaborate with the *Dial*, and of a dozen more anglophone writers. Proust, Croce, Unamuno, Valéry, Aragon, Giraudoux, were among the names listed on his Agency letterhead, along with Yeats, Hueffer, Eliot, Joyce, Lewis, May Sinclair, Williams, Mina Loy, and H.D. In September Thayer would be telling him he was sending in too many good things and asking him to sift his scoops before passing them on. Despite all Thayer's efforts to keep him safely caged it was Pound's input in its first years that was the decisive factor in the *Dial*'s becoming the outstanding international magazine its young editors had wanted it to be. But it was Watson who appreciated Pound's making it modern. Thayer never really accepted either Pound or his modernism.

Ezra and Dorothy took the boat train from London to Paris on the 26th of April 1920. The next day Pound called on Natalie Barney, and on the poets Guy Charles Cros and Charles Vildrac, and enlisted the support of all three for the new *Dial*. On the 28th the Pounds went by train to Venice, intending to spend a month there, then go on to visit Joyce who was now back in Trieste. However, 'the Venetian air' was too much for Dorothy, bringing on a 'quasi-complete disintegration' and forcing a retreat to Sirmione on Lake Garda on May 10. From the 'Hotel Eden' there Pound wrote to Joyce inviting him to join them for a week, ' "on me", as my guest, or whatever the phrase is'. He was also urging Eliot to take his holiday there, hoping for though not expecting a first Eliot–Joyce–Pound 'conjunction'.

'The general state of air, lake, olive trees, food here makes me less diffident in inviting you', he told Joyce. When Dorothy, by now 'considerably recovered', had sketched some watercolours he sent Joyce one of 'her endeavours to convey the colour scheme from the end of the peninsula', saying that 'the water *is* quite as blue at times as the bluest part of the paint'. In the same spirit he assured Quinn that 'This lake is one of the really good things on the planet...It does everything...from deep sea lobster black green to lavender and old lace.' He was back in his earthly paradise, and was contemplating it with the discriminating eye of an artist. 'Here at least / nothing is / changed', he had written in a notebook on his second day, after some lines rediscovering Catullus's timeless Sirmio:

> The smell of hay / neath the olives
> & the fauns singing / against the frogs / in the night

He himself had greatly changed though from the young visionary of 'The Flame' whose 'soul...became translucent' and slipped the bonds of earth in the blue of 'Sapphire Benacus'. There had been little or none of that vapouring off into the ineffable in the first of the three trial cantos; and now the realism was unalloyed as he sketched a paradise proved immediately upon the senses:

> mountains as if painted / on silk
> long flow of smoky water
> olive grey in the near / far the smoke grey / of rock slide
> salmon pink wings of fish hawk
> casting grey shadows in water
> Church tower like / one-eyed great goose
> craning out of the olive grove

With some slight revisions those lines, dated '6/6/1920' in the notebook, would appear in May 1922 at the end of the canto that would become canto 2.

Joyce wrote that he would accept Pound's invitation, but on the day he intended to set out a railway accident closed the line between Trieste and Venice, and after that express trains were cancelled because of strikes. Italy was in a turmoil of railway and postal strikes. Joyce then wrote a long letter in which he said: that he had to get away from Trieste and now intended to escape with his family to Ireland—perhaps they should think of meeting in London; that he had no clothes and could not buy any—he was wearing his son's boots (which were too large) and cast-off suit (which was too narrow in the shoulders); that he was being sunk by the worsening exchange rate; that he must finish *Ulysses* in quiet 'even if I sell off the furniture I have here'. 'This is a very poetical epistle', he concluded, 'Do not imagine that it is a subtly worded request for secondhand clothing.'

Pound replied at once, suggesting that he stop off at Sirmio until June 25 and then proceed to Ireland. He could not 'manage a full invitation to the full family', but would gladly contribute 1,000 lire to 'break the back of a fortnights expenses here'. He had found two good rooms with lake view and all meals—details of menu provided—at the Albergo de la Pace which would cost just 56 lire per day for the four of them. Pound himself was living at the rate of 20 lire or a dollar a day. More letters crossed, conveying in one direction Pound's fixed idea that they must meet and in the other Joyce's indecisions and revisions. Then, on June 8, Joyce did arrive at Desenzano, bringing his son Giorgio 'to act as a lightning conductor' because he feared thunderstorms, and was there met by Pound and carried by boat across the lake to Sirmio.

Joyce's first impression of Pound was of 'a large bundle of unpredictable electricity', 'a miracle of ebulliency, gusto, and help'. Pound, for his part, saw through 'the first shell of cantankerous Irishman' to 'the real man ... the sensitive', and thence to 'the genius: the registration of realities on ... the delicate temperament of the early poems'. All his concern was for the genius, and for Joyce's doing the right thing by it. He approved his being 'stubborn enough to know his job & stick to it', that is, his refusing to let anything, such as 'writing stray articles for cash', get in the way of his finishing off *Ulysses*. Pound was just then interrupting his contemplations of the earthly paradise in order to write '96 sheets' of 'premature reminiscences' for the *New Age*, his 'Indiscretions, or Une revue de deux mondes', a highly mannered family memoir in twelve instalments undertaken because Orage wanted copy and he needed cash. They discussed the problems of publishing *Ulysses* and Joyce's personal predicaments, and it was decided that he should try Paris as a place to live and write. After two days Joyce returned to Trieste to prepare for the move, taking with him a suit of Pound's and a pair of his boots, which he later said were too small, and with some of his cash, possibly the 1,000 lire Pound had offered to contribute. As to Pound's poetry, Joyce then and thereafter maintained 'discrete silence re everything save Mauberley, and one discrete sentence re/ that'.

Ezra and Dorothy left Sirmione with Joyce on June 10. A strike started half an hour after they got to Milan, '& many trains stopped where they were at the stroke of 12'. 'I came out of Italy on a tram-car & reckon the next man will come out in a cab'—so Pound wrote from Paris to Thayer and to Quinn, as an indication of the state of public affairs in Italy at that time. 'That was the year of the strikes', he would record in canto 28, 'When we came up toward Chiasso / By the last on the narrow-guage, / Then by tramway from Como'. They evidently had time at Chiasso while waiting to get on through Switzerland for Pound to observe some of the company in the station buffet, particularly 'the lady who loved bullfights / With her eight trunks and her captured hidalgo', and 'the old woman from Kansas, / Solid Kansas', whose 'daughter had married that Swiss / Who kept the buffet', and who 'sat as if waiting for the train for Topeka'.

In Paris the Pounds stayed again at the Hotel Elysée in the rue de Beaune. 'Paris, the paradise of artists irrespective of their merit or demerit', Pound wrote in a letter for the *Dial*, 'Conversation still exists there, and at least one "salon où l'on cause",' and gardens 'within two stones-throw of the river'. The salon was Natalie Barney's, and there in her garden with its elegant round classical temple Pound began his quest for 'literature for export' to the *Dial*.

Within a fortnight he had secured: a selection of pages from Proust's new book; a 'monopoly on trans[lation] of unpub[lished] work' of de Gourmont; translation and journal publication rights for *Belphégor*, a critique of French culture by Julien Benda, 'the best mind here' and 'a fine disinfectant' of decadence; 'an excellent prose sketch' from Valéry, 'Soirée chez M. Teste', which Natalie Barney would translate; a reminiscence of Mallarmé; modern verse in the style of Pound's own *Lustra* from Paul Morand, a young diplomat and a sound guide to what was new in French writing. He made contact with 'the young and very ferocious' *dadaists*, and mentioned Apollinaire, André Breton, and Picabia. He also gave ear, though more for his own satisfaction than as part of his active service for the *Dial*, to old M. l'Abbé Rousselot whose phonoscope 'with its two fine horn-point recording needles', which had proved useful in locating submarines and 'boche cannon', was providing 'the scientific justification of *vers libre*' and 'proofs that a lot of "rules" and "laws" of prosody as taught in the text-books have no sort of relation to spoken reality'.

Possibly his 'richest half hour' was in the painter 'Vlaminck's studio: Vlaminck impassive, presenting the company with the seat of his breeches, enormous, like the gable end of a barn; Cros, as usual, quiet as brook water moving over a smooth-sanded bottom, and Vanderpyl booming and crackling' with his 'dictum that "a painter, thunder of the thunders of god, is a great stupid brute sweating paint"'. Vlaminck also wrote verse, and his simple realism, Pound decided, was worth 'all the rhetoric that has been spouted during the past six years; all the official publications about the "land fit for heroes" and the safe place for democracy.' And his friend the Flemish poet, novelist, and art critic Fritz Vanderpyl was another 'fine human object', 'perched reading on his balcony, his head like a round dreaming cannon-ball atop the stubby structure of his person; "*obèse*" as the foreign legion discovered him to be after months of quandary as to how to feed him to cannon'.

Probably his worst hours were spent chasing the *permis-de-séjour* Americans needed if they were staying more than fifteen days in Paris. He wrote to the Paris edition of the *New York Herald* to warn American travellers that whereas the year before the American consulate would give you a visa and send you round to the Prefecture to have it stamped *without* also giving you the letter the Prefecture required, this year their little game was to tell you that a letter was *not* required, which was true, but only if you could wait eighty days for the Prefecture's stamp. Otherwise, this year as last, after you had sweated for hours in the queue at the Prefecture you would be sent back to the consulate and would then have to queue interminably all over again in the 'verminous, tedious, ill-ventilated' Prefecture. He wanted America and its 'late noble Allies' to have diplomatic words with each other about these 'bureaucratic imbecilities'.

The Joyce family reached Paris on July 7 or 8. Pound had arranged for them to put up at a private hotel in the rue de l'Université not far from his own hotel, and now set himself wholeheartedly and energetically to establish Joyce in Paris. He introduced him to everyone whom he ought to know or who ought to know him, generally with a view to forwarding the writing of the final episodes of *Ulysses* and securing recognition for the writer and his work. Joyce too was interested only in what would serve those ends. Taken to one of Natalie Barney's *soirées* at which Valéry happened to be present, his only contribution to the conversation was to say that he found Racine and Corneille unbearable. Asked on another occasion whom he thought the greatest contemporary writers in English he could think of none apart from himself. Sophisticated Paris and its artists and writers meant nothing to him, except as they might afford practical support of one kind or another.

On July 10 Pound took Joyce to meet his poet friend André Spire, and there Sylvia Beach, who had recently opened her bookshop Shakespeare & Co., went up to him and asked 'Is this the great James Joyce?' The next day he turned up at her bookshop, 'wearing a dark blue serge suit, a black felt hat on the back of his head, and, on his narrow feet, not so very white sneakers' or tennis shoes. He told her of his problems: 'finding a roof to put over the heads of four people; feeding and clothing them; and finishing *Ulysses*'. Thereafter Shakespeare & Co. became his social seat in Paris, and Miss Beach helped him in all sorts of ways, most of all by bringing out *Ulysses* in 1922 when publication was impossible in England and the United States.

By the time he returned to London, just two weeks after Joyce's arrival, Pound had persuaded John Rodker's mother-in-law, Mme Ludmilla Bloch-Savitsky, to translate *A Portrait of the Artist as a Young Man* into French; he had enlisted Jenny Serruys, a literary agent, in the cause of assisting Joyce practically, morally, and financially, and she had undertaken to translate *Exiles* so that it might be staged in Paris; and he had set going a press campaign to make Paris know that a great writer was among them.

Back in London he found a pair of second-hand brown shoes to meet Joyce's need, and asked Eliot, who was taking his holiday in France with Wyndham Lewis and would be meeting Joyce in Paris, to convey the shoes to him. Eliot and Lewis put up as Pound had at the Hotel Elysée, and there about 6.00 p.m. on Sunday the 15th of August 1920 Pound's three 'men of 1914' met for the first time, with their electric impresario, publicist, patron-finder, agent, editor, and universal sponsor represented by a largish brown paper parcel placed, in Lewis's telling, on a tawdry 'Second Empire marble table, standing upon gilt eagles' claws in the centre of the apartment'. This could have been one of the high moments in the story of modernism, but, alas, the only (and therefore oft and uncritically replayed) record is Lewis's burlesque account in *Blasting and Bombardiering*. Lewis sets the scene as a clash of rivalrous egos, sardonically portraying the affected indifference of Joyce and himself to each other's art, and their assuming set poses to impress each other, he the cold-eyed observer of absurdities and Joyce the mechanical stage dandy. Eliot hands over the parcel, and Joyce, 'overcoming the elegant reluctance of a certain undisguised fatigue', enquires, 'Ah! is this the parcel?', and Eliot admits that it is. Comedy of Joyce 'attempting to untie the crafty housewifely knots of the cunning old Ezra'.

At last the strings were cut. A little gingerly Joyce unrolled the slovenly swaddlings of damp British brown paper in which the good-hearted American had packed up what he had put inside. Thereupon, along with some nondescript garments for the trunk—there were no trousers I believe—a fairly presentable pair of *old brown shoes* stood revealed, in the centre of the bourgeois French table.

Joyce, in denial, manifests polite surprise, disdain; the others, keeping their countenances, remaining self-possessed, silently sympathize. How ridiculous of the good-hearted American, born after all in a half-savage country, to have sent a pair of old shoes to Joyce with his polished airs! Possibly Lewis did not know that it might well have been Pound's suit that Joyce was wearing, and Pound's money he would be spending when he insisted on paying for their convivial dinner that evening. But then Lewis himself had drawn heavily on Pound's unstinting generosity. When one thinks how much all three owed to Pound's efforts on behalf of their creative work and their welfare Lewis's comically reductive account becomes just sadly, blankly ungrateful. Had Pound been there in person there would in all probability have been a high-spirited celebration of their powers, plans, possibly a new manifesto or a programme for a new journal, or a scheme to endow the best writers and artists. He would have been trying to organize them into a new vortex—and they would have resisted, each one of them now too individual, too concentrated on the demands of their own creative enterprise, to be drawn into any concerted action. Their time as 'the men of 1914' had passed. Pound's vortex was breaking up.

'... out of the dead land'

Ezra and Dorothy were back in London by 21 July 1920. Pound's 'chief cash reason' for returning then was the £10 a month he thought he was assured of for doing theatre reviews for the *Athenæum*. When he received a letter from Murry on the 28th informing him that someone else now had the job he took the letter round to show Eliot, and was 'very low' about it, as Eliot reported to Lewis. What made it worse was that while he was away the *New Age* had been forced to reduce its format and Orage had decided to kill off 'B. H. Dias'. He told Quinn 'I am apparently destined to live on £200 per year'—that would have been his salary from the *Dial*, which was working out at about £17.50 per month. Probably he would have been earning as much again at that moment, from his 'Island of Paris' letters and other contributions to the *Dial*, from 'Atheling's' fortnightly column in the *New Age*, and from royalties on his books. But then the cost of living in England was going up faster than the exchange value of the dollar—the cost of living was about twice what it had been in 1917—and the loss of the *Athenæum*'s £10 a month and of Dias's guineas left him lamenting to Quinn that his 'grandiose scheme' for leveraging a sum 'to lure T. S. E. out of his bank' was now off.[3] He had wanted to set Eliot free from the bank so that, like Joyce, he could devote his best energies to 'a longer and more serious work'. That suggests that he probably knew no later than the summer of 1920 that Eliot was struggling to write what would become, with his assistance, *The Waste Land*.

---

[3] The idea had been that Pound would put up £50 p.a. and get Quinn and others to make matching contributions. Pound had asked Eliot in June how much he would need to enable him to leave the bank, and Eliot had replied, 'I want £800 a year at least, and must provide for old age' (*TSEL* 385).

Eliot actually considered himself 'very fortunate in having got into the bank and being so highly thought of there'. From his point of view it was rather Pound's situation that needed to be remedied. 'I am worried as to what is to become of him', he had confided to Quinn at the beginning of the year. He had been able to use his 'influence to get Lewis into the *Athenæum*', but 'the majority of the *Athenæum* contributors belong to a small set that dislikes Pound'. In fact 'Pound's lack of tact has done him great harm' in general—

there is now no organ of any importance in which he can express himself, and he is becoming forgotten. It is not enough for him to publish a volume of verse once a year—or no matter how often—for it will simply not be reviewed and will be killed by silence. . . . People like Osbert Sitwell are much more prominent than Pound, simply because they are always reviewed.

In January 1920 Pound himself had declared that he was 'frozen out of everything' in England, except the *New Age*. He told his father that Steed, the enlightened editor of *The Times*, had said 'he would be delighted to have my "collaboration"', and that they had 'agreed that music was the only safe and possible subject I cd. treat without causing riots'; but Steed had not 'guaged the extent of possible oppositions', and nothing came of the idea. Things were even worse in America. He had believed, in January, that 'there is not one editorial office in the U.S. that wdn't be relieved by my demise'.

His trouble was that, as Herbert Read put it, 'He was not made for compromise or cooperation'. Since being taken on by the *Dial* in March he had been doing his best to meet Thayer's wishes, yet he could not help rubbing him up the wrong way given their 'irreparable divergencies of opinion'. When he suggested that the *Dial* should have some declared editorial policy or programme, for example 'that precision of language is a good thing', and 'that art and literature aim at "truth" or "exactitude" . . . *not* at getting an audience', Thayer brushed the idea aside with 'I don't care for programmes anyhow'; and he wrote that he dared not accept a 'corking' story by Philippe Soupault that Pound had sent in, 'because of the delicate stomachs of our compatriots'. Pound as ever wanted 'the few dozen intelligent men' to be seen 'as a besieged garrison making some sort of fight against public imbecility', but Thayer, who did not see the world that way, simply felt more and more besieged by Pound. He would terminate his appointment the following spring.

Eliot had been partly right about Pound's work being killed by getting no reviews. *Quia Pauper Amavi*, *Hugh Selwyn Mauberley*, and *Poems 1918–21* did receive some notice, and one very favourable and perceptive review-article by Pound's good friend May Sinclair in the *English Review* and *North American Review*. Still, they did not receive nearly as much attention as they deserved; and there were the notices intended to kill them off. *Mauberley* was given only a very brief review in the *Times Literary Supplement*, to the effect that 'The poems of this beautifully printed book...are needlessly obscure', and that if the author would only stop trying to mystify his 'small circle of readers' 'his poems would be sweeter and more effective'. Reviewing *Quia Pauper Amavi* in the *Observer* in January Robert Nichols, having found nothing to redeem 'Three Cantos' and the 'Propertius', had concluded that 'In himself Mr Pound is not, never has been and almost, I might hazard, never will be, a poet.' Lewis protested, in a letter to the editor, that the review was 'suffocating and malignant rubbish'—

part of the same blind conservatism, hatred of a living thing, that men of letters, 'true and honest ones', painters and musicians, of this community have to bear with when attempting to break through the hybrid social intellectual ring to something that is a matter purely of the imagination or intelligence, and not mixed with officialdom or social attitudes.

It was a typically robust attack on the common enemy, though unlikely to win anyone over to Pound's cause. In July Lewis would be planning a new magazine of art and literature with Eliot and, rather to Eliot's embarrassment, not mentioning it to Pound.

Some who had been his friends were also hostile to Pound's recent work. John Gould Fletcher, whom Pound had befriended in the early days of *Imagisme* and who had since attached himself to Amy Lowell, wrote a survey of contemporary American poetry in Harold Monro's monthly *Chapbook* in May 1920. While saluting the early poetry up to 1912, and finding the best of it in *Exultations*, Fletcher rejected as 'almost valueless' everything apart from *Cathay* which Pound had done since then. He wondered how 'the hand which wrote' 'Sestina Altaforte', 'Ballad of the Goodly Fere', 'Sestina for Ysolt' and 'Francesca' 'could ever have descended to the trumpery smartness of "Homage to Propertius" or to the dull pedantry of "Three Cantos"'. 'He can only get life out of books', was Fletcher's explanation, 'from the life about him he can obtain nothing.' The best he could say for Pound was that he had been, before losing his way among contemporary things, an inspiring influence on 'a whole host of modern American poets'.

That was just what troubled his old friend William Carlos Williams. 'E. P. is the best enemy United States verse has', he charged in the 'Prologue' to *Kora in Hell: Improvisations* (1920). Williams was hammering out his homemade and very advanced poetics, which had rather more in common with Pound's than he would ever admit. He was after a strictly American poetry that would catch the native truth of things in themselves, and in their relations, as they appeared to a mind free of all received ideas and associations; and he feared the foreign influence of Pound's—and of Eliot's—'parodies of the middle ages, Dante and *langue d'oc*'. Let them pursue their conventional vision of perfection to London if they must, but 'confine them in hell', he thundered, 'for their paretic assumption that there is no alternative to their own groove'. 'My dear old Hugger-scrunch', Pound retorted, 'Un po di justicia!! Or rather: you're a liar'—

You lay back, you let me have the whole stinking sweat of providing the mechanical means for letting through the new movement, i.e. scrap for the mot juste, for honest clear statement in verse.

Then you punk out cursing me for not being in two places at once, and for 'seeing no alternative to my own groove'.

Which is bilge, just sloppy inaccurate bilge. And you can 'take it back' when you get round to doing so. . . .

If choose to write about a decaying empire, will do so, and be damned to you. But can't see that it constitutes enmity to your work or to that of anyone else who writes honestly, whether in U. S. or Nigeria.

In this counterattack Pound hurled at Williams, in vigorous vernacular, details of his warrings in *Poetry,* and generally, to get rid of bad writing in America and 'to make a place for the real thing'. 'I really can't do the whole show', he ended up, 'Can you keep up some push of American stuff'— 'Have written to the Dial that you are the best thing in the country'.

Williams's 'Prologue' brought to the surface what Pound had been thinking about his own situation:

AND now that there is no longer any intellectual *life* in England save what centers in this eight by ten pentagonal room; now that Remy and Henry are gone and Yeats faded, and NO literary publication whatever extant in England, save what 'we' print (Egoist and Ovid Press)

The question remains whether I have to give up every shred of comfort, every scrap of my personal life, and 'gravitate' to a New York which wants me as little now as it did ten and fifteen years ago.

Whether, from the medical point of view it is massochism for me even to stay here, instead of shifting to Paris. . . .

Have I a country at all . . . now that Mouquin is no more . . . ?

'Mouquin' had been a French restaurant in New York before the war, and Pound and Williams both cherished memories of it. The mention of it in that passage provides a nostalgic resolution to the uncertainties—as if civilized food and conversation were his true country.

Pound put the question to John Quinn in September of 1920, 'Has the time come, or is it coming, when I can return to America?' It was with a view to earning his living there by lecturing that he had reopened earlier that year the matter of his uncompleted doctorate at the University of Pennsylvania. Behind his question to Quinn was again the extraordinary conviction that he was, and indeed had been for some time, the sole entrepreneur of intellectual renewal in England—an outrageous delusion, one might think, until one thinks of his part in what has endured from those years.[4] 'What it comes down to', he wrote,

is that I have 'run' what intellectual life there is here, for the past six years, and now that les maitres, les vieux, are gone I dont see the point in ramming art against the dead mentality of England; if one has the activity in one's own hands, one might conceivably get better results from a more alive, if less sophisticated, milieu.

Quinn, as much out of his own prejudices and contempt for the cultural condition of America as out of concern for Pound, warned him off, telling him that it was no place for a poet, that there was too much to irritate and annoy the fine artist that he was. He would find no Lewises, no Eliots, no Joyces or Yeatses, 'no art that would interest . . . No first rate man of letters. No pleasant coterie.' He offered to subsidize Pound so that he could work where he pleased, to which Pound replied, 'I think Eliot is the first man to be taken off the wreckage', since 'After all I am a free man; not incarcerated for the greater part of the day, all day and every day'.

All the same, impatient as ever to be 'building a civilization', he was having to come to terms with the fact that he could not do it in England. Naturally, he blamed England. 'After twelve years residence I at last and tardily begin to feel the full weight and extent of the British insensitivity to, and irritation with, mental agility in any and every form'. There he was reviewing Cocteau's *Poésies 1917–1920* in the *Dial*, and finding in them 'the quality of perceptive intelligence, or of intellectual sensitivity' for lack of which 'the British official poetry of the past fifteen years has been born dead'. Paris generally 'is alive', he wrote in a letter to an American review, is 'conscious that civilization ought to exist, annoyed that it has been interrupted for five years'. But then 'I return to London, and am immersed in the aroma of death. . . . Britain is not annoyed at the suspension of civilization'.

---

[4] D. H. Lawrence, as a novelist, and Virginia Woolf, would be his two major misses.

The symptoms of intellectual death were the 'dead language...still almost ubiquitous in the verse of the "Georgian poets"'; 'an aversion from the precise word, a hatred of investigation, a dislike of exact valuation' among the 'highbrow' journalists; and the fear and suppression of creative energies—as in the hostile reactions to Eliot's *Prufrock* and to *BLAST*, in the censorship of *Lustra* and *Ulysses*—and the suppression of vital ideas such as those of C. H. Douglas. Pound attributed the failure of the Asquith government during the war, and the making a muddle of the Empire after it, to the same 'horror of exact statement' which was the blight of its official, Georgian, poetry. And he saw the British Empire lapsing into the condition of the Austro-Hungarian Empire in 1913, becoming the oppressor *par excellence*, because the British press would not broadcast Douglas's ideas. The corruption of the press was systematic: 'Here the political and financial criminal...aware that anything like honest speech is dangerous to him', puts 'in command of the press' 'bribed knaves and carefully selected boobies (these latter often pleasant and university trained)',

Hence the tendency to want the lyric boy, the simple poet whom they can pity and patronise and who will never inconveniently *see* anything he isn't intended to.

According to Stock it was while he was still in England, in 1920, that Pound drafted his 'hell cantos', in which he expressed a scathing conviction that England was rotting away and that its political, religious, and intellectual classes had defected from and were obstructing the light of honest intelligence.

'Ten years ago', he wrote, 'I should have advised, and did advise, other American writers to come to England for the sake of their work'. Now, however, 'the young American who wants external stimulant for his thought, would do better to turn his attention to Paris—despite the fact that the actual study of his own language can not be continued in that city, and that the study of his own language is of inestimable importance.' As for himself, 'at the present moment there is no *literary* reason for my not leaving the country', and no reason at all for 'being implicated in the débâcle of her intellect and of her literature'.

What had happened to Yeats and Hueffer, and to Lewis and Eliot? 'Mr Yeats has retired to Oxford, Mr Hueffer to Sussex', he noted in the autumn of 1920, 'Mr Eliot wastes his time in a bank; Mr Lewis is painting'. Pound went up to Oxford to visit Yeats, and was pleased that Yeats appeared 'to approve rather vigorously of parts of Mauberley'; but his opinion of Yeats's work was still that it was 'narrative and reminiscent' when not 'enveloped in celto-spiritist fog'. He went down to visit Hueffer and Stella Bowen at their smallholding in Sussex where Hueffer, along with rearing prize pigs and goats was writing, among other things, *Thus to Revisit*, his reminiscences of writers he had known. Pound was getting instalments of that book published in the *Dial*, and a fairly busy correspondence was going on between them, largely to do with complications arising from Pound's attempting to act as agent for both Hueffer and the *Dial* at the same time. They were also carrying on their old vorticist *vs.* impressionist argument. Pound offered to resolve the matter by saying that he backed Hueffer's impressionism, but wanted 'to put a vortex or concentration point inside each bunch of impressionism and thereby give it a sort of intensity, and goatish ability to butt'. There Pound was returning Hueffer's joke in naming his male goat 'Penny', because 'he facially resembled (but was not) POUND, Ezra'. At the same time he was indicating why he did not rate Hueffer's writing as a creative force. He had implied in a review earlier in 1920 that his best work, as in *The Heart of the Country* (1906), was behind him. And the sketch, among Mauberley's contacts, of 'the stylist' retired from the world's contentions to a quiet life in the country, was so near to Hueffer's outward situation as to appear to write him off. Pound could not know that growing in the stylist's mind was the best English novel of the Great War, a work of wide-angled and deep truth-telling that would cut to the heart of the war and culminate in a brilliantly written act of post-war reconstruction based on his life in that Sussex country cottage. In the case of Yeats he could not have known either, but might have guessed if he had been paying closer attention, that his major poems were still to come, and that Yeats was very actively and intensely engaged in creating a foundation myth for a renewed Ireland freed from British rule.

What art was Pound himself creating to ram against 'the dead mentality of England'? His *Mauberley* was more diagnosis and surgery than cure; and so too were his *Propertius* and *Lustra*. For something to bring about a revival one would have to look to the new cantos of the long poem which he was only just getting under way. 'The Fourth Canto' established a method by which the live intelligence could contend for enlightenment in human affairs, and made a start on the epic task of sorting out behaviours which make for a fuller life from those which are deadening. Now in cantos 5–6–7 he was descending deeper into the realities of the historical record in which the light of intelligence prevails only rarely and fitfully, with his quest for that light still the dynamic principle. One might say that that quest is the 'vortex or concentration point inside each bunch of impressionism'.

'The Fifth Canto', as it was titled in 1921, opens with a rather intense passage of densely detailed composition. This was certainly new creation, and a new kind of creation, or at least a speeding up of the method of 'The Fourth Canto'. The whole canto will move rather quickly from lost Ecbatan through ancient Greece and Rome to a medieval troubadour's tale, and then to the Borgias and Medicis of the Italian Renaissance. ('The Sixth Canto' will be concerned with Eleanor of Aquitaine and her time; and the 'Seventh' with contemporary death and decadence.) Time is insisted upon, and that vision, and love, and the cultivation of the earth are time-bound: that the vision of splendour flits and fades, that light and love fade, that vine stocks will lie untended and what is loved be unfruitful. The streets of Ecbatan are patterned upon the stars but filled with an armed crowd 'Rushing on populous business'—as if the timeless ideal were contradicted by the energetic hustle of life. The 'celestial Nile' cuts 'low barren land', but here 'Old men and camels [work] the water-wheels' so that the rain from heaven can make it fertile. The light from heaven, according to Iamblichus, is One and all things derive from it; and Dante's image of 'the souls ascending' heavenwards like a scatter of sparks has them caught up again into that divine light. But to the living eye the pure light breaks into its many colours, 'Topaz...three sorts of blue', or again 'Gold-yellow, saffron'. Things tend to break down from their visionary perfection into the complexities of life as we know it. Thus the troubadour Poicebot is given the land and knighthood and wife that he desires, but 'lust of travel' takes him away into Spain, and on his return 'lust of woman' takes him to a brothel, where he finds his wife, seduced and abandoned in his absence by a knight out of England. So it goes—the troubadour love-ethic has given way to lusts of one kind and another. In the tale of Pierre de Maensac the Trojan war is pettily played out again as a story of possessiveness and adultery. In Italy, in 1497, a Borgia, son of a Pope, is murdered; in 1537 Alessandro Medici is murdered by his cousin Lorenzo— he had been warned in dreams and by an astrologer but lacked the will to save himself. The historian, Varchi, pondering these facts, concluded only that the murderer at least had shown fearsome resolve. And the poets of the time, Barabello, Mozarello, Fracastor and the rest, went on writing the usual elegant nothings. The light of intelligence had pretty well gone out, except in Varchi, and he could not get past the material evidence.

'The Sixth Canto'—in 1921 Pound had yet to find its concentrated final form—goes back in time to twelfth-century Aquitaine, and to Eleanor who both kept up its high courtly culture and brought about its wars. She married the King of France, Louis VII; and when he divorced her married Henry II of England. The canto portrays her in these relations rather than as the powerful epicentre of Aquitaine, so that she is first a cause

405

of scandal, being suspected of adultery with the paynim Saladin during Louis' crusade in the Holy Land, and thereafter a cause of strife about the ownership of lands. The free-spirited noblewoman is treated as if she were owned by her husbands, and valued by them for what she owned. Outside her court material values prevail. But in her own realm she is a force for liberty and generous love. The canto, in its early form, closes with a prayer to her from the troubadour Bernart de Ventadorn. He greets her as a fount of joy on her return to Aquitaine—this was when Louis had sent her back—and tells her of his love for the Lady of Ventadorn, whose husband in a jealous rage has shut her up in his castle's dungeon. For her sake he has removed himself to Poitiers, and now asks Eleanor to vouch for his being there, 'That he may free her, / who sheds such light in air'. So the enlightened love of beauty shines out for a moment against the blind possessiveness which makes for abuse and war.

Pound was quite right to think 'The Seventh Canto' the best thing he had done—a bare outline of its themes can do no justice at all to the boldness and assurance of its composition. The canto begins with a series of examples of the art of the telling word, out of Homer, Ovid, Dante and de Born, and finally Flaubert, the master of that art. Yet the details Flaubert gives are not so much 'luminous details' as notations of a certain bourgeois style and taste. And in the description of what might be a London club done in the manner of Henry James the imagination of the artist is altogether immersed in the hollow materialism of the age. James himself, saluted in Dante's manner as an honoured master encountered among the dead, is recognized by his 'drinking the tone of things', a precisely judicious phrase. The poet then, visiting Margaret Cravens' old apartment, tries to call back her beautiful spirit in Flaubert's fashion, (or James's, or Hueffer's indeed), by heaping up 'factual data', things that give the tone of the woman—'Low ceiling and the Erard and the silver . . . The pannier of the desk, cloth top sunk in'. But these mementos do not satisfy an enduring passion which 'seeks the living'; and recalling how Arnaut Daniel would recreate from memory the image of his absent lady, so that he might see her again—'e quel remir' is the pivotal line at the heart of the canto—he projects in imagination a dancer, 'Nicea', as a warm and moving presence. This 'Passion to breed a form in shimmer of rain-blur', to assert live energies even if only in imagination, is contrasted at length with the spiritless old men in the club, 'Thin husks I had known as men', their 'Words like the locust-shells, moved by no inner being'. Varchi's Lorenzo, is more alive, 'more full of flames and voices'; 'Nicea' is 'a more living shell'. So the dead who by the force of what they were in life live still in the mind have more *virtu* than the living in whom there is no inner being, no force of will. And that inner being, that *virtu*, is what the poet is after.

The old men with their 'dead dry talk, gassed out' can stand well enough for what Pound thought of England's 'dead mentality' in 1920. Against that he was setting his own will to create live forms; and not to submit to the death of England nor to be merely a passive register of it; not to be a Propertius or a Mauberley. He would direct against that loss of energizing will and purpose the force of his own vision born of passionate desire and need; he would re-imagine and re-create his world by realizing both what it actually was and what it had in it to become. He would do whatever a poet of genius could do to refashion the mentality of his world.

He was quite well aware that minds were not easily changed by new ideas and visions. 'One of the most illuminating hours of my life', he recalled in 1937, 'was that spent in conversation with Griffith, the [leader] of Sinn Fein'. That would have been in October 1921, 'the time of the Armistice when the Irish delegates had been invited to London with a guarantee of immunity' for the negotiations over Irish independence. 'We were in his room to avoid the detectives who infested the hotel', and Pound was trying to persuade Griffith to take up Douglas's economic ideas in the new Irish Free State. Then, 'At a certain point Griffith said: "All you say is true. But I can't move 'em with a cold thing like economics".' That remark would stay with Pound for the rest of his life, as a constant reminder that intelligence by itself did not bring about change, that it counted for very little without the will to change. How to 'move'em' became a basic preoccupation in everything he did thereafter, both as a poet and as a prose propagandist.

He might well have reflected on that problem when he and Dorothy, while staying at Lacock Abbey in Wiltshire for a few days in September 1920, climbed 'over attic rafters' into its tower room, and contemplated the copy of Henry III's revision of the Magna Carta made for the County of Wiltshire and 'left there in 1225', now with 'dead flies thick over' it, 'forgotten, oh quite forgotten'. The Magna Carta, roughly equivalent to the American Declaration of Independence, Constitution and Bill of Rights, had become the basis of such rights and liberties as were allowed the individual in England but only after long and bitter battles in the perennial war.

Another thing Ezra and Dorothy did that September was to help Eliot correct the proofs of *The Sacred Wood*, a collection of essays written for the *Egoist*, the *Athenæum* and the *Times Literary Supplement*. Pound regarded

407

it as a very noble and courageous attempt to pierce the Chinese wall of English stupidity, while regretting that it involved Eliot disguising himself as an old-fashioned gentleman-professor. Curse the country, he wrote, where, in order to get into print a few clear dissociations of ideas, it is necessary to wrap them up in the funereal style of the *Times Literary Supplement*.

In October serial publication of *Ulysses* in the *Little Review* was finally terminated. Although four previous issues of the magazine had been banned by the U.S. Post Office on its account the editresses had continued to print further instalments; but now 'Nausikaa', the episode of Bloom and Gertie MacDowell on the beach, had not only been seized by the Post Office but was to be prosecuted by the New York Society for the Prevention of Vice. Quinn agreed to defend the *Little Review*, really in order to keep the way open for the complete work to be published as a book. Pound took a surprisingly detached view of the case. He too thought that what mattered was that the whole work should be published, and that the *Little Review* was showing a lack of common sense in agreeing with Joyce's unreasonable insistence that nothing whatsoever should be toned down or expurgated in the parts they were publishing. The justification for the things that might shock or offend, Pound maintained, was in the whole; and he himself would have made certain changes in the magazine version to safeguard the whole. His belief in the freedom of the press did not extend, he assured Quinn, to 'people of no tact...behav[ing] foolishly'—it 'requires common sense to break a law advantageously'. And then there was Joyce's 'mania for martyrdom...the christian attitude: they want to drive an idea into people by getting crucified'. 'Being the noble victim' was not his idea of how to spread enlightenment.

Pound was hopeful that the *Dial* was coming good as the magazine in which the best that it was *possible* to publish in the United States would now appear. The November number, he told Thayer, was the 'high water mark of magazine publishing in Anglo-American or English language up to present...AT LAST a magazine that I can read!!' That number contained Eliot's 'The Possibility of a Poetic Drama' from *The Sacred Wood*; ten poems by Yeats from *Michael Robartes and the Dancer*, including 'Easter, 1916' and 'The Second Coming'—'Yeats in *form*', Pound remarked to Thayer; 'Three Poems' by H.D.; and from Pound himself an 'Island of Paris' letter, an instalment of his translation of De Gourmont's 'Dust for Sparrows', and his translation of a note on Mallarmé. He was bothered only by an essay on 'Walt Whitman's Love Affairs'—'awful [Keats and] Fanny Brawne sob stuff', the misguided biographer having devoted himself to digging up 'the life' rather than attend to 'the quality of [the] man's work'.

H.D.'s poems—'Phaedra Remembers Crete', 'Phaedra Rebukes Hippolyta' and 'Helios'—prompted a kind of valediction:

touch of real thing, *in spots*. No longer stamina enough to stand criticism ... This not crit. of you for printing the poems—but of my boyhood's friend—génie—et maintenant—malheureusement—femme de lettres / / part conceit—part nervous breakdown / / But damn it all the *real* thing is there *in* the poems / / which is assez scarce. So far as I can see the *quantum* is exactly what it was in 1912—nothing added—nothing learned—no development possible / /

'Suppose we ought to be thankful for what there is', he added as an afterthought, 'A touch in her, in Williams—a touch of something very different in T.S.E., & elsewhere desolation'.

In November 'Aetheling' was enthusiastically commending Roland Hayes, 'the celebrated Negro tenor', who besides having a beautiful voice sang the words so that they could be understood, and in every song 'moves from a main concept' with a 'splendid grip on the rhythm-sweep' of the whole. 'Atheling' also noted that a young violinist, Olga Rudge, 'charmed by the delicate firmness of her fiddling'.

'A fellow alumnus' of Hamilton College looked him up in December, and wrote to a friend that he and Pound and another Hamiltonian had enjoyed a convivial Christmas dinner together.

On December 27 he wrote to his parents: 'We are in action of closing up; have presumably rented the flat; and are in some sort of trajectory toward Orange or Avignon.' They were subletting the flat to Agnes Bedford, and leaving books and papers and the clavichord in her care. Where exactly they were going to was still to be decided—it would be neither Orange nor Avignon; and whether they would be returning or not was unclear. The only certain facts were that they were leaving England for some time; and that packed in Pound's suitcase were the makings of the score of *Le Testament de Villon*, and drafts for the continuation of his 'poem of some length'.

Orage farewelled Pound in his 'Readers and Writers' column in the *New Age* in mid-January 1921, with a judicial summing up of his career in England and a damning prognostication:

Mr. Ezra Pound has recently gone abroad, perhaps for one year, perhaps for two, perhaps for good. Following the old and, in my opinion, the bad example first set by a man of letters, Landor, Mr. Pound has shaken the dust of London from his feet with not too emphatic a gesture of disgust, but, at least, without gratitude to this country. I can perfectly well understand, even if I find it difficult to approve.

Mr. Pound has been an exhilarating influence for culture in England; he has left his mark upon more than one of the arts, upon literature, music, poetry and sculpture; and quite a number of men and movements owe their initiation to his self-sacrificing stimulus; among them being relatively popular successes as well as failures. With all this, however, Mr. Pound, like so many others who have striven for the advancement of intelligence and culture in England, has made more enemies than friends. Much of the Press has been deliberately closed by cabal to him; his books have for some time been ignored or written down; and he himself has been compelled to live on much less than would support a navvy. His fate, as I have said, is not unusual . . . by and large England hates men of culture until they are dead.

'All the same', Orage then wrote, 'it is here or nowhere that the most advanced trenches of the spirit are to be found; and it is here, I believe, that the enemy will have to be defeated.' Pound had gone to France, he remarked severely, and it was to be expected that sooner or later he would find himself in Paris; but from Paris, even with Pound in it, no advance was to be expected. Paris would teach Pound nothing, and learn nothing from him.

It should be explained that Orage was now looking to Ouspensky's school of occult wisdom and its form of 'psycho-analysis' to realize 'the new Europe and the new world'; and it was because Paris had yet to be converted to that religion, and because Pound was as unenthusiastic about worshipping the unconscious as he was about Yeats's occult revelations, that Orage could expect no contribution from either to the progress of mankind. Orage himself, in 1922, would give up the *New Age* and move to France as a disciple of Gurdjieff.

From Paris in May Pound wrote to Ford: 'one seems rather to have emerged from the murk of England a riveder le stelle', *to see the stars at last*, as Dante said as he emerged from his hell.

ABBREVIATIONS

The Principal Writings of Ezra Pound (1885–1972)

Arranged by date of publication, thus providing an outline of Pound's writing career. Place of publication is London unless otherwise indicated. Where editions differ the date of the one referred to in the notes is given in **bold type**.

ALS	*A Lume Spento* (Venice: privately printed, 1908). Included in *A Lume Spento and Other Early Poems* (New York: New Directions, 1965; repr. Faber & Faber, **1965)**. Also in *CEP*
QY	*A Quinzaine for this Yule* (privately printed, 1908; repr. for Elkin Mathews, 1908)
Personae	*Personae of Ezra Pound* (Elkin Mathews, 1909)
Exultations	*Exultations of Ezra Pound* (Elkin Mathews, 1909)
Provença	*Provença* (Boston: Small Maynard, 1910)
SR	*The Spirit of Romance* (London and New York: J. M. Dent & Sons, 1910; new edn., London: Peter Owen, **1952**, New York: New Directions, 1953)
Canzoni	*Canzoni of Ezra Pound* (Elkin Mathews, 1911)
Ripostes	*Ripostes of Ezra Pound* (Stephen Swift, 1912—sheets then taken over by Elkin Mathews; Boston: Small Maynard, 1913)
Imagistes	*Des Imagistes, An Anthology* (New York: Albert and Charles Boni; London: The Poetry Bookshop, 1914)
Cathay	*Cathay* (Elkin Mathews, 1915)
Cathol Ant	*Catholic Anthology: 1914–1915* (Elkin Mathews, 1915)
PM	*Patria Mia* [1912–13] (Chicago: Ralph Fletcher Seymour, 1950; new edn., with 'The Treatise on Harmony' (Peter Owen, **1962**)
GB	*Gaudier-Brzeska: A Memoir* (London and New York: John Lane, 1916; new edn. Hessle: The Marvell Press, **1960** and New York: New Directions, 1961)
Lustra (1916)	*Lustra of Ezra Pound* (privately printed, 1916; abridged edn., Elkin Mathews, **1916**)
Lustra (1917)	*Lustra of Ezra Pound with Earlier Poems* [and 'Three Cantos'] (New York: privately printed, 1917; ordinary edn. [without 'The Temperaments'], Alfred A. Knopf, **1917**)
Noh	*'Noh' or Accomplishment: A Study of the Classical Stage of Japan* by Ernest Fenollosa and Ezra Pound (Macmillan & Co. Ltd, 1916; New York: Alfred A. Knopf, 1917; included in *T* 1953; new edn., New York: New Directions, **1959**)

PD *(1918)*   *Pavannes and Divisions* (New York: Alfred A. Knopf, 1918). [See PD *(1958)*]

QPA   *Quia Pauper Amavi* (The Egoist Ltd., 1919). Includes *Homage to Sextus Propertius*

HSP   *Homage to Sextus Propertius*. Repr. from *QPA*, with some alterations, in *P 1918-21*, *P (1926)*, and in all later editions of the collected shorter poems; published as a book in 1934 by Faber & Faber; published with *HSM* as *Diptych Rome-London* (New York: New Directions, 1958)

Instigations   *Instigations of Ezra Pound together with An Essay on the Chinese Written Character by Ernest Fenollosa* (New York: Boni and Liveright, 1920)

HSM   *Hugh Selwyn Mauberley by E. P.* (The Ovid Press, 1920)

Umbra   *Umbra: The Early Poems of Ezra Pound* (Elkin Mathews, 1920)

P *1918–21*   *Poems 1918–21 Including Three Portraits and Four Cantos* (New York: Boni and Liveright, 1921)

NPL   *The Natural Philosophy of Love* by Remy de Gourmont, Translated with a Postscript by Ezra Pound (New York: Boni and Liveright, 1922; new edn. London: The Casanova Society, **1926**)

Antheil   *Antheil and The Treatise on Harmony* (Paris: Three Mountains Press, 1924; new edn., Chicago: Pascal Covici, 1927)

XVI Cantos   *A Draft of XVI Cantos of Ezra Pound for the Beginning of a Poem of some Length*, with Initials by Henry Strater (Paris: Three Mountains Press, 1925)

P *(1926)*   *Personae: The Collected Poems of Ezra Pound* (New York: Boni and Liveright, 1926)

Ta Hio   *Ta Hio, The Great Learning*, [later version in *Confucius* as 'The Great Digest'], (Seattle: University of Washington Bookstore, 1928; new edn., Stanley Nott, 1936; repr. New York: New Directions, 1939)

Cantos *17–27*   *A Draft of the Cantos 17–27 of Ezra Pound*, with Initials by Gladys Hynes, (John Rodker, 1928)

SP *(1928)*   *Ezra Pound: Selected Poems*, ed. with an introduction by T. S. Eliot (Faber & Gwyer, 1928)

XXX Cantos   *A Draft of XXX Cantos* (Paris: Hours Press, 1930)

Rime   *Guido Cavalcanti Rime* (Genova: Edizione Marsano S.A., 1932)

Profile   *Profile: An Anthology Collected in MCMXXXI*, ed. EP (Milan: Giovanni Scheiwiller, 1932)

Active Anth   *Active Anthology*, ed. EP (Faber & Faber, 1933)

ABCE   *ABC of Economics* (Faber & Faber, 1933)

ABCR   *ABC of Reading* (George Routledge & Sons Ltd., 1934; New Haven: Yale University Press, 1934; new edition, Faber & Faber, **1951**; repr. New Directions, 1951)

MIN	*Make It New: Essays by Ezra Pound* (Faber & Faber, 1934; repr. New Haven: Yale University Press, 1935)
XXXI–XLI	*Eleven New Cantos XXXI–XLI* (New York: Farrar & Rinehart, 1934; Faber & Faber, **1935**)
J/M	*Jefferson and/or Mussolini: L'Idea Statale–Fascism as I have seen it... Volitionist Economics* (Stanley Nott, 1935; New York: Liveright Publishing Corp., 1936)
CWC	*The Chinese Written Character as a Medium for Poetry* (Stanley Nott, 1936; new edition San Francisco: City Lights Books, **1964**)
PE	*Polite Essays* (Faber & Faber, 1937)
XLII–LI	*The Fifth Decad of Cantos* (Faber & Faber, **1937**; New York: Farrar & Rinehart, 1937)
GK	*Guide to Kulchur* (Faber & Faber, 1938; new edn., Norfolk, Conn.: New Directions, 1952; repr. Peter Owen Ltd., **1952)**
LII–LXXI	*Cantos LII–LXXI* (Faber & Faber, **1940**; Norfolk, Conn.: New Directions, 1940)
Pisan	*The Pisan Cantos* (New York: New Directions, 1948; Faber & Faber, **1949)**
L (1950)	*The Letters of Ezra Pound 1907-1941*, ed. D. D. Paige (New York: Harcourt Brace, 1950; reissued as *The Selected Letters of Ezra Pound 1907-1941* by Faber & Faber, 1971)
L (1951)	*The Letters of Ezra Pound 1907-1941*, ed. D. D. Paige (Faber & Faber, **1951**). This differs in both contents and pagination from *L (1950)*, but letters can be identified in either edition by date and recipient.
Elektra	*Elektra. A Play by Ezra Pound and Rudd Fleming* [composed 1949], ed. Richard Reid (Princeton, NJ: Princeton University Press, 1989)
Analects	*Confucian Analects* (New York: Square $ Series, 1951; Peter Owen, **1956**)
Confucius	*Confucius: The Great Digest & Unwobbling Pivot*, trans. E. P. (New York: New Directions, 1951; repr. Peter Owen, 1952)
T	*The Translations of Ezra Pound* (Faber & Faber, 1953; repr. New York: New Directions, 1953; enlarged edn. **1964**)
CA	*The Classic Anthology Defined by Confucius*, trans. E. P. (Cambridge, Mass.: Harvard University Press, 1954; repr. Faber & Faber, 1955)
LE	*Literary Essays of Ezra Pound*, ed. T. S. Eliot (Faber & Faber, 1954; repr. Norfolk, Conn: New Directions, 1954)
Rock-Drill	*Section: Rock Drill, 85–95 de los cantares* (Milano: All'Insegna del Pesce d'Oro, 1955; repr. New York: New Directions, 1956; also Faber & Faber, 1957)
SWT	*Sophokles: Women of Trachis*, A version by Ezra Pound (Neville Spearman, 1956; repr. New York: New Directions, 1957)

PD *(1958)*   *Pavannes and Divagations* (Norfolk, Conn: New Directions, 1958; repr. Peter Owen, 1960)

Thrones   *Thrones: 96–109 de los cantares* (Milano: All'Insegna del Pesce d'Oro, 1959; repr. New York: New Directions, 1959; also Faber & Faber, 1960)

Impact   *Impact: Essays on Ignorance and the Decline of American Civilization*, ed. Noel Stock (Chicago: Henry Regnery Company, 1960)

CC   *Confucius to Cummings: An Anthology of Poetry*, ed. EP & Marcella Spann (New York: New Directions, 1964)

EP/JJ   *Pound/Joyce: The Letters of Ezra Pound to James Joyce, with Pound's Essays on Joyce*, ed. Forrest Read (New York: New Directions, 1967; repr. Faber & Faber, 1967)

CX–CXVII   *Drafts & Fragments of Cantos CX–CXVII* (New York: New Directions, 1969; Faber & Faber, 1970)

Cantos   *The Cantos of Ezra Pound*. References, in the form of canto number/page number (as 20/89), are to the New Directions collected edition of 1970 as reprinted in the Faber 'Revised Collected Edition (Cantos 1–117)' published in **1975**. The two volumes of *A Companion to the Cantos of Ezra Pound* ed. Carroll F. Terrell (Berkeley: University of California Press, 1980, 1984) are keyed to this text. [For later printings of the *Cantos* add, for those which include cantos 72 and 73, 14 to the page number from *Pisan Cantos* on; and to those which include in addition EP's English version of canto 72 add 20.]

S Pr   *Selected Prose 1909–1965*, ed. William Cookson (Faber & Faber, **1973**)

S Pr (US)   *Selected Prose 1909–65*; ed. William Cookson (New York: New Directions, 1973)—omits 'Statues of Gods' and 'Treatise on Harmony', but adds 'Patria Mia'

CEP   *Collected Early Poems of Ezra Pound*, ed. Michael John King (New York: New Directions, 1976; repr. Faber & Faber, 1977)

EP&M   *Ezra Pound and Music: The Complete Criticism*, ed. R. Murray Schafer (New York: New Directions, 1977; repr. Faber & Faber, 1978)

Radio   *'Ezra Pound Speaking': Radio Speeches of World War II*, ed. Leonard W. Doob (Westport, Conn.: Greenwood Press, 1978)

EP&VA   *Ezra Pound and The Visual Arts*, ed. Harriet Zinnes (New York: New Directions, 1980)

EP/Ibb   *Letters to Ibbotson, 1935–1952*, ed. Vittoria I. Mondolfo and Margaret Hurley (Orono, Maine: National Poetry Foundation, 1979)

P/F   *Pound/Ford: The Story of a Literary Friendship*, ed. Brita Lindberg-Seyersted (New York: New Directions, 1982; repr. Faber & Faber, 1982)

Cav   *Pound's Cavalcanti: An edition of the translations, notes and essays* by David Anderson (Princeton, NJ: Princeton University Press, 1983)

EP/JT	*Letters to John Theobald*, ed. Donald Pearce and Herbert Schneidau (Redding Ridge, CT: Black Swan Books, 1984)
I Cantos	*I Cantos*, a cura di Mary de Rachewiltz (Milano: Arnoldo Mondadori Editore, 1985)—Italian translation with corrected English text *en face*, and substantial commentary.
EP/DS	*Ezra Pound and Dorothy Shakespear: Their Letters 1909–1914*, ed. Omar Pound and A. Walton Litz (New York: New Directions, 1984; repr. Faber & Faber, 1985)
EP/WL	*Pound/Lewis: The Letters of Ezra Pound and Wyndham Lewis*, ed. Timothy Materer (New York: New Directions, 1985; repr. Faber and Faber 1985)
EP/LZ	*Pound/Zukofsky: Selected Letters of Ezra Pound and Louis Zukofsky*, ed. Barry Ahearn (New York: New Directions, 1987; repr. Faber and Faber 1987)
EP&J	*Ezra Pound & Japan: Letters & Essays*, ed. Sanehide Kodama (Redding Ridge, CT: Black Swan Books, 1987)
Plays	*Plays Modelled on the Noh (1916)*, ed. Donald C. Gallup (Toledo: The Friends of the University of Toledo Libraries, 1987)
EP/MC	*Ezra Pound and Margaret Cravens: A Tragic Friendship 1910–1912*, ed. Omar Pound and Robert Spoo (Durham, NC: Duke University Press, 1988)
EP/LR	*Pound/The Little Review: The Letters of Ezra Pound to Margaret Anderson*—The Little Review *Correspondence*, ed. Thomas L. Scott, Melvin J. Friedman with the assistance of Jackson R. Bryer (New York: New Directions, 1988)
P (1990)	*Personae: The Shorter Poems of Ezra Pound*, A Revised Edition Prepared by Lea Baechler and A. Walton Litz (New York: New Directions, 1990)
P&P	*Ezra Pound's Poetry and Prose: Contributions to Periodicals*, prefaced and arranged by Lea Baechler, A. Walton Litz and James Longenbach, 10 vols. [Addenda and Index in vol. XI] (New York & London: Garland Publishing Inc., 1991)
EP/JQ	*The Selected Letters of Ezra Pound to John Quinn*, ed. Timothy Materer (Durham, NC: Duke University Press, 1991)
WT	*A Walking Tour in Southern France: Ezra Pound among the Troubadours*, ed. Richard Sieburth (New York: New Directions, 1992)
Cathay/Catai	*Antiche poesie cinesi*, [a trilingual Chinese-English-Italian edition of *Cathay*], a cura di Alessandra C. Lavagnino e Maria Rita Masci (Torino: Giulio Einaudi Editore, 1993)
EP/ACH	*The Letters of Ezra Pound to Alice Corbin Henderson*, ed. Ira B. Nadel (Austin: University of Texas Press, 1993)

EP/JL	*Ezra Pound and James Laughlin: Selected Letters*, ed. David M. Gordon (New York: W. W. Norton, 1994)
EP/Dial	*Pound, Thayer, Watson and **The Dial**: A Story in Letters*, ed. Walter Sutton (Gainesville, FL.: University Press of Florida, 1994)
EP/BC	*Ezra Pound and Senator Bronson Cutting: A Political Corespondence 1930–1935*, ed. E. P. Walkiewicz and Hugh Witemeyer (Albuquerque: University of New Mexico Press, 1995)
EP/WCW	*Pound/Williams: Selected Letters of Ezra Pound and William Carlos Williams*, ed. Hugh Witemeyer (New York: New Directions, 1996)
EP/EEC	*Pound/Cummings: The Correspondence of Ezra Pound and E. E. Cummings*, ed. Barry Ahearn (Ann Arbor: University of Michigan Press, 1996)
EP/GT	*'Dear Uncle George': The Correspondence between Ezra Pound and Congressman [George] Tinkham of Massachusetts*, ed. Philip J. Burns (Orono, Maine: National Poetry Foundation, 1996)
MA	*Machine Art and Other Writings*, ed. Maria Luisa Ardizzone (Durham: Duke University Press, 1996)
EP/ORA	*'I Cease Not to Yowl': Ezra Pound's Letters to Olivia Rossetti Agresti*, ed. Demetres P. Tryphonopoulos and Leon Surette (Urbana: University of Illinois Press, 1998)
EP/DP	*Ezra and Dorothy Pound: Letters in Captivity, 1945–1946*, ed. Omar Pound and Robert Spoo (New York: Oxford University Press, 1999)
EP/WB	*The Correspondence of Ezra Pound and Senator William Borah*, ed. Sarah C. Holmes (Urbana: University of Illinois Press, 2001)
Cant postumi	*Canti postumi*, a cura di Massimo Bacigalupo (Milano: Arnoldo Mondadori, 2002)
P&T	*Ezra Pound: Poems and Translations* [selected by Richard Sieburth] (New York: The Library of America, 2003)
Cavalcanti	*Cavalcanti. A sung dramedy in three acts*, the full score ed. Robert Hughes and Margaret Fisher, in Robert Hughes and Margaret Fisher, *Cavalcanti: A Perspective on the Music of Ezra Pound* (*CPMEP*), (Emeryville, CA: Second Evening Art, 2003)
CVW	*Complete Violin Works of Ezra Pound*, ed. with commentary by Robert Hughes, introduction by Margaret Fisher, (Emeryville, CA: Second Evening Art, 2004)
Moscardino	Enrico Pea, *Moscardino*, translated from the Italian by EP, (New York: Archipelago Books, 2004)

Collis	Margaret Fisher, *The Recovery of Ezra Pound's Third Opera: 'Collis O Heliconii'* [includes performance edition] (Emeryville, CA: Second Evening Art, 2005)

Writings by Others

Abbreviations are used only for books referred to frequently throughout the notes. For all other books and articles full details are given at the first mention, and a recognizable shortened form is used thereafter.

B&B	Wyndham Lewis, *Blasting & Bombardiering* (1937), (Calder & Boyars, **1967**)
Carpenter: 1988	Humphrey Carpenter, *A Serious Character: The Life of Ezra Pound* (Faber & Faber, 1988)
ET	H[ilda] D[oolittle], *End to Torment: A Memoir of Ezra Pound*, ed. Norman Holmes Pearson and Michael King (New York: New Directions, 1979; Manchester: Carcanet New Press, **1980**)
Etruscan Gate	Dorothy Shakespear Pound, *Etruscan Gate: A Notebook with Drawings and Watercolours*, ed. Moelwyn Merchant (Exeter: The Rougemont Press, 1971)
Foster: 1997	R. F. Foster, *W. B. Yeats: A Life. I. The Apprentice Mage 1865–1914* (Oxford: Oxford University Press, 1997)
Foster: 2003	R. F. Foster, *W. B. Yeats: A Life. II: The Arch-Poet 1915–1939* (Oxford: Oxford University Press, 2003)
Gallup: 1983	Donald Gallup, *Ezra Pound: A Bibliography* (Charlottesville: University Press of Virginia, 1983)
Homberger: 1972	Eric Homberger, ed., *Ezra Pound: The Critical Heritage* (Routledge and Kegan Paul, 1972)
Hutchins	Patricia Hutchins, *Ezra Pound's Kensington* (Faber & Faber, 1965)
Makin: 1985	*Pound's Cantos* (George Allen & Unwin, 1985)
Nelson	James G. Nelson, *Elkin Mathews* (Madison: University of Wisconsin Press, 1989)
Norman: 1960	Charles Norman, *Ezra Pound* (New York: Macmillan, 1960)
Stock: 1970	Noel Stock, *The Life of Ezra Pound* (Routledge and Kegan Paul, 1970)
Stock: 1976	Noel Stock, *Ezra Pound's Pennsylvania* (Toledo: The Friends of the University of Toledo Libraries, 1976)
Terrell: *Companion*	*A Companion to the Cantos of Ezra Pound*, 2 vols. (Berkeley: University of California Press, 1980, 1984)

TSEL	*The Letters of T. S. Eliot*, vol. I: *1898–1922*, ed. Valerie Eliot (Faber & Faber; New York: Harcourt Brace, 1988)
Wilhelm: 1985	J. J. Wilhelm, *The American Roots of Ezra Pound* (New York: Garland, 1985)
Wilhelm: 1990	J. J. Wilhelm, *Ezra Pound in London and Paris, 1908–1925* (University Park: Pennsylvania State University Press, 1990)

Other Abbreviations

AB	Agnes Bedford
ACH	Alice Corbin Henderson
Beinecke	Yale Collection of American Literature, Beinecke Rare Book and Manuscript Library, Yale University
Dial	*The Dial* (eds. Scofield Thayer, Sibley Watson, Marianne Moore, New York, 1920–29)
DM	Dora Marsden
DP	Dorothy Shakespear Pound [DS up to 1914]
DS	Dorothy Shakespear
Egoist	*The Egoist* (1914–19)
EP	Ezra Loomis [Weston] Pound
FMF	Ford Madox Ford [FMH up to 1919]
FMH	Ford Madox Hueffer
G-B	Henri Gaudier-Brzeska
Hamilton	Ezra Pound Collection, Special Collections, Burke Library, Hamilton College, Clinton NY.
HD	Hilda Doolittle
HHS	Henry Hope Shakespear
HLP	Homer Loomis Pound
HM	Harriet Monroe
IB	Iris Barry
HRC	Ezra Pound Collection, Harry Ransom Humanities Research Center, The University of Texas at Austin
IWP	Isabel Weston Pound
JJ	James Joyce
JQ	John Quinn
Lilly	Ezra Pound Manuscript Collections, The Lilly Library, Indiana University, Bloomington, Indiana
LR	*The Little Review* (1914–29)
MC	Margaret Cravens
MCA	Margaret C. Anderson
NA	*The New Age* (ed. A. R. Orage, 1907–23)
NEW	*New English Weekly*
NF	*The New Freewoman* (1913)
OS	Olivia Shakespear

Pai	*Paideuma.* A Journal Devoted to Ezra Pound Scholarship (1972–2002)
Poetry	*Poetry: A Magazine of Verse* (Chicago, 1912–36)
TSE	Thomas Stearns Eliot
UPenn	Manuscript Collections, Rare Book & Manuscript Library, University of Pennsylvania
VBJ	Viola Baxter Jordan
WBY	W. B. Yeats
WCW	William Carlos Williams
WL	Wyndham Lewis
WR	Walter Rummel

NOTES

1. BORN IN THE USA

For most of the information in this chapter I am indebted to the researches of Carl Gatter and J. J. Wilhelm. The Carl W. Gatter collection of materials relating to the Pounds and Wyncote is held in the Department of Special Collections of the Rare Book & Manuscript Library of the University of Pennsylvania, Philadelphia (UPenn Ms. Coll. 182). Noel Stock's *Ezra Pound's Pennsylvania* (Toledo: The Friends of the University of Toledo Libraries, 1976) is 'compiled for the most part from Mr Carl Gatter's researches into original sources and documents'. J. J. Wilhelm's more wide-ranging researches were first published (in part) in *Paideuma: A Journal devoted to Pound studies* [12.1 (1983) 55–87; 12.2-3 (1983) 305–47]; then in *The American Roots of Ezra Pound* (New York: Garland, 1985), with corrigenda and addenda in *Pai* 17.2-3 (1988) 239–44. Pound's own pseudo-Jamesian account of his background and early years was published as *Indiscretions* in 1920, reprinted in *Pavannes and Divagations* (1958). Another important source is Jerome Kavka, MD, 'Ezra Pound's Personal History: A Transcript, 1946', in *Pai* 20.1-2 (1991) 143–85—a record of what Pound said to Kavka in St Elizabeth's in Washington, DC. For detailed accounts of grandfather Thaddeus C. Pound's career see Mary de Rachewiltz, 'T.C.P.'s Heritage', *Helix* [Melbourne] nos.13 & 14 (1983) 1–9; and Wendy Stallard Flory, *The American Ezra Pound* (New Haven: Yale University Press, 1989), pp. 16–22. Pound's father's memories of his early years were published as *Small Boy: The Wisconsin Childhood of Homer L. Pound*, ed. Alec Marsh (Hailey, Idaho: Ezra Pound Association, 2003). For related passages in *Cantos*: re. Grandfather Thaddeus, see cantos 22 and 28; re. Westons, see cantos 62, 74, 80; for a glimpse of life in Fernbrook Avenue, see canto 81; re. Aunt Frank's grand tour, see cantos 74 and 84.

3 'And in his extreme old age': EP, 'The Revolt of Intelligence: VIII', *NA* XXVI.18 (4 Mar. 1920) 287.
5 'artists, writers': Wilhelm: 1985, 37.
  Much later Ezra recorded: in 'Indiscretions', *PD (1958)* 42.
  She wrote verse and prose to him: Kavka, 147. Cf. also 'Ezra Pound: An Interview', *Paris Review* 28 (1962) 31.
  She wanted him to write: Kavka, 147.
6 'respect for tradition': Kavka, 148.
  estate agent's description: cutting of advertisement dated 23 June 1927 in Pound (Homer) folder, Box 13, Pound MSS II, Lilly.
  His mother has dressed him: Cf. 'My damned mother made me wear my hair in curls—the attempt to make me the object of beauty and the masculine protest' (Kavka, 151).
  being called 'professor': Kavka, 152.
  Mrs P. T. Barnum: [EP] letter to Dallam Simpson [n.d., c.1948–50] (HRC).
  a limerick: printed in Carpenter: 1988, p. 36. Since EP told Carl Gatter in a letter in 1959, 'Believe the Times Chron/has butt one POEM, the earliest and POLITICAL'— see Carl Gatter, 'Ezra Pound in Wyncote', unpublished ts., p. 13 (UPenn Ms. Coll. 182)—the discovery of this limerick confirms the suspicions of Stock, Wilhelm et al. that the unsigned 'Ezra on the Strike', which appeared in the *Times-Chronicle* Nov. 8 1902, was not by EP.
7 unusual harmony: Kavka, 148.

'Homer explained': from Gatter, Stock: 1976, 13.

'a nationwide group': Wilhelm's words, Wilhelm: 1985, 74.

planted a row of fruit trees: from Gatter, Stock: 1976, 7.

8 'high society': from Gatter, Stock: 1976, 8.

She did flower painting: Kavka, 147.

It was Isabel's habit: Carl Gatter, 'Ezra Pound in Wyncote', unpublished ts., p. 9 (UPenn Ms. Coll. 182).

photograph in the Academy Catalogue: reproduction in Stock: 1976, 25.

forming fours: cf. 'Take a boy of Quaker stock, put him into a military school at the age of 12 and keep him there till he gets into a university, and if he later turns out to be a writer, musician, etc., it seems unlikely that he will have been enamoured of forming fours. At any rate the present writer was not. It is hardly possible to over-emphasise the degree in which I was not' (EP, 'The State Should Move like a Dance', *British Union Quarterly* II.4 (Oct. / Dec. 1938) 44.

'it was old Spencer': *Cantos* 80 / 52.

'worth more than grammar': *GK* 145.

9 a Pear's Soap advertisement: in an unpublished review [*c*.1908?] of a reissue of *Eighteen Hundred and Eleven* by Anna Laetitia Barbauld, EP satirically observed that 'the art of the Pears Soap Annual might seem to be the very eidolon of the national aspiration pictorially!' (ms., UPenn Ms. Coll. 182).

Aunt Frank's regular habits: 'Indiscretions' in *PD (1958)* 9.

A house in Washington: Kavka, 148.

a list of dates and places: in Poetry notebook 1 (Beinecke). Further details in Wilhelm: 1988, 240.

10 visit to His Majesty's Mint: 'Indiscretions' in *PD (1958)* 45–6.

'wide and white-bodiced': 'Indiscretions' in *PD (1958)* 6.

'The new proprietors' and 'Just no more Italians': Stock: 1976, 11; alsoWilhelm: 1985, 73—see pp. 73–6 for his discussion of this matter.

They let their home: from Gatter, Stock: 1976, 31 and 33.

the *Times-Chronicle* reported: Wilhelm: 1985, 74.

a full printed page: copy in Carl Gatter collection (UPenn Ms. Coll. 182).

11 'Dear Ma': EP to IWP, 1 Oct. 1895: (Beinecke).

12 verse thank-you letter: in EP to HLP, 6 Sept. [1898] (Beinecke).

academy's catalogue: copy in Carl Gatter collection (UPenn Ms. Coll. 182).

'well-taught his Latin': *LE* 249.

13 'boring': Kavka, 148.

He already knew: 'How I Began', *T.P.'s Weekly*, London, XXI.552 (6 June 1913) 707. Cf. also *EP/ACH* 4; 'Date Line' (1934), *LE* 77–8; and 'An Autobiographical Outline' and 'An Interview', *Paris Review* 28 (1962) [18] and 32.

'I want to write': quoted by Emily Mitchell Wallace, 'Penn's Poet Friends', *The Pennsylvania Gazette*, Feb. 1973, p. 33.

2. IN A WORLD OF BOOKS

College of Liberal Arts, University of Pennsylvania: 1901–1903

For access to materials in the Rare Book & Manuscript Library of the University of Pennsylvania I am grateful to Nancy M. Shawcross, Curator of Manuscripts, and to Grant Yoder. The Rare Book & Manuscript Library houses the Ezra Pound Research Collection, 1916–1948 (UPenn Ms. Coll. 183). It also has a copy of Emily Mitchell Wallace's very useful essay, 'Penn's Poet Friends', from *The Pennsylvania Gazette* of Feb. 1973.

14   '**Entered U.P. Penn'**: *EP to LU: nine letters written to Louis Untermeyer by Ezra Pound*, ed. J.A.Robbins (Bloomington: Indiana University Press, 1963), p. 15.
'**In this search**': 'How I Began'.
One of his professors dismissed: Wallace, 'Penn's Poet Friends', p. 33.
a humbug or a genius: Felix Schelling letter to Wharton Barker in 1920 (UPenn Ms. Coll. 183).
not there 'for the unusual man': Wallace, 'Penn's Poet Friends', p. 36.
a 'counter irritant': EP to Warburg, 26 Jan. [1934] (Beinecke).
McDaniel noted: Stock: 1976, 30.

15   **he could still recall**: Wallace, 'Penn's Poet Friends', p. 35.
His grades: details from Wilhelm: 1985, 121–2
'**cantankerous ... curiosity**': EP's own words, letter to Roy F. Nichols, 8 Apr. 1935, printed in *Memorial: Herman Vandenburg Ames* (Philadelphia: University of Pennsylvania Press, 1936), pp. 20–22.
'**across the grain**': EP to Warburg, 26 Jan. [1934] (Beinecke).
only on the strength of his Latin: EP interviews, *Paris Review* 28 (1962) 32; Kavka, 'Ezra Pound's Personal History', *Pai* 20.1–2 (1991) 152.
German ... 'stupid': Peter Demetz, 'Ezra Pound's German Studies', *Germanic Review* XXXI (1956) [279].
his transcript: copy (together with tabular view of course requirements) in Carl Gatter collection (UPenn Ms. Coll. 182).

16   **no-one 'with a view of literature'**: *LE* 15.
a 'coherent interest': *EP to LU* 15.
'**dynamic content**': EP, 'How I Began'.
In a celebrated production: Stock: 1976, 37.
teased by the other students ... 'Lilly' Pound: record of the Arts and Science Class of '05, p. 126, copy in Carl Gatter collection (UPenn Ms. Coll. 182).
oft-related incident: see e.g. Carpenter: 1988, 38.

17   **His descriptions**: the material in this paragraph and the two following is drawn from chapters 11 and 12 of WCW's *Autobiography* (1951) (New York: New Directions,1967); WCW, *I Wanted to Write a Poem* (Jonathan Cape, 1967), pp. 17–20, 24; *Interviews with WCW* ed. Linda Wagner (New York: New Directions, 1976) pp. 15, 81; 'Ezra Pound: His Exile as Another Poet Sees It', *New York Evening Post Literary Review* VII.1 (19 Feb. 1927), as in Homberger: 1972, pp. 224–5; *Selected Letters of WCW* ed. John C. Thirlwall (New York: McDowell, Obolensky, 1957), p. 6.
opera written down: 'I took the whole Villon work down from Ezra's singing and performances on the piano'—Agnes Bedford to Dorothy Pound, 19 Nov. 1967, as cited in Robert Hughes and Margaret Fisher, *Cavalcanti: A Perspective on the Music of Ezra Pound* (Emeryville, CA: Second Evening Art, 2003), p. 20. On the matter of Pound's ear see 'Appendix: "Tone Deaf"', ibid., pp. 183–6.

Hamilton College, Class of '05

For access to materials at Hamilton College I am gratefully indebted to Ralph Stenstrom, former Librarian, and Frank K. Lorenz, former Curator of Special Collections. In the Ezra Pound Collection of the Daniel Burke Library are copies of Pound's academic transcript; of the College *Registers* of 1903 and 1904 which give details of the Faculty, courses and course requirements; Frank K. Lorenz's informative essays, *Ezra Pound at Hamilton College: A Summing Up: 1905–1969* (n.d.)—a closely printed pamphlet— and 'Hamilton and the Poet: Centennial Observations' in *Hamilton* (Fall/Winter 1985)

12–16; also Junius D. Meeker's eight-page, closely-typed letter of Feb. 9 1972 to Walter Pilkington, the then Librarian, giving his recollections of Pound when they were 'on the Hill together'. Pound's letters to his parents are with the Beinecke Library's Ezra Pound Papers.

18   'about 54 miles': EP to HLP, 11 June [1903] (Beinecke).
    Clinton: details from *Encyclopaedia Britannica* (11th edn., New York, 1910), vol. 6, p. 530.
19   the College sternly disbelieved: *Hamilton College Register 1904*, p. 22.
    'the slough of philology': *SR* 7.
20   'did *not* want to be bothered': Lorenz: 1985, 15.
21   a product and a record: see, for one instance, John Leigh, 'Shepard, Pound, and Bertran de Born', *Pai* 14.2–3 (1985) 332–9.
    Pound's mature judgement: 'A Visiting Card', *S Pr* 289.
    'modes of expression': *LE* 101–2.
    stories told of the troubadours: EP's copy of Ida Farnell, *The Lives of the Troubadours* (David Nutt, 1896), is inscribed 'E. W. Pound / May '05'. Now in HRC.
22   by the end of June 1904: as indicated in his copy of Dante's *Opere*, now in HRC.
    some markings in Pound's copy: these are in the three volumes of the Temple Classics edition of the *Divine Comedy* which EP acquired in 'March 1904'. Now in HRC.
    worked into the *Cantos*: see cantos 6, 29, and 36.
23   finishing [*Sordello*] in November: EP to IWP [4 Nov. 1904] (Beinecke).
    In 1938 he would mock: *GK* 222–3.See also *SR* 140–1, and cp. *Phaedrus* 247c and 249c.
    'still mostly college boy': EP to IWP [?3 Mar. 1905] (Beinecke).
    They would smoke and talk...Ossian: from a letter, 'certainly written by Ibbotson', cited in Wilhelm: 1985, 132.
    'Seafarer': on Pound's version see Michael Alexander, *The Poetic Achievement of Ezra Pound* (Faber & Faber, 1979), pp. 66–79; and Fred C. Robinson, '"The Might of the North": Pound's Anglo-Saxon Studies and "The Seafarer"', *Yale Review* 71.2 (1982) 199–224.
    Beowulf, stayed in his ear: see *ABCR* 54–5.
24   the conception of a long poem: details from 'Ezra Pound: An Interview', *Paris Review* 28 (1962) 23–4; *EP/Ibb.*114; Norman: 1960, 356; Hugh Kenner, *The Pound Era* (Berkeley: University of California Press, 1971), p. 354; Giovanni Giovannini, *Ezra Pound and Dante* (Nijmegen: Dekker & Van de Vegt, 1961), p. 9.
    'man dominated by his passions': from related context in *SR* 129.
    'example of genius in a woman': EP to Sophie Brzeska, cited by Timothy Materer, *Vortex: Pound, Eliot and Lewis* (Ithaca: Cornell University Press, 1979), pp. 72–3.
    was reputed: some details from *Encyclopaedia Britannica* (11th edn.), vol. 23, pp. 665–7.
    fine amor and 'as Propertius put it': *LE* 103—cp. *De Vulgari Eloquentia* I.ix.
    'I beg you not to think': for full letter see A. David Moody, 'Dante as the Young Pound's Virgil', *Agenda* 34, 3–4 (1996/97) 66–68.
25   One room mate remembered: Lorenz, *EP at Hamilton* [n.p.].
    'a fellow here': EP to HLP [20 Sept. 1903] (Beinecke).
    'pleasant memories': EP to IWP [?16 Aug. 1904] (Beinecke).
    'broke out': EP to HLP [20 Nov. 1904] (Beinecke).
    'I don't suppose': EP to IWP [17 Nov. 1904] (Beinecke).
26   a 'prospect': EP to IWP [?28 Jan.–1 Feb. 1905] (Beinecke).
    'rough housing': EP to IWP [?11 Feb. 1905] (Beinecke).

Junius D. Meeker...recalled: in letter to Walter Pilkington, Feb. 9 1972 (Hamilton).

On one of his escapes: information in this paragraph is from (a) EP's letters to his parents; (b) EP letter to William Carlos Williams, Feb. 6 [1907], *EP/WCW* 6; (c) letters of Viola Baxter Jordan to EP in Beinecke Pound Papers—'The Kiss' is with the letters.

'beautiful and sympathetic': WCW, *Autobiography*, p. 96.

'My very dearest first love': VBJ to EP, 6 Oct. 1935 (Beinecke).

27 'Please don't part my name': EP to IWP [?28 Sept. 1904] (Beinecke).

Graduate School of Arts and Sciences: '05-'07

27 He wondered if he might teach: Carpenter: 1988, 58.

his MA courses: letter dated 3 Apr. 1961 from Mrs Adrian V. Rake to J. Albert Robbins drawn from 'the records of the various departments', carbon copy in UPenn Ms. Coll. 183.

remembered Rennert: in *Cantos* 20/89 and 94/652.

28 [Rennert] responding: letter to EP, 8 Dec. 1911 (Beinecke).

made him feel nausea and disgust: EP to Felix E. Schelling, 16 Jan. 1907, *L (1951)* 35.

definite presentation: see, for example, *LE* 7, 31, and 33.

But McDaniel: based on *GK* 215–16.

He sailed from New York: details in this and the following paragraph are from EP's letters to his parents (Beinecke); from EP letter to Viola Baxter, 9 May 1906 (Beinecke), published with notes as a keepsake by Yale University Library, 1985; Stock: 1970, 29; 'Burgos, a Dream City of Old Castile', *Book News Monthly* XXV.2 (Oct. 1906) 91–4.

'ordered the University library': EP to HLP, 5 June [1906] (Beinecke).

Velasquez: see *GK* 110–11.

29 loafing around old bookshops and finding Ghero: from note with 'College Essays' (Beinecke).

Ghero's great collection: see 'Raphaelite Latin', *Book News Monthly* XXV.1 (Sept. 1906) [31]-4, and 'M. Antonius Flaminius and John Keats: a Kinship in Genius', *Book News Monthly* XXVI.5 (Jan. 1908) [445]-7.

a new book on...the troubadours: see 'Interesting French Publications', *Book News Monthly* XXV.1 (Sept. 1906) 54–5.

What he was writing: e.g. a draft of 'From Syria' (see *CEP* 92–3), a transla-tion from the Provençal, is dated 'Madrid. May 1906'; a draft of 'Capilupus Sends Greetings to Grotus' (*CEP* 266), from the Ghero collection, is dated 'Paris '06'.

Details of courses: letter dated 3 Apr. 1961 from Mrs Adrian V. Rake to J. Albert Robbins drawn from 'the records of the various departments', carbon copy in UPenn Ms. Coll. 183; also Wilhelm: 1985, 152.

courses in the English Department: from Wilhelm: 1985, 152.

spat 'with nearly everybody': EP to [Lewis] Burtron Hessler, 2 June 1907 (HRC). [note: HRC lists Hessler as 'Bertram'.]

in 'drill manual' fashion: Emily Mitchell Wallace, 'Penn's Poet Friends', p. 35; and see EP, 'How to Read', *LE* 15.

would never forgive him: EP to Wharton Barker, 26 Aug. 1920 (Beinecke).

he had enjoyed the poetry: Wilhelm: 1985, 154.

Child...'real love of letters': EP to Robert E. Spiller, 28 Apr. 1946 (UPenn Ms. Coll. 183).

Shaw better than Shakespeare: H.D., *ET*, p. 14, and EP to Wharton Barker, 26 Aug. 1920 (Beinecke).

'would be turning the pages': WCW, 'Ezra Pound: His Exile as Another Poet Sees It', as extracted in *Ezra Pound: The Critical Heritage*, ed. Eric Homberger (Routledge and Kegan Paul, 1972), p. 225.

the strange letter: *L (1951)* 35.

30   draft of an essay: with 'College Essays' (Beinecke).

'to waste no more of his time': in ts., 'Are our riming and our essays to be confined', with 'College Notes' (Beinecke).

'a remarkably idle student': Felix Schelling to Hugo Rennert in 1920 (UPenn Ms. Coll. 183).

'resigned': EP to Wharton Barker, 26 Aug. 1920 (Beinecke). In 1930, in an unfinished draft essay, 'How to Write', EP said that he had 'resigned from other literary courses because it seemed to me that the quantity of material one was expected or "told" to read was so infinitely in excess of the quantity one could in the given time possibly read with any thought or real understanding' (*MA* 102).

'a poor thing without backbone': EP to HLP, 1 Feb. 1920 (Beinecke).

Schelling told him: in ts., 'Are our riming and our essays to be confined', with 'College Notes' (Beinecke).

31   Pound's answer: EP to Wharton Barker, 26 Aug. 1920 (Beinecke).

his study of Lope de Vega's: with 'College Notes' (Beinecke); and see *SR* 203–6.

32   comparison of Martial and Ovid: with 'College Essays' (Beinecke). Pound's observation would highlight the passage (46 lines out of 644) in which Ovid's invective is furthest from Martial's.

Metastasio, 'the Golden Age': 'M. Antonius Flaminius and John Keats, a Kinship in Genius', *Book News Monthly* XXVI.6 (Feb. 1908) 447.

'misfit': ibid., p. [445].

In June 1907: paragraph based on EP to [Lewis] Burtron Hessler, 2 June 1907 (HRC); and on verses among 'College Notes' (Beinecke)—lines are from 'to my professors', 'Baa Baaa', 'Corny: a ode', 'The Logical Conclusion', 'Goal'.

seeking academic recognition: details in this paragraph drawn from—EP to Schelling, 17 Nov. 1916, *L* 151–3; EP's letters to Homer Pound, Feb.–May 1920 (Beinecke); letters from Schelling to Rennert and to Wharton Barker in 1920, with Pound—Schelling correspondence (UPenn Ms. Coll. 183); EP to Wharton Barker, 26 Aug. 1920 (Beinecke); EP letters of 25 Nov. 1931 and 21 Jan. 1932, respectively to 'Professor of Romance Languages' and E. B. Williams, Acting Chairman Department of Romanic Languages, University of Pennsylvania, with Williams' replies, 8 Dec., 1931 and 19 Mar. 1932 (UPenn Ms. Coll. 183); Wallace: 1973, 35; Wilhelm: 1985, 154; EP, 'Text Books', *Impact*, p. 264.

33   true defender of live learning: see EP, 'How to Read', *LE* 15–20.

3. FIRST POEMS: 1901–1908

Dryad

For both background and as direct sources see H.D.'s mythobiographical fictions *Paint It Today* (written 1921) and *Her* (written 1927); and her 'memoir of Ezra Pound', *End to Torment* (written 1958; published New York: New Directions, 1979, and Manchester: Carcanet New Press, **1980**). Pound's 'Hilda's Book' is appended to those editions of *ET*, and is included in *P&T*. Factual information from Wilhelm: 1985, and Janice S. Robinson, *H.D.: The Life and Work of an American Poet* (Boston: Houghton Mifflin, 1982). References are not given for poems included in the collected editions of Pound's shorter poems from 1926.

35   'Sestina for Ysolt': in *Exultations* (1909), *CEP* 114.

an unpublished poem ("You lie"): among early verse associated with 'Hilda's Book' (Beinecke).

'She hath some tree-born spirit': 'Rendez-vous' in 'Hilda's Book', *ET* 84.

She had wanted him: *Her* (Virago Press, 1984), pp. 63–70.

identifying with natural phenomona: on this see A. D. Moody, 'H.D. "Imagiste": An Elemental Mind', *Agenda* 25.3–4 (1987 / 8) 77–96.

36   'the perfection of the fiery moment': *ET* 11, and see pp. 3–19 for further details.

'nothing but a nomad': Norman: 1960, p. 5.

37   'the great deep symbol': unpublished ts. review of *The Children's Crusade* among 'College Essays' (Beinecke).

'in its Ariel, or Séraphita stage': *ET* 52.

'The Summons': *CEP* 261–3.

an unfinished draft ('The Beatrice face'), and 'Jan. 1908 . . . draft': respectively 'Orbi Cantum Primum' (typescript), and 'It befell that wearied with much study' (manuscript), in Beinecke; both printed in A. David Moody, 'Dante as the Young Pound's Virgil . . . Some Early Drafts & Fragments', *Agenda* 34.3–4 (1997) 65–88.

38   'her authentic intellectual progenitor' etc.: see *Her* 63–70 (chap. VII).

'"Deh! nuvoletta"': see Pound's translation of Dante's Ballata II in *Canzoni* (*CEP* 151).

39   'a hectic, adolescent': *Paint It Today* (New York: New York University Press, 1992), p. 7.

Katherine Ruth Heyman

Factual information concerning KRH drawn from Faubion Bowers, 'Memoir within Memoirs', *Pai* 2.1 (1973) [53]-66; Wilhelm: 1985: 133–5, and *Pai* 17.2–3 (1988) 242, 243.

39   some of Pound's critics: notably Demetres C. Tryphonopoulos—see his *The Celestial Tradition* (Waterloo: Wilfred Laurier University Press, 1992), pp. 60–5.

Hilda, jealously sensing: *Her* 109.

'the lady dwelling': 'Scriptor Ignotus' (*CEP* 25–6).

'To Baltasare Levy: Zionist': ts. in Mary Moore [Cross] Letters from Ezra Pound, Box 2, fo. 81 (UPenn Ms. Coll. 181).

That summer he was hearing her: EP to IWP [Sept. 1904] (Beinecke).

he took Hilda with him: *Her* 133–9.

40   'Blake's Rainbow': original ts. in Beinecke, reproduced in part in *Agenda* 34.3–4 (1997) 68–71.

'conversing with Paradise': William Blake, 'A Vision of the Last Judgment', *The Complete Writings of William Blake*, ed. Geoffrey Keynes (Oxford: Oxford University Press, 1966) p. 609.

'another draft': 'Orbi Cantum Primum', as in *Agenda* 34.3–4 (1997) 77.

'The Meeting of the Winds': ts. among 'College Notes' (Beinecke).

'comes a wonder woman': from ts., 'Body only when surrendered to law', among 'College Essays' (Beinecke).

an early notebook: Poetry Notebook 2, fos. 180, 178, 177, 176 (Beinecke).

41   to 'keep till we are both very old': EP to Mary Moore [? Oct. 1907], numbered 27 (UPenn Ms. Coll. 181).

'1904 Pound': Bowers, 'Memoir', *Pai* 2.1 (1973) 66.

he would refer to K.R.H.: e.g. in letters to Mary Moore [24 Dec. 1908] and [Mar. 1909] (UPenn Ms. Coll. 181); letter to Viola Baxter from London [early 1909] (Beinecke).

Aesthetics

41   a letter ... to Viola Baxter: published in 'Letters to Viola Baxter Jordan', ed. Donald Gallup, *Pai* 1.1 (1972) 109.

The love of beauty: my paraphrase from ts., 'Body only when surrendered to law', among 'College Essays' (Beinecke).

The passionate experience of music: EP to Viola Baxter, 24 Sept. 1907 (Beinecke).

seeing 'the dawn's reflexion': from draft essay in 'San Trovaso Notebook', as published in *CEP* 322. See also 'Aube of the West Dawn. Venetian June', *CEP* 63, and dedication of *QY*, 'To The Aube of the West Dawn'.

42   Dionysus and Eleusis: from ts. note, 'The Cosmic sense', among 'College Essays' (Beinecke).

essay dated July 31 '07: 'Are our riming and our essays to be confined', ts., among 'College Essays' (Beinecke).

'One read Fiona Macleod': 'Lionel Johnson' (1915), *LE* 367.

'celebrated aesthetic publisher': EP, 'The Death of Vorticism', *LR* V.10 / 11 (1919) 45.

Mosher rejected: Mosher to EP, 6 Aug. 1905 (Beinecke).

'the reveries of the imagining mind': Fiona Macleod, 'Foam of the Past', *Poems and Dramas* (William Heinemann, 1911), pp. 99, 104.

'a visionary passion': from the epigraph (source not given) prefixed by the editor and publisher, Thomas B. Mosher, to 'A Little Garland of Celtic Verse', *The Bibelot* VI.8 (Aug. 1900) [260].

'I give you [in my verse]': EP to Viola Baxter [Oct. 24 1907], as in Gallup, *Pai* 1.1 (1972) 109.

43   Ernest Rhys wrote: 'The New Mysticism', *The Bibelot* VIII.11 (Nov. 1902) 373-[403]—both 'mythopoeic' (373) and 'one with ... moves' (398) are quoted from Fiona Macleod.

Others saw the aesthetic movement: e.g. F. W. Myers, 'Rossetti and the Religion of Beauty', *The Bibelot* VIII.10 (Oct. 1902) 339-[67]; and see the extract from Arthur Symons's *The Symbolist Movement in Literature* (1899) prefixed to 'Lyrics from "The Hills of Dream"' [by Fiona Macleod], *The Bibelot* VI.12 (Dec. 1900): 'in speaking to us so intimately, so solemnly, as only religion had hitherto spoken to us, [literature] becomes itself a kind of religion, with all the duties and responsibilities of the sacred ritual.'

'The idealist': from 'Philadelphia, Apr.' [?1907], a set of loose sheets of notepad paper in pencil manuscript, among 'College Essays' (Beinecke).

'Autumnus': *CEP* 249.

'In Tempore Senectutis': *CEP* 21 and 50.

'When I read Dowson': ts. among 'College Notes' (Beinecke).

44   'Revolt–Against the Crepuscular Spirit in Modern Poetry': *CEP* 96–7.

'Make-strong old dreams': see final poem in *ALS*, (*CEP* 52), and dedication page of *Personae* (*CEP* [77]).

'Grace Before Song': *CEP* 7.

He told Viola Baxter: in letter of [24 Oct. 1907], as in Gallup, *Pai* 1.1 (1972) 109.

'Dawn Song': *CEP* 204.

Thirty years later he still recalled: 'When Will School Books ... ?', *Delphian Quarterly* XX.2 (Apr. 1937) 16.

45   Yet he acknowledged: ts. 'Note on Literature', fo. '4' of review of Marcel Schwob's *Children's Crusade*, among 'College Essays' (Beinecke).

False starts

45 **at least three attempts**: the three earliest drafts towards his epic as discussed in this section were published in Moody, '... Some Early Drafts and Fragments', *Agenda* 34.3–4 (1997) 65–88.

'**gathering ore**': ts. fragment among 'College Notes' (Beinecke). Another ts. among 'College Verse' ('As Michael once being commanded') has the variant, 'Seeking all books for virtue and to melt that same to gold in that great flame himself'.

'**Images in his Imagination**': William Blake, 'A Vision of the Last Judgment', *The Complete Writings of William Blake*, ed. Geoffrey Keynes (1966), p. 609.

46 **Pound appears to have judged**: in ts. 'As Michael once being commanded' among 'College Verse' (Beinecke).

47 '**My own prejudices**': *EP/WCW* 9.

48 **He identified**: in 'Have i not, O Walt Whitman', ts. among 'College Verse' (Beinecke).

that rhyme would hobble: cf. 'As Michael once being commanded' among 'College Verse' (Beinecke): 'As the tinkling mockery of Homunculous Mandrake / So is the tittle-babble of ryme'.

'**Browning's dialect**': EP to Douglas MacPherson, 1 June [1940] (Beinecke).

His marking of the metre: on typescript copy of 'Verbum hominium' sent to Mary Moore, numbered 84 (UPenn Ms. Coll. 181).

'**rules of Spanish**': *EP/WCW* 8.

'**We have had enough of metric**': [fo. 110], Poetry Notebook 2 (Beinecke).

'**Always the spirit within**': from fragment, 'I lay on my back and stretched', numbered 83 in Mary Moore Cross collection (UPenn Ms. Coll. 181).

49 '**Dante and Browning**': [fo. 110], Poetry Notebook 2 (Beinecke).

he would come to see: in 'T. S. Eliot' (1917), *LE* 419–20.

'A Lume Spento'

49 **In 1908**: details re. *A Lume Spento* from Gallup: 1983, 3–4. The whole collection, with reproduction of title-page and dedication, is in *CEP* [1]-52.

50 '**Note Precedent to "La Fraisne"**': when the poem was reprinted in *Personae* (1909) and *Umbra* (1920) the note was detached and placed at the end of each volume; in *P (1926)* it was omitted altogether.

'**the man is half- or whole mad**': *EP/WCW* 10.

51 '**to make a mood**': *SR* 85.

dominated by their passions: cf. *SR* 129.

epic of judgement: from the title of James J. Wilhelm's *Dante and Pound: The Epic of Judgement* (Orono, Maine: University of Maine Press, 1974).

52 **the two imitations of Villon**: 'Villonaud for this Yule' and 'A Villonaud. Ballad of the Gibbet'.

Swinburne's Villon: ten ballads from *Poems and Ballads* 2nd series were printed in *The Bibelot* V.7 (July 1899).

53 **by whom ... possessed**: 'Histrion' (*CEP* 71), first published in *QY* in 1908, gives a pertinent account of this.

Madison Cawein: mentioned by EP, along with Carman and Hovey and Vance Cheney, as American poets he was aware of about 1900, in 'Ezra Pound: An Interview', *Paris Review* 28 (1962) 36.

'**balderdash**': EP's note added in *Lustra (1917)* 171. See also EP to JQ, 4 Oct. 1917: 'Simply, I got hold of a rhythm ... I shall probably never get that rhythm again' (*EP/JQ* 131).

'**stale creampuffs**': 'Foreword (1964)', *ALS* (1965) [7].

in an essay...in **1908**: 'M. Antonius Flaminus and John Keats: A Kinship in Genius', *Book News Monthly* XXVI.6 (Feb. 1908) [445]-447.

4. HELL AND DELIVERANCE

The gadfly

55 The letter about 'art and ecstasy': EP to Viola Baxter [Oct. 24 1907], as in Gallup, *Pai* 1.1 (1972) 109–10.
   in imitation of Whistler's: see H.D., *ET* 23. In the letter to Viola EP wrote, 'you must get "The Ten O'Clock lecture" in Mr Whistler's "Gentle Art of Making enemies".'
   Whistler's witty riposte: much of my account is from Richard Dorment and Margaret F. MacDonald, *James McNeill Whistler* (London: Tate Gallery Publications, 1994), pp. 136–7 and 176–7.
   'being born an American': *PM* 35.
56 **'Who bear the brunt'**: 'To Whistler, American' [*Poetry*, 1912], *P (1990)* 249.
   H.D.'s recording: *ET* 23.
   'political verse-lampoons': *ET* 64 n. 23.

Wabash College, Crawfordsville, Indiana

I am indebted to Wilhelm: 1985 for information concerning Mary Moore and 'The Crawfordsville Incident'; also to Tim Redman, paper delivered at the 17th International Ezra Pound Conference, 15 July 1997. EP's letters to Mary Moore (UPenn Ms. Coll. 181) are the primary resource. For a mixed bag of memories supplied fifty years after the event by persons who had known Pound at Wabash see James E. Rader, 'The Value of Testimony: Pound at Wabash', *Pai* 13.1 (1984) [67]-130.

56 **Crawfordsville and Wabash College**: details from *Encyclopaedia Britannica* (11th edn., New York, 1910), vol. 7, p. 386.
   'physically as fit a youth': Stanley K. Wilson, in a letter to 'The Bear Garden' column of the *New York Sun* in Mar. 1932—from cutting in a scrapbook in the possession of Mary de Rachewiltz.
57 **one especially enchanted night**: EP to 'Mardhu', no. 1 in series (UPenn Ms. Coll. 181).
   Mary had thought: her letter dated 1 June 1970 to Carl Gatter (UPenn Ms. Coll. 182).
   He would have '57 men...': unless otherwise indicated this paragraph and the one following are based on EP's letters to Mary Moore (UPenn Ms. Coll. 181).
   'paralyzed and in a wheelchair': according to John Tytell, *Ezra Pound: The Solitary Volcano* (Bloomsbury, 1987), p. 32.
59 **Pound's several versions**: his letters to Mary Moore, nos. 17 and 37 (UPenn Ms. Coll. 181); letter of 11 Nov. 1907 to Lewis Burtron Hessler, HRC—cited Stock: 1970, p. 41 and Wilhelm: 1985, p. 171; 'having spent the evening'—letter of 27 Mar. 1959 to James Rader, in Rader: 1984, 108; 'I was sacked'—letter of 12 Apr. 1955 to Ingrid Davies (HRC). The letter to Ingrid Davies refers to the second incident which occurred in Jan. or Feb. 1908, but which is often conflated with the first incident. A possible cause of confusion is that Mary S. Young's letter to Mackintosh exonerating Pound for the November incident was actually written in mid-February to help out with the second incident. Both her letter and Mackintosh's note are dated 15 Feb. 1908.

60 relished the Paris address: EP to Hessler, 11 Nov. 1907 (HRC).
'almost felt alive': EP to Mary Moore, no. 37 (UPenn Ms. Coll. 181).
'Ten years of life': 'Three Cantos. II', *QPA* 27.
According to Wilhelm: Wilhelm: 1985, 177.
Pound's 'great solace': *PM* 59.
studied Dante's metre: L. R. Lind in his unpublished ts., 'My Friendship with Ezra Pound: An Epistolary Memoir' (Lilly, Lind MSS).
his 'kin of the spirit': 'In Durance'.
sketched the great epic: Pound's third attempt, 'It befell that wearied with much study', is dated on the MSS 'Jan 19 [1908]'.
the official version: Wilhelm: 1985, pp. 181–2, citing James Osborne and Theodore Gronert, *Wabash College: The First Hundred Years*, pp. 291–2.
another account: Viola Baylis [Wildman] to James Rader, cited Wilhelm: 1985, 176.

61 invited to resign: the crisis may have come in mid-January—*The Wabash*, the College paper, noted Pound's absence from Chapel on each day from Jan. 13 to 19 in a manner to suggest that something was up.
'Have had a bust up': EP to HLP [17 Feb. 1908] (Beinecke).
The following two letters to his father are undated.

5. OUTWARD AND AWAY

62 Did young Ezra's poems: Norman: 1960, 24–5.
Ezra urged Hilda: H.D., *ET* 15–19; Wilhelm: 1985, 185–90.
fiery kisses were renewed: *ET* 54.
burn Ezra's letters: *ET* 38.
By the 23rd: details from EP letters to parents (Beinecke), and to Mary Moore (UPenn Ms. Coll. 181).
In the *Pisan Cantos*: 74 / 432.

63 as he wrote to KRH: letter [possibly a draft not sent?] (Beinecke).
by sea to Genoa: EP to Dorothy Pound from Venice [31 Mar. 1923] (Lilly).
'comfortably fixed': EP postcard to HLP, postmarked 28 [Apr. 1908] (Beinecke).
In Gibraltar he had prayed: 'The Rune', *CEP* 242.
the sun of Venice: 'Alma Sol Veneziae', *CEP* 246, and 'San Vio. June', *CEP* 233.
in its waters and silence: 'Night Litany', *CEP* 60–1.
'Old powers risen': 'San Vio. June', *CEP* 233.
'Lord Gloom': 'Roundel for Arms', *CEP* 234.
dreams to be gathered: 'Purveyors General', *CEP* 61–2.
'For the Triumph of the Arts': *CEP* 244–5.
'Lucifer Caditurus': *CEP* 66.

64 It was cheering to reflect: 'Prelude: Over the OgniSanti', *CEP* 59.
'All art': draft of an essay in San Trovaso Notebook, *CEP* 322.
'Try first on "Outlook"': EP to HLP, 26 May [1908] (Beinecke).
'Whang—Boom': EP to HLP [?July 1908] (Beinecke).
'The American reprint': EP to IWP [June 1908] (Beinecke).

65 rarity value: see Gallup: 1983, 4.
'You needn't worry about "affinities"': EP to HLP [before 27 Aug. 1908] (Beinecke).
a series of articles: EP to IWP, May [1908] (Beinecke).
a small puff: 'The Event of the Coming Piano Season', *New York Herald*, Paris (21 June 1908) 9.
'As to what do I do': EP to HLP, 20 July [1908] (Beinecke).
It becomes clear: details, down to and including 'Of course it was only a question', all from EP letters to his parents, May–July 1908 (Beinecke).

66   **Dr Robertson and Miss Norton**: details from EP to his parents, May 1908 (Beinecke).
chuck the … proofs: *Cantos* 76 / 460.
distribution list: inside back cover of notebook 'At San Trovaso' (Beinecke).
Whiteside: Pound wrote of his 'making American art' and of his colour being 'undeniably right', in a letter to IWP from Venice in May [1908] (Beinecke).
poem for K.R.H.: 'Nel Biancheggiar' [= in the whitening, the fore-dawn], *CEP* 72.

67   **'copies of the first edition'**: EP to HLP, 18 June [1908] (Beinecke).

6. LONDON 1908–1910

A stiff white collar

68   **'EP arrived'**: DP MS note, added to EP ts. fragment to Peter Russell [?1951] (HRC).
worn by Henry James: e.g. the Sargent portrait in the National Portrait Gallery, London.
£3: EP in 'How I Began'.
from a pawnbroker: EP to Hutchins, Hutchins: 1965, 57.
Islington lodging house: EP in 'Through Alien Eyes. II', *NA* XII.12 (23 Jan. 1913) 275.
Mrs Joy's boarding-house: EP to HLP [Sept. 1908] (Beinecke); see also Carpenter: 1988, 100.
lent him ten shillings: EP to Hutchins, Hutchins, 57.
He gave her: according to the distribution list inside back cover of notebook 'At San Trovaso' (Beinecke).
to endorse his application: Hutchins, 49 n.

69   **winter underwear**: EP to HLP from London [Sept. or Oct. 1908], on notepaper with printed heading 'EZRA POUND / 861 Ponte S. Vio—Venice' (Beinecke).
'a Walt Whitman': 'What I Feel About Walt Whitman', an essay dated Feb. 1 1909, not published by EP but incorporated into Herbert Bergman, 'Ezra Pound and Walt Whitman', *American Literature* XXVII.1 (Mar. 1955) [56]-61.
'my lyric personality': EP to HLP, 8 Mar. [1909] (Beinecke).
'to drive Whitman': EP, 'What I Feel About Walt Whitman'.
his English hosts: paragraph based mainly on Ford Madox Hueffer / Ford's memoirs, *Thus to Revisit* (Chapman & Hall, 1921), pp. 166–9, *Return to Yesterday* (New York: Liveright, 1932), pp. 356–7, 373–5, 409; also Douglas Goldring, *South Lodge* (Constable, 1943), pp. 46–9.

70   **'soothing personal effacement'**: Ford Madox Hueffer, *The Soul of London* (Alston Rivers, 1905), pp. 115, 112.
assuring his parents: paragraph based on EP to HLP, 27 Aug. [1908] [?1–3 Sept. 1908], and 9 Jan. [1909] (Beinecke).

71   **sources of income**: EP to HLP, 27 Aug. 1908 (Beinecke).
Smith: Stock: 1976, 75–6, citing EP note for 1968 reprint of *SR*.
'between engagements': Wilhelm: 1990, 9, citing EP to Mary Moore, 24 Dec. 1908.
'Wild and haunting stuff': as in Homberger: 1972, 2.
'seriously considering a reprint': EP to HLP [Sept. 1908] (Beinecke).

72   **a cheque from Dr Mackintosh**: EP to HLP, 27 Aug. [1908] (Beinecke).
'a regular routine diet': ibid.
'solus at Pagani's': EP to HLP [end of Nov. 1908] (Beinecke).
A letter to his mother: EP to IWP [Nov. 1908] (Beinecke).

73   **fifty-five people**: EP to IWP, 19 Jan. [1909] (Beinecke).
course of six lectures: details in this paragraph mainly from Stock: 1970, 58–9.

Dr Penniman's 'drill manual': see p. 29 above.
74 **told Harriet Monroe**: Harriet Monroe, 'Ezra Pound', *Poetry* XXVI (May 1925) 90.
Mathews: details in this paragraph drawn from James G. Nelson, *Elkin Mathews* (Madison: University of Wisconsin Press, 1989), pp. 5–6 and Appendix D.
'celebrated aesthetic publisher': see p. 42 above.
'turned his shelves over': EP to HLP, 11 Feb. [1909] (Beinecke).

'A Quinzaine for This Yule'

A Quinzaine for This Yule was reprinted in *A Lume Spento and Other Early Poems* in 1965 by New Directions in New York and Faber & Faber in London; and in *CEP* (with 'To T. H. The Amphora' displaced from third last to last, and the misprint 'works' for 'words' in the fourth from last line of 'Sandalphon').

75 'introductory matter': EP to HLP [Sept. 1908] (Beinecke).
told his father: EP to HLP, 23 Dec. [1908] (Beinecke). Punctuation has been slightly altered.
'The Venetian stuff': EP to HLP, Aug. 27 [1908] (Beinecke).
'the little bit (two Inches wide) of Ivory': *Jane Austen's Letters* ed. R. W. Chapman (Oxford: Oxford University Press, second edition 1952), p. 469.
76 **in the whitening**: EP's translation in letter to HLP [Feb. 1909] (Beinecke).
those other notes: see pp. 40–1 above.
77 **the ecstasy of the soul in ascent**: see p. 41 above.
78 **in** *The Pisan Cantos*: see 80 / 498.
Beddoes' poetry: EP's comments drawn from 'Beddoes and Chronology' (1913), as reprinted in *S Pr* 348–51.
his 1907 essay: see p. 42 above.
80 **Miss Heyman took thirty**: distribution details from EP's list inside front cover of 'San Trovaso' notebook (Beinecke).
Pound suggested: Nelson, *Elkin Mathews*, 134 and 274 n. 8, citing EP to Mathews, n.d., Yale.
'Mr Windham': George Wyndham, influential man of letters 'who gained his chief distinction in political life' (T. S. Eliot—see his 'A Romantic Aristocrat' in *The Sacred Wood*).
appreciative notes: see Homberger: 1972, 5.
Pound and Manning: details in this paragraph, including quotations, taken from Jonathan Marwil, 'Combative Companions' in *Ezra Pound in Melbourne, Helix 13 / 14* (1983) 9–15. On Fairfax see Hugh Witemeyer, 'James Griffyth Fairfax and Ezra Pound in Edwardian London', *English Literature in Transition 1880–1920* 42.3 (1999) 243–64.
81 **a crowded week**: EP to IWP [1 Feb. 1909] (Beinecke).
Sir Edward Sullivan: (1852–1928), born and educated in Ireland, called to the Bar 1888, published *Dante's Comedy in English Prose. I: Hell* (1893).
Maurice Hewlett: see *Pisan Cantos* 74 / 433, 80 / 515.
82 **Laurence Binyon**: see *Cantos* 80 / 506–7, also 87 / 572.
'one of the gang': EP to his parents [21 Feb. 1909] (Beinecke).
'impartially imbued': EP, '"Siena me fe"; disfecemi Maremma', *HSM*.
'the other attractions': EP to HLP, 11 Feb. [1909] (Beinecke).
The Poets' Club: information from A. R. Jones, *The Life and Opinions of Thomas Ernest Hulme* (Gollancz, 1960), pp. 29–30.
failed to impress: details from EP to HLP [? Apr. 1909 (Beinecke).
83 **Hewlett's commendation**: Stock: 1970, 60.
'May Sinclair's belief': EP to HLP, 8 Mar. [1909] (Beinecke).
'It is very pleasant': EP to IWP, 15 Mar. [1909] (Beinecke).

rather decently: EP to HLP [Feb. 1909] (Beinecke).
'Being in the gang': EP to HLP, 8 Mar. [1909] (Beinecke).
'not yet a celebrity': EP to HLP [Feb. 1909] (Beinecke).

'The Dawn' and Dorothy

83   Thursday the 18th: EP to HLP [Feb. 1909] (Beinecke).
84   a sighting: EP to HLP [end Nov. 1908] (Beinecke).
'on the same hearth rugs' and 'they tell me': EP to Mary Moore, Mar. 1909, numbered 61 (UPenn Ms. Coll. 181).
'At first he was shy' and all quotations in this paragraph: DS, notebook 16 Feb. 1909, *EP/DS* 3.
85   a 'prose & verse sequence': EP to MC, 9 May 1910, *EP/MC* 33.
'Extracts from ... "*The Dawn*"': these are printed in *EP/DS* 362–8.
a folder of drafts: YCAL MSS 43, Box 106, folder 4439 (Beinecke).
Dorothy's notebook entries: *EP/DS* 5–6.
86   'White Poppy': 'Planh', *EP/DS* 8—also *CEP* 126.
'meant to me a friendship': DS to EP, 30 Aug. 1911, *EP/DS* 42.
31 *Oct.* 1909: *EP/DS* 9.
March 1910 entries: *EP/DS* 16–17.
87   'If the artist must marry': EP to IWP, 1 Jan. 1910 (Beinecke).
'Ezra kept a candle': WCW, *Autobiography* 116.

'Personae of Ezra Pound'

87   'Six months ago': EP to Mary Moore, Mar. 1909 (UPenn Ms. Coll. 181).
'Mathews is publishing': EP to WCW [Feb. or Mar. 1909], *EP/WCW* 13.
'Well mother mine': EP to IWP, 19 Jan. [1909] (Beinecke).
'No literature is made': EP to HLP [? Mar.–Apr. 1909] (Beinecke).
89   epigraph from the *Vita Nuova*: from section IX.
90   'trailing clouds': 'Ode: Intimations of Immortality from Recollections of Early Childhood'.
Ovid tells his story: in *Metamorphoses* Bk. XIII.
Beatrice: in *Paradiso* I.67–9 et seq.
91   'the equation': EP to HLP [? Sept. 1909] (Beinecke).
'Revolt': discussed above pp. 43–4.
reviews: sources are Homberger: 1972, 43–60; Norman: 1960, 37; Robert A. Corrigan, 'A Yankee in King Edward's Court: The Critical Response to Ezra Pound's Early Verse', *Pai* 1.2 (1972) 232–5.
92   Edward Thomas in *The English Review*: 'Two Poets', *English Review* II (June 1909) 627–32, as in Homberger: 1972, 50–53.
93   Flint found an answer: in review of *Exultations*, 'Verse', *NA* VI (6 Jan. 1910) 233–4, as in Homberger: 1972, 64–6.
'Now as to my rhythmic principles': EP to Floyd Dell, 20 Jan. 1911, as edited by G. Thomas Tanselle, 'Two Early Letters of Ezra Pound', *American Literature* XXXIV.1 (Mar. 1962) 114–19 (pp. 115–17).
94   'Mr Ton': 'Mr Welkin Mark's New Poet', *Punch, or the London Charivari* CXXXVI (June 23 1909) 449, as in Homberger 1972: 6 and 29 n. 4.
'our best writers': R. B. Cunninghame Graham, 'Letter to the Editor', *Saturday Review of Politics, Literature, Science and Art* CVIII (27 Nov. 1909) 662, as in Corrigan *Pai* 1.2 (1972) 234.

Yeats

94   'I want to strike': EP to HLP, 30 Apr. [1909] (Beinecke).
    'Ballad of the Goodly Fere': EP's account is in 'How I Began' (1913).
95   'strongest thing in english': EP to HLP [Apr. 1909] (Beinecke). Pound's allusion is to Oscar Wilde's 'The Ballad of Reading Gaol' (1898).
    'the bloody sestina': EP to DS, 22 Apr. 1910, *EP/DS* 21; see also 'How I Began'.
    'blood curdling': EP to HLP, n.d. [Apr. 1909] (Beinecke).
    Tour Eiffel: The Hotel-Restaurant de la Tour Eiffel was at 1 Percy St., off Tottenham Court Rd., W.1.
    screened off the poets' table: such is the legend, though in Flint's account the other diners were 'on the other side of our screen' when EP performed—F. S. Flint, review of *Ripostes* in *Poetry and Drama* I (Mar. 1913) 60–2, as in Homberger: 1972, 97.
    '30 odd' poems: EP to HLP [June 1909] (Beinecke).
    had him 'nailed': EP to HLP, 8 Mar. [1909] (Beinecke).
    'had about five hours': EP to HLP, 30 Apr. [1909] (Beinecke).
    a courtly invitation: for WBY's note dated 8 May 1909 see Carpenter: 1988, 119.
96   **other regular evenings**: details from EP to HLP [?May 1909] (Beinecke).
    'habit of dining': EP to Peter Russell, n.d. (HRC).
    'If young men funk': EP to James Taylor Dunn, 12 Apr. 1938, *L (1951)* 401.
    T. E. Hulme's group: details from A. R. Jones, *The Life and Opinions of Thomas Ernest Hulme*, p. 31.
    Wanting an intuitive poetry: see 'A Lecture on Modern Poetry', *Collected Writings of T. E. Hulme*, ed. Karen Csengeri (Oxford: Clarendon Press, 1994), pp. 49–56.
    as collected by Pound: in *Ripostes* (1912) and in *P* (1926).
97   **would claim in 1915**: see 'Documents on Imagism from the Papers of F. S. Flint', *the Review* no. 15 (Apr. 1965) 39–40.
    as gospel: notably A. R. Jones.
    Flint himself had recognized: see above p. 93.
    had no time for his Bergsonizing: 'his evenings were diluted with crap like Bergson', EP, 'This Hulme Business', *Townsman* II.5 (Jan. 1939) 15. EP also shows his respect there.
98   'of meeting a man': *LE* 383.
    remembered in the *Cantos*: Tancred at 82/524–5, Fitzgerald at 92/618 and 7/27.
    'journalisms & poetizes' and other details: EP to HLP, 2 Aug. [1909] (Beinecke).
    Colum: remembered at 80/496 ('O woman shapely as a swan') from 'I shall not die for thee', included in EP's anthologies *Profile* (1932) and *CC* (1964).
    'Egyptian plays': *The Beloved of Hathor & The Shrine of the Golden Hawk* (1902).
    'sympathetic to the speaking voice': Florence Farr in dedication of her *The Music of Speech* to WBY, cited Norman: 1960, 47.
    'a nerve-destroying crooning': Foster: 1997, 257.
    'working at Psaltary' settings: EP to HLP, 2 Aug. [1909] (Beinecke).
99   **Yeats came to think**: WBY to Lady Gregory, 10 Dec. 1909, *The Letters of W. B. Yeats*, ed. Allan Wade (London: Hart-Davis, 1954), p. 543.
    couldn't hold a tune: see above p. 17.
    'tone deaf': EP to IWP, 17 Aug. [1909] (Beinecke).
    'organ of a tree toad': EP to James Joyce, 2 June 1920, *EP/JJ* 173.
    'As Yeats is the greatest': EP to HLP [May 1909] (Beinecke).
    'Yeats left this morning': EP to IWP, 1 Jan. 1910 (Beinecke).
    'a solitary volcano': EP to HLP from Lake Garda [? May 1910] (Beinecke).

he was being noticed: *The Pennsylvanian*, Philadelphia, Saturday 21 Nov. 1903—photocopy in Carl Gatter collection (UPenn Ms. Coll. 182).

'Blake's Rainbow': '... Some Early Drafts and Fragments', *Agenda* 34.3–4 (1997) 69–71, 75.

100 **'Plans?'**: EP to HLP [May 1909] (Beinecke).

'3/6 per week': Hutchins: 1965, 57.

'You know I have never': EP to IWP, 17 Aug. [1909] (Beinecke).

'Dear Mother': EP to IWP [30 Jan. 1910] (Beinecke).

constructing ... an opera: EP to IWP, Easter [= Apr. 1909] (Beinecke).

a 'News Note': in Homberger: 1972, 60.

'It's a long road': EP to HLP, 30 July [1909] (Beinecke).

'I should never think': EP to IWP, 19 Sept. 1909 (Beinecke).

101 **'My mind'**: EP to IWP, 23 Feb. [1910] (Beinecke).

'The Dawn': information from Nelson 143 and 275–6 n. 37; *EP/MC* 34–5; and *EP/DS* 361ff.

'Exultations of Ezra Pound'

101 **Mathews agreed**: information in this paragraph from Nelson 141–2; Stock: 1970, 71.

102 **'The collection as a whole'**: EP to Viola Baxter [Jordan] from Swarthmore [summer 1910] (Beinecke).

103 **'In a man's complete work'**: EP to his parents [1908/9], cited in Bruce Fogelman, *Shapes of Power: The Development of Ezra Pound's Poetic Sequences* (Ann Arbor: UMI Research Press, 1988), p. 112.

a 'tirade': see below pp. 129–31.

104 **a definite structure**: Fogelman, *Shapes of Power*, 120–3 gives an alternative account.

Dante's sonnet: translated in Dante Gabriel Rossetti, *Works* ed. W. M. Rossetti (Ellis, 1911), p. 361.

105 **letter to Floyd Dell**: on R. M. S. *Mauretania* stationery [Feb. 1911], as edited by Tanselle, 'Two Early Letters of Ezra Pound', *American Literature* XXXIV.1 (Mar. 1962). 118.

106 **'syntactical simplicity' and the 'image' in 'the early Yeats'**: EP., 'This Hulme Business', *Townsman* II.5 (Jan. 1939) 15.

107 **in the provençal mode**: hear, for example, the fine performance of Faidit's lament for Richard by Gérard Zuchetto and his Troubadours Arts Ensemble on CD Trob'Art TR 001.

'Mr Pound's verses': as in Homberger: 1972, 61.

108 **'I shall never forget'**: Edgar Jepson, *Memoirs of an Edwardian and Neo-Georgian.* (Richards, 1937), p. 140—as cited in Wilhelm: 1990, 28.

'Oh I do humble myself': Edward Thomas to Gordon Bottomley, 12 June 1909, extracted in Homberger: 1972, 36–7.

'met Scott-James': EP to HLP, 24 Sept. 1909 (Beinecke).

'Ezra Pound's second book': Edward Thomas to Gordon Bottomley, 14 Dec. 1909, extracted in Homberger: 1972, 37.

An anonymous reviewer: sources for pp. 113–14 are Homberger: 1972, 7, 61–6; Corrigan, '... The Critical Response to Ezra Pound's Early Verse', *Pai* 1.2 72) 235–7; and Stock: 1970, 75.

110 **'The Simon Zelotes ballad'**: EP to HLP, 24 Oct. [1909]—mistakenly placed as [1908]—(Beinecke).

'Colourless notice': EP to HLP [end of Dec. 1909] (Beinecke).

Ford Madox Hueffer

110 **'The critical LIGHT'**: EP, 'This Hulme Business', *Townsman* II.5 (Jan. 1939) 15.
111 **Hueffer's idea**: paragraph drawn from Ford Madox Hueffer, 'On the Functions of the Arts in the Republic', *The Critical Attitude* (Duckworth, 1911), pp. 25–51—quotations from pp. 27–8, 29, 32–4.
       'One of the best minds': EP to Hugh Kenner, postmarked 18 Mar. 1951 (HRC).
       'that poetry should be': EP, 'The Prose Tradition in Verse', *LE* 373.
112 **'held that French clarity'**: EP, 'Ford Madox (Hueffer) Ford; Obit', *S Pr* 431–2.
       'mad about writing': FMH, 'The Poet's Eye', *NF* I.6 (1 Sept. 1913) 108.
       'not with the bodily vision': EP to WCW [21 Oct. 1908], *EP/WCW* 9.
       'Direct treatment': EP, 'A Retrospect', *LE* 3.
       'characteristic exaggerations': cp. 'the province of the imaginative writer is by exaggeration due to his particular character—by characteristic exaggeration, in fact—precisely to awaken thought. That is to say, that is his utilitarian function in the republic . . . '—Ford Madox Hueffer, 'On the Functions of the Arts in the Republic', op. cit., p. 32.
       Hueffer (by then Ford) . . . stated: in *Return to Yesterday* (New York: Liveright, 1932), pp. 373–5, 356–7.
113 **'as a joke'**: Stock: 1970, 71.
       variant version: from the Gollancz 1931 edition as in Carpenter: 1988, 131.
       the story of . . . the floral decorations: see and compare Norman: 1960, 57; Hutchins 94; Carpenter: 1988, 134; Wilhelm: 1990, 8.
       'had a way of knowing': R. A. Scott-James, cited in Max Saunders, *Ford Madox Ford: A Dual Life* (Oxford: Oxford University Press, 1996) I, 239. My brief account of Violet Hunt is from Saunders' pp. [238]–42.
114 **Douglas Goldring . . . wrote**: in *South Lodge* (Constable, 1943), pp. 46–8.
       according to Ford: *Return to Yesterday*, p. 373.
       wrote to Hueffer: EP to FMH [Nov. 1909], *P/F* 6.
115 **Lawrence thought Pound**: Lawrence to Louie Burrows, 20 Nov. 1909, *The Letters of D. H. Lawrence: Volume 1*, ed. James T. Boulton (Cambridge: Cambridge University Press, 1979), p. 145.
       the first review: *Poetry* II.4 (July 1913) 149–51.
       the other review: 'In Metre', *NF* I.6 (1 Sept. 1913) 113.
       in the *Pisan Cantos*: 82 / 525. Cp. *LE* 371.
       needed to be persuaded: Douglas Goldring, *South Lodge*, p. 49.
       'NEVER': EP's comment to Patricia Hutchins, Hutchins 94 (footnote).
116 **'Hueffer & Miss Hunt'**: EP to his parents, 24 Oct. [1909]—mistakenly placed as [1908]—(Beinecke).
       Private lectures: detail from Jonathan Marwil, 'Combative Companions' in *Ezra Pound in Melbourne, Helix 13/14* (1983) 12.
       lecture . . . to the Poets' Club: details from Stock: 1970, 79.
       Dorothy . . . told Noel Stock: Stock: 1970, 73.
       'fog': EP to HLP, 14 Nov. [1909] (Beinecke).
       'imbibing': EP to IWP, 4 Nov. 1909 (Beinecke).
       twenty-one lectures: the synopsis of 'A Course of Lectures on Mediaeval Literature' is reproduced on p. 21 of *EP/DS*.
117 **Having started**: details of writing *SR* from EP's letters to his parents between Sept. 1909 and 23 Feb. 1910, and from Stock: 1970.
       'The book consists of': unsigned notice, *Nation* XLII (2 Mar. 1910) 221, as in Homberger: 1972, 67.
118 **of the same mind still**: cp. pp. 31, 32 above.

'their myths': *SR* 223.
'In the poems': *SR* 227.
'The art of the troubadours': *SR* 101.
'the one immortal tale': *SR* 79; its 'antithesis': *SR* 83.

119   'the songs of deed': *SR* 66.
'unquenchable spirit': *SR* 67.
'practical fighting man': *SR* 73.
'Modern interest': *SR* 218.
'He is a lurid canto': *SR* 177.
'sought to hang his song': *SR* 166.

120   Dante's 'four senses': *SR* 127.
Ovid writes of the gods: *SR* 15.
the metric of the *Pervigilium*: *SR* 18–19.
'the culture of Provence': *SR* 39.
Dante took him as the type: *SR* 23–4.
'language beyond metaphor': *SR* 33; on Daniel's *maestria* in general pp. 26–38.

121   'An effect': *SR* 113.
Dante's 'onomatopoeia' . . . purely technical notes: *SR* 160–1.
The analysis of Dante's: *SR* 158–9.
'two blending thoughts': *SR* 177.

A tirade on the epic

121–3   This 'scrawl' of eight numbered pages, while evidently written for his mother, is not in the form of a letter and is undated. Beinecke assigns it to around July 1909.

'Our renaissance in the egg'

123   to learn from Yeats: EP to Denis Goacher, 20 Oct. 1954 (HRC).
'Dante and I': 'To Guido Cavalcanti', *CEP* 142.
'less subtle than Dante': *SR* 110.
'POET / out of a Job': EP to IWP, Feb. 11 [1910] (Beinecke).
His private class: EP to HLP, Feb. 5 [1910] (Beinecke).
'Harmless variety': EP to IWP, Feb. 11 [1910] (Beinecke). The proofs would have been for the 'Canzoni' in the Jan. and Apr. numbers of the *English Review*.
applied to teach: Stock: 1970, 82.

124   Williams: paragraph drawn from WCW, *Autobiography* pp. 113–17 (chap. 20).
The day before he left: details from EP to his parents, Mar. 22 [1910] (Beinecke).
'Ezra has gone': *EP/DS* 17.
Margaret Lanier Cravens: details from 'Introduction', *EP/MC* [1]–7.
'all out of the Arabian Nights': EP to MC [23–25 Mar. 1910], *EP/MC* 10–11.
'a sort of sign': EP to MC [28 Mar. 1910], *EP/MC* 12.

125   From 'Hotel Eden': paragraph based on EP's letters to MC in Mar., Apr., and May 1910, *EP/MC* 14–37.
snow-capped mountains to the north: EP wrote thus enthusiastically about Garda to his parents [Apr. 1910] (Beinecke). See also 'Prolegomena' (1912), *LE* 9.
'Nature herself's turned metaphysical': 'The Flame', *CEP* 172.
expressed concern: EP to MC, 3 and 12 Apr. [1910], *EP/MC* 17, 23.
told his father: editors' note, *EP/MC* 13.
'to attend to nothing': EP to MC [28 Mar. 1910], *EP/MC* 12.
'a vague idea': EP to MC, 5 Apr. [1910], *EP/MC* 19.
wrote to Olivia Shakespear: EP to OS [15 Apr. 1910] *EP/DS* 18–20.

Writing to Bynner: EP to Witter Bynner [Apr. 1910] (Kenner Archive, HRC).
126 'the first time I ever saw colour': DP to Noel Stock, Stock: 1970, 86.
about 'to get drunk': EP to MC [14 May 1910], *EP/MC* 36.
Lawrence talked with him: Lawrence to Grace Crawford, 24 June 1910, *The Letters of D. H. Lawrence: Volume 1*, pp. 165–6.
making himself unbearable: see above p. 17.
Dorothy wrote: DS to EP [13 June 1910], *EP/DS* 23.

7. PATRIA MIA

The exile's mission

127 'All America': EP from Sirmione to Mary Moore, n.d.—numbered 65 in series—with her pencilled comment (UPenn Ms. Coll. 181).
'The country seems': EP to MC, 30 June 1910, *EP/MC* 41.
'first on Waverly Place': Wilhelm: 1990, 57.
she felt out of things: see editors' notes *EP/MC* 40.
engrossed with Prokofiev: Wilhelm: 1990, 59.
According to Williams: WCW told the story first in his 'Prologue' dated 1 Sept. 1918 to *Kora in Hell: Improvisations* (1920); repeated it in his *Autobiography* pp. 91–2; and again in *I Wanted to Write a Poem* (1958) p. 20.
128 Pound did not remember: EP to WCW, 11 Sept. [1920], *EP/WCW* 41.
he would remember: Stock: 1970, 90, citing EP to John Quinn, 9 Mar. 1915, *EP/JQ* 20.
'financial end of the game': EP to HLP from 164 Waverly Place, n.d. (Beinecke).
Wadsworth cousins: Wilhelm: 1990, 63.
Barnard Club: EP to MC, 27 Nov. [1910], *EP/MC* 60 and 62 (note).
calling on artists: Stock: 1976, 78.
taken to the theatre: Stock: 1970, 92, and *EP/MC* 51 (editors' note).
attended a meeting: Norman: 1960, 68.
met the writers: Stock: 1970, 93–4.
J. B. Yeats told: J. B. Yeats to WBY, 11 Feb. 1911, Homberger: 1972, 76.
'An American Poet': Stock: 1970, 78.
'jealous of the fact': Stock: 1970, 79.
his 'sudden fame': Stock: 1970, 78.
'the American poet': Stock: 1970, 92.
129 'We began the examination': Homberger: 1970, 75–6.
H. L. Mencken and Floyd Dell: Floyd Dell's review in *Chicago Evening News* of 6 Jan. 1911, and Mencken's in *Smart Set* in Apr., are in Homberger: 1972, 70–74.
Pound was grateful: EP to Floyd Dell, 20 Jan. 1911, Tanselle, 'Two Early Letters of Ezra Pound', 117.
only one man: though I go on to speculate that this might have been Walter Rummel, I note that EP wrote to MC, 'I've found one man, Dramatic Edtr. of the telegraph, who feels poetry, writes it as well as he has time to & wants the best' (*EP/MC* 60). He also wrote, that he had 'greatly enjoyed . . . a chorus by Mr Robert Gilbert Welsh' [footnote, *Poetry Review* I.10 (Oct. 1912) 481]. On that chorus, see 'Patria Mia. V', *NA* XI.23 (3 Oct. 1912) 539–40.
Dorothy's impression, 'Walter & I': *EP/DS* 35, 38.
130 an 'awakening' and 'Swarthmore': Rummel letters to EP, Sept. 1911 (on board R.M.S. *Saxonia*), and 20 Oct. 1911, cited in editors' note *EP/MC* 52.

'had a grand piano': H.D., *ET* 17–18.

'Here people's deep': EP to MC [18 Oct. 1910], *EP/MC* 54.

'I have found me an eyrie': EP to MC, 2 Nov. [1910], *EP/MC* 55.

'a "college of the Arts"': ibid.

'a paradise of the arts': EP to MC [10 Jan. 1911], *EP/MC* 63.

'The events of a life': EP to MC, 30 June 1910, *EP/MC* 41–2.

131   Yeats's 'new lyrics', and reading Swinburne: ibid. In a later letter EP cites 'No Second Troy' as an instance of Yeats's new spirit.

'the imminence': 'Patria Mia. I', *NA* XI. 19 (5 Sept. 1912) 445.

'A Risorgimento': 'Patria Mia. V', *NA* XI, 23 (3 Oct. 1912) 539.

its Dark Ages: ibid.

'the mire of commerce': 'Patria Mia. II', *NA* XI. 20 (12 Sept. 1912) 466.

132   'We need conspirators': EP to MC, 27 Nov. [1910], *EP/MC* 60.

In more diplomatic terms: 'Patria Mia. VII', *NA* XI. 25 (17 Oct. 1912) 587–8.

'the best minds': 'America: Chances and Remedies. V', *NA* XIII. 5 (29 May 1913) 116.

Black Mountain experiment: see Martin Duberman, *Black Mountain: An Exploration in Community* [1933–1956] (Wildwood House, 1974).

exemplary masters: this paragraph is drawn from 'Patria Mia. VIII', *NA* XI. 26 (24 Oct. 1912) 611–12.

'to wrench': 'To Whistler, American', *P*(1990) 249.

he was no artist': EP to Floyd Dell, Jan. 20 1911, Tanselle, 'Two Early Letters', 115–6.

'master of the forces': 'Patria Mia. VIII', *NA* XI. 26 (24 Oct. 1912) 611.

never 'owned a copy': EP to Floyd Dell, 20 Jan. 1911, Tanselle, 115–6.

133   He wanted New York City: see 'N. Y.', first collected in *Ripostes* (1912). The subscript, 'Madison Ave., 1910', was added in *Umbra* (1920).

'the surging crowd': 'Patria Mia. II', *NA* XI. 20 (12 Sept. 1912) 466.

Risvegliaménto: 'America: Chances and Remedies. I', *NA* XIII. 1 (1 May 1913) 9.

He had an idea: paragraph based on 'The Wisdom of Poetry', *Forum* XLVII. 4 (Apr. 1912), 497–501—in *S Pr* 329–32; 'America: Chances and Remedies. I', *NA* XIII. 1 (1 May 1913) 9–10; 'America: Chances and Remedies. VI', *NA* XIII. 6 (5 June 1913) 143; *SR* 128, 131 etc.; 'Introduction' [Nov. 15, 1910] to Cavalcanti poems, *T* 19–24; 'From Chebar', *CEP* 269–72.

Dorothy

134   Dorothy wrote: DS to EP [13 July 1911], *EP/DS* 34–5.

In August 1910: from D's notebook, *EP/DS* 24–5.

In November: from D's notebook, *EP/DS* 26.

135   a brief note: DS to EP, Nov. 1910, *EP/DS* 26–7.

The following May: from Dorothy's notebook, 7 May 1911, *EP/DS* 32.

her thank-you letter: DS to EP [13 July 1911], *EP/DS* 34–5.

Pound's allowed reply: EP to DS from Lake Garda [16 July 1911], *EP/DS* 37–8.

'Canzoni'

'hyper-aesthesia': EP to Elkin Mathews, 30 May 1916, *EP/JJ* 285.

'account of the mystic cult': see above p. 126.

136   two sorts of *canzoni*: see *SR* 88–89.

137   'a high mass': note among 'College Notes' (Beinecke), evidently a draft for the cancelled note at end of the proofs for *Canzoni*—see *CEP* 305. Cp. *SR* 89.

meets Daniel's spirit: *Paradiso* XXVI.136–48.

138   'Only I knew her': Frederic Manning, *Poems* (John Murray, 1910), p. 39.

He had praised: EP to IWP [Oct. 1909] (Beinecke); EP note to Hueffer [Nov. 1909], *P/F* 6.

'Man is in love': W. B. Yeats, 'Nineteen Hundred and Nineteen' (*The Tower*).

139   'to serve that love': EP's cancelled note at end of *Canzoni* proofs—see *CEP* 305.

'rather to be sung': note to 'Canzon: The Spear' in *English Review* IV.2 (Jan. 1910) 195. In a proof copy of *Canzoni* given by Pound to Brigit Patmore and now with his 'Works' in HRC, he wrote indications for musical accompaniment for several of the poems, thus 'strings' for 'Canzon: The Spear', 'plucked strings' for 'Canzon: To be sung beneath a window', 'bowed strings and muted [*illegible word*] for 'Canzone: The Vision', 'canta voce' for 'Ballatetta, and 'chor' for 'Era Mea'. For 'Rome' he wrote 'spoken quality / in organum'.

'It tells how Dante': *SR* 113–15.

141   the programme: see above pp. 118–19.

to fill out the scheme: see EP to DS [16 July 1911], *EP/DS* 38.

142   'overstrained & morbid': ibid.

143   no longer good for: see above p. 41.

a piano accompaniment: *Three Songs of Ezra Pound for a Voice with Instrumental Accompaniment* by Walter Morse Rummel: I. Madrigale II. Au bal masqué III. Aria (Augener, 1911). In 1913 a setting of 'The Return' was added.

'flame beneath the waters': compare 'love ... Glowing like flame beneath thin jade' in 'Canzon: The Spear', and with the variation in 'Canzon: To be sung beneath a window'.

145   his father and his mother: 'Introduction' (1910) to Cavalcanti poems, *T* 20. See also 'Cavalcanti', *LE* 193–4.

'lingua morta': EP to Thayer, 24 Oct. 1920, *EP/Dial* 171.

146   the light of the world: in an unpublished MS [*c*.1910?], headed 'Art and Religion: A Profession of Faith', EP wrote: 'There is one spirit of light, one holy ghost manifesting itself throughout the world and for these manifestations we have many names ... Can you give any better definition of the sincere artist save this, "a man drunk with love of gods chief attributes, beauty and truth, a seeker after the divine essence".... / The arts are channels for the divine light ...' (Beinecke).

147   'a little altar of stones': DS to EP [13 July 1911], *EP/DS* 35. In a letter from Lake Garda dated 12 Apr. 1913 EP told DS 'your altar is still pink slablet uppermost' (*EP/DS* 199).

148   'Dawn Song': see above p. 44.

put herself into the picture: H. D., *ET* pp. 38–9.

'a beautiful tradition': see above p. 121.

149   'Epilogue': *CEP* 209.

The five would have been: according to EP to Harriet Monroe, Dec. [1912], *L* 45–6.

Critics in England: see Homberger: 1972, 77–85.

'Redondillas': *CEP* 215–22.

150   'Whatever I may seem': EP to HLP [Feb. 1911] (Beinecke).

'I have my work': EP to IWP [Feb. 1911] (Beinecke).

'long dullness': EP to MC [4 Feb. 1911], *EP/MC* 64.

revivified: EP to IWP [Mar. 1911] (Beinecke).

in Paris: EP to IWP, 3 Mar. 1911 (Beinecke).

gross earnings: EP to Margaret Anderson, 27 Sept. 1917, *EP/LR* 130. See also *EP/JQ* 20.

8. PRELUDE IN PARIS

153   let Miss Cravens know: EP to MC, 25 Feb. [1911], *EP/MC* 66.

'Concerts-Chaigneau': all details from *EP/MC* 157–8.

portraits: reproduced *EP/MC* 72, 73. In 1983 the originals were in Madison, Indiana. EP told Joyce that his portrait was 'painted by an amiable jew who substituted a good deal of his own face for the gentile parts of my own' (*EP/JJ* 35).

154 **the songs of the troubadours**: paragraph based on Rummel's 'Preface' (1912) in *Hesternae Rosae, Serta II / Neuf Chansons de Troubadours des XIIième et XIIIième Siècles*.... (London, Paris and Boston: Augener Ltd. [1913]. See also 'I Gather the Limbs of Osiris ...X. On Music', *S Pr* 35–8.

his work with Florence Farr: see above p. 98.

without **Rummel's piano**: see Michael Ingham, 'Pound and music', *Cambridge Companion to Ezra Pound*, ed. Ira B. Nadel (Cambridge: Cambridge University Press, 1999), p. 243. Ingham, in his previous paragraph, unaccountably states that Pound failed to see that the best guess as to how to interpret the songs rhythmically was to have 'the text alone determine the hierarchy of durations'—though that was precisely what Pound did see.

introduction to his translation of Cavalcanti: now in *T* 17–25.

had finished it in M.C.'s apartment: see Robert Spoo, 'Pound's Cavalcanti and Cravens' Carducci', *Pai* 20.1–2 (1991) 83.

155 **his July 1907 essay**: see above p. 42.

156 **an 'Étude'**: *Umbra* 128.

Shepard ... congratulated: letter to EP [1912] (Hamilton).

Yeats and Fairy Belief: Foster: 1997, 439–40.

Notre Dame: see *Cantos* 83 / 528, and explication by Jeff Twitchell, 'A Church Note', *Pai* 15.2 / 3 (1986) 135–40.

'a gutless lot': EP to HLP [? Apr. 1911) (Beinecke).

Arnold Bennett: details from ibid.; see also Wilhelm: 1990, 68.

At the Salon des Indépendants: EP to HLP (? Apr. 1911) (Beinecke).

some Cézannes: EP to IWP [16 May 1911] (Beinecke).

157 **remarked the column**: see *Cantos* 78 / 480.

Hueffer in Giessen: details from *P/F* 7–9.

'the living tongue': EP, 'Ford Madox (Hueffer) Ford: Obit' (1939), in *S Pr* 431–2.

9. 1911–1912: Settling In

Of heaven and the ground under it

158 **'It was time'**: EP to MC from '2a, Granville Place / Portman Square, W.' [22 Aug. 1911], *EP/MC* 85.

'his own proper corner': EP to MC from '10 Church Walk / Kensington', 6 Nov. [1911], *EP/MC* 97.

spinet and grand piano: mentioned by EP in letter to DS, *EP/DS* 44.

According to the *New Age*: details from issues dated Aug. 17, 24 and 31 1911.

'The strike carefully avoided': EP to MC [22 Aug. 1911], *EP/MC* 85.

Yeats ... the Irish Players: Foster: 1997, 441 ff.; EP to MC [29 Sept. 1911], *EP/MC* 90.

Hueffer ... 'to be married', and May Sinclair: EP to MC [22 Aug. 1911], *EP/MC* 85.

Elkin Mathews ... to dinner: EP to IWP, 11 Sept. [1911]' (Beinecke).

159 **'a horrible cough'**: EP to MC [22 Aug. 1911], *EP/MC* 85.

Dorothy was away: details of her and EP's movements from *EP/DS*.

no way they could meet: see DS to EP [2] Sept. 1911, *EP/DS* 46.

G. R. S. Mead: information in this paragraph and footnote drawn from *EP/DS* 62 and 351 (editorial notes).

'I know so many people': *GK* 226 (punctuation slightly adjusted)—cp. canto 76 / 446.

'to find out whether I know': EP to DS [22 Sept. 1911], *EP/DS* 63.
'went to conduct an inquisition': EP to MC [6 Oct. 1911], *EP/MC* 95.
canto 46: 46 / 232.

160   **Alfred Orage**: information in this paragraph and footnote drawn from EP's 'Obituary: A. R. Orage' (*NEW* 15 Nov. 1934), in *S Pr* 407–9; Tom Steele, *Alfred Orage
and the Leeds Arts Club 1893–1923* (Aldershot and Brookfield: Scolar Press / Gower
Publishing Company, 1990); Philip Mairet, *A. R. Orage: A Memoir* (Dent, 1936).
'new contemplative and imaginative order', 'co-operate with': from the first issue of
the *New Age*, as cited in Mairet: 1936, 43.
feet on the ground: cp. 98 / 685—'But the lot of 'em, Yeats, Possum and Wyndham / had no ground beneath 'em. / Orage had'—and the variant at 102 / 728—
'. . . had no ground to stand on'.

A passive engagement

This section is based for the most part on materials in *Ezra Pound and Dorothy Shakespear:
Their Letters 1909–1914*, ed. Omar Pound and A. Walton Litz; and mainly on the letters
exchanged between July 1911 and May 1912. Most of the letters in this period are from
Dorothy to Ezra: there are about 40 from her, and only 5 from him. However, it is evident
from Dorothy's letters that Ezra sent her many more than are here. It is probable that
Dorothy burnt some of his letters at the time; and it is known that in her later years, when
she had the whole correspondence in her possession, she destroyed some letters or parts of
letters, including some of her own. The material record, then, is certainly incomplete; and
what remains is what Dorothy chose to preserve.

160   **'that one short time'**: from Dorothy's notebook, 7 May 1911, *EP/DS* 32.
161   **'Thank you'**: DS note to EP 24 July 1911, *EP/DS* 40.
'Don't write too often': DS to EP [12 Sept. 1911], *EP/DS* 57.
'Yours came': DS to EP, 16 Sept. 1911, *EP/DS* 59.
'Silet': the first poem in *Ripostes* (1912).
'I suppose': DS to EP, 26 Aug. 1911, *EP/DS* 41.
In her next: DS to EP, 30 Aug. 1911, *EP/DS* 41.
'they won't work': DS to EP [2] Sept. 1911, *EP/DS* 46.
162   **'What distresses me'**: OS to EP [?1 Sept. 1911], *EP/DS* 49.
'You are very lovely': EP to DS [10 Sept. 1911], *EP/DS* 55.
'Δώρια': first published in Feb. 1912, then in *Ripostes*; also in *Des Imagistes*.
163   **'I am loving you'**: DS to EP [12 Sept. 1911], *EP/DS* 56.
'I go to London': DS to EP, 23 Sept. 1911, *EP/DS* 65.
'you had better come early': DS to EP [26 Sept. 1911], *EP/DS* 66.
hats, 'a £1,000 a year': DS to EP [28 Sept. 1911], in *EP/MC* 88.
by verse alone: EP to MC, 27 Nov. 1911, *EP/MC* 101.
'My dear: Yes': DS to EP [10 Oct. 1911], *EP/DS* 71.
Mr Shakespear was taken: this paragraph is based on HHS letters to EP [12 Oct.]
and 16 Oct. 1911, *EP/DS* 72 and 73–4; and on HHS to HLP, 28 Nov. 1911, *EP/DS*
75.
164   **'I am, as you may have surmized'**: EP to HLP, Oct. 13 [1911] (Beinecke).
'the Shakespears': EP to MC, 27 Nov. 1911, *EP/MC* 101.
'Dearest: No': DS to EP [2 Nov. 1911], *EP/DS* 77.
'No—of course': DS to EP [8 May 1912], *EP/DS* 96.
applied again to Mr Shakespear: this paragraph is based on (a) EP to HHS [12 Mar.
1912], *EP/DS* 87; (b) DS to EP [19 Mar. 1912], *EP/DS* 89.
165   **'a feminine life'**: OS to EP, 13 Sept. 1912, *EP/DS* 154.
it got on her nerves: paragraph drawn from OS to EP, 13 Sept. 1912, *EP/DS* 153–4.

'I'm to be let in': EP to DS [14 Sept. 1912], *EP/DS* 155.
'Once a week': DS to EP, 15 Sept. [1912], *EP/DS* 157.
166 'young, revolutionary poet': see p. 114. above.
'a whole volley of liberations': see p. 131 above.
'a graceful bending': see p. 58 above.
'As for the rest': EP to DS [28 Oct. 1911], *EP/DS* 76.

The work of genius

167 'I have received orders': EP to HLP, Oct. 13 [1911] (Beinecke).
'to earn at least': see EP to MC, 27 Nov. 1911, *EP/MC* 100–2.
'the backbone': EP to MC, 6 Nov. [1911], *EP/MC* 98.
He had received: details from EP letters to MC of 6, 18 and 27 Nov. 1911, and from editorial notes, *EP/MC* 98–103.
fees from his lectures: see *EP/DS* 88n and 89; *EP/MC* 90 and 91 n.
'And none of these things': EP to MC, 27 Nov. 1911, *EP/MC* 101.
'I don't any more need': ibid.
his long poem: EP to MC [2 Jan. 1912], *EP/MC* 105; and see *EP/DS* 82.
'Apparuit': first published (with 'The Return') in *English Review* XI.3 (June 1912), then in *Ripostes* and all later collected editions of EP's poems.
'his one comfort': EP to DS [22 Sept. 1911], *EP/DS* 63.
'I'm keeping my head': EP to MC [29 Sept. 1911], *EP/MC* 89.
168 Writing in 'quantity': sentence based on EP to MC [29 Sept. 1911], *EP/MC* 90, and EP to DS [22 Sept. 1911], *EP/DS* 63–4.
Catullus...in Pound's judgement: see EP's 'Notes on Elizabethan Classicists', *LE* 230. For EP's version of Catullus 51 see *EP/DS* 54 n.
169 as retold by Pater: in chap. 5 of *Marius the Epicurean*.
Yeats... 'read them to us': DS to EP, 12 June [1912], *EP/DS* 110–11.
'The mastery of any art': 'Prologomena' (sic), *Poetry Review*, London, I.2 (Feb. 1912) 74—reprinted as part of 'A Retrospect', *LE* 10.
'rid of the first froth': 'I Gather the Limbs of Osiris...IX. On Technique', *NA* X.13 (25 Jan. 1912), 298; in *S Pr* 35.
'I Gather the Limbs of Osiris': series of twelve articles published weekly in *NA* from 30 Nov. 1911 to 22 Feb. 1912; the prose essays were reprinted, but not the translations, as 'Part One' of *S Pr*.
'It has been complained': 'Prologomena', *Poetry Review*, London, I.2 (Feb. 1912) 73—reprinted as part of 'A Retrospect', *LE* 9.
170 'a unity of intention': 'I Gather the Limbs of Osiris...XI', *NA* X.16 (15 Feb. 1912), 370; in *S Pr* 41.
'luminous details': paragraph drawn from 'I Gather the Limbs of Osiris...[II]. A Rather Dull Introduction', *NA* X.6 (7 Dec. 1911), 130–1; in *S Pr* 21–4.
Burckhardt: for the passage in question see Jacob Burckhardt, *The Civilization of the Renaissance in Italy* (Allen & Unwin Ltd., 'Published by the Phaidon Press': 1944), pp. 46–7.
a prose book...on the Renaissance: mentioned by EP in letters to DS and MC—see *EP/DS* 38, 43 and 45 n., 56; *EP/MC* 90.
virtu of Cavalcanti: see p. 155 above.
the specifically 'English' quality: cf. 'I Gather the Limbs of Osiris...[II]. A Rather Dull Introduction', *NA* X.6 (7 Dec. 1911), 131; in *S Pr* 24. See also 'Patria Mia. XI', *NA* XII.2 (14 Nov. 1912), 33—in *PM* 45.
perceptive intelligence: 'I Gather the Limbs of Osiris...IV. A Beginning', *NA* X.8 (21 Dec. 1911), 180; in *S Pr* 27–8.

'Seafarer'...text: on 18 Nov. 1911 EP told MC he was 'off for an anglo-Saxon mss at the [British] museum', *EP/MC* 100. The original manuscript of 'The Seafarer' was not in the B.M.—which does have the manuscript of *Beowulf*—but he would have found there authoritative transcriptions and editions of the text.

171   a recording: made at Harvard, 17 May 1939, released on cassette by Harvard University Press in 1978, in the series 'The Poet's Voice...Selected and Edited by Stratis Haviaras'.

a 'major persona': note, 'Main outline of EP's work to date', *Umbra* 128.

Arnaut Daniel: paragraph drawn from 'I Gather the Limbs of Osiris...IV. A Beginning', *NA* X.8 (21 Dec. 1911), 178–80; in *S Pr* 25–8.

'matchless': R. Murray Schafer, 'Introduction', *EP&M* 9.

not of the first importance: see EP to DS [16 July 1911], *EP/DS* 38.

technique...really matters: see e.g. 'I Gather the Limbs of Osiris...IX. On Technique', *NA* X.13 (25 Jan. 1912), 298; in *S Pr* 31–5; 'A Retrospect', *LE* 3–12; 'The Wisdom of Poetry', *Forum* XLVII.4 (Apr. 1912) 497–501, in *S Pr* 329–32.

'at the very crux': 'I Gather the Limbs of Osiris...XI', *NA* X.16 (15 Feb. 1912), 369; in *S Pr* 41.

'tone-leading': 'I Gather the Limbs of Osiris...X. On Music', *NA* X.15 (8 Feb. 1912), 344; in *S Pr* 39.

'only after a long struggle': 'Prologomena', *Poetry Review*, London, I.2 (Feb. 1912) 73—in 'A Retrospect', *LE* 9.

'English verse of the future': 'I Gather the Limbs of Osiris...IX. On Technique', *NA* X.13 (25 Jan. 1912), 298; in *S Pr* 33.

172   'harder and saner': this sentence and the next from 'Prologomena'—in 'A Retrospect', *LE* 12.

'The artist discriminates': 'I Gather the Limbs of Osiris...IX. On Technique', *NA* X.13 (25 Jan. 1912), 298; in *S Pr* 33.

as Hueffer had: see above p. 111.

'the analytical geometer', 'the abstract mathematician': 'The Wisdom of Poetry', *Forum* XLVII.4 (Apr. 1912) 500; in *S Pr* 332.

'set moods, set ideas': my sentence is based on ibid. 498; *S Pr* 330. Pound cites 'Melody which most doth draw' from Dante.

'Ripostes of Ezra Pound'

172   'The only man': 'In the Wounds (Memoriam A. R. Orage)', *Criterion* XIV.56 (Apr. 1935), as reprinted in *S Pr* 420.

173   to '"boom"' *Canzoni*: EP to MC [29 Sept. 1911], *EP/MC* 90.

'scarcely more than a notice': EP to Harriet Monroe [18] Aug. [1912], *L (1951)* 43.

'the artistic triumph': EP to WCW [29 Nov. 1912], *EP/WCW* 19.

reviewer in *TLS*: Homberger: 1972, 94–5, from *TLS* no. 570 (12 Dec. 1912) 508. Homberger identifies the reviewer as Harold Child.

Flint's review: Homberger: 1972, 95–6, from *Poetry and Drama* I (Mar. 1913) 60–2. EP wrote to DS [8 Jan. 1913], 'Flint is doing an intelligent article on me chiefly at my own dictation' (*EP/DS* 179). Flint also wrote at EP's dictation the article on 'Imagisme' published in *Poetry* I.6 (Mar. 1913) 198–200.

176   '"historicaly out of place': EP to WCW [29 Nov. 1912], *EP/WCW* 18.

177   'at the hour of the Saviour's agony': EBB's headnote to 'The Dead Pan'.

a stronger suggestion: put forward by John Espey in 'Some Notes on "The Return"', *Pai* 15.1 (Spring 1986) 39.

178   'sublimated': as noted and responded to by EP in letter to WCW [29 Nov. 1912], *EP/WCW* 19.

'This is where I belong'

178   '**"Time's bitter flood"**': from Yeats's 'The Lover pleads with his Friend for Old Friends', in *The Wind Among the Reeds*.
  '**things that are familiars**': from the last line of 'Sub Mare'.
  '**the beastly town**': EP to MC, 6 Nov. [1911], *EP/MC* 98.
  '**I suppose this is where I belong**': EP to MC, 27 Nov. 1911, *EP/MC* 102.

179   **Hulme . . . *salon***: details from Alun R. Jones, *The Life and Opinions of T. E. Hulme* (Victor Gollancz, 1960), pp. 91–8.
  hid herself in Ceylon: cf. W. B. Yeats, 'All Souls' Night', ll.41–50; also EP, *Cantos* 28/136 (as 'Loica').
  invited to contribute: see Norman: 1960, 81–2—Norman cites Marsh's account.
  '**what's left of a nunnery**': EP to IWP, 24 Dec. [1911] (Beinecke).
  '**they passed the car**': *Cantos* 80/515.
  '**glared at each other**': EP to IWP [Feb. 1912] (Beinecke).
  '**quite delightful**': EP to HLP, 14 Mar. 1912 (Beinecke).
  '**still more**': EP to HLP [Mar. 1912] (Beinecke).
  '**unforgettable**' **conversation**: EP, 'Henry James' (1918), *LE* 295.

180   **Sordello**: *Purgatorio* VI, 58 ff.
  '**the tone of things**': *Cantos* 7/24.
  Brigit Patmore: this paragraph based on *My Friends when Young: The Memoirs of Brigit Patmore*, ed. with an introduction by Derek Patmore (Heinemann, 1968), pp. 60–2.
  Hilda Doolittle: in her 'memoir of Ezra Pound', *End to Torment*, drafted in 1958, H.D. wrote that Pound had said to her when she was newly in England, 'Let's be engaged—don't tell . . .', don't tell someone, but 'not just then Dorothy' (*ET* 30). She also made it appear that Pound had been telling people that they were engaged, and declared that Walter Rummel had said to her, 'I think I ought to tell you, though I promised Mrs Shakespear not to,—don't let her know or anyone. But there is an understanding. Ezra is to marry Dorothy Shakespear. He shouldn't tell other people or imply to other people that he—that you—'(*ET* 18). H.D. contrived to put these things into the record while at the same time creating the sense that she had been so traumatized by what Rummel told her that she couldn't say exactly what had been said or when it might have been said. The time must have been the autumn and early winter of 1911–12. But what she writes is not in accord with known facts, and I know of no independent evidence to support her statements. There was indeed an 'understanding', but it was strictly between Ezra and Dorothy; moreover, we know that Mrs Shakespear was against it, and would have been relieved to have Ezra take up with someone else. It is most unlikely that Rummel knew of the understanding from Mrs Shakespear, as H.D.'s report could imply. It is also unlikely that Pound would have been putting it about that he was engaged to Hilda at the very time that he was formally seeking her parents' consent to marry Dorothy. And the implication that Dorothy was not 'just then' on the scene is simply absurd. Again, who were the people he was supposedly telling that he was engaged to Hilda? The South Lodge crowd appear to have known of his 'engagement' to Dorothy— Olivia Shakespear was concerned about that, probably because she had heard it was being talked of. Margaret Cravens knew of it, and so did his parents to whom H.D. was still writing. If H.D. needed to be told that would indicate that she was not then at all close to Pound. Altogether, I am not persuaded of the objective truth of her memories. Whatever the facts, they appear to have been reworked in accord with her persistent rendering of Ezra as a George who 'kissed the girls and made them cry'.
  Frances Gregg: details from H.D., *ET* 8, 18; and editors' note in *EP/MC* 109–10.

'in return for being ressurrected': EP to IWP, 21 Feb. 1912 (Beinecke).

'by the kind permission': this and details of the lectures from a flier reproduced *EP/DS* 89.

181   a note from Dorothy: DS to EP [19 Mar. 1912], *EP/DS* 89–90.

hear Marinetti lecture: a report in *The Times* of 21 Mar. 1912 is given in *EP/DS* 90 n.; see also *Futurist Manifestos*, ed. Umbro Apollonio (Thames and Hudson,1973), pp. 20–3.

a strange incident: my account is based mainly on *ET* 8–9, supplemented (for the last sentence) from Wilhelm: 1990, 102—Wilhelm's source is Kenneth Hopkins, *The Powys Brothers* (Phoenix, 1967), p. 34. H.D. gave a quite different account of this incident in *Asphodel*, an autobiographical fiction (following on from *Her*) which she first drafted in 1921–2 but chose never to publish. In this version (*Asphodel* 83–8) 'George', the Pound character, does know what Frances Gregg is really up to, because she has told him herself while misleading 'Hermione'. 'George' then prevents 'Hermione' going on the honeymoon by telling her that Frances is really going off with Powys and that the marriage is simply one of convenience to cover that up. Since H.D. explicitly declared that she did not want *Asphodel* to be published, but did write *End to Torment* for the record, we must accept the later version as the one she intended to make known, and that means that this earlier version must have been a fabrication. There is no problem about that if only we remember that H.D. did not pretend to objective veracity in *Asphodel*. There is a problem though when critics choose to present her fictions as if they were facts.

Margaret Cravens was kind...It has been suggested: see editors' note in *EP/MC* 109–10. The editors appear to be relying here on what H.D. wrote in *Asphodel*.

10. IN THE STEPS OF THE TROUBADOURS

The principal sources for this chapter are: *A Walking Tour in Southern France: Ezra Pound among the Troubadours*, ed. and introduced by Richard Sieburth [*WT*]; '"The Walk There is Good Poetry": The Missing Rochechouart Notebook of Pound's 1912 Walking Tour' [ed. and introduced by] A. David Moody in *Pai* 29.3 (Winter 2000) 235–41; Carl Baedeker, *Southern France...Handbook for Travellers*, 5th edn. (Leipsic: Karl Baedeker, 1907); *Les Vies des Troubadours*, Textes réunis et traduits par Margarita Egan (Paris: Union Générale d'Éditions, 1985), based on the critical edition of Jean Boutière and A. H. Schutz, *Biographies des Troubadours* (Toulouse: Privat, 1950); *Ezra Pound and Margaret Cravens: A Tragic Friendship 1910–1912*, ed. Omar Pound and Robert Spoo [*EP/MC*].

182   saw a good deal of MC: according to Walter Rummel, *EP/MC* 117.

'Vidal was': EP, 'Troubadours: Their Sorts and Conditions', *LE* 95—the essay was originally published in *Quarterly Review* CCXIX.437 (Oct. 1913) 426–40.

conviction formed at Hamilton: see p. 21 above.

'a life like our own': EP, 'Troubadours: Their Sorts and Conditions', *LE* 101.

'En Bertran's old layout': EP, 'Provincia Deserta' (collected in *Lustra* in 1916).

183   Poitiers: this paragraph and the next based on EP's notes and drafts, *WT* 3–7.

184   Hueffer's trilogy: Ford Madox Hueffer, *The Soul of London: A Survey of a Modern City*; *The Heart of the Country: A Survey of a Modern Land*; *The Spirit of the People: An Analysis of the English Mind* (Alston Rivers, 1905; 1906; 1907).

unwanted nostalgia: cf. *WT* 22: 'going my way amid this ruin & beauty it is hard for me at times not to fall into the melancholy that is gone, & this is not the emotion that I care to cultivate'.

Angoulême: details from *WT* 6–7, and Baedeker.

'with American boots': *WT* 77.

Chalais: paragraph based on *WT* 10–11.

185 'At Vieux Mareuil': *WT* 16.
Brantôme...to Périgeux: *WT* 17–19.
'lost the road': *WT* 23.
'a huge red-bearded peasant': EP, 'Possibilities of Civilization: What the Small Town Can Do' (1936); in *Impact* 77; 'finished courtesy' is from *WT* 31.
Hautefort: *WT* 22. In Sieburth's arrangement of the scattered manuscript materials EP appears to have gone to Excideuil after Hautefort, but EP wrote that when he lost his way around Blis-et-Born he was going from Périgeux to Excideuil (*Impact* 77), and the Michelin map shows the sense of that.

186 'Dompna Soisebuda': EP's first version was 'Na Audiart', in *A Lume Spento* (1908); 'Dompna pois de me no'us cal', in *Lustra* (1916) is a closer and more complete rendering. In a note 'On "Near Perigord"' accompanying that poem when it appeared in *Poetry* VII.3 (Dec. 1915), EP wrote: 'as to the possibility of a political intrigue behind the apparent love poem we have no evidence save that offered by my own observation of the geography of Perigord and Limoges' (*P&P* II, 124).
'Near Perigord' in 1913: EP to HLP, 3 June 1913, as in *L*(1951) 57.
to St Yrieix: *WT* 29, 28.
'Richard Coeur de Lion': *WT* 29.
his left shin: *WT* 30.
'How sane he was': '"The Walk There is Good Poetry": The Missing Rochechouart Notebook of Pound's 1912 Walking Tour', *Pai* 29.3 (Winter 2000) 240–1.

187 'Dear Ezra': *EP/MC* 116–17.
'just to say': *EP/MC* 114–15.
'Marguerite called': WR to EP, 2 June 1912, *EP/MC* 117.
'Sadness and nobility': EP to DS [10 June 1912], *EP/DS* 109.

188 'There is to be no funeral': EP to DS [18 June 1912], *EP/DS* 118.
'His Vision of a Certain Lady': published in *Blast* no. 1, then as 'Post Mortem Conspectu' in *P (1926)*.
Others...reacted differently: see Martha Ullman West, 'Lady with Poet: Margaret Cravens and Ezra Pound', *Helix* [Melbourne] nos. 13 and 14 (1983) 15–22, an article based on the unpublished memoirs of Alice Woods Ullman, wife of the painter commissioned by MC to do portraits of herself and EP. Appendix 3 of *EP/MC* gives Alice Woods Ullman's fictional reconstruction of the suicide in Paris of a young American woman, upon the editorial assumption that 'Most of the details correspond exactly to the death of Margaret Cravens'. There is also H.D.'s fictional account in *Asphodel* (pp. 88–105), part of which is given in *EP/MC* as Appendix 2. As well as including these fictions in their edition, the editors of *EP/MC* make use of them in their commentary on pp. 110 and 112–14—and also on pp. 67 and 20. These memoirs and autobiographical fictions, patently prejudiced and unreliable in the case of Alice Woods Ullman, frankly true only to her own psychodrama in the case of H.D., should not be taken as evidence of what might or might not have happened between MC and EP.
she had known for some time: see for example EP's letter to MC, 27 Nov. 1911, *EP/MC* 101.
'Hardly anyone has known': MC to WR [1 June 1912], *EP/MC* 115.
'She wanted': EP to ACH [Dec. 1912/Jan. 1913], *EP/ACH* 8.

189 two-thirds of her trust income: according to the calculations of the editors, *EP/MC* 6.
'tried more than the rest': WR to DS, 5 June 1912, *EP/MC* 118–19.
'doubtful' and 'in reality I feel': Drusilla Cravens to EP [? 19 June 1912], *EP/MC* 125.
'the blooming opus': EP to DS [16 June 1912], *EP/DS* 113.
'Chap. I of "op 411"': EP to DS [24 June 1912], *EP/DS* 122.
The second chapter: EP to DS [26 June 1912], *EP/DS* 125.

190 'not so thick with ghosts': *WT* 35.
his 'proper land' etc.: *WT* 39.
Gourdon: *WT* 40.
'a 30 mile sprint': EP to DS, 5 July 1912, *EP/DS* 130.
'such a day' and rest of paragraph: *WT* 42–3.
The fresco: *WT* 43–4.
In Toulouse: *WT* 45.
191 'two days before schedule': EP letter to DS, 5 July 1912, *EP/DS* 130.
'heading for Carcassonne': *WT* 50.
Roquefixade: *WT* 50.
'One may lie on the earth': *WT* 48.
Quillan to Axat: *WT* 51–2; Baedeker p. 186.
Carcassonne: Baedeker p. 102; *WT* 53; cf. 'Piere Vidal Old' (in *Exultations* [1909]).
192 Capestang: *WT* 58.
'too hot to move', 'irredeemably hideous': *WT* 59.
a strange mood came over him: quotations from *WT* 60–2.
Arles, Nîmes, Beaucaire, Tarascon: details from *WT* 64–71, and EP letter to DS,
July 1912, *EP/DS* 131.
'for the sake of the open country' and Allègre: *WT* 73–5; *Cantos* 802.
'already full of London': *WT* 76.
193 'A rain storm': *WT* 77.
'the top of the walk': EP, 'The Gypsy' (in *Lustra*).
Wordsworth's strange encounters: e.g. in 'Resolution and Independence', 'Guilt and
Sorrow, or Incidents upon Salisbury Plain', and throughout *The Prelude*.
194 noted the times of trains: *WT* 77.
back in Paris: details from EP to DS [23 July 1912] and 27 July, *EP/DS* 136 and 137.
'to crib some . . . chapters': EP to DS [23 July 1912], *EP/DS* 136.
'This prose book': EP to DS [13 Aug. 1912], *EP/DS* 142.
Hueffer told him: EP to DS [14 Sept. 1912], *EP/DS* 155.
'the book is about done': EP to DS [17 Sept. 1912], *EP/DS* 158.
'I've hung about the 1st 1/3rd': EP to DS [23 Sept. 1912], *EP/DS* 161.
'Patria Mia' and 'Gironde': EP to DS [1 Oct. 1912], *EP/DS* 162; also *EP/DS* 122 n.,
citing EP to IWP of 2 Oct. 1912.
'a damn rotten prose thing': EP to ACH [? Dec. 1912], *EP/ACH* 3.
'Prose has a commercial value': ibid.
'Provincia Deserta': in *Lustra*.

11. STIRRING THINGS UP: 1912–1913

Embroidery and vortex

196 delighted to see him: DS to EP, 14 July 1912, *EP/DS* 135.
'Don't bother': EP to DS, 27 [July] 1912, *EP/DS* 137.
what she was sketching: details from DS letters to EP, 10 Aug.–5 Oct. 1912, *EP/DS*
140–64.
Pound's letters: details from EP to DS, 9 Aug.–23 Sept. 1912, *EP/DS* 138–161.
197 'the only oasis in this waste of ennui': cp. Baudelaire, 'Le Voyage' VII.
Olivia's letter: OS to EP, 13 Sept. 1912, *EP/DS* 153–4. See p. 165 above.
'to be let in': EP to DS [14 Sept. 1912], *EP/DS* 155. In the same letter EP mentions
having written the two 'modern epigrams', 'The Tea Shop' and 'The Bath Tub' —the
latter first published in Dec. 1913, the former in *Lustra* (1916).
not impressed: EP to IWP, 24 Dec. [1912], *L (1951)* 66. [Paige's dating is mistaken.]

'It is very stupid': EP to DS [9 May 1913], *EP/DS* 227.

'will need some Jap prints': DS to EP [13 May 1913], *EP/DS* 230.

'The boredom': DS to EP [24 May 1913], *EP/DS* 231. In my judgement this note would have been sent earlier than the letter of the same date—though the editors of *EP/DS* place it after the letter.

198   'My dear': DS to EP [24 May 1913], *EP/DS* 230.

'Don't you know': DS to EP [10 June 1913], *EP/DS* 232.

sent her a poem: EP to DS [14 June 1913], *EP/DS* 233. First published in *Poetry* and in *NF* 1913 as 'The Choice', then in *Lustra* as 'Preference'. Omitted from 1926 and later *Personae*—text in *CEP* 279.

'Dearest': DS to EP [14 June 1913], *EP/DS* 234.

'My very dear': DS to EP [25 June 1913], *EP/DS* 235.

'you can not': EP to DS [June 1913], *EP/DS* 235.

'You might come in': DS to EP [30 June 1913], *EP/DS* 235.

'Bien': EP to DS [30 June 1913], *EP/DS* 236.

199   'a more lovely colour': DS to EP [1 Aug. 1913], *EP/DS* 237.

'doing some ... wool work': DS to EP [31 Aug. 1913], *EP/DS* 247.

'I am not in the least sure': EP to DS [1 Sept. 1913], *EP/DS* 248.

'Doesn't energy': DS to EP [4 Sept. 1913], *EP/DS* 249.

'No! that is *preciso*': EP to DS [5 Sept. 1913], *EP/DS* 251.

to experiment in colour: EP to DS [1 Sept. 1913], *EP/DS* 248.

One thing and another

199   his own '"Tuesday evenings"': details from EP to HLP [3 Sept. 1912] (Beinecke); and Patmore, *My Friends when Young*, p. 67.

200   Tagore: this and the next paragraph drawn from EP, 'Tagore's Poems', *Poetry* I.3 (Dec. 1912) 92–4; EP, 'Rabindranath Tagore', *Fortnightly Review* XCIII (n.s.). 555 (1 Mar. 1913) 571–9; EP to DS [1 Oct. 1912], *EP/DS* 162; EP to Harriet Monroe, 22 Apr. 1913, *L (1951)* 55.

'these prose translations': W. B. Yeats, 'Introduction', *Gitanjali* by Rabindranath Tagore (Macmillan, 1913), p. vii.

talked ... about the spirit world: see, e.g., EP to DS [8 Jan. 1913], *EP/DS* 180.

kept him with him till two: EP to DS [22 Dec. 1912], *EP/DS* 166.

201   to go over 'The Two Kings': details from EP to DS [2 Jan. 1913], *EP/DS* 175; Richard Ellmann, *Eminent Domain* (New York: Oxford University Press, 1967), p. 66— Ellmann cites WBY's letter to Lady Gregory.

'I learned from him': WBY, post-script dated '1924' to 'Blake's Illustrations to Dante', *Essays and Introductions* (Macmillan, 1961), 145.

the Cuala Press proof: now in the Beinecke EP Papers.

'an old fashioned thing': EP to ACH [14 Oct. 1913], *EP/ACH* 58.

he wrote of it in *Poetry*: EP, 'The Later Yeats', *Poetry* IV.2 (May 1914) 64–9.

'huge wad', 'will be SPARED': EP to IWP [Feb.–Mar. 1913] (Beinecke).

'a delightful old-world letter': EP to Harriet Monroe, 22 Oct. [1912], *L (1951)* 47. See also F. G. Atkinson, 'Ezra Pound's Reply to an "Old-World" Letter', *American Literature* XLVI.3 (Nov. 1974) [357]-359—in *P&P* X.123–5.

Swift & Co. liquidation: details from Gallup: 1983, 15; Carpenter: 1988, 194–5.

204   'stand to the guns': EP to HLP, 10 Oct. 1912 (Beinecke).

'So we procede': EP to HLP, 3 Dec. (1912) (Beinecke).

His earnings: EP to HLP, 13 Dec. 1912 (Beinecke).

read a paper ... Cambridge: details from Stock: 1970, 123.

'in Mrs Fowler's ... drawing room': details from editors' notes, *EP/DS* 178–9.

'Eva has ordered': EP to DS [21 Jan. 1913], *EP/DS* 183.

invited to Oxford: details from Stock: 1970, 131, and *Cantos* 74 / 444–5.

'by kind permission of Lady Low': details from Omar Pound, 'Addenda for [*EP/DS*]', *Pai* 15.2–3 (1986) [239].

205   pleased with his setting: EP to HLP [18 Apr. 1913] (Beinecke).

in the cellar of the 'Chatelet': details from EP, 'The Approach to Paris: I', *NA* XIII.19 (4 Sept. 1913) 551–2; 'Remy de Gourmont' (1915), *S Pr* 386; *Cantos* 77 / 129, 80 / 506.

'the younger energies': EP to ACH [? Apr. 1913], *EP/ACH* 40.

'You are secretary': EP to Flint, 10 Apr. 1913 (HRC).

'the industrial tyrannies': EP, 'The Black Crusade' [letter], *NA* XII.3 (21 Nov. 1912) 69.

'A million men': EP, 'Through Alien Eyes. III', *NA* XII.13 (30 Jan. 1913) 300.

206   'Dear Mr Abercrombie': EP's letter as recalled by John Gould Fletcher, *Autobiography*, [originally published as *Life is My Song* (1937)], ed. Lucas Carpenter (Fayetteville: University of Arkansas Press, 1988), p. 76. Wilhelm: 1990, 117–18, cites John Cournos' account of the incident.

Taking on the contemporary

206   the artists ... 'who can know at first hand': from 'The Rest'.

'I mate': from 'Tenzone'.

207   'Dawn enters': 'The Garret'.

'O generation': from 'Salutation'.

'the tyranny': from 'Commission'.

'Go and dance': from 'Salutation the Second'. 'Mr Strachey'—John St. Loe Strachey, editor of *The Spectator*—was named 'in the classic Latin manner' as 'the type of male prude' (EP to HLP, 3 June 1913, *L* 58). When Manning advised EP 'to placate Strachey' his response was a derisive 'oh là là' (*EP/DS* 180). Not long after, Strachey rejected one of Manning's poems as 'improper' (*EP/DS* 191). The line was omitted by Faber & Faber in their edition of *Personae* (1952)—probably not at EP's request.

208   'with nothing archaic': from 'Salutation the Second'.

'Go, my songs': 'Ité'.

Sophocles' Herakles: see *SWT*, EP's version of *The Women of Trachis*, particularly p. 50.

xenia: Martial Bk. XIII.

lustra: EP gave the polite 'elementary dictionary' definition of *Lustrum* on the verso of the separate title leaf for *Lustra* in *P* (*1926*). He expected the reader to know that the word also meant 'a brothel' (*EP/LR* 191).

209   'Irritation': EP, 'The Approach to Paris.VI', *NA* XIII.24 (9 Oct. 1913) 694–5. Cp. pp. 29–30 above.

as Whitman might: cp. 'Song of Myself' sect. 6 ('A child said *What is the grass?*'). In *Poetry* 'A Pact' ('I make a pact with you, Walt Whitman') immediately preceded 'In a Station of the Metro'.

over a year: EP, 'How I Began', *T. P.'s Weekly* XXI.552 (6 June 1913) 707.

Making enemies in 'The New Age'

209   'For the welfare': 'Patria Mia. V', *NA* XI.23 (3 Oct. 1912) 540.

comfortable if rather musty, 'perched on the rotten shell', a heap of iron filings, etc.: EP, 'Though Alien Eyes. I', *NA* XII.11 (16 Jan. 1913) 252.

not 'the Paradiso Terrestre': EP to IWP [Jan. 1914], *L (1951)* 68.

Rome in its decadence: 'Though Alien Eyes. III', *NA* XII.13 (30 Jan. 1913) 300.

210   its social arrangements: 'Patria Mia. IX', *NA* XI.27 (31 Oct. 1912) 635–6.
sense of property: 'Though Alien Eyes. I', *NA* XII.11 (16 Jan. 1913) 252.
finest authors: 'Though Alien Eyes. III', *NA* XII.13 (30 Jan. 1913) 300.
more advanced in Paris: 'The Approach to Paris.VII', *NA* XIII.25 (16 Oct. 1913) 728.
the cafés of Paris: 'The Approach to Paris. I', *NA* XIII.19 (4 Sept. 1913) 551.
'your society women': 'Though Alien Eyes. IV', *NA* XII.14 (6 Feb. 1913) 324.
'Our women': ibid.

211   'the intellectual life': 'The Approach to Paris. I', *NA* XIII.19 (4 Sept. 1913) 551.
Writing as 'R.H.C.': 'Readers and Writers', *NA* XIII.20 (11 Sept. 1913) 573.
Pound challenged: '"The Approach to Paris"' [letter], *NA* XIII.21 (18 Sept. 1913) 615.
'Pindarism': 'R.H.C.', 'Readers and Writers', *NA* XIII.21 (18 Sept. 1913) 602.
'for the most part': 'The Approach to Paris.VII', *NA* XIII.25 (16 Oct. 1913) 728.
review of *Ripostes*: *NA* XII.22 (3 Apr. 1913) 533
Orage now went for Pound: *NA* XIII.26 (23 Oct. 1913) 761.
In a later issue: *NA* XIV.2 (13 Nov. 1913) 51.

212   'the editor is a good fellow': EP to IWP [Nov. 1913], *L (1951)* 63.

Making a renaissance in 'Poetry'

This section is indebted to: Harriet Monroe, *A Poet's Life* (New York: Macmillan, 1938); Ellen Williams, *Harriet Monroe and the Poetry Renaissance* (Urbana: University of Illinois Press, 1977); Ann Massa, 'Ezra Pound to Harriet Monroe: Two Unpublished Letters', *Pai* 16.1–2 (1987) [33]-47; *The Letters of Ezra Pound to Alice Corbin Henderson*, ed, Ira Nadel (1993) [*EP/ACH*]; Naoyuki Date, 'Ezra Pound's Editorship of the American "Little Magazines", 1912–19' (University of York Ph.D. dissertation, 2005).

212   'dead as mutton': EP to Harriet Monroe, 7 Nov. 1913, *L (1951)* 61.
'nothing alive here': EP to ACH, 20 Jan. [1913], *EP/ACH* 17–18.
spelt out for their readers: EP, 'Editorial Comment/Status Rerum' [with dateline '*London, Dec. 10, 1912*'], *Poetry* I.4 (Jan. 1913) 123–7.
'no man now living': 'Patria Mia. IV', *NA* XI.22 (26 Sept. 1912) 515–6. See further 'Patria Mia. V', *NA* XI.23 (3 Oct. 1912) 539–40.
Poetry promised: paragraph drawn from HM's circular letter to poets, as in *The Poetry Review* [London] I.10 (Oct. 1912) viii, and (with a few deletions) in Monroe, *A Poet's Life*, pp. 251–2; also from her article, 'Modern American Poetry', in same number of *The Poetry Review*, pp. 469, 472.

213   He was interested: EP to HM [18] Aug. [1912], *L (1951)* 43–4.
'over-grip for the future': EP to IWP, 2 Oct. [1912] (Beinecke).
valued his criticism: e.g. see Monroe, *A Poet's Life*, p. 268.
'Controversy': HM, 'The Audience. II', *Poetry* I.2 (Nov. 1912) 31.

214   'the guiding sense': EP to HM [18] Aug. [1912], *L (1951)* 44.
'time for carving': 'A Pact', first published with 'Contemporania', *Poetry* Apr. 1913.
'My idea of our policy': EP to HM [24] Sept. [1912], *L (1951)* 45.
'an international standard': EP to HM, 26 Oct. 1912, *EP/ACH* 67.
'a universal standard': EP to HM, 7 Nov. 1912, *L (1951)* 62.
'The worst betrayal': EP to HM, 22 Oct. 1912, *L (1951)* 46.
could be the best: paragraph drawn from EP to ACH, 20 Jan. [1913], *EP/ACH* 19–20.
'wrathful correspondents': Monroe, *A Poet's Life*, p. 289.
explained the insult: in EP to ACH [? 10 Feb. 1913], *EP/ACH* 33. See also EP to HM, 22 Oct. 1912, *L (1951)* 46.

215   'Mr Pound is not the first': Monroe, *A Poet's Life*, pp. 289–90.
He told her what was wrong: paragraph based on Ann Massa, 'Ezra Pound to Harriet Monroe', drawing on the two unpublished letters as given there from EP to HM,

dated (by H.M.) May 1915 and 5 June 1915 (originals in *Poetry* files, Joseph Regenstein Library, University of Chicago).

'the best critic living': Monroe, *A Poet's Life*, p. 266.

216   'the sort of American stuff': EP to HM [Oct. 1912], *L (1951)* 45.

'A Few Don'ts': included in 'A Retrospect', *LE* 4–7 (ending with '. . . *Mais d'abord il faut être un poète'*).

an 'Ars Poetica', 'returned msss.': EP to ACH, 20 Jan. [1913], *EP/ACH* 19.

'instructions to neophytes': EP to HM, 30 Mar. 1913, *L (1951)* 55.

'the younger American poets': EP, 'The Perfect Poet' [letter], *Daily News and Leader* [London] (8 Apr. 1914) 4.

'he learned the proper treatment': EP to HM, Mar. 1913, *L (1951)* 52.

took him six months: EP, 'Small Magazines', *English Journal (College Edition)* XIX.9 (Nov. 1930) 693.

'VURRY Amur'k'n': EP to ACH, Mar. 1913, *L (1951)* 49.

Williams: see 'A Selection from *The Tempers*', with Introductory Note by EP, *The Poetry Review* [London] I.10 (Oct. 1912) 481–4; EP to HM, Mar. 1913, *L (1951)* 50; EP to WCW, 26 May 1913, *EP/WCW* 21; EP review of *The Tempers*, *NF* I.12 (1 Dec. 1913) 227; Williams, *Harriet Monroe*, pp. 56–9.

had reservations, Orrick Johns: see e.g. EP to ACH, 13 Apr. 1914 and [? Jan. 1915], *EP/ACH* 77–8 and 92–4; also Williams, *Harriet Monroe*, p. 55.

'howling need of training': EP to HM, Mar. 1913, *L (1951)* 50.

'a possible feat': EP to HM, 30 Mar. 1913, *L (1951)* 54.

'All the Yeats': EP to ACH, 14 Oct. 1913, *EP/ACH* 55–8.

'please take over': EP to FMH, Nov. 1913, *EP/FMF* 21.

217   Hueffer then wrote: ibid.

'I don't think you have yet tried': EP to HM, 8 Dec. 1913, *L (1951)* 64.

Individualism in 'The New Freewoman'

This section is indebted to: Les Garner, *A Brave and Beautiful Spirit: Dora Marsden 1882–1960* (Aldershot: Avebury, 1990); Jane Lidderdale and Mary Nicholson, *Dear Miss Weaver: Harriet Shaw Weaver, 1876–1961* (Faber & Faber, 1970); Bruce Clarke, 'Dora Marsden and Ezra Pound: *The New Freewoman* and "The Serious Artist"', *Contemporary Literature* XXXIII.1 (1992) [91]-112; Robert von Hallberg, 'Libertarian Imagism', *Modernism/modernity* II.2 (1995) 63–79. See also Bruce Clarke, *Dora Marsden and Early Modernism: Gender, Individualism, Science*, (Ann Arbor: University of Michigan Press, 1996).

217   Pound offered: what follows in this paragraph is drawn from two EP letters to Dora Marsden, n.d. [? Aug. 1913], as given in Clarke, 'Dora Marsden and Ezra Pound', pp. 99–100. That Fletcher was the 'anonymous donor' is known from *EP/DS* 238 and *EP/ACH* 57; see also Fletcher's *Autobiography* (1988), p. 66.

He wrote home: EP to IWP [Aug. 1913] (Beinecke).

218   'taken charge': EP to HM, 13 Aug. 1913, *L (1951)* 58.

'as our, or at least my', 'the official organ': EP to ACH [?Aug. 1913] and 8–9 Aug. 1913, *EP/ACH* 50 and 52.

'more or less running': EP to ACH, 14 Oct. 1913, *EP/ACH* 57.

'The advantage': EP to Milton Bronner, 24 Sept. 1913 (HRC).

Dora Marsden: biographical details drawn mainly from Garner, *A Brave and Beautiful Spirit*.

219   became . . . *The Egoist*: those who would have it that EP on his own or with some other male contributors forced the new title upon the unwilling editress are wholly mistaken both about the fact of the matter and about her character. The title was of Marsden's own choosing, for reasons that are apparent in her writings from *The Freewoman* on; if there was manipulation, it appears to have been on her part in

having the male contributors write a letter requesting the change she had already decided on; and it is a gross misestimation of her to think she could have been coerced by her contributors.

The Ego and His Own: the translation by Steven T. Byington, a regular contributor to *NF*, had a regular quarter-page advertisement in the review featuring the *NF*'s own recommendation: 'The most powerful work that has ever emerged from a single human mind'.

'the Ego is the only': from the *Morning Post* review as cited in the advertisement.

her philosophical convictions: this and the following two paragraphs are based on Dora Marsden's articles in *NF* and *Egoist*, in particular: 'The Lean Kind' and 'Views and Comments', *NF* I.1 (15 June 1913) [1]-5; 'Intellect and Culture' and 'Views and Comments', *NF* I.2 (1 July 1913) [21]-25; 'Democracy', *NF* I.3 (15 July 1913) [41]-43; 'Views and Comments', *NF* I.4 (1 Aug. 1913) 65; 'Thinking and Thought', *NF* I.5 (15 Aug. 1913) [81]-83; 'Concerning the Beautiful', *NF* I.6 (1 Sept. 1913) [101]-104; 'The Art of the Future', *NF* I.10 (1 Nov. 1913) [181]-183; 'Beauty and the Senses', *NF* I.11 (15 Nov. 1913) [201]-203; '"I AM"', *Egoist* II.1 (1Jan. 1915) [1]-4; 'The Gentle Art of "Appreciation"', *Egoist* II.8 (2 Aug. 1915) [117]-120. DM's two series of articles on 'Lingual Psychology' and 'The Science of Signs' which appeared in *Egoist* from July 1916 are also of great interest.

220   'the life of the race': 'I Gather the Limbs of Osiris.X', *S Pr* 38.

learn to say 'I': cf. 'Ortus', among 'The Contemporania of EP'.

221   'an eternal state of mind': 'Religio, or The Child's Guide to Knowledge', *NF* I.9 (15 Oct. 1913) 176; repr. *PD (1918)*, *PD (1958)*, *S Pr* 47–8.

'cultural brain-rot': [DM], 'Views and Comments', *NF* I.3 (15 July 1913) 44.

didn't read them: DM to Harriet Shaw Weaver, Nov. 1913, in Lidderdale and Nicholson, *Dear Miss Weaver*, p. 73.

'gassing about art': EP to DM, as cited in Clarke, 'Dora Marsden and Ezra Pound', p. 109.

de Gourmont: quotations taken from EP, 'Remy de Gourmont' (1919), *LE* 340–5, 355. EP also wrote 'the truth is the individual' in 'I Gather the Limbs of Osiris.IX', *S Pr* 33.

The 'Imagiste' vortex

222   'began certainly': EP to Harriet Monroe, 13 Sept. 1913, as cited Monroe, *A Poet's Life*, p. 267—date from Williams, *Harriet Monroe*, p. 39. EP first used the term 'Imagiste' in a letter to HM, 18 Aug. 1912 (*L (1951)* 44).

as appended to *Ripostes*: see pp. 101 and 190 above.

'a group of ardent Hellenists': *Poetry* I.2 (Nov. 1912) 65.

'Hellenism & vers libre': EP to ACH [Dec. 1912 ?], *EP/ACH* 4.

the guiding principles: F. S. Flint, 'Imagisme', *Poetry* I.6 (Mar. 1913) 198–200.

Pound's forty things: 'A Few Don'ts by an Imagiste', ibid. 200–6. EP once referred to his 'Don'ts' as 'a series of about forty cautions to beginners' ('Vorticism' (1914)—see *GB* 84.)

223   'the affectation of "Imagiste"': HD to HM, 24 Oct. 1913, as cited by Williams, *Harriet Monroe*, p. 41 n. 18. Williams also cites Aldington's scratching out 'R. A. Imagiste' on the typescript of a poem submitted to *Poetry* about the same time and writing instead 'Richard Aldington'.

'was really in opposition': EP to Flint, 30 Jan. 1921, as given in Wallace Martin, 'Three Letters on Imagism', *Helix* 13 & 14 (1983) 29.

Amy Lowell . . . discovered: see Monroe, *A Poet's Life*, pp. 275–8.

to visit Oxford: see EP to DS [25 Aug. 1913], *EP/DS* 245.

224 **Amy Lowell's take-over**: see EP's letters to her July–Oct. 1914, *L (1951)* 77–85.
preface to *Some Imagist Poets*: quotations from the preface reprinted as 'Appendix C' in *Imagist Poetry* ed. Peter Jones (Harmondsworth: Penguin Books, 1972), pp. 134–6.
turned down Miss Lowell's first offer: EP to Amy Lowell, 1 Aug. 1914, *L (1951)* 77–8. For EP's considered views on AL see *EP/LR* 91–2, 116–17.
'dilutation': EP used the word of some of H.D.'s post-*Imagiste* poems, spoilt, he supposed, by 'the flow-contamination of Amy and Fletcher', in letter to MCA [? Aug.] 1917, *L (1951)* 169. In 1955 D. G. Bridson prepared a radio script based on EP's letters to Aldington and called it 'Origins, Formation, Dilutation and Dispersal' of the Imagist movement (unbroadcast, unpublished BBC script) (Bridson MSS, Lilly).
'floppy degeneration': EP to Flint, 30 Jan. 1921, as given in Martin, 'Three Letters on Imagism', p. 28. [Martin gives 'fluffy', where I read the original in HRC as 'floppy'.]
'You had the energy': F. S. Flint to EP, 3 July 1915, in Christopher Middleton, 'Documents on Imagism from the Papers of F. S. Flint', *the Review* no. 15 (Apr. 1965) 42. Also in *The Imagist Revolution 1908–1918*, A Keepsake (Austin: Harry Ransom Humanities Research Center, 1992).
a *blague*: for Fletcher's account see his *Autobiography* (1988) 151–5; Stock: 1970, 164 adds some details, including the menu. See also Wilhelm: 1990, 160–2.
somewhat spherical: cf. 'Gaudier's eye on the telluric mass of Miss Lowell', *Cantos* 77/ 469.

225 **the official history**: F. S. Flint, 'The History of Imagism', *Egoist* II.5 (1 May 1915) 70–1.
didn't much care for theorizing: see, e.g., 'Prolegomena' (1912), *LE* 9.
'the natural object': 'Credo', *LE* 9.
'the precise instant': 'Vorticism' (1914), *GB* 89.
'universe of fluid force': *SR* 92–3.

226 **'imagism was formulated'**: 'Écrevisse?', *Il Mare* XXVI.1253 (18 Mar. 1933) 3, translated from EP's Italian by Tim Redman, 'Pound's Italian Journalism', *Helix* 13 & 14 (1983) 118.
exemplary *Imagiste* poem: 'Vortex, Pound', *Blast* 1 (20 June 1914) 154. EP cited it again in 1933, in 'Écrevisse?' (previous note).
'Image REFERS': EP to H. B. Parkes, 29 Jan. [1933 ?] (UPenn Ms. Coll. 183). After 'outside' EP added, 'ref/Witgenstein'.
'The real': cf. EP to DS [21 Apr. 1913], *EP/DS* 206.
'The Serious Artist': collected in *LE* 41–57.

227 **Dora Marsden took issue**: particularly in 'The Art of the Future', *NF* I.10 (1 Nov. 1913) [181]-183.
'having spasms': EP to DS, 23 Sept. 1913, *EP/DS* 260.
'There must be intense emotion': EP to ACH, 8, 9 Aug. 1913, *EP/ACH* 53.
emotional energy…compression: see EP to F. S. Flint, 30 Jan. 1921, as given in Martin, 'Three Letters on Imagism', p. 29.
Emotion is: this sentence and the next from 'Affirmations. IV. As for Imagisme', *NA* XVI.13 (28 Jan. 1915) 349–50.
'complex': 'A Few Don'ts', *LE* 4.
Bernard Hart: what follows in this paragraph is from *The Psychology of Insanity* (Cambridge: at the University Press, 1912; 4th edn., 1930), esp. pp. 59–64.

228 **'The strength of the arts'**: 'America: Chances and Remedies', *NA* XIII.1 (1 May 1913) 10.
'thought-seed': 'Obstructivity', *Apple (of Beauty and Discord)* I.3 (July/ Sept. 1920) 168, 170.
'thoughts are in them': *SR* 92–3.

'order-giving vibrations': 'Affirmations, IV. As for Imagisme', *NA* XVI.13 (28 Jan. 1915) 350.

229 'Go in fear of abstractions': 'A Few Don'ts', *LE* 5.

'to fit the formula': EP, in a letter to Aldington, wrote that he had omitted from *Des Imagistes* 'everything of my own not within the formula'—cited in D.G.Bridson's BBC radio script, 'Origins, Formation, Dilutation and Dispersal' (Bridson MSS, Lilly).

DM against abstractions: see 'Concerning the Beautiful', *NF* I.6 (1 Sept. 1913) [101]- 104; 'The Art of the Future', *NF* I.10 (1 Nov. 1913) 183.

'a definite process': DM, 'Intellect and Culture', *NF* I.2 (1 July 1913) 23.

'Images': DM, 'The Gentle Art of "Appreciation"', *Egoist* II.8 (2 Aug. 1915) 118.

construct its own self: see e.g. DM, 'The Science of Signs. XVII: Truth. iv. The Measure of Authority', *Egoist* VI.3 (July 1919) 33–8.

declared war on words: DM, '"I AM"', *Egoist* II.1 (1 Jan. 1915) [1]-4.

230 Dora Marsden retired: information re DM's later life from Les Garner, *A Brave and Beautiful Spirit.*

'a belief in the vision': *TLS* review, 7 Feb. 1929, as cited in Lidderdale and Nicholson, *Dear Miss Weaver*, p. 287.

'The image': EP, 'Vorticism' (1914), *GB* 92.

'great works of art': ibid.

Hulme's talk: see *EP/LR* 155.

'an attempt to evoke': F. S. Flint, 'Contemporary French Poetry', *Poetry Review* I.8 (Aug. 1912) 355.

231 'The development of art': 'Inner Necessity', extracts from Kandinsky's *Ueber das Geistige in der Kunst*, trans. Edward Wadsworth, *Blast* no. 1 (20 June 1914) 120. For EP's mentions of Kandinsky's book see 'Vortex, Pound', *Blast* no. 1, p. 154; and 'Vorticism' (1914), *GB* 86.

not a complete theory: see EP, 'Small Magazines', *English Journal (College Edition)* XIX.9 (Nov. 1930) 691.

'cult of beauty': 'The Serious Artist' (1913), *LE* 45.

a glib parody: 'R.A.', 'Vates, the Social Reformer', *Des Imagistes*, pp. 59–61.

Hueffer's retort: 'F.M.H.', 'Fragments Addressed by Clearchus H. to Aldi', ibid., p. 62.

232 Hueffer's preface: in *Poetry* II. 5 and 6 (Aug. and Sept. 1913) the title was 'Impressionism'; in *NF* I.6 and 7 (1 and 15 Sept. 1913) the title was 'The Poet's Eye'. The opening was altered when it appeared as 'Preface' to *Collected Poems* by Ford Madox Hueffer (Max Goschen, 1914). For this paragraph see *Collected Poems* pp. 15–17.

'I got out of a train': EP, 'How I Began', *T. P.'s Weekly* XXI.552 (6 June 1913) 707.

Odd ends

232 'Those who have read': EP, unpublished brief review sent to *Poetry* about Dec. 1912, as given in editorial notes in *EP/DS* 168.

233 Frost...ungrateful: see Williams, *Harriet Monroe*, pp. 66–7. Williams cites in particular Frost's letter of July 1913 to Thomas Bird Mosher.

Pound's advice: see EP to MCA [? 6 Nov. 1917], *EP/LR* 143.

a 'tactful' review: I have transferred the word from EP's telling DS that his introduction to the selection from WCW's *The Tempers* in *Poetry Review* I.10 (Oct. 1912) was 'a masterpiece of tactful iniquity'—*EP/DS* 145.

'College of the Arts': details from EP, 'America: Chances and Remedies.V. Proposition III—The College of the Arts', *NA* XIII.5 (29 May 1913) 115–16. See also

EP letter to MC, 2 Nov. [1910], *EP/MC* 54 (pp. 137–8 above refer); and 'Patria Mia. VII', *NA* XI.25 (17 Oct. 1912) 587–8.

'The Angel Club': first announced in *NF* I.5 (15 Aug. 1913) 98; invitation 'To Overmen' in *NF* I.6 (1 Sept. 1913) 120; article explaining its aims, 'The Angel Club' by 'The Chancellor', *NF* I.8 (1 Oct. 1913) 144–5.

Pound responded: letter to the editor, 'The Order of the Brothers Minor', *NF* I.9 (15 Oct. 1913) 176. (A letter from 'The Chancellor' welcoming EP's interest appeared in the following issue, *NF* I.10 (1 Nov. 1913) 199.)

Upward had written: in *The New Word* (Geneva, 1907; A. C. Fifield, 1908) p. 290. EP reviewed that work in 'Allen Upward Serious' *NA* XIV.25 (23 Apr. 1914) 779–80 (repr. *S Pr* 377–82). See A. D. Moody, 'Pound's Allen Upward', *Pai* 4.1(1975) 62–3.

234 'the only modern heresy': EP letter to the editor, 'The Order of the Brothers Minor', *NF* I.9 (15 Oct. 1913) 176.

'good man of Nazareth', 'sinister...Italian': EP to JJ [*c*. June] 1915, *EP/JJ* 35. Manning's 'More like Kh-r-ist and the late James McNeill Whistler every year' reported by EP to Iris Barry, 13 July 1916, *L (1951)* 135.

Ralph Fletcher Seymour and EP's Arnaut Daniel: details from *EP/ACH* 3–19; Gallup: 1983, 446 (E6a); and Seymour's 'Announcement' (Beinecke—also reproduced [reduced] *EP/DS* 199). Concerning the articles on America, see Gallup: 1983, 82 (A63)—the 1913 manuscript was published by Seymour as *Patria Mia* when it 'came to light again in 1950'.

'Lustra' to a publisher: see EP to DS [9 Aug. 1913], *EP/DS* 242.

explain the title: in *P (1926)*, p. [78].

John Cournos: Cournos's observations, in his *Autobiography* (New York: G. P. Putnam's Sons, 1935), taken from Norman: 1960, 108–10.

235 'I assumed': WBY to William Rothenstein, 14 Nov. 1912, as given in Foster: 1997, 475—details from Foster's commentary. *Gitanjali* carried a dedication to Rothenstein.

'although I do not really': 'A Word from Mr Yeats', *Poetry* III.4 (Jan. 1914) 149–50.

spent his £40: details in EP to WCW [19 Dec. 1913], *EP/WCW* 22–3.

12. Going to War: 1913–1915

236 'Brzeska': EP's account of the first meeting, *GB* 44–5, 39–40. On Gaudier see also H. S. Ede, *Savage Messiah* (William Heinemann, 1931), and Evelyn Silber, *Gaudier-Brzeska: Life and Art* (Thames and Hudson, 1996).

'Altaforte': *EP/WCW* 22; *GB* 45, 46.

'*the* coming sculptor': *EP/WCW* 22.

'most absolute case of genius': EP in D. G. Bridson, 'An Interview with Ezra Pound', *New Directions 17*, ed. J. Laughlin (New York: New Directions, 1961), p. 161.

Epstein: details from EP, 'The New Sculpture', *Egoist* I.4 (16 Feb. 1914) 67–8, and 'Exhibition at the Goupil Gallery', *Egoist* I.6 (16 Mar. 1914) 109.

237 'But Lewis's drawing': EP to JQ, 10 Mar. 1916, *EP/JQ* 67.

'the sullen fury': EP, 'Wyndham Lewis', *Egoist* I.12 (15 June 1914) 233.

238 another addition...Upward: EP to DS, 23 Sept. 1913, and [2 Oct. 1913], *EP/DS* 259 and 264. Upward is remembered in *Cantos* 74/437 and 110/781.

'against the crushing dominion': The Chancellor, 'The Angel Club', *NF* I.8 (1 Oct. 1913) 144.

'the forces of intelligence': EP, 'The Divine Mystery', *NF* I.11 (15 Nov. 1913) 207–8.

started him off: EP to IWP, 13 Oct. 1913 (Beinecke).

'China has replaced Greece': EP note, introducing 'The Causes and Remedy of the Poverty of China' by F.T.S., *Egoist* I.6 (16 Mar. 1914) 105. See also *LE* 215: 'this century may find a new Greece in China' (1914).

Upward wrote: 'Sayings of K'ung the Master', Selected, with an introduction, by Allen Upward, *NF* I.10 (1 Nov. 1913) 190.

239 'orient from all quarters': EP to DS [2 Oct. 1913], *EP/DS* 264.

Fenollosa: biographical information from Mary Fenollosa's 'Preface' to *Epochs of Chinese & Japanese Art* by Ernest F. Fenollosa (1912; repr. New York: Dover Publications, Inc., 1963), pp. vii–xxii; see also Akiko Miyake, 'Contemplation East and West', *Pai* 10.3 (1981) 536 (on Fenollosa's Buddhism).

'cared about the poetry': EP to JQ, 17 May 1917, *EP/JQ* 118.

'a book on the Japanese drama': EP to HLP [5 Dec. 1913] (Beinecke).

'that you will become': Mary Fenollosa to EP, 25 Nov. 1913, in *EP&J* 8.

'great opportunity': EP to HLP [5 Dec. 1913] (Beinecke).

'got £40': EP to JQ, 17 May 1917, *EP/JQ* 118.

238 would not have paid: EP, tss. note [on 'The Chinese Written Character'], YCAL MSS 43, Box 101 (Beinecke).

Spirits at Stone Cottage

A principle source of information concerning the three winters Pound was with Yeats at Stone Cottage is James Longenbach's *Stone Cottage: Pound, Yeats and Modernism* (New York: Oxford University Press, 1988).

240 'wild moorland': EP to IWP [Nov. 1913] (Beinecke). Further details from Foster: 1997, 502–6.

He had expected: EP to IWP [early Nov. 1913], *L (1951)* 63.

'a learned companion': WBY to Lady Gregory, cited Longenbach, *Stone Cottage*, p. 37.

'the best winter': Foster: 1997, 506.

'much finer *intime*': EP to WCW [19 Dec. 1913], *EP/WCW* 22.

reading Confucius: 'I read Kung-fu-tsu...and I read ghosts to the eagle [WBY]'—EP to DS [14 Nov. 1913], *EP/DS* 274.

Les Quatre Livres: the fourth book was Mencius.

241 'If a man': *Cantos* 13/58–60. See also EP, 'On the Degrees of Honesty in Various Occidental Religions' (1939), *S Pr* 66.

Nishikigi: for EP's translation see *The Classic Noh Theatre of Japan*, included in *T*.

'we see great characters': 'Fenollosa on the Noh', *T* 280.

an Arran legend: WBY, 'Swedenborg, Mediums and the Desolate Places', *Explorations* (Macmillan, 1962), pp. 64–9. Cp. EP in *T* 226 (footnote), and 236.

242 'hearing...Wordsworth': *Cantos* 83/534.

some have argued: e.g. Longenbach in his *Stone Cottage*, and Leon Surette in *A Light from Eleusis* (Oxford: Oxford University Press, 1979) and *The Birth of Modernism: Ezra Pound, T. S. Eliot, W. B. Yeats, and the Occult* (Montreal: McGill-Queen's University Press, 1993). Demetres Tryphonopoulos in *The Celestial Tradition: a study of Ezra Pound's 'The Cantos'* (Waterloo, Ontario: Wilfred Laurier University Press, 1992), while making much of EP's association with occultists, recognized that there is no evidence of his ever joining any group of them, and also that he was definitely not interested in WBY's ghosts, metempsychoses and the like. See Colin McDowell's magisterial 'Literalists of the Imagination: Pound, Occultism and the Critics', *Pai* 28.2–3 (1999) 7–107; also Colin McDowell and Timothy Materer, 'Gyre and Vortex: W. B. Yeats and Ezra Pound', *Twentieth Century Literature* 31 (1985) 348–67.

De Daemonalitate: first mentioned by EP in 'Note Precedent' to 'La Fraisne'—see p. 51 above. See Longenbach, *Stone Cottage*, pp. 48–9.

Heyman...spiritualism: see Faubion Bowers, 'Memoir within Memoirs', *Pai* 2.1 (1973) 53–66, and Demetres P. Tryphonopoulos, '"That Great Year Epic": Ezra Pound, Katherine Ruth Heyman and H. D.', in *Ezra Pound and America*, ed. Jacqueline Kaye (Macmillan, 1992), pp. 149–65.

Mead: see Tryphonopoulos, *The Celestial Tradition*, pp. 25, 86.

Orage: see A. R. Orage, *Selected Essays and Critical Writings*, ed. Herbert Read and Denis Saurat (Stanley Nott, 1935), pp. 113–14, 179–81.

Yeats was after: see WBY, *Per Amica Silentiae Lunae* (1917), in *Mythologies* (Macmillan, 1962), pp. 319–69.

He was to attribute: in 'Introduction to "A Vision"', *A Vision* (1925) (Macmillan, 1962), pp. 8 ff.

'He will be quite sensible': EP to JQ, 15 Nov. 1918, *EP/JQ* 168.

243 'As the abstract mathematician': in 'The Wisdom of Poetry' (1912), *S Pr* 331–2.

'Have you ever seen': *EP/DS* 3.

occult mystery: 'Shallow minds have been in a measure right in their lust for "secret history", I mean they have been dead right to want it, but shallow in their conception of what it was'—EP, *GK* 264. On the previous page EP connected 'a conspiracy of intelligence' with 'Varchi wanted the facts'.

a fountain of energy: see Allen Upward, *The New Word* (A. C. Fifield, 1908), pp. 194–8.

'"Intellectual vision"': EP to DS [21 Nov. 1913], *EP/DS* 276.

'not with the bodily vision': EP to WCW [21 Oct. 1908], *EP/WCW* 9.

'before embarking': EP to IWP [Mar. 1912] (Beinecke). See also *EP/DS* 118–9.

'funny symboliste trappings': EP, 'Remy de Gourmont', *LE* 340, citing *Inferno* III, 18.

244 'You will hate', 'should quarrel': WBY, *A Vision* (1962), pp. 28, 3.

Homage to Blunt: details from *Cantos* 81/522; EP to F. S. Flint, n.d. (HRC); Richard Aldington, 'Presentation to Mr. W. S. Blunt', *Egoist* I.3 (2 Feb. 1914) 56–7; EP, 'Homage to Wilfred Blunt', *Poetry* III.6 (Mar. 1914) 220–3; Mohammad Y. Shaheen, 'Pound and Blunt: Homage for Apathy', *Pai* 12.2–3 (1983) 281–7; Foster: 1997, 509–10. Masefield and Manning were to be in the party, but are not in the photograph.

Blunt's diary: entries for 18 and 19 Jan., 25 Mar. and 19 July 1914, from Shaheen, 'Pound and Blunt', pp. 284–7.

245 'To have, with decency': *Cantos* 81/522.

'a great peacock', 'would not eat ham': *Cantos* 85/533–4.

A marriage

246 On the 21st: this paragraph based on letters and editorial matter in *EP/DS* 304–39, and on a copy of the marriage certificate (HRC).

'it is settled': EP to IWP [early Nov. 1913], *L (1951)* 63.

'never had £300': EP to JQ, 4 and 5 July 1922, *EP/JQ* 209–10.

247 Olivia went bail: Carpenter: 1988, 236 states that OS was the legal tenant.

Ezra had scruples: the letters exchanged between EP and HHS, 16 and 19 Feb. 1914, are given in *EP/DS* 307–9.

248 'we must get that right': HHS to EP, 17 Mar. 1914, *EP/DS* 331.

249 'what you talked of': DS to EP, 21 Mar. [1914], *EP/DS* 333.

5 Holland Place Chambers: details from Wyndham Lewis, *Self Condemned* (1954), (Santa Barbara: Black Sparrow Press, 1983), pp. 5–6; EP to DS [28 Feb. and Mar. 1914], *EP/DS* 310, 315, 316; Stock: 1970, 155.

'the tiny quintangle': EP to Ingrid Davies, 2 Apr. 1955 (HRC).

triangular oak table: Wilhelm: 1990 [152], writes that EP 'designed' the table. In 1970 DP pasted a note on the underside of the table, now in the possession of Omar and Elizabeth Pound, saying, 'This table was bought by Ezra Pound, used for typing Cantos and all correspondence 1914–1920' (communication from Elizabeth Pound).

he knew better: see p. 57 above.

'I can't do a thing': DS to EP, 9 Mar. [1914], *EP/DS* 321. See *Cantos* 81 / 518.

'pan-cakes': EP to IWP [March 1914] (Beinecke).

'excellently': WL, *B&B* 277.

wedding presents: EP to DS [10 Mar. 1914], *EP/DS* 322; Wilhelm: 1990, 154.

'much too much': DS to EP [7 Mar. 1914], EP to DS [10 Mar. 1914], *EP/DS* 319, 323.

250 'deathless music': EP to WBY, '9 / 11 / 14' (HRC)—published in 'Letters to William Butler Yeats' ed. C. F. Terrell, *Antæus* 21 / 22 (1976) 34, repr. *P&P* X, 134.

Gaudier's bust of EP: details from *GB* 47–50; *EP/DS* 315, 323; Silber, *Gaudier-Brzeska* 43, 269–70. Hueffer put the bust in the garden at South Lodge, where it stayed until EP had it removed to Rapallo in the '30s. For a time it was on his roof terrace, 'the stone eyes gazing seaward'; and it was with him after 1958 at Brunnenburg in the Tyrol. Now in Raymond and Patsy Nasher Sculpture Museum, Dallas.

'I hereby declare': DP to EP [June–July 1917] (Lilly).

evidence…financial security: e.g. a ts. note for Olga Rudge [1960s], YCAL MSS 53, Box 34, folder 791 (Beinecke). See also EP, 'Suffragettes', *Egoist* I.13 (1 July 1914) 255: 'If a family of two have two hundred or even one hundred pounds a year of more or less regular income, they can live as befits rational literate animals. If they have children, or if they have too many, they sink.'

sexually unawakened, 'a beautiful picture': respectively HD and Daniel Cory, as cited by Carpenter: 1988, 239–41.

'beautiful and clever': WBY to EP, 8 Mar. 1914, as cited by the editors, *EP/DS* 332.

wrote in 1912: in 'Patria Mia. IX', *NA* XI.27 (31 Oct. 1912) 635–6.

251 'Exhausted by': 'Introduction' to 'Cavalcanti Poems', *T* 19–20.

'Love-Song to Eunoë': now in *CEP* 285.

252 'My invaluable': EP to WL [before July 1915], *EP/WL* 12.

'literary men's wives': WBY to Augusta Gregory, 24 Nov. 1913, cited Foster: 1997, 509.

'Dresden china': WBY to Mabel Beardsley, 15 Jan. 1915, cited Ann Saddlemyer, *Becoming George: The Life of Mrs W. B. Yeats* (Oxford: Oxford University Press, 2002), p. 76.

'Snow Scene': 'D. . . . has done one design, snow', EP to WL, Jan. 1915, *EP/WL* 9.

As an artist: a sampling of DS's work was published as *Etruscan Gate: A Notebook with Drawings and Watercolours*, ed. Moelwyn Merchant (Exeter: The Rougemont Press, 1971). See also *Vorticism and its allies* (London: Arts Council of Great Britain, 1974), pp. 33 and 94–5.

a notebook: now in Beinecke as 'notebook 7'. Dorothy may have been unfamiliar with the use of books in the British Museum, but she had visited the Print Room frequently in Feb. and Mar. 1913—possibly to make sketches of the Chinese works there (see *EP/DS* 177).

an alien: Ellen Wilkinson M. P. wrote to DP on 5 July 1929 on House of Commons notepaper: 'I have, on two occasions, introduced the Bill to grant to English women married to aliens the right to their own nationality, but it did not proceed further than the first reading' (Beinecke Pound MSS II).

The BLAST vortex

253 T. E. Hulme lecture: printed as 'Modern Art and Its Philosophy' in *Collected Writings of T. E. Hulme*, ed. Karen Csengeri (Oxford: Clarendon Press, 1994), pp. 268–85.

according to Lechmere: my paraphrase of Stock: 1970, 159.

suspended . . . in Soho Square: WL, *B&B* 36. There are other more detailed accounts of the episode.

Pound's account: EP, 'The New Sculpture', *Egoist* I.4 (16 Feb. 1914) 67–8.

254 Hulme did say: op.cit., 268 ff., and 284 (on Epstein).

among equals: 'The pleasure of the vorticist movement was to find onself at last *inter pares.*'—'Ezra Pound Files Exceptions', *Reedy's Mirror* XXV.32 (18 Aug. 1916) 535.

Epstein and form: 'Affirmations. III. Jacob Epstein', *NA* XVI.12 (21 Jan. 1915) 311–12.

Of Vorticist art in general: 'Affirmations. II. Vorticism', *NA* XVI.11 (14 Jan. 1915) 277–8.

255 'fire-eating': WL in *Time and Western Man*, cited Peter Ackroyd, *Ezra Pound and his World* (Thames and Hudson, 1980), p. 37.

Vorticism . . . Lewis's: see 'Ezra Pound Files Exceptions'.

a movement of individuals: see *GB* 94, and 'Edward Wadsworth, Vorticist', *Egoist* I.6 (15 Aug. 1914) 307.

'accelerated impressionism': EP, 'Vortex. Pound', *BLAST* no. 1 (June 1914) 154.

mentioning it in his letters: see *EP/DS* 311, 315, 316; *EP/JJ* 26.

256 Pound's particular: see Wilhelm: 1990, 148.

'nice blasty poems': EP to DS [Mar. 1914], *EP/DS* 316.

'Chinese crackers': WL in *Time and Western Man*, cited Ackroyd, *Ezra Pound and his World*, p. 37.

'The vortex': EP, 'Vortex. Pound', *BLAST* no. 1 (June 1914) 153–4.

257 'the dominant cell': EP, 'The Approach to Paris. III', *NA* XIII.21 (18 Sept. 1913) 608; 'Study in French Poets' (1918), *Instigations* 70, *MIN* 211.

not a mere receiver: see EP, 'The New Sculpture', *Egoist* I.4 (16 Feb. 1914) 67; 'Affirmations. IV. As for Imagisme', *NA* XVI.13 (28 Jan. 1915), 349–50.

'think of him': EP, 'Vortex. Pound', *BLAST* no. 1 (June 1914) 153.

'unassimilable and aggressive': WL, *B&B* 275.

'restless, turbulent': 'Edward Wadsworth, Vorticist', *Egoist* I.6 (15 Aug. 1914) 306.

'not unintelligible': [Orage], 'Readers and Writers', *NA* XV.10 (9 July 1914) 229. [Orage thought better of *BLAST* no. 2—it gave him an understanding of Vorticism, and at least Lewis could write: see *NA* XVII.13 (29 July 1915) 309.]

'stamps a man': Prothero's letter of 22 Oct. is given in Stock: 1970, 162.

The coming of war

258 'atavism': EP, 'Chronicles', *BLAST* no. 2 (July 1915) 86; letter to HM, 9 Nov. [1914], *L (1951)* 88.

Lewis went up: see WL, 'The Crowd Master. 1914. London, July', *BLAST* no. 2 (July 1915) 94–102, and *B&B* 56 ff.

'a triumph . . . mass-murder': WL, *B&B* 84–5.

259 casualties: Muriel Ciolkowska, 'Fighting Paris', *Egoist* II.2 (1 Feb. 1915) 29.

'no other news': EP to HLP, 7 Sept. 1914 (Beinecke).

'found a new good poet': EP to HLP [Oct. 1914] (Beinecke).

'London not yet dynamited': EP to HLP, 24 Oct. 1914 (Beinecke).

'Cracow in flames': EP to IWP [? Nov. 1914] (Beinecke).

some fine stuff, 'War losing interest': EP to HLP [? Nov. 1914] (Beinecke).

'a good little book': EP to HLP, 20 Dec. 1914 (Beinecke).

'topics of the moment': EP to HM, 9 Nov. [1914], *L (1951)* 86–8.

Gaudier was writing: Gaudier's letters from the front are edited by EP in *GB* 55–74.

'Human masses': 'Vortex Gaudier-Brzeska', *BLAST* no. 2 (July 1915) 33–4. [Gaudier apparently wrote 'projectors', which I have taken to mean 'projectiles'.]

260 'thoughts of an artist': Hueffer's comment cited by EP, *GB* 28.

'I again indulged': G-B to EP, '14 / 3 / 1915', *GB* 61.
'They depict': G-B to EP, 'Dec. 18th', *GB* 58.
'a gruesome place': G-B to EP [June 1915], *GB* 63–4.

261   'A great spirit': *GB* 17.

did volunteer: EP in letter to Milton Bronner [1915 or 1916] (HRC), said he had volunteered three times but there was 'no foreign legion' [as in France].

'carrying rifles': EP to HM, 15 Sept. 1914, cited Longenbach, *Stone Cottage*, p. 114.

'Be still': 'War verse' (1914), *P (1990)*, p. 253—not published by EP.

'abbreviated': 'Poem: Abbreviated from the Conversation of Mr. T. E. H.', *Catholic Anthology* (1915); in *CEP* 286.

262   to 'erect *The Times*': EP, 'Wyndham Lewis', *Egoist* I.12 (15 June 1914) 234.

'This war': '1915: Feb.', *P (1990)*, pp. 253–4.

Poets in a world at war: 'Cathay'

262   'to make a great age': EP, 'Affirmations. I. Arnold Dolmetsch', *NA* XVI. 10 (7 Jan. 1915) 247.

263   Wyndham Lewis . . . Mr Asquith: WL, *B&B* 50–5.

'relation of the state': see '"The Age Demanded"', *HSM*.

'movement of individuals': 'Edward Wadsworth, Vorticist', *Egoist* I.6 (15 Aug. 1914) 306.

Orage's refusing: see *EP/JQ* 23 and *EP/JJ* 43 n. 9.

'College of the Arts': [EP], 'Preliminary Announcement', *Egoist* I.21 (2 Nov. 1914) 413–14.

264   'no light': EP to HM, 31 Jan. 1915—cited Longenbach, *Stone Cottage*, p. 118.

They were reading: details in the paragraph from EP letters to his parents, '16 / 1 / 15', 'Feb. 1st' and 'Feb. 12th' [1915] (Beinecke); Longenbach, *Stone Cottage* p. 120; Wilhelm: 1990, 173; Foster: 1997, 527.

'We poets': WBY, 'A Reason for Keeping Silent' (1916), given in Longenbach, *Stone Cottage*, p. 118—collected, in a revised version, as 'On being asked for a War Poem' in *The Wild Swans at Coole* (1919).

'Meditations in Time of Civil War': see part V in particular, but the entire poem is relevant here.

265   'sketches': see 'Main outline of E.P.'s work to date', *Umbra*, p. 128.

'a desire personally to insult': WBY as reported by Richard Aldington, 'Presentation to Mr. W. S. Blunt', *Egoist* I.3 (2 Feb. 1914) 57.

history of . . . *Dubliners*: see EP, 'A Curious History', *Egoist* I.2 (15 Jan. 1914) 26–7, repr. *EP/JJ* 20–3.

'the best poem': see EP to HM, 30 Sept. and 9 Nov. [1914], 31 Jan. [1915], *L (1951)* 80, 85, 92–3.

tariff on books: EP to ACH, 29 Mar. 1915, *EP/ACH* 97–8.

'Salutation the Third': as in *BLAST* no. 1, p. 45.

'I cling to the spar': 'Et Faim Sallir Le Loup Des Boys', *BLAST* no. 2, p. 22; *CEP* 284.

266   'if I give': Gallup: 1983, 17 gives the end-note to *Cathay*.

267   'Petrarchan': EP, 'The Renaissance' (1915), *LE* 218: 'Liu Ch'e, Chu Yuan, Chia I, and the great *vers libre* writers before the Petrarchan age of Li Po, are a treasury to which the next century may look for as great a stimulus as the renaissance had from the Greeks.' See also *LE* 24 (Petrarch and Virgil). Further mentions of Petrarch can be found via *LE* index.

'major persona': see 'Main outline of E.P.'s work to date', *Umbra*, p. 128.

'Song of the Bowmen of Shu': for EP's later version see *CA* no. 167 (p. 86).

269   a clear design: strictly speaking, the design first appeared in *P (1926)*—in *Cathay* (1915) 'The Jewel-Stairs Grievance' was placed after 'The River-Merchant's Wife'.

Note also that *Cathay* (1915) ended with 'South Folk in Cold Country'—the four poems which now follow it were first added in *Lustra* (1916).

'**Lament of the Frontier Guard**': in some editions the penultimate line reads 'With Rihaku's name forgotten'—instead of 'Rihoku' (*Lustra* and *P (1926)*, or 'Riboku' (Fenollosa notebook). 'Riboku', the name of a general, would be the correct reading, but the misprint 'Rihaku' was a fortunate lapse.

270   '**the whole man**': EP to Thomas Bird Mosher, 3 Dec. 1914, cited Ronald Bush, 'Pound and Li Po: What Becomes a Man', *Ezra Pound Among the Poets* ed. George Bornstein (Chicago: University of Chicago Press, 1985), p. 42.

271   '**doom-eager**': EP, 'Patria Mia. XI', *NA* XII.2 (14 Nov. 1912) 33.

'**the pity of war**': see Wilfred Owen, 'Preface' for his War Poems.

'**passive suffering**': WBY, 'Introduction', *Oxford Book of Modern Verse 1892–1935* (1936), p. xxxiv.

Finding himself

271   **Hueffer full of praise**: FMH, 'From China to Peru', *Outlook* 35 (19 June 1915) 800–1—repr. (with excisions) in *P/F* 24–6.

272   **Orage judged**: review repr. Homberger: 1972, 110–11.

Wyndham Lewis's colonel: see WL to EP, 'June 22 / 16', and EP to WL, '24 / 6 / 16', *EP/WL* 38, 39.

Eliot's brochure: *Ezra Pound: His Metric and Poetry* (1917), reprinted in *To Criticize the Critic* (Faber and Faber, 1965)—on *Cathay* see pp. 180–1.

'**the inventor**': TSE, 'Introduction', *Ezra Pound: Selected Poems*, ed. TSE (Faber & Gwyer, 1928), p. xvi.

a start on the language: 'Dorothy is learning Chinese', EP to WCW [19 Dec. 1913], *EP/WCW* 22. Omar Pound informed Zhaoming Qian 'that he keeps a notebook of his mother showing she was learning Chinese' (Zhaoming Qian, *Orientalism and Modernism: The Legacy of China in Pound and Williams* (Durham: Duke University Press, 1995), p. 189 n. 6).

273   '*crimson or / vermilion*': lines from Fenollosa's notes for 'Exile's Letter', as transcribed by Ronald Bush, 'Pound and Li Po', *Ezra Pound Among the Poets* ed. Bornstein, p. 54.

'**good translation**': TSE, 'Introduction', *Ezra Pound: Selected Poems* ed. TSE, p. xiv.

274   '**acknowledged guide**': EP to HM [31 Jan. 1915], *L (1951)* 90.

'**unacknowledged legislators**': P. B. Shelley in *A Defence of Poetry* (1821).

13. SHAPING AN INTELLIGENCE UNIT: 1915–1916

276   **There were Zeppelins**: paragraph based on unpublished letters, DP to EP, 8 and 10 Sept. 1915; EP to DP, 8 and 11 Sept. 1915 (Lilly).

She was enjoying: DP to EP, 10 Sept. 1915 (Lilly).

On July 21: paragraph from here based on unpublished letters of EP to DP, 21 and 22 July 1915 (Lilly).

277   '**very fine**': EP to DP, 8 Sept. 1915 (Lilly).

three 'political' notes: i.e. 'American Chaos' [I, II], *NA* XVII. 19, 20 (9, 16 Sept. 1915) 449, 471; 'This Super-Neutrality', *NA* XVII. 25 (21 Oct. 1915) 595. In this connection see also 'The Net American Loss', written early 1915, first published in 'Ezra Pound on America and World War I', presented by Timothy Materer, *Pai* 18.1–2 (1989) 204–11. This paragraph and the one following are mostly drawn from these four articles. Also relevant is the series 'What America has to Live Down . . . I–VI', in *NA*, Aug. and Sept. 1918.

'The struggle at Ypres': EP to HM, May 1915, cited Longenbach, *Stone Cottage*, p. 120.

'civilization against barbarism': EP to HM, 5 June 1915, cited Longenbach, *Stone Cottage*, p. 123.

278   believed with Flaubert: see 'American Chaos. II', *NA* XVII.20 (16 Sept. 1915) 471.

'temporarily off': EP to ACH [15 June 1916], *EP/ACH* 151.

'moribund': letter to MCA, date not given, as in Margaret Anderson, *My Thirty Years War: The Autobiography, beginnings and battles to 1930* (New York: Horizon Press, 1969), p. 172.

'too damn soft': EP to JQ, given as '4 June [1918]' in *L (1951)* 197, but actually part of EP to JQ, 3 Apr. [1918]—see *EP/JJ* 132n; 'celtic' is from EP to Iris Barry, 9 Sept. 1916, 'Letters to a Young Poet', ed. D. D. Paige, *Changing World* 7 (1949) 36 [*P&P* VIII, 416].

'idealism': EP to JQ, 10 Jan. 1918, *EP/JQ* 139.

'a party of intelligence': EP, 'James Joyce: At Last the Novel Appears', *Egoist* IV. 2 (Feb. 1917) 21.

'American collectors': 'Affirmations. III. Jacob Epstein', *NA* XVI.12 (21 Jan. 1915) 312.

John Quinn: details in rest of paragraph from Timothy Materer's 'Introduction. From Henry James to Ezra Pound: John Quinn and the Art of Patronage', *EP/JQ* 1–4. For further information see B. L. Reid, *The Man from New York: John Quinn and His Friends* (New York: Oxford University Press, 1968).

'If there were more like you': EP to JQ [9 Mar. 1915], *EP/JQ* 20.

279   'tools, time and food': ibid. 23.

'the face a triangle': EP to JQ, 18 Apr. 1915, *EP/JQ* 26.

'Decent publicity', 'a well illustrated memoir': EP to JQ, 13 July 1915, *EP/JQ* 30, 29.

title to Gaudier's estate: on this see *EP/JQ* 68–70.

Henry Moore: see Silber, *Gaudier-Brzeska*, 139.

Caring for Wyndham Lewis and James Joyce

279   'two men of genius': EP to ACH, 9 Aug. 1915, *EP/ACH* 120.

280   'too flighty': EP to JQ, 3 Sept. 1916, *EP/JQ* 76 [in editorial note re TSE].

washed his hands: EP to ACH, 9 Aug. 1915, *EP/ACH* 118–19.

'only advance': EP to ACH, 20 Dec. 1916, *EP/ACH* 171.

'led to *Paterson*': WCW, *Autobiography* (1967), pp. 60–1.

a contemporary reviewer: Arthur Waugh, 'The New Poetry', *Quarterly Review* 226 (Oct. 1916) 365–86, as cited by Carpenter: 1988, 282–3. For Pound's retort see 'Drunken Helots and Mr Eliot', *Egoist* IV.5 (June 1917) 72–4.

Francis Meynell: see Stock: 1970, 191.

sales: of the 500 copies printed some were still unsold 'as late as Apr. 1936' (Gallup: 1983, 141).

Joyce: paragraph based on Forrest Read's presentation of correspondence between EP, JJ, WBY and Gosse in June and July 1915, *EP/JJ* 34–40; and on Richard Ellmann's account of the episode, which gives further letters from WBY and JJ, *James Joyce* (New York: Oxford University Press, 1959), pp. 401–5.

281   Lewis: paragraph based on correspondence between EP and WL between Aug. 1915 and 1 Jan. 1916, *EP/WL* 14–22.

just £42 10s.: detail from Stock: 1970, 187.

'THIS IS': EP to WL [Dec. 1915], *EP/WL* 18.

'raising £20': EP to WL, 1 Jan. 1916, *EP/WL* 22.

Joyce's *Portrait*: details in this paragraph drawn from Ellmann, *Joyce*, pp. 413–17; from *EP/JJ* 59–75; and from *EP/JQ* 59–64.

'with blank spaces': EP to JJ, 16 Mar. 1916, *EP/JJ* 74.

'Judging from': EP to JJ, 31 Jan. 1916, *EP/JJ* 68.

'much pleased': EP to JQ, 26 Feb. 1916, *EP/JQ* 60–1.

282   'a tired head': EP to JJ [between 6 and 12] Sept. 1915, *EP/JJ* 46.

an article: 'Mr James Joyce and the Modern Stage', *Drama*, Chicago, VI.21 (Feb. 1916) 122–32.

he was worried: see EP to JJ, 31 Jan. 1916, *EP/JJ* 67.

could not afford London: EP to JJ, 12 Jan. 1916, *EP/JJ* 62.

up in London: EP to JQ, *c.*19 Jan. 1916, *EP/JQ* 58.

Lewis: details from his correspondence with EP between Mar. and June 1916, *EP/WL* 26–40.

'that you should be covered': EP to WL, '24/6/16', *EP/WL* 39.

283   About the same time: details in this paragraph drawn mainly from *EP/JJ* 75–82. The Civil List award was not a pension but a single grant (see *L (1951)* 157).

'I do a good deal': EP to JJ, 1 June 1916, *EP/JJ* 76.

Joyce ... whose habit: see, for example, Ellmann, *Joyce*, pp. 420 ff.

'with the most absolute': WL to EP, 8 July 1916, *EP/WL* 45.

'*No one*': EP to WL [July 1916], *EP/WL* 46.

'Descend with me': WL to EP, 17 July 1916, *EP/WL* 49.

284   a little embarrassing': EP to WL [n.d.], *EP/WL* 51.

another £100: see EP to JQ, 31 Dec. 1916, *EP/JQ* 90.

'no longer on my mind': EP to JJ, 1 and 2 Sept. 1916, *EP/JJ* 82.

'no longer feel responsible': EP to JQ, 3 Sept. 1916, *EP/JQ* 76 [in editorial note re. TSE].

'At the present moment': EP to ACH, 30 Aug. 1916, *EP/ACH* 167.

'I shall devote': EP to JJ, 1 and 2 Sept. 1916, *EP/JJ* 82.

'income for year': EP to JJ, 13 Nov. 1916, *EP/JJ* 84.

to pay the rent: EP to ACH, 23 Jan. 1917, *EP/ACH* 181.

'Cadging': EP to JJ, 13 Nov. 1916, *EP/JJ* 84.

clear his debts: EP to ACH, 23 Jan. 1917, *EP/ACH* 181.

'Lustra of Ezra Pound': the censor censored

285   'the entire text': Nelson, *Elkin Mathews*, 159. Further details in this paragraph are drawn from Nelson pp. 158–65 and 278–80. See also Forrest Read's 'Appendix A', *EP/ JJ* 277–86; and Homberger: 1972, 121–4. 'April or early May' is my deduction from the fact that EP told Kate Buss, in a letter dated 9 Mar. 1916, 'I shan't publish again here until after the war' (*L (1951)* 120).

set of proofs: now in HRC.

'like the Greek statues': EP to Mathews, 2 June 1916, *EP/JJ* 286.

'Salutation the Second' and 'Commission': see above pp. 206–8.

'insults to the world': see above p. 265.

distinguished authors: EP to H. L. Mencken, 17 Mar. 1915, *L (1951)* 100.

'human beings': EP to Mathews, 30 May 1916, *EP/JJ* 284. See also EP to HM, 5 June 1916, *L (1951)* 131.

286   'Even certain smaller poems': EP to Mathews, 30 May 1916, *EP/JJ* 285.

'more or less proportioned': see above p. 103.

'complete service': see *Noh.* 9–12. For 'a sort of musical construction' see 'The Classical Stage of Japan', *Drama*, Chicago, V.18 (1915) 224.

a post card: see Homberger: 1972, 121–2, and *EP/JJ* 277. Forrest Read and Homberger both take the p.c. to be from Mathews's 'reader', but this would mean that Mathews engaged a reader only after having the poems set up in print since the comments are keyed to the proof page numbers. (One can deduce which poems are being referred to from the page numbers, and also from the way several of the comments pick up on words in the poems.) I take the p.c. to be from the firm of Clowes; and Pound told Quinn, 2 Dec. 1918, that Mathews had told him that "Wm. Archyballed Clowes"—W.C.K.'s first cousin and also a managing director in the firm—"was responsible for the trouble over Lustra" (Nelson, *Elkin Mathews*, p. 278 n. 94).

287 **Pound denied**: what follows in this paragraph and the next is mostly drawn from EP's two long letters to Mathews [*c*. 29] May 1916, and 30 May 1916, *EP/JJ* 278–82 and 282–6.

' "through the ordinary channels" ': 'Meditatio', *Egoist* III.3 (1 Mar. 1916) 37.
'Now that the novel': quoted in EP's draft 'Note' included in letter to Mathews [*c*. 29] May 1916, *EP/JJ* 280. The 'Préface' is printed in the original in *LE* 416–17.

288 **Birrell confirmed**: Birrell to Mathews, 31 May 1916, cited in Nelson, p. 161.
'other considerations': Mathews to Birrell, 31 May 1916, cited in Nelson, p. 162.
Mathews . . . list: see Homberger: 1972, 123–4, and Nelson, pp. 162–3.
'The New Cake of Soap': for EP's defence of this squib see EP to JQ, 21 Aug. 1917, *L (1951)* 170–1.
'very beautiful Normande cocotte': compare 'Simulacra', in which the penultimate line read, 'Why does the really handsome young prostitute approach me in Sackville Street'; but in this case EP said he didn't mind changing it to 'the really handsome young woman', and so it stands to this day.

289 'The minute': EP to JQ, 27 July 1916, *EP/JQ* 76–8.
'persecution mania': EP to Milton Bronner [May 1916] (HRC).
'This much': EP to Mathews [*c*. 29] May 1916, *EP/JJ* 279.

290 'The Temperaments': this was included, out of position in a blank space at the end of the *Lustra* section, in Quinn's private edition of the New York *Lustra* (1917).
'poems a grown man': EP to JQ, 24 Jan. 1917, *L (1951)* 156.
'some right': EP to Iris Barry, June 1916, *L (1951)* 132.

Dialogues at Stone Cottage

290 **housekeeping**: WBY's remark, cited Longenbach, *Stone Cottage*, p. 184.
'brrring': EP to JQ, 26 Feb. 1916, *EP/JQ* 61.
Herbert of Cherbury and Landor: EP mentions enjoying reading both with Yeats in a letter to his mother, Dec. 31 [1915] (Beinecke). (Longenbach assigns this letter to 1914, but EP and DP went down from London to Stone Cottage only on 4 Jan. 1915—DP to HLP, 8 Jan. 1915 [Beinecke]. EP begins to mention Landor to his correspondents only during and after Jan. 1916.)
Lord Herbert: Edward, Lord Herbert of Cherbury (1583–1648). His *Autobiography* was first printed by Horace Walpole in 1764, then edited by Sidney Lee in 1886.
'many men's manners': see *Odyssey* I, 3–4, and EP, 'Modern Georgics', *Poetry* V.3 (Dec. 1914) 129.
Imaginary Conversations: in Jan. 1916 EP urged WCW to 'get the ten vols. of Walter Savage Landor' (*EP/WCW* 25)—this would have been the 1891–3 edition of G. C. Crump, with the *Imaginary Conversations* in six volumes, and other important dialogues in prose and verse in the other volumes.

291 'different eras': EP, 'Landor' (1917), *S Pr* 357. See also *LE* 344.
Leo Africanus: some details from Longenbach, *Stone Cottage*, pp. 189–93.
'so tired': EP to ACH, May 5 1916, *EP/ACH* 140.
'the "search for oneself" ': 'Vorticism' (1914), *GB* 85.

292 'although I have never': 'Dialogues of Fontenelle. XII. Bombastes Paracelsus and Molière', *Egoist* IV.5 (June 1917) 71.

'an aristocratic form': 'Introduction by William Butler Yeats to *Certain Noble Plays of Japan* by Pound and Fenollosa', as in *Noh* 151.
'educated': ibid. 155.
'forbidden': ibid. 157.

293 'elaborating': ibid. 162.
'very noble': EP to JQ, 26 Feb. 1916, *EP/JQ* 61.
The Consolations of Matrimony: first published in EP, *Plays Modelled on the Noh (1916)*, ed. Donald C. Gallup (Toledo: The Friends of the University of Toledo Libraries, 1987), pp. 13–22. I know of no certain evidence that this was the play which was to have been performed with *At the Hawk's Well*. However, EP referred to that play as 'a farce', 'a skit', 'a dialogue play', and he told Joyce that it was rejected by the Abbey Theatre in Dublin 'on account of *indecency*' (*EP/JJ* 92), and *Consolations* is the only one of his known 1916 plays to which all those terms could apply.
'celtic noh': EP to IWP, 27 Feb. [1916] (Beinecke).

294 an interlude: Longenbach's account of the incident includes Bridges's letter—*Stone Cottage*, pp. 260–3. See also Stock: 1970, 190.

294 passports: all three are in the Lilly Library Pound Collection.

Works and days

294 'glued': EP to WL [Mar. 1916], *EP/WL* 25.
'immediate activity': EP to Kate Buss, 9 Mar. [1916], *L (1951)* 119–20.

295 'never … so hurried': EP to JJ, 16 Mar. 1916, *EP/JJ* 74.
'nothing but letters', 'raging': EP to ACH, 3 and 5 May 1916, *EP/ACH* 134, 140.
a correspondence course: see EP to Iris Barry, 17 Apr. 1916 to 25 Jan. 1917, *L* 124–60; also 'Letters to a Young Poet', ed. D. D. Paige, *Changing World* 7 (1949) 16–36 [*P&P* VIII, 402–16].
His first question: EP to IB, 17 Apr. 1916, *L (1951)* 124–5.
'In "Impression"': ibid. 125; 'because': EP to IB, 24 Apr. 1916, *L (1951)* 128.
'In "The Fledgling"': EP to IB, 17 Apr. 1916, *L (1951)* 125.
'"Too tender" [in 'Wet Morning']: EP to IB [June 1917], *L (1951)* 131–2.
'a new line': EP to IB, 24 Apr. 1917, *L (1951)* 129.
'I can't read', and further quotations in paragraph: EP to IB, 17 Apr. 1916, *L (1951)* 125–6.

296 'perfectly plain': EP to IB, 13 July 1916, *L (1951)* 135.
They talked: rest of paragraph from IB, 'The Ezra Pound Period', *Bookman* 74.2 (1931) 159.
'KOMPLEAT KULTURE': EP to IB [?20] July 1916, *L (1951)* 137–8. With these letters compare 'The Renaissance. I. The Palette', *Poetry* V.5 (Feb. 1915) 227–33 (in *LE* 214–18).

297 next letter: EP to IB, 27 July 1916, *L (1951)* 139–42.
When she looked back: this paragraph and the one following drawn from IB, 'The Ezra Pound Period', pp. 159–71.

298 Waley would say: 'Arthur Waley in Conversation', a BBC interview with Roy Fuller (1963), in Hugh Kenner Archive (HRC).
The weekly dinners: paragraph drawn from IB, 'The Ezra Pound Period', pp. 162, 168–9.

299 'a free front seat': EP to JJ, 1 and 2 Sept. 1916, *EP/JJ* 82.
en liaison: see Foster: 2003, 27.
'a fitting moment': EP to WL, 28 June 1916, *EP/WL* 44.
proposals: EP to JQ, 3 Aug. 1916, *EP/JQ* 86.
'a number of shots': EP to JQ, 17 May 1917, *EP/JQ* 118.

300 'any man': *GB* 45–6.
Pound reassured: EP to JQ, 29 Feb. 1916, *EP/JQ* 63.
'a renaissance': 'The Renaissance. II', *Poetry* V.6 (Mar. 1915) 285 (in *LE* 220).

Poems of 1915–16, and the measure of realism

300 'trying to decide': EP to ACH, 18 May 1916, *EP/ACH* 145.
'My preference': 'Affirmations: Edgar Lee Masters', *Reedy's Mirror* XXIV.13 (21 May 1915) 10–12; 'without circumlocution' is from 'Webster Ford', *Egoist* II.1 (1 Jan. 1915) 11.
301 'Objectivity': EP to HM, Jan. 1915, *L (1951)* 91.
'subjective things': '*Dubliners* and Mr. James Joyce', *Egoist* I.14 (15 July 1914) 267.
praised ... *Prufrock*: 'T. S. Eliot', *Poetry* X.5 (Aug. 1917) 265, 267; (*LE* 419, 420).
'Lewis ... realism': EP to JQ, 13 July 1916, *EP&VA* 238–9.
the first: 'The Later Yeats', *Poetry* IV.2 (May 1914) 64–9; (*LE* 378–81).
later review: 'Mr. Yeats' New Book', *Poetry* IX.3 (Dec. 1916) 150–1.
Hueffer: this clear but not quite explicit comparison runs through '*Dubliners* and Mr. James Joyce'; 'clarity and precision' is from 'Mr. Hueffer and the Prose Tradition in Verse', *Poetry* IV.3 (June 1914) 120; (*LE* 377).
302 qualified notice: 'List of Books', *LR* IV.4 (Aug. 1917) 9–10; 'you find a man telling the truth' is from 'Webster Ford', *Egoist* II.1 (1 Jan. 1915) 11.
'pearl-pale nuances': 'Mr. Yeats' New Book', *Poetry* IX.3 (Dec. 1916) 150.
'It is very important': all but last sentence of this paragraph from 'James Joyce: At Last the Novel Appears', *Egoist* IV.2 (Feb. 1917) 21–2.
303 'gives us': '*Dubliners* and Mr. James Joyce', *Egoist* I.14 (15 July 1914) 267.
'they are the stuff': 'T. S. Eliot', *Poetry* X.5 (Aug. 1917) 267; (*LE* 420).
'One cannot consider': 'List of Books', *LR* IV.4 (Aug. 1917) 9.
304 about 'as far': Norman: 1960, 444. Norman reports this as having been said by EP in the 1950s of 'Near Perigord', but there must have been a misunderstanding or mistake on someone's part, since it is obviously not true of that poem. It does happen to fit 'Provincia Deserta'.
'Near Perigord': accompanied in *Poetry* VII.3 (Dec. 1915) by a note on 'The historical data'.
'Dompna pois': EP's 1914 version is in *Lustra*; 'Na Audiart' (in *A Lume Spento*) was a quite different imitation.
details wrong: see Peter Makin, *Provence and Pound* (Berkeley: University of California Press, 1978), pp. 18–29.
305 *The Troubadours at Home*: in his note in *Poetry* EP mentions Smith's recounting of 'The traditional scene'.
Dante's de Born: see *Inferno* XXVIII, 118–42.
has Bertrans speak: in *Poetry* this part began 'I loved a woman. The stars fell from heaven. / And always our two natures were in strife.'; in *Lustra* EP deleted those two lines and added speech marks (inverted commas) at the beginning and end of part III. The latter were omitted in (and after) *P (1926)*.
306 'the most vital': 'T. S. Eliot', *Poetry* X.5 (Aug. 1917) 267; (*LE* 419).

'Three Cantos': finding his form

'Three Cantos' first published separately in *Poetry* in June, July and Aug. 1917; then together, considerably revised, in *Lustra* (New York, 1917), and in *Quia Pauper Amavi* (1919). *P (1990)* gives text as in *Poetry*; Library of America *Pound: Poems & Translations* (2003) gives text as in *Lustra (1917)*, with deleted passages from *Poetry* in the notes. My discussion

cites the *Poetry* version, and drafts now in Beinecke. To distinguish 'Three Cantos' from *The Cantos* they are sometimes referred to as the 'ur-Cantos'—I have preferred 'trial cantos'.
'the thing to go on from', 'live form': Interview with Myles Slatin, in ' "Mesmerism": A Study of Ezra Pound's Use of the Poetry of Robert Browning' (Ph.D. diss., Yale University, 1957), p. 263—cited in Christine Froula, *To Write Paradise: Style and Error in Pound's* Cantos (New Haven: Yale University Press, 1984), p. 12.

306   **'best long poem'**: EP to HLP [18 Dec. 1915] (Beinecke). The transcription in Richard Taylor, *Variorum Edition of 'Three Cantos' by Ezra Pound: A Prototype* (Bayreuth: Boomerang Press - Norbert AAS, 1991), p. 11 lacks this phrase.
    'it is a huge': EP to ACH, 9 Aug. 1915, *EP/ACH* 120.
    'cryselephantine': EP to Milton Bronner, 21 Sept. 1915 (HRC).
    'in the Vth canto': EP to HLP [18 Dec. 1915] (Beinecke).
    surviving drafts: now in Beinecke—several fragments are reproduced by Froula.

307   **striking out**: in a copy of *QPA* now in HRC.
    'revised': EP to MCA, 24 May 1917, *EP/LR* 54.
    'pass beyond humanity': EP gives the allusion to Dante, *Paradiso* I, 70, in the original.
    'Aquinas map': EP to Herbert Creekmore, Feb. 1939, *L (1951)* 417.

308   **'had some basis'**: trial canto I.
    he believed: what follows is loosely based on 'Affirmations. I. Arnold Dolmetsch', *NA* XVI.10 (7 Jan. 1917) 246–7.
    as he started: i.e. in 'Three Cantos. I'.
    'the incidents': Robert Browning, 'To J. Milsand, of Dijon' [prefatory letter to] *Sordello*, in *Poetical Works 1833–1864*, ed. Ian Jack (Oxford University Press, 1970), p. [156].

310   **'The theme'**: see Taylor, *Variorum*, p. 13.
    Takasago: EP's translation, not included in *Noh*, was first printed in *EP/ACH* 110–16.

311   **' "she comes" '**: see *Pericles* I.i.
    'single moral conviction': *Noh* 37.
    magnet ... iron filings: EP first used the analogy in 'Through Alien Eyes. I', *NA* XII.11 (16 Jan. 1913) 252; see also, of course, the close of canto 74.

312   **probably made up**: EP first made it up for the start of his 1912 walking tour—see *WT* 5 and III n. 4.
    El Cid: compare *SR* 66–73.
    king '... unjust cause': for EP's account of Lope de Vega's play see *SR* 191–3.
    Ignez: compare *SR* 218–22.
    Fred Vance: see above p. 60.
    'Puvis': Pierre Puvis de Chavannes, late nineteenth-century French painter of mythological allegories (Ronald Bush, *The Genesis of Ezra Pound's Cantos* (Princeton: Princeton University Press, 1976, p. 136). Bush's discussion of 'Three Cantos' (pp. 73–87) is noteworthy.

313   **John Heydon**: see Walter Baumann, 'Secretary of Nature, J. Heydon', in *New Approaches to Ezra Pound*, ed. Eva Hesse (Faber and Faber, 1969), pp. 303–18.
    Ficino's ... 'hotch-potch': *GB* 112.
    Valla: EP's article was 'Affirmations. VI. Analysis of this Decade', *NA* XVI.15 (11 Feb. 1915) 409–11, repr. *GB* 111–17. See also 'The Renaissance' (1914), *LE* 220; and 'Cavalcanti' (1934), *LE* 192.

314   *Odyssey*: citations here are of EP's rendering.
    'dreary': becomes 'dreory' in *XVI Cantos*.
    'Who even dead': 47 / 236.
    Divus' ... version: the volume EP bought is now in HRC.
    'very simple Latin': 'Early Translators of Homer' (1918), *LE* 264.

14 INTO ACTION: 1917–1918

Editor, male, seeks magazine (1912–16)

316 'suicidal': HM to ACH, 9 Apr. 1917, as in *EP/ACH* 194n.
'merely a ragbag': Robert Nichols, 'Poetry and Mr Pound', *Observer*, 11 Jan. 1920, p. 6, as in Homberger: 1972, 166.
'the only person': EP to HM, 21 Aug. 1917, *L (1951)* 173.
'said it was worth doing': EP to ACH, 8 Mar. 1917, *EP/ACH* 198.
'a few hundred': EP, 'Note to Printer' with setting copy for *Poetry* [May 1917], Taylor, *Variorum*, p. 13.
'Great Art': EP to JQ, 10 Jan. 1917, *EP/JQ* 93.
the 'public': from here to end of paragraph from EP to JQ, 27 July 1916, *EP/JQ* 79. Compare EP's 'Imaginary Letters. 1' [Sept. 1917], *PD (1958)* 55–6: 'There is no truce between art and the public.... The taste of the public is always bad...because it is not an individual expression'.
'sheep': cp. EP's epigraph to *GB*, 'Gli uomini vivono in pochi e gli altri son pecorelle' (Niccolo Machiavelli).

317 a magazine: material from EP to JQ, 8–9 Sept. 1916, *EP/JQ* 46–8.
'an international review': Amy Lowell to HM, 15 Sept. 1915, cited by Williams, *Harriet Monroe*, p. 83.
'the faint nuance': this and next sentence from EP to JQ, 21 May 1915, *EP/JQ* 27–8.
flood of ideas: see *EP/JQ* 31–56.
'based on': EP to JQ, 26 Aug. 1915, *EP/JQ* 42.
'a male review': ibid. 41.
'if it would be possible': EP to JQ, 13 Oct. 1915, *EP/JQ* 53–4.
'bundled up': EP to HM, 5 June 1916, *L (1951)* 131.
'foetus': TSE to JQ, 4 Mar. 1918, *TSEL* 223.
'The better stuff': EP to ACH, 5 May 1916, *EP/ACH* 137.

318 'another trial': ibid. 138.
'£120, or so': EP to JQ, 26 Feb. 1916, *EP/JQ* 60–1.
'all for it': EP to JQ, 8 Apr. 1916, *EP/JQ* 71.
'no connection': EP to ACH, 26 Aug. 1916, *EP/ACH* 163–4.
Vortoscope: see *EP&VA* 154–7, 176, 293, 316.
'a dam'd sight': EP to JQ, 13 Oct. 1916, *EP/JQ* 88.
'was surprised': EP to JQ, 17 May 1917, *EP/JQ* 119.
'That about cleans out': EP to ACH, 22 June 1916, *EP/ACH* 154.
Rodker arrested: EP mentions this in a letter to HLP [June 1916] (Beinecke).
Hueffer 'safe': EP to WL [July 1916], *EP/WL* 52.

319 'delivered from the ranks': EP to JQ, 31 Oct. 1916, *EP/JQ* 52.
'buying the remains': ibid.
'still at the front': EP to JQ, 31 Dec. 1916, *EP/JQ* 90.
'young Aldington': ibid.
'chucked school-teaching': EP to ACH, 23 Jan. 1917, *EP/ACH* 181.

Thomas S. Eliot (1914–16)

319 'the best poem': EP to HM, 30 Sept. 1914, *L (1951)* 80.
'in modern life': EP to Henry Ware Eliot, 28 June 1915, *TSEL* 101.
'such a comfort': EP to HM, 30 Sept. 1914, *L (1951)* 80.
Eliot...reported back: TSE to Conrad Aiken, 30 Sept. [1914], *TSEL* 58–9.

320 'hieratically rigid': WL, *B&B* 284.
'introduction to the Dolmetsch family': TSE to EP, 2 Feb. [1915], *TSEL* 86.

320   'been seeing a good deal': TSE to Mrs Jack Gardner, 4 Apr. [1915], *TSEL* 94.
'Prufrock' to *Poetry*: see EP to HM, 31 Jan. 1915, *L (1951)* 92–3.
'except the satisfaction': EP to HLP [? Nov. 1915] (Beinecke).
'Eliot has suddenly married': EP to HLP [30 June 1915] (Beinecke).
'some sort of apologia': Pound's letter to Henry Ware Eliot is in *TSEL* 99–104.
[Note:—'In a private paper written in the sixties', cited by Valerie Eliot in her introduction to her edition of Eliot's letters from this time (*TSEL* xvii), Eliot explained the hasty marriage which had turned out rather badly in terms which could be taken to implicate Pound. It was Pound's 'praise and encouragement' of his poetry, he wrote, and his urging him to stay in England, that had led him to marry as a way of burning his boats. He acknowledged that his heart had not been in the study of philosophy, and that he 'must still have yearned to write poetry'; also that he had been 'happier in England, even in wartime, than [he] had been in America'. All the same, it was under Pound's influence, he implied, that he had persuaded himself that he was in love with Vivienne, when in fact he was not; 'And she persuaded herself (also under the influence of Pound) that she would save the poet by keeping him in England'. However, Pound can hardly have known Vivienne, if indeed he had met her at all before the marriage; and it is hard to see how he could have persuaded either of them to marry the other, even if he had wanted to and they had been so weak as to be influenced by him against their own inclinations. I know of no evidence that he was concerned in any way in the marriage; and there is evidence that should exonerate him. In 1922 Vivienne Eliot wrote in a letter to Richard Aldington: 'once I fought like mad to keep Tom here and stopped his going back to America. I thought I could not marry him unless I was able to keep him here in England' (15? July 1922 (*TSEL* 544)). And Eliot wrote to Pound, also in 1922, 'Vivienne kept me from returning to America' (9 Aug. 1922 (Lilly)).]
'so'z not to 'ave it': EP in letter to Ingrid Davies [Oct. 1955] (HRC).

321   'EPOS on King Bolo': [Note:—T. S. Eliot, *Inventions of the March Hare*, ed. Christopher Ricks (Faber and Faber, 1996), prints stanzas of the King Bolo 'epos', and some other of the bawdy poems which Eliot had drafted along with his serious poems, in a notebook now in the Berg Collection of the New York Public Library. They are on leaves which he cut out of that notebook and gave into Pound's keeping. These 'chançons ithyphallique', as EP labelled them, are now in the Pound archive in Beinecke. With them, in the Fall of 1988 (in YCAL 43, folder 5400 of the then numbering), was a small black hard-covered notebook, containing a fair copy of the full King Bolo or Colombo epic, written in a very neat small hand, together with a considerable number of other similar verses. I should think that it was this fair copy, rather than the miscellaneous drafts and fragments, which EP referred to as 'his earlier EPOS on King Bolo'. In 1994 Donald Gallup told me the notebook was no longer in the Beinecke Pound archive. Ricks did not know of it.]
'I am sorry': TSE to Henry Ware Eliot, 27 Sept. 1915, *TSEL* 117.
Russell reported: Bertrand Russell to Charlotte C. Eliot, 3 Oct. 1915, *TSEL* 119.
'just returned': EP to WL [July 1916], *EP/WL* 52.
'far and away the best': TSE reports the review and Russell's opinion in letter to his mother, 6 Sept. 1916, *TSEL* 149–50.
'swan song': TSE to his brother, Henry Eliot, 6 Sept. 1916, *TSEL* 151.

322   'Pray God': EP to HM, 30 Sept. 1914, *L (1951)* 80.
subsidized: Harriet Shaw Weaver wrote to EP, 7 Sept. 1917, thanking him for £5 towards expenses of printing *Prufrock*. (Lilly). See also *TSEL* 170.
promoted: EP reviewed *Prufrock and Other Observations* in *Egoist* in June, and in *LR* and *Poetry* in Aug. 1917.
a new start: TSE's poems of 1917, first collected in *Poems* (Hogarth Press, 1919) and *Ara Vos Prec* (Ovid Press, 1920), now under 'Poems—1920' in his *Collected Poems*.

rigour of rhyme: see EP, 'Harold Monro', *PE*. 14.
'compact fighting sheet': EP to JQ, 3 Sept. 1916, *EP/JQ* 76 (cited in note).

'The Little Review' and the Great War: arrival of new force

In this section I have benefited from Naoyuki Date's Ph.D. dissertation, 'Ezra Pound's Editorship of the American "Little Magazines", 1912–19' (University of York, 2005).

323 'Want Ad.': MCA in *LR* III.6 (Sept. 1916) [1].
Might he come: see EP to MCA, 29 Nov. 1916, *EP/LR* 4–5.
'of books': MCA, *LR* I.1 (Mar. 1914) 2.
'French individualism': EP to MCA, 29 Nov. 1916, *EP/LR* 4–5.
'a stronger party': EP to MCA, 5 Nov. 1917, *EP/LR* 138. See also EP to ACH, 14 June 1917, *EP/ACH* 211–14.
a long letter: EP to MCA, 26 Jan. 1917, *EP/LR* 6–12. The letter is drawn on in this and the two following paragraphs.
'four pages': EP to JQ, 8 Feb. 1917, *EP/JQ* 95.
'FOUR writers': EP to Stanley Nott, 24 May 1936 (HRC).
kept secret: EP to MCA, 17 May 1917, *EP/LR* 51.

324 French Poetry: 'A Study of French Modern Poets' filled *LR* IV.10 (Feb. 1918) [3]-61; when it was included in *Instigations*, and in *MIN*, EP added 'Unanimism' from *LR* IV.12 (Apr. 1918), and two further articles from *LR* V.6 (Oct. 1918), 'De Bosschère's study of Elskamp', and 'Albert Mockel and "La Wallonie"'.
had long concerned him: for examples, see EP to JQ, 9 Mar. 1915; EP to ACH, 29 Mar. 1915; 'Tariff and Copyright', *NA* XXIII.22 (26 Sept. 1918) 348–9.
'free circulation': EP, 'Things to Be Done', *Poetry* IX.6 (Mar. 1917) 312.
'most deleterious': EP, 'Copyright and Tariff', *NA* XXIII.23 (3 Oct. 1918) 363.
'for internal freedom': EP, 'On "A Book of Prefaces"', *EP/LR* 158.
'damblasted trouble': EP to Edgar Jepson, 29 May 1917, *L (1951)* 167–8.

325 'current prose': EP, 'Editorial', *LR* IV,1 (May 1917) [3]. EP told ACH, 'the L.R. is a prose affair' (*EP/ACH* 213).
'Most good prose': EP, 'Henry James', in *LE* 324n.
'a highly energised mind': EP, 'Books Current', *Future* II.9 (Sept. 1918) 238.
'Katharsis': EP, 'Le Prix Nobel', *Der Querschnitt*, Berlin, IV.1 (Spring 1924), as in *EP/JJ* 220. See also *GK* 96.
effusive enthusiasm: see MCA's 'Surprise!' announcement in *LR* III.10 (Apr. 1917) 25.
his first editorial: EP, 'Editorial', *LR* IV,1 (May 1917) [3]-6.
'By getting': MCA, *LR* III.10 (Apr. 1917) 25.
the salary: the full salary was £36 p.a.—see *TSEL* 187–8. TSE expected a further £2 per month from the *LR*.
'in Male hands': TSE to his father, 31 Oct. 1917, *TSEL* 204.
'a buttress': EP to JQ, 15 May 1917, *EP/JQ* 112.

326 'to call up': EP to JQ, 17 May 1917, *EP/JQ* 114.
'The point is': EP to MCA, 11 June 1917, *EP/LR* 61. For my insertion, '[of patron and public]', see EP's 'Editorial', *LR* IV,1 (May 1917) 6.
'not food': EP to ACH, 8 Sept. 1917, *EP/ACH* 216.
regular and prompt: see EP to ACH, 14 June 1917, *EP/ACH* 211.
'to start off': EP to MCA, 8 Feb. 1917, *EP/LR* 15.
'in the midst': WL to EP, '6 / 6 / 17', *EP/WL* 73.
'particularly lucky': from here the paragraph is drawn from WL to EP, '8 / 6 / 17', *EP/WL* 73–4. About his wanting the experience, see WL to EP, '19 / 6 / 17', *EP/WL* 79.

327 'too frightful incompatibility': WL to EP [20 Aug. 1917], *EP/WL* 96.
'Nature & my training': WL to EP, 18 Oct. 1917, *EP/WL* 109–10.

'truly <u>not</u> sanguinary': WL to EP, 22 Sept. 1917, *EP/WL* 106.

When the United States declared war: information from A. J. P. Taylor, *The First World War: an illustrated history* (Harmondsworth: Penguin Books, 1966), p. 171.

328   volunteers not wanted: see EP to JQ, 3 Apr. 1917, *EP/JQ* 99–100; and EP to ACH, 24 Apr. 1917, *EP/ACH* 209.

'much gayer mood': EP to JQ, 19 Apr. 1917, *EP/JQ* 106. Details of the 'advance' (in footnote) from A. J. P. Taylor, *English History 1914–45* (Harmondsworth: Penguin Books, 1970), pp. 118–19.

'system of *direct supply*': EP to JQ, 3 Apr. 1917, *EP/JQ* 99–101.

National Service: see letter from EP to G. F. C. Masterman, '26/6/1917', reproduced in *Agenda* 23.3–4 (1985–6) 136.

'shook its head': EP to WL [Aug. 1917], *EP/WL* 93.

From a letter to his father

The ts. letter, in Beinecke, is dated 'Aug. 23 1917'.

330   'the long prose of Hueffer's': i.e. *Women and Men*, which EP considered 'the best thing he has ever done' (*EP/JQ* 121). Max Saunders, *Ford Madox Ford*. I, pp. 335–7, writes that this work of 'sociological impressionism' in which FMH tested 'stereotypes against real acquaintances' was a 'spirited refutation of the misogynistic work of Otto Weininger'.

'The Little Review' and the Great War: the enemy

330   'in action': EP to WL [July 1917], *EP/WL* 83.

'an article a day': EP to WL, 30 Aug. 1917, *EP/WL* 102.

331   'My present existence': EP to WL, 10 Sept. 1917, *EP/WL* 104.

Joyce's eye troubles: see *EP/JJ* 96 ff.

'inharmonic astigmatism': EP to JJ, 17 Mar. 1917, *EP/JJ* 100–1.

autograph letters: EP to JJ, 10 Sept. 1917, *EP/JJ* 126. See also *EP/JQ* 155n.

£50 quarterly: see *EP/JJ* 95.

'His two queer chaps': EP to JQ, 1 Apr. 1917, *EP/JQ* 98.

'Mrs Eliot': EP to MCA, 21 June 1917, *EP/LR* 78.

'with the firm intuito': EP to H. B. Parkes ['early 1930s'], Donald Gallup, *T. S. Eliot & Ezra Pound: Collaborators in Letters* (New Haven: Henry W. Wenning/ C. A. Stonehill, Inc., 1970), p. 11. See also *PD (1958)* 161.

co-authorship: see TSE, *Inventions of the March Hare: Poems 1907–1917*, pp. 365–74.

332   'ignorance': EP, 'Provincialism the Enemy. I', *NA* XXI.11 (12 July 1917) 244.

There were four instalments of 'Provincialism the Enemy', appearing in *NA* 12, 19, 26 July and 2 Aug. 1917. Henry James and Confucius are named in the second instalment, Napoleon in the fourth.

stories, dialogues and imaginary letters: most of these were first collected in *Pavannes and Divisions* (1918), and reprinted in *Pavannes and Divagations* (1958).

'basic propositions': EP to MCA, 11 Apr. 1917, *EP/LR* 26.

'states where': *PD (1958)* 95.

church bells: *PD (1958)* 89. EP complained frequently about this campanolatry.

333   'shores of Gallipoli': *PD (1958)* 92.

'personal morals': *PD (1958)* 94.

'a curious desire': *PD (1958)* 102; 'men are prized': *PD (1958)* 103.

'indicates a state': EP to MCA, 14 Apr. 1918, *EP/LR* 210, 209.

Willa Cather: I am thinking particularly of *My Ántonia* (1918).

'11/11/17': EP to MCA, 11 Nov. 1917, *EP/LR* 148–50.

334 'Look!': Emanuel Carnevali, 'Irritation', *Poetry* XVI (Jan. 1920) 211–21, as in Homberger: 1972, 149.
'Dreiser's fearless': EP, 'Dreiser Protest' [letter to the Editor], *Egoist* IV.2 (Feb. 1917) 30. The 'Protest' with EP's comments, also headed 'Dreiser Protest', appeared in *Egoist* III.10 (Oct. 1916) 159.
'Christianity': EP to H. L. Mencken, 27 Sept. 1916, *L (1951)* 150.
'literature and instruments': EP to JQ, 29 Dec. 1917, *EP/JQ* 132.
'*Every obscene*': EP printed the law in 'The Classics "Escape"', *LR* IV.11 (Mar. 1918) 32–5—his poem 'Cantico del Sole' was attached to this piece.
indecorous and indelicate: in EP to WL [July 1917], *EP/WL* 83; volcano: in EP to MCA, 24 May 1917, *EP/LR* 56.
'Cantleman's Spring Mate': quotations from *A Soldier of Humour and Selected Writings* ed. Raymond Rosenthal (New York: New American Library—A Signet Classic, 1966), p. 113.

335 'no living man': EP, 'The Classics "Escape"', *LR* IV.11 (Mar. 1918) 34.

His several fronts: chronicle

335 'My wife': EP to JJ [6–12] Sept. 1915, *EP/JJ* 45.
'save possibly': EP to JQ, 17 May 1917, *EP/JQ* 117.
'the *energy*': EP to JQ, 6 July 1919, *EP/JQ* 176.

336 'constant readers': EP to JJ, 12 Dec. 1918, *EP/JJ* 148.
'in the paper': EP to ACH, 22 June 1915, *EP/ACH* 107.
'quoted chunks': EP to WL, 17 Aug. 1917, *EP/WL* 95.
'in English, 1733': DP to EP [July] 1917 (Lilly).
'four huge folios': EP to JJ, 18 May 1917, *EP/JJ* 117.
'The Austrians': DP to EP [Oct.? 1917] (Lilly).
'the less I think': EP to MCA, 17 Nov. 1917, *EP/LR* 154.
'God knows': EP to WCW [10 Nov. 1917], *EP/WCW* 30.
'a purge': 'Irony, Laforgue, and Some Satire', *Poetry* XI.2 (Nov. 1917), in *LE* 282; 'Comstocks': ibid. p. 283.
'best substitute': 'Landor (1775–1864)', *Future* II.1 (Nov. 1917), in *S Pr* 354–5.
humanizing classics: 'Elizabethan Classicists', five articles in *Egoist* IV.8–11 and V.1 (Sept. 1917–Jan. 1918), reprinted in *LE* as 'Notes on Elizabethan Classicists'; 'EarlyTranslators of Homer', three articles in *Egoist* V.7–9 (Aug.–Oct. 1918), and 'Hellenist Series', three further articles in *Egoist* V.10, VI.1–2 (Nov./Dec. 1918–Mar./Apr. 1919), reprinted (except for the last of the six) in *LE* as 'Translators of Greek: Early Translators of Homer'.
'Studies in Contemporary Mentality': a series of twenty articles in the *New Age* running from 16 Aug. 1917 to 10 Jan. 1918.
On the *Quiver*: see 'Studies in Contemporary Mentality. VIII.—The Beating Heart of the Magazine', *NA* XXI.24 (11 Oct. 1917) 505–7.

337 'Good customs': 'Studies in Contemporary Mentality. XVII.—The Slightly Shop-Worn', *NA* XXII.9 (27 Dec. 1917) 168.
'Art Notes': these are collected with other writings on art in *EP&VA*.
'Music Notes': these are collected with other writings on music in *EP&M*.
'art and music critiques': EP to HLP, 24 Jan. 1918 (Beinecke).
'irreducible minimum': 'Music. By William Atheling', *NA* XXIII.17 (22 Aug. 1918) 271; *EP&M* 118–19.
'the best performers': cited by Schafer as Pound's 'credo', *EP&M* 62.
'he sympathised': EP on 'Atheling' in *Antheil*, as in *EP&M* 266.

'British Music': Schafer's observation on 'Atheling' and Dolmetsch, *EP&M* 60.

free tickets: mentioned in EP to Ingrid Davies, June 1955 (HRC).

338 'doing ten': EP to JJ, 19 Dec. 1917, *EP/JJ* 129.

'great luck': EP to MCA, 14 Dec. 1917, *EP/LR* 167.

'lascivious': EP to JQ, 30 Dec. 1917, *EP/JQ* 134.

Raymonde Collignon: 'Atheling' first wrote about her in the *NA* of 3 Jan. 1918—see *EP&M* 67–70; for further reviews see ibid. 102, 119, 161, 225.

'a clavichord': 'William Atheling', 'Music', *NA* XXIV.17 (27 Feb. 1919) 281—*EP&M* 161.

'Her art': 'William Atheling', 'Music', *NA* XXII.10 (3 Jan. 1918) 190—*EP&M* 69.

'a new start': EP to JQ, 29 Jan. 1918, *EP/JQ* 140.

told Margaret Anderson: EP to MCA, 20 Feb. 1918, *EP/LR* 186–7.

339 'Feel I must': EP to JQ, 22 Feb. 1918, *EP/JQ* 144.

'Damn': EP to MCA, 22 Feb. 1918, *EP/LR* 190.

'I have spent': EP to MCA, 'Third Letter', 22 Feb. 1918, *EP/LR* 194–5.

'to get more time': EP to WBY, 10 Mar. 1918, 'Letters to William Butler Yeats', ed. C. F. Terrell, *Antaeus* 21/22 (1976) 34–49; (in *P&P* X, 135–6).

It is said: this is in spite of the fact that the source appears to have been the notoriously untrustworthy Francis Stuart, who married Iseult in 1920. Apart from repeating the story among his family and friends, he wrote, in his considerably fictionalized and unreliable autobiography, *Black List, Section H*(1975), published long after her death in 1953, that 'Iseult told him . . . she had become the mistress of the poet Ezra Pound'. Wilhelm: 1990, 196–7, wrote, without further evidence, of 'a passionate love affair' lasting 'from the autumn of 1917 until after the Armistice' [Nov. 1918]—'from the autumn of 1917' at least must be an exaggeration. Foster: 2003, 112, states as if it were a known fact, but without giving any source, that Pound 'rapidly seduced her, probably in early 1918', and that 'he was soon claiming that he would leave Dorothy for her'. His note, p. 691 n. 47, says 'See IG to WBY, 28 Mar. 1918, for her denials', though he gives those denials no weight. A. Norman Jeffares, Anna MacBride White, and Christina Bridgwater, the editors of *Letters to W. B. Yeats and Ezra Pound from Iseult Gonne* (Houndmills: Palgrave Macmillan, 2004), directly misrepresent her denials, declaring them to be a confirmation of what they deny—compare their pages 99 and 134. All that is revealed by Iseult's published letters to Yeats and Pound on this matter is that, in late November and December 1918 when she had just left London to be in Dublin with her mother, she wrote five letters to Pound in which she declared that she loved him and wanted to be with him. The letters also make it clear, however, that Pound was not reciprocating. If he had in fact fallen in love with Iseult and if he had said he would leave Dorothy, as Olga Rudge maintained after his death, then he must have been persuaded by the end of 1918 to disengage and to remain with Dorothy. Stuart, I am told, burnt Pound's letters to Iseult. I leave the matter open.

'he has many women': Joseph Conrad to JQ, 6 Feb. 1918, as in Homberger: 1972,139.

'Yseult': 104/741–2.

340 'a typist': EP to HLP, 18 July 1918 (Beinecke).

kept on by Orage: see EP to MCA [Feb. 1918], *EP/LR* 203.

'political mind': EP to MCA, 28 Feb. 1918, *EP/LR* 200.

'to prevent thought': 'Studies in Contemporary Mentality. XIX', *NA* XXII.11 (10 Jan. 1918) 208–9.

'International Capital': 'Studies in Contemporary Mentality. XVIII', *NA* XXII.10 (3 Jan. 1918) 193.

he looked back: see *EP/LR* 212–14 for EP's 'harangue', published as 'Cooperation (A Note on the Volume Completed)' in *LR* V.3 (July 1918) 54–6, also covering letter to MCA [30 Apr. 1918]. EP's contributions to periodicals amounted to: 30 in 1916, 90 in 1917, 120 in 1918, 90 in 1919.

341   'The old houses': 'Books Current. Joyce', *Future* II.6 (May 1918) 161.

'Am in state': EP to MCA, 23 May 1918, *EP/LR* 221.

'ten years younger': EP to MCA, 4 June 1918, *EP/LR* 228.

'cameos': EP to MCA, 10 June 1918, *EP/LR* 231—see also pp. 223 and 224n.

'MUST STOP': EP to MCA, 9 July 1918, *EP/LR* 240.

'Am flat': EP to JJ, 17 July 1918, *EP/JJ* 144.

'Spanish Influenza': TSE, in a letter dated 7 July 1918, mentioned trying to escape it, and that many were away from his office because of it (*TSEL* 237).

342   **military manoeuvres**: details from EP to JQ, 10–11 Aug. 1918, *EP/JQ* 157–8, and from *TSEL* 240 ff. See also *L (1951)* 206.

'red tape': TSE to JQ, 13 Nov. 1918, *TSEL* 254.

wandered about: EP to JQ, 15 Nov. 1918, *EP/JQ* 166.

'the sense of rhythm': 'William Atheling', 'Music', *NA* XXIV.4 (28 Nov. 1918) 59.

paper restrictions: EP to IWP [15 Nov. 1918]: 'Paper restrictions are about as personal as any public affair can be for me' (Beinecke).

'to see the Lago di Garda': EP to JJ, 22 Nov. 1918, *EP/JJ* 146.

343   'The intelligent man': 'Memorabilia', *LR* V.7 (Nov. 1918) 27.

'meagre allowance': EP to JJ, 12 Dec. 1918, *EP/JJ* 148.

no hope: see EP to HLP, 10 Jan. 1919 (Beinecke).

structure of *Instigations*: in EP's desk copy, now in HRC, there are these indications: against 'In the Vortex': '1914 & 1918'; against the Laforgue 'divagation': 'secolo XIX'; against Voltaire's 'Genesis': 'secolo XVIII'; against 'Arnaut Daniel', 'medievo—nel XX'; against 'Translators of Greek': 'classico—XVI. XVII'.

'for *maestria*': 'A Study in French Poets', *Instigations* 4.

'prepared our era': 'Remy de Gourmont: A Distinction', *Instigations* 169; *LE* 339.

344   'vocation of letters': Van Wyck Brooks, 'A Reviewer's Notebook', *Freeman* I (16 June 1920), as in Homberger: 1972, 189.

'Is nobody aware': James Sibley Watson [as 'W. C. Blum'], 'Super Schoolmaster', *Dial* LXIX (Oct. 1920), as in Homberger: 1972, 193.

into the arms, apparently: see Jeffrey Meyers, 'New Light on Iris Barry', *Pai* 13.2 (1984) 287.

'all *les jeunes*': EP to MCA [? May 1918], *EP/LR* 214.

'the poems too good': EP to Marianne Moore, 16 Dec. 1918, *L (1951)* 202.

wrote to Miss Weaver: EP to Harriet Shaw Weaver, 17 Dec. 1918, *L (1951)* 205.

Miss Moore replied: Marianne Moore to EP, 9 Jan. 1919, *The Selected Letters of Marianne Moore*, ed. Bonnie Costello with Celeste Goodridge and Cristanne Miller (Faber and Faber, 1998), pp. 122–3.

He put it down: EP to Marianne Moore, 1 Feb. 1919, *L (1951)* 208–10 (in part); for the lines not given by Paige (from 'You, my dear correspondent') see the original in Beinecke.

345   'should go': EP to JQ, 3 Apr. 1918, *EP/JQ* 148–9.

'controversy': EP to JQ, 29 Dec. 1917, *EP/JQ* 133.

'Think of your own work': EP to ACH, 5 May 1916, *EP/ACH* 139.

'digging up corpses': EP to JJ, 12 Dec. 1918, *EP/JJ* 148.

'Langue d'Oc' and *'Homage to Sextus Propertius'*

345   'étude', 'major persona': under 'Main outline of E.P.'s work to date', *Umbra* 128.

476

'Langue d'Oc': for a fully contextualized discussion see Helen Dennis, *A New Approach to the Poetry of Ezra Pound Through the Medieval Provençal Aspect* (Lewiston: Edwin Mellen Press, 1996), pp. 133–70.

347 '*Venust*': from the Latin, an adjective from 'Venus'. In *P 1918–21* this stanza, like 'Alba', is set in italic; it is also offset from the rest of the poem.

348 had speculated: see *SR* 94 ff.

'I only, and who elrische': see *LE* 139–42; or *T* 178–81.

as Dante will have him: *Purgatorio* XXVI, 142–4.

'sketches': so defined in 'Main outline of E.P.'s work to date', *Umbra* 128.

349 'the Provençal feeling': EP to Felix E. Schelling, 8 July 1922, *L (1951)* 246–7.

'left foot': EP to HM, Dec. 1918, as in Hugh Kenner, *The Pound Era* (Berkeley: University of California Press, 1972; repr. Faber & Faber, 1972), p. 286.

'if you CAN'T': EP to Iris Barry, 27 July 1916, *L (1951)* 142.

'a new *oeuvre*': EP to HLP, 3 Nov. 1918 (Beinecke).

'last and best': EP to Marianne Moore, 16 Dec. 1918, *L (1951)* 204.

'university manual': see J. W. Mackail, *Latin Literature*, a 'University Manual' (John Murray, 5th impression 1906), pp. 123–30.

350 not a translation: see, for example, EP to Orage [? Apr.] 1919, *L (1951)* 211–13. The issue is most fully discussed by J. P. Sullivan, *Ezra Pound and Sextus Propertius*, (Faber and Faber, 1965). Sullivan gives a variorum text with the Latin *en face*.

'portrait': in *P 1918–21 HSP* was classed as a 'Portrait' with 'Langue d'Oc' and *HSM*.

'relation to life': EP letter to the editor of the *English Journal*, 24 Jan. 1931, *L (1951)* 310.

'my genius': *HSP* V.2; see 'Troubadours—Their Sorts and Conditions' (1913), *LE* 103.

'dance of the intellect': from EP's definition of *logopoeia*—see 'A List of Books', *LR* IV.11 (Mar. 1918) 57; 'How to Read' (1929), *LE* 25; *ABCR* 63. EP discovered this quality in Laforgue and always associated it particularly with him.

351 'an educated freedwoman': from J. P. McCulloch, 'Introduction', *The Poems of Sextus Propertius: a bilingual edition* (Berkeley: University of California Press, 1972), p. 1.

352 That deflection: paragraph based on documents given in Homberger: 1972, 155–71:—W. G. Hale, 'Pegasus Impounded', *Poetry* XIV.1 (Apr. 1919) 52–5; A. R. Orage, 'Readers and Writers', *NA* XXV.10 (3 July 1919) 166–7; EP letter in *NA* XXVI.5 (4 Dec. 1919) 82–3; Robert Nichols, 'Poetry and Mr Pound', *Observer* (11 Jan. 1920) 6; EP, 'Propertius and Mr. Pound', *Observer* (25 Jan. 1920) 5.

353 noise: 'sono' could be rendered more neutrally, but not more literally, as 'sound'—the choice is a matter of tone, and in Pound's Propertius tone is all. 'Sono' does not carry the narrower senses of 'song' or 'music'.

'got to the point': see p. 318 above, in connection with Vortography.

354 'Cat-piss and porcupines!': EP letter, 14 Apr. 1919, to Editor *Poetry* (not published), printed in Williams, *Harriet Monroe*, p. 254.

'as a resignation': HM to EP, 1 Nov. 1919, in Williams p. 258–9.

1917 pamphlet: [Anon.], *Ezra Pound, His Metric and Poetry* (New York: Alfred A. Knopf, 1917), reprinted in TSE, *To Criticize the Critic* (1965).

'struggling beneath': EP, 'Mr Pound and his Poetry', *Athenæum* XCIII.4670 (31 Oct. 1919) 1132. Cp. EP to JQ, 25 Oct. 1919, *L (1951)* 213.

telling...his friends: see TSE to Mary Hutchinson [? 15 June 1919] and [? 9 July 1919], *TSEL* 302–3, 311.

'I value his verse': TSE to JQ, 4 Mar. 1918, *TSEL* 223.

on the dubious ground: see TSE, 'Introduction', *Ezra Pound: Selected Poems*, ed. T. S. Eliot (Faber & Gwyer, 1928), p. xxiii.

'So far as American poetry': Basil Bunting, letter to Massimo Bacigalupo, 20 Mar. 1985, reproduced in *Ezra Pound: Un Poeta a Rapallo*, a cura di Massimo Bacigalupo (Genova: Edizioni San Marco dei Giustiniani, 1985), p. 76.

15 GOODBYE TO ENGLAND: 1919–1920

The smell of french asphalt

355 **killed Vorticism?**: see [EP], 'The Death of Vorticism', *LR* V.10 / 11 (Feb. / Mar. 1919) 45, 48.

Lewis's 'war paintings': see 'B. H. Dias', 'Art Notes. Wyndham Lewis at the Goupil', *NA* XXIV.16 (20 Feb. 1919); also EP, 'War Paintings by Wyndham Lewis', *Nation*, London, XXIV.19 (8 Feb. 1919) 546–7.

356 **Joyce**: details of his income from Ellmann, *Joyce*, pp. 435, 471, 481.

Pound ... struggling: see EP to JJ, 12 Dec. 1918 and 30 May 1919, *EP/JJ* 147,156.

'just to take himself': EP to JQ, 25 Oct. 1919, as cited in *EP/JJ* 161; see also EP to JQ, 24 Nov. 1919, *EP/JQ* 179.

'fahrt, yes': EP to JJ, 10 June 1919, *EP/JJ* 158.

Eliot, in 1919: paragraph based on: (1) TSE to his mother, 29 Mar. 1919, *TSEL* 279–81; (2) TSE to J. H. Woods, 21 Apr. 1919, *TSEL* 284–6; (3) TSE to JQ, 25 Jan. 1920, 357–9. For a fuller discussion see A. David Moody, 'Peregrine in England', *Tracing T. S. Eliot's Spirit: Essays on his poetry and thought* (Cambridge: Cambridge University Press, 1996), pp. 39–47.

357 **'ruined'**: Vivien Eliot to Mary Hutchinson [1 May ? 1919], *TSEL* 289.

'the new dances': TSE to Mary Hutchinson, 4 Mar. 1919, *TSEL* 275.

'experimenting': EP to DP, Mar. 1919 (Lilly).

'boxed in one city': EP, 'July Lamentation', unpublished ts. (Beinecke).

358 **crossed to France**: a source of information concerning this visit to France is 'Catalogue of the Pound Exhibition: Sheffield University, 23 Apr. 1976', in Philip Grover ed., *Ezra Pound*: The London Years: 1908–1920 (New York: AMS Press, 1978), following p. 166.

Natalie Barney: see EP, 'Letters to Natalie Barney', ed. with commentary by Richard Sieburth, *Pai* 5.2 (1976) 281; also 'Indiscretions', *PD (1958)* 5.

Dulac: see Grover. *The London Years*, item 7; and *Cantos* 80 / 503–4. Address from *EP/JJ* 156, 157.

'provincial desolation': this paragraph and the next drawn mainly from the first three articles in the series 'Pastiche. The Regional', *NA* XXV.7, 9, 11 (12, 26 June, 10 July 1919) 124, 156, 188.

'renew [his] retina': EP to JJ, 30 May 1919, *EP/JJ* 156.

a round tour: itinerary from postcards with EP letter to HLP, 30 May 1919 (Beinecke).

359 **Baedeker**: Baedeker, *Southern France: Handbook for Travellers* (1907), pp. 166–7.

'an altar': 48 / 243.

watercolours: one is reproduced, sans colour, in *Etruscan Gate*.

Montségur: mentioned in *Cantos* at 48 / 243, 76 / 452, 80 / 510 and 512, 87 / 574, 101 / 725.

'If that statement': 'Pastiche. The Regional. VII', *NA* XXV.17 (21 Aug. 1919) 284—the following paragraph is also drawn from this article.

360 **'flags flying'**: DP note, Grover, *The London Years*, item 46.

'complete guide': 'Indiscretions', *PD (1958)* 23.

'rucksacked Eliot': EP, 'For T. S. E.', *Sewanee Review* LXXIV.1 (1966) [108].

'to put him through': EP to JQ, 6 Aug. 1919, as in *TSEL* 325 n. 4.

'7 blisters': EP post card to DP, Grover, *The London Years*, item 39.

'le papier Fayard': EP, 'For T. S. E.', *Sewanee Review* LXXIV.1 (1966) [108]. The 'paper' was a treatment for blisters.

'rock drawing': TSE, 'Tradition and the Individual Talent' (1919), in *Selected Essays*, 3rd enlarged edn. (Faber and Faber, 1951), p. 16.

'Cro-Magnon': EP to Ingrid Davies, 12 Aug. 1955 (HRC).

'"the life after death"': the episode is recorded in canto 29 / 145.

361 'not to expect': TSE, 'Dante' (1929), in *Selected Essays* (1951), p. 275.

'faith in life': TSE, 'A Commentary', *Criterion* XII, no. 47 (Jan. 1933) 248.

'said nothing': 13 / 59.

'"But this beats me"': 29 / 145.

unknown *alba*: EP's translation of 'Phebi claro nondum orto iubare' was published as 'Belangal Alba' in the *Hamilton Literary Magazine* in 1905, and revised and reprinted as 'Alba Belingalis' in *Personae* (1909). For a detailed analysis of the *alba* see A. D. Moody, '"Phebi claro" by Starlight', *Modern Language Review* 76.4 (1981) [769]-779.

'Pie faced': EP to JQ, 13 Dec. 1919, *EP/JQ* 180.

clerk also told him: EP, 'The Passport Nuisance', *Nation*, New York, CXXV.3256 (30 Nov. 1927) 600-2.

'The clerk of the 1st': EP, 'Revolt of Intelligence. III', *NA* XXVI.7 (18 Dec. 1919) 107.

362 'brute stupidity': ibid.

He was told: EP, 'Four Steps', *Agenda* XVII.3 / 4 / XVIII.1 (1979 / 1980) 139-40.

'journalistic work': EP's passport issued Sept. 1919 in Paris (Lilly).

'seeking for buried beauty': 7 / 25.

Orage's readiness: see EP to JQ, 25 Oct. 1919, *L (1951)* 213.

'I perceive': 'William Atheling', 'Music', *NA* XXVI.2 (13 Nov. 1919) 28.

'rank bad art': ibid.

'London's first': 'B. H. Dias', 'Art Notes', *NA* XXVI.4 (27 Nov. 1919) 60.

'Lewis's portrait': 'B. H. Dias', 'Art Notes', *NA* XXVI.6 (11 Dec. 1919) 96. (This portrait is lost—left in a taxi, according to WL—but see illust. 43).

'Marius David Adkins': EP gave the full name in a letter to HLP, 15 Oct. 1919 (Beinecke).

'two opulent weeks': EP to JQ, 25 Oct. 1919, *L (1951)* 213.

'Daddies': 'M. D. Adkins', 'The Drama', *Outlook* XLIV. 1132 (11 Oct. 1919) 363.

'chief cruelty': 'M. D. Adkins', 'The Drama. Gilbert and Sullivan', *Outlook* XLIV. 1133 (18 Oct. 1919) 390.

363 'Have had my work': EP to JQ, 25 Oct. 1919, *L (1951)* 213.

'*privately* printed': EP note on proof sent to *Dial*, as in Gallup: 1983, 27.

'basic for all aesthetics': EP to JQ, 10 Jan. 1917, *EP/JQ* 93. Cp. 'a whole basis of aesthetics', EP to Felix E. Schelling, June 1915, *L (1951)* 106

'*The Fourth Canto*', and a new poetic

Unless indicated otherwise the text cited in this section is that of the revised complete *Cantos* (1970, **1975**). The variants from the early texts are not relevant here.

363 'The Chinese Written Character as a Medium for Poetry': there is a very extensive secondary literature devoted to this Fenollosa / Pound essay, much of it debating the degrees of accuracy and error in its account of the Chinese written character. A number of significant contributions to the debate will be found in the files of *Pai* and *Agenda*. Not to be missed by anyone with an interest in the issue is an essay by Arthur Cooper, 'The Poetry of Language-Making: Images and Resonances in the Chinese Script', *Temenos* 7 (1986) [241]-58. The most illuminating study I know of is by François Cheng, *Chinese Poetic Writing* (Bloomington: Indiana University Press,

1982). I am concerned here only with the essence of the Fenollosa essay so far as it advances our understanding of Pound's cantos.

365 'Relations': 'The Chinese Written Character', *Instigations* 377; *CWC* 22. Pound's endorsement was in a footnote, *Instigations* 376; *CWC* 22.
'purely apparitional': EP to HLP [late Oct. 1919] (Beinecke).

366 ' "Ityn, Ityn" ': the reading in the earlier versions.

367 'My Lady's face': EP's version of Cavalcanti's sonnet XXXV, *T* 95.

368 'main form': see EP, 'Arnold Dolmetsch', *Egoist* IV.7 (Aug. 1917) 104–5; and 'William Atheling', 'Music', *NA* XXVIII. 2 (11 Nov. 1920) 21. See also EP, 'Chronicles: III. Lawrence Binyon', *BLAST* 2 (July 1915) 86, where he notes the same principles in Binyon's *The Flight of the Dragon: An essay on the theory and practice of art in China and Japan* (1911): ' "P. 17. Every statue, every picture, is a series of ordered relations, controlled, as the body is controlled in the dance, by the will to express a single idea." '
'permanent basis in humanity': 'Psychology and Troubadours', *SR* 92.

Public affairs

369 'The man of letters': 'Pastiche: The Regional. XVII', *NA* XXVI.2 (13 Nov. 1919) 32.
'stabilising element': 'Pastiche: The Regional. XVIII', *NA* XXVI.3 (20 Nov. 1919) 48.
'Two great obstacles':'The Revolt of Intelligence.VI', *NA* XXVI.11 (15 Jan. 1920) 176.
'All religions are evil': 'Pastiche: The Regional. I', *NA* XXV.7 (12 June 1919) 124.

370 'We write': 'Pastiche: The Regional. XVI', *NA* XXVI.1 (6 Nov. 1919) 16. This would date 'the Struggle' from the time of Luther, and not, surprisingly, from the time of the Cathars.
'We note': ibid.
the following article:'Pastiche: The Regional. XVII', *NA* XXVI.2 (13 Nov. 1919) 32.
commonplace in the *NA*: see Tim Redman, *Ezra Pound and Italian Fascism* (Cambridge: Cambridge University Press, 1991), pp. 39–40, 49; and A. David Moody,' "EP with two-pronged fork of terror and cajolery": The Construction of his Anti- Semitism (up to 1939)', *Pai* 29.3 (Winter 2000) 63–7.

371 regretted that Ireland: see 'The Revolt of Intelligence. III', *NA* XXVI. 7 (18 Dec. 1919)
D'Annunzio: ibid.; also 'The Revolt of Intelligence. [I]', *NA* XXVI. 2 (13 Nov. 1919) 21–2.
agricultural guilds: 'The Revolt of Intelligence. V', *NA* XXVI. 10 (8 Jan. 1920) 153.
'league of *nations*': 'The Revolt of Intelligence. III', *NA* XXVI. 7 (18 Dec. 1919) 106.
'a small committee': 'The Revolt of Intelligence. V', *NA* XXVI. 10 (8 Jan. 1920) 154.
'The function': 'The Revolt of Intelligence. IX', *NA* XXVI. 19 (11 Mar. 1920) 301.
'a centre': 'The Revolt of Intelligence. V', *NA* XXVI. 10 (8 Jan. 1920) 153.

372 C. H. Douglas: information in footnote partly from Kenner, *Pound Era*, 301.
'Einstein of economics': cited by Paul Selver, *Orage and the New Age Circle* (George Allen & Unwin, 1959), p. 76—from an article by Orage reprinted in *NA* (after 1923) from *Commonweal*.
'He was squat': Selver, *Orage*, 28.
'In that case', 'I should have remained': EP, 'Memoirs', *Edge* 3 (Feb. 1957) 16. See EP, 'Obituary: A. R. Orage' (15 Nov. 1934), and 'In the Wounds—Memoriam A. R. Orage' (April 1935), in *S Pr* 407–9, 410–21.
'The major': 46 / 231.

373 'the inalienable right': cited from the 'American Declaration of Independence' by C. H. Douglas, *Economic Democracy* (Cecil Palmer, 1920), pp. 4–5.
'We must build up': ibid. 7.

two reviews: quotations in the rest of this paragraph and in the next are from EP, *'Economic Democracy'*, *LR* VI. 11 (Apr. 1920) 39–42; and ' "Probari ratio" ', *Athenæum* XCIV.4692 (2 Apr. 1920) 445.

374 'profound attack': 'The Revolt of Intelligence. VIII', *NA* XXVI.18 (4 Mar. 1920) 288.
'counterforce': 'The Revolt of Intelligence. IX', *NA* XXVI.19 (11 Mar. 1920) 301.
'Don't imagine': EP, review of *Credit Power and Democracy* by Major C. H. Douglas and A. R. Orage, *Contact* [4] ([Summer 1921]) [1].
'fairly courageous', 'the real mind': EP to HLP, 22 Feb. 1920 (Beinecke).
'intelligent . . . an ass': EP to JQ, 21 Feb. 1920, *EP/JQ* 185.
'The economist consulted': 22 / 101–2.
'invented': EP, 'A Letter from London', *Much Ado* X.9 (1 Apr. 1920) [21]. See also EP to HLP, 22 Feb. 1920 (Beinecke).

375 'the national heritage': this paragraph and the next from EP, 'Masaryk', *NA* XXVI.22 (1 Apr. 1920) 350–1. The sentence of Masaryk beginning 'The recognition', cited by Pound in a slightly different form, is taken from his marked copy of Thomas G. Masaryk, President of the Czech-Slovak Republic, *The New Europe (The Slav Standpoint)* (Eyre and Spottiswoode, 1918), now in HRC.
'A bloated usury': this paragraph from 'Hudson: Poet Strayed into Science', *LR* VII.1 (May / June 1920) 13–17.

376 'the creative': EP, 'Affirmations. V. Gaudier-Brzeska', *NA* XVI.14 (4 Feb. 1915) 382; *GB* 109.

'Hugh Selwyn Mauberley'

This poem has been extensively discussed and debated, and widely differing readings have been advanced. I have profited from the gradual development and accumulation of understanding in the critical tradition, and wish to make here a general acknowledgment of indebtedness to it. There is no room, however, within my necessarily compressed account of the poem for registering either agreements or disagreements with others' approaches.

377 'no more Mauberley': EP to Felix E. Schelling, 8 July 1932, *L (1951)* 248.
' "ANY" non producer': EP to H. B. Parkes, 29 Jan. [? 1933] (UPenn Ms. Coll. 183).
'Mauberley / sure': EP to Basil Bunting [? 1935] (Beinecke).
'first Mauberley's': EP to Scofield Thayer, 15 Aug. 1920, *EP/Dial* 122.
'Mauberley buries': EP (1956), as cited by Thomas E. Connolly, 'Further Notes on *Mauberley*', *Accent* 16 (Winter 1956) 59.
'in each case . . . synthesised': EP to Scofield Thayer, 15 Aug. 1920, *EP/Dial* 122.
'the starting point': EP to AB, 7 June 1920 (Lilly).

379 striking at universals: EP, 'T. S. Eliot' (1917), *LE* 420.
'Salutation the Third': pp. 265–6 above.

384 'Lusty Juventus': see 29 / 142.

385 'translated the ideal': S. Reinach, *Apollo: An Illustrated Manual of the History of Art throughout the Ages* (William Heinemann; New York: Charles Scribner's Sons; new edition, 1907), pp. 189, 191.
in Lord Leconfield's: ibid. 58.

387 'the Mauberley is thin': EP to Thomas Hardy [1921], as printed in 'Ezra Pound and Thomas Hardy', *Southern Review* IV (n.s.). 1 (Jan. 1968) 98.

A pair of old shoes

387 'was done': EP to Thayer, 7 June 1920, *EP/Dial* 39.
'Have done': EP to HLP, 13 Dec. 1919 (Beinecke); 'episode': *EP/Dial* 155.

388 'contains': EP to JQ, 9 Oct. 1920, *EP/JQ* 195–6. *Trois Contes*: Flaubert's 'Un Coeur Simple', 'La Légende de Saint Julien l'Hospitalier', 'Hérodias'.
had instructed Homer: EP to HLP, 22 Nov. 1919 (Beinecke).
collaborating with ... a pianist: *Five Troubadour Songs* ... arranged by Agnes Bedford (Boosey & Co., 1920).
'exact concord': ibid., 'Proem'.
'Chère Agnes': EP to AB, 18 Dec. 1919, in Hughes and Fisher, *Cavalcanti* (*CPMEP*), p.[4].
'The "Frères Humaines"': EP to AB, 18 Dec. 1919 (Lilly)—a sentence not given in Hughes and Fisher.
'from Ezra's singing': AB to DP, 19 Nov. 1967, in Hughes and Fisher, p.[xv].

389 music column ... 15 Apr.: details in the paragraph all from 'Music. By William Atheling', *NA* XXVI.24 (15 Apr. 1920) 387–8.
prompted ... by Eliot: see TSE to JQ, 25 Jan. 1920, *TSEL* 358.
at £10: see EP to JJ, 2 Aug. 1920, *EP/JJ* 183.
'general dislike': EP to JJ, 2 June 1920, *EP/JJ* 174.
'It is doubtful': 'T. J. V.', 'Dramedy', *Athenæum* XCIV.4688 (5 Mar. 1920) 315.

390 *The Government Inspector*: 'T. J. V.', 'Gogol', *Athenæum* XCIV.4695 (23 Apr. 1920) 553.
'might be construed': from Gallup: 1983, 262—note to item C569.
Murry ... let him know: see TSE to WL [28 July 1920], *TSEL* 394.
the *Dial*: information in this paragraph drawn from Walter Sutton's 'Introduction', *EP/Dial* xxi–xxx.
wanted him to know: see Thayer to EP, 8 Mar. 1920, *EP/Dial* 12–13.
would be hospitable: see Thayer to EP, 30 Apr. 1920, *EP/Dial* 25–7.
'As to C. H. Douglas': ibid. 27.

391 'unconventional': Thayer to EP, 21 May 1920, *EP/Dial* 31.
'remember the Post Office': Thayer to EP, 8 Mar. 1920, *EP/Dial* 13.
'use [his] best efforts': EP to Thayer, 24 Mar. 1920, *EP/Dial* 15.
'the few men': ibid.
'BUT you must': ibid. 18.
'Arrangement': ibid.
'trying without': EP to JJ, 8 May 1920, *EP/JJ* 164.
'rather rashly': EP to T. E. Lawrence, 20 Apr. 1920, *L (1951)* 215.
'a convenient way': EP to JQ, 1 June 1920, *EP/JQ* 188.
'printing anything unconventional': Thayer to EP, 21 May 1920, *EP/Dial* 31.

392 'if you think' (and rest of paragraph): EP to Thayer, 7 June 1920, *EP/Dial* 36.
'Paris, Milan': EP to Thayer, 24 Mar. 1920, *EP/Dial* 18.
sift his scoops: see Thayer to EP, 18 Sept. 1920, *EP/Dial* 144.
Pound's input: for a summary statement of his contribution see Sutton's 'Introduction', *EP/Dial* xxi–xxx.
The next day: see EP to Thayer, 29 Apr. 1920, *EP/Dial* 23–4.
'the Venetian air': EP to JJ, 8 May 1920, *EP/JJ* 164.
on May 10: cf. 'in Venice, going to Verona tomorrow', EP to HLP. 9 May 1920 (Beinecke).
'"on me"': EP to JJ, 13 May 1920, *EP/JJ* 165.

393 'The general state': ibid.
'considerably recovered': EP to JJ, 19 May 1920, *EP/JJ* 167.
'This lake': EP to JQ, 1 June 1920, *EP/JQ* 188.
'Here at least': EP, Notebook 1920–?1923 (Beinecke YCAL MSS 53, 34/805). In the lines cited EP spelt 'fauns' as 'fawns'.
'The Flame': see pp. 146–7 above.
Joyce wrote a long letter: see JJ to EP, 31 May 1920, *EP/JJ* 167–9.

394   **Pound replied**: EP to JJ, 2 June 1920, *EP/JJ* 170–2.
      20 lire or a dollar: see EP to JQ, 1 June 1920, *EP/JQ* 188. That would have been the
      rate for one person at the Hotel Eden—Ezra and Dorothy generally each paid their
      own expenses.
      'lightning conductor': JJ to Miss Weaver, 12 July 1920, cited *EP/JJ* 175.
      'a large bundle': Herbert Gorman, *James Joyce* (New York: Farrar & Rinehart, 1939),
      p. 272, as cited by Forrest Read, *EP/JJ* 178.
      'the first shell': EP to JQ, 19 June 1920, *EP/JQ* 189–90.
      '96 sheets': EP to JJ, 2 June 1920, *EP/JJ* 174.
      'premature reminiscences': EP to JQ, 1 June 1920, *EP/JQ* 187.
      a suit of Pound's: details from Ellmann, *Joyce*, p. 494. Ellmann says JJ 'wore the suit
      in Paris'.
      possibly the 1,000 lire: Joyce returned an amount equivalent to that to Pound in Sept.
      or Oct., in spite of Pound's protesting that he should let him 'make at least that small
      contribution to the running expenses of *Ulysses*' (*EP/JJ* 183; see also *EP/JQ* 195).
      'discrete silence': EP to Thomas E. Connolly, 5 Sept. 1955, as in *EP/JJ* 191.
      '& many trains': EP to JQ, 19 June 1920, *EP/JQ* 189; see also EP to Thayer, 16 June
      1920, *EP/Dial* 40.
395   **'When we came up toward Chiasso'**: 28/134–5.
      'Paris, the paradise': EP, 'The Island of Paris: A Letter', *Dial* LXIX.4 (Oct. 1920)
      [406].
      Within a fortnight: details from EP to JQ, 24 June 1920, *EP/JQ* 191–2; and from
      'The Island of Paris: A Letter', *Dial* LXIX.4 (Oct. 1920) 407–10.
      Rousselot: details from 'The Island of Paris: A Letter', *Dial* LXIX.6 (Dec. 1920)
      638–9.
      'richest half hour': details from 'The Island of Paris: A Letter', *Dial* LXIX.5 (Nov.
      1920) 516–18.
396   **wrote to the Paris edition**: EP letter, 'Oh, Those Passports', *New York Herald*, Paris
      (22 July 1920).
      'verminous', 'bureaucratic imbecilities': EP letter in *Much Ado* XI.4 (15 Aug. 1920)
      [11–12].
      July 7 or 8: Ellmann, *Joyce*, p. 496 gives July 8; EP in a letter to Thayer dated 'July 7'
      wrote 'Joyce due from Italy in 20 minutes' (*EP/Dial* 66). Details in this paragraph
      mainly from Ellmann, pp. 499–513.
      'Is this the great': Sylvia Beach, *Shakespeare and Company* (Faber & Faber, 1960),
      pp. 46, 48.
397   **a pair of second-hand brown shoes**: paragraph based on WL's *B&B* 265–70. See also
      TSEL 402.

'. . . . out of the dead land'

398   **'chief cash reason'**: EP to JJ, 2 Aug. 1920, *EP/JJ* 183.
      'very low': TSE to WL [28 July 1920], *TSEL* 394.
      'apparently destined': EP to JQ, 9 Oct. 1920, *EP/JQ* 195.
      earnings: EP received from the *Dial* £35. 14s. 2d. as salary for Sept. and Oct. 1920,
      and a further $90 for 'The Island of Paris'—see *EP/Dial* 172.
      royalties: Stock: 1970, 234 lists some royalty payments.
      cost of living: TSE reckoned his £500 p.a. from the bank was worth only half what
      it would have been four years before (*TSEL* 353). The exchange rate of the US dollar
      had gone from $5 = £1 to below $4 and as low as $3.35 in 1920—partly on account of
      Britain's debt to US banks.
      'grandiose scheme': EP to JQ, 9 Oct. 1920, *EP/JQ* 194–5. See also EP to Thayer, 25
      Nov. 1920, *EP/Dial* 184–5.

The Waste Land: TSE wrote to JQ on 5 Nov. 1919, 'I hope to get started on a poem that I have in mind' (*TSEL* 344); and to his mother, on 18 Dec. 1919, he wrote, 'my New Year's Resolution is "to write a long poem I have had on my mind for a long time"' (*TSEL* 351).

399   '**very fortunate**': TSE to his mother, 6 Jan. 1920, *TSEL* 353.

'**I am worried**': TSE to JQ, 25 Jan. 1920, *TSEL* 358.

'**frozen out**': EP, 'A Letter from London', *Much Ado* X.5 (2 Feb. 1920) [1].

'**would be delighted**': EP to HLP, 14 Jan. 1920 (Beinecke).

'**there is not one**': EP to HLP 21 Jan. 1920 (Beinecke).

'**not made for compromise**': Herbert Read as cited Stock: 1970, 223.

'**irreparable divergencies**': EP to Thayer, 23 Oct. 1920, *EP/Dial* 166.

'**precision of language**': EP to Thayer, 11 Sept. 1920, *EP/Dial* 138.

'**I don't care**': Thayer to EP, 18 Sept. 1920, *EP/Dial* 150.

'**the delicate stomachs**': ibid., 143.

'**the few dozen**': EP to Thayer, 23 Oct. 1920, *EP/Dial* 166.

favourable review: May Sinclair, 'The Reputation of Ezra Pound', *English Review* 30 (Apr. 1920) 326–35; also in *North American Review* CCXI (May 1920) 658–68. (In Homberger: 1972, 177–85.)

400   '**The poems**': *TLS* 963 (1 July 1920) 427—in Homberger: 1972, 194.

'**In himself**': Robert Nichols, 'Poetry and Mr Pound', *Observer*, 11 Jan. 1920, 6—in Homberger: 1972, 167.

'**suffocating and malignant**': WL, 'Mr Ezra Pound', Observer, 18 Jan. 1920, 5—in Homberger: 1972, 168–9.

Eliot's embarrassment: TSE to WL [28 July 1920], *TSEL* 394. The new magazine would have been *The Tyro* (no. 1 published Apr. 1921; no. 2 Mar. 1922).

John Gould Fletcher: for an account of his early friendship with EP see *Life is My Song* (1937), reissued as *The Autobiography of John Gould Fletcher* (1988), pp. 62 ff. For his review—'Some Contemporary Poets', *Chapbook: A Monthly Miscellany* 11 (May 1920) 23–5—see Homberger: 1972, 171–4.

'**E. P. is the best enemy**': WCW, 'Prologue' (1918), *Kora in Hell: Improvisations* (1920), as in WCW, *Imaginations* (MacGibbon & Kee, 1970), 26–7.

401   **in common with Pound's**: compare for example *Imaginations* p. 14 with pp. 381 and 386–7 above.

'**My dear old**': EP to WCW [11 Sept. 1920], *EP/WCW* 36–9.

'**AND now**': ibid. 38–9.

'**Mouquin**': information from editor's note, *EP/WCW* 41.

402   '**Has the time**': EP to JQ, 24 Sept. 1920, *EP/JQ* 193.

uncompleted doctorate: see pp. 32–3 above.

'**no art**': JQ to EP, 21 Oct. 1920, excerpted *EP/JQ* 174.

'**I think Eliot**': EP to JQ, 8 Nov. 1920, *EP/JQ* 203.

'**building a civilization**': ibid.

'**After twelve years**': EP [review of] *Poésies 1917–1920* [by] Jean Cocteau, *Dial* LXX.1 (Jan. 1921) 110.

'**is alive**': 'A Letter from Ezra Pound', *Literary Review* [of the New York *Evening Post*] I.13 (4 Dec. 1920) 26.

'**I return to London**': EP, 'Thames Morasses', *Poetry* XVII.6 (Mar. 1921) 325. Pound was 'sweating at "Thames Morasses"' in Sept. 1920—see *EP/Dial* 153.

403   '**dead language**': ibid., 325–6.

'**horror of exact statement**': 'A Letter from Ezra Pound', *Literary Review*, p. 26.

the oppressor *par excellence*: sentence paraphrased from EP, 'Le major C.-H. Douglas et la situation en Angleterre', *Les Écrits Nouveaux* VIII.8/9 (Aug./Sept. 1921) [143].

'Here the political': 'A Letter from Ezra Pound', *Literary Review*, p. 26.
drafted his 'hell cantos': i.e. cantos 14 and 15—see Stock: 1970, 228.
'Ten years ago': EP, 'Thames Morasses', *Poetry* XVII.6 (Mar. 1921) 327–9.
'Mr Yeats': ibid.
'to approve': EP to HLP [Sept. 1920] (Beinecke).
'narrative and reminiscent': 'A Letter from Ezra Pound', *Literary Review*, p. 26.
'celto-spiritist fog': EP to IWP [Nov. 1919] (Beinecke).

404   'to put a vortex': EP to FMF, 7 Sept. 1920, *P / F* 43.
'Penny': FMF to Isidor Schneider, 14 Sept. 1929, *Letters of Ford Madox Ford*, ed.
Richard M. Ludwig (Princeton, NJ: Princeton University Press,1965), p. 190.
'best work...behind': EP, 'Hudson: Poet Strayed into Science', *LR* VII.1 (May/June
1920) 17. (For Ford's reaction—'Why say...that I am gaga!'—see *P/F* 38.)
best English novel: i.e. *Parade's End* (1924–28)—the culminating part is *Last Post*.
diagnosis...cure: see EP, 'The Serious Artist', *LE* 45.
'The Fifth Canto': cantos 5–6–7 were first published as 'Three Cantos' in *Dial*
LXXI.2 (Aug. 1921) [198]-208; and then in *Poems 1918–21* (1921). 'The Sixth Canto'
would be much altered in *A Draft of XVI Cantos* (1925).

406   'factual data': see EP, 'How to Read', *LE* 26, on the 'heaping up of factual data' in
Flaubert and other nineteenth-century prose works.

407   'One of the most illuminating': EP, 'The Central Problem', *Townsman* IV.13 (Mar.
1941) 13–14. (EP wrote 'Griffiths' for 'Griffith', and, in error, called him 'founder' of
Sinn Fein.) For another account of the meeting see 19/34–5—the 'old kindly professor' was Masaryk, 'the stubby little man' was Griffith. EP, by then based in Paris, was
over in London for a week in October 1921 (EP to HLP, 22 October 1921 [Beinecke]).
'over attic rafters': 80/514–15. On this visit to Lacock Abbey and the charter see also
Omar Pound, 'Canto LXXX: Lacock Abbey and the Charter of 1225', *Pai* 26.2–3
(1997) 227–9.
proofs: see TSE to his mother, 20 Sept. 1920, *TSEL* 408.
Pound regarded: in a note in *Action*, Paris, I.7 (May 1921) 56, EP wrote: '*The Sacred
Wood*, essais de critique par T. S. Eliot, tentative trés noble de percer le mur de
Chine, de la stupidité anglaise. Déguisé en professeur-gentilhomme M. Eliot aborde
les sujets traditionnels avec des manières traditionelles.... tentative courageuse.
Malheur au pays où pour faire imprimer quelques dissociations lucides d'idées il faut
se couvrir des styles du *Times Literary Supplement*, et des pompes funèbres.'

408   *Ulysses* prosecuted: see *EP/JJ* 184–5; and EP to JQ, 31 Oct. 1920, *EP/JQ* 198–201.
'high water mark': EP to Thayer, 8 Nov. 1920, *EP/Dial* 173–6. (EP wrote 'Bawn' for
'Brawne'.)

409   'touch of real thing': ibid. 175–6.
'Aetheling' on Hayes and Rudge: 'Music', *NA* XXVIII.4 (25 Nov. 1920) 44.
'fellow alumnus': see editorial commentary, *EP/Dial* 193.
'We are in action': EP to HLP, 27 Dec. 1920 (Beinecke).
'Mr Ezra Pound': 'R. H. C.', 'Readers and Writers', *NA* XXVIII.11 (13 Jan. 921)
126–7—in Homberger: 1972, 199–202.

410   'one seems rather': EP to FMF, 22 May [1921], *P/F* 58.
The intaglio seal was made for EP by Edmund Dulac, It was stamped in orange-red
on the title-page of the first (unabridged) edition of *Lustra* (1916).

ACKNOWLEDGEMENTS AND
COPYRIGHT NOTICE

When one works on Pound one does not work alone. I have enjoyed support both material and moral, together with encouragement, incitement and provocation, from many persons and institutions, and it is a pleasure to recall what I owe to them and to record my gratitude.

There are the great libraries which collect, conserve, and make available to researchers the vast treasury of Pound's unpublished writings and drafts. I am most grateful for the courteous welcome, the frequent kindness, and the willing and expert assistance accorded me: at Yale University's Beinecke Library—particularly by the late Donald Gallup and by Patricia Willis, Curator of the Yale Collection of American Literature; at the Harry Ransom Humanities Research Center of the University of Texas at Austin—particularly by Thomas F. Staley, its Director, by Cathy Henderson, its Research Librarian, and by Pat Fox, Willard Goodwin and Barbara Smith-Laborde; at the Lilly Library of Indiana University, Bloomington, Indiana—particularly by Saundra Taylor, Curator of Manuscripts, and by Breon Mitchell, now the Lilly Librarian; at the Daniel Burke Library of Hamilton College, Clinton, New York—particularly by Ralph Stenstrom, its then Librarian, by Frank K. Lorenz, its then Curator of Archives, and by the present Couper Librarian, Randall L. Ericson; and at the Rare Book and Manuscript Library of the University of Pennsylvania—particularly by Nancy M. Shawcross, Curator of manuscripts, and by Grant Yoder.

Next I must thank the phalanx of scholars who have edited valuable resources from those archives, to the great benefit of other readers and researchers: D. D. Paige, Richard Reid, Noel Stock, Forrest Read, William Cookson, Eric Homberger, Michael John King, R. Murray Schafer, Leonard W. Doob, Harriet Zinnes, Vittoria I. Mondolfo, Margaret Hurley, Brita Lindberg-Seyersted, David Anderson, Donald Pearce, Herbert Schneidau, Omar Pound, A. Walton Litz, Timothy Materer, Mary de Rachewiltz, Barry Ahearn, Sanehida Kodama, Robert Spoo, Thomas L. Scott, Melvin J. Friedman, Jackson R. Bryer, Lea Baechler, James Longenbach, Richard Sieburth, Richard Taylor, Ira B. Nadel, David M. Gordon, Walter Sutton, Hugh Witemeyer, E. P. Walkiewicz, Philip J. Burns, Maria Luisa Ardizzone, Demetres Tryphonopoulos, Leon Surette, Sarah C. Holmes, Robert Hughes, Margaret Fisher, Massimo Bacigalupo, and Alec Marsh. Here the late Carroll F. Terrell deserves a special honourable mention for his outstanding services to Ezra Pound scholarship, as founding editor of *Paideuma*, compiler of *A Companion to the Cantos of Ezra Pound*, animator of conferences, and generous instigator, supporter, and publisher of others' work, especially that of younger scholars. In another special category is Donald Gallup—his *Ezra Pound: A Bibliography* (1983) is an indispensable resource always at hand. I have reason to be grateful also for Volker Bischoff's

ACKNOWLEDGEMENTS AND COPYRIGHT NOTICE

Ezra Pound Criticism 1905–1985: A Chronological Listing of Publications in English (Marburg, 1991).

The good and useful critics and interpreters of Pound's work are legion, and though it is invidious to single out individuals, I must name a few to whom I feel especially indebted. Foremost is Hugh Kenner, the inventor of literary modernism in his time. Then I would name as they come to mind, each for some particular donation: Donald Davie, Eva Hesse, Hugh Witemeyer, George Kearns, David Gordon, M. L. Rosenthal, Walter Baumann, Ian Bell, Guy Davenport, Christine Brooke-Rose, Jean-Michel Rabaté, Richard Sieburth, Massimo Bacigalupo, Peter Makin, Marjorie Perloff, Michael Alexander, James Longenbach, Wendy Flory, Emily Mitchell Wallace, Kay Davis, Ronald Bush, A. Walton Litz, Tim Redman, William McNaughton, Christine Froula, Peter Nichols, Leonardo Clerici, Leon Surette, Demetres Tryphonopoulos, Luca Gallesi, Maria Luisa Ardizzone, Colin McDowell, Scott Eastham, Robert Hughes, and Margaret Fisher. More generally, I have enjoyed being a member of a lively, contentious and collaborative community of scholars at the biennial International Ezra Pound Conferences, from the first in 1976, and have profited from innumerable discussions in various agreeable settings with fellow scholars and critics.

'Biography, a minor form of fiction', Hugh Kenner wrote somewhere, not altogether dismissively, though with reason; yet, as a biographer, I have been glad to be able to check out the facts of Pound's life against the biographies of Noel Stock, J. J. Wilhelm, and Humphrey Carpenter. Mary de Rachewiltz's memoir, *Discretions: Ezra Pound, Father and Teacher*, has been an inimitable inspiration.

Poets, like those who write about them, (and those who would read them), need publishers. Beyond the copyright acknowledgements below, we must be grateful to Elkin Mathews, Pound's first publisher in London; to Charles Granville, Harriet Shaw Weaver, John Rodker, William Bird, and Nancy Cunard, who brought out his early and wholly uncommercial poetry through their private presses; to Alfred A. Knopf, Boni and Liveright, and Farrar and Rinehart, his first publishers in New York; to Faber and Faber who became his publishers in London after 1933; to Stanley Nott; and above all to James Laughlin whose New Directions became his American publisher, and ultimately the leading publisher of his work. Other publishers helped keep his work in print in his later years, notably Peter Owen of London. In recent years we owe edited collections of his correspondence and prose to the enterprise of a number of American university presses. To Garland Publishing Inc. we owe the invaluable ten-volume collection of Pound's contributions to periodicals. And to the Library of America we owe Richard Sieburth's comprehensive collection of Pound's poems and translations.

There are more personal debts. To Claude Rawson, who started me on this project, and to whom I make sincere apology for its having outgrown his commission. To the late Hugh Kenner for opening his personal Pound archive to me and for generous hospitality. To Hugh Witemeyer for his conversation and kindness. To George and Cleo Kearns, for their hospitality and conversation, and to George in particular for a gift of books from his Pound collection. To Geoffrey Wall, biographer and translator of Flaubert, for his close attention to my prose and for his constructive advice. To Peggy Fox and Declan Spring of New Directions for their extraordinary courtesies and helpfulness. To Omar Pound and Elizabeth Pound for generous permission to quote from Pound's published and unpublished writings and from Dorothy Pound's letters and diary; also for permission to reproduce a design of Dorothy Pound's; and for constructive suggestions. To Mary de Rachewiltz for permission to quote from Pound's published and unpublished writings; for generous practical assistance, including giving access to her library and making freely available her collection of photographs; and for her wholly Poundian principle of placing no restriction on the use of her father's work.

Andrew McNeillie took in the book and gave it the best of homes. I owe much to his warm support, and to the impressive expertise and enthusiasm of all who have worked on the book at Oxford University Press, to Jacqueline Baker, Coleen Hatrick, and Phil Henderson; to Sue Tipping for the design and illustrations, and to Elizabeth Robottom and Eva Nyika for the production. It has been a pleasure also to work with Tom Chandler, my copy-editor, and with Michael Tombs who did the index.

I am grateful to David Finn for permission to reproduce his fine photograph of Gaudier-Brzeska's Hieratic Head of Ezra Pound; and to the Wyndham Lewis Memorial Trust and Helen D'Monte for permission to reproduce Lewis's lost portrait of Ezra Pound and his cover design for *BLAST*. I am grateful for the skilled photographic work of Gordon Smith and Paul Shields of York University's Photographic Unit.

Visits to the archives in the United States were supported by a British Academy Leverhulme Visiting Professorship, and by two British Academy research grants. Yale University's Beinecke Library awarded me its Donald C. Gallup Visiting Fellowship in 1994. The Lilly Library of Indiana University, Bloomington, Indiana awarded me its Everett Helm Visiting Fellowship in 1996. This book owes a great deal of its substance to those grants and awards.

The Latin dedication, which I like to think of as engraved on every copy, means WITH JOANNA, TO AND FOR JOANNA.

489

1991). Copyright © 1991 by The Trustees of the Ezra Pound Literary Property Trust.

Previously unpublished material by Ezra Pound. Copyright © 2007 by Mary de Rachewiltz and Omar S. Pound. Used by permission of New Directions Publishing Corporation.

Previously unpublished letters of Dorothy Shakespear Pound. © 2007 by Omar S. Pound, used by permission of Omar S. Pound.

Excerpts from letters and notebook of Dorothy Shakespear, and cover design for *Ripostes*, by courtesy of Omar S. Pound.

Previously unpublished letters of Homer and Isabel Pound. Copyright 2007 by Mary de Rachewiltz and Omar S. Pound.

Excerpts from Douglas Goldring's *South Lodge*, copyright estate of Patrick Golding, by permission of Douglas Goldring's literary executor, Polly Bird.

Excerpts from published works by H. D. and William Carlos Williams used by permission of New Directions Publishing Corporation and Carcanet Press.

'Oread' by H.D. used by permission of New Directions Publishing Corporation and Carcanet Press. Copyright 1925 by Hilda Doolittle.

I am grateful to the following holders of copyright material who have granted access and permission to quote:

The Beinecke Rare Book and Manuscript Library, Yale University
Daniel Burke Library, Hamilton College
The Harry Ransom Humanities Research Center, The University of Texas at Austin
The Lilly Library, Indiana University, Bloomington, Indiana
Rare Book and Manuscript Library, University of Pennsylvania, Philadelphia

Sources of Illustrations

The majority of the illustrations are reproduced by courtesy of Mary de Rachewiltz, apart from the following:

7, 11, 29 The Yale Collection of American Literature, Beinecke Rare Book and Manuscript Library, Yale University
10 Courtesy of New Directions Publishing Corporation
12 Carl W. Gatter Collection on Ezra Pound, Rare Book & Manuscript Library, University of Pennsylvania
16, 22, 33 Courtesy of Omar Shakespear Pound
32, 35, 43 Courtesy of Wyndham Lewis Memorial Trust
36 National Museum of Wales, Cardiff
38 Courtesy of David Finn
Endpapers Private collection

INDEX

Note: Includes all collections, poems and writings indexed by title.